SAMUEL BUTLER
Prose Observations

SAMUEL BUTLER

Prose Observations

EDITED WITH AN INTRODUCTION
AND COMMENTARY BY
HUGH DE QUEHEN

OXFORD
AT THE CLARENDON PRESS
1979

Oxford University Press, Walton Street, Oxford OX2 6DP

OXFORD LONDON GLASGOW
NEW YORK TORONTO MELBOURNE WELLINGTON
KUALA LUMPUR SINGAPORE HONG KONG TOKYO
DELHI BOMBAY CALCUTTA MADRAS KARACHI
NAIROBI DAR ES SALAAM CAPE TOWN

Published in the United States by
Oxford University Press, New York

© *Oxford University Press 1979*

British Library Cataloguing in Publication Data

Butler, Samuel, b. 1612
    Prose observations. – (Oxford English texts)
    I. Title   II. de Quehen, Hugh   III. Series
    828'.4'08   PR4349.B7   77–30357
ISBN 0–19–812728–6

182598

Printed in Great Britain
at the University Press, Oxford
by Eric Buckley
Printer to the University

FOR
JOHN WILDERS

PREFACE

THIS edition was undertaken in the belief that Butler's surviving manuscripts provide a mass of interesting and often entertaining material hitherto inaccessible or unintelligible to the literary student. In my study of Butler, I soon became aware of the defects in the Cambridge English Classics volumes edited by A. R. Waller and René Lamar. Valuable as these were in making available a printed text of Butler's prose and verse remains, comparison with the manuscript originals in the British Library revealed significant inaccuracies of transcription and substantial omissions of material. The omission, and silent rearrangement, of passages is most serious in Lamar's *Satires and Miscellaneous Poetry and Prose*; but Waller's *Characters and Passages from Note-Books* omits some material and provides no systematic collation of parallel drafts. Waller also assumes, incorrectly, that the British Library folios are bound in their right order and overlooks the fact that some are not in Butler's hand. And his transcription of the manuscript prose is not up to the standard expected of a scholarly text. So to my mind there was no question but the text should be transcribed afresh and edited on modern bibliographical principles.

There was also another manuscript, which had come to light since Waller's edition was published: a commonplace book now in the Philip H. and A. S. W. Rosenbach Foundation Museum in Philadelphia. It was assumed to be largely in Butler's hand, with some material from later sources added by his friend and literary executor William Longueville; but I found when I commenced my editorial work that almost all the entries thought to be Butler's were in fact transcriptions made by Longueville from Butler's manuscript. Many of the transcriptions were valuable none the less, since the originals from which they derived were now lost, and they clearly deserved to be printed, especially an account of a visit to France and a number of reflections on Restoration politics.

In preparing this edition I have followed as closely as the nature of the different material permits the general plan and particular policies of John Wilders in his edition of *Hudibras*, published in this same series in 1967. So the conventions of the textual apparatus and commentary conform to that model, and the commentary aims to be of equal scope and detail. The commentary's deficiencies reflect my own shortcomings, but some allowance may perhaps be made for the difficulties of a first commentator on a seventeenth-century text, especially when its author is so studiously obscure in his allusions. There are no explanatory notes in the Cambridge English Classics volumes, and Robert Thyer, who included a selection of the prose observations in his *Genuine Remains* of 1759, made only very occasional comments. In explaining material largely drawn from the miscellaneous reading habits of another century, one does need the guidance of an early commentator, inevitably more conversant with obvious sources now lost to sight; so one much regrets Thyer's reticence. Nor is it so clear to a modern scholar what aspect of a cited passage most interested Butler, and the length of some of my notes reflects that uncertainty. It is intended that a companion volume of Butler's manuscript verse will follow this present one, and it will include many references back to the prose passages which Butler later redrafted in verse; so quotations from Butler's sources in my commentary on the prose sometimes include matter not directly relevant to the prose passage because the quotation will also serve to elucidate additional details from the source found only in the verse draft.

My success in identifying sources is due in large part to the generous help I have received from my colleagues in English and Classics at University College, Toronto, and from many other scholars who have readily answered my questions over the years. With bibliographical problems I have been much helped by Professor G. E. Bentley, Jr., Professor Desmond Neill, and Professor Allan Pritchard. Invaluable assistance has been given by the director and staff of the Rosenbach Foundation Museum and the librarians at the Bodleian Library and at the British Library, especially in the Department of Manuscripts. I am grateful to the University of Toronto for allowing me a leave of absence to complete my research and to the Canada Council, now Social Sciences and Humanities Research Council of Canada, for a leave fellowship and summer research grants. Permission to publish the manuscript texts and photographs of individual folios was kindly given by the Rosenbach Foundation and the Trustees of the British Library. This book has been published with the help of a grant from the Canadian Federation for the Humanities, using funds provided by the Social Sciences and Humanities Research Council of Canada. I much appreciate the help and guidance of Mr. Philip J. Cercone of the Canadian Federation for the Humanities, who handled the application for the publication grant. The officers of the Oxford University Press gave me much patient advice and encouragement in the preparation and publishing of this book and suggested many improvements in organization and detail. I have finally two special debts of gratitude, to Mr. Basil Greenslade, who supervised my postgraduate study of Butler, and to Dr. John Wilders, whose generous contribution to my work in all its stages I acknowledge as best I can in the dedication.

A. H. de Q.

University College
University of Toronto

CONTENTS

LIST OF ILLUSTRATIONS

SIGLA

B   British Library Add. MS. 32625, Literary remains of Samuel Butler . . . written in Butler's own hand, fos. 236.

C   Manuscript Commonplace Book written in the hand of William Longueville, fos. [84] + 100. Philip H. and A. S. W. Rosenbach Foundation Museum, Philadelphia

GR   *The Genuine Remains in Verse and Prose of Mr. Samuel Butler*, edited by Robert Thyer, 2 vols. 1759.

T   British Library Add. MS. 32626, Transcripts and extracts from original compositions in verse and prose of Samuel Butler, by Robert Thyer, fos. 154.

W   Samuel Butler, *Characters and Passages from Note-Books*, edited by A. R. Waller, Cambridge, 1908.

ABBREVIATIONS

Aristotle	*The Works of Aristotle*, translated into English under the editorship of J. A. Smith and W. D. Ross. 12 vols. Oxford, 1908–52.
Bacon, *Works*	*The Works of Francis Bacon*, edited by J. Spedding, R. L. Ellis, and D. D. Heath, 14 vols. 1857–74.
Baker, *Chronicle*	Sir Richard Baker, *A Chronicle of the Kings of England*, 1653.
Birch, *History*	Thomas Birch, *History of the Royal Society*, 4 vols. 1756–7.
Blackstone, *Commentaries*	Sir William Blackstone, *Commentaries on the Laws of England*, 4 vols. 1765–9.
Bodl.	The Bodleian Library, Oxford.
Burnet, *History*	*Burnet's History of My Own Time* . . . *The Reign of Charles II*, edited by Osmund Airy, 2 vols. Oxford, 1897–1900.
Blount, *Glossographia*	Thomas Blount, *Glossographia; Or, a Dictionary Interpreting All Such Hard Words* . . . *As Are Now Used in Our Refined English Tongue*, 1656.
Cardan, *Opera*	*Hieronymi Cardani* . . . *Opera Omnia*, edited by Charles Spon, 10 vols. Lyons, 1663.
Clarendon, *History*	Edward, Earl of Clarendon, *History of the Rebellion and Civil Wars in England*, edited by W. D. Macray, 6 vols. Oxford, 1888.
Clarendon, *Continuation*	The Continuation of *The Life of Edward Earl of Clarendon* . . . *Written by Himself*, Oxford, 1857.
Cotgrave, *Dictionarie*	Randle Cotgrave, *A Dictionarie of the French and English Tongues*, 1611.
DNB	*The Dictionary of National Biography*.
Dryden, *Works*	*The Works of John Dryden*, edited by E. N. Hooker, H. T. Swedenberg, and V. A. Dearing, [20 vols.] Berkeley and Los Angeles, 1956.
ELH	*A Journal of English Literary History*.
Firth and Rait	*Acts and Ordinances of the Interregnum, 1642–1660*, collected and edited by C. H. Firth and R. S. Rait, 3 vols. 1911.
French Virtuosi I	*A General Collection of Discourses of the Virtuosi of France, upon Questions of All Sorts of Philosophy, and Natural Knowledg*, translated by G. Havers, 1664.

French Virtuosi II	*Another Collection of Philosophical Conferences of the French Virtuosi*, translated by G. Havers and J. Davies, 1665.
HLQ	*The Huntington Library Quarterly.*
Hudibras	Samuel Butler, *Hudibras*, edited by John Wilders, Oxford, 1967.
MLN	*Modern Language Notes.*
MP	*Modern Philology.*
ODEP	*The Oxford Dictionary of English Proverbs*, third edition, revised by F. P. Wilson, Oxford, 1970
OED	*The Oxford English Dictionary.*
Platina, *Lives of the Popes*	*The Lives of the Popes . . . Written Originally in Latine by Baptista Platina . . . and Translated into English, And [Pt. ii] the Same History Continued from the Year 1471. to This Present Time . . . by Paul Rycaut, 1685.*
Plato	*The Dialogues of Plato*, translated by B. Jowett (re-edited by D. J. Allen and H. E. Dale), 4 vols. Oxford, 1953.
Purchas, *Pilgrimage*	Samuel Purchas, *Purchas his Pilgrimage*, 1626.
Purchas, *Pilgrimes*	Samuel Purchas, *Purchas his Pilgrimes*, 4 vols. 1625.
PMLA	*Publications of the Modern Language Association of America.*
P.R.O.	The Public Record Office, London.
RES	*The Review of English Studies.*
de Serres, *Histoire*	Jean de Serres, *Inventaire General de l'Histoire de France*, 2 vols. Geneva, 1632.
Spingarn	*Critical Essays of the Seventeenth Century*, edited by J. E. Spingarn, 3 vols. Oxford, 1908–9.
Sprat, *History*	Thomas Sprat, *History of the Royal Society of London for the Improving of Natural Knowledge*, 1667.
Tilley	Morris Palmer Tilley, *Dictionary of the Proverbs in England in the Sixteenth and Seventeenth Centuries*, Ann Arbor, 1950.
TLS	*The Times Literary Supplement.*
VCH	*The Victoria History of the Counties of England.*

INTRODUCTION

I. *Butler's Manuscript Remains*

IN the years immediately preceding his death on 25 September
1680, Butler lodged in Rose Street, Covent Garden, and an earlier
description of this alley as 'fitt for mechanicks only and persons of
meane qualitie' points clearly to the poet's straitened circumstances.[1] He had, however, one true friend and patron in William
Longueville (1639–1721), a distinguished bencher of the Inner
Temple who lived not far away in Bow Street.[2] 'Mr. *Longueville*',
writes Roger North, 'was the last Patron and Friend that poor old
Butler, the Author of *Hudibras*, had, and, in his old Age, he supported him. Otherwise he might have been literally starved. All, that
Butler could do to recompense him was, to make him his Heir, that
is, give him his Remains; but in loose Papers, and indigested. But
Mr. *Longueville* hath reduced them into Method and Order.'[3]
North's character of Longueville suggests the right qualities to
draw out the taciturn and disappointed older man: Longueville was
talkative, with a love for 'Classic Wit' and the topical application
of Latin sentences, and he was eminent in a profession which had
always fascinated Butler.[4]

Longueville inherited at least the following groups of manuscripts: fair copies of 'The Elephant in the Moon' and other satires;
fair copies of the prose tracts, such as *King Charles's Case* and the
'Prynne–Audland' letters; over two hundred Characters; a collection of miscellaneous prose observations; and a similar collection of
miscellaneous verse. North's phrase 'loose Papers, and indigested'
applies particularly to the two miscellanies, each of which

[1] *Survey of London*, xxxvi, ed. F. W. H. Sheppard, 1970, p. 183. Cf. ibid., p. 268.
[2] Ibid., p. 187.
[3] *Life of Francis North*, 1742, p. 289. The anonymous 'Life' of Butler mentions that
he '*was buryed at the Charge of his good Friend Mr.* L--*vil of the* Temple' (*Hudibras*,
1704, sig. a4ʳ).
[4] North, loc. cit. Many of Longueville's letters survive in the Hatton Correspondence (B.L. Add. MSS. 29555–85); some, dated 1676 to 1688, have been printed
(Camden Soc., 1878).

consisted partly of material classified under different headings, but also of passages jotted down at random for later rewriting in the appropriate classified sections.[1] The classified folios Longueville needed only to arrange in what he felt to be their right order, but the only way to salvage and methodize what was of interest in the remainder was to transcribe. Accordingly Longueville copied some 430 prose passages and a lesser quantity of verse into a quarto manuscript book already half-filled with an English–French dictionary (A–lawrel) which may tentatively be called Butler's.[2] Longueville wrote under 84 headings, and he included passages from Butler's 13 classified sections. Yet the bulk of Longuevilles's prose transcripts do derive from Butler's unclassified folios, a number of which were subsequently lost. Hence Longueville's commonplace book is the sole source for some 180 prose passages, though of no authority for the other 250, of which the originals survive.[3]

It is unfortunate that Longueville began to use his commonplace book for entries from other sources as well. Yet as he became less scrupulous about provenance, he became also less careful of his handwriting; whereas he had previously used a very small neat hand, he now lapsed into a large sprawling one. This, together with the identification of an alternative source, will usually distinguish what is not from Butler, but there are occasionally indeterminate reading notes which Butler could first have taken and Longueville recopied.[4]

On William Longueville's death in 1721 the manuscripts passed to his son Charles. Charles Longueville, also an Inner Templar, was Auditor to Queen Caroline and M.P. for East Looe. John Lockman read him his article 'Hudibras', and Longueville's

---

[1] In the present edition the classified sections of prose are printed on pp. 1–146, and the unclassified prose (plus odd characters, letters, and lists) on pp. 147–246.

[2] The dictionary probably dates from the early 1640s, and, given the different style of writing with very small and often unjoined letters, there are acceptably few variations in letter-forms from Butler's later hand. See the bibliographical description of the commonplace book on pp. lv–lvi.

[3] For a fuller discussion of these interrelated manuscripts and of the editorial problems they pose see A. H. de Quehen, 'Editing Butler's Manuscripts', in *Editing Seventeenth Century Prose*, ed. D. I. B. Smith, Toronto, 1972, pp. 71–93.

[4] For instance, an extract from Seneca on the efficacy of good example (*Epistolae Morales*, xciv. 40–1, Nulla . . . profuisse); when Butler writes on this topic he refers to Seneca (p. 8).

comments are printed as marginal notes to it in Lockman's *General Dictionary*.[1] Charles Longueville died in 1750, having willed the manuscripts specifically to John Clark, his natural son, who inherited the bulk of the estate.[2]

John Clark (or Clarke) was admitted to St. John's College, Cambridge, in 1744, aged 19; he took his B.A. in 1747-8.[3] With his inheritance he moved to Cheshire and purchased land in the parish of Wybunbury, near Nantwich.[4] Soon afterwards Robert Thyer, Chetham's Librarian in Manchester 1732-63, secured Clark's permission to publish a selection from the manuscripts, and his letters show him at work on the edition towards the end of 1754.[5] Thyer's *Genuine Remains in Verse and Prose of Mr. Samuel Butler* was published in two volumes in 1759, the list of subscribers accounting for over eleven hundred copies. The 'one or two more' volumes foreseen by Thyer never materialized; nor did the new edition of *Hudibras* which he intended to illustrate with passages from manuscript.[6] Thyer had, however, transcribed a good many more Characters than the 121 he printed; an additional 66 which survive in his transcripts have, following the loss of Butler's holographs, become a unique source.[7]

Clark lived until 1789, but it is doubtful whether he took the various manuscripts back into his own keeping after Thyer had used them. Zachary Grey made inquiries through Christopher Byron, a Manchester man who had helped him with the notes to his edition of *Hudibras* (1744), and from Byron Grey received the reply that he had 'waited upon Mr. Thyer, and he readily agreed to oblige you with some part of Butler's MSS.; but said the consent

---

[1] 10 vols., 1734–41, vi. 289–99.

[2] Admon. 25 Dec. 1750 and 25 Oct. 1751 (P.R.O.). See also Elizabeth Mompesson (*née* Longueville), prob. 2 Oct. 1751 (P.R.O.).

[3] Venn, *Alumni Cantabrigienses*, I. i. 344.

[4] Clark's certificate of the manuscripts' authenticity given to Thyer in 1754 is dated from the township of Walgherton; Land Tax returns (from 1781) show him resident in the adjacent township of Hough, as does his will, prob. 13 Jan. 1790 (Cheshire County Record Office).

[5] Thyer to Samuel Pegge (Bodl. MS. Eng. lett. d. 43, fos. 403, 407, 409). Thyer published *Proposals* for his edition in 1755.

[6] Letters to Pegge, fo. 409; *Proposals*, p. 4.

[7] B.L. Add. MS. 32626, fos. 82–147. Three of these Characters are in fact transcribed in Longueville's commonplace book as well; see p. xxiv.

of his co-proprietor would be necessary, whom I have not seen (one Mr. Massey)'.[1] Whatever the nature of Thyer's proprietorship, James Massey, into whose family John Clark had married, did certainly come to own all or most of the material; but, as he later wrote to the editor of *Hudibras*, T. R. Nash, 'My son's death rendering me indifferent to any thing of the literary kind, I disposed of the MSS. to Dr. Farmer; they consisted chiefly of characters drawn according to the taste of those times.'[2]

Longueville's commonplace book did not pass to Richard Farmer; Massey gave that to Nash, who made a note of its provenance inside the upper board.[3] In the same place is an armorial book-plate of 'John Somers. Lord Somers': John Sommers Cocks, then Baron and subsequently (from 1821) Earl Sommers; he was married to Nash's daughter and sole heiress. In May 1930 Dr. A. S. W. Rosenbach, then visiting London, bought the commonplace book from P. J. and A. E. Dobell (Bruton Street), and it is now in the collection of the Philip H. and A. S. W. Rosenbach Foundation in Philadelphia.[4]

As to the other manuscripts, Nash wrote that 'what remain of them, still unpublished, are either in the hands of the ingenious Doctor Farmer, of Cambridge, or myself'.[5] Nash does not make it clear, but there is no reason to suppose that he himself owned any holograph compositions; the bulk of them does seem to

---

[1] Letter dated 31 July 1759; in John Nichols, *Literary Illustrations*, 1817–58, iv. 263.

[2] Letter in Treadway Russell Nash, *Supplement to the Collections for the History of Worcestershire*, 1799, p. 72.

[3] 'In the beginning of January 1796 dyed at Rostherne in Cheshire aged 83. James Massey Esq, who gave me this book.' In the Preface to his edition of *Hudibras*, 3 vols., 1793, I. xvii–xviii, Nash speaks also of a manuscript abridgement of Coke upon Littleton, which he had 'purchased of some of our poet's relations, at the Hay, in Brecknockshire'. He takes the hand to be Butler's, but one cannot be certain of that; Nash took Longueville's hand to be Butler's.

[4] The manuscript does not appear in P. J. Dobell's Bruton Street stock-book (MS. Bodl. Dobell Papers, box 85), nor was it advertised for sale. But in a notebook largely concerned with matters arising on his father's death in 1914, P. J. Dobell lists 'Butler' among 'MSS. at Queen's Crescent', where Bertram Dobell had traded (ibid.). The main beneficiary of the third and last Earl Sommers' will, in 1883, was his daughter Lady Henry Somerset (d. 1921), and the manuscript, of which I have found no auction record, may well have been sold privately to Dobell from her library at Reigate Priory, Surrey. If Nash's books were kept together, it certainly was at Reigate; a copy of the Nash *Hudibras*, with the same 'Somers' book-plate as the manuscript, has also a 'Reigate Priory' book-plate (with press-mark) in late nineteenth-century style. This copy is now in Massey College Library, Toronto (Samuel Butler Collection). [5] Preface to *Hudibras*, I. xvi.

have been in the Farmer sale of 1798.[1] The buyer was John Thane, compiler of *British Autography*.[2] Charles Baldwyn drew on the manuscripts for his new edition of the *Genuine Remains* in 1822, and Henry Southern then printed six selections of previously unpublished verse and Characters in the *London Magazine*.[3] The last selection is now the sole source for eight Characters which no longer survive in manuscript.[4] Those apart, the editor of the *London Magazine* need not have had access to manuscript material other than what is now extant; but he could equally well have owned, without using, all the holograph compositions that Butler originally left to William Longueville: verse satires, prose tracts, Characters, and miscellanies. Whatever Southern did have and however he disposed of it, no more than half the total left by Butler survived in the hundred and forty odd folios of miscellaneous verse and hundred odd folios of prose observations which, together with Thyer's transcripts, were purchased for the British Museum at Sotheby's in Ellis's Sales of 1885.

II. *Editions of the Prose Observations*

The only prose observations hitherto included in editions have been taken from the British Library holographs. Thyer's selection in the *Genuine Remains* derives from the neatly written classified

---

[1] '*A large Collection of Materials, by Mr. Samuel Butler, for Hudibras, with many other Poetical Pieces, Original Letters, to and from him, &c.*' (*Bibliotheca Farmeriana: A Catalogue of the . . . Library . . . of the Late Revd. Richard Farmer, D.D.*, 1798, lot 8100).

[2] 3 vols., n.d. See Supplementary Note on p. xxiv.

[3] In 1819 Baldwyn had published an edition of *Hudibras*; in 1820 Southern had contributed an article on 'Butler's Genuine and Spurious Remains' to the *Retrospective Review*, ii. 256–70, of which he was editor and Baldwyn publisher. There is no suggestion in these publications of access to manuscripts. The only enlargement in Baldwyn's *Genuine Remains*, 1822, is the 'Additions to *Hudibras*', i. 260–88, which Thyer in his transcript, *T* 3ʳ–20ᵛ, had abstracted from holograph. Baldwyn's vol. ii was never published; his business failed in 1824. Joseph Booker took up the project, then confined it to a volume of *Genuine Poetical Remains*, 1827, reprinting the verse from Baldwyn's vol. i and adding five Characters for which illustrations had already been cut. For details of 'Butleriana' in the *London Magazine* see Josephine Bauer, 'Some Verse Fragments and Prose *Characters* by Samuel Butler', *MP* xlv (1948), 160–8. Miss Bauer overlooks the fifth of the selections—*Lond. Mag.* IV. xv N.S. (Mar. 1826), 401–6—and is misled in her belief that some of the verse is no longer extant in manuscript. See de Quehen in *Editing Seventeenth Century Prose*, pp. 91–2.

[4] *Lond. Mag.* VI. xxiii N.S. (Nov. 1826), 396–401; repr. Bauer, art. cit. The loss could have resulted from Southern's using Thyer transcriptions as printer's copy, Butler's holographs having already disappeared.

folios, and his indifference to the unclassified material that has survived would account for his passing over other such material which we now know only in Longueville's selection.[1] The relatively difficult hand may be the reason why Thyer made no use of Longueville's commonplace book, even if he had access to it; for his own modest purposes Thyer had no need to look beyond the classified folios in holograph. From those he printed the complete section 'Reason', the one in which Butler sounds most like an Augustan disciple of Locke.[2] He ignored 'Nature' and 'History', where Butler is most the contemporary of Sir Thomas Browne. From other sections, where he chooses passages individually, he chooses most from 'Religion', 'Princes and Government', and 'Criticismes upon Bookes and Authors', in that order. The total 142 passages in the *Genuine Remains* are thus a limited selection, not just in their relatively small number, but also in their restricted range of interest. Moreover, the imposition of eighteenth-century accidentals detracts from the quality of the original versions, and the lack of textual or explanatory notes is an obvious drawback.

There was no further printing of Butler's prose observations until 1908, when A. R. Waller edited the material then in the British Museum in the second of the three 'Cambridge English Classics' volumes of Butler's Works.[3] While Waller's edition is for the most part free of those blatant mistranscriptions which alert a reader, such as 'Truth' for 'Fayth' at the beginning of the seventh passage in 'Religion', its presentation of the text is sufficiently perfunctory and inconsistent to distort the whole pattern of accidentals which an old-spelling edition exists to preserve. As Waller

---

[1] See Appendix A; also de Quehen in *Editing Seventeenth Century Prose*, pp. 83–4. Thyer's selection is in two parts (*GR* i. 393–403 and ii. 466–512); Baldwyn reprints only the first (*GR*, 1822, i. 387–95); Booker in his 1827 edition prints neither.

[2] 'These Thoughts upon a Topic so curious and interesting will give the World a Specimen of *Butler*'s Abilities in the argumentative and philosophical Way; and shew, that he had a Capacity of excelling in the cool and sober Province of *Judgment*, which is to separate and compare Ideas, as much as he has done in the gayer one of *Wit*, which is humorously to associate and assimilate them' (Thyer in *GR* i. 393).

[3] *Characters and Passages from Note-Books*, Cambridge, 1908, pp. 269–480. The first Cambridge volume was *Hudibras*, ed. Waller, 1905; the third *Satires and Miscellaneous Poetry and Prose*, ed. René Lamar, 1928. The deficiencies of the *Satires*, which silently omits and rearranges substantial parts of the manuscript verse, were first noted by Sir Walter Greg ('Hudibrastics', *TLS*, 23 Aug. 1928, p. 605).

explains in his introductory Note, the Press took over a transcript previously made by Edith Morley, 'the further checking of the transcript and the proofs with the original MS has been accomplished mainly by Mr George Brown, . . . and my share in the present volume has been confined . . . to reading the proofs, to correcting certain eccentricities of the scribe . . . wherever I thought that they might prove stumbling-blocks to the reader and to compiling the textual notes'. That Waller performed his part without reference to the manuscript is apparent from 'corrections' in square brackets that in fact give the holograph reading. It is not in these circumstances surprising that his textual notes give a very unsatisfactory account of the manuscript, most notably of the many substantive alterations and parallel drafts. Half-hearted revision of Miss Morley's transcript when the second reader distinguished differently, for example, between initial capitals and miniscules in the holograph would certainly account for the over-all lack of textual uniformity. No one appears to have questioned the order in which folios had been bound or to have noticed that the handwriting (and accidentals) of the first prose folios differs from what follows.[1]

It is of course to Waller's great credit that he did publish a reasonably complete version of the manuscript prose then available. It could, however, have easily been made much better, in legibility as well as in accuracy; for the unclassified material is printed as an appendix in minute type. The 'Cambridge English Classics' volumes have, moreover, neither introduction nor commentary, and their plain text of Butler makes hard reading indeed. Only one more recent edition has included any prose observations; there is a small modernized and annotated selection in the 'Oxford Paperback' Butler.[2] The material from Longueville's commonplace book has never been published, except for illustrative quotations in two useful articles by Norma E. Bentley and one Character, 'Schoolmaster', in Charles W. Daves's collection.[3]

---

[1] See p. xl.

[2] *Hudibras Parts I and II and Selected Other Writings*, ed. John Wilders and Hugh de Quehen, Oxford, 1973, pp. 268–88.

[3] Bentley, '*Hudibras* Butler Abroad', *MLN* lx (1945), 254–9, and 'Another Butler Manuscript', *MP* xlvi (1948), 132–5; Samuel Butler, *Characters*, ed. Daves, Cleveland, 1970, pp. 329–30.

III. *Some Additions to the Published Characters*

The most complete edition of Butler's Characters is that of Charles W. Daves. Thyer printed 121 Characters in the *Genuine Remains*; Waller's edition added 66 from Thyer's unpublished transcripts; Dr. Daves adds the eight discovered in the *London Magazine* by Josephine Bauer and 'Schoolmaster' from Longueville's commonplace book.[1] But further important manuscript material is overlooked by Dr. Daves and is therefore supplied in the present edition. The holographs 'War' and 'A Covetous Man' are printed as Characters for the first time,[2] and the holographs 'Bankrupt', 'Horse-courser', and 'Churchwarden', together with the concluding paragraphs of 'A Modern Politician', appear for the first time in their original form, not in Thyer's versions.[3] That material from Butler's manuscript is printed in full; so is a more accurate transcription of the commonplace book's 'Schoolmaster'.[4] Longueville is a less accurate transcriber than Thyer, but his readings do derive from Butler's holograph independently; so Characters which survive in the commonplace book as well as in Thyer's versions are of some interest for their substantive variants, even though Longueville's text is generally inferior. Appendix B lists the substantive variants in 'A Court-Wit', 'A Lawyer', 'A Dueller', 'An Oppressor', 'A Proselite', and 'An Atheist', and thus completes the textual account of Butler's Characters.

---

[1] See p. xxi and footnotes above. Like Miss Bauer, Dr. Daves overlooks the fifth of the *London Magazine* selections.

[2] 'War' (pp. 238–9 below) is printed by Waller as a piece of unclassified prose, regardless of its form and of Butler's standard Character heading (title in Greek letters, number, and date). 'A Covetous Man' (pp. 222–5), also printed by Waller as unclassified prose, is written in a carelessly formed and hurried hand. 'The Miser', *GR* ii. 341–4, apparently supersedes it, and comparison of the two texts will show how completely Butler rewrote, using largely new material.

[3] The three complete holographs (pp. 237–41) Waller omits without mention. The 'Modern Politician' paragraphs (pp. 218–21) he fails to identify and prints as unclassified prose.

[4] p. 265.

Supplementary Note on *British Autobiography*, p. xxi above. Vol. ii gives the first four lines of a satire in an engraving from holograph since lost ('Upon the Age of Charles II'; *GR*. i. 69); also the subscription with signature of the letter on *B1*ʳ (p. 243 below).

IV. *Butler and His Times*

Butler had been born in February 1613 and educated at King's School, Worcester.[1] His later learning was informally acquired, and the habit of miscellaneous reading is manifest in the prose observations, as is the ambivalent attitude to scholarship that distinguishes a self-taught man. He was forty-seven at the Restoration, too old perhaps to make the most of what the new reign offered. The following year he was holding a stewardship to Richard Vaughan, Earl of Carbery, at Ludlow Castle, but in 1662 had already relinquished this post. The First Part of *Hudibras* was published in December 1662, the Second Part a year later. The poem was a great success; yet Butler felt himself unrewarded and looked back with bitterness to that time when 'the Chanceler Hide' had preferred 'the Rebells', who had money to buy pardons and places, and depressed the Royal Party, 'who had payd so deare for their Loyalty, that they had nothing left but merit the most ungratefull of all Pretences'.[2] Many passages assert that nothing had really changed with the Restoration. While private life might indeed be more private than under 'the Heaven-drivers',[3] integrity remained a disqualification for public office, with the Test Act 'the most Compendious way to exclude all those that have any Conscience, and to take in Such as have None at all'.[4] While morals were different, at least in outward show, and 'Great Persons' now committed iniquity like Absalom 'upon the Tops of Houses',[5] the libertines were just like the 'saints' in their jealousy of educated men: 'The Modern Fals-doctrine of the Court, That Mens Naturall Parts, are rather impaird then improv'd by Study and Learning, is . . . no more then what the Levellers, and Quakers found out before them'.[6] Butler describes a world in which a man of his kind could expect little attention, and his lists of synonyms on the general theme of

---

[1] For a full account of Butler's life see John Wilders, Introduction to *Hudibras*, Oxford, 1967, pp. xiii–xxi.

[2] p. 197 (and cf. p. 190). According to Aubrey and Wood, Clarendon promised Butler employment, which never materialized (*Brief Lives*, ed. Andrew Clark, 2 vols., Oxford, 1898, i. 136; *Athenæ Oxonienses*, 2 vols., 1721, ii. 452–3).

[3] See pp. 242 and 214.   [4] p. 6.

[5] p. 3.   [6] p. 17.

rejection strike one as genuinely personal statements.[1] A draft letter to an unnamed benefactor reminds us, with its fulsome circumlocutions of gratitude, of the poet's dependence upon patronage.[2]

The holograph folio 232[r] is dated 10 October 1665, and there is no evidence to prove that other prose passages predate this. Butler wrote his Characters in the later 1660s,[3] and the frequent appearance of similar ideas or phrases, together with references to books like Sprat's *History of the Royal Society* (1667), suggests that the bulk of the prose observations date from the same period. In the early 1670s Butler turned his attention to verse satires, completing amongst other poems 'The Elephant in the Moon' and the ode to the memory of Claude Duval. The verse holographs include successive drafts for 'a pretty long Satyr upon the Imperfection and Abuse of human Learning';[4] also a collection of verse passages classified under headings in the same way as the classified prose observations.[5] All this material draws on the prose observations, as do the notes Butler added to *Hudibras* Parts I and II in the revised edition of 1674. Butler then returned to the prose observations, arranged the classified folios, and added further material in a distinctly different hand.[6] These additional passages comprise about a quarter of the total number of prose observations. The last entry that can be dated is a response to Rymer's *Tragedies of the Last Age* (published late summer 1677).[7] Butler had by this time completed the Third Part of *Hudibras*, which was on sale at the end of 1677, and in it he draws substantially on the prose observations and the corresponding verse collection. Only one extant folio looks like working manuscript for the poem,[8] but, as noted above, Thyer collected

---

[1] pp. 244–5 and 255. It adds weight to the tradition of Butler's neglect that Longueville twice writes out the couplet from Otway's Prologue to Lee's *Constantine the Great*: 'To thinke how Spencer dye'd, how Cowly mourn'd, / How Butler's faith and service were Return'd' (*C* [iii[r]], also lower endpaper 2[r]; slightly misquoted).

[2] pp. 242–3 (printed for the first time in this edition).

[3] '*As most of these Characters are dated when they were composed, I can inform the curious, that they were chiefly drawn up from 1667 to 1669*' (Thyer in *GR* II. iv). The extant holographs printed on pp. 237–41 below bear dates in October 1667.

[4] Fos. 90[r]–138[v] *passim*. The description is Thyer's (*GR* i. 202).

[5] Fos. 2[r]–82[r].   [6] See pp. xxxix–xl.

[7] See pp. 184–7. This important passage is badly mangled in Waller's text.

[8] Fo. 139[r] (rejected version of Hudibras's visit to the lawyer).

together a number of related passages, most of which pertain to the Third Part.[1] In suggesting where the prose observations may fit into the literary chronology of Butler's life one of course cannot be certain that passages written out at one time did not originate earlier (unless they contain 'late' allusions). Any classified passage, datable by hand, may be a fair copy of an unknown or at least undatable draft; much unclassified holograph has been lost, and what survives is very hard to date by the less careful handwriting.

Butler's commentary on current affairs, which benefits especially from Longueville's commonplace-book passages, reflects the concerns and prejudices of an intelligent observer who, apart from his contact with Buckingham when the Duke employed him in the early 1670s, appears to have had no special access to political information. Butler fears a strong and secretive nonconformist-republican party waiting to re-enact the 1640s, supported as then by the Scots Presbyterians.[2] He is critical of the Established Church, which has gained no popular support; the only people whose faith the bishops have confirmed are the dissenters.[3] Indeed Butler thinks the bishops eager to re-establish Catholicism 'to insure their Spirituall Dignitys' against 'the generall Il will, and Hatred they have contracted from the People, of all Sorts',[4] and he shows, in a long discussion of the 'Strange Art that Emissary-Priests use in making of Proselytes', that he is ready enough to believe in papist plotting (though he doubts the Catholics can 'turne the Government, as well as Particular Persons').[5] His knowledge of Buckingham's Paris negotiations for the *traité simulé* of 1670 must have suggested the dangers of France, and French religion, which the secret Treaty of Dover had in fact already realized: 'The Interests of the King and his Parliament (though they are really the Same) yet by Factions are renderd so different; that hee is constrain in Reason rather to trust to a Treaty with his most Implacable Enemyes: then Venture a Conference with his great Councell.'[6] Instinctively Butler

---

[1] See p. xxi. There are 44 Third-Part passages and only 8 others.

[2] pp. 205, 216–17. Yet this exaggeration is typical even of better-informed men like Pepys (*Diary*, ed. R. C. Latham and W. Matthews, [11 vols.], 1970– , I, Introduction, cxxviii).

[3] pp. 152, 194   [4] pp. 50–1.   [5] pp. 51–4.

[6] p. 282. Factionalism likewise frustrates religion (p. 32).

supports the Crown, maintaining the king's 'Prerogative to Adjorne, prorogue, or Dissolve Parliaments as oft as hee pleases', and asserting that 'The Lawes of the land that give the King power to make warr doe by Consequence give him power to Raise money to mainteine It'.[1] Butler distrusts the motives of M.P.s who will 'lay downe so great a Stock' to buy election;[2] they supply the king with money 'as usurers use to do yong Heirs, to get a hold upon their Estates'.[3] M.P.s are not competent in matters of state, 'the which such Numbers are as Incapable of understanding as managing', and 'they are not Accountable to the people; by whom they are entrusted for any abuse or breach of Trust'.[4] In fact 'There is nothing in Nature more Arbitrary than a Parliament, and yet', adds Butler (to reveal the paradox), 'there is nothing Else that is able to preserve the Nation from being Govern'd by an Arbitrary Power, and confine Authority within a Limited Compass'.[5]

Butler could look at arbitrary power in action when he visited France in the late summer of 1670 as a member of Buckingham's entourage.[6] He is impressed by the freedom of Paris from robbers and the safety of the highways, but notes the debased currency, heavy taxation, meanness of private buildings, and poor quality of goods for sale. The king's public works have grandeur, but are in their context pretentious. Butler was working for Buckingham in June 1673 in the Duke's capacity as Chancellor of the University of Cambridge, and he may well have retained his secretarial post until Buckingham ceased to be Chancellor in July 1674. Except for the Character 'A Duke of Bucks'—which is comment enough—Butler never mentions his employer by name; yet much of what he writes about Court and politics could be related to the Duke's milieu, as, for example, the remarks on buffoonery in 'A Modern Politician'.[7] It is worth noting that Butler comes closest to the style of a Restoration wit in the verse satires, some with 'long' lines, that he concentrated on during this same period in the early 1670s. Anthony Wood suggests Butler had a hand in *The Rehearsal*;[8] Butler quotes

---

[1] pp. 282, 268. [2] pp. 282–3. [3] p. 163.
[4] pp. 283–4. [5] p. 4.
[6] See pp. 248–53. Others in the group were Buckhurst, Sedley, Thomas Sprat, and the actor Joseph Haines (Bentley, '*Hudibras* Butler Abroad', *MLN* lx (1945), 254).
[7] pp. 219–20. [8] *Athenæ Oxonienses*, 1721, ii. 804.

from the play once,[1] but his manuscripts reveal no parallel passages. The only writer with whom some exchange of ideas can be established is Thomas Shadwell; details from one passage in this edition appear more than once in *The Virtuoso*.[2]

ii

While artistic unity is not to be expected in a commonplace collection, there are controlling ideas more or less explicit in these (as in other) writings of Butler's. There is the sense of Nature as a living organism, sharing with its constituent parts the pattern of infancy, maturity, and decay; for 'The Ages of the world are like those of Men'.[3] Butler can look at everything in these terms so that, for example, 'Governments like Natural Bodies have their times of growing Perfection and Declining' and 'All Innovations in Church and State are like new-built Houses, unwholesome to live in, untill they are made healthful, and agreable by time.'[4] The instinct for analogy is essential not just to Butler's witty style, but to his vision of a universe 'every Part of which ha's so rationall a Relation to every other in particular, and the whole in generall; That though it consist of innumerable Pieces and Joynts, there is not the least Flaw imaginable in the whole'.[5] The ultimate guarantor of such a universe is 'the Divine wisdome', which drew a copy of itself in 'the Order of Nature'. From that same 'Divine wisdome' proceeds 'The Original of Reason'.

The human mind is incapable of comprehending God's essence: 'only as hee is a Creator . . . does hee descend to our Capacities', and 'if wee will venture farther. . . wee cheate ourselves with negatives: and Believe wee can discover what God is by telling what hee is not . . . and call Him Immateriall, Immortall, Infinite, &c'.[6]

---

[1] p. 287.
[2] p. 89, l.30–p. 90. l.3; *The Virtuoso*, I. ii, IV. iii, in *Works*, ed. Montague Summers, 5 vols., 1927, iii. 113, 159–60. Shadwell was a pallbearer at Butler's funeral. He must surely be the subject of Butler's poem 'To Thomas . . .' (B 88ʳ; *Satires*, ed. Lamar, p. 146).
[3] p. 203.   [4] pp. 113, 35.
[5] p. 66. For a concise discussion of the 'analogical world-view' see W. R. Elton in *A New Companion to Shakespeare Studies*, ed. Kenneth Muir and S. Schoenbaum, Cambridge, 1971, pp. 180–8.
[6] p. 274.

Hence 'Divinity is a Speculative Science of Finding out Reasons for things that are not within the Reach of Reason, and therefore it multiplys into so many Differences of Opinions, according to the various Tempers of mens wits, and understandings'.[1] This dangerous, disputatious folly, which leads to sectarian violence, is matched only by the *naïveté* of visionaries—Cardan, Nicholas Flammel, Ramón Lull, and other illuminati—who pretend, like Ralpho in *Hudibras*, to transcend the limitations of their faculties by refusing to exercise them at all (like Democritus, 'who is sayd to have put out his own eies, that he might contemplate the better').[2] In Butler's belief, 'the Opinions, and Judgments of Men can have no better, nor other Foundation then that of Nature, from whence they are, or should be derived',[3] and there are ill consequences to pretending otherwise: 'Preaching masters perpetually Cry down Nature . . . and Defame her to arrogate and take to themselves, and their Trade all that is good and virtuous of Gods making.'[4] The antinomian 'Godly' carry dualism a stage further and 'will not admit that Grace and Morality should be the same, . . . Grace in their sense being nothing but a Dispensation for the Defect of Morall virtue'.[5]

When he rejects men's attempts to deal directly, whether by logic or by inspiration, with some higher reality Butler is at one with Sprat and his fellow apologists for the New Science. So too when he asserts that the proper study of a Christian is Nature; 'For that very Inquiry into Nature; the further It goes, will at length bring the most obstinate in spight of their Hearts to an acknowledgment of a first Intelligent Cause: and that is God.'[6] This inquiry proceeds from general agreement about the physical properties of the external world: 'Among so many Millions of Errors, and Mistakes, as are to be found among Authors, I do not remember any one that is grounded upon the Deceit or Misreport of Sense'.[7] Like Locke, Butler finds the real problem of human understanding in our manipulation of ideas rather than in the validity of the initial sense data. The mind must sort together its simple ideas, 'For in the first

[1] p. 212. [2] p. 203. Cf. p. 80 on epicurean chance.
[3] p. 80. See also pp. 7-8. [4] pp. 43-4.
[5] p. 44. [6] p. 273. [7] p. 127.

Characters and single elements of the Creation, we cannot so perfectly read God, as we can where those letters are joynd together, and become words and Sense, as they do in the Rational Distribution of all the Parts of Nature'.[1] The choice of metaphor is significant; for Butler's epistemology corresponds to his theory of literature, the two being brought together in the substantial and crucial passage which begins the section on Reason. The first part of the passage reads:

Reason Is a Faculty of the Minde, whereby she put's the Notions, and Images of things (with their operations, effects, and circumstances) that are confusd in the understanding, into the same order and condition, in which they are really disposd by Nature, or event: The Right Performance of this is cald Truth, to which Reason naturally tend's in a direct line, although she sometime miscarry, and faile by the Subtlety of the Object, or her own Imperfection, and that we call error or Falshood.[2]

Unfortunately 'most men know less then they might, by attempting to know more then they can'; 'There is no Ignorance so Impertinent as that which proceeds from Curiosity and over-understanding of any thing'.[3] Men are fatally in love with their own notions, unwarily confounding those 'Pictures of things in the Imagination' with 'their originals in Nature'.[4] Symptomatic of this is the arbitrary use of language: 'Men commonly in the world have noe regard for thinges how considerable soever, but highly afect words and names that serve only to expresse them . . . And when they undertake to give a Reason for any thing believe they have performd it sufficiently as soone as they have put it into other, though lesse significant expressions . . . Soe when they would redresse any Publique supposd inconvenience, as soone as they have chang'd the Names and outward formalities, believe the Busnes is done'.[5] And the business is done, at least to the extent that 'Nonsense is as well proof against contradiction as Demonstration is, for no man can say more against that which he do's not understand,

---

[1] p. 66.
[2] p. 65. From this Butler proceeds to a definition of wit, which is discussed on p. xxxvi.   [3] pp. 10, 301.
[4] p. 15. Hudibras has this failing (*Hudibras*, I. i. 139–42).
[5] pp. 168–9.

then against that which is manifest'.[1] Only lawyers make the most of nonsense; the other learned professions are handicapped by the delusion that their jargons have some meaning.[2] Writers who 'have the unhappines, or rather Prodigious Vanity to affect an obscurity in their Stiles' resemble 'Fooles and Madmen [that] use to talke to themselves in Publique'; but they seldom miss 'the Admiration of the weake and Ignorant, who are apt to contemne whatsoever they can understand, and admire any thing that they cannot'.[3]

The holograph section on Religion is longer than any other, and religious matters pervade Butler's manuscripts as a whole. His emphasis is on Christian morality and, consistent with that, on rational theology.[4] He adopts the objective scale of certainty suggested by Hooker and insisted upon by William Chillingworth: 'no man can believe any thing but because he do's not know it' and 'the lesse any man knowes the more he hath to believe'.[5] Human perversity will of course prefer belief to knowledge precisely because it is subjective and notional, but 'They that tell us we must lay by reason in matters of Fayth, forget that nothing but reason can tell them soe'. Reason, or 'some implicit thing like reason', must be 'the Ground and foundation of [belief], else noe man living can give an accompt why he is rather of one fayth then another'.[6] This is not to insist on logical proof; for nothing really useful can be demonstrated. 'Inferences, and Inductions, if they are true and Certaine, are commonly of things slight, and Insignificant: But if of thinges Abstruse, and Remote, as often Doubtful and Insignificant themselves'.[7] So the disillusioned sceptic or fideist 'put's out his eies because he cannot [see] so wel as he would'; he rejects probability because, 'like one that squint's', it looks 'severall ways at once'. Butler argues that probability is 'the effect of Reason and discourse' and therefore 'of a nobler Nature then mere Opinion, or implicit Credulity'.[8]

---

[1] p. 8.
[2] On lawyers see pp. 178–9.
[3] pp. 131–2.
[4] Butler's rationalism is anti-Puritan; but he is, first of all, a Protestant, who asserts against the Catholics that good works are 'but an effect' of 'Faith in the Merits of Christ' (p. 49). Yet he can take a broad view of worship—pious intention is what matters, not the form (p. 195).
[5] p. 67.   [6] p. 236.   [7] p. 139.
[8] p. 8.

Just as 'Demonstration is the proper Buss'nes of Knowledg', so is
'Probability of Beliefe, and as there is no certaine Knowledg without Demonstration, so there is no Safe belief without Probability'.[1]
It remains, however, that in questions of the greatest importance
probability may rest on no more than an analogy—like that
between death and birth which suggests to Butler the soul's immortality.[2]

This physico-theology is quite unspecific when it speaks of
nature's 'regular operations'. Particular 'natural questions' seem to
occupy another part of Butler's mind, where the answers given
show little scientific originality. There Butler takes for granted the
traditional theories of elements, of form and matter, of generation
and corruption, and his arguments with Aristotelians are arguments
of emphasis or detail conducted within the encompassing theo-
retical framework, much as Scaliger had argued with Cardan in the
previous century. Butler seems to forget about his own restrictive
theory of knowledge and his disparagement of inference (so vigor-
ously expressed in the attacks on School logic); his theology may be
rational, yet his science is frequently credulous. He was, of course,
one of those men whose middle years had been of necessity preoccupied with politics and religion. He would not, unless perhaps
he had studied medicine, have felt much pressure to rethink the
first principles of a science, whereas in theology that pressure had
been upon every educated man since the Reformation. Even among
professed scientists the secularization of epistemology was still
uncompleted when Butler died. What he says of Bacon, 'not so
much a Naturall Philosopher as a Naturall Historian', could be
said even better of some early contributors to the *Philosophical
Transactions*.[3] The behaviour, and prose style, of a man like
Charleton would have convinced Butler in his natural conservative
distrust of virtuosi. Butler mocks them as fools. He seems compara-
tively unperturbed about the moral implications of their revived
epicureanism; indeed *De Rerum Natura* is an 'excellent poem',
though more perhaps for Lucretius' comments on human psy-
chology than his philosophy and science.[4] As for the planetary

---

[1] p. 9.   [2] p. 211.
[3] p. 280.   [4] See pp. 229, 127.

system, Butler is inclined to think the sun at the centre, but he doubts it can be proven either way.[1]

iii

Much of Butler's activity is in the collection of analogical material: anecdotes and observations which, while not necessarily true or consistent in themselves, will realize satiric truth when yoked as similes to the plain topical statements of a poem or Character. For example: as the heavens' motions may really be earthly, so too may men's heavenly motives.[2] What Butler looks for in his reading is suggested by the two miscellany headings that he uses, 'Contradictions' and 'Inconsistant Opinions'. Perhaps the greatest part of all the manuscript material could be called 'contradictory' or paradoxical. Some paradoxes are simply inherent in the human condition: nature has given beasts leisure without capacity for contemplation, man that capacity without leisure; men of parts lack application, industrious men lack intelligence. More often some degree of human wilfulness is implied: misers accumulate what they cannot enjoy; soldiers, who earn most dangerously, spend most freely; the worst men make the best gaolers; the best saints are made of the worst sinners; the more false a religion is, the more piety it produces; 'No man can possibly do another so much Hurt as hee that ha's oblig'd him.' There are paradoxes of government: monarchy is in practice more a commonwealth, commonwealth more a monarchy; Roman dominion expanded because of an imperfect constitution; armies break the peace to preserve it; princes are governed by their vassals, as masters are by their servants; the reign of St. Louis was more pernicious to his subjects than the reigns of vicious French kings. Behind many paradoxes is the idea that 'extremes use to meet', so that the greatest miseries grow out of the greatest felicities, and conscience 'which at first was nothing but Tendernesse and selfe preservation in time becomes the Greatest Inhumanity in the world to all others'. Whatever is contrary to nature will work against itself and bring on its own proper retribution, 'For Gods Judgments commonly pay men's Crimes in Kind . . . And though wee doe not presently perceive th'effect of

<hr />

[1] See pp. 289, 94–5.   [2] p. 278.

Bad Actions, more then every moment the Growth of a plant; yett they never stand still but evry minute ads something to their encrease; untill at length they produce the fruites to which they were by the Lawes of nature first condemnd.'[1] Butler illustrates the even-handedness of these judgements from the case of those Londoners who, having run away from the Plague, had their houses burnt down by the Fire.[2]

Men are subject to the laws of nature and yet themselves unnatural (as is shown by comparison with the beasts, which 'never meddle beyond their latitude'). Attempts to explain matters invariably compound the contradictions because the innate inconsistencies of the mind assert themselves in abstract thought. The folly of philosophers has, nevertheless, its entertainment value, and Butler introduces one collection of illogical rationalizations with the admission that 'It is not unpleasant to observe how inconsistant the Opinions of the world are, to them selves, and how all Sorts of men doe not only act but say, things cleane Contrary to what they pretend and meane.'[3] Yet this may well be the only pleasure available to the wise, that is moderate men of 'the middle sort', attentive to truth, 'which always lies in *the Mean*'.[4] They are disregarded by the world, which is run by knaves and fools,[5] and their deprivations prompt the question whether they truly are wise. Butler therefore distinguishes 'two sorts of wisemen in the world, the one is of those that are wise in their Tempers, that governe their Actions with a kinde of Prudent Instinct without understanding the reason (unless it be implicitly) of what they doe, and those commonly prosper, and live happily in the world: The other sort is of those that understand the reasons perfectly of all things that concerne themselves, and others, but by the unhappiness of their Temper, cannot prevayle with themselvs to make those advantages of their knowledg and understanding, which other men easily doe without it.'[6] Butler writes, and lived, as one of the latter sort.

The best way to restrain men 'from the Ruine of one another' is 'to make use of their Passions'.[7] Writing, like ruling, requires some subterfuge and equivocation; in that practical sense Butler sees it

---

[1] pp. 288–9.   [2] p. 41.   [3] p. 228.   [4] See p. 4. Cf. p. 14.
[5] See pp. 11, 16.   [6] p. 171.   [7] p. 68.

as rhetorical. Formal rhetoric he condemns along with other arts that have lost sight of the end in their preoccupation with the means,[1] but he does work out a basic theory of his own literary practice. In the first passage of the section on Reason he explains that between truth and falsehood (which he has just defined)

> ly's the Proper Sphere of wit, which though it seeme to incline to falshood, do's it only to give Intelligence to Truth. For as there is a Trick in Arithmetique, By giving a False Number, to finde out a True one, So wit by a certaine slight of the Minde, deliver's things otherwise then they are in Nature, by rendring them greater or lesse then they are in Nature, by rendring them greater or lesse then they really are (which is cald Hyperbole) or by putting them into some other Condition then Nature ever did (as when the Performances of Sensible, and Rationall Beings are applyd to Senseles and Inanimate things, with which the writings of Poets abound) . . .[2]

These false assertions of identity or similarity will relate to nature in such ways as to make the true correspondences manifest. There is no suggestion that a poet's lies are in any way the truths of a golden world; one would scarcely expect that from Butler. Wit and fancy remain, in the familiar metaphor, 'but the Cloaths, and Ornaments of Judgment'.[3] The best dress is the plainest, if 'the excellency of the Sense will beare it'; otherwise lace and embroidery are needed to 'disguise the naturall homeliness of the thing'. Whatever the style, there is no discussing it without reference to content; 'For as Stile is Nothing (as it is taken) but a proper naturall and Significant way of expressing our Conceptions in words, and as it agree's or disagree's with those is either good or Bad; So he that take's it for Good or Bad of it self is very much mistaken'.[4] Moreover, 'Those who imploy their studies only upon Fancy and words, do commonly abate as much in their Reason, and Judgments, as they improve the other way',[5] and this enfeebling preoccupation with expression is apparent to Butler in most of the writing he dislikes: verse plays (especially French ones), 'regular' dramas on the

---

[1] See pp. 136–7, 128, 133. Butler sees an absurdity in the teaching of arts through foreign languages; if the Greek authors excelled it was precisely because 'they had but one language to lay out their witt and Ingenuity upon' (p. 258).

[2] p. 65.   [3] p. 58.   [4] p. 144.   [5] p. 69.

Greek model, 'Romances made on the Scripture', quibbling verses with outmoded puns (or the newfangled turns introduced by Waller), Donne's poems with their random key-changes, and Montaigne's essays with their tipsy impulsiveness.[1] Butler is distrustful of verbal facility, and his own work drafting and revising must have strengthened the conviction that 'The greatest Difficulties are performd by Patience and Industry, not Quicknes of wit.'[2] Jonson was thus able to surpass Shakespeare, just as Virgil had done Ovid.[3]

Butler was of course only one of many professed enemies to the imagination. Like Swift, however, he brings to his attack the animus of a man who knew what imagination was:

When the Imagination is Broken loose from the obedience of Reason, it become's the most disorderd and ungovernd thing in the world: It cheate's the Senses, and rayses the Passions to that prodigious height, that the Strength of the Body (as if it gaind what the Minde loose's) become's more then treble to what it was before. It transport's a man beyond himself, and do's things so far beside the ordinary Course of Nature, and the understanding of the wisest, that as if they had lost their wits too by contagion, it often passe's for possessions of the Devill.[4]

Butler recognizes the creative power of emotion, and he does so, fittingly, in a long part-ironic discussion of malice as the main-spring of satire: 'There is nothing that provokes and sharpens wit like Malice, and Anger si Natura negat facit Indignatio &c And hence perhaps came the first occasion of calling those Raptures Poeticall Fury. . . .'[5] Acknowledging as it does the paradoxes of the mind, Butler's opinion of his art is not inflated or pretentious. A satire as 'a kinde of Knight Errant' is a quixotic anachronism, well meaning but not worldly wise.[6] 'Poetry is a thing that passes in the world upon It's good behaviour. It is like taking of Tobacco or Drinking of Coffee which men doe at first for Company and retaine afterwards by Custome. It is no staple Commodity but passes only

[1] See pp. 138, 253, 248, 146, 184–7, 179, 144, 248, 131, 139.
[2] p. 84.   [3] p. 128.
[4] p. 68. Cf. Swift, *A Tale of a Tub*, ix, in *Prose Writings*, ed. Herbert Davis, 14 vols., Oxford, 1939–68, i. 108–9.
[5] pp. 59–61.   [6] pp. 215–16.

among Those that take it and meetes with as Few that judge rightly of it as all those things doe that have no measure nor weight but fancy to bee examined by.'[1]

Butler's humour is the humour of disillusionment. Yet for all his misanthropy, Butler's prose of the 1660s and 1670s shows a lively and inquiring mind. It shows a further range of reading and observation beyond what we see in *Hudibras*, and while Butler's concerns were in many ways typical of his time, the familiar becomes distinctive when handled by (in Thyer's phrase) 'a writer of so extraordinary and uncommon a turn'. For the student of literature the manuscript prose has a further special interest as the groundwork of composition; for in the corresponding verse drafts prose passages are reshaped and polished for use in future poems. It is hoped that a volume of the manuscript verse, in which that process will be illustrated, will complete the publication of this significant and substantial collection of a major seventeenth-century author's papers.

[1] p. 280.

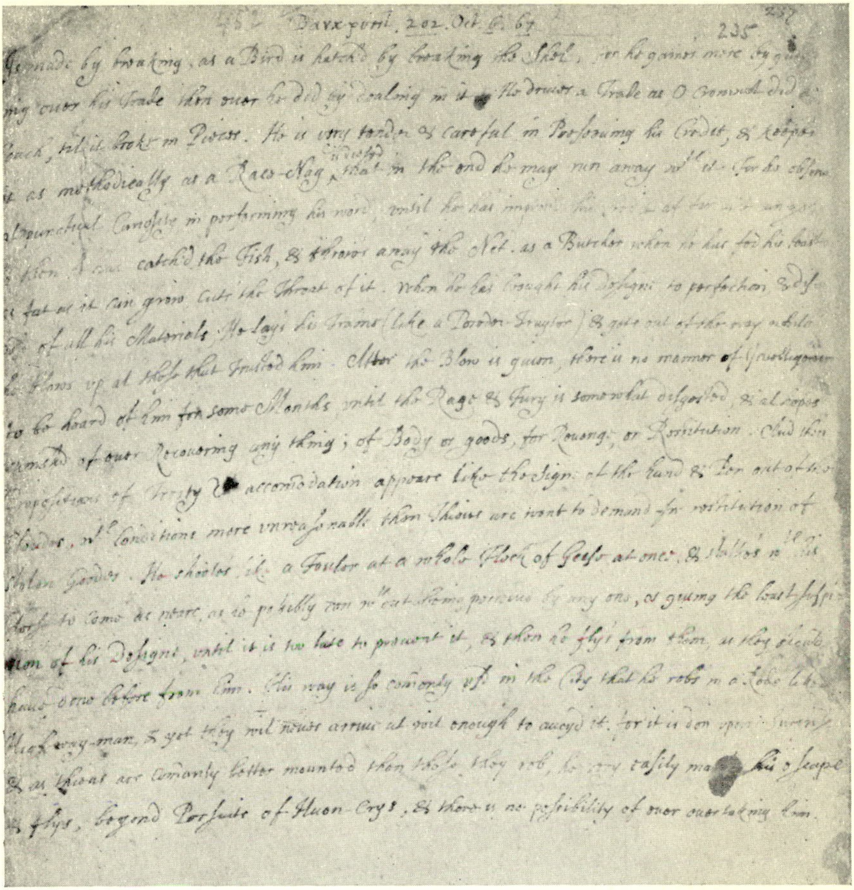

PLATE I. 'Character of a Bankrupt'. Holograph in British Library Add. MS. 32625, fo. 235ʳ.

PLATE II (*overleaf*). From 'Criticismes upon Bookes and Authors'. Holograph in British Library Add. MS. 32625, fo. 202ᵛ. Written in Butler's earlier hand A with the final paragraph added in his later hand B using the sickle-tailed *g* in the words 'managed' and 'agreed'. Marginal notes by Willia   Longueville; crosses by Robert Thyer to mark selections for the *Genuine Remains*.m

p. 2.

He comits as great a fault in Chronologie when in the last two lines of his 8th Satyr he supposes Agamemnon might have taken Methridate above a hundred years before it was in being.

Satyrical wit may seeme to be the most pleasant of all other: Men can not laugh heartily without shewing their Teeth, & therefore the French call a Satyr Dent rant.

Bull & Mistake is not the worst sort of Nonsense for that may proceed from Ingagitance, or Diversion by somthing else: But Metaphysicq or that Nonsense, that is derived from Study & Consideration is the more desperate, as Hippocrates says Sad & Studious Madnes is more in curable, then that which is froliq & Carelesse:

Inferences & Inductions, if they are true & certaine, are commonly of thinges slight, & Insignificant: But if of thinges Abstruse, & Remote, as often Doubtful & Insignificant themselves: & so both waies for the most part serve to very little Purpose.

The virtuosi affect Subtletys & Curiosities in Nature, as Priests do in Divinity, & Lawyers in doing Iustice or Injury.

There are Some Authors that write for fame only: & never have it. That thinke it below them to take Money for their writings, because no body will give it. When all ye Proudest of Professions submit to meaner offices to earne Money. The Divine will not trouble himself to save, or Damne any Soul, unless he is wel pay'd: & then he is indifferent The Physician takes money for writing a recipe whether it Kill or Cure: And the Lawyer will not Draw one Line, nor speake one word whether it preserve or undoe untill he is wel feed for it.

Mons. Mountaigne the Essayist seemes when he wrote to have been either a little warmd wth wine, or Naturally Hotheaded.

All Controversies & Disputations are managed by Polemiq writers, like the Duell between two Rivalls in the Comedy, who had but one sword between them both which they agreed to use by turnes, & he that had it first was to run at the other, who was ingag'd to stand fair, & receive his Thrust, & after to do the same to him again:

Money.

PLATE II (*see caption overleaf*).

TEXTUAL INTRODUCTION

I. *The Prose Folios of Butler's Manuscript*

As explained above in the first section of the Introduction, Butler's manuscript (*B*), B.L. Add. 32625, is all that remains of the holograph compositions bequeathed by the poet to William Longueville. The uncompleted English–French dictionary is of present interest only for Longueville's entries on other folios of that manuscript book, accordingly termed Longueville's commonplace book (*C*) and separately described below.[1] Robert Thyer's transcripts (*T*), B.L. Add. 32626, have been mentioned above,[2] but they contribute nothing to the present text, as they are solely of verse and Characters.

The British Museum bought Butler's manuscript as a bound folio volume in November 1885. Beyond the inference that it was in generally poor condition, no further information about the volume's appearance can be given; in 1964 the leaves were disbound and laminated, then re-bound, mounted on guards, with new boards and covers. If two, or more, pairs of conjunct leaves had previously been gathered, the repairer would need to disjoin the outer pair so that the inner pair could be pasted to a guard. The now disjunct outer leaves would be pasted each to a different guard. There would be no alternative to disjoining leaves, as the old folio order had to be kept.

The prose takes up the latter part of Butler's manuscript; the first 139 folios are largely devoted to verse drafts. Butler worked at the prose in two distinct phases, distinguished by a change in his handwriting.[3] The later hand is smaller and more upright, the letters are not so full and rounded—they are more angular—and the ink is normally much darker and blacker. It is further characterized by the frequent use of a miniscule *g* with a sickle-shaped

---

[1] pp. lv–lx.   [2] pp. xix, xxi.
[3] See pp. xxvi–xxvii, and, for further discussion of the manuscript, de Quehen in *Editing Seventeenth Century Prose*, pp. 73 ff.

tail similar to the tail of the abbreviated -*que* termination which scarcely ever occurs in the earlier hand except in the word *Ægypt*. More subtle variations, mainly in the earlier hand, may be observed in the manuscript and have been taken into account in determining the original arrangement of the folios: for example, the gradation of a more florid formal style in which Butler begins classified groupings into a more hurried working hand. In the rough notes of the unclassified section letters are not carefully formed, and it is not easy to make the earlier–later hand distinction.

The present arrangement of the prose folios is not the original one; so some detailed analysis of the manuscript is necessary. The table on the following pages shows the original pairings of the prose folios before they were rearranged and numbered in the order in which they stand in the British Library manuscript. It is this original arrangement which has, as far as possible, been reconstructed and adopted for the present edition. The two lines allowed in the table for each folio give palaeographical details of the recto and verso of each folio. The folio dimensions and characteristics of the paper are also given.

The first three prose folios (141–3) comprise an eighteenth-century transcriber's list of contents and brief passages he abstracted from lost originals which have been mentioned above. The title [Sundry Thoughts], which was added by Waller, is here retained in square brackets. The sixty-nine folios which follow (144–205) were put together by Butler in thirteen classified groupings: 'Learning and Knowledge', etc. It is within this section that eleven folios have been rearranged for the present edition into their original order, as far as that may be reconstructed. The last thirty-one folios (206–36) are miscellaneous with no inherent order to prompt rearrangement. Except for those of Characters, the headings are unspecific,[1] and the papers and hands are as diverse as the topics of the entries. There are fifteen different watermarks, and only one of them is familiar from the earlier classified prose. Six folios are

---

[1] The only headings Butler uses here are 'Contradictions', on fo. 206 (recto and verso), and 'Inconsistant Opinions', on fos. 232^r, 232^v, and 233^r. 'Inconsistant Opinions' is written in Greek characters, and on fo. 232^v it appears as 'Incongrue and Inconsistant Opinions'. Of the Characters only the four on fos. 235–6 are headed (in the same pseudo-Greek).

wholly or partly taken up by Characters, and nine others are neatly written in an identifiable early or late hand. The rest are of rough notes, in which the date of the hand is especially hard to determine. Some folios, however, were headed with a date by Butler,[1] and further evidence may be gathered from the passages themselves.[2] So, although the evidence on several of the roughly written ones is slighter than one would wish, folios 206–36 can usefully be dated, like the classified ones, early or late with a break coming between at the beginning of the 1670s. The last five folios in the following table are from the earlier part of Butler's manuscript, which is mostly of verse, but as these folios 84^r, 1^r, 86^r, 87^r, and 89^v are exclusively of prose, they are included in this volume, whereas the verse drafts on folio 217^v are excluded from this and reserved for a verse volume.

At the left of the table, solid-line braces link pairs of folios still joined together as single sheets; broken-line braces link separated pairs. Additional folios, blank and subsequently detached, are conjectured to account for unpaired folios in the classified groupings. Col. I shows the British Library foliation, with folios lacking text (and therefore not numbered) designated by the previous folio's number and an asterisk (151*); col. II, numeration by William Longueville; col. III, the division between Butler's earlier hand (**A** for text, **a** for page heading) and later hand (**B** for text, **b** for page heading);[3] col. IV, the number of manuscript lines per page, an asterisk indicating a page only partly filled (fo. 151^v: 28*); col. V, the combined width of the side margins, then the depth of the top margin, each to the nearest centimetre (fo. 146^r: 6–2); col. VI, folio dimensions in millimetres, measured at the widest sections, but averaging out the minor variations of the deckle; col. VII, the

---

[1] Fos. 232^{r,v} (10 and 14 Oct. 1665), 233^r (4 Feb. 1666), 235^r–236^v (6–13 Oct. 1667).

[2] Folios are 'late' which postdate named events or publications in the mid 1670s: fos. 215^v (Burnet's *Relation of a Conference*, 1676), 218^r–219^r (Rymer's *Tragedies of the Last Age*, 1677), 220^r (Clarendon's death, 1674). Folios are 'early' from which passages were transcribed on classified folios written in early handwriting: fos. 212^r, 214^r, 217^v.

[3] In those unclassified folios where the two hands cannot be distinguished, quotation marks around 'A' or 'B' denote rough handwriting dating, according to other evidence, from the respective A or B period.

watermark or countermark (CM), details of each mark being given in the footnotes at the end of the table.[1] The placing of the entries in col. VII corresponds with the mould side of the paper.

I B.L. fo.	II W.L.'s no.	III hand	IV lines per page	V margin size (cm)	VI paper size (mm)	VII watermark or countermark (CM)
[Sundry Thoughts]						
141			16★		314×201	
			—			CM[a]
⌈142			42		317×199	
			42			CM[a]
⌊143			41		317×196	pro patria[a]
			43			
Learning & Knowledge						
⌈146		Aa	34	6–2	313×203	horn[b]
		Ab	34	5–2		
⌊147		Ab	33	6–1	313×201	
		Ab/B	32	5–2		
⌈144		Ab	30	5–2	315×199	
		Aa	35	5–2		
⌊145		Aa	31	5–2	315×198	horn[c]
		Aa/B	30	4–2		
⌈148		Bb	38	5–3	311×196	coat of arms[d]
		Bb	40	4–2		
⌊149		Bb	40	4–2	312×196	
		Bb	33★	4–2		CM[d]
Truth & Falshood						
⌈150	14	Aa	32	7–2	314×199	
	15	Ab	32	6–2		
⌈151	16	Ab	34	5–2	315×201	horn[c]
	17	Aa/B	28★	5–2		
⌊151★		b			315×200	
		b				
⌊...?						

[1] The footnotes cite by serial number the corresponding tracings in Edward Heawood, *Watermarks, Mainly of the 17th and 18th Centuries*, Hilversum, 1950. Where no specific correspondence can be indicated, reference may be made by the name of the mark to that class of marks in Heawood. The dimensions of a mark (in millimetres) are given with relation to the chain lines, the dimension which crosses them being recorded in brackets [18], and the distances from the extremities of the mark to the adjacent chain lines outside the brackets: 4[18]1. Where one or more chain lines pass through the mark, their positions are indicated by division of the measurement in brackets: [21/12] or [9/24/9]. For more detailed explanation of chain-space measurement see Allan Stevenson, 'Paper as Bibliographical Evidence', *Library*, 5th ser., xvii (1962), 200, and G. T. Tanselle, 'The Bibliographical Description of Paper', *Studies in Bibliography*, xxiv (1971), 46–7. Two pairs of twin watermarks are identifiable in Butler's prose folios; they are described in the footnotes under 'b' and '*b*', and 'c' and '*c*', respectively.

I B.L. fo.	II W.L.'s no.	III hand	IV lines per page	V margin size (cm)	VI paper size (mm)	VII watermark or countermark (CM)
Religion						
152	1	Aa	33	4–3	312 × 200	horn[b]
		Ab	36	4–2		
153	2	Ab	34	4–2	313 × 198	
		Ab	35	4–2		
159	8	Aa	36	7–2	313 × 197	
		Ab	33	5–2		
154	3	Ab	32	6–2	314 × 199	
		Ab	33	6–2		horn[b]
155	4	Aa	35	5–2	315 × 201	
		Ab	33	5–2		
156	5	Aa	34	5–2	314 × 200	
		Aa	35	5–2		horn[c]
157	6	Aa	32	4–2	315 × 200	
		Ab	32	4–2		
158	7	Ab	33	4–2	313 × 198	horn[c]
		Bb	39	4–2		
163	12	Bb	41	4–2	307 × 200	
		Bb	38	4–2		
160	9	Bb	42	5–2	307 × 198	horn[e]
		Bb	40	6–2		
161	10	Bb	39	5–2	303 × 198	horn[e]
		Bb	39	4–1		
162	11	Bb	39	4–2	307 × 197	
		Bb	42	4–2		
164	13	Bb	23*	5–3	306 × 198	
		–				
164*		–			307 × 198	
		–				horn[e]
Wit & Folly						
165		Bb	39	4–2	306 × 198	horn[e]
		Bb	35	5–2		
166		Bb	25*	4–2	307 × 198	horn[e]
		Bb	42	4–2		
167		Bb	16*	4–2	307 × 197	
		–				
....?						
Ignorance						
168		Bb	36	5–2	303 × 196	
		Bb	36	4–2		
168*		–			305 × 196	
		–				horn[e]
Reason						
169	11	Aa	32	6–3	314 × 200	
		Ab	34	4–2		
170	12	Ab	32	6–2	314 × 198	
		Ab	32	6–2		horn[b]

I B.L. fo.	II W.L.'s no.	III hand	IV lines per page	V margin size (cm)	VI paper size (mm)	VII watermark or countermark (CM)
Reason (*cont.*)						
171	13	Bb b	30★	4–2	316×199	
171★		b			316×200	
		b				horn^c
Virtue & Vice						
174		Aa	33	6–2	313×200	horn^b
		Ab	35	7–2		
175		Aa	33	5–2	314×198	horn^c
		Aa	28	5–2		
172		Aa/B	35	5–3	315×202	
		Bb	21★	6–2		
173		Bb	42	6–3	313×198	
		–				
Opinion						
176		Aa	34	6–3	314×204	horn ^b
		Ab	34	6–2		
177		Bb b	34★	5–2	312×197	coat of arms^d
177★		b			312×196	
		b				CM^d
?						
Nature						
182		Aa	32	6–4	313×200	horn^b
		Aa	36	4–1		
179		Ab	33	5–2	315×200	
		Ab	32	5–2		
178		Aa	33	6–2	313×202	horn^b
		Ab	35	6–2		
183		Aa	32	6–2	314×199	
		Ab	34	5–2		
180		Aa	33	5–2	313×196	CM^d
		Ab	33	5–3		
181		Ab/B	40	5–2	313×196	
		Bb	41	4–2		coat of arms^d
184		Bb	40	5–2	311×201	
		Bb	27★	5–2		
?						
History						
187		Aa	35	3–3	312×198	horn^b
		Ab	36	3–2		
185		Ab	36	4–2	314×200	
		Ab	34	4–2		
186		Ab	32	5–2	314×200	
		Bb	29★	3–2		
186★		a b			316×199	horn^c

I B.L. fo.	II W.L.'s no.	III hand	IV lines per page	V margin size (cm)	VI paper size (mm)	VII watermark or countermark (CM)
History (*cont.*)						
⌈188		Ab/B	32	4–2	311×197	CM[d]
		Bb	13*	5–2		
⌊188*		b			310×198	
		b				coat of arms[d]
Physique						
⌈189		Bb	33*	4–2	305×197	
⌊..?		–				
Princes & Government						
⌈193		Aa	35	7–2	312×198	
		Ab	33	5–2		
⌊190		Ab	32	6–3	313×199	
		Ab	30	5–2		horn[b]
⌈191		Ab	32	6–3	315×203	
		Ab/B	34	6–2		
⌊192		Ba	38	4–3	315×197	horn[c]
		Bb	37	5–3		
⌈194		Ab/B	33	6–2	310×196	CM[d]
		Ab/B	36	6–2		
⌊195		Bb	42	6–2	315×195	
		Bb	5*	5–2		coat of arms[d]
Criticismes upon Bookes and Authors						
196	1	Aa	33	6–2	313×198	
		Aa	29	5–2		horn[b]
197	2	Ab	33	6–2	313×201	
		Aa	31	5–2		horn[b]
198	3	Aa	32	5–2	313×201	
		Ab	35	5–2		horn[b]
199	4	Ab	35	5–2	313×200	
		Aa	34	4–2		
200	5	Aa	33	6–2	314×200	
		Ab	32	5–2		
201	6	Aa	33	5–2	313×197	
		Aa	30	5–2		
⌈202	7	Ab	34	5–2	314×201	
		Aa/B	34	6–2		
⌈203	8	Bb	44	4–2	315×199	
		Bb	41	4–2		
⌊204	9	Bb	40	4–2	314×198	
		Bb	41	4–2		horn[c]
⌊205	10	Bb	7*	4–2	314×198	
		b				horn[c]
Unclassified Observations						
⌈206		Bb	38	5–2	288×191	
		Bb	40	5–2		
⌊207		B	36	5–2	289×190	
		B	39	4–1		horn[f]

I B.L. fo.	II W.L.'s no.	III hand	IV lines per page	V margin size (cm)	VI paper size (mm)	VII watermark or countermark (CM)
Unclassified Observations (*cont.*)						
⌐208		'B'	37	nil	292 × 181	
		'B'	39	,,		
⌐209		'B'	37	,,	293 × 186	pot[g]
		'B'	36	,,		
⌐210		'B'	39	,,	308 × 193	
		'B'	40	,,		
⌐211		'B'	41	,,	309 × 192	horn[h]
		'B'	40	,,		
⌐212		'A'	37	,,	306 × 192	hat[i]
		'A'	36	,,		
⌐213		'A'	37	,,	306 × 190	
		'A'	39	,,		
214		'Aa'	36	2–1	304 × 198	
		'Aa'	38	2–2		
215		'B'	37	nil	298 × 198	fleur-de-lis[j]
		'B'	39	,,		
216		'B'	43	,,	296 × 177	coat of arms[k]
		'B'	40	,,		
217		'Aa'	38	,,	305 × 197	letters[l]
		–	[verse]			
⌐218		'B'	34	nil	275 × 177	grapes[m]
		'B'	34	,,		
⌐219		'B'	38	,,	273 × 173	
		'B'	37	,,		
⌐220		'B'	42	,,	306 × 196	
		B	39	,,		horn[e]
⌐221		B	39	,,	306 × 195	
		B	43	,,		
⌐222		'B'	43	,,	300 × 189	horn[n]
		'B'	43	,,		
⌐223		'B'	40	,,	300 × 188	
		'B'	42	,,		
⌐224		B	43	,,	311 × 197	CM[o]
		B	47	,,		
⌐225		B	43	,,	311 × 196	
		B	46	,,		horn[o]
⌐226		B	39	,,	310 × 198	
		B	42	,,		CM[o]
⌐227		B	43	,,	312 × 198	horn[o]
		B	42	,,		
228		B	39	4–2	313 × 194	
		B	40	4–2		
229		B	22★	5–2	314 × 195	fleur-de-lis[p]
		–				
⌐230	200	'A'	36	nil	296 × 189	pot[q]
	197	'A'	33	,,		
⌐231	198	'A'	35	,,	296 × 186	
	199	'A'	34	,,		

I B.L. fo.	II W.L.'s no.	III hand	IV lines per page	V margin size (cm)	VI paper size (mm)	VII watermark or countermark (CM)
Unclassified Observations (*cont.*)						
232	143	'Aa'	36	nil	312×195	fleur-de-lis[r]
	144	'Aa'	31	,,		
⌈233		'Aa'	40	,,	306×192	
		'A'	39	,,		
⌊234		'A'	38	,,	308×192	
		'A'	39	,,		hat[i]
⌈235	237	'Aa'	20★	,,	312×198	
	238	'Aa'	31★	,,		pot[s]
⌊236	245	'Aa'	24★	,,	312×195	
	246	'Aa'	21★	,,		
84		'A'	26	,, ⎫		
		–	[verse]	⎬	310×199	
85		–	[,,]	⎭		
1		'A'	15	3–1	106×179	
86	5	'A'	26★	nil	240×198	
	6	–	[verse]			
87	7	–	[,,]		273×205	
		'B'	25	,,		
89	10	–	[verse]	,,	285×223	
		'B'	15★			

[a] pro patria, 105×10[16/25/25/25/17]8, and CM royal cipher 'GR' and bell, 52×17[9/24/9]15

[b] horn (cf. Heawood 2671), 62×13[11/24/14]11

[b] horn (cf. Heawood 2671), 63×13[11/25/9]15

[c] horn (Heawood 2669), 73×8[14/25/11]13

[c] horn (Heawood 2669), 73×12[14/24/14]11

[d] coat of arms (Heawood 344), 93×14[10/23/24/24/11]14, and CM 'IA', 12×4[18]1

[e] horn (Heawood 2670), 62×11[12/24/12]12

[f] horn (cf. Heawood 2670), 62×9[14/24/14]10

[g] pot, 35×16[6/21/2]18

[h] horn (cf. Heawood 2671), 62×13[12/23/10]15

[i] hat (Heawood 2592), 60×17[6/22/24/8/13

[j] fleur-de-lis (Heawood 1658), 70×10[14/25/14]9

[k] coat of arms (Heawood 663), 95×7[19/25/20]6

[l] letters 'FLEG' (?), 18×3[21/23/7]16

[m] grapes, 30×8[16]0

[n] horn (cf. Heawood 2670), 60×12[12/26/11]14

[o] horn (cf. Heawood 2668), 66×14[10/24/9]14, and CM 'IPEIP', 10×4[21/21]1

[p] fleur-de-lis (Heawood 1737), 83×8[15/24/14]9

[q] pot (Heawood 3667), 42×2[18]2

[r] fleur-de-lis (cf. Heawood 1674), 78×12[11/23/5]18

[s] pot (Heywood 3692), 123×7[17/23/14]9

II. *Rearrangement of Folios for This Edition*

This edition prints the material from the classified groups of folios (144–205) according to the order and foldings in which Butler accumulated them. At any time after the completion of a sheet its position in relation to other completed sheets in the grouping could be altered, or its folding reversed; since each prose passage is a self-sufficient unit, such changes of placing or folding would not affect the sense of the passages—unless two folios happened to be linked by a single passage running on.[1] As there is no evidence for attributing the present manuscript order to Butler's deliberate revision, it follows that the first folding and placing of each sheet is the only authoritative guide. Printing the passages according to this first folding and placing of each sheet (or pair of sheets, if gathered) is not exactly the same as printing them in order of composition, since interpolated passages are printed as they occur, however much later than the adjacent passages they may have been written. Furthermore, no attempt is made to alter the relative order of the groupings according to the dates of the first entries.

First foldings and placings are re-established (as shown in the table) by meeting the following bibliographical requirements: (1) folios must be placed as if each sheet were undivided, the reconstructed pairings being consistent with the watermarks and (with such precision as eroded edges allow) the dimensions and tear-patterns of the paper. (2) There can be no alternation of passages in the earlier and later hands; the earlier must precede the later.[2] (3) Variations in either hand should show unbroken development from one folio to the next. (4) The partially blank folios, followed by the blank folios, must be at the end of groupings.[3] (5) Where the arrangement of folios in the earlier hand remains in

---

[1] Such run-ons occur at fos. 148–9, 152–3, 160–1, 166–7, 169–70, 203–4, 218–19, 230–1, 233–4.

[2] But fos. 191–2 and 194–5 must each have been partly written in A, then completed in B; the alternative order 191–194–195–192 offers no improvement. B on fo. 194^r (as on fo. 147^v) represents a brief interpolated passage at the base.

[3] The partially blank folios 166^r and 172^v suggest that Butler wanted to begin the next passages, which are long, on a new page.

doubt, it should be determined on the assumption that a heading in the earlier hand (Aa) identifies the first recto of a folded sheet, and that headings in the later hand (Ab) were subsequently added on other pages.

The original arrangement would have ten less sheets quired in gatherings than the British Library's arrangement, and it may be assumed that the single sheets were gathered together wherever possible when the manuscript was bound. The gathering in three sheets of fos. 196–201 appears an inappropriate first placing, and accumulation by single sheets would be more plausible. Yet for want of specific variations in the hand that gathering is retained for this edition.

In the gatherings, all outer sheets that were intact would have had to be divided in half when the manuscript was first mounted on guards. Many of them may previously have become divided, since all sheets show considerable wear and tear at the fold.

Fos. 220–1 are an ungathered sheet, correctly folded, and the table records that physical arrangement. Yet the passage which concludes fo. 220^r is continued by Butler at the top of fo. 221^v, and he signals this continuation with a pair of asterisks. Hence the text of the present edition adopts the folio order 220^r, 221^v, 220^v, 221^r, thus keeping together all material from fo. 221^v, whatever its chronological status may have been.[1]

III. *The Text of This Edition*

In the marginal references to Butler's manuscript, folio numbers are those of the British Library; Longueville's numeration is omitted for the sake of clarity, but reference can be made to it in the table. The hand in which passages commence and the hand of the heading are identified directly below the folio reference, the same notation being used as in the table (Aa etc.). A change to the later hand is signalled by a marginal B.

---

[1] On the other hand, a short passage at the top of fo. 218^v, after which the long preceding passage is continued, is simply moved to the end of the continuation (p. 187 below).

In the text itself manuscript 'ſ' is changed to 's', and the capitals 'I/J' and 'U/V' are consistently distinguished according to modern usage, as are the miniscules 'u/v'. The corresponding distinctions between 'i' and 'j' are already made by Butler with only occasional exceptions (here normalized). The familiar seventeenth-century contractions, such as *&*, *y^e*, *y^t*, *y^eir*, *w^ch*, *w^th*, *neū* (for*never*), *c̃ on* (for *tion*), *m̃* (for *mm*), and *q̃* (for *que*), are expanded whenever they occur (rather less frequently than the uncontracted forms); but contractions of proper names are retained, since the most appropriate full spelling is not always apparent. Similarly retained are Butler's abbreviated and scantily punctuated references to sources, and his arabic numerals in contexts where verbal or roman forms would now be used.

Where the letters of a word are unambiguous yet malformed, as for instance an additional minim in 'mm', the error is passed over in silence; likewise any manifestly inadvertent repetition of whole letters or of words, whether corrected by Butler or not. While some of these repetitions could occur most readily in copying and thus point to earlier drafts, to record over sixty instances of dittography would distract attention from notes of more certain significance. Manuscript repetitions are preserved in the text wherever there is a possibility of an intentional, though unusual, spelling or construction.

Significant errors or omissions are emended in two distinct ways: (1) where there can be no doubt as to the word intended, the emendation is simply embodied in the text, and the manuscript reading given in a footnote. This includes probable spelling errors when they could cause confusion: e.g. 'melefactors' for 'malefactors' (but not habitual forms such as 'strang' for 'strange'). (2) Where there is doubt as to the word intended, square brackets in the text enclose the interpolated word or letters, and a footnote is provided only if a blot or tear provides evidence for the letters having once been in the manuscript. Where a word is obscured or torn away, and the editor is unable to offer any informed conjecture, a space in the text is marked with square brackets [   ] so as to distinguish the loss of a word, as opposed to a space left blank by Butler between words.

Full points omitted at the ends of paragraphs are silently added, unless the division of the manuscript passage is the editor's decision, in which event the addition (or change) of punctuation is shown in a footnote. Emendations within paragraphs, intended only to prevent difficulties or misinterpretations in reading, are always identified. Since the punctuation marks in the manuscript are very often hard to distinguish, the apparatus includes only those alternatives crucial to the sense. This equally applies to spacing between the elements of compound words, and to hyphenation; alternatives are noted which could alter the emphasis, but in other cases, where such forms as 'himself' or 'him self' are indifferently employed, they are passed over. Multiple points, such as a comma below (and probably intended to replace) a colon, are emended and listed in the footnotes when they do occasionally occur. In such cases, however, and in the more general matter of disjunctive semicolons, intervention by William Longueville cannot be entirely discounted.[1] The slash / is not used by Butler; in this edition it indicates, where necessary, the end of a manuscript line (the point at which a passage runs on between folios or at which text may be lost through fore-edge damage). The double hyphens which Butler prefers in dividing words between lines are represented by single ones wherever divisions are recorded in the footnotes.

One awkward feature of Butler's punctuation is the very frequent use of full points within sentences as if they were commas or semicolons. In this edition these points are emended and listed in the footnotes (or else established as periods, with the first letter of the following word capitalized to begin a new sentence).[2] Brief

---

[1] Especially in the grouping 'Criticismes upon Bookes and Authors', where Longueville adds several underlines, and where the ink shows one semicolon to be his alteration from Butler's comma (p. 138, l. 4, below). In other groupings there are occasional modifications of spelling and grammar which suggest Longueville; for example on p. 73 below, the 'o' added in 'Countries' (l. 35) and a 'they' interworded (l. 8).

[2] These emendations may at times be correcting simple omissions on Butler's part: failure to change or delete the point when adding a continuation to a completed sentence (e.g. p. 63, l. 22), or failure to capitalize at the opening of an intended new sentence.

emphatic underlines may almost always be ascribed with certainty to Longueville; underlines which are definitely Butler's extend through entire passages to record that a fairer copy has been made elsewhere. Hence the presence of all underlines is simply recorded in the footnotes, their actual (as opposed to intended) extent being given to the nearest word.

Except in such cases of crucial punctuation and spacing as are mentioned above (and accordingly recorded in the footnotes), variations between two drafts of the same passage in spelling, capitalization, and punctuation are beyond the scope of this edition's notes; to record such variants would be futile when there is little evidence of Butler consciously emending or preserving accidentals when he recopied drafts. Yet all alterations made by Butler within a draft are necessarily deliberate and must therefore be recorded, unless (as in the case of spelling corrections) they can have no possible bearing on the sense.[1] In recording those alterations where letters are reshaped into other letters, the original word is identified up to and including the letters reshaped, but no attempt is made to conjecture its probable termination: in, for example,

wherever] altered from when B

Butler may originally have written the complete word 'whenever'. But where the alteration is made by interlining, the complete original can of course be given.

The formula altered from covers all kinds of alteration, whether by reshaping, by deletion, or by addition (which last may either precede the writing of the next word or be an interlettering, interwording, or interlineation). Reduction, wherever feasible, to this one familiar formula allows for editorial uncertainty through the qualifiers probably and possibly. Where one word cannot logically be

---

[1] Butler's revision of punctuation—a fact significant in itself—normally strengthens the points. Parentheses are substituted for pairs of commas, and semicolons or colons for single commas. Since it is hard to detect revisions of the latter kind, they are recorded only when it is clear from the inking that a change has been made. The formula lower point altered from is used to avoid conjecture on the priority of the upper point. Some words at first misspelt could, like the accidental repetitions of words, suggest copying from earlier drafts; but Butler makes over four hundred spelling corrections, far too many to record.

expressed as an alteration of another, angle brackets denote the
erasure; the presence of blotted or otherwise illegible characters is
indicated by a space between square brackets. Where an alteration
or interlineation within a recorded variant must be noted, it is
interpolated within square brackets and refers to the immediately
preceding word unless otherwise specified:

> better pleasd [*altered from* plead] with *B* 193ᵛ
> ty'd naked to [naked *altered from* to] the *B* 214ᵛ

Where, occasionally, parentheses have been added across or beside
commas or full points, the purely descriptive formula *superimposed on*
is preferred to *altered from*, unlikely as it is that the original points
were intended to be retained alongside. As for interpolations, the
term *interlined* covers not only those between two manuscript
lines, but also those on a line previously unfilled.

Duplicate or parallel passages are brought together whenever
possible: that is whenever they are not both incorporated in larger,
unrelated passages. When just one of the pair is part of a larger unit,
that is preferred for the printed text unless the other is substan-
tively revised. Content apart, a later date is implied either by the
hand or by presence in the classified groupings; if the alternative
passage in the unclassified section is underlined it is certain to be an
earlier draft. The location of a duplicate is given by folio number in
the footnotes to the printed version, and variants (if substantive or
semi-substantive) are recorded according to the formulae mentioned
above. At the point in the text where the duplicate would occur if
printed, a footnote is given in the style:

> 4. 1–4 *See p. 263, ll. 3–8*

The initial line-reference '4. 1–4' indicates that the duplicate
would occupy (approximately) four lines following l. 4; it has less
words than the six-line printed version on p. 263.

In the unclassified folios there are a number of underlined passages to which nothing in the classified sections corresponds. These
were not necessarily rewritten as prose observations (on folios
since lost); for Butler may have transferred them directly to

Characters or other writings.[1] There are other passages in the manuscript which resemble one another, but differ so much in their wording that they amount to independent essays on a common theme. So even when one is underlined, there is no certainty that the other is the revision, and they would, in any event, defy intelligible collation. Some cross-references will be found,[2] but to cross-reference all passages that resemble one another would overburden the *Commentary*. The *Index of Topics* may help here. It is necessarily selective, but it should assist the student in search of similar passages for stylistic comparison, as well as the reader who wishes to make a quick survey of all Butler's observations on a particular subject.

Appendix A lists selections made by Longueville for his commonplace book (*C*) and by Thyer for the *Genuine Remains* (*GR*). Most *C* and *GR* variants have no place in the textual apparatus as they are manifestly errors, or grammatical corrections, made in transcription or printing (roughly two per passage in *C* and one per passage in *GR*). Any variants, however, which could suggest transcription from an alternative draft no longer extant are recorded in the apparatus.[3] The many misreadings in Waller's text (*W*) are of course ignored; but where the present editor is less than certain about his own printed reading, and a possible alternative is supported by *W*, *C*, or *GR*, that siglum follows the alternative in the apparatus. Occasionally words or letters are obscured by the guards on which folios were mounted in 1964, and here the text necessarily derives from Waller's. For fos. 142–3, where the autograph is not Butler's, all substantive variants in *C* and *GR* are given, since they are equally authoritative transcriptions. In recording *C* and *GR* variants no attempt is made to restore Butler's spellings (except in the cue-words). Capitalization is made uniform with that of the printed text wherever there is exact syntactical correspondence, but not otherwise, and this principle is applied also to variant holograph drafts. Any confusing details of punctuation which do not

---

[1] For example, the underlined passage on 'The Hobbists' (p. 227) reappears in 'A Republican', *ad fin.*, and in 'An Hermetic Philosopher', par. 6 (*GR* ii. 58, 243).

[2] For example, between the underlined passage on p. 231, ll. 19–25, and what is *probably* the revised version on p. 148, l. 23–32.

[3] Material which Butler incorporated in Characters and other prose falls outside the scope of the apparatus, but significant parallels are noted in the *Commentary*.

distinguish the sense of the variant are silently emended, and Longueville's underlining is ignored, as are *GR*'s italics.

IV. *Longueville's Commonplace Book*

Longueville wrote in a quarto manuscript book, the leaves of which measure 188×142 mm. Of the 184 leaves in the book Butler had used eighty-one for his uncompleted English–French dictionary. Longueville used the unfilled last leaf of the dictionary and the remaining hundred leaves of the book. He also wrote on the three leaves preceding the dictionary and on the endpapers and boards. A full description of the book follows:

Paper: pot (sheets at least 376×284 mm.), with flag watermark throughout (similar to Heawood 1372), $70 \times 22[6/28/27]0$. The twin forms of the watermark are clearly distinguishable.

Collation: $4°$. $[1^8 2^6 3{-}12^8 13^6 14{-}23^8 24^4]$, 184 leaves, fos. [i–lxxxiv] 1–99 [100]. There is no watermark, or other, evidence that gatherings [2] and [13] were indeed irregular when made up; nor any manifest loss of written text to confirm the probable alternatives $[2^8(-2_{4.5})]$ and $[13^8(-13_{1.8})]$.

Binding: original calf, rebacked 1974 (the original back, now separately preserved, having five panels, one gilt stamped 'DIC | GALL | MS', the other four stamped with gilt decoration); two upper free endpapers and two lower free endpapers (all from sheets of printed books). The upper endpapers are disjunct, and each has a stub; the lower are conjunct, though also with a stub. The upper endpapers are from [Thomas Heywood,] *Machiavels Ghost* [or *Machiavel*], 1641, half-sheets A1,4 and C1,4 (C1,4 type-setting not the same as in copies from A. M. Clark, *Bibl. of Thomas Heywood*). The lower endpapers are from Charles I, *His Majesties Declaration to All His Loving Subjects. Of the 12 of August. 1642*, Oxford, 1642, sheet E. The book was bound before it was written in.

Contents:

    inside of upper board and endpapers, commonplace entries;

    fos. [i–iii], France and the French;

    fos. [iv–lxxxiv], English–French dictionary;

fo. [lxxxiv], commonplace entries;

fos. 1–99, classified commonplace entries;

fo. [100], index;

endpapers and inside of lower board, commonplace entries.

The English–French Dictionary: an original compilation inasmuch as the words and glosses do not derive exclusively from any one of the published dictionaries in which the English preceded the French (or French and other languages).[1] Some entries are unparalleled in those published works, and the imperfect alphabetical arrangement, together with interpolated additions, is further evidence of originality. But a detailed study of the dictionary has yet to be made.

In the commonplace book section of this edition some exceptions are made to the textual conventions established for Butler's holograph. The folios of *C* have remained as first gathered and bound from blank sheets, and the only numbering on them is that supplied by Longueville. Marginal references accordingly take the form 1^r etc. when relating printed text to folios which Longueville numbered (a sequence of ninety-nine, which comes after Butler's English–French dictionary); the roman numerals in brackets [ ] refer to the preceding sequence of unnumbered folios (which is largely taken up by the unprinted dictionary). All eighty-four of Longueville's section headings are given, but where no passage from a section is printed (either because the material is already printed from *B* or because it is not of Butler's composition), the heading is enclosed in brackets.[2] It will be seen that passages printed from some unheaded pages do not belong under the last preceding heading; this material (and more, which is not of Butler's composition) was simply transcribed on convenient empty pages without regard to classification.[3]

Most *C* passages are written in Longuevilles's very small 'tran-

---

[1] Notably those of Huloet (1572), Barrett (1573 and 1580), Minsheu (1617), Sherwood (in Cotgrave, 1632), Howell (1659–60), and, towards the end of Butler's life, Miege (1677).

[2] Longueville's headings are not always centred above the text; he may simply write the opening topic phrase of the first passage in a larger hand. The status of some less prominent opening phrases is doubtful.

[3] Fos. 30^v, 32^r, 55^v–56^r, 81^{r-v}, 83^v, 96^{r-v}. Fos. 18^v and 43^v anticipate the headings on fos. 19^r and 44^r.

scription hand'. Where the hand is larger or less careful, a later entry is presumed (most often something not by Butler), and for the relatively few of these passages which are printed the difference of hand is recorded in the footnotes. Longueville's habitual pyramids and other multiple points are silently reduced to single full points, but his underlines, while rejected from the printed text as un-Butlerian, are a part of his own writing style and are accordingly recorded in the footnotes (though variant underlines in duplicate passages are ignored). Alterations made by Longueville are not recorded; they reveal some inattentive transcribing, but throw little light on the lost originals. As in the treatment of *B*, contractions of proper names are retained, but the superscription ↵ᴖↄ which Longueville often adds over the end of these contractions is ignored. Accents placed on Latin words are retained; the English word *thô* is rendered *tho'*. The frequent miniscule openings of paragraphs or verse lines are capitalized without comment.

Where *C* includes material from lost originals which is also preserved by Thyer there is no need to print Longueville's versions as alternatives. Comparing the two men's transcriptions from holographs that do survive, one finds Longueville making errors about twice as often and producing a text much less consistent in its accidentals. His spelling, capitalization, and punctuation diverge from the original with all the idiosyncrasy of a seventeenth-century copyist; Thyer's uniform imposition of the later conventions produces no more changes than are found in Longueville and delivers the sense with greater clarity. So Thyer's text of Characters which are also in *C* retains its status; unlike his text of Characters from *B*, which is superseded by the present printing from holograph. Substantive variants in *C* are, however, recorded, as they derive from the lost holographs quite independently of Thyer's readings and thus have a potential authority, notwithstanding Longueville's greater propensity to make mistakes. These variant readings in Characters are collected together in Appendix B; two passages from other lost holographs transcribed by Thyer are simply listed in the footnotes at the points where *C*'s versions occur.[1]

---

[1] From *The Case of King Charles I* (*C* 16ʳ) and 'Observations upon the Long Parliament' (*C* 66ᵛ).

As mentioned above in the introductory account of Butler's remains, the provenance of some *C* material is uncertain. There are some 250 passages known to be Butler's work because the originals are extant in *B*; they are listed in Appendix A. Some 180 passages of which originals do not survive may with confidence be taken as Butler's: they are transcribed together with the 250 of proven authenticity in the same small neat 'transcription hand', and their content, in all but a few instances, confirms the attribution. Those 180 passages make up the *C* text printed in this edition. A few of these passages could be unidentified quotations from other writers, transcribed verbatim by Longueville either from transcriptions of Butler's or directly from the original authors; a few, which do not bear Butler's distinctive stamp, could be of Longueville's own composition. But Longueville's initial purpose was to reduce Butler's remains into method and order; so one presumes that all passages which he transcribed are Butler's, unless there is evidence to the contrary.[1]

Longueville did, however, add a lot of cross-references to passages on other folios of *C* and a few to parallels in *Hudibras*. He also noted parallels in other writers, sometimes just giving a page reference to a book and other times writing a phrase or sentence by way of elucidation. The cross-references suggest Longueville's difficulties in classifying passages which could come under more than one of his chosen headings, but they have nothing to do with the passages as Butler wrote them, and they are therefore ignored in this edition. His references to other writers could be problematic; even if Longueville did not get them from Butler's papers, some of them might derive from his recollection of Butler's conversation. There is, on the other hand, nothing in them which an intelligent and literate man with classical and theological interests could not have come upon in his own course of reading. So there is no reason to print as Butler's what could equally well be Longueville's.

Entries in Longueville's large sprawling later hand may be rejected with some confidence. Many relate to events or publica-

---

[1] Longueville does as a rule identify his quotations, and he will use the notation *SB* where a passage of Butler's must be distinguished from other material. But on *C* 2ᵛ there is a passage from Selden's *Table Talk* ('Presbitery', 1) which is not identified and not unlike Butler in content and tone. This may illustrate the problems of provenance.

tions after Butler's death, and the content of the entries in general differs from that of Butler's reading notes. The emphasis is on sound doctrine and moral advice from contemporary sermons; it has no apparent purpose beyond the personal satisfaction of the transcriber, none of the potential for literary development which characterizes Butler's reading notes. Longueville was at this stage using the book as a commonplace book proper and to a large extent as a devotional digest of morbid commonplaces.

In summary, this edition excludes from its commonplace book text all passages already printed from *B* and all entries identified as quotations from, or references to, other authors (including such references as *vide Chillingworth* interpolated in passages of Butler's). Almost all entries in Longueville's late hand are excluded; what is conceivably Butler's is printed with the note *written in a large hand*.[1] It includes all passages in the small early hand which do not appear elsewhere in Butler or in other authors. Strictly speaking, verse should be excluded, as it is from the *B* section; but the relatively little verse which is extant only in *C*, and therefore has never been published, is included in the section. The textual apparatus simply records the existence in *C* of verse drafts also extant in the authoritative verse folios of *B*. These references to the verse folios of *B* can be of little help to the reader until such time as that manuscript verse is accurately printed (with appropriate folio references). It might, provisionally, seem sensible to give additional references to René Lamar's edition of the verse; but Lamar excludes very many of the verse drafts, and the composite versions which he often prints give no adequate sense of the material as it exists in manuscript. So while the topic, at least, of some *C* verse could be identified by way of Lamar, this would not make up for the confusion created through reference to versions of passages which are not those transcribed by Longueville.[2] References to the *B* folios are, however, essential; otherwise this authentic verse would be reduced to the same status as Longueville's own prose passages, which are silently rejected.

To have printed in an appendix all the rejected material from *C*

---

[1] See pp. 260 and 291.
[2] For some details of Lamar's edition see footnote to p. xxii.

would have satisfied the bibliographical impulse to give a full
account of Longueville's manuscript, but when collected and then
supplemented with editorial notes and comments its bulk proved
out of proportion to its utility. While some of the notes and
references may indeed have come to Longueville by way of Butler,
there is no determining which those are. A brief indication of the
authors drawn on will, however, suggest an over-all difference of
emphasis from that in Butler's own holograph reading notes. There
are some thirty-seven writers on theological subjects, of whom the
following appear more than three times: Tillotson, Sanderson,
Stillingfleet, Edward Yong, Samuel Parker, Edward Bagshaw,
Hales, Jeremy Taylor, Hooker, Sir Matthew Hale, Anthony
Farindon, Barrow. Some thirty other writers, half classical and half
modern, are most often cited with some moral implication, but no
one writer with any frequency.[1] The most substantial entry in *C* is
Butler's apocryphal 'Tragedy of Nero' (fos. 60^r–61^v), in fact selections from the anonymous play *Nero*, published 1624.[2] The extracts,
mostly one or two lines and the longest seven, are taken from
throughout the play; there is nothing in them to imply Butler's
choice rather than Longueville's. The cynical line 'Whom wee doe
hurt; Them wee call Enemies' might attract Butler, but hardly the
sentimental 'if I dye for pittying Pisoes End / There will be some
too, that will pitty mine'; that is more typical of Longueville's
commonplace entries. Either man could have selected the play's
penultimate line 'Thus great Bad men above Them find a Rod', but
Butler would surely have added its bathetic sequel 'People depart,
and say there is a God'. Over all, the assumption that Longueville
selected will account most easily for the lines chosen and for the
lines passed over.

[1] Indeed only the following are mentioned more than once: Sir Harry Marten,
Cardan, Marvell, Cicero, Seneca, Tacitus, Grotius, Montaigne, Jeremy Collier, Lord
Argyle.

[2] In his Preface to *Hudibras*, I. xviii, T. R. Nash wrote, 'I have, in his MS. commonplace book, part of an unfinished tragedy, entitled Nero'. The error became current
in playlists and is perpetuated even after Norma E. Bentley identified the 1624 source
('Another Butler Manuscript', *MP* xlvi (1948), 133).

CLASSIFIED
PROSE OBSERVATIONS FROM
BUTLER'S MANUSCRIPT

[Sundry Thoughts]

If Travellers are allow'd *to Lye* in Recompence of the great
Pains they have taken to bring home strange Stories from
foreign Parts, There is no Reason why *Antiquaries* shoud not
be allow'd that Priviledge, who are but Travellers *in Time*,
and import as strange Stories from *foreign* Ages, with no less
Pains and Labour. And as a Right Traveller is wont to prefer
all Countries he has seen abroad before his own, So does an
Antiquary, all Ages before the Modern.

*p. 1 Anti-
quaries*

5

The More silly and Ridiculous Things are in themselves
the more *sacred and Solemn* Pretences, they require to set them
off.

Religion

10

Christian Charity is a great Impediment to Zeal.

A Client is fain to hire a Lawyer to keep him from the
Injury of other Lawyers—as Christians that travel in Turkey
are forc'd to hire Janizaries, to protect them from the
Insolencies of other Turks.

Law

15

The Mahometan Religion instills Charity into the Professors
of it, to all Sorts of Living Creatures but *Man*, whom it
engages to abhor—especially all those of another Religion.

Religion

19

Most Men owe their *Misfortunes* rather to their Want of
Dishonesty, than Witt.

*p. 2 Mis-
fortunes*

[141r-v] *Fo. 141r, headed* Miscellaneous Observations and Reflections on
various Subjects, *lists Butler's classified sections from* Learning and Knowledge *to*
Criticismes upon Authors, *then* Contradictions. *At the end of this list comes*
Beneficial reflections on Milford Haven (*Printed by Thyer in GR i. 411–18,
but no longer extant in manuscript*). *Fo. 141v is blank.*

8. 1–2 *See p. 201, ll. 3–4*

Happiness   All the Business of this World is but *Diversion,* and all the
Happiness in it, that Mankind is capable of—any thing that
will keep it from reflecting upon the Misery, Vanity, and
Nonsence of it: And whoever can by any Trick keep himself
5 from Thinking of it, is as Wise and Happy as the best Man
in it.

p. 3. Enemy   Men seldom hear of their faults but from their *Enemies,*
which makes that excellent office of Friendship, as Odious, as
the Reproaches of an Envious Adversary.

Religion   It was Queen Mary that establish'd the Protestant *Religion*
11 in England and not Queen Elizabeth, who coud never have
done what she did, if her Sister's barbarous Cruelty in destroying so many poor Innocent Creatures, had not prepar'd
the Nation rather to admitt of any Religion, than That which
15 They saw produce such horrid Inhumanities—The Memory of
which does to this day possess the People with an Abhorrence
and Detestation of it, and will be found the greatest of all
Obstructions, to those who endeavour to introduce it again.

p. 5 Life   The Antient Patriarchs who liv'd the longest Lives, did no
20 doubt live most according to the Course of Nature, before the
World, understood the Various Ways of Luxury, Physick and
142v   Intemperance / which have been since found out: otherwise if
the Date of Mens Lives had naturally decreas'd so fast, They
had in a short time been reduc'd to Nothing at all.

Learning   One Swore that Homer, Aristotle and all the Rest of the
26 Antient Greeks were such Ignorant Fellows that They did not
understand *one word of Latin.*

Popery   The Pope found it Easier to Domineer over the Emperor and
the Greatest Princes of the Christian world at a Distance, than
30 keep his own little Subjects Quiet at Home, where *He was*
better Understood.

Wine   *Wine* had no Share in the Wickedness of those People, who
lived before, and Caused, the Flood.

1 *Marginal note* Happiness] *altered from* Human Life *B*   *Diversion,*] Diversion.
B   10 *marginal note* Religion] *followed by* 27 *B*   25 Homer,] Homer. *B*
27. *1–2 See p. 212, ll. 3–4*   27. *3–4 See p. 165, ll. 23–4*

It is a wonderful silly Distinction that Divines make between getting of Children for Procreation only, and out of natural *Concupiscence*, which was only provided by Nature as a Necessary means to produce the Other, as if it were a Sin to Eat *for Hunger*, but not *for the Support of Life*. Concupis-cence 5

Conversation is *a Glass* for Men to Dress their Minds and Manners by. p. 6. Conversation

He that woud write Well, must not step out of his Way for the most excellent of Wit and Sense, unless it Lye so directly before him, that he coud not possibly avoid it. Learning 10

One Quibble in the Scripture viz *Tu es Petrus*, has done almost as much Mischief to Mankind in General, as all the excellent Precepts of Justice and Morality has been able to do Good upon Particulars, and caus'd more destruction in the world, than all the Heavenly and Peaceful Doctrines have had Power to prevent; and therefore those Preposterous fanatick Mountebanks that cry down Morality for *Dirt*, as they Us'd to call it, throw it all upon the Gospell, where it is so frequently enjoyn'd, as a necessary Christian Duty. p. 4 Religion 15

Great Persons of our Times do, like Absolom when he rebell'd against his Father, commit Iniquity upon the Tops of Houses; that all People may see and take Notice of it. p. 7. Vice 21

This Age will serve to make a very pretty Farce for the Next, if it have any Witt at all to make Use of it.

A whore is but a Painted Sepulchre that holds nothing but Pox and Rotteness within how fair soever it looks on the Outside. 25

Courts of Justice are like Court Cards, which no body wins by, but another looses, according as They are dealt, and commonly there is as much *Chance* in the One as the Other, and no Less shuffling—One Ace beats them all as O. C. did. 143r Justice 30

3 *Concupiscence*,] *Concupiscence. B* 4 Other,] Other. *B* 8 step]
stop *W* 16 prevent;] prevent. *B* 30 Other,] Other. *B*

Charity   Charity does not only begin, but End at Home.

The Best Instrument will make as bad Musick as the Worst if it light in hands that do not understand how to Use it.

Folly   There are more Fools than Knaves in the World, Else the
5   Knaves woud not have enough to live upon.

If it be a Wise Child that knows its own Father, So he is a wise Father that knows his own Child.

Excess   The greatest Drunkards are the worst Judges of Wine—The most Insatiable Leachers the most Ignorant Criticks in
10   Women, and the Greediest Appetites, of the best Cookery of Meats—for Those that Use *Excess* in any Thing never understand the Truth of it, which always lies in *the Mean*.

Learning   They who study Mathematicks only to fix their Minds, and
p. 19   render them the Steadyer to apply to all other Things, as
15   There are many who profess to do, are as wise as Those who think by rowing in Boats, to learn to Swim.

Government   There is nothing in Nature more Arbitrary than a Parliament, and yet there is nothing Else that is able to preserve the Nation from being Govern'd by an Arbitrary Power, and
20   confine Authority within a Limited Compass—As a Prop can make a falling house stand firm, Though it cannot stand of itself, and a Bow make an Arrow Fly, tho' it cannot fly itself.

Religion   The Christian Religion in the primitive times was bred up
p. 20   under the Greatest Tyranny in the World, and was propa-
25   gated by being opprest and persecuted, but in after Times when it was deliver'd, from that Slavery, it naturally inclin'd to be Tyrannical itself, For when the Popes had reduc'd their cruellest Enemies the Roman Emperors, They assum'd a greater and more extravagant Power than the Others ever

19 Power,] Power. *B*   20 Compass—As] Compass, though It has none Itselfe. As *C*   23 times *C: om. B*   25 persecuted *C*: prosecuted *B*   27 itself, For] itself, (as the Jewes did (when they were free) to set up the Religion and Customes of their former Oppressors, th'Ægiptians): For *C*   29 Others] Other *C*

pretended to, as if Religion having serv'd out an Apprentice-
ship to Tyranny, as soon as it was out of its time, had set up
for itself.

All Mens Bodies are like their Estates—whosoever lives   Physick
above his Natural proportion of health in any Enjoyment of   P 21
Life, will in a Small space waste his constitution, and run out   6
his Life before his Time—As many are undone by living above
their Fortunes, but few or None Under. So Thousands dye
of Surfeits for One that Dies of Famine.

The Popes of Rome that made, and Canoniz'd all the Saints   143v
of That Church, coud Seldom or Never make themselves or   Religion
one Another Saints, For there are Fewer Popes in the Rubrick
than there are of any other Sorts of Christians—whether They
were above it, or below it, is not easy to determine—However
it is no great Argument of their Sanctity, when no One shoud   15
have Reason or Confidence enough to consecrate the Memory
of his Predecessor—tho' many of them were of the same
Family—And indeed there are Fewer Good Men in the Cata-
louge of Popes, than there are of any other Princes, in the
Histories of the most Barbarous Nations—and the Lives of   20
Some not inferior to the prodigious Inhumanities of the worst
Pagan Emperors.

Disease and Pain are the Natural Effects of Extravagant   P. 15
Pleasure as Punishment is of Sin.

1 to, as] to) as *B*; unto; Not only over all this World (of which the
emperors claimd, but a part) but extended their Dominion and Authority
over the whole Heavens; when the most proud and insatiable of all their
Predecessours, the pagan princes, were Contented to bee flatterd, into a
Single starr. As *C*   3 itself.] itself; And as at first it was nourished with
the blood of It's own Martyrs (as monkies are sayd to eate up their Own
Tayles) now quite contrary, It delights in Nothing so much, as the Blood
of those that Oppose It; or refuse to submitt to It's most Imperious Commands: like some mastive Dogs, that having tasted blood once; will afterward
kill Sheep, and feed on nothing but only sucking of their Blood. *C*   6–7 out
his] out of his *C*   7 Time—As] Time, But hee who is a better Husband and
spends no more of his naturall strength then hee is able to beare will make
It hold out a great deale longer For as *C*   8 but] and *C*   Under.]
Under; *C*   24 Sin.] Sin. For men's vices and errors are for the most
part payd in Kind and the specifique Remedy of foolish Councells is to bee
Regulated by those that are foolisher, as the Jews for committing Idolatry
were punished by greater Idolaters then Themselves. *C*

Government   As Mad Men are best Cur'd by being Shut up in the Dark,
so the Natural Frenzies of the Rabble are best temper'd by
being kept in Ignorance.

Learning   As small Tyrants are always found to be most Severe, So
5 are all little Criticks the most unmerciful, and never give
Quarter for the least Mistake.

p. 16   No Man can possibly be a Competent Judge of his own
Conceptions, unless he coud have more Reason than he has,
and He that has *less*, is a more unfit Judge of what he has per-
10 form'd than *Himself*, for the Judges of all Courts are wont to Sit
above those who are to be try'd before them, and so shoud all
others do, at least in the Capacity of Reason and Judgment.

Religion   Ovids Metamorphosis was the Legend of the Pagan Church,
and his Fasti, the *Rubrick*, and tho' the Religion was very
15 Silly and Ridiculous, none was Ever better set off.

p. 17 Gov-   As Soon as a Man has taken an Oath against his Conscience
ernment and done his Endeavour to damn himself, He is capable of any
Trust or Employment in the Government; So excellent a
Quality is Perjury to render the most perfidious of Men most
20 fit and proper for publick Charges of the greatest Consequence; and Such as have ever so little restraint laid upon
them by Conscience, or Religion or Natural Integrity are
declared insufficient and unable to hold any Office or publick
Trust in the Nation—and this is the Modern Way of Test as
25 they call it—to take measure of Men's abilities and Faith by
their Alacrity in Swearing—And is indeed the most Compendious way to exclude all those that have any Conscience,
and to take in Such as have None at all.

10 of] in *C*   19 Quality] Qualification *C*   23 or publick] or
Charge of publick *C*   25 it—to] it, tho' as dull as that of lead and Bone
Ashes—to *C*   27 that] *om. C*   27–8 Conscience, and] Conscience or
honesty and *C*   28 to] *om. C*

Ignorance is never so abhominable as when it pretends to wisdom and Learning, for among Bad things those that seeme to be the Best are always the worst: As a Probable Ly is more Dangerous and apt to deceive, then that which is apparently false. So monkeys and Baboones that are between Man and Beast, are worse and more deformd then those Creatures that are all Beast.

It is much easier to Defend then oppose for a little force will put by a thrust of great Strength.

All forcd Constructions of Difficult and learned Nonsense are like planing of Knots in wood, which when they are rough hewn appeare deformd and Crosgraind every way, but when they are smooth'd and polish'd, represent the shapes of Faces, and other figures which to a Strong Imagination may seeme to have been meant, and intended, when they fell out so by chance, and are renderd what they appeare by a Superficiall gloss.

Before the Inventions of Printing and Gun-powder, A Gooses Feathers did the same things in the world, as both these do now. For the Pen disputed Quarrels, and set men together by the eares and the Feather furnishd their Arrows (the only Artillery then in use) with wings to fly as Powder makes Bullets, and do as great execution.

Speculations with wise and knowing Men go for little, untill they are approv'd by Practice and experiment: for commonly they use us as glasses, and deliver that Right in appearance, that proves left in tryal.

It has pleasd Almighty God to allow Man no meanes of Knowledg but by Sense, and Reason collection, Consequence and Demonstration: for whosoever shall enterteine any as Knowledge (though it were true) of which he can give no accompt that hath relation to any of these, I am sure can give none why he should not as well

receive any thing else: and that cannot be don without madnes. Hence it is that the slightest Capacities are soonest taken with the slender appearancies of things, as we see in the People, who upon foolish, and inconsequent Pretences, become highly confident, while
5 sober and solid Judgments move cautiously, and not at all, unless
146ᵛ upon certain or very / probable Groundes. There is no Sayling in
Ab shallow waters, but with flat-bottomd Botes, and Flat Dull wits are easily carryd away with shallow and slight Stuff, while those that have any Ballast of Judgment presently stick fast.

10   Though Probability (like one that squint's) look severall ways at once, it is much better then blinde Fancy, or Credulity, for he that put's out his eies because he cannot [see] so wel as he would, inflicts a just Punishment upon his own Folly. Nonsense is as well proof against contradiction as Demonstration is, for no man can say
15 more against that which he do's not understand, then against that which is manifest. There is a great deale of Difference between that which may be provd, and that which cannot be disprov'd. For though Doubt always attend's Probability, yet in knowing Persons being the effect of Reason and discourse, it is of a nobler
20 Nature then mere Opinion, or implicit Credulity which is but the Apostacy of Doubt. Credulity and Demonstration, are Different ends of Doubt, as health and Death are of Paine; but he that thinkes to cure himselfe of that Malady, by the former deserves it.

25   Subtletys and Mysteries are like Mines hid from the view of Man for his own Benefit: For man never tooke an ownce of Mettle from the vaines of the earth, but he payd as much out of his own vaines for it.

They are in a great Error, who say the Ancients deliverd their
30 Learning and Knowledg in Fables, and Parables, to conceale it from the Profane Rabble, which is so false, that they rather invented those Fables for Illustration, as the only Possible way of conveying their Doctrine to the Capacity of the People. For as (Seneca say's) there are but three ways of teaching any thing, By Reason Precept and
35 Example: Of the first they knew the People utterly incapable. And

for the Second (Precept) being a kinde of Imposition, they observ'd it was very unpleasant to those, who are so naturally fond of their Liberty. But the third Example, being capable of Prodigie and strangnes, and of neare kin to a Ly which they have ever been naturally inclynd to, they knew could not but finde a welcom enter- 5 teinment, at least attention, which was more then they could expect any other way.

Wee ought to have a Care of pressing things to far in Discourse **147^r** which must of necessity render us not only tedious but obscure, and Ab in naturall affection to our own Conceptions wee may believe it to 10 be Sense, yet if it do not appeare so to others, it is not so; there for as soone as we leave to be understood, we begin to talke to no purpose.

It is very probable we do not understand (although we may believe) the Purpose for which wee were created, for if wee are 15 ignorant of the immediate, and nearest Causes of our selves, much more must wee be so of the most remote, The End for which we are, which do's not seeme to bee for our own sakes, more then a Gold-smith make's a Cup for it self to drink in. And to this end we may serve as well, though we know it not, as if we did: For it is not 20 necessary for an Instrument to know it's own use, and it is not unlike if we had been made for our own concernments, the meanes that lead to it would have been ordered more directly to our own Conveniences.

Demonstration is the proper Buss'nes of Knowledg, and Proba- 25 bility of Beliefe, and as there is no certaine Knowledg without Demonstration, so there is no Safe belief without Probability.

The Impertinencies and Impostures of Learning have outgrown the useful Parts of it, as weedes commonly do corn; but weedes being too apt to spring up of themselves, must of necessity become 30 much more fruitful when they are planted as those are.

Wee may learne no less from the Errors and Mistakes of some then from the wisdom, and Knowledg of others, for as other mens harmes make us cautious, so the Miscarriages of others may make us wise.

2 so] *altered from* So *or possibly* to B   11 so;] so B   21 use,] use. B

He that see's another in a wrong way, is so much the nearer to the right himself, and of such Discoveries those are always the best that are made at the charge of others.

The wit of the School-men like the Righteousnes of the Pharises, consisted much in the streining of Knats, and swallowing of Camells. For they that are curious in Subtilties, and ignorant in things of solid Knowledg are but penny-wise, and Pound-foolish.

147ᵛ   He that has less Learning then his Capacity is able to manage,
Ab shall have more use of it then he that has more then he can master.
For no man can possibly have an active, and ready command of that which is too heavy for him.

The understanding of Man hath a Sphære of Activity, beyond which if it be forc'd, it become's unactive, as it do's vigorous by being confin'd. Unless a Vine be Prund it will yeald no Fruite. He that related to the Senate De Coercendis Imperii Terminis, was no unwise States-man. Opinion of Knowledg ha's ever beene one of the Chiefest Causes of Ignorance, for most men know less then they might, by attempting to know more then they can.

They that take Pleasure in Naturall Fooles and Ideots, do it out of kindenes or Flatery to themselves: For as all men delight to see others have less wit, and Knowledg then themselves, so there are many that are never like to enjoy that Pleasure, unless they keepe those of purpose about them that are usefull, and of fit abilitys for it.

Many men that pretend to learning and wit, have the Barbarous Cruelty of those thieves, who cannot be content to rob, unlesse they murther to; For having stollen some things which they esteeme excellent, from others, they cannot believe themselvs Safe, untill they have dispatchd their Reputation, that it may not rise up in Judgment against them, nor be thought fit to owne that, which they have a Desire to entitle themselves to.

It requires a greater Mastery of Art in Painting to fore-shorten

2 himself,] himself. *B*   14 Unless] unless *B*   15 Coercendis] Coercendis.
B   16–18 Opinion . . .] *duplicated B* 234ʳ   16 Opinion] Immoderate Desire
B 234ʳ   18 attempting] endevoring *B* 234ʳ   20 Flatery] *altered from*
Charity *B*

a Limbe exactly, then to draw three at their just Length: and so it is in writing to expresse any thing briefly, and Naturally, then to inlarge and dilate.

Philosophers in their Disputes, use commonly, after some weake B Arguments to conclude, and take what they would have for 5 granted; and upon that, build other Inferences, that hang together like Sale-work, this only passable for it's cheape slightnes.

The Reason why Fooles, and knaves thrive better in the world 144ʳ then wiser and honester men, is because they are nearer to the Ab Generall Temper of mankind, which is nothing but a Mixture of 10 Cheat and Folly, which those that understand and meane better cannot comply with, but entertaine themselves with another kinde of Fooles Paradise of what should be, not what is: while those that know no better take Naturally to it, and get the Start of them.

Ignorance, and knoledge or understanding are the very same to 15 one another; for the greatest Reason in the world signify's no more to those that do not understand it, then error, and want of Reason do's to those that understand better; and perhaps not so much, for he that ha's more reason then others, know's how much they want: but they know nothing of what he has: and that makes them 20 generally the more Confident.

The observations of some men, are like the Sifting of Bakers, that use to retaine the Bran, and let the Floure pass through.

It is both the wisest, and Safest way in the world to keepe at a Convenient Distance with all men: For when Men converse too 25 closely they Commonly (like those that meete in Crowds) offend one another.

He that ha's many Languages to expresse his Thoughts, but no thoughts worth expressing, is like one that can write all hands, but never the better Sense, Or can cast up any Sum of Money, but has 30 none.

The end of all knowledge, is to understand what is Fit to be don;

26 Crowds)] Crowds B   30 Sense,] Sense. B

For to know what ha's been, and what is, and what may be, dos but tend to that.

A man gaine's nothing by being wise (which he may not as wel obteine without it) but only that he is less liable to cheates, and
5 troubled with fewer unnecessary Scruples, then Fooles usually are, which he is faine to allow for, in having his Miscarriages the more taken Notice of, and his Errors render'd the more Ridiculous.

The way to be esteemd Learned, is but only to have a Library, and to bee able to Turne to the Indices, upon any Occasion of
10 shewing great Reading.

144ᵛ   Doing, and Saying and Giving Advice, and taking Advice, and
Aa   understanding and Acting, are all Severall things, and so averse to one another that they seldom or never meet in the same Person. For as Physitians and Lawyers that live by giving others Advice, do
15 seldom make use of it in their own Occasions: So men of greatest understanding and knowledge, do as Seldom make that use of it, for their own Advantages, as they do for the Benefit of others, which being a hard Condition imposd upon them by Nature, deserve's rather to be pitty'd then blam'd. For Nature that in her
20 distributive Justice, indeavors to deal as equally as possibly she can with all men, and never bestow's any Convenience without Allow-ance, would breake her own Rules, if she should confer all her Favours upon any one Person, and not make him abate for it some other way.

25 All wit, and Contemplative Wisdom in the world must of Neces-sity appeare Lazy and Idle, for as it is Performd by Cogitation and thinking, and that cannot be don without a Sedentary Quietnes, together with a Present, and agreable Temper of minde, which no man ha's allways ready at Command, it cannot be avoyded but
30 much time must of necessity be spent to no purpose, or to very little, which might be sav'd if men were always in a fit humor to performe, what they designe and propose to themselves. For the more Curious and subtle Mens Capacitys are, the further they are from being at their own disposing. For though Prophets when they
35 are inspir'd, can foretell things that are to come to pass after many

5 are,] *altered from* are. B   *A different ink begins at this alteration*

Ages, [they] can never presage when they shalbe in the next fit of Predicting, while all Arts and Sciences that are learnd by Rule and Practice, or acquird by habit, are allways ready at the will and pleasure of their owners.

All Men Naturally affect Wit, and as it commonly falls out, in 5 other things, those that are most deny'd it have the greatest inclinations to it. Hence it is that States-men, and Judges (whose Busnes ly's another way) when they would shew their Parts to the best advantage wil venture to appeare Ridiculous to shew a little wit; and when they finde by other mens judgments that they have 10 miscarryd, they use to lay the fault upon the thing and not their own infirmities.

Wit is like Science not of Particulars, but universals, for as Argu- **145^r** ments drawn from Particulars signify little to universal Nature, **Aa** which is the Proper object of Science; So wit that is raysd upon any 15 one Particular Person go's no further unlesse it be from thence extended to all Human Nature.

Heroicall Poetry handle's the slightest, and most Impertinent Follys in the world in a formall Serious and unnaturall way: And Comedy and Burlesque the most Serious in a Frolique, and Gay 20 humor, which has always been found the more apt to instruct, and instill those Truths with Delight into men, which they would not indure, to heare of any other way. And therefore the Ancient Romans cald a School, as we do now a Comedy a Play, and the Greekes Idlenes and Diversion, for if any man should but imitate 25 what these Heroical Authors write in the Practice of his life and Conversation, he would become the most Ridiculous Person in the world, but this Age is far enough from that, for though none ever abounded more with those Images (as they call them) of Moral and Heroicall Virtues, there was never any so opposite to them all in the 30 mode and Custome of life. But if that be true which some have sayd that the best end of Tragedy is but to Cumfort those that are un-fortunate, by seing the greater Infelicities of others, though it may be Naturall, [it] is not at all Heroical.

In all feates of Activity men are understood then to do best when 35 they come nearest breaking their Necks: So in writing, those that come nearest to Nonsense are many times believ'd to write the most wit.

Many things are rather found out by chance then Industry or
5 Designe; as Men sometimes light upon Money, and Jewells in the high Ways, where if they had sought of Purpose, it had been in vaine; So they often hit upon Wit, and Fancy by chance which no Study would ever have suggested, especially if it bee extravagant and Humorous.

10   The Stoicall Necessity and Presbyterian Prædestination are the very same.

145ᵛ   In universities Men are valewd only upon the Accompt of their
Aa   Ingenuity, and Parts, which is seldom found to be observd any where else: For in Courts they are esteem'd only for their Interests,
15 and in Great Cities only for their wealth, and in the Common Standard of the world, for what they assume and appeare, not what they are.

When French Men would say the greatest thing of any great Person of their own Nation, they use to admire him for Having Le
20 Sense Froide, because it is the greatest Rarity among them; who are generally so hot Headed, that very few are capable of arriveing at so great an height of sober understanding, as to be Dull, for so it signify's with all other People.

That which the wise man prayd for of God in Ecclesiastes, to give
25 him neither Riches nor Poverty, is as much to be desird in Conversation and Bus'nes: to have nothing to do with men that are very Rich, or Poore, for the one Sort are Commonly Insolent and Proud, and the other mean, and Contemptible, and those that are between both are commonly the most agreeable.

30   The Authors of our times are so unwilling to finde any thing obstruct the good opinion which they have of themselves, That the most Charitable Christians are not more glad to be reconcild to those that have don them the greatest Injuries, (for feare Animositis

shoud prove an Impediment to their Piety) then they are to their greatest Detractors, and this they call overcoming of Envie.

A great Deale of Lerning is, like a great House, very chargeable to be kept in Repaire, and if it be too big for the owners use, and Occasions, in a small time it fall's to decay, only by being not inhabited (that is) discontinu'd. For no man is the wiser for his Bookes, untill he is above them; and when he is so, the utter neglect of them will in a few yeares, bring him below them again: And as he was at first raysd by them, so he is ruind.

Notions are but Pictures of things in the Imagination of Man, and if they agree with their originals in Nature, they are true, and if not False. And yet some Men are so unwary in their Thoughts, as to confound them and mistake the one for the other, as if the Picture of a Man, were really the Person for whom it was drawn.

Though Adams knowledge cost him Deare, yet his want of knowledge betrayd him to it: for if his eies had been open before he tasted the Forbidden Fruite, He would never have forfeited the whole Orchard of Paradise for one Apple of it; though the Devil and his wife joynd forces against him.

Wisdom pays no Taxes, nor is it rated in the Subsidy-bookes, and therefore has not so much Right to a Share in the Government, as Wealth that contribute's more towards it. It is like hidden Treasure, that is of no use in the Traffique of the world, while it is conceald; and forfeited as soone as it is discoverd. And as knowledge cast Adam out of Paradise, so it do's all those who apply themselves to it, for the more they understand, they do but more plainly perceive, their own wants, and Nakednes, as he did, which before in the State of Ignorance, were hidden from him, untill the eies of his understanding were opened, only to let him see his losses, and the Miseries which he had betrayd himself unto. For the world appeare's a much finer thing to those that understand it not then to those who do, and Fooles injoy their Pleasures with greater Appetite and Gust then those who are more sensible of their vanity, and unwholsomnes.

The ordinary and most laborious Drudgeries of Mens hands are

18 it;] *comma altered from full point* B   22 towards] *altered from* to it B
29 opened] opene'd B

the cheapest of all, and the most Curious, and Ingenious the Dearest: But it prove's quite contrary in the Labors of the Braine, where the Dullest, and most Rugged Studies, as Law, Divinity &c are the most Profitable, and those of the greatest Ingenuity and
5 Knowledge as Philosophy &c of no valew at all.

Though many Men Repine, and Complain to see Fooles Govern, and wisemen obey, They mistake the true Reason of both: For wisdom is no standing Measure in the world more then Folly, and therefore can Pretend to no greater a Priviledge; For Fooles do not govern,
10 as they are Fooles, But as they are Commonly Fortunate, and Rich, and the Greater Number, which is the only standard in all Affaires, of the world. For no mans wisdom is able to give that Security for his Faith to be trusted with a Share in any Government, as the wealth of a Fool can. And 'tis no easy matter sometimes to distin-
15 guish the one from the other, while Pretences will serve as well to satisfy the world as Realities, and some times better, as making a fairer shew. And as among Madmen, He that is most Mad has a Naturall Dominion, and Superiority over all those, that have ever so little more Sense then himself, which they all acknowledge, and
20 submit to: So in the Government of the world, nothing is found to render a Man so fit, for Publique Imployments, as his want of Abilities for them, and nothing to obstruct, and Depresse others more, then the excellence of their Reason and Judgment./For the
148ᵛ
Bb world being a foolish and Bruitish thing in the whole, like a Barbar-
25 ous Nation will not easily indure to be governd any way, but by it's own Lawes, and idle Customes.

There is in all Oratory a Naturall Inclination to overdoing, and Aptnes to forget and transgress the just Limits of what is proper, and fit to be say'd, and no more: For an Orators Tongue, if it do's
30 not run before his wit, seldom faile's to outstrip his Judgment. For all volubility is much more light, and Aiery then Reason and Judgment, and therefore cannot but leave it behinde.

The Greek Tongue is of little use in our times, unless to serve Pedants and mountebanks to smatter withall; to coyne foolish
35 Titles for Medcines, and Bookes of all Languages, and furnish

11 standard] standar'd B   23 Judgment.] Judgment B   24 the] th B

Preachers with Sentences to astonish the Ignorant, and loose time withall in translating it over again into the vulgar and Nonsense. It is in itself a very untoward Language that abound's in a Multitude of Impertinent Declinations Conjugations, Numbers, Times, Anomula's, and formings of verbes, but has little or no Construction. And though no language is so Curious in the Contrivance of long and short vowels, yet they are so confounded by the Accent, that they are render'd of no use at all, And in verse, the Accent is again so confounded by the Quantity of the Syllable, that the Language become's another thing.

The Modern Fals-doctrine of the Court, That Mens Naturall Parts, are rather impaird then improv'd by Study and Learning, is so ridiculously False, that the Design of it is as Plain as the Ignorant Nonsense; and no more then what the Levellers, and Quakers found out before them, that is to bring down all other men (whom they had no possibility to come neare any other way) to an equality with themselves: that no man may be thought to receive any Advantage by that which they with all their Confidence, dare not pretend to. But if there should be any such thinge, they are the most incompetent Judges of it, who are incapable of understanding more then the worst halfe of the whole thing, and that too is their own Case. And the true State of that ly's between Dunce and Dunce, with whom Bookes, or no Bookes make so little Difference, that there is nothing gain'd or lost on either side: But in Persons of Ingenuity and equal Talents, the Advantage is as apparent, as in all Arts and Professions it is between those who have been bred up to any one, and such as are utterly ignorant of it, or which is worse have only learn'd to smatter. And he that do's not know so much as this, deserve's to go to a Physitian, for his Advice in Law, and a Lawyer for his Counsell in Physique. And in this they fall short of their Tutors the Fanatiques, who though they pretend to the same thing; yet are not such Sots to do it upon any Naturall accompt; but by virtue of Dispensations, and Gifts, and Lights, and therefore never undertook to work at one anothers Trades, in which they had never serv'd a Prenticeship. For that were too faire a way for Cheates and Impostors to deal in, and would immediatly, detect their Ignorance and Folly. It is true that some Learned men by their want of

Judgment, and Discretion, will some times do and say things
149ʳ ridiculous to those / Who are utterly ignorant, but he who from
Bb thence take's measure of all others is more Indiscreet then both. For
no man can make another mans want of Reason, his just excuse for
5 not improving his own, but he who would have been as little the
better for it, if he had taken the same Paines. And if there be no Art
to improve the understanding of Man, there can be no Improvment
of any thing else, for it is the understanding only that can improve
any thing, and if it cannot help it selfe, it is below the Ingenuity of
10 Beasts that are capable of being taught to do many things which
Nature never bred them up to. But the Truth of all is; That as it is
easier to cry down any thing then to take the necessary Paines to
understand it, and more glorious to appeare above it, then ever so
skilfull in it; So these men endeavor to make a virtue of Necessity,
15 and dispise their own Deficiences least others should do so, as
Gamsters do their losses, only to keep up their Credit, and make
the world believe they are in a better Condition then they really are,
that they may have the better opportunity to Cheat.

Those who Study, and Practice Mechanicall Artifices, grow
20 excellent by applying themselvs to but one thing, for few men were
ever known to bee considerable at more: But it fal's out quite contrary in contemplative knowledges, For he that is wholly taken up
with any one, is not only Ignorant in all others: But incapable to
Judge rightly of that which he professes. For there go's so much
25 partiality to cause an Addiction to any one alone, that whosoever is
possest with it, is so unable to make any just comparison of it, with
others (by which all Judgment is to be perform'd) that he is at best
but a Flatterer to himself and his own Inclinations.

Nature designe's every thing to it's end, and do's not make all
30 men to one Purpose but dispose's the greatest Part to the ordinary
Bus'nes, and Drudgery of the world, and because the necessitys of
life require the greatest numbers, as she gives the Generality, Capacities equall, to their Imployments, and no farther: So she makes
some to more noble Purposes, for her own Conversation, to trust
35 with her Secrets, and admit to the understanding of many Truths
that are conceald from vulgar Apprehension, and when such men

10 things] thing *B*   14 these] those *W*   31 necessitys] *altered from* necessar
B   32 gives] give *B*   33 farther:] farther,: *B*

meet with those Second Advantages that Art and Study can furnish them withall, they spread into a greater Latitude, and extent, but can never be improv'd to a greater height then Nature at first design'd; as men may grow fatter, and bigger by Plentifull feeding, but never taller then that Stature, that was measur'd out to them at 5 their full growth. And therefor as all knowledg is nothing but a right observation of Nature; He who suppose's he can understand any other way, is in an Error, For there was never but one Tree of Knowledg, and although that was the most Compendious way of attaining it, yet it cost Mankinde all the Study and Paines he has 10 ever since been condemnd to: For Adam might have liv'd still in Paradice, if he could have been contented, to know no more, then God and Nature had allow'd him; but when he would venture beyond his Latitude he was turn'd out to drudge, and labour for his living, and ever since Knowledge, and labour, and Study, are so 15 inseparably joynd together, that there is no way of arriving at the one; without the other, both being two twin-effects of the / same **149ᵛ** Cause. And as the earth was commanded to bring forth thornes and Bb Thistles to supply Adam with labour: There is no Knowledge that is not so fruitfully stockd with Difficulties, that those who are con- 20 demnd to a Contemplative Punishment, shall finde as hard and barren a Soyl to manure, as he did of the earth. And although it has pleasd God and Nature to allow man no way of improving his understanding, but by Study, observation, and Practice; it is the perpetuall Custome of all those who have been deny'd those advan- 25 tages, to perswade themselves that they have no neede of them, rather then be thought to want any thing, and though they finde by experience, that no man can attaine to the understanding of an Ordinary Mechanique Trade untill he ha's spent some time in the Practice of it, yet they believe it may be don, in matters of the 30 greatest Difficulty, and Depth, though it will not hold in the most easy. It is naturall for all men to affect those things most, which they are most incapable of, and never to valew Health so much, as when they are sick: and therefore none set a higher esteeme, upon Learning and Knowledge, then such as have just wit enough to 35 know there is such a thing in the world, and because it is deny'd them, have a greater hankering after it, then those who are most capable to acquire it: And as nature is soe industrious to give herself ease when she is opprest, and render's the greatest paine with

use and Custom tollerable, so she relieves the Necessities of those, who are ashamd to have them known to others, with perswading them they injoy that which of all things they are the most destitute of. And hence it come's that no men are so indefatigable Drudges in
5 all manner of Sciences, as those to whom Nature ha's allow'd the weakest abilities to attaine to any perfection in them: for Dunces are commonly observd to be the hardest Students, as those always prove the most passionate Lovers, that meet with the most Coy and disdainfull Mistresses: For no love-martyr ever hangd himself for a
10 gentle, and tender-hearted Lady. But as such men labour and vex themselves in vaine: so there are others no less unfortunate, who having the greatest assistances of Nature, to attaine to any thing they can propose to themselves, are commonly observd to want industry, as much, as the Industrious do ingenuity: and the sooner
15 they are able to prevayl, the sooner they become indifferent; for all delight is lost in the Injoyment, and Appetite extinguisht in Satisfaction. And therefore are not so much concernd and possest with any thing, as those who pay dearer for it, to whom it appeares a kinde of Novelty, or strange thing, that has a greater power over all
20 men at first, and is more taking, then when it become's familier, and is no news.

1 tollerable,] tollerable. *B*   4 no] *or possibly* noe *B*

A man may be condemnd out of his own mouth, but never acquitted, for his own Testimony is sufficient to serve against him, but not at all for him: The reason is because no man can be supposd to be so much an enemy to his own Preservation, to accuse himself wrongfully, nor any so guilty, but if his own Deniall might bee 5 sufficient to acquit him, he would never be found Guilty, though the Fact were never so manifest.

Authority in the Affayres of Truth is very inconsiderable; For in Trafique men do not consider from whom they receive money, so much as what it is: and if it be adulterate, or clipd, The Reputation 10 of the Payer will not make it Currant.

A man may be deceivd and cheated with Truth, if he want Judgment, no less then with Falshood; as he may stumble, and fall in the right way, for want of care, as wel as in the wrong.

Truth is like that shield that fell from Heaven, upon which the 15 fate of the Commonwelth of Rome depended, and therefore the Romans causd a certaine Number of others to be made so like it, that whosoever should attempt to steal the True one, should hardly hit upon it. So although there be but one Truth that come's from Heaven, there are so many false Counterfets introduc'd by reasons of 20 State that pretend to be it, that nothing is more difficult then to distinguish the true from the false and fictitious. For the Devil of Error doth perpetually transforme him selfe into the shape of the Angel of light Truth, and nothing make's it passe more freely among the Vulgar, then that Mistake that made Ephæstion appeare 25 more like a king then Alexander, because he was braver, and more richly cloathd.

Truth is Scarse so much as a Notion, for it is but the Putting of those Notions of things (in the understanding of Man) into the same order that their Originals are in Nature.   30

o. 1–2 [fo. 150^r] *See p. 136, ll. 16–18*   6 sufficient] sifficient *B*   20 many] ma-/ *B*

150ᵛ   The constancy and Resolution of Martyrs is no Argument of the
Ab   Truth of that which they suffer for (for there have been Martyrs
of all Religions) but of their own Perswasion of it: Although the
People, who commonly mistake one Cause for another, use to under-
5 stand it otherwise: Into whose hearts softned with Pitty, the
Suffrings of others use to make a deep but false Impression: For if
the Punishment be but somewhat severe, the Beholders who know
no limits but extremes if they dislike the Cruelty of the inflictors,
are very apt to condemne every thing else.

10   There is no Doubt but some Secrets in Nature have been discoverd in Dreames (as wel as events foreseene) when the Imagination has had no Conduct of Reason, nor Sense: and yet Dreames are
very improper and unfit ways of discovering Truth.

     I do not believe the Storys of the Legend to be so Ridiculous as
15 some Men thinke them: For though they appeare very vaine and
monstruous, certainely the Inventers had a Purpose to which they
were very Serviceable: For considering how far the Credulity of the
People would reach, they were to fit it with Fables Proportionable,
in which if they had not out don all Possibility, They could never
20 have kept their Beliefe in exercise, nor have been able to keep them
in Awe, whose Perswasion being accustomd to swallow such prodigious Impostures, would become insensible of lesse.

     They that endeaver to redeeme the world from Error and Im-
posture, have a very ungrateful Imployment, for if they do any man
25 good it is against his will, and therefore they must not only reward
but thanke themselves: For as Mad men always hate their Physitians, The People can never endure those, that seeke to recover
them from their deare Dotage.

     Since the knowledg of good and evill are unseperable, it hath
30 pleasd almighty God, that man should know less how to do himselfe
good then he might, lest he should know more how to do others
hurt then is fit for him.

151ʳ   Mens Fortunes and Estates have past through so many cheates,

     8 extremes] *altered from* extremities *B*   11 foreseene)] *probably altered from*
foreseene, *B*   21 Awe,] Awe. *B*

and Impostures before they came to them, that it is a hard matter to Ab
say who has a just Right to any thing; And therefor he that by the
worst meanes gets what he can, is not like to do much wrong, where
there is so little Right, And it is the Bus'nes of Justice, to take from
thieves and cheats what they come unjustly by.   5

The Devil tempt's men to be wicked that he may punish them for
being so.

Curious Disputes, between Men of Different Factions, are the
same Artifices that Charletans use to draw the ignorant multitude
from one another. And therfor as the end they all drive at is indirect, 10
so are the ways they all take to attaine it, by al sorts of little
Fallacies to impose upon one another, and never care to come neare
the Truth, but only in Discovering one anothers Impertinencies,
falsities, and Juglings, but take the same Course to gaine Proselytes
as the Devil dos Soules.   15

Oathes and Obligations in the Affaires of the world are like
Ribbins and Knots in Dressing, that seeme to ty something, but do
not at all. For nothing but interest dos really oblige.

All Great Actions derive one half of their Greatness, from the
meaness of other mens Performances. For when all Particulars meet 20
upon eaven Tearmes, there is seldom any great Difference in the
Success.

The very same thinges that Mountebankes Empiriques and
Quacks are to Learned Physitians, are Pettifoggers to Lawyers, and
Fanatiques to Churches. And the Negligence, Pride, and Ignorance 25
of the Professors of those Faculties are one halfe of the Reasons why
those Impostors pass so Currantly among the Rabble, And the
other is, that as most men gaine more by indirect ways, then Plaine
Dealing, So they have greater incouragements to be more Industrious (as they always prove) then those that are content with honest 30
and moderate Gaines. For there is noe Profession in the world in
which honest and careful Industry will gaine half so much, as the
cheates and Impostures that belong to it.

Gaming is a thing between Diversion and Busnes, Jeast, and **151ᵛ**

14 Juglings,] Juglings. *B*

Aa Earnest. And although it go's by the Name of Sport and Pastime, it always proves to be the most serious of all things, to those that either win or loose very much.

Logitians cannot teach men solid, and substantiall Reason, but 5 only little Tricks and evasions, that are worse then nothing, like stamping on the Flour of a Fenceing school, that go's for nothing upon the Grasse.

Can any thing be more Ridiculous then the Common Custome of most old Men, who the less time they have to live, are the more 10 Solicitous to provide Abundance for the use of it. Tully.

B Truth is too strict and severe to make Parties, and Factions, and want[s] that free latitude to flourish in, which error always usurpe's: For there is too little of it known, to make any great appearance in the world, or beare up against those vast multitude's of errors and 15 Impostures that prevayle every where, like the antient Barbarians, and modern Turkes, that use to invade the civiler part of the world with numerous Forces, and subdue them not by virtu of their courages, or conduct, but the impetuous force of their rude Numbers; beside the greater numbers of Tricks, and Artifices, that 20 Falshood has to support it self, and impose upon truth that has none at all. And though truth be the difficultst thing in the world to be acquainted with, yet when it is once known, it is the playnest, and most easy to be dealt with; that is always constant to it self, and has no variations to be allowd for, nor alterations from its own originall 25 Simplicity, and therefore is the more to be undermin'd by falshood that never deales fairly and openly in the Affayres of the world, but has change of faces and every one proof against all impression. Can personate and act truth and do what it please's in her Name, like the Ægyptian Conjurers though in the Presence of Kings, by whom shee 30 is too often imployd and trusted.

[151*]

11 strict and] *interlined B* (*probably by Longueville*) B and Falshood (b, b) B

19 greater] greater, B   24 its] *interlined* [151*] *Unnumbered folio, with only headings* Truth

Religion

There is a vast Disproportion between Gods Mercy, and his Justice, for the one reaches but to the third or fourth Generation but the other unto thousands.

The Sin of swearing should seem to be greater then any other, for though the Scripture say's God see's no Sin in the Saints, yet it do's not say that he heare's none.

When the Devil tempted Christ, he set him on the highest Pinnacle of the Temple. Great Church Preferments are great Temptations.

The Church of Rome teaches the People Religion, as men teach singing Birdes; Shut them up and keep them Darke.

The Judaical Law was but confirmd, and establishd by Moses for it was in use long before, as appeares by the Distinction of clean and unclean Beasts in the Arke. The Sacrifices of Cain, and Abel. Josephs refusing to commit the Sin of Adultery with Potifars wife before it was forbidden by the 10 Commandments.

God did not make man, until he had finishd the world, and as it were built, and furnishd his house for him.

Fayth is so far from being above Reason and Knowledg, that it is below Ignorance which it depende's upon; for no man can believe, and not be Ignorant, but he may be Ignorant and not believe. Whensoever Reason and Demonstration appear's, Fayth and Ignorance vanish together.

There is no folly, or Madnes so vaine and ridiculous, but if it put it self into the Protection of Piety and Religion, is by the easy credulous and Ignorant reputed Sacred, and not to be touchd. As

---

11 keep them] keep then *B*　　　16 Commandments.] *then interlined:* and the distinction of cleane and uncleane Beasts in Noahs Arke. *B*　　21–2 Whensoever] whensoever *B*

Malefactors in the Church of Rome when they have taken Sanctuary, let their Crimes be ever so heinous, are by no meanes to be brought to Justice, and those that attempt it are excommunicated and deliverd over to the Devil, for offering to Obstruct his Affaires, as
5 long as he proceed's in a Canonicall Regular and ecclesiastical way.

The Turkes accompt mad men Saints, and the Christians dispise them for it and yet esteeme the greatest Madneses in the world Sanctity.

David complaine's that the zeal of Gods house had eaten him up,
10 But the Fanatiques zeale quite contrary is always devouring Gods House.

Repentant Teares are the waters upon which the Spirit of God move's. Malvezzi.

152ᵛ   Princes and States do by Religion as the King of France do's by
Ab   his Salt, make every man that is his Subject take a Quantity of it,
16   whether he use it or not.

The Church of Rome allow's of holy Cheates, and Religious Fraudes in Lying Miracles and false Legends, and of pious Idolatry in worshipping of Images. God forbid's them, but they wilbe wiser,
20 and believe they may be allowd in a christian way.

Because the Scripture says obedience is better then Sacrifice, Sectarys believe the less of it wil serve.

Presbyterians cry down the Common Prayer because there is no Ostentation of Gifts in it, with which the People are most taken, and
25 therefore they esteeme it but as lost time.

The Curiositys of Ceremony in the Church of Rome are like the Painted Glasse in Church windores, designd to keepe out light, not to let it in. And in Italy they keep their Churches Darke, [and] their Congregations Ignorant for Devotion. They call Confession Purging
30 of the Soul, And they use it commonly as men take Purges, to get a better Stomack to their Sins.

19 Images.] *or* Images, *B*   28 [and]] *MS. blotted B*

A Charitable man is an Instrument of Divine Providence, by whose meanes it preserve's the most wretched from Sterving.

Clergy-men when they cannot perswade kings to make Priests Princes, endevor to make Princes believe that they are Priests (as the Bishops did King James that he was Persona mixta) and by that 5 meanes infer that Priests are or ought to be Princes.

The Empire and the Church out of it, have observd the self same Method and order in their Increase, Height, and Decay: For as the Empire was raysd upon the Virtue and Courage of many excellent Persons produc'd by several Ages, and when it came into the 10 Handes of a single Person, did immediatly degenerate into all Lewdnes, Vice and Tyranny imaginable: So the Church that was founded upon the Piety Devotion, and Martyrdom of the Primitive Christians when it came to be setled under the sole Authority of the Popes, did presently fall from it's first Integrity, and grew so highly deboshd 15 from what it was in the beginning, that as the one extremity has already in a manner utterly destroyd the Empire, so the other has very neare equally don the Church; and in Time is like to be the final Ruine of it.

There is Nothing that can so wel enable a man to Judg of those 20 things as the observation of the Nature and Common Practice of Mankinde, by which it will easily appeare to any man of an Indifferent Capacity, and Judgment, that it / is Impossible it should be 153ʳ otherwise: For the effects of True Piety and Devotion are always Ab found among a Few, and never to procced from great Multitudes 25 especially where Power and Interest have to do.

The Catholicks are very devout in observing Lents and Fishdays merely out of Civility and Respect to St Peter who was a Fisherman.

It is no lesse Idolatry to discribe God in a Corporeal Shape to the Eare, then to paint him so to the Eie: The Difference being only in 30 the Sense conveying, not the thing conveyd to the understanding.

Æquivocation is worse then plaine Lying in Matters of Religion, for a lyer intends only to cheat another man, but he that æquivocat's do's at once design to deceive God, and his own Conscience and another man too.

As the expectation of Happines is greater then the Injoyment; So the Apprehension of evil to come is, many Times, greater then the
5 Thing it self. This causes Men in Dispair to make away them selves, and to meet rather then expect that which they feare; Christ himself was so impatient of the Delay of what he was to suffer, that he bid Judas do quickly what he was to do.

Men commonly never Regard their Soules, until they have
10 spoyld their Bodys like our Richard the third, who when he had kild the Brother fell in Love with the Sister.

Heresies may seeme to have contributed much in the Infancy of the Church to the Propagation of it: For it was impossible (speaking of Natural meanes) that the Plaine True and simple way of Christi-
15 anity should be receivd by men of all Tempers, and Inclinations, before they were prepard by use, and education. But Heresies being the Disease of Different Constitutions and Capacitys, could not fayle to infect others of the same Latitude, and tendency, which any of them met with; and so bring them within the Name and verge of
20 Christianity, out of which they could not be ejected, while the Church had no Secular Arme, but the Devil to deliver them over to. But afterward when it had acquir'd Authority to establish or reject what it pleasd; Those opinions it disapprovd were condemn'd and the Persons that obstinatly adhered to them severely punishd, and
25 the rest receivd into the Number of the Orthodox and faythful. So that as Dogs drive in the Straglers of a Flock, though they are none of it themselves, they brought many that were without, into the Pale of the Church, which otherwise might possibly have never
29 come there by any other meanes.

153ᵛ   Omens among the Romans being Part of their Religion, and
Ab   observd by every Person, there could nothing of any great and

3 expectation] *altered from* expectations B   6–8 Christ . . .] *duplicated B*
155ʳ   6–7 Christ himself] Our Savior Christ B 155ʳ   7 so] *om. B* 155ʳ   the]
om. B 155ʳ   7–8 of what . . . that he] in his very being betrayd and therefore B
155ʳ   9–11 *Duplicated and underlined B* 212ʳ   9 commonly] *om. B* 212ʳ
10 our] *om. B* 212ʳ   who when] tha[ ] after B 212ʳ   11 kild] destroyd B
212ʳ   fell in] made B 212ʳ   with] to B 212ʳ   16 education.] education B

Publique concernment fal out, but something (though ever so accidental) must of necessity happen somewhere before it, that might be easily interpreted to foreshew it: Beside many that were forgd and made afterwards, according to that of Livy Dec. 3. L 4. Prodigia multa nunciata sunt. Quæ quo magis credebant simplices 5 et Religiosi Homines eo etiam plura nunciabantur. Such a vaine Delight do Ignorant People take, to heare and tell strange things. And that is the Reason why almost all their Historys do abound with Storys of this kinde.

Poverty and want are greater Temptations then Riches: when 10 our Savior had fasted 40 days, and as many Nights, the Devil thought it the fittest time to attaque him, and St Peter denyd and forswore Christ when he saw him in Affliction. For wealth and Luxury can but Tempt: Necessity compel's.

The enmitys of Religious People would never rise to such a 15 Height, were it not for their mistake, That God is better serv'd with their opinions then their Practices, Opinions being very inconsiderable further then they have influence upon Actions.

The Bigger the Volumes of Conciliators are the less Credit they deserve, for the Difference must of Necessity be very great, where 20 there is so much Difficulty to compound it. Things that have any Natural Relation are easily made to agree.

The Judaicall and Levitical Law was deliverd by God to Moses the Civil Magistrate, and by him to Aaron the Priest.

Roman Catholiques cannot pray without their Tooles, as Beads 25 to pray with, Bookes to pray by, and an Image to pray to. They have so very weake memories, that they are apt to forget Christ if he be but out of sight.

There are two Sorts of People that Profess Religion, The Hypocrites, and those that meane well. The Hypocrites are not only the 30 greater number but the more subtle and Crafty, that profess

---

10 Riches:] Riches, *B*   12 him,] him. *B*   13–14 For . . .] *probably interlined* (*cf. l. 22n*) *B*   21 it.] it, *B*   22 agree.] agree. ⟨For wealth and
Luxury can but tempt, Necessity compell's.⟩ *B*   26 with,] with *B*

Religion as a Trade, and therefore omit noe occasion to make the fayrest shews, and pretend to the greatest Zeale. The wel-meaning are commonly so easy and Simple, that they always suffer themselves to be govern'd by the Hypocrites, who with wrested and misapplyd
5 Texts of Scripture, and pulpit-Sophistry, can easily make them believe any wickednes how inhumane so ever to be a christian Duty.

159ʳ   In the first times of Christian Religion many Saintes were made,
Aa but since the Popes found out a way of selling Sanctity as Princes do honor, and conferring of Benefices in the church triumphant as wel
10 as the militant, they have been very sparing of bestowing that honor upon any but such as left money enough, to go to the charge of it.

Preachers use to turne the Historical part of the Scripture into Fable, and then make Mythologies upon it: And the Morall, and
15 Theologicall into Riddles, and afterward expound them.

There is no better Argument to prove that the Scriptures were written by Divine Inspiration, then that excellent saying of our Savior, If any man will go to Law with thee for thy cloke, give him thy Coate also.

20   The ancient Heathen who knew no True God supplyd that defect with multitudes of false ones, among which they had Deitys of two sorts. The one of things as Jupiter the Aier, that containes and comprehends all things, Juno his wife and Sister the Lower Region of the Aire, and therefor when Ixion made love to her and thought to
25 embrace her, he found she was but a Cloud; Apollo the Sun, Neptune the Sea, Vesta the Earth &c. The other of Notions abstract from matter, as Fortune Pax atque Fides Victoria Virtus, but these were but inferiors, and the first carry'd away all the Devotion, and adoration from them.

30   The Ægyptians that worship'd Onions and Leeke's were more humane then the Catholiques for they forbore to eate that which they ador'd. Porrum et cæpe nefas violare et frangere morsu.

     3 easy] easily *B*   11 charge] charge. *B*   22 sorts.] *altered from* sorts, *B*
as] a *B*   23 things,] things. *B*   25 Sun,] Sun. *B*   27 these] *or possibly*
those *B*   32 ador'd.] ador'd *B*

Homer never makes his Gods and Goddeses appeare to those whom they tooke part withall but when they were in som great Danger and Distresse.

It was the Profuseness of Leo the 10th that gave the first occasion to the reformation of Religion, For when all Sorts of Spirituall exac- 5 tions had been usd to the uttermost, and no New ways left to rayse more money to supply his vast expences, He by sequestring all the Christian world, and putting all men to compound with his Commissioners for their Delinquencys, and Sins, enforcd them to take those Courses which have since engagd halfe the Christian world to 10 take part with them.

Fanatiques suppose there are no Christians in this Age but them- **159ᵛ** selves, because in the Primitive times all but the Appostles and their Ab Proselytes were either Jews or Pagans, and therefor they will endure no church Government but what was then used. As if the Jews, 15 after they had passd through the wildernes, and were setled in the Lands allotted their severall Tribes, should stil believe themselves bound to live in Tents and remove from place to place, because their fore-fathers did so when they were in the wildernes.

Monasterys are but a Kinde of Civill Bedlams where those that 20 would bee otherwise troublesom to the world, are perswaded to shut up themselves.

He that give's to the Poore make's a Begging Present to god almighty in expectation to have ten times as much as it cost him. But he that presents the Rich do's it to buy favour, and pay's before 25 hand for that which he never has: so that Bribing is the evenest way of both.

All the abilities of our moderne Guifted men consist in fantasstique Senseles expressions, and silly affected Phrases, just in such a Stile as the great Turke, and the Persian Sophy use to write, which 30 they believe to be the true Propriety of the Spirit, and highest perfection of all Sanctity. This Canting run's through all Professions and Sorts of men, from the Judge on the Bench, to the Begger in the Stocks, and like a Spell or charme, has a wonderfull operation [on] the

10 those] these *W*   34 Stocks,] Stocks. *B*

Rabble, for they Naturally admire any unusuall words which they do not understand, but would gladly seeme to do, as believing all wisdome as these men do all holines to consist in words. They call their Gifts Dispensations, because they believe God do's dispence
5 with them for any wickednes which they can Commit.

An Hypocrite hide's his Vices, as a Dog do's his meate when his Belly is full; untill he has a fresh Appetite, and then he know's where to treat himself again.

In the Primitive Church when there was no Ecclesiasticall Govern-
10 ment, nor any use of the Civil Power among Christians to re-straine the loose freedom of Opinions, there were more Heresies bred in 2 or 3 hundred yeares, then in 1200 after when there was church Government and Authority to suppress them.

154ʳ The Originall of Sacrificing Living Creatures among the Heathen,
Ab may seeme to proceed from the cheat of Priests, who could not
16 possibly invent a subtler way to become Sharers in the wealth of men, which in those times before the use of Money, consisted only in their Cattle (of which the first Money had both the Stamp and Name) for they burnt, only the Intrailes and Tallow, and took the
20 rest as their fees to themselves, not unlike the Keepers of Parkes in our times who are allowd their fees for every Dere which they kill.

The Differences and Distractions of Mankinde in matters of Religion, do's not proceed from an unaptnes in human Nature to the service of God, but from the Defect, and want of Certainty in
25 the Rules and prescriptions by which they are to apply themselves to it. For all men agree in the end of Religion that God is to be wor-shipd, to which they are by Nature So Powerfully inclin'd, that though they differ only about the manner how, they are impatient of the least opposition that can arise from a Circumstance, and if
30 there were but so much generall Certainty in the Doctrines of Religion as there is in some other knowledges, in which Mankinde may seeme to bee less Concernd, all the world would be of one Church.

The Saints in heaven do not believe in God, and the Devils in Hel

5 they] *om. B*   20 themselves,] themselves. *B*

do, For St Paul say's faith and hope have no Being in Heaven, and
it is written in the Gospel that the Devils believe and tremble.

The Papists that use to hire Penitentiaries that scourge themselvs
for the Sins of others, are very simple if they believe they receive
any Benefit by it: and no less vain then he that believe's another 5
man may take Physique for him.

Almighty God bestow's the inæstimable Treasure of Light upon
us freely, which wee enjoy without any Cost or Trouble of our own,
untill Nature requiring the Reparation of Sleepe, to which it is
unusefull, he remove's it that so pretious a Thing might not be 10
spent to no purpose, and when wee are fit to use it againe, he as
freely restore's it to us.

Certainly Almighty God will not bee so unmercifull (since his 154ᵛ
Mercy is above all his workes) to Mankinde, to expose the eternall Ab
Being of Soules, to the Passion, Interest, and Ignorance, of those that 15
make themselves his Messengers, and do their owne worke in his
Name.

They that Dispute Matters of Fayth into nice Particulars and
Curious Circumstances, do as unwisely as a Geographer that would
undertake to draw a true Map of Terra Incognita by mere Imagina- 20
tion, For though there is such a Part of the Earth, and that not
without Mountaines, and Vallies, and Plaines and Rivers, yet to
attempt the Discription of these, and assigne their Situations, and
Tracts without a view of the Place, is more then Ridiculous.

They that believe God dos not foresee Accidents, because 25
Nothing can be known that is not, and Accidents have no being,
untill they are in Act, are very much mistaken: For Accident is but
a Terme invented to relieve Ignorance of Causes, as Physitians use
to call the strange operations of Plants, and Mineralls Occult Qualities, not that they are without their Causes, but that their Causes 30
are unknown. And indeed there is not any thing in Nature, or event,
that ha's not a Pedegree of Causes, which though obscure to us,
cannot be so to God, who is the first Cause of all things.

Supererogation is no Contemplative Virtue, nor always an active

1 Heaven,] Heaven. *B*   2 tremble] trempble *B*   23 these] those *W*

one; for in war it is a Crime, for he that go's beyond his Commission though with Prosperous Succes, is punishd no less then he that neglect's his Orders, which he that observe's though he miscarry, is justly excus'd. So he that thinke's to please God by forcing his understanding in Disquisition of him, beyond the Limits which he ha's been pleasd to prescribe, beside the loss of his Labour, do's but endeavor to intrude where he is denyd accesse, and prepostorously attempt to serve God by Disobeying of him.

Error as wel as Devotion is the Natural Child of Ignorance, and the elder Brother.

155ʳ That commandement that injoynes all People to honor their
Aa Parents without any exception whether they are good, or bad, do's (no doubt) oblige them to do the same thing to their Native Cuntrys, whether they deserve it, or not: and it is a kinde of Piety to be Partiall, and mistake for the better.

Zeal is of no use without Opposition and Conscience has no way to shew its Tendernesse, but in seeking Occasion to take offence at some thing or other, and the more slight, and triviall the better, for it's strict tendernes, and Innocence appeares to be the greater, and the world will not be apt to suspect the Fayth and Integrity of those, that are severe and scrupulous in small matters.

When Absolom had resolv'd to Rebel against the King his Father, he had no way so proper to put his Designe in execution, as that of pretending to pay a vow which he had made to the Lord.

Hypocritical and Zealous Teachers that Cry down Plays most, are the greatest Actors themselves in the world. For they do not at all indeavor to convince their Hearers, with strength of Reason, and Soundness of Doctrine, but with Laborious vehemence and Noyse, Forc'd Tones, and Fantastique extravagant expressions, to impose upon their Naturall Infirmitys. And those that do not use this way, do that which is as bad, apply to their Ignorance, weaknes, and Passions, with so much Art, and Cuning, that he must be an excellent Actor that is able to come neare them.

3 Orders,] Orders. *B*   17 take] *altered from* shew *B*   24 pretending] petending *B*   32 Cuning] *or* Cunning *B*

All Innovations in Church and State are like new-built Houses, unwholesome to live in, untill they are made healthful, and agreable by time.

Hoc est Corpus meum, is true in a Litteral Sense, For as Bread naturally turne's to Flesh, and wine to bloud; He, to whom all 5 times are present, might very properly say that is, that was to bee.

Joseph is say'd in the Gospell to be a Just man for being kinde or rather mercifull to his wife. Of all morall Virtues Justice only is sayd to go to heaven.

The Practice of the Church of Rome, and that of the Reformation 10 in dealing with Sinners, is like that of a Charletan, and a Learned Physitian in Curing of claps, for as the one will not undertake a Cure unless the Patient wil enter into a Course, and observe Rules, which the other will dispence with, and give him, leave / to go abroad and 155ᵛ follow his occasions (that is such as gave him the Disease) So the Ab Reformd Churches, will not promise forgivenes of Sins, without 16 Repentance and amendment of Life; which the Church of Rome freely dispences withall, and upon mere Confession, and penance perform'd give's them, Pardon, and freedom to do the same things over againe.   20

The greatest Hypocrites may seeme to be the most meritorious of all Professors, for he that can prevayle with himself (in dispight of Nature and the Devil) to do that which is quite contrary to his owne Inclination; and publiquely professe Piety, and devotion, though of all things he has the greatest aversion from it, cannot but 25 seeme to deserve better, then he that do's only comply with the Natural Propensity of his own Temper. For it is a greater Argument of Self-denyall to doe then to forbeare those things which we are Naturally indisposd to.

We do not finde that the Possessions of the Devil have ever don 30 half so much mischief as his mere Temptations.

Rebellion is sayd to be like the Sin of witch-craft, because both are

3. 1–3 *See p. 28, ll. 6–8*   14 leave] *catchword only B*   18 withall,]
withall. *B*

promoted, and manag'd with nothing else but Lyes, and cheates, and Impostures. For civil Armes can neither be raysd, nor maintaind, by honest meanes.

The Gentiles (though they were all Idolaters) prov'd much better
5 Christians then the Jewes, who were bred up in the Service of the True God: And therefor the Apostles presently gave over Preaching to them, and remov'd themselves as far of, as they could. St Paul was glad to appeale to Nero the greatest Tyrant in the world, to
9 deliver himself out of the hands of his Cuntry-men.

156ʳ   The Israelites after Josephs Death were made slaves by the
Aa Ægyptians not for any Sin (that wee heare of) which they had committed, but only for being Poore at first, and after Courtiers to Pharo.

It is a dangerous thing to be too inquisitive, and search too
15 narrowly into a true Religion, for 50000 Bethshemites were destroyd only for looking into the Ark of the Covenant, and ten times as many have been ruind for looking too curiously into that Booke in which that Story is recorded.

Men inflict and suffer Persecution for Religion with equall zeal,
20 and though both pretend to Conscience, both oftentimes are equally mistaken.

They that professe Religion and believe it consist's in frequenting of sermons, do, as if they should say They have a great desire to serve God, but would faine be perswaded to it. Why should any man
25 suppose that he please's God, by patiently hearing an Ignorant fellow render Religion ridiculous?

If the Saints in Heaven retaine any of that tendernes of Charity that can only bring them thether; They may seeme not to enjoy much felicity if they have any sense of that eternall Misery which
30 many of their dearest relations must of Necessity be condemnd to.

The more false any Religion is, the more Industrious the Priests of it are, to keepe the People from prying into the Mysteries of it,

and by that Artifice render them the more zealous, and Confident
in their Ignorance.

Men ought to do in Religion as they do in war: when a Man of
Honor is over-power'd, and must of Necessity render himself up a
Prisoner, Such are always wont to indeavor to do it to some Person 5
of Command and Quality, and not to a mean Scoundrell: So since
all men are oblig'd to be of some Church; it is more honorable (if
there were nothing else in it) to be of that which ha's some Reputation, then such a one as is contemptible, and justly dispisd by all the
best of men.   10

Gathering of Churches is like the Gathering of Grapes of Thornes,
or Figs of thistles; for as those harsh and untractable Plants, seeme
to bee no part of the first Creation, but to come in afterwards with
the Curse, so are all Schismatiques to the Churches which they set
up against.   15

Almost all the Miracles in the Jewish History, from their Deliver- **156ᵛ**
ance from their first slavery by the Plagues of Ægypt, to their Aa
second Captivity in Babilon, were performed by the Distruction,
Ruine, and Calamity of Mankinde. But all those that our Savior
wrought to confirme his Doctrine, quite contrary; By raysing 20
the Dead to life, cureing of Desperate Diseases, Making the Blinde
see, casting out of Devils, and feeding of hungry Multitudes &c,
but never doing harme to any thing, all Suitable to those excellent Lessons of Peace, and Love, and Charity, and Concord, to
which the whole Purpose of all that he did, or sayd, perpetually 25
tended: whosoever therefor do's indeavor to draw Rules, or
Examples for the Practice of Christianity, from the extraordinary
Proceedings of the Jews, must of Necessity make a strange confusion,
and Adulterate mixture of the Christian Religion, by depraving,
and alloying it with that which is so directly averse and contrary to 30
it's own Nature. And as this unnaturall Mixture of two Different
Religions was the first Cause of Dissension among the Apostles,
themselves, and afterwards determin'd and resolv'd against by
them all: Soe there is no Doctrine of Rebellion, that was ever vented
among Christians, that was not reviv'd, and Raysd from this kinde 35
of false and forcd construction.

21 Diseases,] Diseases. *B*

As those that use to take Physique often, do at length finde it has
no operation upon their Bodys: So those that are wont to heare
Sermons often finde that that Spirituall Physique do's not at all
worke with their Souls, and that is one Reason why no sort of men
are lesse Sensible for the most part of those Doctrines which they
are perpetually accustomd unto.

The Romish Religion is best fitted to the Capacitys of the Ignorant Rabble and better secur'd against their wise Inquiries into
it self; Gives the Priests a greater Power over them then any other,
who are so industrious to loose no opportunity of Improving their
Interest, that whosoever is Delighted with Shows, and Sights, and
Strange Stories, and ha's not a great Strength of Naturall Reason
(as such People seldom have) is incapable of ever being redeem'd
from it.

The Popes heretofore usd to send Christian Princes to plant
Religion with the Sword among Pagans, while they with tricks and
Artifices Planted the Pagan at home.

157ʳ
Aa Pharo who was Destroyd for being Hard-hearted, or renderd
Hard hearted to be Destroy'd, was not neare so pertinaciously
obstinate, and incapable of being convincd, by those Prodigious
Miracles, of which he was an eie witness, as the Jews themselves
prov'd afterwards, for whose Deliverance they were purposely
wrought. For after so many miserable Experiments as he had seen
try'd at his own charge, he was at last satisfy'd and glad to give
them leave to Depart: but when he Retracted that, and persu'd
them to his own Distruction, They became so unsatisfy'd with
their own miraculous Deliverance, that they desir'd nothing more
then to return back againe, in so much, that no miracle that was
ever wrought for them, appeare's so prodigious as that of their own
obstinate incredulity.

Priests have found out a way to render the meanest and most vile
of all things (as Rags, and Pieces of Rotten wood, and Bones &c.)
the most Pretious when they are pretended to be the Reliques of
Saintes and are publiquely visited and ador'd.

9 it self;] *comma altered from (or possibly to) full point B*   20 incapable] in-
capble B

Christ commanded the Devil (when he grew so Arrogant to tempt him) to go behind him; But the old Priests taught the People to bid him go before when they exorcisd him with saying avant.

The Religion of the Pagans had its Foundation upon Naturall Philosophy, as the Christian may seeme to have upon Morall. For all those Gods which the Ancients worshipd as Persons, did but Represent the severall Operations of Nature, upon severall Kindes of Matter, which being wrought by an unvisible, and unintelligible Power, the wisest men of those Times could invent no way so fit and proper, to reduce them with Respect and Reverence to the Vulgar Capacity, as by expressing them by the Figures of Men and women (like the Ægyptian Hieroglyphiques, or as Poets and Painters do Virtues and Vices) and by ascribing Divinity to them, to introduce a veneration in the mindes of the Common People, who are apt to contemne any thing that they can understand, and admire nothing but what is above their Capacity, which they would never have receivd upon any other accompt. And therefor with great Piety and Devotion ador'd those Notions / Represented by Statues and Images which they would never have regarded if they had understood. For if they had understood the Naturall Reason of Thunder, they would never have Sacrific'd to Jupiter, to divert it from themselves: For their Capacitys are Naturally too Dul to apprehend any thing that is removd ever so little from outward sense, though it be deriv'd from it. But are wonderfull acute at unriddling of Mysteries, and such things as have no Relation at all to it.

When David put on Sauls Armour, he found it was so heavy for him, that he could do no Feates of Armes in it, because it had the weight of all Sauls Sins upon it, who was a Tyrant, an Oppressor, and a wicked man: So those that put on the Armour, or the Causes of Unjust and wicked Princes, will finde it ly's so heavy upon their Consciences, and Courages, that they can never behave themselves valiently, nor appeare to any purpose untill they have put it of as David did. For though he did nothing but by Divine Assistance, which could have don his Bus'nes as easily in the most unwealdy Armes, as without them, yet it would have nothing to do with any

thing how Innocent so ever of it self, that had any relation to so
wicked a Person.

Ordinary wicked Persons, that have any Impression of Humane
Nature left, never Commit any great Crime, without some aversion,
5 and Dislike, although it be not strong enough to prevale against
the present Motives of utility or Interest, and commonly live and
dy Penitent for it. But the Modern Saint that believe's himself
Priviledg'd, and above Nature, ingage's himself in the most horrid
of all Wickedneses, with so great an Alacrity, and assurance and is
10 so far from Repentance, that he puts them upon the Accompt of
Pious Dutys, and good workes.

An Excomunicate Jew was not sufferd to sit within 4 Cubits of
any other Jew that was not Excommunicate. The Jews that livd
further then 10 days Jorney from Hierusalem, because they could
15 not have timely Notice from the Sanhedrim, were oblig'd to keepe
two holy Days instead of one, that they might be certaine not to
be mistaken. Selden De Call. Heb.

158ᵣ Great Prilates of the Church use to write themselves Providentia
Ab Divina, to assert their Divine Right, but allow Temporall Princes,
20 (from whom they derive all that Right) to be only Dei Gratia, As if
they were introduc'd by the wisdom of God, and Princes only by
his Favour.

The Different ways that the Church of Rome and the Reformed
take to instruct the People, is like the Severall Courses that Butchers
25 use to steare Calves by the Tayles: For as the one blinde's their
eies to make them keepe the Road the better, and the other let's
them see though it do's but render them the more uneasy to be
Driven, and give's them Occasion to run out of the way: Yet that
stragling is more in the Poore Creatures way considering whether
30 he is going, then the others silly running forwards, and the Advantage, or Inconvenience only theirs, that have the Driving of them.

Priests in the Church are the same things with Guards in the
State, for as the Guards keep the Rabble from falling foul upon the
Government, So do [the] others upon Religion. And when both

5 to . . . against] *altered from* with B   29 stragling] stragling. B

revolt, they are equally able to destroy that which they were designd to preserve, and both usually out of pretence of Conscience, but really Interest.

Charity is but the Steward of Beggars, and is only honest and Just in Smal Sums of Single Money: But when she gets good round 5 Sums in her hands, it is always imbezeld, and Diverted to other purposes by her under officers.

Those that lay their own faults to the charge of others, may learne Modesty of the Devil, for when Adam was accusd for his Sin, he layd all the Fault upon his wife, and she upon the Devill, who 10 was more modest (though perhaps not more Guilty) and tooke all upon himself and made no Defence at all.

The Inhabitants of the City of London, who generally had run away from the Plague, and deserted their Houses more then those of the Suburbes, were the next year burnt down by the Fire, and 15 those who had sufferd before under the one Judgment were spar'd by the other.

The Christians borrowd the Custome of Sprinckling Holy-water **158ᵛ** in their Churches, from the Antient Pagans, who usd the very same **Bb** thing, in their Temples; where they had Vasa περιρραντήρια aqua 20 lustrali plena, qua Sacerdotes, aut Æditui, intrantes aspergerent, aut etiam ipsi sese. Lips. in Tacit 527 nec aliunde Delubra derivari vult Asconius quam ab ista in Templorum vasis aqua ad Deluendum.

The Clergy, in the Church of Rome, are supply'd, as the Turkes Janizares, and great Officers of State are, Not out of the Breed of 25 Naturall Turkes, but the Children of Christians. And so are the Romish Priests, not by the Sons of Priests (as such) but those of the Christian Laity. By which Artifice, Both Turkes, and Popes support themselves, by weakning of their Enemies, For such are both the Christians to the Turkes, and the Laity, to the Roman Clergy. 30

The Protestant Religion was not introduc'd by our King Harry's Codpiece (as Papists very foolishly suppose): But by the Codpiece,

---

(and other extravagancy's) of Pope Leo the tenth, whose Luxuries reduc'd him to that Necessity, that he was forc'd to sequester all the Christian World, and grant Commissions to all Clergie-men that would buy them to compound with Whole Provinces, in any
5 kingdom in Europe. Some of which he gave freely away to his Mistrises and Favorites, who sold them to those that would give most; untill the oppression grew Intollerable, by the Avarice of those, who striv'd to improve their Pious Purchaces as high as they could. But were first oppos'd by Martin Luther in Saxony, and from
10 thence grew, all those Alterations which have since Succeeded. When King Harrys Codpiece was so far from being concern'd, that he was busy in writing (or owning) of Polemique Bookes against Luther, in defence of the Pope, for which he confer'd upon him the glorious Title of Defender of the Faith, which he would never have
15 don if he had been infallible.

The Doctrine of the Resurrection was, in Probability, a great Incouragement to the Martyrs, in all Ages, to expose their Bodys to be destroyd, all manner of the most horrid Ways, by their Persecutors; For (like those who suppose themselves shotfree) they believd
20 themselves Proof against all the Attempts of Death: And that to be kill'd was nothing but a certaine way to improve life, and to dy an Infallible Meanes to render themselves Immortall for ever.

The Councell of Trent, which was calld of Purpose to Reforme Errors and Abuses crept into the Christian Religion; which severall
25 Nations had begun of themselves to rectify, was manag'd with so much Fraud, and notorious Fallacies of all the Popes, that reign'd while it sate; That it was not only diverted quite contrary to the end it was designd for, and instead of Reforming, forc'd to confirme all those Errors, and Impostures, which it intended to rectify: But
30 with the abhominable Cheates, and Practices of its Proceedings to render all Future Generall Councels odious; General Councels having been for many yeares before, more terrible to all Popes, then all Infidels, and Emperors, and Gibellins, and other Reformers in the world, Amendment and Newnes of life being to them, one of
35 the worst of Innovations.

163ʳ   A Religion supprest by the State where it is Profest, is always

6 Mistrises] Mʳⁱˢᵉˢ C: Mʳⁱˢᵉˢ or Mʳⁱˢˢ B; Mʳⁱˢˢ W   11 concern'd,] concern'd. B   13 Pope,]Pope. B   34 world,] world. B   36 always] om. C

more zealous, and Devout in it's way (merely by the Naturall Bb
Power of Contradiction,) and more charitable to all of the same Profession, then any (how true, or False soever) that is publiquely
own'd and established. For nothing oblige's nor unite's men more,
then some Common Danger, or Feare of it, that equally concerne's 5
them all; as nothing render's them more careless and Negligent of
their Publique Interest, and one another, then their Presumption of
the Security of it. And allthough the Opinions of the Rabble, are as
weake, and Contemptible as the Power of a Rude Multitude without order, or Discipline; yet most Men are wonderfully Delighted 10
to see great Numbers possest with their own Opinions, how inconsiderable so ever the Persons are.

Religion never made any man in the world Just, or Honest who
had not some foundation for it in his Nature before, For all the
operation it can have upon others, is but Artificiall, and all their 15
conversions prevayle no further upon their Naturall Corruptions,
then to inable them to performe the same unjust and wicked Actions
under other Formes and Dispensations, which their Inclinations
lead them to before, and not seldom render them more barbarous
and Inhumane then they were before, when zeal and Conscience 20
light in their way to serve for Pretences. And this they do in a
manner acknowledge, when saving to them selves all Right and
Title that they may pretend to Grace, They will freely confess
themselves to be Naturally the greatest Monsters in the whole
world and lay all the Fault upon Nature, in which they had no hand 25
themselves; to magnify that in which they had the working out
of their own Salvations. And therefore though Preaching masters
perpetually Cry down Nature (forgetting that shee is [more]
immediatly the worke of God, then any thing else can pretend to
bee) yet if shee did not lay a foundation in the Tempers of Men for 30
them to work upon; all their holding forth, would prove to very little
Purpose, for which most inhumanly they rob her of her Due, and
falsly slander, and Defame her to arrogate and take to themselves,

1 Devout] sincere C   4 nor] and C   7–8 then their . . . of it] then the Freedome
from it C   8 allthough] though C   as] om. C   9 as] and C   11 Numbers
C: Number B   possest with] of C   12 are.] are though such as if their
perswasions were true would bee utterly Incapable of ever receiving any Impression
from Them; as Generally the Vulgar are of all manner of Truth and Reason from the
thicknesse of their Understandings. C   26 themselves] interlined B   27 Salvations.] Salvations B   32 of her] of he B

and their Trade all that is good and virtuous of Gods making.
Our Savior was not so Severe to any Sort of People among the
Jews, as the Scribes and Pharisees who were but Sectaries, and
Fanatiques of that Religion, whom he perpetually brand's with the
5 Names of Hypocrites, condemne's as the worst of Mankind, and
prefer's Publicans and Sinners (which were those kinde of People
our modern Pharisees call the wicked) every where before them;
with whom he vouchsaf'd to converse, but we never heare that he
would have any thing to do with the Zealots of those times.

10   The Godly will not admit that Grace and Morality should be the
same, although there is nothing more true. For then their want of
both would plainly appeare: Grace in their sense being nothing but
a Dispensation for the Defect of Morall virtue, and granted only to
those who are God Almightys especiall Favorites, as Titles of
15 Honor are but Ticketes and Exemptions, to dispence with Men for
want of Reall Honor, or Mandates to inable them to take their
Degrees without doing their Exercises.

      Clergy-men expose the Kingdom of Heaven to sale, That with
the Money they may purchace as much as they can of this world:
20 And therefor they extoll, and magnify the one, as all Chapmen do a
Commodity they desire to Part with, and cry down the other, as all
Buyers are wont to do that which they have the greatest longing to
purchase, only to bring down the Price, and gain the better bargain
by it. And yet in the Generall; The world go's on still as it usd to
25 do And men will never utterly give over the other world for this,
nor this for the other.

163ᵛ   Religion is orderd much more to the Advantage of the Seller then
Bb   the Buyer. It is equally repugnant to Truth, to believe too little, or
too much, though the last extream is allways found to be most
30 frequently usd: and most hurtfull.

      God made Adam in Paradise but one woman, and yet shee be-
tray'd him, by holding correspondence with his only Enemy the
Devill against him. Then what are his fall'n Posterity like to suffer
that have so many?

The Greatest Miseries commonly grow out of the greatest Felicities, as Death was first introduc'd in Paradise.

The First Quarrell and Murther that ever was committed in the world was upon a Fanatique emulation in Religion: when Kain Kill'd the fourth Part of all Mankind, his Brother Abel, merely out of Zeal, for seeing the Truth of his brothers Religious worship preferd before his own: though God himself were Judge. And ever since that time, much about the same Proportion of all Mankinde has constantly been destroyd, by the Rest upon the very same Accompt.

All Idolaters that ever were in the world, were but Fanatique Zealots, and those who were the most Devout, and Pious in their own Sense, the most horrid of all the Rest; For the Jewes that sacrific'd their Children, instead of their Cattle, did it no Doubt, out of extraordinary Zeal, and Transportation. For zeal without knowledge is infinitely more violent, then that which understand's ever so little of it self. And therefore it is not improbable, but those who Sacrifice themselves (if they have not more Reason for it, then wee can understand) are more Blameable for so doing, then those, who do but sacrifice their Children. It is most certaine that no Idolater intend's to erre, or suspect's he do's so: But the more zealous (that is Hot-headed) he is, become's the more Barbarous and Inhumane in his way, not out of any Intent to do evill; but the Contrary Good and to perform his Duty, And his Crime is nothing but want of understanding, and that which Ignorance Naturally Produces, obstinacy.

In all Religions for one Proselyte that is made by Preaching, there are hundreds that are converted, by private Tamperings, and Particular Interests.

The Fanatiques have changd the Method that Christ observd in calling his Apostles, and take a cleane contrary Course, For those that he cal'd left their Trades to follow him (as St Peter did the mending of his Nets) but these men call themselves to follow their Trades and him too. And as St Mathew left his receiving of Money to turn Apostle They turn Apostles, only that they may get in to Receive money. Our Savior commanded the Rich yong man, that

6 brothers] brother *B*

had a Desire to follow him, to sell all he had, and give it to the Poore; These will follow him, without so much as asking his leave, to no other purpose but only to get more. St Paul was stricken Blinde when he was admitted to be an Apostle: But these men intrude of
5 themselves, only because they have more light, and see better then others.

160ʳ   The originall of worshipping Images came (in Probability) from
Bb the Ægyptian Hieroglyphiques, For as the Ægyptians, exprest all their Apprehensions by the Figures of Animals, and Plants, &c
10 which serv'd them for the Charecters of all things, The Ignorant vulgar mistooke them for the things themselves, and hence came their Adoration of Crocodiles, and Cowes, and Dogs, and Birds that devour'd their Serpents and did but Represent some secret Power that was able to do them either great good or Hurt.

15   Though all Matters of Doubt in this world are carryd by most voyces, it is directly Contrary in all the Affaires of the Kingdom of Heaven, in which the smaller Numbers are always prefer'd before the Greater. And therefor the Catholiques have no great reason to vapour of their universality, and Generall Consent.

20   The Romish Sacrifice of the Alter has something of the old Roman Immolation in it, For as the one Sprinkled the Sacrifice with Flowre, the other turne's the Floure into the Sacrifice. They will by no meanes admit the words to beare a Parabolical Sense; Though the Gospell say's Without a Parable he spoke nothing. They make
25 him of wood or stone to worship him, but of Bread to eate him. It looke's like the old way of killing a Slave, and drinking his Bloud, to confirm the Fayth of Conspirators. And when both the old Law, and the Apostles in the New forbad the eating of any thing in the Bloud, because the life was in it, here it is don for that very Reason,
30 Because Christ (who cald himself life) is in it to shew that they will not take his word either in a Plaine or Metaphoricall Sense but only as it serve's their occasions. A strange way of Fulfilling of Types.
    So the Jewes put him to Death for using but a Metaphor, and only
35 borrowing the Name of their Temple, to express the Condition of

21 Immolation] *interlined B*   32–3 A . . . Types] *possibly interlined B*
34–p. 47, l. 5 *Possibly separate passage B*

his Body by, which the Jews would have (right or wrong) understood in a litterall Sense, to accuse and condemne him for it. By
which it plainely appeares that the Jews were the first litterall
Interpreters of Transubstantiation, and Christ himself the First
Martyr that sufferd for it.   5

When our Saviour and his Apostles, were upon Earth, they were
so ill treated that we may thence take a Measure of the wickednes
of this world, and the Naturall Aversion it hath to all Truth, and
Reality in Religion. For though Christs Residence here were to
convert, and convince the world, by the greatest of all Reasons Tru 10
Miracles: Yet wee do not finde, that he had many Proselytes, besides
his own Apostles during his life, and of these the chief of all the rest
denyd, and the only Officer he had, betray'd him. While the very
Devills of Hell, whether he descended after his il usage here, gave
him a better Reception, and obediently deliver'd up those Prisners   15
they had of his, upon the first Demand; as they were the First that
believd in him with feare and trembling, which very few have don
ever since. Beside though the Devill tempted him severall ways and
set him upon the Top of a very high Mountaine where he had a
Prospect of all the world, and after upon a Pinacle of the Temple, as 20
the greater Temptation, yet he did him no Hurt (though he refusd
his offers) but only left him.

All Churches both Catholique, and reformd forbid their Disciples   **160ᵛ**
to be present at one anothers Liturgies, or Divine Services; For   Bb
feare they should be prevayl'd upon to change their severall   25
Religions; where there is no reasonable meanes, nor Probable
occasion offer'd for any such Caution: But give them all Freedome
to heare one anothers Sermons, though intended for nothing so
much as to inveagle, and Draw in one anothers Rabble, as Enemys
in war do so many Head of Cattle out of one anothers Quarters: As 30
if they had agreed on both sides, that there is no man so Silly and
Ignorant, that is not Sermon-Proof.

The Priests that say Mass turn their Backs to the People, and
speak in an unknown Language, that they may neither See, nor
understand what they do, further then the Bowes, and legs that   35
they make; which is no more then Baals Priests usd. For all that wee

11 Miracles:] *or (but more probably altered from)* Miracles, B

know of their way of worship (besides Sacrifices) is that they Bent
the knee; And that is all that the Rabble can possibly understand
of Mass.

The Roman Emperors had no sooner imbrac'd the Christian
5 Religion, but the Bishops of Rome perswaded them to remove the
Seat of the Empire into the East, while they possest themselves of
the chief City and Metropolis of the world Rome. And by this
meanes, in few yeares after, divided the Empire into two Parts,
which weakened it so, That as they exposd the Eastern to be
10 utterly Destroy'd by Infidels, while they incroach'd upon the
Western, they render'd that so Feeble, that it was not able to defend it self against the Invasions of the Barbarous Northern Nations,
untill they had reduc'd that also, into almost as low a Condition.
Meanwhile they made their greatest Advantages of the miserable
15 Calamities of the Christians, who in any Publique Affliction fled to
them (as all Religions use to do to their Temples, and Alters) for
Refuge, or Consolation at least, which brought them in so much
Reverence, and veneration; That it was not uneasy to Improve
their Authority to what Height they pleasd. And when by these
20 Arts they had gaind so much Intrest with the People, that they
were able to contest with Kings; They began with the Emperors
first, and most ungratefully after they had by their Assistance
driven their mortall enemies the Lumbards out of Italy; They never
gave over, untill by Degrees, they had driven the Emperors out
25 also, and had reduc'd them to be their Vassels, to be raysd or Deposd
at their Pleasure; and serve them only as their Guards against the
Turk, The only People who have shar'd with them in Reducing of
Christian Princes, of whom they suffer none (they can help) to injoy
any Power, but only as they serve them for Defence against the
30 Further incroachments of the Infidels. And this is the Constant
Course they have always taken with their Predecessors heretofore,
whom they sent with the Strongest Part of their Subjects into
remote Parts, to fight against Turks, and Saracens, while they
34 incroach'd upon their Power, and Authority at home: And when
161ʳ they miscarri'd abroad (as it always fel out) / sold the Inheritances
Bb of their Crowns from the Right Heires to Usurpers, who would
afford them the best Bargaines of Church-Priviledges, as they did
to our Will: 2 Hen: 1. Stephen. John &c. And as by these Artifices

30 Infidels.] Infidels B   38 Artifices] Arifices B

they grew greater and greater, they still Screwd up the plaine and
Innocent Doctrines of the Christian Religion to an æqual Pitch with
it. And made the Originall Humility Submission, and obedience
serve for the greatest Instruments of Pride Insolence and Tyranny
in the world, by imposing Patience, and long suffering as Christian 5
Duties upon all others, only to advance their own Greatnes, and
unlimited Power.

The Papists do but confess the Protestants to have better Parts
[then] themselves, while they indeavor to undervalew them: For if
their Religion be so false, and Foolish as they pretend, they could 10
never maintaine it against them, and a Truer Cause, if they had
both equall Abilities; much less get Ground of them, as they have
don, ever since the beginning of the Controversy. For men do but
undervalew themselves, that dispise the meaness of those, who are
Able to Contest with them, especially upon unequal Tearmes. 15

The Holyest men that live in Monasterys, have enough to do to
supply those of the same Covent with Supererrogation (who in
Charity ought to be first serv'd) and therefor have very little, or
none at all to Spare for others: So that this Treasury of the Church,
is like a Banke without Money, that is Supply'd merely by it's 20
Credit. And those who trust to it are not certaine to be the better
for it, untill some extraordinary glut of Merits comes in.

The Church of Rome finding by Experience that Faith in the
Merits of Christ was noe Profitable Doctrine (though the Foundation of the Christian Religion) They set up good Workes (though 25
but an effect of that Faith) in opposition to it: And in Few yeares,
arriv'd, by that meanes, at that vast wealth in Religious Indow-
ments, which their Church once possest, and still do's in some
Measure. Yet not contented with this, they found out another
expedient, no less Advantageous, especially to draw in Desperate 30
Sinners (who could expect no forgivenes from the Merits of Christ
by reason of the strictnes of the Conditions, upon which it is to be
obteind) and that was Supererogation which is nothing else but a
Supposd Treasury or Banke of Merits, raysd out of the Overplus of
the Saints Good workes, which they pretend to have the Disposing 35
of; and out of that Stock can, as they see Cause, compound for the

27 at that] that *altered from* a B

Horridst Crimes of the most abhominable Sinners, and Redeem Soules from the Devill (as the Spanish Friers do slaves out of Algiere) though the whole Sense and Doctrine of the Christian Religion do ever so much oppose it. From whence it may in Prob-
5 ability be guesd That nothing is more like to introduce that Religion into this Nation (next a totall conquest of it) as the Sottish vice, and Debauchery of the present Age. For the Church of Rome has made the way to Heaven so much wider, and easier then the Christian Religion will allow it to be; That all Sorts of abhominable and
10 wicked People betake themselves to that Road, as the most safe and Convenient, where they travell with Convoy, and have their Carriadges and Baggage, that is the Burthen of their Sins, and Iniquities
161ᵛ borne at / the easiest Rates. For as all Malefactors live in Perpetuall
Bb Feare of being apprehended, and finde themselves no where so much
15 in Safety and at ease as in a Sanctuary: So the most Inhumane of all Sorts of Sinners can no where else in all the world finde that Protection, and Indulgence which they do in the Church of Rome: In which they have an open and Free Trade between Sins, and Merits, and the Actions (as merchants call them) of both, are So equally
20 ballanc'd, That the Supererogations, and Overdoings of the Saints, are sufficient to adjust, and accompt for the most horrible and Prodigious Crimes of the worst of Sinners (though the Merits of Christ signifyd nothing at all) who can no where else buy Absolution at so low a Price, and insure their Soules (though they venture ever
25 so Desperatly) at so little in the Hundred. In so much that Sin and Debauchery being the most Probable ways of Introduction into that church, they may seem to be the shortest Cut to salvation, and but a Northwest Passage to Heaven.

All the Designes and Practices of Popish Priests upon the Protes-
30 tant Religion, are never in Probability so like to reduce the Church of England to lick up it's old vomit as those of our own Dignitaries at home. For eversince the Church-lands were Sold in the Presbyterian times, they have so terrible an Apprehension that the same thing may be don again, some time or other (especially where there
35 is so late a Precedent for it) that there is nothing they would not submit to, and believe, to insure their Spirituall Dignitys. And as nothing can perform that so certainly as the Introduction of the Romish Religion, that has so great a Power over all Governments

13 Malefactors] Melefactor *or possibly* Malefactor *B*

where it is receivd: So there is no Course, nor meanes, which they would not willingly use, and contribute any thing (but money) to reestablish it here again. And hence it is that in the late Contest between the King and Palament, about Indulgence to be granted to the Catholiques for the free exercise of their Religion as well as the Fanatiques (who were only brought in as Stales) some of the Prælates appeard openly for them in the House of Lords. And this being their certaine Interest, they will never forget, nor omit to promote, especially when it is like to bring with it so great an additionall increase of Power and Revenue. And this they have a further Reason to advance, considering the generall Il will, and Hatred they have contracted from the People, of all Sorts, by their imprudent Demeanure, and the unjust Dealing they have usd since their restoration; beside the Envy they have drawn upon themselves, by the vast Sums of money they have gain'd, and the Few Charitable workes they have don with it. For these officers, and commanders of the Church Militant, are like Souldiers of Fortune that are free to serve on any Side that gives the best Pay.

If the Priests and Clergie of all Religions could but be true to their Common Interest, and preserve themselves united, they would easily subdue all the Rest of Mankinde and governe the world, (as men do Beasts) in spight of all it's greatest Force and opposition. For the Rabble of all Nations do always Naturally take Part against themselves, and preserve a Generall obedience, which no other Power is able to perform.

It is a Strange Art that Emissary-Priests use in making of Proselytes, to finde out those that are fit, and Proper for their Purposes; and avoyd all such as are not, which they will do with that exactnes, as if they had a Ballance to weigh mens Wit, and Reason in, that would turne with the 40th Part of a Graine. For those Fishers of Men are not allowd by their Instructions, to attempt any Man whom they suspect to be too heavy to be pul'd out: And therefore with the Fox in the Fable, they always weigh their Geese, before they will adventure to carry them over a River. And this they will do, with that Curiosity, by observation of Mens Inclinations, and Abilities; That I have known some Converts of so much appearinge Ingenuity and Parts, that it ha's been a hard Matter to an ordinary

30 those] these *W*

observer, to finde out any such Flaw or Blinde side in them, as
would serve a Priest to fix his Engines against: And yet they have
don it with so much Dexterity, that they have not fayld of Success.
Not that they have more wit, or better Parts then others (which
5 they are so farre from, that they seldom incounter with any Adversary in Publique, that is not too hard for them) But whether a Fool
be not most proper to finde out a Fool, as a Thief is to discover a
Thiefe, and a Tarriar to unearth a Fox, so the weaknes of mens
Reason is most apt to prevayle with those of the Same Elevation.
10 Their constant Practice is to make choyce (next to the Ignorant) of
the most Lewd and Vicious Persons that they can finde out whose
understandings are Corrupted with their Debaucherys. Those they
believe make the best Converts, as the best saints are made of the
worst Sinners. And therefor there is scarse a Notorious whore or
15 Baud that escape's them: Partly by reason of the opportunity of
their Conversations, and Partly the wickednes of their Lives, which
make the worst Religions, as well as the worst men most proper
for their Purposes. Nor do they at all indeavor to reforme their
Lives, but only their Judgments and opinions, which no doubt are
20 wonderfully considerable in such People, who by the Integrity of
their Lives and Conversations, cannot but have great Inclinations to
truth, and as great Natural Parts in discerning of Spirits. Another
way they have, which is the same, by which their Church has gotten
the greatest Part of it's vast Revenues, and that is by applying to
25 sick and Dying Persons, especially such as have by wicked meanes
gotten great wealth. These they always finde most willing to compound for their Sins and Purchaces at the easiest rates, and yet had
rather give the more for an Implicit generall Pardon, then be
troubled with the Hard Conditions of Repentance, and Caution for
30 amendment, and Restitution, without which the Christian Religion
do's not pretend to any Power to grant it. As for Compassing of
widdows Houses, and tithing of Mint &c The old Pharises wer but
Bunglers to them. For as one Baud is sayd to do the Service of three
Pimps, so they finde that one Femall Proselyte is more considerable
35 then thrice as many Males. For as they are easier made, being but
the weaker vessels, so that Qualification renders them the more
Devout, Zealous and obstinate in their New opinions: and they
seldom fayle to draw in their Husbands, and as many of their Rela-
162ᵛ tions as they possibly can. / And if they be but talkative, few of their

8 mens] men B   14 Sinners.] Sinners . . B

Gossips escape. In so much as all Impostors in Religion, have never Bb
omitted this Fruitfull way of Propagating False Doctrines, ever
since the Devill first practic'd it upon Eve in Paradice. They have
long had a designe to turne the Government, as well as Particular
Persons, but though the experiment hold in little, it will not do in 5
great, no more then the virtuoso's Trick of Pulling up an old Oake
by the Rootes, with one Finger, yet like a loosing Gamster he cannot indure to thinke of giving over. He steale's Fooles from themselves, as Spirits do children from their Parents, and rather then
fayle he will attaque Footmen and Scullions and for want of better 10
those that are condemnd to be hangd, for he give's in his accompt
by the Head, and reckons by tale, and not by weight. As soone as
he is once got Free of his Covent, He believe's himself Free to all
things else, and his Debaucheries and vices pass upon the Accompt
of his Disguise, as acted, and counterfetted of purpose to conceale 15
himself from being suspected to be a Religious Man. As if Hypocrisy, and Dissimulation were so Naturally inseperable from his
Religion, that he can neither profess nor conceal it, without the
exercise, and Assistance of both. Our Savior calls all those that
only bought and Sold in the Church Thieves, and the Church it self 20
where Trades are Driven, a Den of thieves, though there is no Com-
plaint of their cheating, or overreaching of their Customers, and
therefore he believes, that though it be a sin to buy and sell in the
Church, to cheat and circumvent is meritorious; and hence it is
that they have sanctify'd and canonizd all Cheates and Impostures, 25
that are but in order to their Spirituall Interests. For if it be lawfull
for Princes to cheat their People into their own Preservation, and
for Physitians to delude their Patients into Health, why should it
not be so for Priests to cheat men of their Soules to send them to
Heaven? the only Difference is, that the experiment cannot be try'd 30
in this world, as the other two are, in which wee often finde, that
they sometimes Destroy instead of Preserving, and Kill instead of
Curing, and that Priests do not do so too, we have no assurance but
their own words. And their Busnes is the same with the Temptations of the Devill, to draw in as many as they can to make over 35
their Soules in Trust to them, in which the Devill is a little more
Reasonable; for he is contented with the Reversion of Soules, but
nothing will satisfy a Priest but present Possession. He is no just
Enemy to the Government where he sets up, but a Spy, and therefor

never appeare's in his own Shape but always in Disguise. He
turne's Proselytes as Botchers Doe old Cloaths, the best side out-
wards, and the worst inwards, as they commonly prove themselves
and their Conversions to be upon all experiments that are made of
5 them. And as the Devill never sow's his Tares but in the Night, no
more dos he his Doctrines but in the Dark understandings of the
Ignorant, which he believe's to be the Fruitfullest Soyl of Devotion.

There is nothing in the world that breed's Atheisme like Hypocrisy, and the Licentiousnes of the present Age, owes its originall to
10 nothing so much as the Counterfet Piety of the last. And it is well
for the world, that there is nothing to be gotten by Atheisme; For
if there were, Those who profess God only to affront him for gaines
would with greater Reason and less impudence utterly disown him,
14 if there were nothing to be lost, in the exchange.

164ʳ All men dy the first Day they were Born, As God told Adam,
Bb The Day that thou eatest of the forbidden Fruite, thou shalt certainly Dy. Yet he liv'd some Hundreds of yeares after, but was
counted Dead as soon as he was condemnd to Dy, as he and Eave
were. But the Serpent (though the Author of all the Mischief) was
20 sentenc'd to a lesser Punishment; only to have his Head broken and
eate Dust; Because he broke no Commandement that wee heard
of; and therefor was not Guilty of any Disobedience.

Men ought to manage their vices, and Debaucheries, with great
Caution, when their very prayers to obtaine pardon and forgivenes
25 for them, are commanded to be made in Secret. A man may have a
great Deal of vice in his Nature, but as long as he keep's it to himself out of the Sight of the world, it is none of his, like a covetous
mans Money, which he hoords up, and dare's not make use of,
untill he render's it really none of his own.

30 There is nothing in the world so powrful to destroy any
Religion, as the Publique ill example of those that profess it: For the
People that always learn more by example then Precept, are very
apt to imitate those Courses, which they see publiquely practic'd;
and the greater the Persons are by whom they are taught, the more

19 Mischief)] *superimposed on* Mischief—B   30–p. 55, l. 8 *Duplicated and under-*
lined B 217ʳ   30 any] the Christian *B* 217ʳ   31 example] examples *B* 217ʳ

ingenious and docible they are to improve: The wicked lives of the Heathen Emperors destroyd their own Religion as fast as the Persecutions which they inflicted on the enemies of it to preserve it, propagated the Christian. And although the bloud of the Martyrs be said to have been the seed of the Church, and persecution the ploughs, and Harrows that were usd to plant it, the inhuman Crimes, and wicked impieties of the Pagan Princes were the Dung and impost that improv'd the Soyle into a rich fertility.

[164^v and
164$\star$ blank]

4 And] For *B* 217^r

Bb

    Wit is very chargeable, and not to bee maintaind in it's Necessary
Leasure, and Expences, at an ordinary Rate: It is the worst Trade
in the world to live upon, and a Commodity that no man thinkes he
has neede of, For those who have the least, believe they have as
5 much as the best, and injoy greater Priviledges, for as they are their
own Judges, they are subject to no Censures which they cannot
easily reverse, and it is incredible how much upon that Accompt
they will dispise all the world, which those who have more wit dare
not do, and the more wit they have, are but the more severe to
10 them selves, and their own Performances, and have just confidence
enough to keep them from utterly Renouncing of it, which they
are apt to do upon the Smallest Check, if some thing else then their
own Inclinations did not oppose them in it.

    The Condition of those who are born to Estates, and those who
15 are born only to wit, are very neare the same: For very few of both
know how to make a Right use of either, but generally as the first
live above their Estates, so do the later below their wit; And when
both meete in the same Person, it is seldom seen that either of them
Prospers, while [those] who are born to neither, if they have but
20 Industry (which no man of Wit, or Fortune, is so capable of) do
commonly thrive better in the world then either of them. For as
they are both in their kindes, above the Ordinary alloy of Mankinde
(and do most frequently associate together) they cannot submit to
that Slavery, and Drudgery, which those who have neither, must
25 indure, either to thrive, or get into Preferment. For all that men can
get in this world (setting Fortune aside) is but the Sallary, and Pay
of their Paines, and Drudgery, which fine Wits are no more fit for,
then fine Cloaths to labour, and Sweat in. For Nature when shee
has once given a Man wit, thinke's she has don enough for him; and
30 after leave's him to himself, as she ha's don all Mankinde (in respect
of other Creatures) in Providing them neither Food, nor Cloaths,
nor Armes (as she has don Beasts at her own Charge) but such as
they can invent, and prepare for themselves. And hence it is that

27 Drudgery,] Drudgery. *B*   32 Charge)] *superimposed on* Charge. *B*

Fooles are Commonly so fortunate in the world, and wiser men so unhappy and miserable. To say nothing of the Craft and Subtlety which she ha's given to all helpless Creatures (as Hares, and Foxes) with which they are able to preserve themselves, from being utterly destroy'd by their stronger and Docile Enemies who if they were 5 not assisted by men, would be able to do them very little Harm. Nor is it Improbable, but Fooles may be as Fit for great Imployments, as wiser men, for what they want of wit, and Ingenuity, is Commonly abundantly supply'd with Care and Industry. And wee see dayly such men as have nothing but Formality and Dul gravity 10 to set them of, do rise in Church, and State, sooner to preferment, then those of Freer and Readier Parts. For the Truth is Fooles are much fitter to have the Management of things of Formality, and shew (as the greatest Part of all State-Affayres are) for they do then Naturally, and in earnest, which wise men do but Counterfet and 15 dissemble And so become the more unapt for them.

There are as many Sorts of Fooles, as there are of Dogs; from the largest of Mastives and Irish Greyhounds, to the Smallest of Currs, and Island Shocks, and all equally Fooles as the rest are Dogs. 19

Men that are mad upon many things, are never so extravagant, **165ᵛ** as those who are possest with but one. For one Humor diverts Bb another, and never suffers the Caprich to fix. And as those who apply themselves to many Studies, never become exellent in any one: So those that are Distracted with severall Sorts of Freakes, are never so solidly, and Profoundly mad as those that are wholy taken 25 up with some one Extravagance. For Sottishness and Folly, which is nothing else but Natural Madnes is neither so ridiculous, nor Serious in its way, as that which men fall into by Accident or their own ungovernd Passions. And although a Mad man in his Intervals, is much wiser then a Naturall Fool: yet a Fool (if he be not very 30 Stupid) has (al things Considerd) much the Advantage of him. For Nature never made any thing so bad as the Deviations from her have render'd it : Nor is she more Improv'd by Art, and Ingenuity, then Impayr'd by Artificiall Folly, and Industrious Ignorance. And therefor the Author of Don Quixot, makes Sancho (though a Natural 35 Fool) much more wise and Politique then his Master with all his Study'd, and acquird Abilities.

11 do] *altered from* ri B   27 but . . . Madnes] *interlined B*   36 Fool)]
Fool, *B*

A Blinde Man know's he cannot see, and is glad to be led, though it bee but by a Dog, But hee that is Blinde in his understanding (which is the worst Blindenes of all others) believe's he see's as well as the Best, and Scorne's a Guide, and the more, the more he neede's
5 one. For all Men are very sensible of the Defects of their Senses, but none of their Intellects. For the understanding being Judge of all their Abilities, is either so Partiall to it self, that it is Impossible it should ever discover it's own wants, or else is incapable of Doing it, by being depriv'd of right Information, the only meanes, by which
10 it is to be don.

Few mens wits, and Judgments, (how excellent so ever in their kindes) will ever be brought to stand in Tune together. For good wits do not always Jump. There is no Theft so easy as that of Wit; that is so cheap, it will not beare the Charges of being lock'd up,
15 or look'd after. But though it be less Difficult then to rob an Orchard that is unfenc'd, yet he who think's he can steal Judgment, is as Ridiculous as he that believe's he can run away with the Trees, or because he can steale the Oare, suppose's he can convey away the Mine. For there is no tru wit that is not produc'd by a great Deal of
20 Judgment. For wit and Fancy are but the Cloaths, and Ornaments of Judgment, and when they are Stollen by those whom they will not fit, they serve them to no Purpose, or that which is worse then none, to make them Ridiculous, For almost all Plants, and Animals too degenerate where they are not Naturally produc'd, and he that
25 believe's otherwise of wit, is as ignorant as those silly Indians, that buy Gunpowder of our Merchants, and sow it in the Earth believing it will grow there.

That Providence that Cloaths, and Feede's Beasts, because they know not how to help themselves, Provide's for all Sorts of Fooles,
30 that are æqually in capable of Relieving themselves without it.

166ʳ Though wit be ever so contemptible, to the Ignorant: yet those
Bb who have none of their own Growth, and are forcd to buy it, are

---

11–20 . . . Judgment] *Duplicated and underlined B 222ʳ*   13 Wit;] *comma altered from full point B 165ᵛ*   14 Charges] Charge *B 222ʳ*   15 But] and *altered from* for *B 222ʳ*   then] *altered from* to *B 222ʳ*   16 who] that *B 222ʳ*   17 Trees, *B 222ʳ:* Trees *B 165ᵛ*   18 can steale] can *interlined B 222ʳ*   20–7 wit . . .] *duplicated and underlined B 222ʳ*   23 almost all] Most *altered from* all *B 222ʳ*   25 silly] barbarous *B 222ʳ*   that] who *altered from* th *B 222ʳ*   26 believing] being perswaded *B 222ʳ*   27 there.] there, or those who thought [to] make the Philosophers stone of Pin-dust. *B 222ʳ*

sure to pay Deare for it; although it be the most slight, and Course
of all others, as all things that are made for Sale usually are, to pass
the easier of by their Cheapnes: only Bought wit is the Dearer for
being Vile and Paultry. For a Cheat is worse then a Thiefe, and do's
not only Rob a man of his Goodes (as a thiefe do's) but his Reputa- 5
tion also, and makes him Combine and take Part against himself:
Steale's and convey's him, out of his Reason, and Senses (as Chang-
lings are sayd to be serv'd by witches out of the Cradle) And is not
so Civil as to beg the Tuition of him, but assume's a Power, and
Authority to make himself his Guardian, upon what Tearmes he 10
pleases.

Fooles are always wrangling and Disputing, and the lesse Reason
they have, the more earnest they are in controversy: As beggars are
always Quarrelling about divideing an Almes; And the Paultryest
Trades will higgle more for a Penny, then the Richer will do for a 15
Pound. For those who have but a Little ought to make as much of it
as they can.

All Mad men are Humorists, and wholly possest with some Foolish extravagant Fancy, which they are never to be redeem'd from,
but by the Recovery of their wits, which are commonly so wasted 20
with the violence of the Frenzy, that they are never good for any
thing after. For Madmen are more earnest, and serious, in their
wildest Apprehensions, then those that are in their wits are in their
greatest Probabilities of Reason, So much has error the odds of
Truth wheresoever they meet; That the Kingdom of Darknes is 25
more frequently taken by violence then that of Heaven. For Truth
is so often baffled, and outwitted in the Affaires of the world, that
wisemen are discourag'd to ingage in her Right. For as it was
Crucify'd in the Person of our Saviour (who was truth it self) so it
has been ever since and wilbe to the end of the world. 30

There is nothing that provokes and sharpens wit like Malice, and **166ᵛ**

7 Senses] Senses, *B*   8 Cradle)] Cradle. *B*   12–17 *Duplicated and
underlined B* 222ʳ   15 Penny] Farthing *B* 222ʳ   16 who] that *B* 222ʳ
18–30 *Duplicated and underlined B* 222ʳ   18 Mad men] Madmen *B* 222ʳ
some *B* 222ʳ: soome *B* 166ʳ   21–2 never . . . after] good for nothing else *B*
222ʳ   23 wits are *B* 222ʳ: wits and [*interworded*] are *B* 166ʳ   24 Reason,]
Reason. *B* 222ʳ   25 meet;] meet *B* 222ʳ   28 wisemen] men *B* 222ʳ
30 world.] world. and has no hopes of escaping but either by being proof against
Baking as the three Children were or being [*interlined*] eaten raw in a Den of Lyons
as Daniel was usd. *B* 222ʳ

Bb   Anger si Natura negat facit Indignatio &c And hence perhaps came the first occasion of calling those Raptures Poeticall Fury. For Malice is a kinde of Madnes (For if men run mad for Love, why should they not as well do so for Hate?) And as madmen are sayd to have in
5   their fits double the Strength they had before, so have Malitious men the wit. He who first found out Iambiques; and before with all his wit and Fancy could not prevayle with the Father of his Mistris to keep but his Promise with him; had no sooner turnd his Love into Hate, but he forc'd him with the bitternes of his New Rhimes
10 to hang himself: So much Power has Malice above all other Passions, to highten Wit and Fancy, for malice is Restles, and never finde's ease untill it has vented it self. And therefore Satyrs that are only provok'd with the Madnes and Folly of the world, are found to conteine more wit, and Ingenuity then all other writings whatso-
15 ever, and meet with a better Reception from the world, that is always more delighted to heare the Faults and vices though of itself well describd, then all the Panegyriques that ever were, which are commonly as Dull as they are false, And no man is Delighted with the Flattery of another. Among all Sports and shews that are usd
20 none are so Delightfull as the Military; that do but imitate, and Counterfet Fights. And in Heroicall Poetry, that has nothing to do with Satyr; what is there that do's so much captivate the Reader, as the prodigious Feates of Armes of the Heroes, and the Horrid Distruction they make of their Enemies? There is no sort of Cuning in
25 the world so subtle and Curious, as that which is usd in doing of Mischief: Nor any true wisdom and Politie so ingenious, as the Artifices of Cheates and Impostors. Against which all the wisdom of Laws is so unable to prevail that they will turne all their best and Surest Guards upon themselves, in spight of all the caution and
30 Care which the wisest Governments can possibly contrive. How far more cunning and Crafty have the wits of Men been in finding out that Prodigious variety of Offencive weopons, in comparison of those Few that have invented only for Defence? though their own Preservation ought in Reason to be more Considerable, to them
35 then the Distruction of others. What made the Serpent so subtle, as to out-wit Adam in Paradise, though a Copy drawn from the Original of wisdom it self, but only the Malice of his Designe? so active and Industrious is the Devill to do mischief. For Malice is the Reason of State of Hell, as Charity is of Heaven, and therefor the

39 Heaven,] Heaven. B

Proceedings of both are directly Contrary. For God who made the
world, and all that is in it in six days, was forty Days and Nights too
in Drowning of it, beside so many yeares in executing what he had
resolv'd, whose Punishments extend but to the third or fourth
Generation, but his mercy unto Thousands. Malice is so great an 5
Odds in any Contest between Man and man; that the Law do's not
condemne one man for killing another, for any Reason so much,
as for having Malice Prepensd on his Side: as if it were one of those
Illegall weopons, which the Statute of Stabbing provide's against.
What a Stupendious operation has the Malice of witches (for nothing 10
else Qualify's them to be such,) who if the Laws of the Land are but
true and just, are able to do feates, which the wisest men in the
world are not able to understand? And hence it is that Envie and
Emulation, which is but a kinde of Malice, has power to inable some 14
men to do things which / had otherwise been far above their 167^r
Naturall Abilities. It is not only a wicked vice, but it's own Punish- Bb
ment also: For it always afflict's those more, that beare it, then
those, for whose sakes they indure the slavery to maintaine it. He
who in a Rage threw his Pencill at his Picture, because he could not
please himself in Drawing the Fome of a Mad Dog; came nearer to 20
Nature both in his Performance, and the way of Doing it, then all
his sober study and care could ever have brought him. For all the
best Productions of most Judicious mens Studys proceed from
nothing more, then their Restles vexation of thought which all
Passions naturally produce in the minde, and put the Spirits into a 25
quicker motion then they are capable of in a quiet Temper. But notwithstanding the many Advantages that wit receives from Passion,
there is nothing in Nature so pernicious, and Distructive to all
manner of Judgment: For all Passion is so Partiall and Prepossest
that it is not capable of making a true Judgment of any thing 30
thoughever so Plaine, and Easy. And although there are but few
Passions of the Naturall Temper of Judgment, As Feare Sorrow
Shame &c yet where they Prevayl they are as averse to it, and
sometime more, then those of a direct contrary Nature. For Judgment is like a Ballance that measure's all things by weight, and 35
therefore the more light, and less solid any thing is, the less apt it
is to be examind that way.

[167^v
blank]

The less Judgment any Man ha's, the Better he is perswaded of his owne abilities, because he is not capable of understanding any thing beyond it, and all things how mean so ever, are best to those who know no better: for beside the naturall affection that he has for
5 himself, which go's very farre, the less he is able to improve and mend his Judgment, the higher value he set's upon it, and can no more correct his own false opinions, when he is at his height, then out-grow his own Stature. When he is possest with an Opinion, the less he understand's of it, the more confident and obstinate he is in
10 asserting it, and commonly the more false it is, the better satisfy'd with the Truth of it: As all smatterers take more Pleasure in their Bungling, then great Masters in their best Performances, otherwise they would never indure to take the necessary Paines to arrive at any perfection. All right reason consist's (like Justice) in an impar-
15 tiall examination of all extreames, and giving a right Judgment upon both sides; but he whose latitude is not able to extend so far, but is wholly taken up with any one, will never understand the Truth of either, but must of necessity become the more confident, as a Balance, that ha's a weight put into one Scale only, do's easyly
20 outweigh the other, but prove's nothing at all. And this is the true Reason why al ignorant People, are always so naturally obstinate, in all things which they believe they know, only because they know nothing to the Contrary, for a wooden leg is much stiffer then one that is Naturall, and derive's its use and activity from being flexible
25 and Plyant to all purposes it was designd for. Ignorance has more occasions of Difference then any thing else, as having nothing but crack'd Titles to all it hold's, or pretend's to, and therefore require's the more earnest Prosecution, and if it meet with no Adversary know's not what to do with it self, but is lost, and ha's noe other
30 way to appeare, and shew it's Parts: and this Litigiousnes of Ignorance produce's more Suites in Law then all other mistakes of Right,

2 capable] *altered from* able *B*   11–14 smatterers . . . perfection] *duplicated*
B 175^r   11 smatterers] If smatterers did not *B* 175^r   12 Masters] Artists
do *B* 175^r   Performances, *B* 175^r: Performances. *B* 168^r   otherwise] *om. B* 175^r
13 the] *interlined B* 168^r   necessary] *om. B* 175^r   22 believe] believe. *B*
23 Contrary,] *possibly altered from* Contrary. *B*

and wrong put together, for nothing is more contentious, as men
are more peevish when they are sick and apt to quarrell when they
are drunk, then when they are in perfect minde and memory. All
ingagements and contests are made upon a Supposition, of very
little inequality between both sides, and an ignorant Person believes 5
himself equall to any man that he can provoke to contend with him,
and many times prove's so, for what he want's of Reason, and
ability is abundantly supply'd with heate, and confidence. When a
Man hast lost an eie, he is wont to supply the place of it, with an
Artificiall one of glass which though it cannot see, can make a 10
Shew as if it did, and is proof against al those accidents that use to
destroy true ones. So he that know's nothing, knows as little of
himself, and ha's no more Sense of his own defects then he has of any
thing else / which renders him impregnable against all conviction, 168ᵛ
which no reason can promise it self. And yet as obstinate as it is Bb
against all Truth, there is nothing in Nature so apt, and easy to be 16
imposd upon: For having no foundation of it's own, it is always
prop'd (like a Cripple) with such crutches as are not able to stand of
themselves, And as hee that is blinde, is wont to be led by a child, or
a Dog, or feel out his way with a Staff, that ha's less Sense then him- 20
self: So ignorant Persons are Commonly govern'd by those that have
less understanding then their own, if it be Possible. For all things
are most inclynd to mix with those that are most suitable to their
own Natures, and present conditions, and equalls [have] always the
fairest correspondence either in Conversation or Dealing: For there is 25
a naturall disproportion between Superior, and inferior, that is never
to be reconcil'd, and made perfectly agreeable to either, while both
conceive themselves lessen'd, the one in Condescention, and the
other in Submission. And hence it is that Ignorant Persons are so
averse to be govern'd or advisd by those that are wiser then them- 30
selves; and so easy to comply with such as are nearer to their own
Levell, who commonly can but lead them from one error to another,
but never bring them to indure any truth, how plaine, and manifest
soever. For as Philosophers say, In all Mutations The Subject ought
to be neare of Kin to the new Forme it receive's, so there is so great 35
an aversion between Truth and Error, that whatsoever inclines to
the one, is very uneasily brought to be reconcild to the other.
Ignorance is easily possest with any opinion, that is but strange and
monstrous, and receive's the one for rare and curious, and the other

8 When] when B   21 those] thos B   22 own,] own. B

as extraordinary, and not vulgarly understood, and the fewer objections it is able to make against any thing, the easier it is induc'd to
give credit to it, and the more obstinate to be disswaded from it.
For Prepossession is more then nine Poynts of the Law with it, and
5 whatsoever foolish suggestion it first meete's with, is sure to be first
serv'd, and the more perverse it is, the more pertinaciously adhear'd
to (as Burs will stick closer to any thing they can fasten upon then
better Plants) and will not indure Advice for feare of being thought
to be governd, which of all things it naturally abhor's, though it is
10 utterly incapable of being free; For al Barbarous People have ever
been slaves, and never in any possible condition to be governd any
other way; and is no more to be prevayl'd by Truth and Reason
then any other bruit Beast: But whatsoever ha's a specifique virtue
to worke upon hope or Feare, has a great influence upon it, provided
15 there be nothing of Truth in it, to which it has a naturall Antipathy,
and will not indure unless it be so disguis'd that it is not to be
distinguish'd from a Ly. Otherwise it is never to be reduc'd; but
like the madman in the Acts of the Apostles, that beat seaven men
for offering to dispossess him of his Devill, it fal's foul upon all those,
20 who indeavour to cure it of it's Deare Frenzie.

[168*
blank]

7–8 to (as . . . Plants)] *superimposed on* to. as . . . Plants, *B*   9 abhor's,]
possibly altered from abhor's. *B*   17 Otherwise] otherwise *B*   19 dispossess]
disposse's *B*

Is a Faculty of the Minde, whereby she put's the Notions, and Images of things (with their operations, effects, and circumstances) that are confusd in the understanding, into the same order and condition, in which they are really disposd by Nature, or event: The Right Performance of this is cald Truth, to which Reason naturally tend's in a direct line, although she sometime miscarry, and faile by the Subtlety of the Object, or her own Imperfection, and that we call error or Falshood. Betweene this, and Truth, ly's the Proper Sphere of wit, which though it seeme to incline to falshood, do's it only to give Intelligence to Truth. For as there is a Trick in Arithmetique, By giving a False Number, to finde out a True one, So wit by a certaine slight of the Minde, deliver's things otherwise then they are in Nature, by rendring them greater or lesse then they really are (which is cald Hyperbole) or by putting them into some other Condition then Nature ever did (as when the Performances of Sensible, and Rationall Beings are applyd to Senseles and Inanimate things, with which the writings of Poets abound) But when it imploys those things which it borrows of Falshood, to the Benefit and advantage of Truth, as in Allegories, Fables, and Apologues, it is of excellent use, as making a Deeper impression into the mindes of Men then if the same Truths were plainely deliverd. So likewise it becomes as pernicious, when it take's that from Truth which it use's in the service of Error and Falshood; as when it wrest's things from their right meaning to a Sense that was never intended.

Reason is the only Helme of the understanding, the Imagination is but the Sayle, apt to receive, and be carryd away with every winde of vanity, unles it be stear'd by the Former. And although like the Lodestone, it have some Variations, it is the only Cumpas Man ha's to Sayl by, nor is it to be contemn'd, because it sometimes lead's him upon a Rock; that is but accidentall, and he is more apt to hit upon those without it. For all the variations of Reason, that

169ᵛ do not proceed / From the Disproportion of Mens wits, which can
Ab never be reduc'd to a standard, are rather imposd by Passion, Concernment, Melancholy, Custome, and Education, (which very few
can ever redeeme themselves from) then intended by Nature. And
5 for the Cheats, and Impostures that are wrought by it, They are no
other, then the greatest Blessings which God and Nature have
bestowd upon Mankinde are usually made serviceable to; And if we
will disclame Reason, for being no better dealt with; I doe not Know
how we can excuse the Gospel, Physique, wealth, Liberty, wine,
10 and Love, which were destin'd to the Happines, and wel-being of
man, but most commonly become the Fatall Causes of his Ruine
and Distruction.

The Original of Reason proceede's from the Divine wisdome, by
which the Order and Disposition of the Universe was immediatly
15 contrived, every Part of which ha's so rationall a Relation to every
other in particular, and the whole in generall; That though it consist of innumerable Pieces and Joynts, there is not the least Flaw
imaginable in the whole. Hence it follows, That the Order of
Nature is but a Copie which the Divine wisdome has drawn of it
20 self, and committed to the Custody of Nature, of which she is so
constant, and Faythfull an observer, that her very Deviations and
Miscarriages are Arguments of her Loyalty to it: For in those, she
is as rationally obedient to her Instructions, as in her regular operations, and by preserving the Religion of Causes (wheresoever they
25 meete) inviolate, though with the miscarriadge of the intended effect
(as if she kild the child, to save the Mother) dos but tell us, that she
had rather fayl of her own Purposes, and make Monsters, or Destroy
Mankinde, then digress the least minute from those Rules which
the Divine Pleasure has prescribd her. This Booke of Nature, Man
30 only of all Mortall Creatures, has the Honor, and Priviledge to read,
which lead's him immediatly to God, and is the greatest Demonstration he hath given of himself to Nature; and the nearest visible
Accesse to his Divine Presence Humanity is capable of. For in the
first Characters and single elements of the Creation, we cannot so
35 perfectly read God, as we can where those letters are joynd together,
and become words and Sense, as they do in the Rational Distribu-
170ʳ tion of all the Parts of Nature. This order is the universall / Apostle

of the whole world that perpetually preaches God to mankinde (and Ab
to mankinde only) every where, and ha's hardly found any Nation
so Barbarous, where some have not become Proselytes, and for
others nothing but this can encounter with them upon their owne
groundes; This is the foundation of all Religion, for no man that is 5
not certaine there is a God can possibly believe or put his trust
in him.

Faith can determine nothing of Reason, but Reason can of Faith,
and therefore if Faith be above Reason (as some will have it) it
must be reason only that can make it appeare to be so; For Faith can 10
never do it: So that Fayth is beholden to Reason for this Præroga-
tive, and sure it cannot be much above that from which it receive's
it's Credit. Faith cannot define Reason, but Reason can Faith, and
therefore it should seeme to be the lardger, as the Comprehending
must be greater then that it comprehend's. But howsoever wee 15
should grant it to be above Reason, certainly the lesse it is above it,
it is justly esteem'd the better; else Divines and Schoolmen of all
Ages would never have taken so much paines as they have to bring
it as neare to reason as they can, if it had been better at a Distance.
The very being of fayth depends upon Reason, for no Irrational 20
Creature is capable of it: and if we will not allow this, we must of
necessity acknowledg that it depend upon ignorance, which is
worse, for no man can believe any thing but because he do's not
know it. But Fayth allways differs from itself according as it falls
upon Persons: For that which is one mans fayth may be another 25
mans knowledg. So that the lesse any man knowes the more he hath
to believe.

There is nothing that can pretend to Judge of Reason, but only
itself, And therefore they that suppose they can Say most against
it, are forcd (like Juellers who are wont to beate true Diamond to 30
pouder to cut and polish false ones with their Dust) to make use of
it against it self, if they will ever say any thing against it, that can
pretend / to be to any Purpose. But in this they cheate themselves, 170ᵛ
as well as others, For if they that can say most against Reason, do Ab
it without Reason they deserve to be neglected: And if they do 35
it with reason, (as they can never do it with any thing else) they

1 mankinde (and] *probably altered from* mankinde and B   2 only)] *superimposed on*
only, B   3 Proselytes,] Proselytes. B   23 worse,] worse. B

disprove themselves: for they use it while they disclame it, and
with as much inconsistance and Contradiction, as if a man should
tell me he cannot speake.

There is a great deal of Difference betweene those Actions that
5 Reason performe's freely, and of her own accord; and those wherein
she is prescribd to and forcd: The former being commonly cleare,
and open, and the other obscure and intricate, as the Streame of a
River differ's from the Pipes of an Aqueduct: For when Opinion that
should wayt upon Reason, do's govern and dictate to it, the dis-
10 order is so preposterous, and the Restraint so ungratefull to reason
(that like a Conjurer must not stir out of a Circle) that commonly
her best performances, are but canting, and imposture. When the
Imagination is Broken loose from the obedience of Reason, it
become's the most disorderd and ungovernd thing in the world: It
15 cheate's the Senses, and rayses the Passions to that prodigious
height, that the Strength of the Body (as if it gaind what the Minde
loose's) become's more then treble to what it was before. It transport's a man beyond himself, and do's things so far beside the
ordinary Course of Nature, and the understanding of the wisest,
20 that as if they had lost their wits too by contagion, it often passe's
for possessions of the Devill.

They that layd the first Foundation of the Civill Life, did very
well consider, that the Reason of Mankinde was generally so slight,
and feeble, that it would not serve, for a Reine to hold them in from
25 the Ruine of one another; and therefor they judg'd it best to make
use of their Passions, which have always a greater Power over them,
and by imposing necessary Cheats upon their hopes and Feares,
keepe them within those limits, which no Principles of Reason or
29 Nature could do.

171ʳ   Men without Reason are much worse then Beasts, Because they
Bb   want the End of their Creation, and fall short of that which give's
them their Being; which Beasts do not, but are Relievd for that
Defect, by another way of Instinct, which is nothing but a Kinde of
Implicit Reason, that without understanding why, direct's them, to
35 do, or forbeare those thinges that are agreeable, or hurtfull to their
Particular Natures: while a Fool is but Half-man, and Half-beast, is
deprivd of the Advantages of both, and ha's the Benefit of Neither.

11 out] of *B*

There is nothing more Necessary, and usefull to Reason then Distinguishing, and therefore the word Discretion signifys nothing else; And yet there is nothing that is render'd so much the Cause of Ignorance, Error, and Nonsense as School distinctions: For no Distinctions can be good, but those that are so plaine, that they make themselves. For the best things when they are abusd become the worst.

Those who imploy their studies only upon Fancy and words, do commonly abate as much in their Reason, and Judgments, as they improve the other way; For unless they make Truth and observation the Ground and Foundation, or rather the end of their Studys, and use Fancy, and Stile only as Instrumentall, to expresse their Conceptions the more easily, and Naturally, they are noe wiser then an Artificer that mistake's his Tooles, for that which they only serve to worke upon. For those who propose Wit, and Fancy for their end, and take in sense and Reason only as circumstantiall and on the by, judge as extravagantly as those who believe themselves Rich, because they can cast up ever so great Sums of Money, but have not one Penny. And that is one Reason why such men are commonly the most unapt in things that require Judgment and Reason. For those who mistake their ends, do but shoot Powder that makes a noyse, but aime's at nothing—sequitur Corvos testaque lutoque.

Reason and understanding can only preserve a Man from being imposd upon, by the various cheates of the world, but will not cure him when he is Sick, nor Protect him against Misfortunes, nor inrich him when he is in want, and out of Imployment.

If Reason be the only note of Distinction between the Immortality and Mortalitie of the Soules of Men and Beasts; It is strange that this Reason should be of no use to men, in the Concernments of their eternall Being, but that all should be manag'd by the Imagination, with which Beasts are not unfurnish'd, and therefore may seem capable of Immortality, since they only want that, which man ha's no advantage by, Reason.

[171ᵛ, 171★]

3 else;] else,. *B*   yet ... that] *altered from* yet nothing that *altered from* yet that *B*   4 School distinctions] School-distinctions *W*   14 Artificer] Artificers *B*   25 Sick,] Sick. *B*   [171ᵛ, 171★] *Only headings* Reason (b, b, b)

Aa

Vices like weedes grow by being neglected; but Virtues like Herbes degenerat and grow wild, if there be not care taken of them. Both render a man equally contemptible when they are openly profest, and gloryd in. For Virtue looses it self and turne's
5 vice in doing that which is contrary to its own Nature: for many virtues may become vices, by being ill managd, but no one vice by any meanes a Virtue.

Pleasures have the Same Operation upon the understanding that sweet meates have upon the Pallat, the one being renderd as
10 unapt to Judge of the True State of things, as the other is of Tasts.

The first undertakers in all great Attempts commonly miscarry, and leave the Advantages of their Losses to those that come after them. As 30 of the Best Popes were Martyr'd to lay a foundation
15 for the greatness, and Power of their Successors.

The world is always the same, and ha's the same things don in it equally in all Ages, and vicissitudes although under different modes, and Characters: As the Sea though it be always in Motion is always the same, and neither grow's greater, nor lesser, for what
20 it loose's by being streitned in one Place, it recover's again by encroaching upon another. The greatest extravagancys in the world are things that ever have been and ever wilbe, and to reforme them is but to put them into another way, and perhaps a worse, and not to alter their Nature.

25 No mans Reputation is safe, where Slander is become a Trade, and rayling a Commodity, where men may get a living by defaming others, and eat upon any mans Credit that has any reputation to loose: where a Scribler at once satisfys his Itch of writeing, his Petulancy Malice or envy and his Necessity.

30 The Gold and Silver mines in the west Indies were taken by

8 Operation] *altered from* Operations B

the Spaniards from the Natives, the most harmless and Innocent users of wealth in the whole world, who had neither Ambition, Avarice nor Luxury, to which they have ever since beene Service-able. For the Spaniards have made them Instruments of the same cruelty and Tyranny in this Part of the world which they used 5 there / in depriving the Right owners of them: for they have ever **174ᵛ** since been but the Treasurys of Death and Distruction to man- Ab kinde.

In Natural things the offence and Punishment are joynd together, as he that put's his finger into the fire is presently burnt: So in 10 Morals, he that commits any wickednes, is instantly punishd with the dislike of his owne minde, for not only good deeds, but bad reward themselves.

Men in the upper Region of the Aire would be in the same condition that Fishes are in the nether, when being taken out of 15 their Native Element the water, they gape a while and labour to repair their Spirits, but presently dy.

Greatnes and Basenes of minde indure Injurys Afflictions and Affronts so equally that it is a hard matter to distinguish which is the True Cause, and sometimes perhaps both may at once Con- 20 tribute to the same effect.

He that is punish'd for talking is a Foole: But he that is sufferd to talke freely of all Persons Publique or Private, is more contemp-tible, and excusd as one that is not worth Punishing.

Though Flattery be but a Kinde of Civill Complement, and 25 Address, yet nothing has don more Mischief, nor been the Cause of greater Cruelties in the world.

When a Shepheard cannot keep his Sheepe from stragling, he is wont to set a Dog upon them: So when we will not keep within our Duty, Providence Commonly set's some wicked Person upon us, to 30 reduce us.

The world is so vile a thing, that Providence commonly makes

5 world] w[ ]d B   12 minde,] minde. B

Fooles, and Knaves happy, and good men miserable in it, to let us know, there is no great Difference between Happines and misery here.

Those Courts of Justice that pretend most to equity and Con-
5 science do always use the least of both. And the Judges at Law use to prefer the Security of Judgments before Statutes (which have allways been esteemd the Surer) only because they gaine nothing by Statutes, but much by Judgments.

Those who make it their Bus'nes to cheat others, do sometimes
10 put tricks upon themselves, else al Knaverys would always be prosperous.

175ʳ   There is no Reward in this world, for Modesty Obedience and
Aa Submission, but impunity (and not that always) But whosoever will assume, and pretend to greater Abilitys in any Profession then
15 all others, shall never want admirers, and followers among the Ignorant, And therefor this is the Constant Rode of all Impostors. For every man is apt to believe himself so much wiser then another, as he can with more Confidence pretend to understand that which neither of them do's, not can do. And therefor many men when they
20 heare any thing which they are utterly Ignorant of, are loath to inquire what it mean's, for feare of being discoverd not to understand more then they do. For he that submits to all men, shall meete with few that will not be as ready to assume.

As Thornes and Brambles though they are the Curse of the
25 earth, are yet the Fittest to make Hedges: So the worst of men are the most Proper to be made Jaylers.

In vicious Courts men of any Goodnes, or worth would appeare but Libels, and Lampoones upon the Rest: For the more there are to share in Infamy with Great Persons, the less fall's to the Parti-
30 cular accompt of any one.

As if the world were not vaine enough of it self, wee Derive our

---

7 allways] allway *W*   Surer)] Surer, *B*   10 Knaverys] *probably altered from*
Knavery *B*   13 impunity (and] *probably altered from* impunity and *B*
16 Ignorant,] Ignorant *B*   Rode] Rede *W*   19. 1–3 *See p. 62, ll. 11–14*

Delights from those things that are vainer then it: As Plays, Maskes, Romances, Pictures, New fashions, Excess &c, For as we were begotten with a Caprich, so we endevour to live up to it.

As in Carnevals All People use to take their Leaves of Flesh, as if they were glad to part with it, and indeavor by Surfets to render 5 the Quarrell irreconcilable; yet after a while they are impatient to be at it again: So is it with all men in their Resolutions of leaving those things which they have been accustomd unto.

Good men are the better for having been miserable, and in Affliction and bad men the worse. 10

The world is more beholden to Fooles then wisemen, for they 175ᵛ maintaine the greatest Part of it, that would be in a very Sad Aa Condition, but for the Encouragment, it perpetually receive's from them. All the great and Honorable Professions, and most of the Richest, and Right worshipfull Mysteries would have very 15 little to do without their Custom, and the constant Imployment which they never fayl to receive from them. For Prodigality and Luxury, and vanity are great Consumers, not only of themselves, but of all Commoditys of the growth of any Nation, which (as Men of Politiques affirme) is the only way to distribute, and Propagate 20 trade among all People. And although those extravagant Follys are Distructive allways to those that use them (and to those only) yet they are very beneficiall to all others that have to do with them. And when their Disorders produce Diseases and Infirmities in their Bodys or Estates, imploy two Professions to manage and 25 governe them, to their own best advantages. And as for those Fooles whose Natural weaknes, and want of Reason render's them Credulous, and apt to devoure any thing that is imposd upon them, by those that have ever so little more wit, or rather Craft, then themselves, There are innumerable Impostors that live upon them, 30 as the varieties of Folly and Ignorance are Infinite. And although those two Different Sorts of Follys disdaine one anothers extrava- gancies, in their severall ways, yet both tend to the same end and Purpose, which is nothing but what Philosophers affirmd so long since. That All men are born to live and Dy for the Service of their 35 Native Countries.

8 they] *interworded* B

172ʳ　　All Bad men are levellers, for when they finde it impossible to
Aa　attaine to the Reputation of those that are esteemd, for being good
and Virtuous, they use all false Arts, and by ugly Aspersions, and
slanders indeavour to cry them down to an equality of Infamy with
5　themselves.

It is an Argument of great Generosity to be cheated, for as
Princes are cald Invincible that have never been overcome, So he
that is supposd to be capable of being by any extravagancies,
exhausted, can never appeare great and magnificent.

10　　All the Pleasures of our Lives are not worth one houre's feare of
Death to those that are timorous and Fainthearted.

B　　Virtue and vice are not so inconsistent, but they are frequently
found to unite in the same Person: That all the contrariety that is
supposd to be in them, is only in Speculation, and seldom appeare's
15　in the Practice, like Convenience, and Inconvenience that are very
hard to be parted. The greatest Difference is that virtue, is but the
outside, and vice the Lineing, that men weare next their Bodys, for
ease and convenience. So that the one is but for shew, and the other
for use.

20　　Virtue, as it is commonly understood in women, signify's
nothing else but Chastity, and Honor only not being whores: As
if that Sex were capable of no other morality, but a mere Negative
Continence. Those who have this virtue, believe it is sufficient to
compound for any fault, or Defect whatsoever, and are commonly
25　so humorous, and uneasy upon that accompt, as if they had Parted
with their Right, and resolv'd to Repaire themselves some other
way: or had taken out Letters of Repriesall, to recover their Losses
upon all they can light upon; and Revenge themselves, as Eunuchs
do their Disabilities with Il-nature, and the Hatred of all Mankind.
30　When no virtue can be Sullen, and Proud upon it's own Accompt,
but it degenerate's into something worse then that which it strove
to avoyd.

All the Doctrines of Philosophers, and Tutors tend only to keep
yong Men from being vicious too soon, before they come to yeares

of Discretion, and Judgment to manage their vices to the least
Disadvantage. For Mens vices, like their Estates, ought to bee
order'd by their Guardians, when they are under Age, and not left
in their own Power.

Virtue is so neare reduc'd to nothing that the very Name is 5
become Pædantique.

Wine is the greatest Flatterer in the world, to those that are
vainglorious, that by perswading them they want nothing, bring's
them further into reall wants, not only of money but Courage, wit,
and Reason &c. And therefor the Curse of God is often in the Scrip- 10
tures exprest by making men Drunk with the Cup of his wrath.

Pride and Insolence is as Naturall to those that are great and 172ᵛ
Rich, as Humility is to those that are poor and Miserable: And as Bb
the Conditions of Men rise or fall; So do's their Humility, or Pride,
exactly hold the same Proportion, and both these do Naturally 15
produce all the Pitty, and envy in the world: For no man is envy'd
so much for his happines, as the Odious Pride, and vanity it bring's
with it nor pittyd so much for his unhappines, as the gentlenes and
Submission it naturally produce's.

Wealth Honor and Advancement conferd upon old Men, are 20
but Rattles to still them when they grow twice Children. Their
Aftermarth or Autumnall Spring in any kinde of extravagance is
worse, (because more unnaturall) then the earliest Freakes of
Youth.

Men are most usefull to themselves, according as they are so 25
to others: For he whom no man ha's need of, has most need of all
others, and is just so far from being able to help himself, as he is incapable of helping others. The Hands are the most useful Members
of the Body, that do not only labour to maintaine it, but feed it like
a Child; Fight in Defence of all the rest, and naturally expose them- 30
selves against any blow that is aym'd at any other Part though
with their own inevitable ruine, and all this because they have

10 Reason &c.] Reason. &c B   12–19 *Duplicated and underlined B* 223ʳ
18 unhappines] wants B 223ʳ   32 ruine,] ruine. B   they have] *altered from*
it has B

so necessary a Dependance upon the Body, that without it's safety they cannot subsist.

Men are not so apt to be Diverted from Truth and Reason by those things they dislike, as those they are pleasd, and delighted
5 withall.

173ʳ   It is esteem'd a great virtue in some Men, That they have never
Bb been observ'd to censure, or speake ill (true or false) of any man: Which is such a kinde of Moral Virtue, as Justice, and Impartiality is in a Judge, to whom Right and Wrong are all one. For it is an ill
10 Argument of the Judgment or Integrity of any Man, That he is indifferent to all others, good, or Bad; as he must be who make's no Distinction. For either he must want Reason to understand the Difference, or Integrity to take Notice of it: And if all men should do so, there would be no Difference betwene Good and Bad, and
15 True and False in all the Affaires of Mankinde. For it is impossible for any man to approve of any thing that is good, that do's not at the same Rate dislike the Contrary. But this do's Commonly proceed from two Contrary extreames, either of stupid inadvertency, or overmuch Caution, And such men may be sayd to have lost
20 Paradise for nothing, without being able to discerne between Good and Evill; And as they are for the Bad in not being against them, So they are against the Good in not being truly for them, which such Newters can never be, and therefor are not unjustly in the great Affaires of the world, hated by both sides. For Neutrality
25 between Good and Bad, naturally turnes to the Bad, as the Conversation of sick men in Contagious Diseases, may infect those that are sound, whom the Society of all the Sound men in the world can never Cure. In the Scripture no Men are sayd so expresly to be hated by God as those who call Good Evill, and Evill Good: and to
30 such none can come nearer, then those who in their Discourse make no Difference between the one and the other. Physique is not an Art of understanding Health, but Diseases, and by that meanes chiefly become's usefull to Mankinde. Nor is the world so well understood by observation of the little Good that is in it, as the
35 Prodigious variety of Wickednes Folly and madness with which it is Possest. Nor has all the wisdom of the Law, any way to provide for the safety and preservation of Mankind, but in being severe to

21 Evill;] *comma altered from full point B*   30 nearer,] nearer. *B*

mens Crimes, without any regard at all to their virtues, further then mere impunity. So that if Censure be Bad of it self, all Religions, and Governments in the world must be so, that cannot subsist without it. All the Fault ly's in the Injustice and Error of Censure, not in the thing it self; more then a Ly which is nothing 5 but a mistake or Forgery of Truth, ought to be Charg'd upon Truth it self. For Conscience is nothing but a just Censure of a mans self. And the Censure of the world a just Punishment, that like Gods Judgments fall's inevitably upon all those that do ill, against which no Prerogative nor Power upon Earth can protect 10 the Greatest, and is indeed the only thing that can keep the most potent in aw, and serve to abate that stupendious vanity, and Insolence, which Flattery (the perpetuall Slave of Greatnes) dos always produce. For some whom Death and Judgment could not terrify, the Shame of the world and feare of Infamy ha's reduc'd. 15 For he that is proof against Shame, is free of all the Trades and mysteries of Iniquity in this world and cannot fayle of Preferment in that which is next to it, and is but a Colony and Plantation of this, and some Bandittis of the world above.

[173ᵛ
blank]

1 further] *or possibly* farther B   9 ill,] ill. B   11 Greatest,] Greatest. B

Aa

Though our Opinions commonly deceive us; yet they are certaine enough in the Valew of our own Happines, for he that dos not finde that in his own Perswasion, shall never meet it any where else.

5   Gold and Silver that governe all the opinions that govern the world are of little use to any other purpose, and yet are valu'd at the highest rates: But Iron and Steel that serve the world to so many excellent and necessary uses, have but a cheap and low price set upon them.

10   There are but few Truths in the world, but Millions of Errors and falsities, which prevayle with the Opinion of the world, and as the Major Part easily outvote, and overpower all the most reall, and cleare Truths in Nature, which afterwards appeare ridiculous to the Rabble, in whose wise opinion, the greatest absurditys 15 seeme graceful and becominge like flat Noses and great Lips among the mores: And as those Mores breake the Gristles of their childrens Noses that they may grow more flat and deformd then Nature meant them, So are men broken and bred up to those il favourd opinions in their infancys by use and Custome, which otherwise 20 Nature had never inclin'd them to, if they had been wholy left to her.

A credulous Person is like a Pitcher born by the eares, empty of it selfe, but apt to hold whatsoever is put in it.

No man is apt to have so meane an opinion of himself, as to 25 believe he is capable of being Flatterd, or if he were that he is so weake and easy, that any man should presume to attempt it.

Opinion and conjecture are often at a loss in the Discovery of Truth and so often upon a False Sent, that wee are more beholden to chance for the Invention of many noble Knowledges, which else

18 il favourd] *or possibly* il-favourd *B*

we had never enjoyd; for certainly the use of the Loadstone had
never been found out by that wit and Ingenuity, that is not able
to unriddle it, now it is found out.

Wee ought to have a great Care of our Publique Account of
those things which we either love or Delight in: for they appeare in 5
one shape to us, and to others in another. So general Assertions
ought to be sparingly usd, for though they hold in many things,
'tis strange if they do not fayle in some.

It is a most ridiculous Opinion that a Circle is a Fortification for 176ᵛ
a Conjurer, and so impregnable that a whole Legion of Devils Ab
cannot storm him in his worke.   11

Birds are taken with pipes that imitate their own voyces, and
men with those sayings that are most agreable to their own
opinions.

If the French Nobility, and Gentry should follow our Fashions, 15
and send their children over to learne our Language, and receive
their education from us; we should have as glorious an Opinion of
ourselvs, and as mean a valew of them, as they have of us: and therefor we have no reason to blame them, but our own folly for it.

Although very few men in the world are Content with their own 20
Fortunes, and Estates, but would gladly change on any tearmes
for the least advantage; yet no man was ever unsatisfyd with his
own understanding (especially if it were Defective) but always
believd himself (how unreasonably so ever) to be as wel provided
that way, as any of his Neighbors. For Ignorance is one of those 25
Infirmitys that are Insensible, and though it be ever so desperatly
sick, feeles no Paine, nor want of Health at all.

Those ordinary Formes of Speech which are now accompted Profane and Irreligious, came up at first from the manner of expression
usd by Religious, and Devout People. For when they usd out 30
of Scruple, and tendernes of Conscience, to ascribe nothing to
themselves, but all to god Almighty, and therefore when they
undertooke to perform any thing, usd to say they would do it by

26 Insensible,] Insensible. *B*   27 Paine,] Paine. *B*

Gods help or Permission, or for Brevity By God, That afterwards being usd by all People upon all Occasions, became to be esteemd Profanation and Swearing, and an odious Sin. And that which is now accounted most horrible to affirme any thing by the wounds,
5 and Bloud of God was then but a more serious and Comprehensive way of Asseveration, and meant nothing but by the Virtue and merits of the Death of our Saviour. Hence it is, that what was once the most pious and Civil way of speaking, is now become the most
9 impious, and wicked.

177ʳ They who suppose the world was made by chance (as Epicurus
Bb &c, did) do but acknowledge, that the Foundation of that Opinion must be so too: For if it bee possible for all things to fall into so excellent an Order, by trying infinite experiments in Vacuo from all eternity, it follow's, that That Opinion can Proceed from
15 Nothing but mere chance, and therefore can have no Reason to depend upon, and consequently all that we finde by experiment to be constantly true and Certaine do's but fall out to be so by chance: For the Opinions, and Judgments of Men can have no better, nor other Foundation then that of Nature, from whence they are, or
20 should be derived, if they are true; but if False from Error and Mistake, the Common Productions of Chance and Accident. For the Minde and understanding of Man is but a Mirror, that receive's, and Represents, the Images of those Objects that Nature set's before it at a just Distance, as far as it is able to receive them, and
25 therefore the more remote things are, the more uncapable it is to enterteine them; and if it ever hap to be in the Right, it is like a lucky cast at Dice, but by mere chance, and Hap-hazzard.

Men are not so much concernd in the Opinions they hold whether they are true, or false, as they appeare to be: But having
30 once declard themselves, Their Reputation becom's ingagd, to maintaine what they have once affirmd, right, or wrong; That thay may not be discover'd by others (whatsoever they think themselves) to have been in an Error. Like Hectors, who believe themselves bound in poynt of Honor, to maintaine (when they are
35 Sober) whatsoever they have don amiss when they were Drunk. And therefore men of honor are in Probability the most like to take the worst Courses (if no other will Serve) to vindicate that

1 God,] God. *B*   11 did)] did; *B*   31 what they] whathey *B*

Reputation, the Loss of which is So grievious to them, and the
shame so Intollerable.

All Reformations of Religion seldom extend further then the
mere opinions of Men. The amendment of their Lives, and Conversations, are equally unregarded by al Churches how much so ever ₅
they Differ in Doctrine, and Discipline: And though all the Reformation our Savior preach'd to the world, was only Repentance, and
Amendment of life, without taking any Notice at all of Mens
Opinions and Judgments; yet all Christian Churches take the
Contrary Course, and believe Religion more concern'd in one ₁₀
erroneous Opinion, then all the most Inhuman, and impious Actions in the world. And therefor the Punishments of the Inquisition
that ha's Jurisdiction only over mens opinions (or some in Order to
them) are more Cruell, Severe, and arbitrary, then those that are,
by other Courts, inflicted on the greatest Criminalls. For the ₁₅
greatest Sins are capable of Pardon, but the least Heresy, without
Recantation and Penance of none.

[177ᵛ,
177*]

[177ᵛ, 177*] *Only headings* Opinion (b, b, b)

Nature made women timorous, that they might not by encountring Dangers expose the Breed of Mankinde with which they
are intrusted for so many moneths, to those hazards which courage
often engages men to.

5   The eare can heare further upon a Level then the eie can see, for
wee can heare Guns further of at Sea then wee can see: And yet in
looking upwards the eie can see Stars at a greater distance, then the
eare can heare any thing.

If the Intellect be so cleare, and Infallible as the Philosophers
10 would have it, why do's it perpetually submit to the Judgment,
and Arbitration of Sense? as in the Mathematiques the Principles
whereof are Intellectuall and Abstract, and yet they can produce no
conclusions that will pass for certaine and True untill they have
past the Test of Sense, And in cases that cannot be determind by
15 Sense, why dos this Oracle of the Intellect borrow collaterall
Precedents, and Paralels from such as may be, if it dos not believe
the Sense more Authenticall then it self? for the Intellect cannot
persue any thing beyond the reach of Sense, but by observing the
Instructions which it receiv's from Sense, for there is nothing in the
20 Intellect that it did not either receive immediatly from the Sense
or by Tradition and at second hand as by collection and Consequence, and if there be any incertainty in the first, there must be
much more in the other.

There is no Creature so much a Slave to his own Condition as
25 man, that owes his Being to Fancy and his wel-being to Fortune;
That is made by the Sun to be burnt up with his Rays, or betrayd
by him to the Cold; that is exposd Naked to all the Crueltys of
Heaven and earth, beside those greater that men inflict upon one
182ᵛ another. That is sentencd / to the horrid execution of Death, with
Aa so much uncertainty of his after-condition, that the Differences of
31 Men about the next Life, become their greatest Troubles in this,

where though their best Certaintys are but Hopes and beliefs, yet
every man is so confident, that he is ready to beat out any mans
Braines that do not agree with his owne. That hath all his pleasures
imaginary, and his Paines Reall, His Calamitys and Afflictions that
come of them selves, but his emoluments and Security not without 5
great Care and Industry. That is forcd to drudge for that Food and
Cloathing which other creatures receive freely from the Bounty of
Nature.

The eie among thousands of objects can make choyce of any one
to peruse, and lay by the rest, but the eare cannot do so among 10
many soundes, for they mix together and become one great confusd Noyse. So the eare ha's one advantage of the eie that can see
but on way at once, as it turn's it self, but the eare can heare
every way without moving it self towards the sound.

Insects and vermine of æquivocall Generation increase and 15
multiply much faster then those that are producd the more
noble, and deliberate way of Nature.

Things that ly far of the Sense, are lessend to the understanding
as remote objects are to the eie.

Nature ha's planted in Man so strong a Desire of Society, that 20
when all other pleasures leave him, that only stay's with him.
This may be observd in Persons condemnd to dy, who being forsaken of all other consolations, finde some in the company of those
that are to suffer with them.

It is not improbable that the Globe of the earth do always 25
increase and grow Bigger, for it's own Productions returning still
with more then they receivd from her (that is those Parts of the
Sun and water that are in all Animals, and vegetables) must of
necessity ad to her bulke. As appeare's by the forc'd Grounds about
all great Cities, and the Stumps of Trees found some fathoms under 30
ground in Marshy Lands, Stoppages of the Currents of Rivers,
&c; for the cloudes being drawne from the Sea, and cast upon the
Land, and there turnd into Plants, do never return again.

The Virtuosi affirme that the Sun do's not go equal at all times

31 Lands,] Lands B   Rivers,] Rivers. B   32 &c;] &c B

in his Diurnal Course, but sometime faster and sometime slower in the same space of Time, in so much that their Pendulum-clocks are able to correct him, and when they are made with allowance for his variations, will go true with him all the yeare.

179ʳ The Ignorance of Naturall Causes make's many things passe Ab for Miracles that are not so, and when they are once reputed Miraculous, The many who are always inclind to favour strang things do their endevour to make as much of them as they can.

There is no living Creature in the world but nature ha's made some other to destroy it, to let us know, That Nothing can be secure, that has not some care to preserve it self, and avoyd those dangers that it is naturally subject unto.

The Moone performes her Diurnal Course slower though her monthly faster then the Sun, because her Motion North and South being much wider then that of the Sun she cannot so soone perform her motion east and west.

The greatest Difficulties are performd by Patience and Industry, not Quicknes of wit. The Braine is sayd by Philosophers to be the Coldest part of the Body and we finde that the Noses of Dogs where their Sagacity ly's are always Cold.

A Fig-tree will beare fruite though it never blossom.

A whale that is Naturally thick-sighted is always guided by a small fish called Musculus, that swims before and give's his Notice of Rocks that ly in his way.

A Load-stone looses all his Magnetique Virtu being placd neare a Diamond.

Numbers can have nothing to do (though some Philosophers have believd otherwise) in the workes of Nature, where heat and moysture govern most, and are never measurd by Number.

All the workes of Nature are Miracles, and nothing make's them

2 Time,] *possibly altered from* Time. B

appeare otherwise but our Familiarity with them, for there is
nothing in Nature but being rightly considerd, would carry us,
beyond admiration, to amazement: But these wonders are methodi-
call, and confin'd to order, to which they are so constant and Certaine, that the Ignorance of Mankinde account's nothing Miracu- 5
lous but the Deviations or diversions of them.

It is the Method of Nature in all her Productions to proceed by
gentle and easy Degrees, and when she make's any thing excellent,
and lasting, she is commonly the longer about it: For all things
decay after the Rate of their growth, and weare out with the same 10
Pace they arrivd at their Perfection. She never uses Violence but
when she destroy's.

There are some things Naturally performd by Birds and Beasts 179ᵛ
that may seeme rather to proceed from Divine Revelation then any Ab
thing that is don by Man: For wee finde by experience, That Birds 15
can keep an accompt of the Time they sit untill their yonge ones
are hatchd, without the knowledg of Numbers: They can cross
the Seas without a Card or Cumpass, and passe directly from one
Cuntry to another, according as they have occasion to fly, or follow
Summer, or winter. That they foreknow Stormes, and Tempests 20
long before they come. That Dogs can finde out a way which they
never went before, without a Guide, or knowledg of the Meridian,
or Pole, for many Miles: which Pidgeons in the East can do for
many hundreds: with aboundance of others no less strang and
wonderfull which wee frequently meet with in Bookes, to which if 25
a Man could perform any thing equal it would not fayl to perswade
the world, he could not possibly do it without divine Revelation.

If the Minde or Soul of Man can observe the Errors and miscarriages of Nature, and finde out ways of it selfe to relieve her, which
she could not do her selfe: It may seeme to be an Argument, that it 30
is derivd from some thing above her: For Nature cannot give that
which she hath not.

Phancy and Memory are like the Right and left hand, And as the
more active the one is the other is the less: So they that have

ready Memories are observ'd to have dull Phansies, and they that have ready Phancies for the most part bad Memories.

There is no Plant in Nature so humble as a Vine, that creep's upon the earth and will not rayse it self untill it finde something to
5 support it. That comes behinde almost all other in putting foorth its Buds, and will not expose them to the open Aire, untill all the Colds of winter are past: And yet it beare's a fruite that for might and Power has held competition with Kings, and Truth. That make's no shew at all when it is in the flowr, but hide's its blossom
10 with thick and shady leaves.

Snayles and Fleas are reported by Virtuosos to see through Naturall Tubes and perspectives. For their eies grow on the ends of their Hornes.

Nature perhaps entended Horses should beare Burthens, but
15 she never meant they should load themselves.

178ʳ   The Specificall Principles of things may seeme to proceed from
Aa the Matter, and not from the Universall Forme, which being Simple ha's not so fair a Pretence to that infinite Variety as the Matter which is as infinitely Various: For wee see the same clod being
20 warm'd by the same Sun-beames, do's produce both Plants and animals of Severall and Different Kindes.

Nature do's not trust us in this world without a Guard upon us, For wee are rather kept within the Limits of it, by the Feare of Death, then the Love of Life: and certainly no Man would endure
25 the Calamities of this world, if the Passage out of it were not so horrid to human Nature.

The Generall Humor, and Genius of every Nation takes a Particular Delight in the Bewty of some one Part of women, as wee may finde by observing their Poętry. For the English most comonly

30   The least graine of Corne is bigger in Potentia then the whole Earth, For we can easily comprehend the Bounds and Limits of the Earth but the Imagination of Man know's not where to determine the extent of that Multiplying Power.

8–10 That . . .] *interlined* B

It may seeme not Improbable, That all the Light wee see is by
Reflection, For in the Night wee perceive no Light of the Sun,
but only as it is reflected by the Moone and Stars, though it be
equally disposd every where above the Shadow of the Earth. And it
is no more strange that it should shine and not light but by reflec- 5
tion, then that it should shine and not heat but by the same meanes,
which appeares most certaine by the Coldnes of the upper Regions
of the Aire, through which the Sun-beames pass without imparting
any light at all.

I cannot imagine upon what account The Intelligible world 10
came to be receivd among Philosophers, nor the Cælestiall, as they
understand it. If wee must meddle with any thing so much above
us, The most probable way is to believe the Stars to be other
worlds, for the reason of the Peripatetiques that they do not consist
of Elementary Matter, because they are Incorruptible is very 15
slight, and / weake and may be as truly sayd of the earth, where 178ᵛ
there is no corruption but of Particulars, the whole being always Ab
the same.

Occasion in the Affayres of the world, is like the seasons of the
yeare in Nature, for the Planting growth and Maturity of things 20
which if wee forget or confound all our Labour is in vaine.

Nature is very Bountifull of her Preciousest Treasure, that's
Necessary, or usefull to Mans life; But sparing of that which is
only serviceable to our Pleasures.

The Minde of Man is the only overseer of the workes of Nature 25
in this world, That can observe her mistakes, and in some things
understand the Reasons of that which she seeme's to do Mechanically, and if she be at a loss in others, it is only her want of Perfection, for her Abilities are limited, and if she could comprehend all
things she were not a Soul but a God. 30

All things were hidden in the first Matter, as a Bird is in an
Egge; But now it is hidden in all things, as an Egge is in a Bird.

12 it. If] it, if *B*   16 slight,] slight. *B*   25-30 *Duplicated B* 182ʳ
25 of the workes] *om. B* 182ʳ   25-6 Nature in] Nature of all Creatures in *B* 182ʳ
27 Reasons] Reason *B* 182ʳ   27-8 Mechanically, *B* 182ʳ: Mechanically.
B 178ᵛ   28-9 her . . . Perfection] a Difference in Degree *B* 182ʳ   29 com-
prehend] understand *B* 182ʳ   30 a God] somthing greater *B* 182ʳ

The Beames of the Sun move down-wards towards the Earth empty: and upwards when they are Laden with exhalations: as water in the Inside of the Earth move's upwards towards the Tops of Mountaines, where the Heads of great Rivers are usually found, 5 and downwards on the outside.

The Thumbe is equal in strength, to all the four Fingers of the hand.

Animal Vital and Rational are Distinctions of Functions only, and are no more real then a standing, sitting or talking Body is 3 10 Bodys.

It may appeare strange that evill Angells should have a larger Priviledge to do mischief then good ones have to relieve Mankinde: For if the Devil have Power to compact with wicked Persons, and witches, to destroy and hurt, it is probable that good Angels have 15 as much to combine with holy and Religious Persons, for their Preservation, (which was never heard of in our times) else the one must have more Power, or will to hurt, then the other has to help. Nature ha's given Beasts of Prey, more of Strength, to hurt and destroy, but less wit and cunning then she has bestowd upon the 20 weaker to defend themselves for hares and foxes would be too Cunning for Dogs did not the wit of man take their Parts.

183ʳ   If a man remove his fingers out of that Order in which Nature
Aa   ha's planted them, and place the Second before the first, they will give him a false accompt by doubling the Single object they both 25 touch upon at the same time. So if he remove his eie out of the levell of it's Seate, it will presently multiply whatsoever is within his view.

As Great Persons use to give Liverys to their Inferior Servants, and leave the better sort to cloath themselves, as they please: So 30 God and Nature have furnish'd every Species of Creatures with a Naturall Sute of the same stuff, but only Man the chiefest of them, who is left at liberty to fit himself according to his own choyce.

4 found,] found. *B*   16 Preservation, (which was] Preservation, which (was
B   18 to hurt] *altered from* but le *B*   31 only] ony *B*   32 who is]
who⟨m he h⟩ is *B*

All Flowers are but the Cradles of Seede, of which Nature seeme's to have a very great regard, in that shee is so curious of their ornament, in bestowing so much Bewty and sweetnes upon them.

Elephants, that are the Tallest of all Beasts, have their Teeth (that are their Armes) growing downwards, as more proper for all incounters, that they can have with enemies that are not so Tall: And the Tuskes of Boares that are lower (commonly) then their Adversaries, grow upwards for the more convenience in their Fights.

The head ought to be kept warme, because Nature has cloathd no other Part of Man.

Yong Vipers (in the Belly of the Dam) have egs in their own bellys. The male ha's a double Penis and a Forked Tongue. The Femall is sayd, when they ingender to bite of his Head, for which the yong ones in Revenge eate their ways out of her Belly.

All sorts of Bruite Beasts, and Foul, and Fish are commonly taken with Baytes layd to allure their Appetites to food; and only man with provocations apply'd, to his Fancy, or Concupiscence.

Every Living Creature may seeme to have been made by a severall Nature; For there is no one, that was not created to distroy, or be distroyd by some other.

The Apprehension of a violent Death is more terrible then that of one, that is Naturall, although the former is many times much easier.

Black women decay sooner then those that are fair, and the Fayr **183ᵛ** sooner then the Brown. Ab

The smallest Sands in the River Sein appeare in a Microscope to be all Snayl-shels. As the Egs in the Rows of Fishes to have little fishes in them. And the Blew Tarnish upon Plums, to be Animals.

---

12 other] othe *B*   13 Dam)] *superimposed on* Dam, *B*   14 bellys.] bellys *B*
15 Head,] Head. *B*

So in the Bloud of men in Fevers, and in vineger, little Animals are discoverd by the same Instrument. And in the Livers of Rotten sheep Butchers use to finde little Fishes.

No good Orenges have ever been observ'd to grow above a Day
5 Jorny from the Sea, nor good Tobacco in any Cuntry neare it. Great Sholes of Herrings make toward the Shore to cast their Spaune.

Cold Iron beaten hard with an hammer becomes Magneticall.

Old glass will rot as we see it often in Church windores full of
10 holes.

There is in Oxfordshire (or somewhere thereabout) a Quarry of Freestone of so strange a Nature, that if it be layd in the walls of a Building east and west and as it grew in the Earth, it become's hard and durable against Time and weather. But if it be put in any
15 other Position, it presently decay's and moulders away. Of the Truth of this the Lord Cravans house at Causham is a present example, that though it be lately built already decays. And the New Theater at Oxford that is built of the same Stone with regard to the manner it lay in the Pit, continue's firme, and is like to do so.

20 Nature has provided that old men should be unfit for Love, or getting of Children, because they are not like to live long enough to breed them up.

No Maggots are observd to breed in walnuts (as they do in others) perhaps because of the Bitter skins that inclose but the
25 Shell and Kernell.

Those Sparkes of Fire that are beaten out of a Flint by a Steele, being receiv'd upon a clean Paper, do appear in a Microscope to be glassy, and to receive, and reflect the Light.

180ʳ If pease be sowed in the Increase of the moone, they wil never
Aa leave blooming. Heyd p. 43. If wood be Cut after the Sun decline's
31 from us, until he Comes to the Æquinoctial it wil never grow

5 Sea,] Sea. *B*   8. 1 *See p. 96, ll. 11–12*   13 grew] grow *W*

againe. (idem ibid) The Reason is because when the Sun is Past the
Autumnal æquinox, The Sap retire's into the Rootes of Trees, and
before the Sun returne's to draw it up again, that part of the Stump
that is cut become's mortifyd, with the Cold, and so hardned, that
the Sap can finde no Passage through it, without any relation to 5
the stars at all.

Chronical Diseases follow the Course of the Sun, and acute of
the Moone.

All the most Intense Artificiall Heats in the world, can never
make a Counterfet Stone so hard, as the gentle soft Heat of Nature 10
dos a Rubie or a Diamond.

Some men Suppose that the Soul of Man is like the Radicall
Moysture in Plants, which Philosophers affirme can never be destroyd by fire, but there will a Salt be left in the Ashes of it that may
be brought to vitrification but no further. 15

Man has an absolute Power over Fate in all things that concerne
his own Distruction, but none at all in those that Relate to his own
Happines, in which his greatest care and Industry is many times
defeated by an unfortunate Accident.

Men never see Spectres and Apparitions, but in the Darke, when 20
their eies are in the worst Capacity of Discerning, and their Fancies
in the best of apprehending.

Nature take's a longer time to produce great and large Animals,
then those of a lesser Size. An Elephant is sayd to bee two yeares in
the Belly of the Dam: Horses, and Cows &c little lesse then one 25
(and seldom produce more then one at once) while Bitches, and
Cats, and Rabbet, and all the lesser Sorts of Living Creatures are
produc'd in a few months, (and many at the same time) and Insects
of æquivocall generation in great Numbers in a Few Days. 29

All Beasts of Prey have most of the Male, and those that are **180ᵛ**
prey'd upon of the Female, and therefore are more Salacious then Ab
the other; for we do not finde that a Lion, or wolf, or Tiger require
so many Femals as a Bull, or Ram, or Goate, and therefore do not
multiply So Numerously.

Those Philosophers and Mathematicians are mistaken who say that the Moone goe's further without the Tropiques then the Sun, for as she move's lower then the Sun, she seeme's to come nearer to the Horizon, and consequently to have a greater Declination then the Sun, when they both Stop at the very same Degree.

It is one Argument, That Antipathys are commonly Phantastique, and Affected; Since no man was ever observd to have an Antipathy to Wolves, or Foxes or Hares, though they persue them to death for the Damages which they are wont to Cause, nor to Horses nor Houndes, because it is a kinde of mode for all men to pretend to delight in Riding and Hunting. But only to Cats and Pigs, upon the old Accompt of the first being turnd into witches and the other Possest by the Devil.

Iron is an extraction of Clay, and Glasse of Sand, and that may Seeme to be the Reason why Glass is so brittle, and Iron so tough, like the matter which they were produc'd of.

It is a great Question among Virtuosos, whether Timber do shrink in length or not.

The Backs of all Fishes are very neare of the Cullour of the Water that they are bred in, to avoyd the Discovery of those that prey upon them. As the Antients usd to cullour those Boates that they usd for Discovery, and Dy the Sayles, and the Garments of the mariners that went in them, of the Cullour of the Sea.

When the Eies of Birds are blinded they are sayd naturally to fly upwards, and the more blinde and Ignorant men are, the more they are always apt to aspire, either to the Top of this world or some other above it.

181ʳ
Ab The Hair of the Heads of all Beasts grows upwards and that of men downwards, who have vertices, and beasts none.

B
31 The Sun drawing neare the vernall Equinox drive's the Cold before him towards the North, which is one Cause why the first Approaches of the Spring are so exceedingly cold, and the beginings of winter so warme, when the Sun is at a greater Southern Latitude.

All yong Animals by stirring themselves in Sport, and Play, improve their growth by conveying the Nourishment by motion, with greater Facility to the severall Parts. So yong Trees mov'd by the winde, grow the Faster, untill they have attaynd to a firme Solidity, and then they resist them, and leave only their weaker 5 Bows and Branches to be exercisd, and improv'd by the Same Agitation. And therfor it may be one Reason, why underwoods never grow great, not only because the Sun and Raine is kept from them, but also this exercise of the windes.

The Tradition That the Earth will in the End be destroyd by 10 Fire, is not Improbable in Nature. For as the Sea has visibly, and apparently in few yeares Decay'd, and left many Havens some Miles from the Shore in almost all Cuntrys that border upon it, It follow's that in length of time (supposing the same order of Nature still continuing) it must of Necessity be utterly exhausted: And then 15 there being no moysture left to produce and preserve Plants, all vegetables wilbe naturally Dry'd and renderd Combustible, and inevitably set on fire by the Beames of the Sun. And as at the Floud, when the Sea had all those vast Quantitys of water, which are since spent, The Earth was perhap's Naturally Drown'd: so when it 20 has too little, it will probably be as Naturally burnt. Nor is it improbable that what the Sea loose's, the Earth gaine's, and therefore Dayly grow's bigger, for as the greatest Part if not all the Supply of Matter in all Naturall Productions, Come's from the Sun, and the Sea, the Fountaines of all Heat and Moysture (For all 25 Places that ly too remote from the Sea, to receive a Constant share of Raine, become Desarts, and produce nothing) So little or nothing of that moysture, is ever return'd back againe from whence it came, but resolv'd into earth, as all Naturall Bodys by corruption are, and so must of Necessity ad perpetually to the Bulke of the Earth. As 30 we see about all great and Antient Cities the Earth increast some yeards in Depth (Notwithstanding the vast Quantitys of Materialls that are taken out of it for the uses of building) And in all Fens,

11 For as the] For the *C*   15 of Necessity] *om. C*   15–16 then there] there then *C*   16 and preserve] *om. C*   Plants, all] Plants and quench the Heat of the Sun, all *C*   24 Supply] Supplyes *C*   Come's] are *C*   24–5 the Sun, and] *om. C*   25 Fountaines] Fountaine *C*   Heat and] *om. C*   Moysture *C*: Moysture. *B*   26 the Sea] it *C*   a] *om. C*   share] and necessary Supplyes *C*   28 that moysture] it *C*   29 but resolv'd] but all that proceeded from moysture is resolv'd *C*   31 Cities the] Cities (the *B*   32–3 (Notwithstanding . . . building)] *om. C*   33 building)] *superimposed on* building. *B*

and Marshes, and woodlands uninhabited, a great deal more.
Beside the Raines carry a great deal of Earth from the Tops of
Mountaines down into vallys, which may be one Reason why
the Adriatique Sea has lost so much of its antient Shore, lying in
5 the midst of so many Mountaines.

An Animal is nothing else but a House for the Spirits of the world
to inhabite, which the Form rayse's out of the Matter; And
therefor they differ as other Edifices do, of which Some are Pallaces,
and some but Cottages, according as the Supply of Materialls are,
10 upon which the Spirits are to work.

181ᵛ   The Tides of the Sea may seeme to be causd by the Motion of
Bb   the Earth, for if it always move's Eastward (as some believe) it
cause's the great Ocean to move westward, untill it meete's with
the opposite motion (for all the opposite Parts of a wheele in motion
15 move contrary to one another) and then the great Bulke of the Sea
turne's back againe. What operation the moone ha's upon the Sea,
may in Probability, bee collected from the Course shee keepe's
with the Sun. Nor is there any way so likely to conceive how the
Sea should have such variety of Currents, but as this great Motion
20 meet's with variety of Diversions, as we see the winde do's among
Mountaines. All the Motions that wee can observe great Bodys of
Water naturally to have proceed either from the Declivity of the
Earth, or the Impulse of violent windes; But the Tides are far from
having any of those Causes, for they move equally Backwards, and
25 Forwards, almost as equally with or against both. Whatsoever it is,
it must be something of Prodigious Force, that can move so great
a weight as that of the Sea: And if the Influence of the Moon can
do it (as some believe) it is probable that the Influence of the Sun,
being so many times more Powrfull, may have the same operation
30 upon the Earth. As for the Reasons some give for the Rapid motion
of the Sun, from the Quick motion of Light, that appeare's at any
Distance ([at] which it may be seen) the very instant it is lighted,
that do's not at all concern the Diurnall Motion of the Body of the
Sun, For a Torch that appeares at a great Distance the Same mo-
35 ment it is held up: yet if it be carryd from one Place to another, dos
not appeare to move faster, but rather slower (by reason of the

2 Beside . . . carry] the Raine carryes C   3 vallys] the vally C
21 Mountaines.] Mountaines, B   24 those] these W

Distance) then the Person that beares it. And if the Body of the
Sun did move with that velocity (as it must of Necessity to pass so
vast a Space) it must by the Same Necessity, draw a Tayle after it
like a Comet; which it do's not, and therefor in Probability stands
still. And if the Rest of the Planets do not do so, it is because they 5
are only Illuminated by the Sun, and therefor not subject to any
such Impression by their Quick Motions through the Æther, more
then the most violent windes are able to move the Sun-beames,
when it shine's upon the Earth. And therefore they who affirme the
Sun to be the Same with our Artificiall Fire, are mistaken for then 10
the Sun-beames would be as lyable to be mov'd by the Aire, as our
Fire is. The Truth is though our Fire be made of the Beames of the
Sun, yet it is mixt with grosser Matter which render's it not so
fine, and Pure as those Rayes are Naturally of themselves, and consequently subject to the Impulse of Grosser Bodies. But if any man 15
shall suppose from hence that the Sunne being of so Pure a Substance, and passing (how rapid soever) through the Pure Æther,
is not capable of meeting with that opposition, that can cause him
to change his Figure, yet we see that Comets which pass through
as pure and subtle an Aire, do never theless draw Tayles after them, 20
of many thousand Miles in length. And if the Sun can draw out of
the Sea that vast Quantity of water that is conteind in the Clouds,
and out of the Earth, all Plants and Trees of the largest size all
tending towards it self, It is not Improbable but it may with less
Difficulty, cause the Earth to turn Round towards it self, being 25
equally poysd in the Aire, and no Impediment that we know of to
stop it's Circulation.

Nature has order'd it so, That Parents have a great Inclination **184ʳ**
to the Love of their Children, because they cannot subsist without **Bb**
it: But takes no course that children should Love their Parents, 30
because they have no such neede of it.

All the Influences of the fixt Stars, Constellations, and the Rest
of the Planets are no more considerable to those of the Sun alone,
then all their Light together is able to compare with his alone.

It is no uneasy thing to prove, That all men go Naturally on 35
their Heads, because the Rootes of the Nerves, that give Motion to

17 Æther,] Æther. B   30 takes] take B

the whole Body, are plac'd in the Head, by which all the Members are agitated, as the wheeles of a watch are by the Spring.

All Bewty, and the Ornaments of it, are Naturally designd for the outsides of things, and not their inward Parts; For if the Inside of the Bewtifullest Creature in the World were turnd outward, nothing could appeare more Gastly, and horrible: And so it is in all the Affaires of the world, by which Nature seeme's to provide for the Decency, and comlines (at least) of the world, but leave's it to it self in all other matters.

The Streits of Gibralter are too narrow to let the Great Ocean in and out: And therefore they have little or no Tides in the Mediterranean Sea, whose extent is too large to bee supply'd, or emitted, at so streit a Passage.

Women are Naturally most fond, of the Children of their first Husbands, and Men of those of their second wives, for whose sakes they frequently neglect those of the first, And therefore women are always more severe, and Cruel Mothers-in-Law, then Men are Step-fathers; who are many times more kinde to their wive's children then their own, Whose Mothers are Dead, and cannot use, the Naturall Arts they have to turn their Husbands Inclinations which way they please.

They who delight in Bus'nes, are in their Naturall Tempers slaves, to whom Drudgery properly belong's. And as such men are generally Covetous; So the Antients were of opinion that all those who were inclind to that vice, were naturally Slaves, because they labour and drudge not for themselves but others: And though they often understand not who those are: yet they have no more Power to Dispose of any thing they have gain'd for their own Injoyment then the wretchedest Slaves in Turky. But perpetually Condemne themselves to gather Wealth, as slaves do in the Mines of Potosy, For nothing but their own drudgery and the pleasure and Injoyment of they know not whom. For Labour and Paines are so Naturally

9 other] othe B   11–12 no . . . Sea] duplicated [There are no . . .] B 183ᵛ
14–21 Duplicated and underlined B 223ʳ   14 Naturally] always B 223ʳ
17 Mothers-in-Law] Mothers in Law altered from Mother in Laws B 223ʳ   30 themselves] themselve B

ungratefull; That God himself blest the Day in which he rested
from his worke, And therefor he inflicted immediate Labour, and
Drudgery (as a greater Punishment then Death the End of it) upon
Adam for his Disobedience. And when the Jewes provokd him to
the highest, he did not destroy them utterly, but sent them into 5
Captivity, where they might suffer a more grievious Affliction then
Dying in Defence of their Cuntry, The Drudgery of Slaves. It was
the worst part of Adams Curse to till the earth that was renderd
Barren of purpose to finde him the more Toyl, and Labour. Yet
that was nothing to the additionall Curse which man ha's layd upon 10
himself, to dig into the Bowells of the Earth for mettles, not to
earn a Living but a thousand ways of Death.

If Raines are most frequent in Places neare the Sea, It is strange, **184ᵛ**
That Spaine that is almost incompast by the great Ocean, and the Bb
Streits, Italy in the middle of three Seas, and all Africk that Border's 15
upon the Ocean, should be so exceeding Dry, that they seeme to
want Raine, which England, and Ireland, too much abound with
while all the Ilands of the Mediterranean are so destitute of it:
That Cyprus is sayd to have been forsaken by the Inhabitants for
want of Raine, having been 18 continuall yeares without one Show'r. 20
And in Ægypt that ly's between the mediterranean, and Red Seas,
it never raine's nor were there ever so much as Clouds seen, in the
Iland of the Rhodes, as the Antients report, And wee are told that
in the Ilands of the west Indies, they have seldom any Raine but a
Constant moyst Aire. 25

The western Coasts of Spain and England, that ly open to the
Great Ocean, and the violence of the west-windes, are full of
Mountaines, as if the waters at the Floud, or the Creation had
setled there in Stormes, and renderd the Land so uneaven by the
Impetuous Fury of Tempest, and every Hill were but a Congeald 30
Wave.

7–12 It . . .] *duplicated and underlined B* 223ᵛ   8 Curse to till] Curse at the
Fall to be a Husbandman, and till *B* 223ᵛ   11 mettles, *B* 223ᵛ: mettles. *B*
184ʳ   12 a Living] a poore Living *B* 223ᵛ   of] to *B* 223ᵛ   13–25 *Duplicated and underlined B* 223ᵛ   13 most . . . neare] causd by the Nearenes
of *B* 223ᵛ   15 Streits,] Streits. *B* 184ᵛ, 223ᵛ   22 were there ever] *altered
from* are there seldom or never *B* 223ᵛ   so much as] *interlined B* 223ᵛ   23 report,] report,. *B* 184ᵛ   wee . . . that] *om. B* 223ᵛ   24 Raine] Raines
B 223ᵛ

Although the Sun makes all things in Nature, yet he seemes to do it Mechanically, like a great Engine, that do's not understand what it do's: For if it had that Prodigious wit and Judgment to invent and order all things in Nature, as it pleaseth, it would not
5 fayl so often in Particulars, as wee finde it do's, nor miscarry in it's Designes, by the interruptions of that which seeme's to be mere chance, and in its Power to divert. And therefor it may seem to be imployd by some greater Power, that set's it on work with Rules to observe, as it always do's with so much Care in the Generall,
10 that it is not at leisure to use the same Industry in every Particular.

It is a Question whether Horses do not see, or imagine they see something (like Balaams Ass) when they start at Poasts that never did them Hurt, and take them for some thing that ha's don: though wee cannot fancy, what it should be, nor Guess what it is that
15 put's them into so horrible a Terror, as when they are sayd to be ridden by Hags in the Stable.

Planetæ, quia sunt propè, non Scintillant. Arist. Poster. Lib. 1us.

14 be,] be. *B*

Pope Paul the 2d (a venetian by birth, and bred a Merchant)
Declared all those Heretiques that should in earnest, or in Jeast,
pronounce the word Academy, or university. De Serres p. 920.

The Ages wherein our Henry the 5th, 6th, and Edward the 4th
lived and some yeares since, were much more given to Rebuses and 5
Devises then the modern, the Reason I suppose to be the Disuse of
Tilting.

Guicciardine write's that the walls of Bologna were blown up in
the Aier so high that the Soldiers within and without the Town,
could see one another under it &c. which was not Possible to be 10
don, for the smoke of the Pouder could not but cast a mist before
their eies, too thick to be seen through.

The Roman Historians (as Livy, Salust and Tacitus &c) use no
Passion nor Partiality in Discribing the Actions of those Parties
they dislike or favour, but commonly bring in some eminent 15
Persons then in Action, who in their Orations or Counsels freely
discover the Good, and evil both of the one and the other Faction, in
which they seeme to spare neither, but only to regard Truth. Much
unlike the Historians of our Times, who very indiscreetly use
to discover their own Inclinations, and having made themselves 20
Parties, do justly deserve the misbeleife of their Readers.

In Persia those that appeal to the Emperor himself, put on
vest's of white Paper when they deliver their Petitions: To signify
The Agravation of their Injury is not to be describd but in as much
Paper as wil cover their whole Bodys. Ricault p 46. 25
Quære whether the Persians use white Paper, for they write
always upon Green.

The Frenchmen have in late Ages been always beaten out of
their Conquests by the People they subdu'd, being Impatient of

4 5th,] 5th. B   15 favour,] favour. B   25 Ricault p 46.] *interlined* B

their Insolence and Tyranny. As in Constantinople, Sicely, Naples, Millaine Flanders &c.

The Spaniards overcame the Americans, by wearing the Shapes of Lyons, Dragons, Tigers, Beares, and Devils in their Helmets, which the Poore Ignorant Creatures took for their Heads and faces, and had not courage to endure the sight of them.

Childeric the 2d king of France began his Reign well, but ended it ill, contrary to his Predecessor chilperic, who began it ill and ended it well.

Charles Martel was Bastard to Pepin Maistre Du Palais, by Apayde a Concubine which he kept in his wifs time.

In France those great Lords that have Haut Justice, or Regal Power within their own limits, use to distinguish their Qualitys as Dukes from Earls &c by the Fashion of their Gallowses. Cotgrave in the word Gibet.

187ᵛ They that affirm the Northern Cuntrys to abound with People
Ab more then the South, because great Multitudes have from thence invaded the warmer Climats, as Goths Vandals, Huns &c Do not consider what great Numbers of People fled from the Romans Northward as they extended their Conquests that way, and by that meanes renderd those Parts exceedingly Populous, from whence many yeares after they dischargd themselves (in the Declination of the Empire) upon the South: for since those times wee do not finde them to abound with such Numerous Breedes.

Queene Elizabeth placd Officers at every Gate in London, to cut the Ruffs of all men that past, that were above a Nayl of a yeard deep, and break their Rapiers that were above a yard long.

Buck a Herald and Antiquary wrot the life of Richard the third with partiality because he founded the Heralds Colledg.

Charles the 5t caused Prayers to be Publiquely made in all his Dominions, for the Popes Delivery, whom he himself held in Prison, and might have deliverd when he pleasd: So our H: 7th

caused his Spies and Intelligencers whom he sent abroad as Fugi-
tives, and pretended Revolters to be solemnly cursd with Bel,
Book, and Candle, at Paules.

When the Saxons had driven the Brittanns into the western Parts
of this Ile, It is more then Probable, That many (especially those 5
that profest Religion and Learning, and were therefore most unfit
for war) fled for their greater Security into Ireland, (As the Veneti
did into those Ilands of the Adriatique Sea, when Attila invaded
Italy) and carryd with them that Learning and Knowledg which
the Romans had in so many yeares planted here; For when it was 10
utterly extinguishd in this Iland, it flourishd at so high a Rate
in Ireland, That after Peace had reduc'd the Saxons themselves to
christianity and Civility, they were forc'd to send their Children
to be instructed in Religion and Learning into Ireland.

The Roman Emperors gave the Eagle for their Armes, untill the 15
Division of the Empire into East and western, and then the Spred-
Eagle with 2 heads come in.

The Story of Godfry of Bullen Routing six hundred thousand
Saracens in one Battle, after he had taken Hierusalem and was
crownd King of it, was like the painting of the Saracens heads, 20
bigger and more terrible then the life: For it is incredible they
should be able to bring so many men together, considering what
Numbers had been slaine before, besides those vast Multitudes
dispersd in Afrique, and those not many yeares before destroyd
by Charles Martel.   25

The Modern Jews in stormes, and Tempests use to set open **185ʳ**
their windores to let their Messias in.   **Ab**

When a Turk happens to meet with an Emir (or one of Mahomets

4 had driven] invaded *C*   4–5 into . . . Ile] *om. C*   5 more then] very
C   5–7 (especially . . . war)] *om. C*   7 for . . . Security] *om. C*   Ire-
land] forrain Countries to avoyd the fury of their Arms *C*   9 and carryd]
and some, if not most into Ireland who carryd *C*   and Knowledg] *om. C*
10 in . . . yeares] *om. C*   For . . . was] which (when the Saxons had *C*   11
extinguishd in] extinguishd it in *C*   Iland, it] Isle) *C*   12 in Ireland] there
C   12–13 after . . . forc'd] most of those nations among the Northern people
had introducd Barbarisme beginning to recover a little Civility, were glad *C*

kindred) Drunk, he will take of his green Turbant, kiss it with great Reverence, lay it by, and then beat him without Mercy.

William Marise the Son of Jeffery Marise an Irish Nobleman was condemnd for Piracy 1265 in the Reigne of Henry the 3d, was 5 hangd drawn and Quartred, and is the first example of that kinde of Punishment wee finde in history.

Brunhault wife to Sigebert king of Mets or Austracy committed more murthers, and other horrid crimes; and built more Churches and Monasterys, and gave them greater endowments then any 10 christian Queen before or since. St Gregory writ many Epistles to her, in all which he highly extols her Piety and Prudence. She was afterward condemnd to be ty'd to the Tayl of a wild Horse, and so was Dragd and torn in pieces. De Serres p 81.

The little kingdom of Yvetot (and indeed the least that ever 15 was in the world) in that part of France which was afterward cald Normandy, was erected on this occasion. Clotair the first (of the first Race of French kings) upon good Fryday kild Gautier De Yvetot in his own chappel at Masse, some write that he might with more freedome enjoy his wife; Pope Eugenius being highly 20 incensd with Clotair for this murther, commanded him (under paine of Excommunication) to make Reparation to the Relations of Gautier, who therefore presently absolv'd and free'd the Lords of Yvetot from all future Homage, Service, and obedience to the Crown of France. And hence that little Territory assumd the Title 25 and Prerogative of a kingdom, which it enjoyd for many yeares, until it was changd into the Name of a Principality, which the Famely of Bellay enjoys to this day. id. p 65.

Although the Tribunes of the People (among the ancient Romans) had a vast and almost unlimited Power, yet it did 30 never extend to the raysing of Armies though frequent Tumults [happend], in which themselfes for the most part perished.

The Popes of Rome, to avoyd the Infamy that befell Pope Joane,

7-13 *Duplicated B* 214ᵛ   9 and Monasterys] *om*. B 214ᵛ   10 christian] *om*.
B 214ᵛ   writ] wrot B 214ᵛ   11 all] *om*. B 214ᵛ   12 ty'd to] ty'd naked
[*altered possibly from* to t] to B 214ᵛ   27 day.] day B   29 Romans)] Romans
B   30 the] the. B   31 [happend]] happend C

forbeare ever since to go in Procession in the Same Street; as if that
Disaster had depended [rather] upon the Place then time in which
it fel out, for if she had been at the high Alter, at the same time,
the same thing had befallen; And all ensuing Popes might with as
much reason have forborn to say Mass there any more; But while 5
they provided for the Prevention of Infamy that was never like to
befall againe they preservd the memory of one that was past alive,
which otherwise perhaps had dy'd long since, And that with no
more / Discretion then if the Succeeding Popes who have more 185ᵛ
Testimonys then their owne, of their Manhood, should feare if they Ab
came into the same Street againe in Procession, they should be 11
deliverd of Children.

The Ægyptian Dervises have Sainted the Horse of St George,
and plac'd him in Paradise, with the Ass that Christ rod upon, The
Camel of Mahomet, and the Dog of the Seaven Sleepers. Rycaut 15
p 139.

I do not remember in all History any one good thing that ever
was don by the People, in any government, but millions of bad
ones.

Historys are full of more and more strange things foretold by 20
Aruspicie and Augury in all Ages of the Antients, then by Astrolo-
gie though the former were as undoubted Cheates, as the Lying
Miracles among the Christians.

Astrologie, Necromancy, Geomancy, Pyromancy, chiromancy
and Metaposcopie were all but Fanaticismes in the old Greek and 25
Roman Superstitions, and that which was perhaps as Sottish,
Augury, Aruspicy and Omens Orthodox and Establishd: From
whence wee may rationally inferre, that all those were but severall
Cheates obtruded upon the Ignorance of the Rabble and the most
sottish, and improbable being nearest to the vulgar Capacity 30
prevayld above all the Rest, and are still Continued.

The Shepherds of England, and France to the Number of 30000,
in our Harry the 3ds time, met to make a voyadge to the holy
Land, but they in a smal time dispersd themselves.

33 to the] to *altered from* into B

Constantine in removing the Seat of the Empire eastward was the first cause of the Distruction of Rome, and all the western Provinces, by exposing them to the Invasion of those vast multitudes of Northern People, without any reliefe but at so great a Distance, [and] this was don by the Artifices of the Popes who at first setting up under the Empire did afterwards in all ages indevour to supplant it. But as the church of Rome first became Catholique and universall by depending upon the Empire, which was then falsly supposd to be so, Since the empire is devided into severall kingdoms and governments, why the Church should not be so to, no reason can be given.

Osporco, or Hogsface being made Pope, and displeasd with the homeliness of his Name, causd himself to be cald Sergius, and gave a begining to that Custome observd by all Popes ever since of Changing their Names at their Elections, as if all that were to Succeed, were to have ill Names.

186ʳ Cato uticensis lent his wife (after he had Children by her) to
Ab his Friend Hortensius, to beare him issue, and after his Death tooke her home again.

A Græcian Prince of the Family of Constantine the great, came (of late times) into Italy, and sold Titles of Honor, by whole sale, to all that would buy them. At Ferrara he made sale of a great Part of the Turkes Dominions, for which he receivd great Sums of money. Comment upon Zecca Rapito.

Diogenes being taken by Pirats at Sea, and brought into Crete to be sold for a Slave, directed the Cryer to proclame, That if any man wanted a Master to govern him, there was one to be sold. Seing a very ill Archer shoote at a marke, he went and stood before it, because he would not be hit. He dy'd by eating a Raw Cowsheel.

The Popes contributed as much to the Distruction of the Empire, as the Goths and Vandals, and Huns. And the Seditions and Tumults of the People of Rome about their elections, was one

of the chiefest Causes of Increasing their Power, and Authority, to
that height which it afterwards grew to.

The Turkes are wont to force their Prisoners to drinke wine,
and drub them if they refuse it; that when they are Drunke, they
may give them occasion to discover the Truth of what Quality, or 5
Condition they are; and accordingly rayse their Ransoms; or if
they have any Designes, induce them by fair or foule meanes in
their Drinke to discover it.

The Tartarian women before they were marryd usd to prostitute
themselves to all men, and from every one, they had to do with, to 10
receive some Small Trifle, which they wore publiquely about their
Necks, as a Certificate of their Merits: and she that could shew
most of these, was reputed the most deserving, and had the fayrest
pretences to a great, and Rich husband. And our modern Ladys,
who appear in the greatest Bravery, to Testify the greatnes of 15
their Performances, do the same thing.

The Goths and vandals were reduc'd to Civility themselves, by
destroying it in all others where their Armes prevayld.

Mem: Henry the 4th of France his Hunting Apparition at
Fountainbleau. De Serres p. 760.   20

In all our Wars with France, the French never overcame the **186ᵛ**
English in any one great Battle; But the English were always Bb
victorious, though with far inferior Numbers and all other Advantages. They were often too hard for us [in] small Parties, and sur-
prises, and in such Incounters at length (with our own Dissentions at 25
home) drove us out of their Cuntry under the Conduct of a woman;
which whether it were a greater shame for them or us is hard to
determine: Howsoever it agree's perfectly with that Charecter
which the Antients give of them. That whensoever they are
worsted (as they had long been in those times) they have less 30
Courage then women, and therefor were Naturally reducd to
fight under the Ensignes of the Pucel.

In the second Lateran Councell in the yeare 1215 Transubstantiation was first canoniz'd in the Crowd. Brevint p 169.

4-5 they may] they *altered from* that B   5 may] make B   6 Ransoms;]
Ransoms. B   20 Fountainbleau.] Fountainbleau B

The Saxons, Danes, and Normans That heretofore successively conquer'd Britaine, were all of one Originall, and came all at severall times from Denmarke.

Caligula had a Statue which was every day Drest in the same
5 Habit that he wore himself.

When K H 8th had dissolv'd all Monasteries, and turnd the Friers out to grass, they overspred the whole Nation as Chaucers Friers did Hell: And having nothing to live upon but begging, wheresoever they came to aske an Almes, they raysd so much
10 Compassion in the Common People, by bewayling the miserable condition they were in (though the Freedom they injoy'd, and the Plenty they liv'd in, by the Charity of all People, pleasd many of them much better, then the Strictnes of their former Lives) that they were in Probability like to rayse Insurrections, if the King
15 and Parlament had not made the Statute of vagabonds against them, and by that meanes sent them from Cunstable to Cunstable, to the Severall Places of their Births, where they were kept from stragling about the Cuntry, to infect the People with dislike of the Government.

20 Epistles Dedicatory began in the time of Ptolomæus Philadelphus.

Crucifying was the most painfull of all Punishments that ever were invented, for it kild with a most grievous, and yet a lingring Torture, to put to Death with more Paine.

25 No man was capable of being a Persian Magus that was not begotten by a Son upon his owne Mother. Avenimenti D'Erasto p 153.

[186*]

188ʳ The Antient Britaines having been beaten out of their Cuntry
Ab by the Saxons, and the weakest and most impotent flying into the
30 mountaines for Protection; They had leasure to reflect upon [the]

7 they] the B　　　12 Charity] Chari[ ] B　　　22 Crucifying] Crucif[ ]g B
[186*] Only headings History (a, b)

great losses, and the Cruelties they had sufferd from their enemies, which produc'd so great a chagrin, and ill humor in the whole Nation: that all their Posterity after so many Ages have a Tincture of it to this day. And that is certainly the Reason why they are generally so passionate and Cholerique.   5

Bodin admires Guicciardine for the best of Historians, and cals him Parens Historiæ, but in the end of his Encomion discovere's the true Reason of it, when commending his Ingenuity and Candor, he say's he was so just to Truth, that speaking of the Original of the French Pox he take's the Scandal of that Nation, and very   10 impartially lay's it upon the Neapolitans.

Tully may seeme to have been a good Naturd man, because he defended far greater Numbers then he accusd, and writ very many of his familier Epistles in the behalfe of Men in Distresse, and no doubt was as honest as it is possible for a Statesman to bee.   15

The Italians hate the French naturally, as the French do the English, and both for the same Reason, for having been a little too ruggedly handled by the Ancestors of both, although many Ages since.

Men have sayld round about the Earth East and west severall   20 times and yet know nothing of the Longitude: But North and South is impossible and yet there is nothing more certainly known then the Latitude.

The Scripture set's no ill Character upon Solomon for having   B such a large Number of Concubines; but deliver's it only as an   25 Argument of his Greatnes and magnificence, But lay's a greater blame upon his wife, who did him more mischief then all his Mistresses, in Perswading him to change his Religion for Idolatry, in his Doating old age.

The 70 Disciples, that Christ sent abroad to Preach, went in the   30 Habits of the Philosophers of those times, with Scrips, and Staves, and course Habits, that scarse coverd their Nakedness, not unlike some orders of Friers of our Times; Only the Philosophers profest

22 known] know *B*

no Mortification, nor Piety, nor Devotion, but only pretended to wisdom, as Friers do to Holines and both much at the same Rate, of Folly, and Hypocrisy.

188ᵛ　William the Conquerer destroyd the Cuntry, and turnd it into
Bb　Forrest, that entertaind him at his Landinge, that it might never
6　be in a Condition to do so to any other Invader, for to oblige, or Disoblige Princes, is equally Dangerous to those who have Power to do both.

　　Those 7 Cities of Greece that strove which should be the Native
10　Place of Homers Birth, Did themselves, and him, no great Honor (though they designd nothing else) For they did but Declare, That either He was in his Lifetime, so obscure, Or they so Barbarous, as not to take Notice of him, till so many yeares after his Death.

　　The Indians of Moabar allow of no mans Testimony that drinke's
15　wine, or goes to sea. Marco Polo. 117.

　　The Rabbins interpret Sampsons grinding in a Mill to serve the Philistians to signify ploughing with their Heifers.

[188*]

14–17 *Duplicated and underlined B* 217ʳ　　16 to serve] for *B* 217ʳ　　17 signify] mean *B* 217ʳ　　[188*] *Only headings* History (b, b)

Mountebankes and Quacks who have to do with the Meaner Rabble are faine to set up their Bills, and in them allow a larger Dose of Lying, and vapouring, and pretend to greater Cures, then any Learned Physitian will undertake to performe, who having to do with People of better Quality, and understanding, hath not that 5 Necessity to brag, and Ly, as those who have nothing else to introduce them: For having past the Test by their studyes and Degrees, it is sufficient to satisfy those that have but ordinary Sense, and Reason that they cannot but understand more in their Professions, then those that are utterly Ignorant. 10

Christ told the woman whom he Cur'd, That her Faith had made her well; But the Faith of Patients in the Doctors, and Empiriques of our times, is often found to be the Cause of their Distruction.

Among all Diseases incident to Mankind, Three Parts of Four 15 are so Naturally curable (except in Epidemical Maladys) that they recover of themselves (especially in Places where there are Few Physitians) And of that 4th, one half at least miscarry, either by Disorder, or want of Necessary Help, and Care, or too much: So that there is but one 8th that is Naturally Mortall. As for the Rest, 20 whatsoever Course is usd, either by Applycation of Med'cines that do no hurt, or charmes that do as little Good; The Cure never fayle's to be Imputed (though don by Nature) to that which was last usd. And that is one Reason, why there are so great varietys of Medcines (especially among Empriques, and old women) for one, 25 and the same Disease, Of all which not one Perhaps ever wrought the Effect; But only hapned to be applyd at that time, when Nature was doing her own worke; and so carryd the Credit of the Cure from her. While the best and most proper Medcines in Nature, being applyd to incurable Diseases, are as falsly supposd to Kill, 30 and as idly layd by, as the other are receiv'd.

Physitians believe themselves discharg'd from keeping the

26 Disease,] Disease .. B

Counsels of their Patients in Scandalous Diseases, as long as they
are not payd for their Cures, that they may gaine Reputation at
lest, if nothing else, for the Paines they have taken.

Chirurgions that cut men of the Stone, use to carry stones in
5 their Pockets, to pretend to pull out of mens Bladders, where they
finde none, that they may not be discover'd to have beene mistaken, As those who use to open Dead Bodies, are wont to counterfet the signes of those Diseases in their Inward Parts, with which
they had before declard them to be affected only to save their
10 Credit, and Deceive the world.

[189ᵛ
blank]

        3 lest] best *W*

Those that depose Princes, and set up others on their Thrones, do after a while finde themselves so much mistaken and unsatisfyd in their New Masters, though of their own election, that they afterwards desire nothing more then the Restauration of those whom they pul'd down before. This appeares by our own Histories of Edw. 2. Rich. 2. Hen 6. Rich. 3. Ed. 4. Hen. 7. Though the fault perhaps ha's not been in the New-raysd, nor old Deposd Prince, but their own insatiable expectations and perpetuall desires of Change. For H. 6. was a most Virtuous, and Religious Prince and such a one as could never upon his own account, disoblige his People, and yet he came to a most unhappy end.

A Tyrant is a Monster or Prodigy born to the Distruction of the best men, as among the Antients, when a Cow calfd a monster, great numbers of Cattle, that were fair, and perfect in their kinde, were presently sacrificd to expiate and avert the ominous Portent.

Dull-witted Persons are commonly the fittest Instruments for wise men to imploy, if they have but sense enough to observe Directions, the Speculation of such into the Reason of Affayrs being unsafe, and their knowledge of why or to what end they act, as unnecessary as it is for a Saw to know what it Cut's.

Publique Actions are like watches that have fine Cases of Gold, or Silver, with a windore of Christall to see the Pretences, but the Movement is of Baser Mettle, and the Original of all (the Spring) a Crooked piece of Steel: So in the Affaires of State, The solemn Professions of Religion, Justice, and Liberty are but Pretences to conceale Ambition, Rapine, and usefull Cheate.

Princes that make choyce of their officers our of affection, Fancy, and Inclination; or because they are usefull, and Serviceable to their Pleasures, or Vices, and not for their fitnes and abilitys for their Imployments, must of necessity be ill servd. For such men

17 observe] *altered from* be B

never regard the Interests and utilitys of their Masters, because they were never regarded by themselves, as the Causes of their Preferment, but apply them selves to that which first raysd them, Their Humors, Fancys or Infirmitys, as all things are nourishd by
5 that which bred them.

If Princes could not confer Merit as well as advancement on their Favorites, the world would be many times mightily mistaken.

193ᵛ There is no better way to Judge of the Naturall Temper of any
Ab Nation then by the severity of their Criminall Punishments, For
10 where great Cruelty is used, there must be great, and incorrigible offences to cause it: And therefor Impaling, Breaking on the wheel, Boyling in Oyle, and Torturing before Conviction, which are never usd with us, may seeme to be Arguments, That the English Nation is not naturally inclin'd to such Barbarous Crimes, as
15 others are, where such Punishments are necessary to preserve the Publique Peace.

The kings of Great Britaine put the Armes of France always before those of England in their Coynes, though in the Inscription France is always written after Scotland.

20 Weake Princes are commonly dispisd themselves, and yet those they do but favour, much esteemd and applyd to.

The wisdom of the Law consist's most in admitting all the Petty mean, and reall Injustices in the world, to avoyd Imaginary great ones that may perhaps fall out; and though it be sayd to bee the
25 wisdom of many ages the Knavery of them all is grown up along with it.

The Greatnes of the Nobility and Gentry of France depend's upon more meane and little Supports then that of the English. As their keeping of Publique Ovens, as some Lords do, and force all
30 their Tenants to pay for the Baking of their bread. Permitting none to keepe Bulls but themselves, and takeing money of their Villaines for the bulling of their Cowes.

The chiefest Art of Government is to convert the Ignorance,

4 Infirmitys,] Infirmitys,. *B*   16. 1–5 *See p. 115, ll. 3–5*   18 Coynes,] Coynes. *B*   24–6 though . . .] The law is both the wisdome and Knavery of many Ages grown up together. *C*

Folly, and Madness of Mankinde (as much as may be) to their own
good, which can never be don, by telling them Truth and Reason,
or using any direct meanes; but by little Tricks and Divises (as
they cure Madmen) that worke upon their Hopes and Feares to
which their Ignorance naturally incline's them. 5

Governments like Natural Bodys have their times of growing 190ʳ
Perfection and Declining, and according to their Constitutions, Ab
some hold out longer, and some decay sooner then other, but all
in their beginings and infancies are subject to so many Infirmities
and Imperfections, that what Solomon sayd of a Monarchy, Wo to 10
that Kingdom whose Prince is a Child, may be more justly sayd of
a new Republique and wee may with as much reason say, Wo be to
that People that live under a yong Government; for as both must
of Necessity be under Tutors, Protectors, and Keepers of Liberties,
untill they can give the world an accompt that they are able to 15
govern of themselves (which a Prince do's in fewer yeares then a
Republique can in Ages) the People always suffer under so many
Lords and Masters, and though a Foundation of Liberty be layd
the Fruition of it is for after Ages, like the Planting of trees, whose
shade and fruite is only to be enjoyd by Posterity: For what Protec- 20
tion can a Nation have from a Government, that must it self be
protected? That must maintaine Guards, and Armes at their own
charge, to keepe themselves in obedience, that is, Slavery, untill in
Process of time by slow degrees, that which was rugged at first
become's gentle and easy. For as that which was Tyranny at first 25
do's in time become Liberty, So there is no Liberty but in the
beginning was Tyranny. All unripe fruite is harsh and they that
live in New built Houses, are apt to catch Diseases and infirmities.
Nor is it possible to settle any Government by a Modell that shall
hold, as men contrive Ships and Buildings: For Governments are 30
made like Naturall Productions by Degrees according as their
Materials are brought in by time, and those Parts of it that are
unagreeable to their Nature, cast of. No two Nations in the world
have exactly the same Government, nor all Places the same in
any one. 35

Governments managd by unwise Ministers miscarry like Ships
that perish in Shallow waters.

13 Government;] Government. *B*   26 Liberty,] Liberty. *B*

190ᵛ   That Justice that is sayd to establish the Throne of a Prince,
Ab   consist's no less in the Justnes of his Title, then the Just administration of his Government, for an unjust Title cannot be supported
but by unjust meanes. And for want of this all our late usurpations
5 miscarrid.

Princes ought to give their Subjects as much of the Shadow of
Liberty as they can for their lives, but as little of the Reality of it,
if they regard the safety of themselves or their People.

The Ambition of some men, and the wants of others are the
10 ordinary causes of all Civil wars.

All Princes are sayd by Lawyers, not to be able to do Injury,
because they are above the Punishment of it: But when they have
lost that Prerogative, the Injuries they do, become greater then
those that are committed by private Persons. For it is to no purpose
15 to take notice of the wrongs they do, as longe as they cannot be
cald to an account.

He that fights against his Prince want's the Humanity of a Dog,
that being a Creature intended by Nature for the service of Mankinde, will not be brought to do any thing so averse to the morality
20 which all those ought to have, whom he is designd to live under,
as by any meanes to fall upon his Master.

He that keepe's a watchfull or vigilant eie upon that mans
Interest whom he is to treate withall, and observe's it as the
Cumpasse that generally all men steare by, shall hardly be deceivd
25 with fair Pretences.

Principles of Justice, and Right have chiefly relation to the
general Good of Mankinde, and therefore have so weake an
Influence upon Particulars, that they give Place to the meanest
and most unworthy of Private Interests.

30 The Deserts of Good men do not produce so bad effects being
unrewarded as the Crimes of evill men unpunishd: For good men
are but discouragd but the bad become more perverse and wicked.

3 Government,] Government. B   4 And] and B

Rebellions are always found to be most Frequent under weake Princes.

Rebels have been used in this kingdom like Sinners in the **191ᵉ** kingdom of Heaven, where there is more Rejoycing over one Ab Sinner then forty Just men that need no Repentance. 5

When Princes and Great Persons dy, as their Bodys use to be opend and the Soundnes or infirmitys of their Inward Parts exposd to a strict Scrutiny: So are their Actions, and abilitys, and the Integrity, folly or wickednes of their Lives freely layd open to the view of their severest enemies, and reduc'd to the Inquisition, and 10 Censures of the meanest of their Inferiors.

It is Safer for a Prince to tollerate all Sorts of Debauchery, rather then Seditious meetings in Conventicles: As those that have the Stone, the Gout or Consumptions are not shut up, because their Diseases are only hurtfull to themselves; But those that have any 15 Contagious Maladys, that are apt to spread, and infect Multitudes, are with all Care to be shut up, and kept from Conversing with others, whom their Distempers may indanger, and in time Propagate among the People.

The worst Governments are the Best, when they light in good 20 Hands, and the Best the worst when they fall into bad ones. So the worst Governments are always the most chargeable, and cost the People Dearest: As all men in Courts of Judicature, pay more for the wrongs that are don them then the Right.

If the Christian Roman Emperors had made themselves Bishops 25 of Rome, as their Predecessors the Pagans very wisely did, they might perhaps have preservd the Empire to themselves, and their Posterity to this day: But by trusting the Popes with that unlimited Power over the Consciences of all men, they deprivd them selves of the greatest Part of their Power, and Authority. 30

1–2 *Added in a different ink* B   3–5 *Duplicated* B 84ʳ, 193ᵛ; *underlined* B 84ʳ
3 Rebels . . . kingdom] The Present Government do's by the late Rebels B 193ᵛ
Sinners in] *om.* B 193ᵛ   4 where . . . over] that is better pleasd with the
Conversion of B 193ᵛ   5 then . . . men] then ninety nine Righteous Persons
B 193ᵛ   Repentance.] Repentance. when Perhaps our Converts esteeme their
Reconciliation no better then an Apostacy. B 193ᵛ   16 are] *om.* B

The two best of all the Roman Emperors, Titus and Marcus Aurelius, were so unhappy as to have the one a whore to his mother, and the other to his wife.

The Emperor Vitellius usd to invite himselfe to two Dinners in one Day. Sueton.

191ᵛ
Ab The vices of Tyrants run in a Circle and produce one another. Begin with Luxury, and Prodigality, which cannot be supply'd but by Rapine. Rapine produces Hate in the People, and that Hate Feare in the Prince, Feare Cruelty, Cruelty Dispair, and Dispair Distruction.

When our Edward the 4th had raysd a very great Army to invade France, at the Request of the Parlament, who had given him vast Sums of Money, to beare the charges of it, Hee carryd over with him 12 of the most Powrfull men in the House of Commons, out of Respect (as he pretended) to the Parlament, and to make use of the Advice of those (in the management of the war) who were to supply the expences of it. But really out of Designe to inforce the French king to buy his Peace as deare as was possible, and put both that money and what the Parlament had given him into his Purse. And to bring this the easier about: He gave private Orders to all his Quartermasters to dispose of those members (to whom in Publique he alway shewd a very great Respect) in the worst Quarters they could possibly finde out in all their march, That when he came to treat with the French, Those Parlament men (tir'd with the Inconveniences they perpetually indur'd) were the most importunate Soliciters with the King to make Peace with the Enemy, which after much Importunity he at length as only at their Request condiscended unto and made them his Instruments to beg that of him, which though he eversomuch desir'd, he knew not how to effect any other way. De Serres.

B Princes that have lost their Credit, and Reputation, are like Merchants, inevitably destind to Ruine: For all Men immediatly call in their Loyalty, and Respect from the First, as they do their Money from the Later.

Crafty Princes use to Imploy the most Covetous, and Insolent

17 expences] *altered from* Charges B   31–4 *Duplicated and underlined B* 223ᵛ
35–p. 117, l. 18 *Duplicated and underlined B* 222ᵛ

Stats-men, they can possibly select out of all their subjects, That when they are become odious by oppressing, and discontenting their People, they may acquire the opinion of Justice, by making them Sacrifices to the Publique Hate, and inrich themselves by Confiscating the Estates they have gain'd by Robbing them and 5 their Subjects.

For if Governments were manag'd to the Best Advantages, of the 192ʳ Joynt Interests of Prince and People, it would not be so often out Ba of order, nor so Difficult, to be Preserv'd as it is, where Men had rather hazard the Ruine of all, by perpetuall Practizing of little 10 Tricks, and Cheates, then Trust to plaine Honesty and Integrity: And by Dividing the Publique Interest, and ingageing the one Part to prey upon the other, had rather inrich themselves suddenly by sharing in the Spoyles of both, then fayrly, and Softly gain twice as much with Justice Honor and Safety. So unwise are all 15 Wicked men, that had rather Comply with their own Inclynations then their Security, and venture all, to gaine a little their own way, then indure to be honest at a far greater Rate.

All wise Princes have ever usd to instill into their People, a Contempt, and Hatred of Forraine Nations, to render them the 20 more united among themselves. For those who are perswaded that another Nation is wiser, or valianter then themselves, do really make them such. And a Prince, that admires Forrainers, and dis- pise's his Native Subjects, cannot possibly finde out a nearer way to ruine his own Interest, and at the same time do's but instruct 25 them to undervalew him; For all Nations and the greatest Part of Particular Persons, do naturally believe themselves undervalewd by the Immoderate Prayses of others, although they are true, and have no way so ready to relieve themselves, as by contemning his Judgment who preferd others before them, and how just so ever it 30 bee, had rather believe him mistaken then themselves. And although it be a vice in Particular Persons to overvalew their own Abilities, it is not so in greate Multitudes, whose false Perswasions have a greater Power over them then those that are true. And therefore all Great Generalls of Armies in their Speeches to their 35

---

1 Stats-men] Statesmen B 222ᵛ   8 Joynt Interests] Joynt-Interest B 222ᵛ
17 a little B 222ᵛ: alittle B 192ʳ   35–p. 118, l. 3 all . . . Enemys] duplicated B 198ᵛ:
It is the Constant Method of all Generalls Orations before Battles to vapour and
undervalew the enemy, and magnify themselves.

Souldiers before great Battles, have always one Constant Common Place to encourage them by magnifying their own valour, and disdaining the Cowardise, and weaknes of their Enemys; For Panique Courages may be raysd as well as Panique Feares, and although the Reason of both be equally insignificant, yet the Effects are Prodigiously different. And hence it is that the Spaniards who believe themselves (though falsly) to be the best Soldiers in the world, have sometimes prov'd much better then they Naturally are, and without that Proud Conceipt of themselves, had been found much worse. The Chineses whom some believe to be the most Ingenious People in the world, were so carefull to avoyd the Infection of Strangers, that they would suffer none to enter into their Cuntry, but brought their Goodes to the Frontiers, to trade with Merchants that came from al Parts to traffick with them. The Jewes disdain'd all Nations but themselves, And held it a Sin and breach of their Law to converse with them, and by that meanes raysd the Grandure of their little Cuntry much above it's intrinsique valew. The Greeks and Romans esteemd all Nations Barbarous but themselves, and while they did so easily subdu'd them: But when the later began to make Forrainers free of Rome, and receivd their Customes and manners into the mode they were in a short time Ruined by those very People as soon as they began to esteem them, whom they had always vanquish'd as long as they disdaind.

192ᵛ All Governments are in their Managements so equall, that no **Bb** one has the advantage of another, unless in Speculation, and in that **26** there is no convenience that any Particular Modell can Pretend to, but is as liable to as great Inconveniences some other way: In so much, that the worst of all Governments in Speculation (that is Tyranny) is found to be the best in the Hands of Excellent Princes, who receive no advantage from the Greatness of their Pow'r, but only a larger Latitude to do Good to their Subjects, which the best Constituted Formes, that is, the most Limited, do but deprive them of, and ty them up from Doing Good as well as Hurt.

Though Common wealths are so much worse rewarders of those that serve them best, that many have perishd for nothing but the overgreatnes of their Merits; yet they are generally better

serv'd then Princes, that give the greatest incouragements both of
Honor and Profit, not only to themselves, but their Posterity. In
which Republiques are so Defective, That the Greatest that ever
was (the Roman) had not Power to make the most Deserving
Plebeian, a Patrician: And were so far from being able to confer the ₅
Honor of Nobility on any that were not born to it, That if a great
or Rich Plebeian adopted a Patritian his Heir, He lost all the Honor
and Priviledges of his Birth.

Princes have great Reason to be allow'd Flatterers to adore them
to their Faces, because they are more exposd to the Infamy and ₁₀
Detraction of the world then the Meanest of their Subjects: otherwise they would be dealt with very unequally, to be bound to all
the Infamy, true, or false, that can be layd upon them, and not be
allowd an equall freedom of Prayse to qualify it, for though he
may be abusd at any man's Pleasure he Cannot be flatterd without ₁₅
his own.

As the meanest virtues of Excellent Princes do really deserve
greater Admiration then the Highest of any Private Person can
possibly arrive at; because they do not only pas through Greater
Difficulties, but extend to greater Numbers, and oblige the world ₂₀
more: So are their vices more odious, and give a worse example to
mankinde, then the most horrid of any Private Person can possibly
do. And therefore one of the most Antient Religions that we finde
in the world, was nothing but the worship and Adoration of some
excellent Princes after they were Dead, whom Posterity made ₂₅
Gods, And by Custome first, and Interest after, obligd all men to
adore. And hence it is that the Romans built Temples, and Alters,
to the Dead Emperors, which though it may seem strange to us,
was no New thing to them, but according to the Doctrine and
Practice of their Religion in the most pure and Primitive times. ₃₀

Princes whose ordinary Money is Silver, and Gold, are like
Persons of Quality that are serv'd in Plate; But those that coyne
base Money, are like those of Inferior condition, that are serv'd in
Pewter and baser Mettles.

---

6 it,] it! *B*   31–4 *Duplicated and underlined B* 223ʳ   32 Persons *B* 223ʳ:
Person *B* 192ᵛ   34 Pewter . . . Mettles] Brass, and Pewter *B* 223ʳ   Mettles]
Mattles *B* 192ᵛ

194 **r**   He that supposes he may be a Statesman without understanding
Ab the Humors, Dispositions, Tempers, and Abilities of all men that
he has to doe withall, and some knowledge of the Historys of past
times, is as much mistaken as he that thinke's to be an able Physi-
5 tian, without understanding Anatomy, and the Constitution of
mens Bodys, and the Truth of their Infirmities, that he may know
how to apply his Remedys accordingly. And as it is far more usefull
to unriddle the true State of Diseases then of Health, So it is to
discover the Infirmities and weaknesses of men, then their Abilities,
10 and Perfections, and to make observations upon the Nature of Sick
men then those that are Sound.

The ill Constitution of the Roman Commonwealth may seeme
to have contributed very much to the great Increase of their
Empire. For the Temper of their Government being such as would
15 not indure one yeare's Peace, but those Perpetuall Factions (that
Naturally grew out of it) betweene the Nobility and the People
always broke out into Tumults, and Civil wars, They were compeld
to divert that inconvenience (for nothing else Could) to carry
their Armes abroad. And though they attempted many Reforma-
20 tions, and try'd a world of experiments, they all provd in vaine and
worse then to no purpose.

The kings Money is like one that is committed close-Prisoner:
All those that have any Relation to it by Right, are kept from it,
and those only admitted that come to betray it.

25 There is no Difference betweene a Government that is manag'd
by Law, and one that is maintayn'd by Force, but that the one
oppresse's in a Gentle, and the other in a Rugged way.

Princes that have the Command of other men, have lesse freedom themselves then the meanest of their subjects, and are ty'd
30 to greater Reservations and forbearances then the rest of mankinde.
For just so much Respect as they shew to the Publique opinion of
the world, wil the world have of them, and no more.

B   Princes that govern unwisely, are commonly punishd with as
foolish and Ignorant Rebells, that pay them in kinde.

10 Perfections,] Perfections. *B*

If the Power of our House of Commons were in any one Single 194ᵛ
Person, it would easily devour all the Rest, and convert them into Ab
it self, as it did when it was but in few handes, for the Power of
the Purse has naturally a greater Command then any other. But
nothing keepe's it within its Boundes so much as being devided 5
among so many Persons of equall Shares, who like all Crowds do
but hinder one another in all things that they undertake. For an
Army of all Commanders would be in a worse condition then one
that has none at all, And though Solomon say's in many Counsellers
there is strength, it is but like that of a Beast that know's not how 10
to make use of it.

Among all the Arts of Government, There is none more consider- B
able (though commonly less regarded) then that Knowledge and
Judgement in Persons, that is requisite to make a true choyce of
mens Abilitys, and Fitnes for those Imployments, to which they 15
are design'd, which is of so great Consequence that it is Impossible,
that any thing in the Affaires of Princes should succeed well without it: And so certainly prosperous where it is well don; That some
Princes of the weakest Talents only by the Fortunate choyce of
their Ministers, have reignd in as great Prosperity, and Happines, 20
as those of greater wisdom, and Politie in the worlds esteeme, who
have either neglected, or Mistaken this most necessary Part of the
management of all their Affaires. For it is an ill Signe of a Skilful
Artificer That he do's not know how to make Choyce of his
Tooles, the chiefe thing, which all those who are arrivd, at any 25
Perfection in any Art, are most Curious in; and all Bunglers neglect:
For he that do's not weigh the Ballance, before he examine's any
thing in it, shall have but a bad Accompt of what he proposes to
himself. Where the People have the Choyce of their Officers, the
very opposition and faction, that is usd in all their Elections, do's 30
for the most Part produce a better Scruteny of men's Abilities, then
Princes use; who commonly do it merely out of Favour, or the
False Perswasion of Favorites.

Taking of Counsel is like taking of Physique, and as in Physique
no man ought to consider the pleasing of his Pallate, and Gust: No 35
more ought he to refuse those counsels (if he expect any good from

4 other.] other B   18 it:] it; B   19 Talents only] Talents ⟨by⟩ only B
25 Tooles,] Tooles. B   36 those counsels] interlined B

them) that do not please his Humor, as most men commonly do, and never finde the Mischief they do themselves untill it is too late. For pleasing Counsels are generally the worst sorts of Flatteries, and seldom fayl to ruine all those, who naturally incline to them; as few Men ever attaine to that excellency of Reason, and Judgment that is requisite, to make them Proof against their Pleasing Insinuations.

195ʳ
Bb The greatest Empire that ever was (the Roman) increasd by, not only tollerating, but Imbraceing the Religions of all Cuntrys they had Conquerd. But when they were grown up to their Height, and began to persecute the Christian Religion (as they seldom did any other) they declin'd, untill afterward becoming Christians themselves, and then persecuting all others, they fell by Degrees to that little, that is now left of them.

Among the many Arguments of the worth and Bravery of our Ed. 3d one, and that no meane one, was the great kindenes and Affection he had for his excellent Son the Black Prince: whose Death he tooke so grievously that in a short time, it causd his own: When other Princes of less virtue, and consequently more inclin'd to envy, would rather have remov'd him out of the world, before his time, then indur'd the Sight of that glory, which he had justly purchac'd to himselfe: As many other kings have don both before, and since, esteeming the virtue and merits of their Heires, not only a Blemish, and ecclips, of their own; but dangerous to the Safety, and free Enjoyment of their Crownes, and Empire. For men are sayd to have overcome Envy, not only because their Actions are grown too big for the Emulation of those, who are mean enough to be capable of Envy: But because they are themselves above all Causes of Enviing others: or else so much below it, that they have no pretence, or Title to any thing that can deserve it.

The Preferment of Fooles, and undeserving Persons, is not so much an Honor to them, as Infamy and Dishonor to those that Rayse them: For when a Prince confer's Honor on those, that do not Deserve it, He throw's it away out of his own Stock, and leave's himself so much the lesse, as he part's with to those that want merit to pretend to it; and by that ill Husbandry, in time leave's himself none at all, to pay those to whom it is Due. For though a

Prince be sayd to be the Fountaine of Honor, it is easily exhausted, when he let's it run lavishly, without Care, and Consideration, like a Coronation-Cunduit to intoxicate the Rabble, and Run in the Canell.

Statesmen do commonly crowd themselves into great Imploy- 5
ments, rather out of their Itch, and Inclination to be medling in Affayres; then their Abilities to understand, and manage them. For they intrude, and Presse themselves into Bus'nes with greater Importunity, then those, who are much fitter for it: And commonly the more uncapable they are of it, the more they hanker, and longe 10
for it, As all men Naturally desire those things most, that are most deny'd them. Yet they have one advantage, above those that are wiser, and that of no meane importance; For no man can guess, nor Imagine, beforehand, what Course they will probably take in any Busnes that occur's, when tis not uneasy to foresee, by their Inter- 15
ests, what wiser men are like in Reason to designe. But as Houses are oftener set on fire by chance, and Negligence, then Designe, so are Governments by the Ignorance and sottishnes of those who have the management of them, and both are no way so easy to be extinguishd as by being blown-up.   20

Princes and Governours have great Reason to avoy'd and depress 195ᵛ
Men of Penetrating and smart wits, especially if they have Integ- Bb
rity, and Honesty. For the Imprudence and extravagancy of their Actions are not fit to be exposd to the view and censure of such men, to whom they cannot but appeare in their most Deformd and 25
Sottish Charecters.

8 intrude] intru'de *B*   20 extinguishd] extingushd *B*   26. 1–2 *In Longueville's hand and well spaced off from l. 26:* 2 Instit. p. 207/9. Minister Regis in E. 1. his time taken for a Judge of the Realme *B*

He that believes in the Scriptures is mistaken if he therefore thinkes he believe's in God; For the Scriptures are not the immediate word of God, for they were written by Men, though dictated by Divine Revelation; of which since we have no Testimony but
5 their own; nor any other Assurance, we do not believe them because they are the word of God; for wee must believe them, before we believe that which wee receive only from them. And if we belive [in] God, because wee believe them, we believe in him, but at the second hand; and build the Foundation of our Fayth in
10 God, upon our Fayth in Men. So if we imagine we believe in God because we believe in the Scriptures, we deceive our selves; for if I tell a man something of a third Person which he believe's, he do's not believe that third Person, but mee that tel it him.

He that appeares to be of no Religion may perhaps be as much
15 a wel-willer to Dishonesty as a Religious Person, but can never have so much Power to commit any great, or considerable mischife; For he that bespeake's every mans Distrust, shall hardly be able ever to deceive any. If such Men intend any hurt to Mankinde, they are very unwise to deprive themselves of the Power of acting it;
20 and loose so many advantages which the mere Pretence of Religion would put into their handes. For the Saint and the Hypocrite are so very like, that they passe all the world over undistinguishd: the difference being only in the Inside of which we have no guess, (until it be too late) but by Symptomes that commonly bely both.
25 All wee are sure of, is; that the Hypocrites are the greater Number, more devoutly zealous in appearance; and much more crafty then those that are in earnest.

Guevara Antiquary to Charles the 5t in his Epistle to him speake's of an old Coyn of an Ægyptian King, the Ancientest that
30 ever he saw, that had a Latin Inscription upon it. Much like the Stagg some yeares since sayd to be kild, that had a Coller found

---

21 For . . . Hypocrite] *underlined by Longueville B*   24 bely both] *underlined by Longueville B*

about his neck with an English Rhime written in it by Julius
Cæsar.

Preachers may seeme to be the greatest Truants in the world, for   **196ᵛ**
they skip over the Noble Booke of Nature, and since they cannot   Aa
understand it, most ignorantly rayle at it.   5

Physick may seeme to be much honester then Law in the
Practice, for a Physitian ha's to do but with one man (in relation to
himself) at a time, and may cure him without Poysoning another:
But a Lawyer cannot do one man good, without indevouring at
least to hurt another; for if it were Possible for him to confine him-   10
self always to the Right side, he would hurt himself instead of his
Client, which no Lawyer was ever known to do.

When two or three speake a forraine Language together in
company with others who do not understand it, They would have
all they say pass for witte, for whatsoever any one of them say's,   15
the rest allways applaud.

Lawyers have no kindenes for the Statute-Law, but take all
occasions to depress it, and advance the Common-Law, because it
give's them a greater Latitude to do what they please, and is more
capable of serving all purposes, without being understood by any   20
but themselves: Just as the Catholiques do by the Scripture which
they do not love to heare of; but prefer Tradition, as the more
certaine, because it never fayles to serve all Occasions that can fall
out, much better then that which is written and so publiquely
known; that it is impossible to corrupt or falsify it, to comply   25
with all Advantages, as they may do by Tradition. And therefor
they are forc'd to interpret the Scripture not by the sense and meaning of the words, but the Custome and Practice of the Church,
otherwise no booke in the world could say more against them.

Wee had perhaps never heard of Nero's Bumbast way of writing   30
but for Persius whose Stile came nearest to it, of any Author then
living. For Torva Mimaloniis &c. and Costam longo subduximus
Apenino are not much worse then Quantas robusti Carminis offas, &c.

1 English Rhime] *underlined by Longueville* B   21 themselves:] themselves; B
33 Apenino] e *possibly altered to* p B   worse] *altered from* better B

197ʳ They that call living Princes Divi in imitation (as they suppose)
Ab of the Romans, commit a gross Error; for the Antients never gave
that Title to any before they were Dead and Canonizd.

No less mistake are they guilty of who writing Epitaphs in our
5 times usually inscribe them Viatori in imitation of the old Romans,
which they have no reason to do; for the Tombes of this age are
commonly in churches, and the Romans usd that Forme because
theirs were ever in the high-ways; by which Travellers past.

The like error may be observd in Lucretius (lib 1us p 11a) who
10 make's the Moysture that hangs on Stones an Instance of his
vacuum, which rather proceed's from their Solidity, that wanting
pores do's rather keepe it out then let it out.

Persius also commits a very great Absurdity, when laying the
Scæne of his 4th Satyr in Greece, and bringing in Socrates reproving
15 a yong States-man, he make's him call the Græcians Quirites.

Allegories are only usefull when they serve as Instances, to
illustrate Some obscure Truth: But when a Truth, Plaine enough,
is forcd to Serve an Allegory, it is a præposterous mistake of the
End of it; which is to make obscure things Plaine, not Plaine things
20 obscure; and is no less foolish, then if wee should looke upon things
that ly before us with a Perspective, which is so far from assisting
the sight, that it utterly obstructs it; beside the Preposterous
Difficulty of forcing things against their Naturall inclinations,
which at the best do's but discover how much wit a man may have
25 to no purpose; there being no such Argument of a slight minde as
an elaborate Triffle.

He that would write obscure to the People neede's write nothing
but plaine Reason, and Sense, then which Nothing can be more
Mysterious to them. For those to whom Mysterious things are
30 plaine, plain Things must be mysterious.

4–8 *Duplicated and underlined roughly B* 232ʳ: Wee direct the Epitaphs upon Tombes
in Churches, Viatori [*altered possibly from* to], because the Ancients who placd their
Tombes in the high-ways did soe: And divide our writing into Booke's Tomes and
Sections having nothing of the same reason that they had to doe soe.   12. 1–3
See p. 138, *ll.* 14–16 (*to which marginal cross-reference by Longueville p.* 7b. *here refers*)
15 Quirites] *underlined by Longueville* B   18 an] *altered from* all B   20–2 no...
obstructs it] *underlined by Longueville* B   22 it;] it. B   29–30 For . . .]
underlined by Longueville B   29 whom Mysterious] whom Myst[ ]rious B

They that have but a little wit are commonly like those that cry **197ᵛ**
things in the Streets, who if they have but a Groatsworth of Aa
Rotten or stinking stuff, every body that comes nigh shalbe sure
to heare of it, while those that drive a rich noble Trade, make no
Noyse of it.   5

They are much mistaken who Say the Minde of Man performes
any thing wholly without the Senses, because in Dreames and
meditation when the minde is Busy, the Senses are lockd up. For
that is no further true, then that the Minde do's then worke upon
that, which it had before receivd from the Senses; and we may as 10
well say the Stomach dos something without the Mouth, because it
concocts, and digest's when wee do not eate, which it never could
do if wee had not eaten before.

Among so many Millions of Errors, and Mistakes, as are to be
found among Authors, I do not remember any one that is grounded 15
upon the Deceit or Misreport of Sense: For I never met with any
man, that would undertake to prove, that objects are really lessend
by Distance because they appeare to be so.

When the Rude Antients heard their own voyces in Solitary
woodes repeated by the Eccho, and could see no Person appeare, 20
They supposd there were certaine invisible Inhabitants whom they
cald Faunes and Satyrs, and lest they should be unprovided of
Ladys and Mistreses they devisd Nymphs Driades, and Hama-
dryades for them. This appeares by Lucret lib 4us p 95.

Hard Students, and great Artists are commonly most Ignorant 25
in those things that border upon their Arts, and Professions. As
Priests and Lawyers of Morality, Practicall Men of Speculation,
and the Speculative of Practice.

Lucretius is mistaken in saying the Memory sleepe's with the
Body, for wee only, or at least for the most Part, dreame of thinges 30
that are suggested by the Memory, and if that were fast a sleep no
man could remember his Dreames. There is nothing that sleepe's
soundly but only Reason and the Senses that are the Informers
of it.

198^r   Men of the quickest apprehensions, and aptest Geniuses to any
Aa thing they undertake, do not always prove the greatest Masters in
it. For there is more Patience and Flegme required in those that
attaine to any Degree of Perfection, then is commonly found in the
5 Temper of active, and ready wits, that soone tire and will not hold
out; as the swiftest Race-horse will not perform a longe Jorney so
well as a sturdy dull Jade. Hence it is that Virgil who wanted much
of that Natural easines of wit that Ovid had, did nevertheless with
hard Labour and long Study in the end, arrive at a higher perfection
10 then the other with all his Dexterity of wit, but less Industry could
attaine to. The same we may observe of Johnson, and Shakespeare.
For he that is able to thinke long and Judg well wil be sure to finde
out better things then another man can hit upon suddenly, though
of more quick and ready Parts, which is commonly but chance and
15 the other Art and Judgment.

The Aristotelian Philosophy is like a Virtuoso's watch that
Controwles the Sun.

A logician, Gramarian, and Rhetorician never come to understand the true end of their Arts, untill they have layd them by, as
20 those that have learnd to swim, give over the bladders that they
learnd by.

Some men have declard against Aristotle not so much because
he was in an error as because he was in Authority.

He that would hit the Mark he levels at must shut one eie, and
25 take his aime with the other: So he that would attaine to perfection
in any one Study, must lay by all his other Ingenuity, and apply
himself wholly to that which he proposes.

The Sceptique Philosopher that sayd wit was not Invention, nor
Similitude, nor apt Metaphor; but inference, Induction &c might,

6 Race-horse] *or* Racehorse B   11 to.] to:. *B*   12 For . . . well]
underlined by Longueville B   well] *altered probably by Longueville to* well, *B*   14–15
which . . .] *underlined by Longueville B*   16 watch] *altered probably by
Longueville to* watch, *B*   19 by,] *altered probably by Longueville to* by; *B*
22 Aristotle] *altered probably by Longueville to* Aristotle, *B*   23 error] *altered
probably by Longueville to* error, *B*   24 at] *altered probably by Longueville to* at, *B*
29 &c] *altered probably by Longueville to* &c; *B*

as wel have sayd that a Jewel is not all Diamond or Rubie, but gold and enamell. But the Truth is, every man would gladly have it that which he believe's he has most of himself, and not that he wants.

He that apply's himself to understand things that are not to be known, uses his wit and Industry like the edg of a Toole that is 5 Cut upon a thing that is too hard for it; beside his loss of Labour he dos but render it more blunt and dull then it was before.

The Invention of the Vibration of a Pendulum was intended to 198ᵛ settle a certaine Measure of Continuity all the world over, which Ab should have its foundation in Nature. For by swinging a weight at 10 the end of a String, and calculating how long the Vibration (by the motion of the Sun) would last in proportion to the length of the String, and weight of the Pendulum They thought to reduce it back again, and from any part of Time calculate or compute the length of any string that must necessarily vibrate exactly in so 15 much space. So that if a man should ask in China for a Quarter of an Howr of Sattin, or Taffaty they would know perfectly what it meant. And all the world learne a new way to measure things no more by the yard, foot, or inch, but by the Hower, Quarter and Minute.   20

Scholastique Disputations are like Running at Tilt hertofore with Crackd Launces.

Tis Strange that the Lacedemonians who were so thrifty of their words should call themselves by so long a Name.

He that engage's himself in any thing without consideration, 25 and after undertake's to maintaine it by Reason, do's like a cleane Beast that swallows first and Chaw's after.

They that admire Cæsars dexterity in dictating to three secretaries at once do not consider it was a thing of Art rather then Nature, for so great was the Industry of the Ancient Orators 30

    2–3 But . . .] *underlined by Longueville B*   2 But] but *B*   that] *altered probably by Longueville to* that, *B*   4–5 that are . . . known] *underlined by Longueville B*   5 known,] *altered probably by Longueville to* known; *B*   edg] edg. *B*   Toole] *altered probably by Longueville to* Toole, *B*   22. 1–2 *See p.* 117, *l.* 35–*p.* 118, *l.* 3 all . . . Enemys

812728   F

(amonge whom he was noe meane one) that they provided not only Common Places, and materialls of Sense for all Occasions, but formes of expression pertinent to all Purposes which they cal'd Supellex, as appeares by M. Seneca.

5   Men take so much Delight in lying that Truth is sometime forcd to disguise her self in the habit of Falshood to get enterteinment as in Fables and Apologues frequently usd by the Ancients, and in this she is not at all unjust, for Falshood do's very commonly usurp her Person.

10   Fancy is (like Caligula) an excellent Servant to reason and judgment but the most unfit thing in the world to governe.

Publique æstimation commonly neglects substantiall things and cry's up the slight and Frivolous; Like the winde that passes over 14 solid bodys and beares up Dust and feathers.

199ʳ Lucretius erre's in saying All heavy things do not Naturally Ab incline downwards, because Trees and all Plants, in their growth, tend upwards which is a great mistake, for they are not heavy as they grow, growth being nothing but an Addition of light Parts that move upwards, but being intercepted and fixt, do afterwards 20 become heavy.

The Spanish Poets are excellent disigners of Comedy but very ill writers as it falls out commonly in Painting.

Tedious Polemique writers are more severe to their Readers then those they contend with.

25   Dr Sp:s Dedication of his Book to Cl: is not unlike what Marco Polo relate's of the Tartars, that they never eate, nor drinke, but they spill some of it on the ground, as an offering to the Devil.

Ja: Howell write's that the Neopolitans in Massanellos Rebellion rung the great Bell backwards and shot the King of Spain's Picture 30 through and through.

3 but . . . expression] *underlined by Longueville B*   4 Supellex,] Supellex. B   15 erre's] *underlined by Longueville B*   22 writers] *altered possibly by Longueville to* writers; *B*   23 Readers] *altered possibly by Longueville to* Readers, B   29 backwards] *altered possibly by Longueville to* backwards; *B*   Picture] Pictue *B*

Lucretius is mistaken in saying that the effluvias of things pass in an Instant through the greatest Distances, because the stars appeare suddenly as soone as the Cloudes are remov'd; Lib 4 p 87. which is don by a perpetual rather then a sudden emanation.

The writings of the Antients are like their Coynes, Those that 5 have any lasting and Naturall Sense, and wit in them, are like Medals of gold or Silver, and beare a value among all men in all times, And those that have little or none, are like those of Brasse, that have only a value among a few, that esteeme them merely for their Antiquity. 10

Dr Don's writings are like voluntary or Prælude in which a man is not ty'd to any particular Designe of Air; but may change his key or moode at pleasure: So his compositions seeme to have been written without any particular Scope.

They that write Plays in Rime tell us that the language of 15 Comedie ought to be common Discourse, such as men speake in familiar conversation: as if verse were so.

Our moderne Authors write Playes as they feed hogs in West-phalia, where but one eate's pease, or akornes, and all the rest feed upon his and one anothers excrement. So the Spaniard first 20 invents and Designes Play's, the French borrow it from them and the English from the French.

Some writers have the unhappines, or rather Prodigious Vanity **199ᵛ** to affect an obscurity in their Stiles, indevouring by all meanes not **Aa** to be understood, but rather like witches to cast a mist before the 25 eies of their Readers. These are Owles of Athens only in avoyding the Light; which they do, not so much in regard of the Profoundnes of what they deliver, which is commonly very vulgar and slight when it is understood, but appeare's very learned, when it is disguisd in darke and insignificant expressions. To write not to be 30 understood is no less vaine then to speake not to be heard; Fooles and Madmen use to talke to themselves in Publique, and he that

publishes that which he would have no Man understand but himself do's the same thing. These are like Citizens that commonly
choose the Darkest streets to set up in, or make false lights that
the Spots and Steines of their Stuffs may not be perceived. But they
have another Marke at which this folly always ayme's and seldom
misse's of, the Admiration of the weake and Ignorant, who are
apt to contemne whatsoever they can understand, and admire any
thing that they cannot.

There is a kinde of Physiognomy in the Titles of Bookes no less
then in the faces of men, by which a Skilful Observer will as well
know what to expect from the one as the other.

Some men are of such Hardy understandings that they disdaine
to take notice of any thing that is capable of being understood, but
perpetually apply themselves to occult and abstruse knowledges
(like Knights Errant in Romances that fight with Giants, and
besiege Inchanted Castles) and the more weake and unable they
are to encounter Difficulties the more obstinately they are bent
upon them, untill they become the most Irrational of all Mankinde:
For their perpetuall drudging about things hard and obscure, or
Mystical, has the same operation upon their understandings that
hard Labour ha's upon the hand, which it do's not render Plyant
and agile, but stiff and num'd, For while with mere Fancy and
Conjecture, they gaze upon things far off and uncertaine, they
oversee that which ly's nearer and more concerns them.

The Ridiculous wits of our times have that indulgent Ignorance
to themselvs, that they never impute any thing that is fixt upon
them (how apparently true so ever) to their own faults, but ascribe
it wholy to the envy or malice of others, as Fanatiques do their
Just Punishments, and call them Persecutions for Righteousnes,
inflicted by the wicked.

200ʳ Aristotle thought to reduce Nature to his own Notions, rather
Aa then to suite them agreable to her; and studied her more in the
metaphysiques of his own Braine, then her own certaine operations;
As if his chiefest care had been to make his Systemes of her rather

4 perceived.] perceived B   16–18 and the . . . them] *underlined by Longueville
B*   29 Punishments] Punishment B

Artificiall then true, and to agree among themselves very prettily, but perhaps without any great regard to Truth or Nature. This made him So over-Artificiall, that some have believd the use and Profit men receive from his writings will not beare the Charges of the Paines and Study that must be bestowd upon them.   5

It is a common Manner of Souldiers to commend the Valour of an Enemy, whom they have beaten; for in doing so, they do but commend themselves: For all that Virtue which they can possibly intitle such an Adversary to (and much more) do's but become due to themselves, by whom it was outdon. This is a Custome much in   10 use with learned men in Disputes and controversies, who commonly begin their Confutations with the Prayses of their Antagonists (like Cuntry-fellows, who use to shake hands, before they breake one anothers heads) and extoll him in the Præface, whom they intend to ruine in the Booke: For they know such prayses are   15 but lent, or rather put out to use, which they purpose shalbe payd back againe with interest. For he that cry's up the Learning and Knowledg of one whom he afterward take's upon him to correct, and confute, do's but profess his own to be greater.

So Scaliger in the Præface to his Exercitations which he wrot of   20 Purpose to win that Reputation from Cardan which he had gaind in the opinion of the world; admire's him for the greatest wit that ever livd in any age, as knowing that man must of necessity be held a greater that was able to detect his Errors and Mistakes.

There is a Perpetuall Civil war in the Commonwealth of Learn-   25 ing which ha's no less fair Pretences on all sides, then Politique Quarrels; For as those commonly pretend Religion Law and Liberty: So do these Truth, Reason, and the opposition of Error; when really it is nothing but the advantage of their own little interest, and the Contradiction of one another. For like Bowlers if   30 one ly nearer the Jack (Truth) then another can expect to lay himself, his next bus'nes is to knock him away.

There is nothing that do's confound the understanding more **200ᵛ** then an over-curious Method; so too much Light dazle's the eies.   Ab

---

3 that . . . believd] *underlined by Longueville B*   13 shake] skake *B*
20-4 *Marginal rule drawn for emphasis by Longueville B*   31 (Truth)] *probably altered by Longueville from* Truth *B*   34 Method;] Method. *B*

They are in an Error who thinke the minde of Man can pass through the greatest Distances of Space in an Instant: For the Images of things most remote are always ready in the understanding, where she can easily turne from one to another without
5 stirring out of the Place, more then the eie doth out of the Head, when it beholds things far of.

The Reasons and Arguments of Chymists are like their operations upon Mettles, They give a Tincture of Truth upon Error, and Falshood as they do, of Gold and Silver upon Copper, but it
10 will not indure the Test. They are not more reservd and Cautious in concealing the Discipline of their Mystery from one another, then Nature is in hiding hers from them all, and it is probable, This is all they imitate her in. For the Dark and Secret Cavernes of the earth, which she only trusts with her Counsells, are not more
15 obscure then those Cabals of Canting to which they commit theirs. Nature in her Operations of Mineralls workes so close and retir'd that it is impossible to learne her Trade of her, For it is to no purpose to know her Principles and Ingredients (if wee could go so far) while we are Ignorant (as wee must ever be) of their Prepara-
20 tion and Dose, with the Temper of her heat, and the order and steps of her Proceeding, with other Circumstances, without a perfect knowledg of which, all the rest is in vaine, and no man living can possibly imitate her. For though in the Generation of Animals, the Dullest Creaturs are furnishd with Materials and can project, yet
25 it will produce nothing out of the proper Matrix, but monsters.

There can be nothing obscure in any Booke but by the Ignorance of the writer or the Reader. And when many Readers of excellent and known abilitis concur in the Ignorance of some obscure writer, it is easy to guess on which side the fault ly's. Things of the most
30 pure and refin'd Nature, are always most obedient to light, as glass, and Diamonds; the later of which receives a great loss from the least cloud or Foulnes, and there is no reason why it should bee otherwise in mens reason and Sense.

201ʳ
Aa   Raymund Lully interpret's Kabal (out of the Arabique) to signify Scientia Superabundans, and no doubt it is a very super-

---

12 This] *altered from or possibly to* That B   31 receives] *altered from* receive B
32 or] of *W*   Foulnes,] Foulnes. *B*

fluous Thinge; His Ars Brevis is a Divice to pack up knowledg in a Small case (like a Paire of Twises) of Nine Letters, which being set upon Magnitudo, Bonitas, Quomodo &c (like Shopkeepers Markes) will suddenly instruct the most Ignorant in all Manner of Learning. This his Commentator Cornelius Agrippa (being very Partiall to this 5 Vanity of Science) strains so hard to make good, that he affirmes of his owne knowledg (in spight of Reason, or Probability) that Illitterate and Decrepit old men, with Boys of Ten yeares of Age, have, in a short Space, been inabled, by this Sole Art to dispute with the wisest Doctors of his Times in all manner of Learning. 10

But this is no more to be believd then the Story of Cardan, and Nicholas Flamell, who by buying two guilt Books of two Strangers whom they met by Accident, became immediatly learned; the first in the Latine Tongue, of which he was utterly Ignorant before; and the other, by the help of a Jew, and St James in the 15 Philosophers Stone. But I wonder who was ever the wiser for his 12 Principles in a Circle, like the figures on a Dial? Or why I cannot as well understand there are 5 Senses, when I am told so; as by seeing them written upon Crosse-Triangles, which are no more to be regarded then Pyramids and Alters in verse. But these are but 20 the Conceptions of wearyd Melancholy, like the Images which a Sick or Idle Fancy will observe in the fire, or such as Cardan saw upon a wall.

The Author of the History of the Gresham-Society report's that the Guanches, a People of the Race of the old Inhabitants of the 25 Canary-Iles do use to head their Darts with Butter hardned in the Sun: That they whistle so loud that they may be heard at five miles distance.

Scaliger say's, that the shape of every thing is contain'd in every thing, For a Sculptor that cut's what Image he pleases out of a 30 Stone, and any other out of that, do's but remove the Disguise that cover'd that figure which was really there before: which is false, for it was not there before it was made so; Figure being nothing but the Position of outward Parts, and therefore cannot be

imputed to any thing internall. This and the wonders that may be
performd by a streit Line, are much like.

201ᵛ   The writers of our Times are much mistaken, who believe they
 Aa   may be allowd to write that, which is unfit for them to speak, and
  5   therefore they use a Dialect and Sense Different from that which
men use in Civil Conversation, as if the Language and account of
thinges deliverd in Bookes ought to be different from that of men
that write them. Or that men might assume a Priviledg, to Publish
things so extravagant of themselves or others in Print to all the
 10   world (only backd by a ridiculous Custome) which modesty would
not permit them to owne or heare in Private. This is frequent in
Dedications and Prayses of Authors, in which as if Self love had
usurpd that Priviledge of Love—Dicere quæ puduit, scribere
jussit amor—They wil assume and own as due, those lavish Prayses
 15   of themselves, in Publique, which another Custome will not indure
them to heare sayd in private to their faces. But as mens eies are
out of order when they see double, So are their understandings
when they make more of a thinge then is in it; for a man must
make his Friend Ridiculous, when he ha's made himself so, by
 20   saying extravagant things of him; as he may commend his enemy
by undervaluing of him indiscreetly.

In the Alphabet no letter ha's any Naturall Right to stand
before another but V. might as well have taken place of all the Rest
as A. But Custome has been pleasd to order it otherwise; and if wee
 25   should go about to alter that ranke: the Reformation would be as
troublesome as ridiculous.

Those that Professe the Instrumentall Arts as Grammar Rhetorique and Logique, are like organ-makers, that understand all the
inward Fabrique of the Bellows, Pipes, and Registers, and can tell
 30   when any thing is out of order and how to mend it, and yet cannot
play so well as one that know's nothing but the keys. They use to
make senseles and impertinent Reflections upon things, and having
fitted them with as insignificant Tearmes, they passe for learning,

14 amor—] amor. *B*   16–18 mens . . . it] *duplicated B* 150ʳ   16 eies]
braines *B* 150ʳ   17 they . . . So] their eies see double, and so *B* 150ʳ   18 it;]
it. *B*   25–6 the . . .] *underlined by Longueville B*   30–1 and yet . . . keys]
underlined by Longueville B

which every man is to take Notice of at his peril, and he that can
expound them is a Master.

Ben: Johnson in saying (in one of his Prologues) All Gall and **202ʳ**
Coprace from his Inke he drayneth; only a little Salt remaineth &c Ab
would in these more Censorious times be chargd with a kinde of 5
Nonsense, for though Gall and Cop'race be usd in Inke Salt
never was.

Cambden speaking of an Antiquary that plac'd the Trinobantes
in Yorkshire, say's the too much love of his Cuntry deceivd him,
as if his Cuntry receiv'd any advantage by it.   10

Dr Bates pag. 52 2dæ Partis Elenchi Motuum, cal's a Bridge of
Boates Pons Sublicius; and ad Salivam facere to please.

Commentators usd to expound English Bookes with Latin and
Greeke Annotations.

Glanvile of Witchcraft. pag. 75 confesse's that he makes the 15
Objections himself which he Answer's, in these words, I am sure
I have suggested much more against what I defend, then ever I
heard, or saw in any that opposd it: And yet rayle's at the Impious
Proposers of such Suggestions, and makes them guilty of Misprision
of Sin against the Holy Ghost, forgetting what he had sayd of him- 20
self before.

My writings are not set of with the Ostentation of Prologue,
Epilogue nor Preface, nor Sophisticated with Songs, and Dances,
nor Musique nor fine women between the Cantos; Nor have any
thing to commend them but the Plaine Downrightnes of the 25
Sense.

It is as easy to pervert in Disputation what is sayd to the Purpose,
as if one should say 2 and 4 make's 6, to make him say 2 times 4
make's 6.

3 Prologues)] Prologues B   6–7 Salt never was] *underlined by Longueville B*
11 Motuum,] Motuum. B   12 Sublicius;] *comma altered from full point B*
18–21 *Marginal brace drawn for emphasis by Longueville B*   20 forgetting] *underlined*
by Longueville B   27–8 . . . as] *underlined by Longueville B*   27 Purpose,]
altered probably by Longueville to Purpose; B   28 6,] 6. B

It is much easier to write Plays in Verse then Prose, as it is
harder to imitate Nature then any Deviation from her; and Prose
require's a more Proper and Natural Sense, and expression then
verse, that ha's something in the Stamp and Coyne, to answer for
5 the Allay, and want of Intrinsique Value.

Mr D: approve's of no Satyr but that which is written against
the Gods; No doubt a very Ingenious way, because we are very
well acquainted with their crimes, and have excellent opportunitys
to make observations of their humours, and to be severe to their
10 Ignorance and Folly, as Satyrs use to bee to those extravagancys in
men.

Juvenal proposes the Argument of his Satyrs to be Votum Timor
Ira &c but afterwards say's nothing of any of them.

202ᵛ   He commits as great a fault in Chronologie when in the last two
Aa lines of his 6t Satyre he supposes Agamemnon might have taken
16 Methridate above 5 hundred yeares before it was in being.

Satyrical wit may seeme to be the most pleasant of all other:
Men cannot laugh heartily without shewing their Teeth, and therefore the French call a Satyr Dent riant.

20 Bull and Mistake is not the worst sort of Nonsense for that
may proceed from Incogitance, or Diversion by somthing else:
But Metaphysique or that Nonsense, that is derivd from Study and

1 It is] They [the French] find it C   then Prose, as] then in Prose; for C   Prose,]
altered probably by Longueville to Prose; B   1–2 is harder] is much harder C
4 verse,] *altered by Longueville to* verse; B   4–5 that . . .] *underlined by Longue-*
ville B   5 of Intrinsique] of the Intrinsique C   12–13 *Duplicated B* 232ʳ
12 proposes] in his first Satyr sets downe B 232ʳ   his . . . be] all the rest, which he
say's shalbe—B 232ʳ   13 &c but afterwards] Voluptas, ∴Gaudia˙˙ Discursus
—and never after B 232ʳ   nothing] any thing at all B 232ʳ   any of] any one of
B 232ʳ   14–16 *Duplicated B* 197ʳ (*to which marginal cross-reference by Longueville* p.
2ᵃ *here refers*), 233ᵛ   14–15 He . . . Satyre] *om. B* 233ᵛ   He . . . lines] Nor
is Juvenal altogether free who about the end B 197ʳ   15 he] *om. B* 197ʳ; Juvenal
B 233ᵛ supposes Agamemnon] supposes that Agamemnon B 233ᵛ   16 Methridate above 5] that Antidote which Mithridates invented soe many B 233ᵛ   above]
though he livd [though *to end of draft underlined by Longueville*] B 197ʳ   before
. . .] after he was dead, in these wordes—Si prægustarit Atrides Pontica tèr victi
cautus medicamina Regis B 233ᵛ   in being] invented B 197ʳ   19 Dent riant]
underlined by Longueville B

Consideration is the more Desperate, as Hippocrates says Sad and Studious Madnes is more incurable, then that which is frolique and Careless.

Inferences, and Inductions, if they are true and Certaine, are commonly of things slight, and Insignificant: But if of thinges 5 Abstruse, and Remote, as often Doubtful and Insignificant themselves: and so both waies for the most part serve to very little Purpose.

The Virtuosi affect Subletys and Curiosities in Nature, as Priests do in Divinity, and Lawyers in doing Justice or Injury. 10

There are Some Authors that write for fame only: and never have it. That thinke it below them to take Money for their writings, because no body will give it. When all the Proudest of Professions submit to meaner offices to earne Money. The Divine will not trouble himself, to save, or Damne any Soul, unless he be wel 15 payd, and then he is indifferent. The Physitian take's money for writing a recipe whether it Kill, or Cure: And the Lawyer wil not draw one Line, nor speake one word, whether it preserve or undo until he is wel feed for it.

Mounsieur Mountaigne the Essayist, seeme's when he wrot to 20 have been either a little warm'd with wine, or Naturally Hotheaded.

All Controversies, and Disputations are managed by Polemique B writers, like the Duell between two Rivalls in the Comedy, who had but one sword between them both, which they agreed to use 25 by turnes, and he that had it first, was to run at the other, who was ingag'd to stand fair, and receive his Thrust, and after to do the same to him againe.

Though all Prefaces are perpetually addres'd to the Gentle 203ʳ Readers, yet the Authors use them no more Gentilely, and Civilly, Bb

4–8 *Duplicated and underlined B* 217ᵛ   4 Inductions] *altered from* Deductions *B*   6 Remote, as] Remote, they are as *B* 217ᵛ   14 *Marginal note* Money. *added by Longueville B*   16 indifferent.] indifferent *B*   17 writing] *altered from* drawing *B*   20 Mounsieur] Mouˢ *or possibly* Monˢ *B*

then Quakers are wont to entertaine those whom they make their Applications to. For let the Gentle Reader be a Person of ever so great Quality, yet he receive's him, with no more Respect, nor treat's him with better Language then the Quakers thou and thee; A preposterous way of Insinuating into the Favour of a Gentle Reader, or making of Apologies, and Excuses before hand, though that be the whole Designe and Purpose, for the most Part of all Præfaces.

Those who write Bookes against one another, do but Play a Prize in Defaming one another, in which nothing is to be gotten by either of them but Infamy. For as to Fence with foyles (that can do no great hurt) is an Exercise for all men of ever so great Quality to Practice; So to play Prizes, is only fit for meane and inferior People to use, who expose themselves to blows and wounds, for the Sport of the Rabble, only to Purchace their Approbation of their Abilities and a little Intrest in their ways, and among their Parties, with the expence of their Bloud and Sometime, Lives. Those who rayle at one another in Print, encounter like the Fight of Rams, whose Hornes are but Foyles, and Rebated. And that beast that tilt's with greatest Force, give's as much of the Blow to himself, as he do's to his Enemy, and receive's as much Hurt as he give's, if their Foreheads are equally Hard, which are the only weapons, that are usd by both sides, (men and Beasts) in those Rancounters, and the Hardest has always the Oddes.

Disputes are commonly so ill manag'd, that whosoever is able to judge impartially, will certainly finde, upon the whole matter, that Both sides are in the wrong: For their Partiality is so great, that there [is] no Medium to reconcile, the Infamy, Scandalls, and Fallacies they unjustly lay upon one another, but by dividing it æqually between both; and just at that Rate their Controversys are to be Decided: For they always Part, as they met to no Purpose, and the wisest and justest Course, those that are unconcern'd can take, is that which a Sottish Juryman proposd, to hang half, and save half, without giving themselves the Trouble to examine any

13 to play Prizes, is] *underlined by Longueville B*   18–24 Those . . .] *dupli-cated and underlined B* 222ʳ   18 who] that *B* 222ʳ   in Print] *om. B* 222ʳ   20–1 give's . . . Enemy] *underlined by Longueville B* 203ʳ   23 weopons *B* 222ʳ: woepens *B* 203ʳ   24 Rancounters] incounters *B* 222ʳ   27 that . . .wrong] *underlined by Longueville B*

Particulars at all. The more Regular, and Formall Disputes are, they are Commonly the more impertinent and Ridiculous, like Fenceing by the Mathematiques: For whosoever cannot understand Reason, untill it is put into Moode and Figure, is as great a Bungler as he that cannot read without Spelling, nor write without Construing every word. For Scholastical Disputes do Commonly lay by the Question, and scuffle about the Art of Logique in which both sides tyre themselves in putting by those Thrusts, that are wide enough from hitting of themselves.

All the Pretences that Geomancy ha's to tell Truth, are nothing but the very same that Gamesters call Fancying, and believe to be the Cause why they throw in, or out, according as they Fancy right, or wrong. And both are perform'd the same way, By judging by spots set down at Random, not unlike those upon the Dice, that are thrown as much at Random, by those who use no tricks, but play fairly. But as Tricks are found to be the surest ways to win, so is Cheat of Predicting, when they foretell nothing but what they knew before. All the rest is the same in both, mere Chance, which sometimes do's greater things then all the Art and Cunning in the world, and one lucky Hit is sufficient to excuse a thousand miscarriages. Nor is the Name less Silly and Impertinent, then the Thing, For why they should call Fancy that has nothing to do with the Earth Geomancy, none but he that understand's the Nonsense of the thing can guess.

The Heroicall Poetry of the old Bards of Wales and Ireland (and perhap all other Barberous Nations) who at publique Solemnities, were wont to sing the Prayses of their valiant Ancestors, was the Originall of all the more Elegant Greeke and Roman Epique Poems.

The old Greeke Poets make Minerva the Goddess of wisdom not to be born of a woman, but the Braine of the greatest of all the Gods.

The Quantity of Syllables in Latine, and Greek Poetry was not introducd by Custome, and Poeticall Licence: but has its Foundation in Nature. For those Syllables, that by reason of their frequent

---

1–9 *Marginal rule drawn for emphasis by Longueville B*   3–6 For . . . word]
underlined by Longueville B   18 knew] know *W*   21 then] *altered from* fo *B*

and doubled Consonants, are hard to be pronounc'd, are Naturally long, and those that are easy, as naturally Short. And therefore who write's ruggedly do's but put himselfe, to the unnecessary trouble, and Drudgery of Rhime to no purpose.

5   All Authors of all Sorts of Bookes about Queen Elizabeths time, usd to excuse themselves in their Epistles and Dedications and Præfaces for writing plainly, and not using Scholastical Tearms and Rhetoricall Phrases, which are since found to be the Fopperys, and impertinent Follys of all writers. So certaine it is, that some men
10 may do better by being below, as well as others by being above all Phantastique and Ridiculous Impertinencys.

Abondance of Rules, and Tedious Methods are designd more for the Advantage of the Teacher then the Learner, As no Man can want any thing, in another mans trade, but he that supplys him,
15 make's the most Considerable Profit of it: And therefore those who are bound Prentises to any trade, are slaves and servants to those that teach them for so many yeares, and do their Busnes for them, before they can be Free, and admitted to make any Benefit of their own.

20 As Printers put their Erratas always at the Ends of Bookes, and Lawyers bring writs of Error at the ends of Suites: So men Commonly never see their Errors, and Mistakes untill the End of the Busnes, when it often prove's too late to repayr, and amend them.

It is not Difficult to guess when any Mans Learning is grown too
25 Heavy for his Naturall Parts. For he that is more Confident of those things which he take's up only upon trust, then Industrious to know the Reason of them, which Partiality, and Prepossession will not permit him to do, is not like to take a Right Course to understand the Truth of any thing: and when he ascribe's more to the
30 Authority, then the true Reason of Bookes, it is a Signe that he has had too much of them, and more then he knows how to manage to the best advantage. For as Men who are past their Height and decline, do naturally come to be in the Same Degree, as they were when they were but Learners (to whom a Resignd beliefe is

17 many] *altered probably by Longueville from* may B   23 amend] *or possibly* ⟨am⟩end B

Necessary) it is an Argument that those who believe all they Read
without Examination, are not in a much better condition then
meare Learners, and do but go back the very same way, by which
they improvd before. Beside when they impute more to their own
Studys, and undertakings then is really in them, it is a Signe they 5
have overstraynd their Judgments in heaving at that which is too
hard for them. So Mr Hobs believd that if his De cive, had been
Printed but a yeare sooner, it would have prevented all our Civill
wars. And the Anatomist who supposd that Nature contrivd the
Inward Parts of all Men into one Position, only that there might be 10
Truth, and Certainty in Anatomy; As if all Men were made of
Purpose to be Dissected. Or he who durst never go through a Gate
in Oxford, because there was an old / Prophesy of a Stone in it, that **204ʳ**
should fall and kill the Greatest Philosopher in the world. These Bb
are the Customes of very many Learned Men, that prevayle upon 15
them, by being too much Possest with any thing they apply to,
untill like old and over fond Lovers they come to doate.

The Spanish Romancers make all Gallant Moores (who are
Frequently their Subjects) in the end to turne Christians, and all
Heroique Christians (Knights and Ladys) to enter into Religious 20
Orders, instead of Marrying; Only to Complement, and Flatter
the Church, to get the Priests Leading voyces of Applause, who
otherwise would not fayle [not only] to stop the Printing of their
workes (which none but they have Powr to licence) but forbid
their Penitents to read their unsanctifyd Apocryphas in Manu- 25
script.

Most Men of Learning have the same Judgement, and Opinion
of Latin and Greek Authors, as they had when they were Children,
and were taught to read them at School, to understand the Languages they wrot in, and not the Truth of their Reason, and Sense, 30
of which they were then incapable: And because they found them
excellently usefull for the Learning of words, believe they are so
for all things else.

The Rabins interpret that Place in Genesis The woman gave mee

5 then . . . them] *underlined by Longueville B*   14 world.] world,. *B*
16 being too] being ⟨pos⟩ too *B*   24–5 but forbid their Penitents] *underlined by*
Longueville B   27–33 *Marginal rule drawn for emphasis by Longueville B*

of the Tree &c to signify that she beate him with a Cudgell of the wood of that Tree, untill he did eate of the Fruite of it.

There is Scarse any one thing, in which men are generally more apt to mistake, then in their Censure of Stiles: For as Stile is Noth-
5 ing (as it is taken) but a proper naturall and Significant way of expressing our Conceptions in words, and as it agree's or disagree's with those is either good or Bad; So he that take's it for Good or Bad of it self is very much mistaken, and erroneously takes the musique for the Instrument it is playd upon, and according as that
10 is in or out of tune, commend's, or Cry's down the Composition; For though good things may be blemish'd by being ill Deliverd, yet that which is Bad of it self, can never be renderd good, by any language of it self. And although the Plainest, and most Significant Stile be undoubtedly the best, yet it is only so where the excellency
15 of the Sense will beare it; as it is a superfluous thing to lace or imbroder that which is Richer without it. But where the Sense is vulgar, and common it do's require something extraordinary in the expression, to set it of with a greater Grace, and disguise the naturall homeliness of the thing, and (if it be possible) to render it
20 as becoming, as if it were naturally so of it self: For that which is old, and worn out, may be made new, by a new way of expression, or Application, and no less witty, then if it were Fresh and never heard of before. But this is Impossible to be don in Some Arguments and no way but in one fashion of writing.

25 There are two ways of Quibling, the one with words, and the other with Sense; Like the Figuræ Dictionis, et Figuræ Sententiæ, in Rhetorique. The first is don by shewing Tricks with words of the Same Sound, but Different Senses: And the other by expressing of Sense by Contradiction, and Riddle. Of this Mr Waller, was the
30 first most Copious Author, and ha's so infected our moderne writers of Heroiques with it, that they can hardly write any other way, and if at any time they indeavour to do it, like Horses that are put out of their Pace, they presently fall naturally into it againe. Trotto d'Asino dura poco.

7 those] these W   9 according] altered from accord by Longueville B
11 For . . . Deliverd] underlined by Longueville B   14-15 yet . . . beare it]
underlined by Longueville B   15 it;] comma altered from full point B   16 imbro-
der] altered to imbroider by Longueville B   23 But . . . Arguments] underlined
by Longueville B   26 et] & B; and GR, W

Those treatises that are dayly publish'd upon all sorts of Learn- **204ᵛ**
ing, are, for the most part, nothing else but Notes and Collections **Bb**
gather'd by Ignorant Novices in those Studys, and Professions;
Who like all Smatterers admiring that most which they least
understand, believe that the same things that please them best, 5
out of their want of Judgement, will have the same effect upon all
the world.

The Critiques of Quarrells, are wiser then those of Polemique
Disputes, For all the Learned Sages of the Blade, unanimously
agree, that no man is bound by the Law of Armes, or Honor to 10
answer a Challenge from his Inferior in Quality: while the other
more Peevish, and Furious Hectors of Controversy, thinke themselves oblig'd (only because there is less Danger in it) to answer
all the most ridiculous Fooles in the world, that shall object any
thing against them. 15

A Fiddle is more Delightfull to the Eare, then any Sound of
words without excellent Sense, and New: For no News is so naturally pleasant (to those who understand it) as that of Sense. For
then only it instructs with Pleasure, and is most apt to stay with
us: when what we knew before passe's away unminded, and un- 20
regarded, like News that we had heard before, and neither care to
heare, nor tell.

Before the Invention of Printing, Those who transcrib'd Bookes
writ such excellent Hands that though they abbreviated all long
words, and some of five or six letters into two, yet they were more 25
legible then the hands of most writers in our times. And yet
Abbreviations were (no doubt) in those times, one of the greatest
Causes of the Corruptions of all Bookes; when the Ignorant copyers
understood less of what they transcribd, then our Setters of letters
in the Press do of what they Print: But our mistakes are capable of 30
amendment by the Care of Correctors, which those who did
rather ingross then write, were depriv'd of, lest by blotting out
and mending the Errors of words, they should spoyle the Bewty

3 those] *or* these *B*   9–10 all . . . agree] they pronounce *C*   10–11 to
.. . Quality] *underlined by Longueville B*   11 in Quality] *om. C*   12 more
. . . Controversy] *om. C*   13 (only . . . it)] *om. C*   23 Bookes] Booke *B*
28 Ignorant] Ignorant, *B*

and Fairnes of the Booke: which was no inconsiderable thing in the Sale.

Among all the writings of the Antients, we finde that none have been transmitted to posterity so Perfect, and Intire as the workes of
5 the Poets; For Homer, and most of the Greeks of any esteeme with them are transferd without any considerable miscarriage unto our times. And of the Latins, Virgill and Ovid and Horace (and more then all Juvenal and Lucretius) and all others of the best Quality with them, as perfect as they left them: when there is very little
10 of History, though ever so excellent in the Kinde, but what is maym'd, and has lost the one half of it self. By which it should seem that Poetry was in greater esteeme with them: For nothing could preserve it safer then other writings but the greater Number of Copys that were extant, which naturally infer's a greater Number
15 of Readers. For they would never have been at the charge, and trouble, to transcribe so many, if they had not had an equall vend for them.

They are very weake Critiques who suppose a Poet that write's a Play, ought (like one that ride's Post with a Halter about his
20 Neck) to bring all his Designe, and contriveance within so many Howrs, or else be hangd for it. As if things of greater Importance, and much more to the Purpose, were to be omitted for a mere Curiosity, which few or none but the Capricchious take notice of.

205ʳ   It is strange that among the many ways that Impostors have
Bb   found out to predict by, none have of late times attempted to do
26   it by Quibling and Clinching when it is as Rationall, a way and Naturall as any other, and comes nearer to the Custome of the Antients, and the Devills Oracles. For if Astrology be rightly considerd, Almost all those operations ascribed to the Planets,
30 Constellations, and Signes in the Zodiaque, are deriv'd from their Names and not their Natures, which agree no more then the Figures of those Stars doe with the Shapes of those Creatures that are forc'd to represent them.
[205ᵛ]

Contradictions 206^r

Bb

There is nothing extraordinary and unusuall that the world
pretend's to, but it ha's some thing extravagant in it, that is
directly contrary to what it professe's: As the most Passionate
Love, by Jeolousy become's mixt with the most implacable Hate;
The Greatest Fancy with Madnes. The Greatest Perfection in any 5
one Knowledge, with Ignorance in all other, and those that nearest
border upon it. Like Summum Jus, Summa Injuria. The Tendrest
Consciences with the most horrible Impieties. For when Health it
self is at the Highest, it is (as Hippocrates say's) most apt to fall
into Sicknes. And Dreames the more earnest they are, are the 10
nearer to waking.

Simon Magus was destroyd for offering to give the Apostles
money, and Ananias, and his wife for indevouring to conceal it
from them.

The most Difficult Professions in the world, are the easiest to be 15
assumd and with lesse Study Practic'd by Impostures, and men of
the weakest Parts, as Divinity, Politiques, Commands in war,
Physique, Poetry &c while the meanest and merely Mechanicall
are never to be attaynd without great Industry, labour and Paines.
So the greater any Imployment is, the easier it is to be performd: 20
As it is easier to be a Judge then a Counseller. For all the Drudgery
and weight ly's upon Inferior Managers. The greatest Difficulty
they have is to carry themselves uprightly, like Dancers upon the
Ropes, with Justice and Moderation, and all the Rest of their
Dutys, and Abilities will do their Busnes of themselves without 25
any great Trouble, or Paines.

---

3 professe's:] professe's B   12–14 *Duplicated B* 155^v   13 and his wife]
om. B 155^v

The unjust Jealousys of Husbands have made more Cookolds then all their Care and Vigilance have prevented.

Antiquity abrogate's Laws (the most necessary things among mankinde) only becaus they are old, But sets a value upon things 5 of no use at all for the very same reason, which prevaile with as little reason, above modern things that are usefull with men of that humor, and Inclination.

Though Distance of Place do's naturally diminish all objects to the Sense, yet the Effect is contrary in Fame, and Report, that 10 increase the more, the further they are of, either in Distance of Time or Place.

No men need less then those who desire most, Nor have less use for wealth, then those who are most insatiable in acquiring it: For the end of all Riches is nothing else but to provide for all 15 Occasions of Spending, and those that can put no Bounds to their Greedines of getting, are commonly most averse, and incapable in their Naturall Inclinations of all manner of expence: and only out of humor, like Children, long for that, which they know not what to do with, when they have it.

20   The Proverb say's happy is the Son whose Father goes to the Devill: But he that visits the sins of the Fathers upon the Children, to the third, and 4th Generation dilivers another Doctrine.

206ᵛ   I have known some Professors of Religion who had perpetually
Bb   nothing but the Name of God, and the Lord, and Conscience, and
25   Religion in their mouths; And yet would never venture the loss of one Penny for either; but get as much as they could by all. And at the same time have seen some Persons, whom by their Discourse, no man would guess (after a yeares conversation) to have any concernment at all for Religion; and yet would rather loose all they 30 had, and their lives too, then indure to do any thing against their Consciences; which the other would imbrace with all Alacrity, for a Small Reward, under the Pretence of Piety.

There is nothing more Delightfull and Agreeable to human

9 Sense,] Sense. B   22 another] a nother B

Nature then to Love, and nothing more unpleasant, and uneasy then to Hate: And yet Hatred is alway prosecuted with greater violence, and earnestnes upon the slightest occasion given, then Love upon the greatest obligations imaginable: whether the Returnes are more chargeable to be performd, or the Revenge more 5 Pleasant to those who believe themselves injurd I cannot tell.

Charity is the chiefest of all Christian virtues, without which all the Rest signify nothing, For Faith and Hope can only bring us on our way to the Confines of this world: But Charity is not only our Convoy to heaven, but ingag'd to stay with us there for ever. And 10 yet there is not any sort of Religious People in the world, that will not renounce, and Disclame, this Necessary Cause of Salvation, for mere Triffles of the slightest moment imaginable, Nay, will most preposterously indeavor to secure their eternall Happines, by destroying that, without which it is never to be obteyn'd. From 15 hence are all their Spirituall Quarrells Deriv'd, and such Puntillios of opinion, that though more nice and Peevish then those of Love, and Honor in Romances, are yet maintayn'd with such Animositys, as if heaven were to be purchac'd no way, but that which is the most certaine and infallible of all others to loose it. 20

A Judge that takes Bribes of both sides is not so unjust as a Counceller that takes fees of both sides; For a Judge being equally poysd may be upright, but a Lawyer can hardly do it without betraying one Party to the other.

French-men are the filthiest Eaters in the world, but the clean- 25 lyest Drinkers, For though they delight to eate stinking Foule, drest the nastiest Greacy way Imaginable yet they wash their Glasses every time they Drinke, according to

> For they that can feed, on Carrion and Stinke,
> Yet wash their Glasses as oft as they Drink. 30

He that make's more of any thing then is really in it, Is a greater Bungler then he that performe's less then it will beare; For such a Man is in a way of Improveing, as the most excellent in all knowledges were before they arivd at their Height: But he that

---

5 performd,] performd. *B*   28 Drinke,] Drinke. *B*   29–30 *Editor's lineation*

overdo's any thing, go's back, and still grow's worse and worse;
For the Defect is in his Judgment, which when it is once over-
straind can never recover it's strength again.

Those Constitutions of Men that have least of Naturall Heat, are
5 the Aptest to bee inflam'd into Feavers.

207ʳ   There are more wise men governd by Fooles, then Fooles by
B   wise men.

Little families always lay clame to be the chief of the name, and
pretend the great ones to be of the yonger house.

10   The Italians are the fondest adorers of their woemen in the
world, and yet no nation keepe's them in greater Subjection and
slavery.

By the Lawes of Nature The Strongest have an undoubted
Power to command the weaker, But in Religion and the Civill life,
15 The wisest and Ablest are faine to comply and submit to the weakest and most Ignorant, for their own Quiet and convenience.

The Curse upon the Jews that Banishd them their own Cuntry
and dispersd them all the world over, has been so far from doing
them any hurt, that if the Felicitys of this world signify any thing,
20 (as they pretend to nothing else) they have thrivd the better for it.
For that which they live and dy in hopes of, to have their Nation
some time or other restord to their Native Cuntry, would be so far
from doing them good, that if they were in earnest they have
wealth enough to purchace it twenty times over, but that it would
25 not only yeald them nothing, but Cost them more then a thousand
in the hundred, which make's them rather stay for a Messias who
they believe is better able to make bargaines then them selves,
though they are the Cunningst Merchants and Brokers in the
world.

30   Lawyers who are for the most Part, the worst Linguists of all

4–5 *Duplicated B* 183ᵛ   8–9 *Duplicated and underlined B* 217ʳ   8 lay
clame] pretend *B* 217ʳ   9 pretend the] *om. B* 217ʳ   10–12 *Duplicated B*
217ʳ   10 of *B* 217ʳ: or *B* 207ʳ   13 The] Thre *B*   14 Religion] *altered
om* the *or* tho *B*   25 then] the *B*   28 Cunningst] Cunnings *B*

Men and as Incompetent Judges of Stile, are yet the greatest Critiques of words, and assume a Powr to interpret them which way they please.

There are more Men kild by Medcines then the Diseases they are intended to Cure. And more Curd by chance, then Reason and certaine Designe. For one Disease sometimes prove's a better Medcine to another then any that the ablest Doctor know's how to prescribe.

King James his Zeal against Popery was as much his Interest as his Judgment and Inclination, for nothing in the world contributed more to his enjoyment of the English Crowne, as his Mother from whom he derivd his Right, lost hers and her life too, for being of a Contrary Perswasion.

French Men who are believ'd by themselves and others to be the best makers of Adresse in the world, are worst qualifyd of all men for it, if it were not for their Native Confidence, which is all they have to shew for it, and serves them instead of other reall Abilities.

Honest Counsels, like Honest Men are commonly the most unfortunate and worse receivd then those that are the most Pernicious.

The late thorough Reformation, though pretended and Designd to force the Protestant Religion further off from Popery then it was before establishd did propagate it more, then thrice soe many yeares had don before, and by indevoring to destroy the Church of England, Recruited that of Rome, more then all their Seminarys, and Pouder Plots could have don, if they had taken effect, or any other Course imaginable, beside the vast Numbers of Sectaries and Fanatiques, which the zealous Reformers ingendred by equivocall Generation, to devour, and Prey upon themselves. And in the end were but Reducd to their old Conventicles and in a worse Condition then they were before, And if there had been Priests and Jesuites among them (as some believd) they could not possibly have

---

6 Disease sometimes] Disease do's sometimes *B*   a] *interlined B*   12 hers]
altered from the Crown *B*   and] ⟨and⟩ *B*   17 it,] it. *B*   29 devour . . . them-
selves] *underlined by Longueville B*   31 Priests] Priest *B*

don the Pope better Service and Religion in generall more mischief then they did.

The Pagan Religion though in appearance the most Phantastique of all others, came nearer to Nature (from whence it derivd at first) then any other way of worship, in the world; for it intended nothing, but the adoration of the Sun, though veyld under different Names, and Symbolical Ceremonys; And for Saints they worshipd the Aire the Earth, The Sea, and Planets; as Subordinate Parts of Nature to their great Deity the Sun.

Beasts that have no Apprehension of Death that wee can perceive, live more according to Nature, and some Brutes are better qualifyd with those things that wee call Virtues in our selves then men who professe the Greatest Mortifications, and deny themselves no pleasure of life, which perhaps is not so easy to be obteynd any other way.

Nothing conduce's more to the quiet injoyment of this world as the perswasion of Rewards or Punishments to be expected for management of it in the next.

The less Judgment any Man has, the less reason he has to dislike any thing he do's and the more Confidence to applaud it. For when a man has more wit then his Judgment and Discretion will hold, it run's over and spil's most abhominably.

Our Bishops have Bishop'd none but their own Dissenters the Fanatiques, and confirm'd in the former ill Opinion they had of them heretofore.

Souldiers whose Profession tend's Naturally to destroy Peace, and all things that belong to it, are the only Men that are able to preserve it, and although it's Busness is to put all things out of order but it self, yet when they are so, nothing else can set them right again. There is no Profession so easy, for like Mechaniques

---

4 whence] whenc *altered from* which B   5 world;] world. B   8 Subordinate] *altered from* inferior B   11–12 Brutes . . . things] *interworded (in one-word space initially left blank) and interlined* B   13 men] *altered from* those B   21 Judgment] Judgmen B   30 easy,] easy. B

they are able to practice the first Minute they are put to the Trade,
And all the Difficulty is to teach the most Stupid Beast in the world
a Multitude, to shew tricks, and manage like a great Horse; War
is the Rudest and most Barbarous thing, in the world, yet nothing
is more confin'd to Rules and Order, which to transgres ever so 5
little, though for the better, is pernicious, and unpuni'st in one
particular prove's distructive to the whole. Ther is nothing that
requires less ingenuity nor more, for all the necessary Judgment ly's
in the generall and the Invention and Fancy in his Councell: the
rest is but clockworks that go's as it is set.   10

The Breed of Mankind is Naturally less able to help it selfe as **208**ʳ
soon as they are producd into the world, then those of any other 'B'
Creatures: And Divines say so are all men, by the Assistance that
Nature gives them, untill they are New-born, and Rectifyd by the
Supernatural and Divine Improvment of Grace from above.   15

Geometry is the only Science, that it hath pleasd God hitherto
to bestow on Mankind. Hobs Leviathan Cap 4 p. 15.

Men usd to apply their fingers of one or both hands to those
things they desird to keepe accompt of; And thence it proceeded
that now our Numeral words are but Ten in any Language. idem.   20

Germans Authors of Gentry, and Herauldry which is found in
no Cuntry, where it hath not been Planted by them. idem.

The life of Man is like a Candle, that either Burnes out of self,
or is put out by Accident. ℬ.

If Mankind were but Immortal what wickednes would it for-   25
beare to Commit, that in this wretched Condition, is not Deterd
from attempting these horrible Impieties.

Law is but a Rule, and Equity an Exception to it.

His Grandfather when he came to be —— was forcd to change the

4 is the] the *om. B*   in the] *altered from* yet B   6 one] on B   8 requires]
requir[ ] / B   11 Breed] *or possibly* Brood B   17 Hobs . . . 15.] *probably*
interlined B   27 these] *or* those B

Religion He had been bred up in to conform to that of his People because he found it Impossible otherwise to Injoy the Crown. But he thinke's to do it a way quite Contrary, and to acquire the —— by a way that would utterly Deprive him of it, if he had it.

5   Fire is in Its Nature Invisible, for it was never seen but in Something that Burnes unless in Flints, which the Antients may seeme to have meant by Elementall Fire, for it was nonsense in any other apprehension.

Water's the clepsydra of the world.

10   Reliques, Crosses, Holy-water. Fumes, Spels, Charms, Exorcisms, Whips. Pictures. Crucifixes. Beades. Medals. Rosaries. Charecters. Circles. Antimagique. Censers. Indulgences Bel. Booke. and Candle. Grimoires. Curses. Bead rols. Inchantments. Coules. Pixes.

15   He was Begotten in Sodomy. Son of an Arse.

Monsters are cal'd so from being showne.

The Jewish women were so wide That their Husbands were sayd to go into them.

It is a Dangerous thing to flesh men as you may see in the little
20   French Lawyer in the 3d Act about the 4th or 5t Sceane, who being by Accident fleshd beat all those who had beaten him before in all his life time; So the last Duke of Burgundy cald Charls the bold &c In the Body of the Epigram.

There is a kinde of Fatall Necessity that Causes all great Towns
25   to increase Bigger Perpetually, For the next Grounds that border upon the Buildings being by the multitude of Inhabitants trodden down and renderd of no valew, the owners are necessitated to get leave to build them &c.

---

3 acquire] acqure *B*   4 Deprive] Deprve *B*   9 *Written on the same line as l.*
8 *B*   clepsydra] *possibly altered to* Clepsydra *B*   17–18 *Interlined B*
17 Husbands were] Husbands we *B*   18 into] *or* in / to *B*   22 of] o[ ] *B*
23 In . . .] *possibly a separate passage B*

The Fortunes of Sir W. C. and his Brother, strangely raysd, by **208ᵛ**
being of the same Name with one, who had no Name of his owne, **'B'**
And did but Reward them for having made use of theirs.

There is Pedler's Latin, as wel as Pedlers French.

French men now are the same thing to the English Nation, the 5
Jews were heretofore, or the Greeks to the old Romans, only
Liberall Arts, and Sciences exepted.

As Sleep was intended by Nature, to Repair, and Restore her
Defects, so our last Sleeps have the same effects upon our Soules,
and Bodys, when they are divided as when they were united, and 10
conjoynd together.

It was none of the Meanest of Domitians Tyrannys, That he
hated Learned Men and Banish'd all Philosophers from Rome,
as the most unfit of all men for his Inhuman Purposes. As the Lady
that made a Lampoon upon him, complaind, when she faithfully 15
foretold the vengeance that befel him afterwards.

The Historian of Gresham Colledge, Indevors to Cry down
Oratory and Declamation, while He uses nothing else.

Wee finde little Mention of Pictures to the Life of the Antients.
But nothing frequenter, then their Statues, which were sayd to be 20
more Numerous in Old Rome then the Living People.

Perhaps There may be the Same natural Harmony, and Discord
in Cullors among themselves, as there is in Musical Notes, which
the French virtuosi have made some Observations upon, in their
Reflexions upon the mixtures of Cullors in Pictures: And if our 25
Abler Greshamites would but undertake, they might (no doubt) in
time, not only, Discover many Rare Secrets in Nature, but be Able
to Prick Notes, and Sing 'em, in Cullors only; As Heraulds can (at
the same Price, and Ease) Blazon Coates of Arms, from Planets, and

---

5 *Editor's paragraph*   8 Sleep] Sleep. *B*   9 Defects,] Defects. *B*
10 and Bodys] and .. Bodys *B*   18 Declamation,] Declamation. *B*   22 natural]
interlined B   26 Greshamites] Grsshamites *B*   27–28 but . . . only] *under-lined by Longueville B*

Pretious Stones, with Fields of Gold and Silver, down to Red
Lattices, and Dogs turds Proper. Beside it might serve for an
Excellent New way to convey Intelligence and such as can never
be Discoverd, as Musical Notes, and Figures have been

5   when Statesmens Cifers have been Song or Fidled,
              and yet by cuning cabalist unriddled.

      All the Gallantry of Cloaths began with Figleaves, and was
brought to Perfection with Mulbery Leavs.

      The holy Ghost that first fel upon the Apostles in the Shape of
10 Cloven Tongues, Did but tell them, that they should speak all
Languages which before they never had been taught to understand,
and by that miraculous meanes convert Some of all Sorts, to the
Christian Faith, and disperse it over all the Face of the Earth, as the
Division of Tongues had made all mankind to do at the Building of
15 Babilon: so Punctuall is Divine Justice to cure the wounds it has
inflicted, like the weapon-Salve, by the same way and method that
it usd before to give them.

209ʳ   Spanish Morisco, or Irish Fingalian, [were] more Proper for
'B' Cheats to Cant and Juggle with, to amuse the Rabble then to con-
20 taine the Principles of so great a Science and all with more Brevity
then a Shorthand Alphabet and more anomalous then a Conjurers
Presto begon, or Hum and Buz: And yet the Ignorance of this Insignificant Jabbering renders all the Professors of Law utterly incapable of arriveing at any Perfection in the Mystery. So certaine it
25 is that a Science that is composd of nothing else but Rules, should
have nothing Regular in its Institution. And the Greatest verbosity
in the world should begin with the Study of no Language, or at
least with the Study of so rude and Barbarous a Dialect as is worse
then None. For as they Render the Latin insignificant by Dashing
30 and sinking the Last Syllable of every word: So they debauch the
French as Impertinently, by over-pronouncing every letter in a

2 Proper.] Proper / B   5–6 *Editor's lineation*   7–8 *Duplicated B*
227ᵛ   7 Figleaves] Fig-leaves B 227ᵛ   8 Mulbery leavs] Mulbery-leavs
B 227ᵛ   9 Apostles] Apostle B   11 been] [ ]en B   13 over all]
over the all B   24–26 So . . . Institution] *underlined by Longueville B*
25 composd of] *interlined B*   27 should begin with] *altered from* has its original
from B   30 debauch] *altered from* render B   31 Impertinently] *altered from*
Impertinent B

word, which that Nation is wont purposely to omit to avoyd the harshnes of the Sound, and so Disguise and alter what they steal or Borrow from other Nations, that the Right owners understand nothing of their own Goods and Chattles, when they chance to light upon them again. And yet they are so Nice and scruplous to omit no 5 formal Circumstance though but in the Addition to a Name (as Squire for Knight and Knight for Baronet) that the least Error or Mistake make's the whole Busnes, many times, miscarry and Abate; While Real Errors in the Names of things in Question, as unum vestigium Anglice a Footstoole, is excusd by the Anglice and Passes 10 for good in Law and latin. In somuch that I have heard some esteemd no mean Sages in the Law, Affirme that the greatest Security Men have to the Titles of their Estates is that their Evidences are in their own Power and Keeping which if they were but Publiquely exposd not one in twenty, would hold out for Good in Law, which 15 is one Reason they are wont to Produce in Parlaments against Publique Registers in al Counties, which they would never do, if they believd themselves, That they would multiply Suits in Law by being layd open To evry mans view and Censure. And all this is the tru Reason why they have advancd so little in their Profession that 20 their best Authors and Oracles of their Knowledge and Science, are only such as livd heretofore in the most Ignorant, and Barbarous Ages. And the only man of their Profession who undertook to Advance all other Arts, and Sciences, could ad nothing to his own, as others Famous men since by attempting things beyond their 25 Latitude have Sufficient shewn their Ignorance, and want of Judg-ment, and thrown away all that Fame and Reputation, (by dabling in other Professions) which they Purchacd Right or wrong in their own. 29

The Greatest Concern of Meum and Tuum, Ly's in Hoc est **209**^v
Corpus Meum. 'B'

No doubt weavers and other Artificers have as many Famous Authors among them in their Severall ways, as the Learned, though the Memory of their Famous Men is better Preservd by Dealing in

5 scruplous] *or* scrupelous *B*   10 vestigium] *altered from* scabellum *B*
11 and latin] *interlined B*   13 of] *altered from* to *B*   17–18 which . . . them-
selves] *underlined by Longueville B*   18 by] *altered from* be *B*   24 own,]
own *B*   27 away] aw[   ] *B*   29. 1 [fo. 209^v] ⟨G after N is to be
Pronounct in one Syllable⟩ *B*

writings then the others that only Passe by Tradition from Hand to Hand, and are in a Short time forgoten.

If you had but considerd how much wit and Reason go's to Civility and Good Manners as wel as Nature and Morality: you would never have trusted one that is voyd of all.

Whether there be a Supererrogation of Merits in the Saints as the Church of Rome Hold's, is too Silly, to be made a Question without the Allowance of Reasons that are not to be ownd: But that there is a Supererrogation of wickednes and Damnation in the world, is too manyfest, to be doubted.

He would not be in his Coat at the Day of Judgment.——will so cudgel him, He had better ly still in the Grave, and never Rise.

Singing and a voyce are but winde Musique.

It is wel for the English Nation, That our Common-Lawyers do not understand the Idiom, and Propriety of the Latin-Tongue, for If they did, they would be furnist with more Ambiguitys in the Syntaxis and Construction of it, such as Aio te Æacida Romanos &c Then they would ever be able to determine. But by dealing in a Language which they do not understand, and by Dashing and abreviating the last Syllables of all words, in which the whole Sence of that Language only consist's, They Preserve the old Simplicity of Speaking Barbarously, But meaning more fairly then they are aware. For Having agreed upon a Use and Signification of words though ever So Diffrent from their Original Sense and Meaning, The Skilfullest Lawyers in that Tongue are so far from having any Advantage over the most Ignorant, that they are faine to submit and Conforme to their allowd-of Errors. The same things, and worse may be sayd of their French, a mere Fustian Jargon which no Part of Mankind meddles with, but themselves, whom it serve's only for Tearmes of Art, though words of noe manner of Intention; and yet is sufficient to Containe in so short, and rude a Compass, the greatest, and most Difficult Curiositys, (as they say) of all Human

Sense and Reason, like Lullys Ars brevis which none but children or those who had been twice such, Ignorant old Dotards were ever the wiser for, And yet those of the Dullest Capacitys are able to instruct themselves in, without the Assistance of a Tutor: a Broken Gibberish that has no Part of Speech in it, like Spanish morisco.   5

One that has a Strange old-fashiond understanding.   **210ʳ**
                                                                        'B'

Complainants are the greatest Persecutors.

Evry man, that live's to it, is twice a child but the first is much better then the last, for there is hope he may outlive the first but never the last.   10

One that's Inimitable at deposing and the Ablest of all men.

The English who were before a Sober Nation learnd Drunkennes of the Duch by assisting them in the wars of the Low Cuntrys. Baker p 518.

He that has a House and fishponds in a Park dwels like a Mouse 15 in a cheese, and in a smal time without a great Estate, eate's himself out of it.

Printers finde by experience that one Murther is worth two Monsters, and at least three walking Spirits. For the Consequence of Murther is hanging, with which the Rabble is wonderfully de- 20 lighted. But where Murthers and walking Spirits meet, there is no other Narrative can come neare it.

Dryden weighs Poets in the Virtuoso's Scales that will turne with the hundredth part of a Graine, as Curiously as Juvenals Lady-Pædantesse   25

> Committit vates, et comparat inde Maronem
> Atque alia parte, in trutina suspendit Homerum.

He complaynd of B Johnson for stealing 40 Sceanes out of Plautus.—
Set a Thief to finde out a Thief.

---

3 for,] for. *B*   4 in,] in: *B*   Tutor:] Tutor *B*   6 understanding.]
understanding *B*   7 *Editor's paragraph*   9 outlive the] outlive ⟨that but⟩
the *B*   20 of] *altered from* is *B*   24 Graine,] Graine. *B*   26-7 *Interlined*
alongside l. 25 *B*   28-9 *Interlined below ll.* 25-7 *B*

Our Saviour wore his Coate without a Seame because he would have nothing to do with a Tayler. The Jewes in any Publique Calamity tore their Garments to signify their Detestation of him, And Elias when he was taken up to heaven, left his Mantle behinde
5 because it was made by a Tayler and therefore not fit to be carryd up to Heaven.

There is no one Originall Author of any one Science among the Antients known to the world (and therefore they were faine to father all Mechanique Inventions upon some God or other) for the
10 old Philosophers stole all their Doctrines from some others that were before them, as Plato from Epichamus and as Diognes Laertius say's, Homer stole his Poems out of the Temple of Vulcan in Ægypt where they were kept, and sayd to have been written by a woman, and from him and Ennius Virgil is sayd to have stolen his. Nor did
15 they so much as improve what they found, which the modernes have don to admiration, Charlton excepted who has only drawn bad Copies of Excellent originals.

The most Prodigious of all Miserable Sinners use to flock to Jubilees to pertake of those Indulgences, which are not to be
20 dispenc'd at any other time and occasion and of such as those, and Ignorant Fops is that great Concourse of People generally made up.

One that can raise 10000 Pepper-Cornes by the yeare upon Demand.

The Pleasure of having narrowly escapd the Gallows is so great
25 that malefactors never remember the horrid feares that went before it, more then Gamsters do the Agonys of Loosing, compard to the extacys of wining, and therefore both Rogues are the easier inclynd to run the same hazards again.

There is no Prince that would deny his Subjects Liberty of Con-
30 science if it were in his Power to grant it, without violating the Law of selve-preservation; for it being the Nature of all Sects (like other

2 Tayler.] Tayler *B*   3 him,] him *B*   8 world (and] *superimposed on* world, and *B*   9 some] *altered from* the *B*   other)] *superimposed on* other, *B* 10 Doctrines] *altered from* Opinions *B*   14 his.] his *B*   16 admiration,] admiration / *B*   22–3 *Added on the same line as l.* 21 *B*   22 One] one *B* 27 wining,] wining. *B*   Rogues] *interlined B*

vermine) to increase and multiply, there is no Religion that can become the most Numerous but do's Naturally incline to suppress or destroy all others, and to give way to that, is to take part with such as indevour to subvert the Government.   4

Mr Hobs his Doctrine that advise's evry man to understand and **210ᵛ**
unriddle all others by comparing them with himself, is very false: 'B'
for whosoever do's it Justly and syncerely shall finde thousands of things but good, or Bad that are not in himself at all.

There is nothing more Ridiculous then the Friendships of Club-Caballers, for as they have all the same Designes, to make their own 10
Particular Advantages, whosoever has the good Fortune to get any thing, is condemn'd and abhominated by all the Rest, as if they lost, what he has acquir'd. And he in Return disdaine's and Scornes them as much.

The Grӕcians were such great Drinkers, that the Antientest of 15
their Philosophers and Divines (who were not unlike the British and Gallique Bards) made the Founders of their Noblest Families, to be the Sons of Rivers, and their finest Ladies Nimphs of Lakes and Fountaines.

There is no Question but the Commonwealth of the Romans was 20
the worst constituted Government of all others, and yet it had the Advantage of all in acquiring the Greatest Empire that ever was. And this their owne perpetuall Divisions at home produc'd, which (arising from the evill Constitution of their Government) renderd them incapable of preserving Peace at home longer, then they were 25
diverted by Foraine wars. And therefore when they had no wars abroad they always fell in to Civill wars or Tumults, untill the greatest and last, reduc'd their Government into an absolut Tyranny.

Poets that write to the Stage, and Mountebanks that Quack to it, 30
use the same Course in Disparaging, and perpetuall Rayling at all others of the same profession with themselves.

4 such as] *altered from* that B   Government] Governm[   ] B   5 evry]
altered probably from al B   7 syncerely] sycerely B   12 all] as B
14 much] muc[ ] B   23 And] and B   26 wars.] wars B   27 Tumults,]
Tumults. B   31 Disparaging, and] Disparaging ⟨and Rayling⟩, and B

Naturall in the Sense of the People signifys Foolish and Ignorant and unnatural wicked.

Presbytery is but a Religion of the French Fashion, as the greatest part of all our vanities and Follys are, as well as our Cloaths, and it
5 came to us from Scotland which has in all ages Correspondence with France against England, but never did us so much mischief as when they introducd that.

In all our wars with France, wee never had so great advantage by our Leagues with Burgundy and other Neighboring Princes, as the
10 French gain'd by the Asistance of the Scots, who were always True and Constant to them, and implacable Enemies to us, while our forrain Cofederates never fayld to betray us. And yet the English, when they were well conducted, were able at the same time, not only to incounter, but subdue all three together, though the Scots
15 sent such great supplys into France, that they obtain Priviledges beyond the Natives, and always ingagd here upon our Backs.

If the king had but half so many legitimate Sons, as he has illegitimate it would be farre more Pernicious to the Nation, for it would lay in Provision for Rebellion and allterations of Governments
20 for many hundreds of years: as may be observd by the effects of that Numerous Issue of our Edward the third.

Ovids Metamorphosis was when it was first written a wondrous Pious and Religious Book And no less designd to improve the Interests of Piety and Religion in those times, then Legend, and
25 other Ecclesiasticall Historys have been since: For as the Poet indeavors to deterr men from Impiety by the example of those who for their Irreligion have been turnd into Beasts and Trees and Stones &c So do the other indeavor to rayse men as much above Humanity
29 by as strange and miraculous Stories.

211ʳ   Æsop taught the world Morality a better way then Ovid who
'B'   turnd men into Beasts and trees to make them wise. But Æsop

3 a] *interlined* B   6 England,] *altered from* England. B   6–7 but . . .]
interlined B   13 able] abler W   17 has] has: B   27 Beasts] Birds W
28 men] *altered from* them B

turnd Beasts and Trees into Men, and make's them say wiser things
then they could do before their first or second Transformation, or
Conversion.

Great Counsels have always been tender of taking Notice of the
Personall Imperfections, or Extravagancys of Princes untill they 5
grow intollerable to the Publique, and then they break out with all
Impetuous violence imaginable and evry Man strive's who shall
aggravate them most: and the more modest and reservd they were
before they become the more Implacable.

Libels and Lampoones are but a kinde of Morall Representations 10
that only Rally and Rhime Treason, for which they are Commonly
Contemn'd and slighted, as things in Jeast, though they do more
hurt then all the Dull earnest of vulgar Mutiners; for they spread
like News, and all Pretenders to wit, and Intelligence hold it a
Disparagment to their Parts to be unfurnishd of them, in which all 15
men seeme to bee so much concernd, that nothing passes so safely
under the Rose, and Seal of Secresy (for though they pass through
so many hands, the Right Authors are seldom or never Discoverd)
But all men keepe Counsel more true and faithfully then those who
are bound by the strictest Oaths, and among the Rest, many (no 20
doubt) who are obligd by oath to reveale them. For as they are but
Prologues to all Tragedies or Comedys of State, So they are fitted to
the Humors of all People who are to sit as Judges, or Spectators of
the following Acts and Sceanes. And as they are more True then
Panigyriques so they are capable of doing Princes more good, (for 25
Panegyriques being nothing but Polite Flattery never did any) if
rightly considerd, and like Charmes easily Cure those Fantastique
Distempers in Governments, which being neglected grow too stub-
born to obey any but as Rigid Medecines.

This Parlament ha's supplyd the k—— with money, as usurers 30
use to do yong Heirs, to get a hold upon their Estates, which they
believe they now have, and therefore will venture no more money
till they have an accompt of what ha's been already receivd. In the

7 evry] ev'ry *W*   12 slighted,] slighted. *B*   13 Mutiners;] Mutiners.
B   17 Secresy (for] *superimposed on* Secresy; for *B*   18 Discoverd)] *super-*
imposed on Discoverd. *B*   20 bound . . . Oaths] *underlined by Longueville B*
21 by oath] *interlined B*   27 and] *altered from* for *B*

mean time the Nation is like to be in the Condition of those Tenants, who when their differing Landlords disput their Titles, are wont to be distrain'd by both sides: and which soever prevayle's, they are sure to the Arrieres and Costs and Damages of all. For though Parlaments may defend the Liberties and Rights of the People against the Incroachments of Princes, as the Saxons did the Britans against the Picts, and all Mercenarys have ever don to those they have protected, yet if they get those Liberties once into their own Hands, they cannot possibly be so certainly and inevitably utterly destroyd any other way. For it is a Contradiction against the Nature of Liberty to be safe in the Handes, or Disposing of any one Power (More then the Poores Box is under one Churchwardens Key). And therefore when the long Parlament last had it, they were forcd to Juggle and Convey it into the Imaginary Custody of the invisible Keepers of the Liberties that is their own, where it was no Safer then it was before: for Oliver found it out though invisible and got it from them, And the Rump, from him, and the Safty from them, but no Powr was able to keepe it, for like Sejanus his Horse it was always fatally Distructive to all those who had the vanity and Ambition to become owners of it.

The long Parlament to secure the Liberties of the People from themselves, hid them in the invisible Hands of those Fayries the Keepers of the Libertys. But Oliver stormd [the] Inchanted Castle, and tooke the Lady into his own Protection, &c.

211ᵛ Cleargy-men cannot abide that lay-men should meddle with their **'B'** Trade, or offer to interpret Scripture, lest having no shares in the Advantages of their Profession they should lessen the Interests of it.

As the Goaths and Vandalls destroyd Civility, before they learnd it: so did the Saxons roote out the Christian Religion of the Britans, and afterwards became the most Zealous Professors of it, as appeares by vast Numbers of Monasterys which they founded, in which a greater Number of their Kings and Queenes and Princes and Nobility, renouncd the world and livd Monastique lives.

2 to] be B   4 Arrieres and] *interlined* B   7 to] *interlined* B   8 protected,] protected) B   12 Power (More] *superimposed on* Power, More B   12–13 More . . . Key] *underlined by Longueville* B   15 invisible] *interlined* B   16 found . . . invisible] *interlined* B   16–17 invisible and] invis[   ] B   17 them,] them B   23 stormd] storm[   ] B   [the]] *MS. damaged* B   26 Trade,] Trade. B   28 learnd] leärd B   30 it,] it. B

God Almighty do's not oblige men to be Religious for his owne sake but for theirs that by interposing his Authority he might ingage them to be good and Just, and especially kinde to one another, for it is below that Reverence that is due to his Divine Majesty to suppose that he can be concernd in their weak and insignificant Opinions, further then they conduce to their own Peace, and Quietnes.

There were never any Twins produc'd in Egs, that I could heare of.

Sir I am your Organum Animatum that is (according to Aristotle), your humble Servant.

A Footman is a Jument, and a Porter a two legd Beast of Carriage.

Sir are you you or your Brother? A. Sir I am my Brother. Q. your Pardon. Pray tell your Brother I would speak with you.

Colebert might better have deriv'd his Name from Collibertus a Quondam fellow servant then from Coluber.

Like him that greasd his File to make it Cut the easier, such is a Rugged mans Civilitie.

Leachery in our times is like a Dutch Reconning, not according to the value of the Treat, but the Quality of the Person treated.

> The gay and Pleasant Seasons of the yeare
> Maintain the Rigid and Severe.

The Ancients did wisely to discribe the Furys in the Persons of women.

Those who have attempted to deal in universalls, never perform any thing, as universall Charecters Languages, Medcins, and measures all met with the same success that is none at all; for as universalls are never producd nor dy, nec cruintur nec intereunt, and

Aristotle says they prove nothing, so they never come to any thing, and in probability never will.

It is the Nature of almost all Men to indure nothing against their own Humours, and rather indanger their Safety, then submit to any thing against their Inclinations, unless compeld by Necessity or force. And those Princes that use such Courses teach their Subjects by their example to take more Liberty then perhaps they otherwise would have don, and when they have once contracted a Sullen aversenes to the Government they live under, they will rather expose themselfes to the greatest Dangers imaginable, then contribute the smallest matter to their own Defence and preservation, though in nothing so Prodigall and lavish as in maintaining whatsoever they have a will and Inclination to. And this never appeard more then in the late Civill warr by the [great complaints] that were made against the Shipmoney before, and the vast Sums brought in voluntarily [   ] to rayse [levies] against the Government.

212^r   All Apologies, and publique Defences of Private Persons com-
'A'   monly doe them more hurt then Good, for the world is always apt and inclind to take Part with the worst Sense, and as in Signing of writings he that take's of the Seale, is alway understood to put it on, Soe he that endeavors to excuse himselfe openly, for somthing that is but secretly suspected, and not commonly knowne, doe's but divulge it, and expose himselfe to more and harder Censures then he could possibly have incurd by being Silent.

Catholiques glory much in the Antiquity of their Church, and yet there is noe Religion of Christians more unlike the most antient then theirs. The moderne Fanatiques dispise Antiquity, cry up new lights, and yet perhapes come nearest to the outward forme of the Primitive times.

The world is soe naturally wicked that the best things of it are

11 preservation,] preservation. *B*   12 though] *altered from* And th *B*   as] and *B*   14, 16 *Parentheses*] *MS. damaged B*   15 before,] before. *B*   16 voluntarily] volu[ ]tarily *B*   Government] Govermnent *B*   16. 1–3 [fo. 212^r] *See p. 28, ll. 9–11*   17–p. 167, l. 3 *Underlined lightly B*   17 *Editor's paragraph*   20 alway] always *W*   23 more and] *interlined B*   24 Silent.] Silent: *B*   25 *Editor's paragraph*   28 forme] forms *W*   30 *Editor's paragraph*

forcd to depend upon the evill. Most of the most noble Monuments
of Piety and Devotion, were erected at first for expiation of some
horrid Crimes of the Founders.

Hypocrisie is the most odious of all Sins and yet it is soe necessary
in Church affaires that nothing can be don without it.   5

The greatest Estimation that wisdom and knowledg have depends most upon the Ignorance of those that doe not understand
what it is. If the true Reasons of all great Affayrs were commonly
known, they would appeare soe slight and triviall, that the Rabble
would Scorne and dispise that which with reverence they now 10
submit to.

There can be noe great Glory that is not purchacd by the opposition, removeal or distruction of some great evill, and without that,
the other had never been. What would Physique or Law signify if
there were noe Diseases, nor Injurys in the world? what were all the 15
Curious Inventions, and rare manefactures in the world worth, if it
were not for the Vanity, Pride, Avarice, Curiosity or wants of men?
what use would there be of wealth, if there were noe such things as
Ambition Covetousnes and Luxury? what were Truth and Reason
good for, if there were noe Frauds and Falsitys to discover?   20

In the time of the Apostles, wee finde that the greatest part of
those that were present, and eie witnesses of the miracles which
they wrought, continued obstinate, and unconvincd, while those
that only heard them related were converted by thousands at a time.

If the Thiefe that was Crucifyd with Christ, had not committed 25
that robbery for which he was condemd, he had not had the
happines (for any thing wee know) to have been so soone in
Paradice.

There are more that perish by having too much, then too little, for thousands dy of Luxury and Surfets for one that starve's or dy's of famine.

Noe men are more unsatiable at getting of Riches then those that are the most sparing, and easiest satisfyd in the use of it.

5   The more Pleasure men enjoy the lesse Sensible they are of it, and when they have lost all Appetite to it, there is noe way soe certaine to recover it againe as by abstinence, and to obtaine what they would have, by avoyding it.

All those that are of a Profession, seldom make use of that them-
10 selves which they prescribe to others, as Lawyers goe seldomest of all men to Law, Physitians as seldom take Physique themselves, and Preachers that undertake to teach other men, Piety and holinesse of life, doe most seldom rayse any use to themselves out of their owne Doctrine, but dispence with them selves for having noe thing to
15 doe with that which they presse soe earnestly upon others.

212ᵛ   Men commonly in the world have noe regard for thinges how
'A' considerable soever, but highly afect words and names that serve only to expresse them, have an earnest Desire to be thought wise and Learned, and good, and Pious, but care not at all to be soe
20 indeed, call themselves evry mans Servant and desire to appeare useful and obliging to all they converse with, but of all thinges in the world, abhor to be really soe. And when they undertake to give a Reason for any thing believe they have performd it sufficiently as soone as they have put it into other, though lesse significant expres-
25 sions, and the more obscure these are, believe them to be the more learned although in that, which they call Learning, for one Notion that is obscure by haveing a remote Sense, there are hundreds that are soe for haveing none at all. Those That are calld by ignominious Names which they doe not deserve, and consequently can suffer
30 nothing by them, are neverthelesse more concernd and provokd, then those are to whom they are due, and never light in vaine, as if

3 *Editor's paragraph*   5 *Editor's paragraph*   7 recover] *altered from* recovery *B*   11 Law, Physitians] Law, ⟨and⟩ Physitians *B*   17 afect words] afect ⟨the⟩ words *B*   and names] *interlined B*   20 indeed,] indeed. *B*
21 useful] *altered from* Civill *B*   25 these] *altered from or possibly to* they *B*
28 ignominious] ign[ ]minious *B*   30 neverthelesse] never the lesse *W*

a man could be wounded that is impenetrable, and he that is naked unhurt. Soe when they would redresse any Publique supposd inconvenience, as soone as they have chang'd the Names and outward formalities, believe the Busnes is done; as our Reformers when they abolishd Episcopacy Roote and branch; They set up Presbytery in ⁵ the Roome of it with ten times more power and opportunity, of doing the same things, which they sought to remedy and secure the Nation against in suppressing Bishops.

The more usefull and necessary things are, the lesse they are generally esteem'd, and the cheaper the Labours of those valu'd ₁₀ that are imploy'd about them, as Agriculture Building, and most of the usefullest manifactures (without which humane life would want many Conveniences) are accompted noe better then Drudgeries, while any thing that is of noe use but to satisfy the Humor Caprich, vanity or mistake or Pleasure of the world is in great esteeme, and ₁₅ noe reward thought too much for those that spend their time and study about them.

In the times of the late Civil warre, I remember most men were more curious nice and scrupulous of subscribing the Engagement though but a Civill Promise, and such as they were compeld by ₂₀ necessity to observe and performe without that obligation, which extended noe further then to live quietly under the present government as long as it should continue soe establishd; then they were of taking and breaking the Covenant, though a solemne vow made to Almighty God. ₂₅

Thieves, and Robbers are more true and faythfull to one another, and just among themselves, though bound by noe obligation, then other Partners and dealers in lawfull Callings can be compeld to with all the Authority and rigor of Law and Justice.

Some write that Apelles drew a Picture of a Boy bearing a bunch ₃₀

1 is impenetrable] is ⟨unhurt and⟩ impenetrable *B*   1–2 naked unhurt] naked ⟨and wounded⟩ unhurt *B*   5 abolishd] *or possibly* abolist; abolis[ ] *B*   9–17 *Underlined roughly B Editor's paragraph*   13 Drudgeries,] Drudgeries. *B* 17 about] abou[ ] *B*   18 *Editor's paragraph*   19 more] *interlined B*   curious nice] curious ⟨and⟩ nice *B*   subscribing] *altered from* taking *B*   Engagement] *probably altered from* Covenant *B*   22 the] *altered from* that *B*   23 establishd;] *comma altered from full point B*   25 God.] God: *B*   26–p. 170, l. 7 *Underlined roughly B*   26 *Editor's paragraph*   30 *Editor's paragraph*

of Grapes soe Naturally to the life, that Birds mistaken flew upon the Table to peck at them. If it be true the Boy was not soe well drawne as the Grapes, otherwise the Birds would have been afrayd to come soe neare him.

5   Estridges and Peacocks that have the finest feathers, fly worst of all other Birds, and fishes that have the finest painted [scales] have noe eies to see them.

213ʳ   The Turkish Historys report that when Soliman the Emperor had
'A'   commanded his Son Mustapha to be strangled, and his Mutes were
10   slow in the performance of soe Cruel a Task that he lookd through a windore in his Tent, and with furious words calld upon them to dispatch, which was very strang if they could not heare. If fishes cannot heare how could Lucullus his Lamprys come to hand when they were cald by their Names? or Arion in the Fable charme the
15   Dolphin to carry him on his Back?

    Among Goverments Monarchy has in the manage and practice of it more of Commonwelth, and Commonwelth more of Monarchy, then either have of what they are cald. For noe Monarch can possibly Governe alone, but must of Necessity submit and be ruled
20 by the advice, and Counsell of others; And in the Senates of Republiques some one Commonly governes all the rest, and has that really in power, which Princes have but in Name. Soe in the Church of Rome The Pope who is the absolutest Monarch in the whole world owe's all his Power to a forme of Comonwelth, for he come's to it by
25 election noe otherwise then the Duke of Venice do's to his; and though he Stile's himselfe Gods Servants Servant, lay's clame to a Dominion over the whole world.

    They that say the world grows worse and worse, are very much mistaken, for Adam who had but one Commandment to keep broke
30 that, and Cain slew his brother Abel when there was but two of them to share the whole world.

2 If] if B   5 *Editor's paragraph*   6 Birds,] Birds. B   [scales]]
MS. damaged B   10 through] throug[ ] / B   16–22 . . . in the] *underlined B Editor's paragraph*   17–18 Monarchy,] Monarchy. B   19 submit and]
interlined B   20 the Senates] the *interlined B*   22 Princes] Pri[ ] B
26 Gods] *altered from* the B   28–p. 171, l. 4 *Underlined B*   29 *Editor's paragraph*   30 that,] that. B

The nearer men come to Truth, and yet misse of it, the more dangerous their mistake's are, as a Clock that goe's too fast or slow but a little, is apter to deceive, then one that goe's soe notoriously false that nobody regard's it.

Men of great, ready, and luxuriant wits, doe frequently prove more ridiculous then those that are dull, and stupid, and only for want of Judgment which never flourishe's but where it grow's naturally of it selfe, and will not endure to be planted: for there are two sorts of wisemen in the world, the one is of those that are wise in their Tempers, that governe their Actions with a kinde of Prudent Instinct without understanding the reason (unlesse it be implicitly) of what they doe, and those commonly prosper, and live happily in the world: The other sort is of those that understand the reasons perfectly of all things that concerne themselves, and others, but by the unhappiness of their Temper, cannot prevayle with themselvs to make those advantages of their knowledg and understanding, which other men easily doe without it.

The best Laws are made of the worst manners, and the best Lawyers of the worst men. The best Pictures of the worst faces, and the best Cider of the worst Apples. The best Astrologers of the worst Mathematicians, and the best Schoolmen of the worst Schollers. The best Preachers of the worst Divines, and the best Knights of the worst Gentlemen, The best Medcines of the worst Diseases.

The old Pagan Greekes and Romans thought there was noe such way to pacify their Angry Gods, as by publique Playes and Sports; The Jews and Christiens tooke the Contrary Course, and endeavord to make their Peace by strict Penances, fasts, and Punishements inflicted on themselves. The first supposd the Gods were best pleasd with that which they found best pleasd themselves.

There are more Baudy Pictures made of Lucrece, the Martyr of chastity, then ever were of all the Common Prostitutes of all Ages and Nations in the whole world.

1 *Editor's paragraph*   5 *Editor's paragraph*   9 wisemen] wiseemen *altered from* wisdom B   18-24 *Underlined B Editor's paragraph*   21 Mathematicians] Mathematician B   25 *Editor's paragraph*   27 tooke] [ ]ooke B   31-3 *Added in a different ink B Editor's paragraph*   31 more] more. B   and Nations] *altered from* in the B

213ᵛ   Covetous Persons store up Riches to noe purpose but to satisfy
'A'   their Avarice that has noe end, and afflict themselves to possess
that which they are utterly incapable of ever obteining: that is,
Satisfaction. And Soe covetous men are counted Rich though they
5   make noe use at al of their welth, And those times cald the most
ancient in which the world was yongest.

The windes are sayd to sit when they are always in motion, and
Sundials to go when they are fixt to a Place and never stir out of it.

The Scripture says that the President and High Priest Herod and
10   Pilat durst not apprehend Christ openly for feare of the People. And
yet when he was condemnd, and it was referrd to the People
whether he or a Thief should be repreevd, they all (according to
their usual way of proceeding) preferd the Thief and cryd Crucifige.

Cookolds love their wive's children of other men's begetting
15   commonly much better then real Parents doe their own, with al
their Natural Affection.

Great and Notorious Cheates, that doe their busnes to the Purpose, and grow rich by their frauds and Impostures, rather gain
then loose Credit by it, for men are trusted and esteemd in the
20   world by what they have, not what they are.

All Coates of Armes were Defencive, and worn only upon Shields,
and though the ancient use of them is now given over, and men
fight in Querpo, yet the Honor of all Feates of Armes is charg'd
upon them, and those that have done gallant things now, are
25   rewarded with additional bearings in their Shields, which are reputed more honorable in our Times, for serving only at funerals,
then they were when they preservd the lives of men.

o. 1–2 [fo. 213ᵛ] *See p. 175, ll. 16–17*   1 *Editor's paragraph*   Persons] Person *B*
purpose] *altered from* end *B*   3 that which] that ⟨of⟩ which *B*   obteining]]
obteining. *B*   4 And Soe] And ⟨as those times are [those times are *altered
from* that is] cald the Golden Age in which there was noe Gold at all in use⟩ Soe *B*
5 those] *or possibly* these *B*   times] *altered from* Days *B*   most] *interlined B*   6
ancient in] ancient ⟨times⟩ in *B*   in which] *altered from* when *B*   7 *Editor's
paragraph*   always] alway[ ] *B*   9 *Editor's paragraph*   President] Presiden *B*
10 And] and *B*   13 proceeding)] proceeding[ ] *B*   14 *Editor's paragraph*
15 real] *altered from* true *B*   17 *Editor's paragraph*   18 rich] ric[ ] *B*
21 *Editor's paragraph*   and *W*: [ ] *B*   25 with additional] with ⟨an⟩ additional
B   26 more *W*: m[ ] *B*   27 lives] live[ ] *B*

Most of al ancient Military Titles of honor, are derivd from the Names of Common Soldiers and not Commanders, For Knight and Squire are but the appellations of Common men, and Baron is somewhat lesse, and Count but fellow Soldier, and Duke noe more then a file-leader.

A wanton, Idle Peace Naturally produces war, and war is never Quiet until it Beate's it selfe into Peace again.

All the Curious Disputes and Controversies Divine and human in the world are never in possibility to be Determind, but by those that understand nothing at al of them, and for the most part never soe much as heard they were in being, That is Armies.

Noe Man of war is ever thought fit to have the chardg and command of other mens lives, until he has made it appeare that he care's not a Straw for his own.

Navigation the only Art that Almighty God himself taught Mankinde for the Preservation of it self, is since perverted to a quite Contrary Purpose and renderd the most dreadful way of Distruction, that ever was Practicd in the world.

Insects and Serpents the feeblest of all kindes of animals, destroy more certainly then the Fiercest Beasts of Prey; for the wounds of Scorpions Tarantulas Vipers and Rattle-snakes, &c are more difficult to be cur'd then those of Lions and Tigers. For smal vermin are arm'd with Poysons, and great Beasts with force.

The greatest Sea's are always the Calmest, and the smallest Straights, and Gulphs soonest stird with stormes, and most dangerously armd with hidden rocks that ly in ambush to devour what the fierce windes and fiercer waves cast upon them.

The Papists say they believe as the Church believs, and the **214ʳ**

1 *Editor's paragraph*   3–4 somewhat *W*: some[   ] *B*   4 Count but] Count ⟨is⟩ but *B*   Soldier,] Soldier. *B*   and Duke] and *interlined B*   Duke noe] Duke ⟨indeed and Marques are the Names⟩ noe *B*   5 file-leader.] file-leader; *B*   6 *Editor's paragraph*   8 *Editor's paragraph*   human] huma[ ] *B*   12–14 *Underlined roughly B Editor's paragraph*   13 mens] me[ ] *B*   14. 1–5 *See p. 175, ll. 25–8*   15 *Editor's paragraph*   17 dreadful] dreadf[ ] *B*   19 *Editor's paragraph*   20 wounds] wound[ ] *B*   21 Vipers] *interlined B*   Rattle-snakes, &c] Rattle-snakes, ⟨are⟩ &c *B*   22 Lions] Lion[ ] *B*   24 *Editor's paragraph*   25–6 dangerously] dangerou[ ] *B*   27 waves] wave *B*; wavs *W*

'Aa' Protestant's laugh at them for it; but do the very same thing themselves; all the Difference is, the first believe by wholesale, and the
last by Retaile. The Papists believe some thing, but they know not
what. The Protestant believ's this, or that, but he know's not what
5 it is. The Papist believ's what he cannot understand without
examination: The Protestant will examine (though he cannot understand) before he wil believe: So that though they differ in words,
they agree in the same thing. The Protestant will not allow the
Scripture to be read in an unknown Tongue, but is content to have
10 it read in an unknown Sense, which is all one. They wil not have
God discribd to the eie in any corporeall Shape, but are willing he
should be expresd to the eare, by several Parts of mans Body, as it
is frequently found in the Scripture.

Among our Perrs of the Realme, Those that have Honors entayld
15 on their Posterity, are cald, Lords Temporal, That is for the Time
being: And those that have it only for their Lives Lords Spiritual
in opposition to the other.

All things lessen to the eie at distance, but increase to the Fancy
at the greater Distance both of Time or Place; For wee admire
20 little things of the Antients, or Moderns that are far off, and
Contemne and Disdaine greater of our own.

Men of the greatest wisdom and those that apply themselves
most to it, commonly make least use of it to their own Purposes:
As those that apply themselves wholy to be Rich, The greater
25 wealth they attaine to, the less use they make of it themselves. But
lay it up for those that come after them, as Learned men do their
knowledges in those writings which they leave behinde them.

The Governments of women are commonly more Masculine then
those of men: For women delight in the Conversation and Practices
30 of men; and men of women. This appeare's by the management of
State Affayrs in the Reigns of Queen Elizabeth, Catharine De
Medices Regent of France, and the Princes of Parma in the Low
Cuntrys, compard with the best of any other Christian Princes of
those times.

35   Men that were born in poore, and barren Cuntrys have commonly

---

1 *Marginal note* 'Aa'] *fo.* headed Contradictions *B*   6–7 understand)] *super-*
imposed on understand, *B*   10 They] *altered from* The *B*   25 attaine to]
altered from gaine *B*   35–p. 175, l. 2 *Duplicated and underlined roughly B* 233ʳ
35 Men] Those *B* 233ʳ   were] are *B* 233ʳ   35–p. 175, l. 1 commonly a] *om. B* 233ʳ

a greater kindenes for their Native Soyles (as the Scotch and welch &c) then those that had their Birth in Rich ones.

No Age ever abounded more with Heroical Poetry then the present, and yet there was never any wherein fewer Heroicall Actions were performd; Nor any though the most Barberous, ever so averse to the Practice of those examples which are dayly set before their eies. That the Best of Romances are now esteemd no better then Palmerins &c.

Fooles are more Serious and Confident in their most gross mistakes and errors, then wise men are in the most probable Truths.

The wisest men in the world are commonly the most foolish in it, and the most foolish the wisest; for the first neglects himself, and all his own conveniences to understand all things: And the last is neither capable nor careful to know any thing but what concerne's himself, and therefore apply's himself wholly to that.

Summarys that Containe most things are always shortest themselves.

We have a more sensible apprehension of Cuntrys Cities and Places which we have only read or heard of, then those wee dayly see and live upon; for although things at a great Distance lessen and vanish to the eie; they do increase by fame and Report to the eare, and the imagination, and the further off in time or place they are, the more admirable they appear in comparison with those things which wee are dayly conversant withall.

No Mechanique Profession is more disdaind then that of Taylers, and yet it should seeme to deserve the greatest honor, for it was first practicd by God almighty him self, for wee read in the Scripture, that he made cloaths for Adam and Eve of the skins of Beasts.

1 Soyles] Soyle *B* 233^r   1–2 (as . . . &c)] *om. B* 233^r   2 had] owe *B* 233^r   in Rich ones] to nobler regions *B* 233^r   11 wisest;] wisest. *B*   15. 1–2 *See p. 184, ll. 6–8*   16–17 *Duplicated B* 213^v   18 We] W[ ] *B*   24 things] th[ ]ngs *B*   25–8 *Duplicated B* 213^v   25 No . . . Taylers] A Taylers Trad is vulgarly most disdaind of any *B* 213^v   26 it . . . honor] there is none more necessary nor any [*interlined*] soe ancient *B* 213^v   27–8 first . . .] instituted like Matrimony in Paradice, and usd by God himselfe next after he made woeman to ma[ke] her and her husband Coats of Skins, after they had try'd to fit themselvs with suites of figleavs *B* 213^v   28. 1–7 *See p. 102, ll. 7–13*

The worst of Emperors have commonly in their first Accesess to Empire appeard Eccellent Princes, but afterward became inhumane Tyrants, as Caligula, Nero, Domitian &c. And the Best of Princes begun their Reigns with the ill opinion and expectation of the world and some Crueltys, untill they had renderd themselves Secure, and afterward prov'd most excellent gentle and benigne Princes, As Augustus, Titus &c.

No Sect of Philosophers ever lasted so long, or propagated so far as that of Pythagoras, although perhaps one of the most extravagant and Sensles of all others.

There is a Trick in Arithmetique by giving a false Number, to finde out a true one. So there is no way to come nearer to Truth then by Fable Allegories and apologues that have no truth at all in them.

Insects are more industrious then Nobler Creatures, and come nearer to the Politie of man in the manner of their Government then either Beasts or Birds or Fishes. For Bees and Ants seem to manage their affayrs with little less reason of State, and more Justice then men, being wholy free from those Distractions which the vices of Avarice Pride and Ambition produce in a Governments.

215ʳ   As for his Similitude between a Great Rich man and a great
'B'   Genius (by which I do not understand what he meanes unless it be his own Talent) It may pass well enough if he will but allowe that such men are oftner cheated and abusd then those of lesser abilitis but it is an ill signe of a Rich man to borrow, and steal, and take up upon Trust all that he can, and the one is as like to breake in his Parts as the other in his Fortune.

The Government never grew extravagant untill the old Party of Reformers began to be worne out.

If St Paules Doctrine, That the unbelieving Husband is sav'd by the Believing wife &c be true; It is the safest way for those to marry that are of Different Religions.

1–7 *Duplicated B* 233ᵛ   1 of Emperors] Princes *B* 233ᵛ   1–3 commonly . . . as] beene the best in the beginings of their Reignes as Tiberius [*interlined*], *B* 233ᵛ 3–6 of . . . Princes] the worst *B* 233ᵛ   7 Titus *B* 233ᵛ: Titus. *B* 214ᵛ   &c] and others *B* 233ᵛ   17 Fishes.] Fishes *B*   19 men,] men. *B*   26 can,] can. *B*

When evry Body, that is, all the Rabble is in a Religion, it is a Shame to Own it.

The Pride of Valets and wayting women is a kinde of Flattery to their Masters and Ladys who take it for nothing but a vainglorious Conceipt of the Happines of their Services.   5

The Insolence and Pride of Clergiemen, serve among the Ignorant, for virtus to improve the Dignity of their Profession.

The habit of Cardinals is as Effeminate as that of whores, and therefore they are the more Proper to be Mayds of Honor to the whore of Babilon.   10

One that was Jealous of his mother.

Now they have establishd their Factory of votes.

Cats are never found to be mad, But Dogs frequently, but no Creature so much as man.

He is an Implacable Enemy to all those who have less or more   15
Impudence then himself As if his own Forehead were the only Standard of Impudence, which the French call Intrepidity. And is bound to the Ilbehavior.

A Pimpes very Imployment is Flattery, And if he have any Guift in Secrecy, He is esteemd, as the Turks do one that is both   20
Eunuch and Mute, as a Person of a Double Capacity.

A Huntsman is but an Auxiliary Hound.

Layd by the Eares in the Pillory.

One of the 9 unworthys.

He fel in Love with a widdow of his own making.   25

11 mother.] mother *B*   12 *Editor's paragraph*   their] thiir *B*   19 *Editor's*
paragraph   21 Person] Per / [ ]on *B*   22 *Editor's paragraph*   23 *Edi-*
tor's paragraph   Pillory.] Pillory *B*   24 *Editor's paragraph*   25 *Editor's*
paragraph

Some outlying whimsy of Bedlam that being tame and Harmles is sufferd to go at Liberty.

The Church of Rome is the mother Church of all the Fanatique Religions in the world, For when they had Corrupted and Debauchd
5 the Christian Religion into the greatest Sottishness and Knavery imaginable, that those who had but any kinde of Sense or Honesty would have nothing to do with it, The hot-headed Fooles came in Afterwards, and ran it into so great an extreame, that they pretend all the Papists do, in the most Careless and spontaneous Actions
10 [which] is to be avoyded by all the Rest of mankinde.

Let the Subtlest men in the world say what they can against wit, it fa[lls as] naturally upon those that have none.

No man ever studyd the Law for its own Sake, but in Contemplation of the [   ] and Preferment that is to be obteynd by those
15 who arrive at any Perfection in [it].

215ᵛ   In all Nations, and Ages, more Persons have been Ruind, and
'B'   undon and destroyd as the Antients Prophets were for fore telling of Truths that have afterwards come to pass, then for venting of Lyes, and the Impostures in the world which the greatest part of
20 Mankinde live and thrive by.

What dos the Right-hand Gaine by being more Active, and useful then the left; But only more Labour and Paines.

If Lawyers understood the Latine tongue Critically, they would finde more occasions to pervert and wrest the Sense of it then now
25 they have, for by applying the meaninge of an Adjective whose construction perfectly agree's with two substantives to which of them they please, they would create matter for perpetual Controversy. The same may be sayd of verbes, whose Syllables have the same letters though different Significations of Time which
30 would furnish them with everlasting Hints to wrangle. All [this]

3 all] a B   5 Knavery] Knavey B   7 it,] it. B   extreame,]
[ ]treame. B   pretend] pretend. B   9 Actions] Acti[ ] B   10, 12, 14,
15 Parentheses] MS. damaged B   12 fa[lls as]] fastens W   naturally] [ ]turally
B   14 the] th[ ] B   18 come to] come-to B   27–8 Controversy. The]
Controversy the B

their Ignorance in Construction, and Dashing the last Syllables of all words (in which the sense and meaning chiefly Ly's) dos only prevent. The like may be inferd from their Barbarous French, which passes well enough among themselves, who have agreed upon it but would spoyl all if it signifyd any thinge else: Like Canting 5 among Beggars, By which it appeare[s] they study in Nonsense, and practice in Sense and Reason, as the Tearms of all Arts are generally Nonsense that signify nothing, or very improperly what they are Meant to do, and are more Difficult to be learn'd then the things they are designd to teach.   10

Mr Wray and Coleman Durst not have undertaken to Dispute with Dr Stil: or B: if they had been either Priests or Regulars of the Church of R. in Publique, without the Licence and Priviledge from their Superiors.

Romances made on the Scripture, are worse then Burlesque and 15 Travestees, because they are Further off Truth, for those Signify nothing, unlesse they containe Smart Truths which the others never do, unless by construction and Inferrence which is made by those who Admire them, like the Interpretations of Dreames of that kinde. And only teach Truth and Morality the furthest way about, 20 And like a French Ragust is but Sauce to Bones. The Parish clearks of London that Acted all the Bible over at Clerken-wel (from whence it tooke that Name) were excellent in that kinde, as the Jesuits Schollers that invented the Devill with two Loggerheads are at present, and the Dutch Roderigos, which are their Operas, and 25 only Serve to Render the Scripture ridiculous (tho they Lay it falsely upon others) by reducing it all to Fiction. A little Philosophy wil serve to Qualify a Romancer (which is oftener taken to signify a Lier then in any other Sense) [and] he that can belive it possible in Nature, for Virtuosos to make Viages to the moone, is fit [to be] 30 a Philosopher of Gotham, as wel as Gresham. For Fancy in Philosophy, would no doubt be [   ] improvd by travelling to the Moon that at this Distance is able to Produce such ingenious [   ], and inable Romancers to cry down Reason and Sense and wit and

---

22 Clerken-wel (from] *superimposed on* Clerken-wel, from *B*   25 Operas,] Operas. *B*   26 ridiculous] ri[ ]iculous *B*   28 wil] [ ]l *B*   29, 30, 32, 33,
p. 180, l. 1 *Parentheses*] *MS. damaged B*   30 fit [to be]] fit ⟨to⟩ [ ] *B*
31 Gotham, as] Gotham, and *B*   33 ingenious] ingenio[ ] *B*

Judgment, by the Names of [   ]s, to advance Geniuses, universall Tradition, and Sotticismes. He that undertook to anatomize
the Muscles of the minde: or the modern French Virtuosos, that
pretend to understand what Pictures thinke, had much such a
5 kinde of Taske, and with the same success.

216ʳ   There is no Man who has taken the Paines to Learn the Greek
'B' Tongue at School, But when he come's to understand better
things, is not much taken up with it, unles He be a Dunce, or a
Schoolmaster to whom only it is necessary, and usefull.

10   Those who play upon the Organs or Virginals, have the Advantage of those that play upon Lutes, &c. for they have the use of one
Finger and a Thumbe more then the others have, and with the
same Touch do both stop and strike.

     The most Inhuman Monsters of all Men do many times Prove
15 none of [the] worst Husbands to their wives, nor fathers to their
Children, For they wil Raven like the fiercest of other wild Beast's
to maintaine their yong, and not only venture their Bodys to the
Hangman but their Soules to the Devill, to leave them, (though
perhaps none of their own) the best Advantages they can make
20 of Both.

     There were more Colledges and Schooles founded in Universitys,
and all the Nation over, For the Incouragment and Increase of
Learning, when there was hardly any such thing in the world, then
have been (or are ever like to be) since it has been Improvd. For
25 the Ignoranter all Ages have been, the greater esteem they have
had, for the little Smatterings of the Present Pretenders, And the
more Learned they have grown ever since, the less has Learning
been Regarded in the general. And therefore wee finde that the
Greatest Number of those who have founded Grammar Schooles,
30 or been Benefactors to the Endowments of Colleges, are such as
those whose Names are written upon the wals of Hospitalls (to
Draw in others) and understood as little in themselves of the

---

2 anatomize the] ana[   ]e B   4 understand what] un[   ]t B
4 thinke,] thinke. B   6 has] interlined B   11 that] altered from who B   &c.]
altered from and St B   15 to their] to altered probably from fo B   nor] altered from
and B   16 wil] interlined B   22 Nation] Nati / B   24 been (or] superimposed on been, or B   28 general.] general B   30 the] interlined B   are] as B

Learning of those men, to whom they were So Bountiful, as the others felt the Necessitys of those People whom they provided for. So the Errors and Mistakes of the Antients, when they were Receivd into Schooles in the Ignorant Ages, and became the greatest Part of their Support, and al their Learning, have been 5 fortifyd as well as their Industry and Bungling wayes of Reasoning could amount to; For they have not only made a Canting Language of Purpose, to Juggle with various Significations of words, but introducd a world of Impertinent Distinctions, and as Idle Metaphysicall Notions, to face Truth out of England, and Pass in the 10 Disguise of Profound Learning among the Ignorant, and Render Artificiall Nonsense Impregnable, because nothing apperes more Learnedly Solid to those who do not understand the vanity and Idlenes of it. By this meanes they can Maintaine long Disputes without the least expence of Reason, and Sense on both sides, which 15 is not to be don in Sober Sadnes any other way. For as Fenceing masters when they exercise their Schollers use to stamp upon the Bords, and make a Dreadful Noyse, to make a Pass with their Blunted Foyles, which is of no use when they come to fight in the Field: So do they with their Pedantique Fustian, that is as Ridicu- 20 lous, and of no use in all the Serious Affaires of Mankind and Right ways of Reasoning.

The K. of France take's the Government upon himselfe by the Grant, and never puts his Subjects to the Trouble of giving their voyces at the Elections of their Officers, nor to serve upon Jurys, 25 nor so much as to Run the Hazard of keeping their own money, who have nothing to do all the yeare but only of fasting days, which they observe all together, in order to their great General Feast in the other world. 29

If God Almighty had found those Rigors that are Imposd by 216ᵛ Priests necessary to every Mans æternal Happines, He would 'B' have made all Men in the world of one and the same Constitution of Body, that do's Naturally produce those severe effects, and wee might predestinate and Determine the Fate of mens Soules, more Rationally by their Complexions, and Faces then their Opinions as 35

2 for.] for B   11 among] among. B   16 way.] way B   16–17 Fenceing masters] altered from Fencemas B   23 upon] upn B   27 of] altered from to keep B   33 those] interlined B

Presbyterians use, who most preposterously make mens opinions the Standart of their Present and future Condition, though nothing can be more Inconsiderable to both. But Opinion is the only thing that all Churches in the world looke after, and because it has the Greatest Influence to promote their owne Interests, Ridiculously perswade themselves, it has the same Dominion over all the other Concernments of Mankind, when nothing is more vaine and False of it selfe, to all other Purposes, but only that of their own Trade.

Tis a Fatall Crisis in a Government when Ruling and obeying become to have Contrary Interests, and have perpetuall Jealousies and Designes to intrap and betray one another. For then the Publique Peace and Politie, is in a Speculative State of Civill war, which cannot long faile to break out into open Rebellion or Slavery; and Destroy both sides.

The Spanish Souldiers in the Low Cuntrys had been so usd to mutinyes, that they became a Part of their Military Discipline, and were managed with Set-termes, of Turning out their Officers, and setting up Elects (as they calld them) in their Places, who were ty'd to Certaine Rules, to govern their Tumultuous Disorders by, which other wise would have immediatly Ruind of themselves, but by being strictly observd among them selves continud some yeares before they could be Reducd.

A Man may have a Great Deal of Reason, and yet be noe more concernd in the use of it for his own Purposes, then an Avaritious Person that has a great deal of Money, but not Power to make use of it for his own necessary occations; Beside some Men have it not always about them especially upon a Sudden Occasion, and then it is the same as if they had it not at all; But nothing renders it so utterly unusefull as Passion, to which it ha's a Naturall Antipathy, and is absolutely inconsistent—For Passion is but a kind of Dry Drunkennes, and as far from Sobriety, as the most Debauch'd, and so much the worse as it is more Natural. For though a Madman have twice the Strength that he had before he lost his wits; yet one that is Drunke, has as much less then he had when he was Sober.

I suspect ——s' Parts upon one Accompt, as much as his other Disingenuites, and that is that his Speeches are better then his Lettres which shews that his Judgment is better at extempore then upon fit deliberation, of which Temper of understanding, though I have known many; I never yet found any good and Solid. And the Truth is there was never any Man of Excellent understanding whose Morals and Practices were not of the same Quality, though millions of others, whose Craft and Subtlety in the Ordinary affairs of the world is Sufficient; but as it often put's them upon Attempts without fair means and ends, it sometimes distroys them for nothing. And the fault of all ly's in a Corrupt understanding that is the original of all.

The Richest and most pretious of all Perfumes are but the Impostumes or excrements of wild beasts, or Fishes.

When the Richest cloaths were worne (as in King James his time) they were made after the most ugly and deformd fashions.

The Femals of Human Creatures are always ready to generate, and the Males seldome Contrary to all other Animals, whose Males are allways ready and femals seldom.

A stag is bravely armd, but has no Courage to make use of his weopens, and his Safety depending upon his Speed in Flying, they are but an Impediment to him.

The Goths and vandalls were never reduc'd to Civility themselves untill they had destroyd it in all other Nations.

Men inflict and suffer Persecution with equall zeal, and although both pretend to Conscience, both many times are equally mistaken.

We grow weary of those things (and perhaps soonest) which we most desire.

There are more Bastards begotten in Matrimony then out of it,

---

1 other] *interlined B*   8 Subtlety] Subtly *B* affairs] affair / *B*   9 Sufficient;] Sufficient. *B*   10 sometimes] *altered from* of *B*   13–14 *Interlined B*   14 beasts] beast *B*   14. 1–3 *See p. 150, ll. 10–12*   15 *Editor's paragraph* When] when *B*   24 other] othe *B*   25 *Editor's paragraph* suffer] seffer *B*   27 *Editor's paragraph* We] we *B*   29 *Editor's paragraph* it,] it. *B*

and more Servants that govern their Masters then Masters their Servants.

Pillers, that were at first but the Props of Cottages became afterwards to be the most bewtiful and magnificent Parts of Structures.

5   Tis Strange that the French who have the worst Appetites in the world, should be esteemd the best Cookes. And that they who have no Good Horses bred in their own Cuntry, should yet affect Horsmanship above any other Nation.

As Bad manners are the Causes of Good Lawes, So great incon-
10 veniences have always produc'd the greatest Advantages. The Pox and Scabs of the French People ha's put them in a way of using the greatest clenlynes in their Cups and glasses, and handling of their meate: And there is no other Reason why the Duch are so extraordinary neat and cleanly in their Towns and houses, but only the
15 unwholsomnes of the Aire, and naturall Durtines of the Cuntry, which if they were not provided against, would be apt to produce Contagious Diseases. For where there is any thing excellently well contriv'd for the generall Benefit of the Place, it is commonly nothing else but the remedy of some Defect.

20 Pleasures to those that have no Inclination to them are more uneasy then Labour and Paines and so are all glorys to those that are not vainglorious.

Some Men delight in things for no other reason but because they
24 are ugly, and Infamous.

[217ᵛ]

218ʳ   One Scripture is Enough for all Men to submit their Reason and
'B' Judgments to without Examination, and not to make a kinde of Canonical Philosophy, to Impose upon their understandings with

3 *Editor's paragraph*   5 *Editor's paragraph*   6–8 And . . .]
duplicated B 214ᵛ: France produces the worst Horses in the world and the best
Horsemen.   9 *Editor's paragraph*   10 Advantages.] Advantages, *altered
from* Conveniences B   12 clenlynes] *altered from* clens B   15 naturall
Durtines] *altered from* nasty Durtines *altered from* nastines B; naturall nasty Durtines *W*   20 *Editor's paragraph*   21 glorys] *altered from* glorious B
23 *Editor's paragraph*   Some] *interlined B*   24. 1–2 *See p. 150, ll. 8–9*
24. 3–6 *See p. 108, ll. 14–17*   24. 7–19 *See p. 54, l. 30–p. 55, l. 8*   [217ᵛ]
Verse drafts B

Authority instead of Sense and believe the Best Modern Observations (that is the best experienc't and most Antient) to be but
merely Apocryphall, by a Silly mistake of the yonger and Rawer
Ages of the world for the most Grave and Knowing, as if all Mankind, like some Particular Men, were twice Children, and the last 5
Infancy the worst, when tis Apparent by thousands of Instances,
what Excellent Discoverys have been found out since, of which
those they falsly call the Antients were utterly Ignorant. The same
may be sayd of Tragedy and Comedy, which, if they are Properly
cald Imagines et Spectacula Humanæ vitæ why they should be 10
confind to Persone mezzane that are neither very good nor very Bad
like the Garnishing of Dishes and not the Food, is as useles and
Insipid, or why they should be reducd only to Foolish Pitty and
infeasible Terror, and instead of Instructing the understanding, the
only end to which they should be designd. To humour two such 15
childish Passions only, is as Sottish and Ridiculous For they could
hardly have found out two things so inconsistent in the Nature,
and tyd to such Impossible Conditions, To terrify men, without
Punishing their Crimes in others, (which all Laws provid for in
their publique Executions) only because they are Incapable of Pitty, 20
As if the Laws should forbid men to be Hangd, till they are prepard,
and fitted for it, Or others who have deservd the same Punishments,
and are only proper to be terrifyd, did not finde the same Fellow-
feeling and Compassion of them for their own Sakes, by which it
Plainly appeares, that Pitty, and Terror can never possibly meet, 25
but in the worst and most criminall, which therefor they have very
Judiciously Banishd the Stage. But to make the Nonsence more
Compleat, They will not suffer Delinquents to be Punishd in
Tragedys for their own faults, but some Mistake or oversight of
their Ancesters, like the Jews eating of Sour Grapes against all 30
Principles of Reason and Justice, only to make them capable of
Pitty, and the Spectators of Terror, to avoyd that which is in no
mans Powr to Prevent.

3 Apocryphall,] Apocryphall. *B*   4 Knowing,] Knowing. *B*   5 Chil-
dren] *altered from* a Child *B*   6 worst,] worst. *B*   8 were] we[ ] *B*
10 et] & *B*; and *W*   11 Persone] *altered from* Persona *B*   12 useles]
altered from Silly *B*   13 reducd] rducd *B*   14–15 the only end] *interlined B*
15 be designd.] be ⟨only⟩ designd *B*   17 Nature] *altered from* Same Subject *B*
19 provid] proved *W*   20–7 Pitty, As . . . it, Or . . . Stage.] Pitty.* Or [*altered from* As if] . . . Stage.* As . . . it. [As . . . it *underlined*] *B, W* (*cf. p.* 191, *ll.* 7–8 *n*)
28 Delinquents] *altered from* men *B*   29 faults] *altered from* sakes *B*   33. 1–3
[fo. 218ᵛ] *See p.* 187, *ll. 5–7*

218ᵛ   For if the Lewdest of all their Gods (whom their Poets make
'B'   Lewd enough) take part against the Poor Offender, or have but
some old Pique to his Family, it is enough for the Spectators to
Pitty the Innocent Criminal, and terrify others from being born of
5   such wicked Parents: a most Just and Excellent Law of Tragedy
(no doubt) strictly observd by the Antients, and therefore ought
to be so by the moderns upon paine of Being Proceeded against,
as Stage-nonconformists; when all the Absurditys of all the later
writers put together, will not amount to halfe the Sottishness of
10   this Regular and Judicious Nonsense which wil not admit of so
much truth or Resemblance of Nature in it, as is Capable of
Morality, though tru History be utterly forbidden Tragedy as wel
as Comedy as less convenient to Morality, then Fable and mere
fiction, where th'Inhumanest Actions of Mankind can only be
15   Punishd in Effigie, like the Tragedy of Pyramus and Thisbe, where
the Spectators are desird not to be terrifyd at the Lyon, that was
really no tru Lion but only Flute the Bellows mender in Disguise
&c. These two Magots of Terror and Pitty are very untowardly
Put together, as the only Ends of Tragedy For as no Affliction can
20   terrify others from the like, but where it is Justly Deservd, So none
can move Compassion, that is not Injustly incurd, both which are
Provided against in the Persone Mezzane, who it seeme's are neither
fit to Represent Good, or Bad men in Tragedy and Serve to no
Purpose at all, either in order to Terror or Compassion of which
25   when they are capable of the one, they are utterly voyd of the other.
For the very Good by their frequent Misfortunes are only apt to
move Pitty, and the very Bad Terror and for that very Reason
preposterously forbidden to be introduc'd in Tragedy directly contrary to those supposd Ends of it; And if this be not a Plain and
30   Manifest Contradiction of themselves as wel as Common Reason
I cannot Imagine what is. All Ends of Tragedy are condemnd to be
unfortunate; and certainly tis more agreable to Reason as wel as
219ʳ   Human Instruction, that men should be Punishd for their Crimes
'B'   (as they are in all Nations) to deterre others, from Comitting the

---

5 Parents:] Parents *B*   6 strictly observd] *altered from* observd strictly *B*
7 Being] Bing *B*   8 Stage-nonconformists;] Stage-nonconformists . . *B*
10 Judicious] *altered from* wel contrivd *B*   11 Resemblance] Resemblanc /
B   12 though] *altered from* for *B*   be] *probably altered from* is *B*   14 th'Inhu-
manest] th Inhumanest *B*   18 &c.] &c *B*   20 Deservd,] Deservd. *B*
22 Mezzane,] Mezzane. *B*   neither] neithe *B*   24 all,] all. *B*   28–9 con-
trary] contratry *B*   it] *altered from* Tragedy *B*   30 wel as] wel a *B*

like, then to suffer wrongfully for no Purpose, but to Raise So
Impertinent, and Childish a Passion in the Spectators, as Idle and
Insignificant Pitty—that Gives no Relief at all to the Innocent
Sufferrer, but Rather aggravat's his Misfortunes.

[Why Poets should allow of none but Persone Mezzane to be ₅
admitted upon the Stage: who are the Only Persons themselvs that
are debard all Mediocrity, is somthing awkward.]

Gifts and wit are but a kind of Hotheadednes, that Renders those
that are Possest with it, better at Extempore, then Premeditation,
and therefore such men are wont to Speak better, and more In- ₁₀
geniously then they are Able to write, and the more Suddenly the
Better, but if they come to Consider, the longer they think, it always
proves the worse, For their Judgments are of so Feeble a Temper,
that they cannot hold out, but turn Edge at the Second thought,
and if they venture further, it still Proves worse, and worse, as all ₁₅
things at their Height Naturally Decline.
And this is the Reason why Orators Poets, and Fanatiques are
such Ill Masters of Reason, for they have not Patience nor Temper
to Consider long on any thing but rather at first to take up any
thing though ever so unreasonable, which sooner becomes a Habit ₂₀
in them then others, which afterwards is never to be gotten out
again. As Spots and Staines are never to be taken out [of] fine and
weake stufs, though they may bee out of stronger that wil indure
more paines Rubbing, and vexation.

Davids Tongue was not like to be very voluble, if it could speak ₂₅
noe fluenter then a Jew was Able to write, whose Charasters
Require so many Strokes of the Pen, and Hang so ill together only
to avoyd Abreviations, that it seeme's to be a Language to be
written with the slowest Dispatch of al others, and most uneasy
to be written, unless they had a way of Shorthand which I never ₃₀
heard of. Their Letters have something of our Court and Chancery
Hand which is never to be written speedily by the ablest Clerk;
Besides their Drawing their Lines from the Right Hand to the Left

1 to suffer wrongfully] *interlined B*   2 in] *probably altered from* as B
5–7 *Written at the top of* fo. 218ᵛ (*p. 185, ll. 33. 1–3*) *and separated by a horizontal rule
from p. 186, l. 1* B   9 it] *altered from* them B   15 and worse,] and worse. B
21 which afterwards is] which is afterwards is B   24 paines Rubbing,] paines
⟨and⟩ Rubbing. B   33 Drawing] Dawing B

seeme's to be unnaturall, being directly averse to all the ways of Drawing and Sculpture, usd by all other Nations, And though wee are forcd to Print the same way, It is no small Impediment, to the Easines and certainty of that usefull Invention. The Hebrews are
5 more Curious of their Letters Then their words, and their words, then the Sense and meaning of them and their Pricks then both, which makes them differ so much about their Radixes that some of them interpret the same word A Horse which others Render a House, to say nothing of their Grammar, which construs Is and
10 was and shalbe for all one. A Great Argument of the Imperfection of that Antient Language which is always Supplyd in our English Translations of the Bible, beside a world of other expletives, which are no Part of the Scripture.

219ᵛ   All Humorists hate their own Inclinations in others, which
'B'   renders them so easy to be flatterd and cheated, by all that can but
16   Dissemble and comply with their Extravagancies.

All the Stars that twinkle, seeme to be flames, and consequently Suns and those that do not, other worlds, like the Moon who when shin[ing] ever so bright is never seene to twinck as the Sun do's.

20   There is no Religion in the world, that Deboches the Reason and understandings of Men, so much as Popery, For the Reformation was introducd upon the Accompt of Reason, But Papisme crept in by stealth in the Darkest times, like a Thief in the Night: they themselves cannot tell when nor how. And by forceing all things
25 out of the Course of Nature where only Human Reason is in its Sphere of Activity, and Prefering Story and Mi[racles] which are never to be understood, nor Prov'd, They Reducd all their followers to that slavery of thinking, That they are ready to Receive any falshood that is imposd upon them, and nothing upon any true
30 Accompt, though ever so Rationall. Hence it is that they are so apt to tell, and believe Lys, and have no other Measure to judge of any thing, but as it stands in Relation to the Church of Rome, and make any thing Good, or Bad, according as it comply's or stand's in opposition to that. From this want of Judgment it is, That all

2 Drawing] Drawn B   6 both,] both. B   9 House,] House. B
11 Language]Languag B   19 shin[ing]] shees W   ever] eve B   25 where]
whe B; who W   29 that] this B   30 they are so] they so B   31–2 any
thing,] any thing., B   34 Judgment] Judgmen / B

their Plots and Designes are so Ridiculously Silly and weak that though they Perpetually Miscarry, they wil never Give them over.

The Apostles and Evangelists might believe in Christ whom they knew and converst with, and were eie-witnesses of his Miracles, But al others do but Beleive in them, and what they affirm of him to be tru, and mistake themselves if they think they believe in him, unles it be at second Hand, As the Jews did, when they perswaded themselves that they Believd in God the Creator of Heaven and Earth, when Really they did but believe in Moses, who told them he was So, and Discribd the History of the Creation.

All Divines that marry, are (like Citizens) commonly Henpeckt by their Comfortable Importances, For a woman can be no meet Helper to a Priest in his Calling and Profession, and to marry her, is but a kinde of Entring her into holy Orders, and as much Spirituall Incest for a Daughter to Marry her Ghostly Father, as it is in the Church of Rome, for a Man to marry his God-daughter, whom he undertook to answer for at her Baptisme. And if they are Transubstantiated into one Flesh, which of them has the Care of Soules, none but a School-man can Determine.

One that could tell what Sort of Fanatiques naturally turn Papists, what Athiests &c as easily as what kindes of Putrifyd Flesh produce any Sorts of Insects, For Fanatiques are but severall specieses of Magots, that never continue long what they are, but turne to something else by equivocall Generation. And are not such in Religion only but in all other things that they may not mistake that for Spirituall, which is nothing but the naturall temper of their constitutions, and the effect of their Intellectual Complexions; for they have the very same Affectation, Ignorance, obstinacy, and Self-conceit in all things else how inconsiderable soever that they under take. And therefore their Revelations of other matters are not like to be true that are so false of themselves, and those Gifts which they bestow upon themselves no better then Begging Presents, to bring them in Returne, more then they are worth, which is lesse then nothing.

2 over.] ove / B   5 affirm] affirm B   6 tru,] tru. B   22 any] altered from all B   24 And] altered from For Fanatiques B   27 Complexions;] Complexions. B   30 And] and B

—— would have been one of the best husbands in the world if
he had lighted upon a good wife, and such a one as he could have
liked, for he that can be so constant to —— that bring him Children,
would have been as much where he had a greater obligation. And
this unhappines among many other, the Nation ows to the Ambition
and perfidiousnes of the Chanceller, who prevayld with the Sheep
to make a League with wolves, against their old Guardians, that
in time himselfe might become the Head of it. For when he had
enterd the Poynt before, what he did afterward, was but in order
to binde his man, that lay open to too many Blots: But the Divine
Justice would not suffer him to live in any Condition in that Nation
which he had so much injurd; for his first Banishment being for his
Loyalty he could never indure it afterward, but was at last banishd
for his Apostacy, and dy'd an excommunicate of his Cuntry and
Morality if not the Christian Religion, and Humanity. There can
be no greater Punishment to an Ambitious man then to fall from
what he was by indeavoring to be greater, and therefore no doubt,
a Private life more plagud him then his Gout.

The old Greek Poets that invented the Fables of the Metamorphosis had no Designe to express Naturall Philosophy, or teach
Morality by them as Mythologists would perswade us, For nothing
can be more unagreable to Nature, or insignificant to the other
purpose; but they seeme to have no other end, but that which the
Authors of the Legend since have proposd to themselfs, to amuse
men with Stories of Miracles, and fright them in to a Reverend
Awe of Religion, or Superstition. And Ovids Metamorphosis was
no doubt a very Pious worke and did no less Service to the Pagan
Church, then his Rubrique of their Holydays, to which it servd as
the Legend dos to the Saints day's in the modern Roman Calender.

That Prince who live's above his Revenues, and below his Dignity, has as hard a Province As a Marchant that spends above his
Estate, and ha's no Credit, especially if he expects his Supply's
from his people, who will charge all his extravagant expenses upon
their own Accompt, and believe they pay for all; and grutch him
that which is his owne. And the more he takes of them to relieve
his wants, the less they wilbe sure to pay him in obedience, and

9 before,] before *B*   10 Blots:] Blots· *B*   12 injurd;] injurd. *B*   21 us,]
us *B*   23 purpose;] purpose. *B*   31 Province] Provin *B*   35 And] and *B*

subjection, that what he gaines one way, he looses another, and much more, for Money do's always goe hand in hand with Credit and Reputation, but never go's before, nor come's after it. And when he has lost all Authority, their next Bus'nes is to accuse him, for assuming more then is his Due, and to binde him up with Laws   5 as thieves do those they Rob, and use him insolently for having noe more about him.

For as Princes while they are great and Powrfull can do no wrong,   **221** So when they decline, and grow low they can do no Right; for   'B' their good or Bad Actions are equally odious to their People, as soon   10 as their Persons, and management of Affaires begin to be dislik'd; and whether they mean well or ill, it is always taken in the worst Sense, and they have the Prerogative only to be judg'd before they are heard or understood.

Astrologers are in a great Error, who ignorantly mistake Genesis   15 for the moment of a Mans Birth, when it properly signify's the Instant of his Begetting, between which and his production there is 9 monthes Difference, and if there be any Probability in their Art may seeme the fittest and properest time, for the Influences of the Stars to worke upon when the matter is most capable of their   20 Subtle Impressions, for as they receive apparant Qualifications in their Body's, from those of their Parents, whose very imaginations have been found to imprint Signatures upon them in the wombe, before they are brought to perfection, but never at their Birth, nor after they are born, So if those feebler and more remote operations   25 produce any effect at all, it is as unseasonable, to assigne it to the Birth as to thinke to improve or alter Corn after it is Ripe. And as the good or Bad Growth of Corn depend's, much if not most, upon the Season of the yeare, and the condition of the weather in which it was Sown; without any regard to the Position of Stars, So if   30 there bee any such trick in Nature, the Act of Generation cannot but bee the seasonablest time for influences to do their Busness, and the wisest way to predict, to draw a Scheame of the weather in which the feate was don, which is both a more immediate Cause, and of more Sensible Operation, of alterations in the Body of Man,   35

4 their] *probably altered from the B*   5 then] [ ]hen B   Laws] *or possibly*
Lawe / B   7-8 him. For] him.* *For B (*cf. p. 185, ll. 20-7 n*)   11 dislik'd;]
dislik'd. B   12 they] the B   18 Art] Arts W   25 born,] born. B
31 bee] be W

then any far-fet Magique of the Stars, that is further of from Sense and understanding then any thing else. By which it appeare's that a weather-cock, or weather glass is like to prove a better Instrument to their Purposes then an Astrolabe or Jacobs-staf. And if they were but so wise as some men's Cornes and Aches are to foretell the change of weather (which they all ways undertake but never perform) they would have more reason for their Pretences then they have yet been able to produce.

Genesis is but the Getting of Children, and Exodus the Running away for it. In the Scotch translation Genesis is renderd the Buke of Swiving.

Those Children that are begotten in the day, are commonly born in the day, and those in the Night by night: for Nature for the most part keepe's a Punctuall accompt of time: and that is one reason, why more are born in the Night then by Day, when men are commonly diverted by many other occasions. And in great Cities men are often in Drink before they goe to Bed which make's the Children they get prove soe foolish, beside the mothers longing for ridiculous extravagancies, when they are great while in diviseing what to long for, that's hard to be had to try how much Naturall Affection a Cuckold may have to none of his own issue.

For if Princes are lawfully marryd by Proxy, why should not others have their Children as legally begotten the same way? And as all Empire (some hold) was at first deriv'd from Paternall Authority, He who ha's that Dominion over other mens children, is a greater Person, then he that can pretend to none but over those that are of his own simple begetting. Before the Reformation, all Priests and Friers were cald fathers by the Layety (as they are still in al Catholique Nations) only because having no wives of their own, they got all other men's children, and yet nobility, and Gentility was never in higher esteem then it was in those times, and is at this day where that Course is taken.

220ʳ   As many Inheritances are Disposd of by Physitians as by Lawyers,

---

5 but] *interlined B*   6–7 weather (which . . . perform)] *superimposed on* weather which . . . perform, *B*   15 Day,] Day. *B*   18 foolish,] foolish,. *B*
25 over . . . children] *interlined B*   mens] men *B*   27 own] *interlined B*
30 nobility,] nobility. *B*

for if a Doctor wilbe content to kill moderately and sometimes spare 'B'
a Life, for his Credit, though he loose by it, he may thrive in his
way, but if he give's no Quarter, his Practice will not long hold out.

How can Lawyers have [a] clean Hand that eate their Meat
without Trenchers, or Napkins. 5

Some Divines and Philosophers have found out I know not where,
nor how, That Angels converse by Intuition, and understand one
another without Speaking, whereby it seemes There is always a
great Silence in Heaven, as well as in St John's time; and perhaps
that is no mean Contribution to the Happines of it, as talking is 10
one of the greatest causes of the Disorders of this world.

Truth can be no older then the Creation of Man, but Lyes are of
greater Antiquity eversince the Fall of Lucifer, when he became
the Father of Lyes.

The Natives of America, before the Spanyard invaded them, 15
injoyd the same Happines of life which the Poets fancy of the
Golden Age; To which they may pretend a fairer Title by the vast
abundance of Gold which they possest, although they had no need,
because no use of.

Priests had a brave time, when all the Rest of Mankind were 20
Fooles, and they the only Knaves.

He that lay's his Designes too far of, is like one that shootes
before he is within a just distance of his Mark, and more remote
then his Artillery can reach.

Ignorant and Sottish People are never to be prevayld upon, by 25
those who have the greatest abilities of Reason, but by such as [are]
nearest to their own Latitude, and have but ever so little more
Sense and Capacity, as Duckes are never to be Drawn into a Decoy
but by other Ducks, of their own kinde.

Benefit's oblige but one sort of People (and that the least of all) 30

---

11 world.] *spaced off on the same line* Tooth from ὁδούς B   27 nearest] *altered
from* neare B   30 People (and] *superimposed on* People, and B

the Just and Gratefull; To all others who are more to one then can
be easily accompted; they Naturally turne to Injuries, and dis-
obligations and are seldom otherwise then as such Returnd.

The Pox go's under as many borrowd Names of other Diseases,
5 as whores that give it do of other women.

Princes cannot be waited upon on Free-cost, nor serv'd by any
but such as are able to beare their own Charges, for their Necessary
Occasions frequently stand in neede of such only who have no
Dependance but upon their services; and have no other way to
10 better or maintaine their Condition so well as in being obsequious
and Faythfull to them.

Although the Management of almost all the Busnesse in the
world may appeare very extravagant and Ridiculous, yet whosoever consider's it Rightly will finde that it cannot be avoyded,
15 nor possibly be don any other way.

There are Infinite evident Demonstrations of the Prodigious
wisdom and Ingenuity usd in the Creation and Fabrique of the
world but the Providentiall Government of it dos not so plainly
appeare, but still there is reason enough for some men to suppose,
20 that all those Affares that fall out in the Civill management of it,
are but the Effects of it's own Nature.

The Bishops have been so far from converting their Enemys to
a better opinion of the Church, since their Restoration then they
had before, that those are the only People they have confirmd in
25 their former Faith, beside many new Proselites they have begotten
of the same Perswasion.

221ʳ   There is nothing that can improve Human Nature so neare to
B Divinity as knowledg. This was the first opinion in the world, when
Adam and Eve believd that to know Good and Evill was to be like
30 God; And as Lucifer fell from Heaven for indeavoring to be as great

2–3 disobligations] *or possibly* disobligatives *B*   4–5 *Duplicated B* 226ʳ
4 under] by *B* 226ʳ   borrowd] *om. B* 226ʳ   of other Diseases] *om. B* 226ʳ   5
as whores] as the whores *B* 226ʳ   that . . .] do that dispence it *B* 226ʳ
6 on] *altered from* by *B*   9 their services] *altered from* themselves *B*
18 Government] Governmet *B*

as God, So did Adam for Attempting to be as wise; whereby it should seem that man was not created Rationall, but bought his knowledge with the Forfeiture of all his other Priviledges.

There are as many (if not more) Living Creatures in the Sea, as on the Land and more wealth where there is no use of it.   5

All Sorts of Forrainers come into this Ile as poore as if they had been wract at Sea, and cast up upon it; but finde such kinde Enterteinment among the Natives, that they never care to leave it, and return home again.

Why should not Religion as well as Morality be insinuated by   10
Fables and Apologues? and Those Rites, and ways of Divine Adoration, that are founded upon false and Mistaken Grounds, being well meant and Piously intended, not be as acceptable, as if they were true, and rightly assumd; as long as they are as well meant and really believd to be true, and orthodox by those who use them? for   15
a too Scrupulous inquiry after mere Speculative Truth, in Performing Actions of Duty and obedience (which Naturally do not admit of Dispute) may be as Superstitious, and of worse Consequence, then those Ceremonys, and Formes (if they were mistaken) which they Quarrel and take offence at.   20

Fanatiques in Religion are the same things, that Fops and Humorists are in the world, that do all things out of Caprich and Affectation, And like Papists do not pray but say their Howrs, and yet condemne them for it.

Clergie-men are severe to Bigots as well as Athiests, and would   25
have all men have Religion enough to serve their own Interests, and no more.

It is apter to Raine in great Cities, then in Open Cuntries; For the clouds that are driven over them by the windes, or inclination of the Atmosphere, are easier dissolvd by the Heat of the Chimnies,   30
then in other Places, where the Aire is not so warme; and this I

1 wise;] wise B   6 as if] af if B   14–15 meant . . . them?] meant?
. . . them, B   19 Formes (if] *altered from* Formes which B   22 world,]
world. B   25 are severe] are as severe B   31 warme;] worme. B

have often observd, that When it has Raynd in the Streets, it has at the same time been dry in the Fields.

Wit in a Traveller is like Money, He who carry's but a little out with him, brings none back again.

5   Wit takes Naturally to Debauchery, make's men Free and Open Hearted, Complesant, and Frolique, to delight in Conversation, and that which is the Inducement to it, wine; which as it set's fallse valewes upon all things, blow's it up into the Greatest extravagancies.

10   A spruce Gallant take's his cloaths for the better Part of his Redemption; For as Adam after his Fall among his other Defects found himself Naked (of which he appeard to be most Sensible and hid himself) So his Restoration from that Calamity, and Improvment of it into Bravery, cannot but apeare to him to be his greatest
15   Indulgence.

The Modern Extravagance of Gallanting, is imputed wholly to the men when the greatest part of the Fault is causd by the ill Humor, Caprich, Passion and perpetuall Provocation of wives, that Serve for Foyles to set of the Temptations of other women, whereby
20   it appeares that men have a Double Provocation to it, and both from women, who have but one from them.

Alas poor man he is Dead stil.

222ʳ   Like a Beast with a bord on his Hornes hee can only push down
'B'   but not goare.

25   There is no man so unsafe as he that is too Great, or too Proud to be told Truth, or have his Errors taken Notice of.

Popery made the Christian Religion a Fable, and Reformation by discovering that cheat, will in time bring it to Nothing.

No man can Imagine how vendible and Current Commoditys
30   Flattery and Pimping are.

4 with] wit B   8 things] thing B   19 women,] women. B   22 *Spaced off from left-hand margin B*   22. 1–16 [fo. 222ʳ] *See p. 59, ll. 18–30*   23–4 *Interlined B*   26 Truth,] Truth. B   27–8 *Interlined B*

The Chanceler Hide having layd his Dessignes at the Kings
Restoration to depress the Royall Party (who had payd so deare
for their Loyalty, that they had nothing left but merit the most
ungratefull of all Pretences, to pay for new Imployments, in the
Government) and to advance the Rebells who had not only money 5
to buy Pardons but Places of the Greatest trust and Profit in the
Nation, not only preferd (before all others) the most perfidious,
to the greatest Secresys and Trusts in the State, but Justifyd the
most pernicious of all their False Doctrines by which they had don
so much mischief before, and made their Preferments pas for Dis- 10
pensations and outgoings of Providence, that had utterly exposd
and disownd them before.

That Cruelty of the Grand Signor in destroying all his Brothers 222ᵛ
as soon as he comes to the Crown, that is so abhominated by all 'B'
other Nations, is if rightly consider'd, not so inhuman and Bar- 15
barous as we suppose it, for there was never any one life that was
taken away upon that accompt, but has preserv'd many thousands
that otherwise had been inevitably cast away, besides the certaine
Ruine of that Empire, which must of necessity have fallen out
many yeares Since. For their Religion allowing Plurality of wives, 20
which must consequently produce great Numbers of Children, and
little Distinction made between the legitimate and others (especially where Merit is so much Regarded, that there [is] no other
way to advancement, and by it the highest Preferments ly open
to the meanest) It is impossible to preserve the Empire in Peace 25
at home and avoyd perpetuall Civil wars, any other way. For
though many Sons may be a kinde of Security to a monarke during
his life time, yet after his Death nothing is found more pernicious
to the People. And this wee finde tru, by the History of our Ed.
3 who having more Sons then any of our Kings before or Since, 30
furnisht the Nation with severall pretenders to the Crowne and
a Constant Civill warre for above 200 years, and ended with the
Distruction of all the Heires Male of that Family, and introducing
of another.

5 advance the] advance ⟨and trust⟩ the B   not only] ⟨not only⟩ B   7 preferd (before] preferd (⟨them⟩ before B   8 State,] State. B   10 pas
for] *interlined B*   12. 1–6 *See p. 59, ll. 12–17*   12. 7–16 *See p. 58,*
ll. 11–20   12. 17–23 *See p. 140, ll. 18–24*   12. 25–33 *See p. 58, ll.*
20–7   15 other] other. B   18 that otherwise] that ⟨had⟩ otherwise B
22–3 others (especially] *superimposed on* others, especially B   32 200] *altered*
from 500 B

The Age that H 8 livd in occupyd Reformation in, and this is in a fair way to occupy it out again.

Preachers are more audaciously Impious then other men that dare denounce against the Sins of other men, and never feare their own
5 Sodoms and Gomorrha's should rise up in Judgment against them, for there is no Condemnation so certaine as that which come's out of a Criminalls owne Mouth, and that kinde of confession never fayles of hanginge.

There is nothing more Importune and petulant then the Solicit-
10 ing of fooles, for fooles are the best Solicitors in the world.

The Invention of Pilleries was to expose the Faces of Notorious offenders to publique view, that all men may take notice of their Faces, and avoyd them. As in France they use to cause all Male-factors when they are first brought into a Prison to be ty'd in
15 Chaires with their Heads and Faces bare, that all the keepers may observe and take Notice of their Particular visages, and Markes, in their Outward men, and Ages (which are all carefully set down in a Register) not only to prevent all Attempts to Escape in Dis-guises, but if that should chance to fall out, to know how to seeke
20 after them again.

If a man were really the worse for being evill Spoken of behinde his Back, it were Impossible for any Man to live in the world, But Nature has so orderd it, that the most venemous Serpents can bite and sting nothing at a Distance that they cannot touch, and fasten
25 upon, and the mortall'st poyson hurt none but those that apply and take it in to themselves. For Detraction is like witchcraft that always strives to do mischief to the Absent, but if either were effectuall, or could do but so much hurt to others as it often do's to those that use it, the world would be quite another thing, and
30 in little time, Nothing.

223ʳ   There is nothing in Nature that has so great a Power over the

---

1–2 *Interlined B*   7 Mouth,] Mouth. *B*   9–10 *Interlined B*   10. 1–19
See p. 116, l. 35–p. 117, l. 18   13 Faces,] Faces. *B*   14 be] by *B*   19 out,]
out. *B*   22 But] *altered from* for *B*   23 can bite] can ⟨hurt and⟩ bite *B*
24 at a Distance] *interlined B*

Minde of man and governs there so like a God as Conscience 'B'
rightly qualifyd, nor any thing so like the Devill, as that which is
false, and mistaken, and erroneous, for then it is worse then the
Possessions of Evill Spirits, which are seldom observd to do much
to others, but there is no Mischief and Distruction which wicked, 5
and Deluded Conscience is not always ready to attempt. For as
there is no Folly so extravagant as that which believes it self to be
wise and knowing, so there is no Impiety so horrible as that which
supposes it self to be Godlines and Christian Duty: for then of a
Spirituall Calenture, and hot Fit of Zeal it turn's to the Plague and 10
destroys all that come neare it. This is that Devill that assume's
the Shape of an Angell, and having Disguisd its Nature, indeavors
to change its Name too, and calls it selfe Tenderness, and Feare
and holy Jealousy, in stead of Obstinacy, Pride and Insolence, as
all Impostors use to change their Names to disguise their cheates, 15
as well as Popes do it to Declare and profes their Holines. Conscience is like the Magistrates Sword that Protects in a Goodman's
hand, but destroys in a Bad mans.

A Virtuoso sayd That the Spring of a Watch that was wound up
with a Fals Lutestring would never go True more then a False 20
string would stand in Tune upon an Instrument.

The Spring of a Watch that puts all the wheeles in motion, and
is the life and Soule of that Curious Engine, is not seen it self, but
shut up close in the Barrell (as Diogenes was) as if it did nothing
at all when nothing can be don without it. So do the chief Managers 25
of great Affaires, that imploy others in the Mechanical parts of
Bus'nes, but never appeare themselves.

Sir P. Neal being rated in a Publique Tax, the Sixt Part of an
Estate he had, complaind it was too much, and desird he might
be relievd and pay but a fift. 30
The Story of his being of the Jury at the Tryal of the lifeguard
man that kild a Coach man.

1 of man] *interlined B*   4 Possessions] Possssions B   5 Mischief]
Michief B   10 Fit] F[ ]t B   13 too,] too. B   16 and profes] *interlined*
B   18. 1–8 *See p. 96, ll. 14–21*   22 *Editor's paragraph*   Watch] Wat'ch B
motion,] motion. B   23 Engine,] Engine. B   28 rated] *altered from* ceasd B
29 it] is B   30 be] *om.* B   fift.] fift. . B   31–2 *Interlined B*   *Editor's*
paragraph   32. 1–4 *See p. 119, ll. 31–4*

This Pope for his Supine Negligence had a Painted Poppy fix[ed] upon Pasquill with Papa vero written upon it, for Papavero to intimate his Sleepines.

Cleargy men have no wit and very little or noe Sense untill they come to encounter with some other Party of the Same Religion, where their Interests differ, and then they are implacable and give no Quarter to the most inconsiderable mistake, although the whole Designe and End of the Religion they Contend about, be directly Contrary Patience, and Charity: And although they maintaine their little Interests with the greatest Animositys in the world, yet if they finde them like to become a Prey, they presently joyn with the Strongest side, and like Lipsius his Dogge share with those whom they opposd before in Dividing of that, which they indeavord with the utmost of their powr to secure to themselves. But in matters of no Contest in which their wits are not ingag'd by their Gaines or losses, they are always found to be very Dull and Insignificant.

Fanatiques are worse then the Devill, for he never do's any hurt to Mankinde without a Commission from God, But a Fanatique when he do's the greatest mischiefs in the world has no Authority for it but what he forges and gives himself; And Certainely when Jobes Integrity was to be try'd, he would not have been so Civill to aske Leave to throw down his House, and destroy his Children and his Cattle, but would have don it of his own Authority, and taken a thriftier Course, to destroy his Children only, and sav'd his House and Cattle for his own use; for Certainly no Conscience was ever So Sour'd as that which has been burnt with Zeal.

Fooles are always allarmd and frighted with things they do not understand as horses start at Posts in the Darke.

Clergymen are like Scavengers that pollute and Defile their own Soules and Consciences in clensing those of other men.

Covetous men prescribe no end to themselves in getting of

1–3 *Interlined B*   3. 1–8 *See p. 75, ll. 12–19*   4–17 *Underlined B*
13 whom . . . before] *interlined B*   14. themselves.] themselves *B*   20–1 has
. . . it] *interlined B*   20 no] *altered from* none, *B*   26 use;] use. *B*
26–7 Certainly . . .] *underlined B*   28–9 *Interlined B*   30–p. 201, l. 7
Underlined B   30 pollute] *altered from* Durty *B*   32–p. 201, l. 2 *Interlined B*

Money because it is to no end. For they have not the Hearts to make use of it.

Good Natures finde a great deal of Pleasure in Pitty, and Compassion.

One that make's more Noyse then an Empty Dung-cart. 5

The fellow that in a Storme at Sea Read Matrimony in the Common Prayer.

The Reverend Judges are the greatest Swordmen of the Nation, for they are allways Seconds to one Side or both, and never fayle to have the better of which side they please to take. 10

All Cheates and Knaves thrive no less then Honest men by keeping of their words, untill they finde a fit opportunity to breake them. And honest men are Ruind by ingageing Carelesly to perform what they really intend in the mindes they are in, but afterward neglect it. 15

Dr Wil: has set up Common Prayer only for the Visitation of the Sick and Burial of the Dead that is in it.

The Auspicia of weake Princes are always unfortunate.

The History of the Romans wars with the Græcians compar'd with those of Carthage that fell out much about the same time 20 apeare the paultriest little things in the world, that it is unpleasant to read them (in Livie) both together.

The Common People have no more Proper Notions of the Deity then Beasts have, and therefor are apt to receive any that are instild into them. 25

3–4 *Duplicated with marginal note* Good Nature *B* 142ʳ   3 Natures finde] Nature findes *B* 142ʳ   3–4 Pitty, and Compassion] having Compassion of the Miseries of others *B* 142ʳ   5 *Interlined B*   5. 1–4 *See p. 116, ll. 31–4*   5. 5–8 *See p. 44, ll. 27–30*   6 *Editor's paragraph*   11 then] *altered from* by *B* 14 what they] they *om. B*   in,] in. *B*   16–17 *Interlined B*   18. 1–12 *See p. 97, ll. 13–25*   20 that . . . time] *interlined B*   25. 1–6 *See p. 97, ll. 7–12*

No Man can be, or at least appeare to be ill-humord but for want of wit and Reason.

An Humorist is the same thing in Civility and Conversation, as a Cross-knave is in Bus'nes, and it is equally troublesome to
5 have any thing to do with the one as the other.

224ʳ   Those who have nothing of their own, but venture their lives
B for what they get, do after spend it most Prodigally, and the more Danger it cost them, throw it away the more extravagantly: as if it were unreasonable to preserve that which had brought them
10 in Perill of their Lives, and therefor the wisest Course is to be the Soonest rid of it, though the want of it will bring them into the same danger again, as those who have escapd hanging are never quiet untill they have tryd the same experiment the second time. For most men are so far from taking warning by their own Deliver-
15 ances, that they are rather encourag'd to attempt the same things againe, and though a burnt Child be sayd to dread the Fire most men want that wholsom Reason and understanding.

Ignorance is not so much a want of Learning and Knowledge, as an incapacity of it, or a Naturall Stupidity and weakness, that is
20 by no Art or Industry to be Cured; For there have been many Men of great understanding without any Learning at all, and many Learned Men very Ignorant, as skill in Fencing do's not make valiant, nor valour skilfull. But nothing can be don where Nature do's not allow a Free Supply, who can do nothing herself without
25 Materials, and [if] where those fayle her workes prove imperfect and Defective, much more must that do that has no foundation but what shee lay's: And therefore Art when it do's not receive it's whole support, and Instruction from her can produce nothing but Imposture, and Delusion, as shee do's Monsters and Prodigies,
30 when her supply's fayl to be duly brought in.

Wit and Fancy are light and Airey, but Judgment weighty, as wee do not Sound the Depth of the Sea with Boys that will swim upon the Top of it, but Plumets of lead that will sinke to the Bottom: All Sorts of Tricks and Rotines in Knowledg are easily

4 Bus'nes] Bu'snes *B*   10 wisest] wises *B*   12 again,] again *B*
17 wholsom] *interlined B*   25 those] these *W*   33 Plumets] Plume'ts *B*;
Plum'ets *W*

learnd, but there is no way to attain to that which is perfectly, and excellent, but with great Study and Paines, and as great Naturall wit and Judgment.

All Speculative Men, by living Retir'd, want the Readines and Adress of the Practicall; as the Practicall do the Knowledge of their Bookes and Studies, and both differ but as the Roman Velites did from their Heavy Armd Triarii.

The way of attaining Mysticall Knowledges is equally extravagant with that Sottish Story of Democritus who is sayd to have put out his own eies, that he might contemplate the better; An excellent Preparative to his Discovery of the worlds being made by the Accidentall Rancounter of Atoms in vacuo, which no Man could ever have hit upon, that had not been mad enough to put out his owne eies upon any accompt whatsoever. Neverthelesse this Freake of the Philosopher [was received] with great Reverence and Admiration by the Learned, as many others of the same kinde are, and no less celebrated then Socrates his Dying for his Religion, or Induring to be beaten by his wife, in which he was but a Confesser of Virtue, but in the other a Pagan Schismatique, and Martyr to his own opinion.

The Ages of the world are like those of Men, and agree as truly as that Paralel which L. Florus make's of the severall Ages of the Roman Republique with the Ages of a Man: And as all men naturally improve still in their Strength and understanding untill they arrive at their height, and then after a certaine Pause, as Naturally decay by the same Degrees: Just so it is with the world, whose Infancy and youth, must in Probability have the same weaknes and Defects which we finde in men of the same Condition. But when the world wilbe at it's Height and how long continue so, and when decay we know nothing; only we are sure wee come after its Infancy and youth for many Reasons, and consequently are nearer its maturity. And therefore those modern Humorists, that prefer the yonger Ages of the world to the Present that has had not only a greater experience, but a more stayd Temper, are

2 as great] as great. *B*   12 by] be *B*   29 it's] *altered probably from* the *B*
30 nothing;] nothing *B*   31 consequently] *altered from* therefore *B*
32 Humorists,] Humorists. *B*

sufficiently mistaken, and if they had livd in those times which they now so much admire, would much more have undervalewd them, for those that were before.

224ᵛ The Law has not so many nice and Curious Subtleties to furnish
B with Perpetuall Disputes and wrangling as Priests have found out,
6 to debauch and Corrupt the native Simplicity of the Christian Religion. That no thing can be sayd ever so plaine and easy, but they will turn it with their Juggling Distinctions, into what Sense, or Nonsense they please and make it, either Pious, or Impious,
10 Hereticall or Orthodox, true or False, according as it serve's the Present occasion; and all to no Purpose but to propagate Contention, and wrest Religion, from the great, and chief end it was at first designd for. And it is not improbable, but they taught the Lawyers this Curious Mischief, when they had the Management of
15 the highest Court of Justice, and by that meanes, layd a Foundation to pervert Justice and Conscience, as they have since don Humanity and Christian Charity. That no Spider ever spun his web with that Curious Niceity to intangle Flys, as they have don more Tricks out of their own noddles to insnare the weake, and Ignorant, that
20 have not wit enough to break through them. By this meanes they are able to rayse and maintaine Quarrels world without end, beyond all Possibility of Peace or accommodation, which are never to be introducd this way that tend's directly contrary to it, and can no more be reconcild then the war between the Elements by which
25 Nature subsists, as all Particular Churches do by this mutuall Dissention, and all directly contrary to the whole Designe and Interest of that Religion for which they pretend to be so zealously concernd, as if they had rather destroy all Religion then not have it their own way. And when by this ill managment of Religion, and setting it
30 against it self they have renderd it unuseful to the ends it was design'd for, and given occasion to some to suspect, that they who can make what use of it, they please, may perhaps have made it themselves, they exclame against them as Atheists, and forget that if there are any such, they are for the most part none but such as
35 they have bred up and taught to be so, by making Religion perpetually Contradict it self, and recant those things in their Practices

---

7 no thing] nothing *W*   15 highest] higest *B*   Justice,] Justice. *B*
20 them.] them *B*   23 it,] it. *B*   29 ill managment] ill-managment *W*
34 there] their *B*

before all the world, which they professe and own before god. For
though God made Religion, as Princes and Goverments do Laws,
yet those who have the management, and interpreting of both,
will make what they please of either. Nor is it probable that the
Laws of God, should fare better then those of Magistrates, who 5
are present to oversee their execution, while the Ministers of the
other, are left wholly to themselves in this world and only accomptable in the next.

The old Parlament-Party preserve themselves united as the Jews
do all the world over, out of hopes to their antient kingdom again, 10
as the other do to their late Commonwealth. For as those who
have escapd any great Danger together, where they have come of
with better successe then they deservd or could expect, have
greater Indearement's to one another (and the more reall the more
heynous their Crimes have been) then those who have sufferd upon 15
an undeservd accompt, so are they more Industrious to arme themselves against that vengeance which they know too well they have
deservd from Justice, and by keeping themselves united be better
able to defend themselves against it, and beare that infamy the
better (by still owning their old Pretences) which otherwise would 20
fall too heavy upon them, if they were less Numerous to support it
and if the times should alter, and an opportune Revolution happen,
they may be in a Redines to revive the good old Cause again, and
make better use of that experience which they have gaind by their
former miscarryadges, and by that meanes being more wise, cannot 25
but be more able, by those observations they have since made, to
carry on the work with better Success, and bring their Designes
upon the Church and State to full perfection.

Men of Different Parties, and Factions are never so good as they
make themselves nor bad as they are renderd by their opposites, 30
and therefore they easily deceive those that Consider but one thing
at once.

The Reason why Great Persons have the Gout and other
Diseases in greater extremity then those of a meaner Condition,
is because they are apter to take Physique, and try the experiments 35
of Medcines upon themselves, then those that have not so much

Money to spare, nor occasion to be applyd unto, and drawn in by Quacks and Empiriques.

Most of the Cheates in Law, are but to get time and a Repreeve from Justice when she cannot be further prevayld upon, and there-
fore men regard the Laws of God so little, because they believe they have so long a Reprive from their execution, as they are the less concernd in Death, because they know not when it wil come.

225ʳ   The comandment that injoyne's us to honor our Fathers and
B   Mothers do's not bid us do so to our Grandfathers, and Grand-
10   mothers, nor unkles nor Aunts, nor any other of our Relations.

When a Man Dy's all Actions in Law dy with him, and so should all other Quarrels and Animosities, for although the Infamous memory of the Dead like hanging Malefactors in Chaines, serve's for the Good of the Living to deter others from doing the like (and
15   he that is very notoriously Infamous is usd at his Death like a Traytor has his Heart and inward Parts puld out and burnt, and his head and quarters exposd upon some eminent Place) yet he that is not very Scandalous, though we never heard good of him in his life time, will pass as well in funerall Sermons, Burnt wine,
20   and mortality-Rings as the Best, and if his executors will go to the charge of it, may pray upon a Tombe and be belyd in an Epitaph, without any great Inconvenience.

There is so natural a Charme in all Civility and Complacence, that if it were not for that disguise Flattery would never pass in
25   the world upon any other accompt.

No man can possibly do another so much Hurt as hee that ha's oblig'd him. For as all Creditors are Tyrants to those who owe them Money, and hold their liberty only at their Mercy, who are never Satisfy'd with Legall Interest; So is no Obliger with Just,
30   and Reasonable Returnes, but as if the Bonds were forfeited, indeavor to take their Advantage, untill as the Greediest usurers, loose all by over-exaction; So they force others to breake out into open Ingratitude, and relieve themselves by paying nothing, or

---

1 applyd] apply *B*   12 Animosities,] Animosities. *B*   13 Malefactors]
Malectors *B*   24 disguise] disguis- / *B*

compounding for a Small Matter like Bankrupts. For those who do either Benefits or Injurys to others, do commonly never forgive either the one, or the other.

There is nothing ever so wise and Just of it self, but when it come's to be fitted to the Capacity of the Rabble it must like 5 Childrens Physique be disguisd with something else, which may perhaps defeat the virtue and operation of it, and render it utterly unusefull to the end it was designd for. For the Corruption of that little Reason that mankind is capable of, which is the constant Talent of the vulgar, is worse then the Instinct of Beasts that never 10 meddle beyond their own Latitude.

Why should not getting of clap's or Bastards, pass for as sufficient a Penance for Incontinence, as whipping do's in Monasterys, especially of their own Laying on?

Our Savior was of no Profession, neither Priest, nor Lawyer, nor 15 Merchant (as Mahomet was) nor Physitian, though he had more to do with their Trade then any other, not that he usd their Methods or Medcines: But seldom or never undertooke to cure any Disease, untill he had both seen and touchd the Patient, though he could have cur'd the Infirmity as well without it, which some 20 of our modern Doctors will undertake to performe, by touching only of their Fees, who from his example ought to learne what care they should use, before they meddle with the lives of men untill they have sufficiently informd themselves, and considerd all Particulars.   25

Customes that are made by Reason out of Minde, in time out of minde become Laws, and Lawes that were made with the greatest care and Consideration, in time are renderd of no use, but unmake and antiquate themselves: For time that ratify's the Silliest Customes, abrogate's and antiquates the wisest Laws. For Laws are 30 but the Instruments of Government, and as such are apt to be out of order, and spoyld and made useless, according as they light in

8–11 the Corruption . . .] *duplicated B* 139ᵛ   8 of that] of the *W, B* 139ᵛ
9 which is] *om. B* 139ᵛ   11 own] *om. B* 139ᵛ   13 in Monasterys] in
⟨the⟩ Monasterys *B*   22 their] *altered from* his *B*   Fees,] Fees. *B*
24 themselves,] themselves. *B*   29–30 For . . . Laws.] *duplicated B* 139ᵛ
30 and antiquates] *om. B* 139ᵛ   Laws.] Laws *B* 225ʳ

ill, or ignorant hands and though they are made with ever so great Prudence, and Caution, are easily diverted in the Practice, by the Dishonesty of those who have the Interpretation, and management of them.

5   When the Cheats and Impostures that are acted under the Cloke of Religion, have discoverd the Hypocrisy and superstition of one Age, The next comonly (that know's no meane) runs into as extravagant an extreame of Impiety and Profanenes.

225ᵛ   Antiquaries are but Travellers in time, and something worse
B   then those who wander over severall Forrane Cuntrys, for the
11   Difference is Antiquaries only travell by the Book, and take up all their Relations upon Trust, which the other have their eies and Senses to attest, and yet will Impose unmercifuly by which wee may guess how far those (who have nothing but Report, and that
15   by the great variation of Customes and Languages subject to be mistaken) are to be Credited, if they were true which wee have the same Reason to doubt as the Storys of our modern Travellers, which appeare so strangely extravagant.

We finde Antiquaries generally most concernd and delighted
20   with the Admiration of those Inventions of the Antients that are utterly lost, and consequently unknown, as if that very loss were an Argument, of their Excellency, when it is rather of the Contrary. For the world is not so apt to neglect and loose any thing that is found true and usefull to Mankinde, as those that are false and
25   Frivolous [which] in a short time perish Naturally of themselves. For among those Multitudes of foolish Bookes which we finde mentiond by antient Authors, only for being such, there is not one transferd to Posterity, while the greatest part of all those they admir'd and commended are preserv'd and still extant, and if they
30   are not all Perfect, but some have some considerable Parts dismemberd and lost, no man in Reason can suppose they sufferd that because they were better then those that remaine: but it is rather to be imputed to the many hazards they were exposd to by the Barbarousnes and Ignorance of succeeding Ages and the mistake

5 Impostures] Imopostures B   10 Forrane] *interlined B*   14 far] for B
15 variation] variations *W*   18 extravagant] e / vagant B   19 *Editor's paragraph*   concernd and] concernd ⟨with⟩ and B   24 Mankinde,] Mankinde. B
25 [which]] *probably* in B; which *W*   26 which] w / B   28 Posterity,] Posterity. B

of Priests, who guelded and mutilated many Passages in them right
or wrong, supposeing them to be disagreable to the Religion of
their times. Beside the inconvenient way of publishing the Bookes
and writings of those ages, in severall Small Rolls of Paper and
Parchment, for the convenient managment of them in Reading, 5
(which was the cause of their Dividing them into Booke and
Sections &c) by which meanes they were more difficult to be kept
together, or in Boords wax'd over which were as incapable of containing any great Bulk: and the few Copies that could be extant
by mere writing, especially when that Trade could not but be 10
almost decayd by the Confusions and wars of succeeding times.
For if the Antients had had but the good Fortune (among their
other Prodigious Inventions to which all the modern compard
signify nothing with men of Antiquity) to finde out but our way
of binding of Bookes (though they had never arrivd at Printing) 15
the world had never sufferd the loss, nor they lost the Credit of
many excellent writings, which are now (in probability) never to
be recoverd, when since the Arts of Printing and binding it is
impossible, that any thing that is worth preserving, should ever
utterly miscarry. 20

Lawyers who do their Busnes only with words, are the worst
furnishd of all men, For the original Language in which their
Science is written, has neither Grammar nor Syntax, nor Idiom, in
so much that the language of the Richest Men, has no advantage of
being Refin'd above that of Beggars and this perhaps may be one 25
Reason why it is so perpetually subject to Controversy: Like the
originall of the Bible, which by reason of its Antiquity is incapable
of being perfectly understood, and therefore exposd to all manner
of Constructions. The Greatest Convenience of it is, that it is very
short and easy to be Learned as all Barbarous Languages are that 30
have no Rules. For Rules are more usefull to preserve a Language in
its Purity, then to learn it: and therefore Children who are incapable
of them, learn any tunge with greater ease by Rote, then those who
are taught the most Artificiall ways. As for their Latin it has no
Advantage of their Mother-tongue, but only that it is more Cop- 35
ious in Barbarismes, and can turn any language into itself, with a

1 Priests] Priest B   5 managment] manag / ment B   17 probability]
probabilty B   35 Mother-tongue] Mother tongue W   36 itself, with]
itself, ⟨only⟩ with B

Dash only on [the] last Syllable, though in those only al the
Sense of Proper Latin wholly consist's. Yet when they come to
speake at the Bar, they want no Store nor Supply of words, as if
their Studys had been the same with the exercises of those who
5 run Races, and allways Practice in heavy shoes, that when they
come to the Contest and tryall of Skill, they may feel their legs the
lighter.

Stationers deal with all those who write Bookes, as Receivers of
Stollen Goods do with Thieves: Give them what they please and
10 make no Conscience of cheating them of all, if they do not use the
greater Caution in making their Bargaines.

226ʳ   He findes no way to conceal himself and his own Iniquitys from
B   the thicksighted vulgar, more certaine, then by perpetuall seeming
to detest and abhominate all freedom in others, as Renegades are
15 always observd to be more severe to those of their former Religion,
then Naturall Turkes, Not that they like one Profession better or
worse then another, but to instill a Perswasion into their New
Brethren, that their Conversion was Syncere, and in earnest, and
Partly to be Revengd for that ill Opinion, which they know, those
20 whom they have deserted, must of necessity have of them.

So neare of kin are all Cheats and Impostures, that the very same
Lineaments and Features may easily be observd to appear in them
all. Sir T N's Agnition.

Toby Rustick perswaded the king that it was foul weather when
25 it was very Fair; and all the Rest of his Servants make him believe
it is fair, when it is filthy and Foull, to carry him abroad.

All the Pleasures of Luxury or Avarice, or any other Delightfull
vice, And the Greatest Part Of all the Imployments, and Busnes of

2 Latin wholly] Latin ⟨ly's⟩ wholly B   consist's] consis'ts B   10 they]
the B   14–18 Renegades . . . earnest] *duplicated* [*probably* Renegados . . .] B
155ᵛ   15 always] *om.* B 155ᵛ   severe to] severe, and cruel to B 155ᵛ
Religion] Professions B 155ᵛ   16–17 Profession . . . worse] Religion more B
155ᵛ   17 another, but] another (for those Conversions are commonly
made for necessity or Convenience) but B 155ᵛ   a Perswasion] *om.* B 155ᵛ
18 that . . . earnest] an Opinion of their zeale and Syncerity in their new
Conversions B 155ᵛ   21 *Editor's paragraph*   23 Sir . . .] *spaced off from
preceding words* B   24 it] is B

this world, serve only to divert Man from Reflecting too much upon the Misery, Fraylty, and vanity of his Condition in this world, and the Horrid Conclusion of all Death.

The Nature of a Narrative require's nothing but a Plaine, and Methodical Accompt of Matter of Fact Without Reflections, and witty observations on the by, which are more Proper for Discourses, and Repartees.

He that seriously considers, the Miraculous ways of our Coming into this world, and how much wee are Surprisd with our selves, will finde Reason to thinke, That our Departure out of it, is not the last Change of Condition that wee are to expect, though wee understand not the Particulars, more then we did what was Design'd for us, before wee were Born, when we were less capable of guessing, at our Future Condition, then we are now at what may hereafter concern us. And though wee have noe certaine apprehension of it, That may proceed from the Nature of the thing it self which may be so different from all Analogy with this world (where our understanding is limited and confind) That we have no Notions in our Mindes, to Represent it, more then we had in the wombe of the Nature of Human Life, or what we had to do or suffer in it, thoughe we were capable of Contributing our own Indevours to our Entrance into it, and make use of that meanes as soon as we are in it, which Nature had before provided for us.

The Lawes of God prohibit some things only for being Il-naturd, and have no other kinde of Injustice in them, as Boyling a kid, in the Dams Milk, Muzzling the Ox that treads out the Corne &c., To tell us that any Sort of Cruelty, and Hard-heartednes is Displeasing to the Divine Nature, that is sayd to be Gentle and Mercifull.

I do now begin to finde my self Naturally inclin'd to cast up an Accompt with Death, what the true valew of any thing Really come's to.

There is Nothing that can Prevayl more to perswade a Man to

3. 1–2 *See p. 194, ll. 4–5*   11 expect,] expect. *B*   12 understand not] understand ⟨the⟩ not *B*   13 Born,] Born. *B*   16 it self] is self *B*   20 Life,] Life. *B*   25 have] *interlined B*   33 Prevayl] Prevayl. *B*

be an Athiest, as to see such unreasonable Beasts pretend to Religion.

Divines may perswade the world that the Husband and wife are one Flesh, but they will never prove that they are of one Minde.

5   The Prodigal Son was Punishd in kinde, and condemnd to keep hogs, for being a Cully that usd to keepe Sows and Pigs before.

226ᵛ   Divinity is a Speculative Science of Finding out Reasons for
B   things that are not within the Reach of Reason, and therefore it multiplys into so many Differences of Opinions, according to the
10   various Tempers of mens wits, and understandings, which afterwards sort themselvs in to Sects, as all other things in Nature unite, when they meet with others of the same kinde. And though all equally pretend to Truth, which their Contradictions Render Impossible yet evry one is able to draw in others of the same
15   Capacity, and Inclination, and believe's it has Reason enough to Distroy all others, that fall within its Power, and refuse to submit and conform: But the more they lay claime to Truth, the less they are to be Regarded, as Experiments that have the fayrest title to Natural Truth, Have more Lys chargd on their Accompt then any
20   thing else, that cannot lay clame to so great a Certainty. But there is nothing prevayles so much, as a Generall Fancy among them all, of an Implicit Supernatural Influence (of which they have no certaine notion) that conducts their understandings, they know not how, which way it pleases. And upon this they father all their
25   Naturall Defects of Reason and Judgment and wicked Inclinations to things of the Horridst Condition Imaginable. As if their Sottish Ignorance and Inhumane Actions, were but Possessions of the Deity, though they have all the Charecter of those and worse which the Devil is so much revild and exorcisd for.

30   The French tongue though derivd from the Latin, is most unpleasant to those who understand both, and not unlike that Barbarous Canting which those use who do not understand the

---

3–4 *Duplicated (with marginal note* Marriage) *B* 142ᵛ   3 Divines . . . Husband]
Tho' Man *B* 142ᵛ   3–4 are one] are said to be but one *B* 142ᵛ   4 but] *om.*
B 142ᵛ   prove . . . are] be found to be always *B* 142ᵛ   8 it] *interlined B*
30 French tongue] *or possibly* French-tongue *B*

Sense and Propriety of a Language, and such in Probability it was
at first when they receivd it from the old Romans. And therefore
the Italian which the Northern Barbarians receivd more immediatly
from the Roman originall upon the Place, come's nearer to the
Latine, then that which was introduc'd at a greater Distance.   5

Whosoever first found out the Carving of Images, were the
first Authors of Idolatry, for when they shewd the Ignorant
Rabble, the Shapes of things Different in Proportion, and the figure
of Parts, from those that Nature Produces, and they had not wit
and Reason enough, to conceive how they should become such it   10
was not uneasy to perswade them into any opinion of their super-
naturall beings, and make them pay for being taught to adore and
feare them according as they were made believe it was in their
Power to do them either good or evill.

The Greatest Heates of Summer, and Colds of Winter, are my 15
Springs, and Falls of the Leaf, in which I take naturall Physique, by
Sweating Evacuations, or necessary Restringences.

Incontinence is a less Scandalous Sin in Clergy-men then Drinking, because it is manag'd with greater Privacy, then the other
Iniquity, which is apt to expose them to greater Freedom, and   20
tempt them naturally, to venture too far, without their Necessary
Guard of Hypocrisy, without which they are in perpetuall Danger
of being Discoverd, that is to say, undon. The Flesh has a greater
Advantage against the Spirit, in zealots then any other Sort of men,
For their natural inclinations that can Indure nothing that is settled, 25
and injoynd, must of Necessity possess them, with as great and
earnest longings to breake Commandements and violate the Laws
of God with the same zeal and eagernes as they do the Laws of the
Land. For that extraordinary and supercilious Reservdnes which he
always puts on in Publique, is not to conceal nothing, but hide 30
something else that is worse, from the sight of the world. For he
that is Innocent is not so apt to stand always upon his Guard, as
one that is guilty and perpetually in fear of being discoverd. And
therefore this outward stiff Mortification dos really appear to be
but a kinde of Spiritual Carnevall, in which all men are allowd to 35
use all manner of Freedom under a Vizard.

2 Romans.] Romans B   22 they] the B   30 puts] put / B   36 Free-
dom] Freedon B   36. 1 *Illegible rough notes written previously with folio inverted* B

227ʳ   Socrates was wont to stand whole Days and Nights in one
B Posture unmovd, as some Indian Fanatiques are found to do, in our
times, all their Lives, which is no great Argument of the wisdom of
the Philosopher.

5   The Scripture says God made Man in his own Image, and therefore evry man makes God as like himself as he can, and fashions
him according to his own naturall Temper, or the Custome of the
Place where he has been bred, and not the true Reasons of his
Essence and being.

10   Hee who sets a very high valew upon himself, has the less need
to be esteemd by others.

A Hero was nothing but a fellow of a greate Stature and strong
Limbes, who was able to carry a heavier Load of Armes on his
Back, and strike harder Blows, then those of a lesser Size; and ther-
15 for since the Invention of Guns came up; there can bee no true
Hero in great Fights, for all mens Abilitys are so leveld by Gun-
shot, that a Dwarf, may do as heroique Feats of Armes that way as
a Gyant, and if he be a good Markesman, be too hard for the
stoutest Hector and Achilles too.

20   Let the Debaucheries of this Age be ever so great and Scandalous, they Ruine none but such who may avoyd them if they please
and if they wil not, are but justly punishd for their want of Reason,
the Naturall effect of all Infatuation: But the former Religious
Debaucheries were more Pernicious, that comprehended all People,
25 and no man was wise or honest enough to preserve himself from
Distruction, that was but suspected to be such, or thought to
feele the weight of his Burthen, that is, Disaffected to his own
Oppression, or own the Naturall Priviledg of wormes, when they
are troad upon, to turn, about.

30   There was never any Ingenious man in the world that utterly
forbore Drinkeing, that is commonly the greatest vice of very

3 Lives,] Lives. B   6 God as] God ⟨in his own⟩ as B   can,] can. B
7 or] altered from and B   8 and] interlined B   14 Size;] Size. B   16–17 Gun-
shot, that] Gun-shot,—that B   18 Gyant,] Gyant. B   20–1 Scandalous]
Sandalous B   29 troad] or possibly tread B   31 that is] that it is B

witty men, or very fooles, as all extreames use to meet, but seldom
falls upon the middle Sorts of both, of whom their Sobriety renders
multitudes worse then Naturall Fooles; and perpetually makes the
virtuosi or learned Sorts of men Naturally turne Pedants, which the
Freedom of Conversation in Drinking as naturally redeemes them 5
from. And therefore the Antient Greek Philosophers and modern
German Mechaniques have been found to improve their Inventions, and Parts that way more then any other, and to outdo all
the Soberer Persons, and Nations, in the world for the more ab-
stemious, Italians, and Spaniards, are not more inferior to them in 10
Drinking then they are in all other Arts and Sciences.

That monster of Bishops, the Bishop of Munster.

Men do things out of Custome and Example only for want of
Reason, which whosoever has, will meet with Many Occasions
that will often divert him, not only from the Customes of the 15
world, which are for the most part fitted to the Capacity of the
Rabble, but from such as he has bene bred and usd to himself.

The Prince of Conde in the Reignes of Charles the ninth, was
never Quiet but when he was either in the Head of an Army or
the other end of a whore. 20

As all Feats of Activity are the more admird, the nearer they
come to Danger, so is all Speculative wit the nearer it come's to
Nonsense.

A Satyr is a kinde of Knight Errant that goe's upon Adventures,
to Relieve the Distressed Damsel Virtue, and Redeeme Honor out 25
of Inchanted Castles, And opprest Truth, and Reason out of the
Captivity of Gyants and Magitians: and though his meaning be
very honest, yet some believe he is no wiser then those wandring
Heros usd to be, though his Performances and Atchievments be
ever so Renownd and Heroicall. And as those worthys if they Livd 30

---

1 extreames] extreame *B* 4 Pedants,] Pedants. *B* 8 outdo] out do *W*
12 *Interlined B* monster] moster *B* 17 bene] *interlined B* bred and] bred
⟨to⟩ [*interlined*] and *B* bred] *or possibly* brede *or* bredd *B* 20 other end] *altered*
from Arse *B* 25 and] *altered from or possibly* to to *B* 26 Castles,] Castles. *B*
30 ever] eve *B* 30–p. 216, l. 4 those . . .] *duplicated B* 139ᵛ 30 those
worthys] An Antique Knight Errant *B* 139ᵛ they] he *B* 139ᵛ

in our Days, would hardly be able to Defend themselves against the Laws against vagabonds, so our modern Satyr has enough to do, to secure himselfe against the Penaltys of Scandalum Magnatum, 4 and Libells.

227ᵛ   The Great Error of the French Kings Pallace the Louver in Paris
B is that the most magnificent Roomes of State, and the Stables, and Houses of the meanest offices, are all of one Peice, and built after the same manner, which the Dong and filth that is dayly thrown out (especially being in France) renders most Nasty and loathsom.

10   The king of France is the Greatest Affecter of Glory in the world, and the —— on the contrary as great a Neglecter of it, and both in the wrong as all extremes are, and in the end are very like to have the same Fate, as they would have the same Interests.

If the modern Scots could but ingage the two houses of Parla-
15 ment of England to take their Parts No doubt they would immed-iatly rebel againe: For it is only the Feare of them, and the yet Fresh Memory of how they have been lately inslavd that keeps them in their Present obedience. And to that omen I say amen.

Queen Elizabeth was not so much concernd for the Death of the
20 Queen of Scots as she seemd to bee for the Queen's sake, As for the Dangerous Example she had made to the Interest of all Soveraine Princes: to suffer one to be brought to tryall and condemnd, and beheaded, which not long after broke out, in the Reign of her Grandson and will stand upon Record, for a Precedent to deal with
25 all Future Princes, that shall attempt to invade the Rights of their Subjects, or prove so weake, as to have such Pretences how false soever imposd upon them. For to be Guilty, or capable of being put upon for such, is all one to those who are not able to defend their own Innocence. And both those sad Examples we owe to the
30 Barbarous Infidelity of the Scotch Presbyterians, who upon the

1 Days] times B 139ᵛ   themselves] himself B 139ᵛ   2 Laws against] Laws made against B 139ᵛ   2-4 so . . .] underlined B 139ᵛ   2 Satyr has] Satyrs have B 139ᵛ   3 secure himselfe] defend them selvs B 139ᵛ
5 Pallace the] Pallace th B   Louver] or possibly Louv⟨e⟩r B; Louvre W   6 magnificent] magnifice[ ] B   9 France)] Fra / B   14 two houses of] interlined B   18 And . . .] and . . . interlined (possibly a separate passage) B
23 beheaded,] beheaded. B

first occasion, wilbe ready to Act a third, and so forth to the end
of the world and desire nothing more then to venture the Experiment again, and indevor to mend it, by avoyding those errors,
which they suppose were the Causes why they fayld before.

Many a Man ha's been Murthred, that would have Dy'd perhaps 5
within a Day or two, of a Naturall Disease, and yet that never
excusd the Murtherer, if he were discoverd.

As Frenchmen are sayd to furnish their Librarys by the yeard
So their Bookes are written by the yeard, for a Nation that is so
much given to talke cannot but abound as much in writing and 10
Scribling, and to as little Purpose.

The Papists may as wel maintaine that a Cup is wine, because
the Scripture say's Drinke of this Cup, as that the wine is bloud:
There is a great Deal of Difference betwen Drinke of this Cup: and
Drinke off this Cup.   15

Learning is like a Great House that Requires a Great charge to
keepe it in constant Repair.

To be Really of the Church of Rome, is to believe not one word
of the Christian Religion, which No Pope, nor Cardinal for some
Hundreds of yeares are believd (by those that knew them best) to 20
have don, and he that Reade's their Lives written by their own
Creatures will finde little reason to doubt. And if it be the True
Church of God the Devill has his Chappell of Ease in the Metropoli-
tan of it, and those very Oracles which he hearetofore Deliverd at
Delphos are now given out of the Infallible Chaire.   25

Sandwitch was burnt and Drownd himself for using the Spanish
Duke with his wife and Daughter in the same Manner. So Crom-
wels and Bradshaws Heads were Cut of after they were Dead and
Buried, for cutting of the kings Head some yeares before.

10 writing] writing— B   14 a great] agreat B   16 Requires] Require B
21 don,] don. B   23 God] Good B   23–4 Metropolitan of] Metropolitan
⟨State⟩ [altered from Chair] of or possibly Metropolitan State [or ⟨Chair⟩ [or Chair]
altered from State] of B   25. 1–2 See p. 156, ll. 7–8   26–9 Duplicated
and underlined B 87ʳ   27–8 Manner. So Cromwels] Manner and Oliver B 87ʳ
28 were Cut] were om. B 87ʳ   29 cutting . . .] being the Chiefe Instruments
of using the king in the same manner B 87ʳ

[from A Modern Politician]

The best parents, who are commonly the worst men, have
naturally a tender kindenes for their Children, only because they
believe they are Part of themselves, which shew's that self-love is
the Originall of all others; and the Foundation of that great Law of
5 Nature Self-preservation, for no man ever destroyd himself wilfully,
that had not first left of to Love himself. And therefor a mans self
is the proper object of his Love, which is never so well imploy'd,
as when it is kept within its own Confines and not sufferd to Strag-
gle. For every man is just so much a Slave as he is concernd in the
10 will, Inclinations or Fortunes of another: or ha's any thing of
himself, out of his own Power to dispose of. And therefore he is
resolv'd never to trust any man with that kindenes, which he
take's up of himself, unless he has such security, as is most certaine
to yeald him double Interest: for he that do's otherwise is but a
15 Jew, and a Turke to himself, which is much worse then to be so to
all the world beside. For a mans best Friends will never forgive him
the wrongs he do's himself, although they were don merely for
their sakes. For Friends are only Friends to those who have no
neede of them, and when they have, become no longer friends. Like
20 the Leave's of trees, that cloath the woods in heat of Summer,
when they have no need of warmth, and leave them naked when
Cold winter come's, and since there are so few that prove otherwise, it is not wisdom to rely on any.

He is of opinion that no men are so fit to be imployd and trusted,
25 as Fooles, or Knaves, for the first understand no Right, the others
regard none, and whensoever there fall's out an Occasion, that may
prove of great importance, if the infamy and Danger of the Dishonesty were not too apparent, they are the only persons that are
fit for the undertaking. For they are both equally greedy of imploy-
30 ment, the one out of an Itch to be thought able, and the other
honest enough to be trusted as by use and Practice, they sometimes
prove: For the generall Busnes of the world, ly's for the most part
in Rotines, and Formes, of which none are so exact observers as
those who understand nothing else to divert them, as Carters use
35 to blinde their Fore-horses on both sides, that they may see only
forwards and so keep the Road the better; and men that aime at a
Marke use to shut one eie that they may see the Surer with the

27 infamy and] *interlined B*   32 generall] (*or* general) *altered from* greatest B

other. And if Fooles are not notorious they have far more persons
to deal with of their own elevation (who understand one another
better) then they have of those that are above them, which renders
them fitter for many busnesses then wiser men, and they believe
themselves to be so for all: For no man ever thought himself a   5
Foole that was one, So confident do's their Ignorance naturally
render them, and confidence is no Contemptible Qualification in
the management of human affaires, and as blinde-men have secret
Artifices and tricks to supply that defect, and finde out their ways,
which those who have their eies and are but hood-winkd, are utterly   10
unable to do: So Fooles have always little Crafts, and Fraudes in all
their transactions, which wiser men would never have / thought   228ᵛ
upon, and by those they frequently arrive at very great wealth,   B
and as great success in all their undertaking's. For all fooles are but
feble and impotent knaves, that have as Strong and vehement   15
Inclinations to all Sorts of Dishonesty, as the most notorious of
those Ingineres, but want Abilities to put them in Practice, and as
they are always found to be the most obstinate, and intractable
People, to be prevayld upon by reason or Conscience: So they are
as easy to submit to their Superiors (that is) Knaves, by whom they   20
are always observ'd to be govern'd; as all Corparations are wont
to choose their Magistrates out of their own members. As for
knaves they are commonly true enough to their own Interests, and
while they gaine by their imployments wilbe carefull not to disserve
those who can turn them out when they please, what tricks soever   25
they put upon others, which commonly those by whom they are
intrusted share in underhand: And therefor such men prove more
usefull to them in their Designes of gaine, and Profit, then those
whose Consciences and reason will not permit them to take that
Latitude. And since Buffonery is and has always been so delightfull   30
to great Persons, he hold's him very improvident, that is to seeke in
a quality so induceing, that he cannot at least serve for want of a
better, especially since it is so easy that the greatest Part of the
Difficulty ly's in Confidence and he that can but stand fair, and
give aime to those that are Gamsters do's not always loose his   35
Labour, but many times becomes well esteem'd for his Generous
and bold demeanure, and a lucky Repartee, hit upon by chance may
be the making of a man. This is the only modern way of Running

at Tilt, with which great Persons are so delighted, to see men incounter one another, and break Jests as they did Lances heretofore, and he that has the best Beaver to his Helmet, has the greatest advantage, and as the former past upon the Accompt of valour, so
5 do's the later on the Score of wit, though neither perhaps have any great reason for their Pretences, especially the later, that depend's much upon Confidence, which is Commonly a great Support to wit, and therefore beleevd to be it's betters, that ought to take place of it, as all men are greater then their Dependences. So
10 pleasant it is to see men lessen one another, and strive who shall shew himself the most ill natur'd, and most ill mannerd. As in Cuffing all Blows are aym'd at the Face: so it fare's in those Rancounters, where he that weares the toughest leather on his visage, come's of with the Victory, though he has ever so much the
15 Disadvantage upon all other accompts. For a Buffon is like a mad Dog, that has a worme in his Tongue, which make's him bite at all that light in his way, and as he can do nothing alone, but must have somebody to set him, what he may throw at; He that do's perform that office with the greatest Freedom, and is contented to
20 be laugh'd at to give his Patrone pleasure, cannot but be understood to have don very good Service, and consequently deserve to be well rewarded: as a mountebanks Pudding that is content to be cut and slashd and burnt and poysond, without which his Master can shew no Tricks, deserve's to have a considerable share in his
25 Gaines.

229ʳ As for the meaness of those ways which some may think too
B base to be imploy'd to so excellent an end, that import's nothing, for what dislike soever the world conceive's against any mans undertakings, if they do but succeed, and prosper, it will easily
30 recant it's error, and applaud what it condemn'd before, and therefor all wise men have ever justly esteem'd it a great virtue to disdaine the false valews it commonly set's upon all things, and which it self is so apt to retract. For as those who go uphill, use to stoop, and bow their Bodys forward, and some times creep upon their
35 Hands, and those that descend go upright: So the lower a man stoopes, and submit's in these indearing offices, the more Sure and certaine, he is to rise, and the more upright he carry's himself in other matters, the more like in Probability to ruine. And this he believe's to be a wiser course for any man to take then to trouble

23 slashd] shashd B   37 rise,] rise. B

himself withe the knowledge of Arts or Armes, for the one do's but bring a man an unnecessary trouble and the other as unnecessary Danger: And the shortest and more easy way to attaine to both, is to dispise all other men and believe as steadfastly in himself as he can, a better and more certaine Course, then that of Merits.   5

What he gaine's wickedly he spend's as vainly, for he hold's it the greatest Happines that a Man is Capable of to deny himself nothing that his Desires can propose to him but rather to improve his enjoyments by glorying in his vices: For glory being one end of almost all the bus'nes of this world; He who omit's that in the 10 enjoyment of himself, and his Pleasures, loose's the greatest part of his Delight: And therefor the felicity which he supposes other men apprehend he recieves in the relish of his Luxuries, is more delight-full to him then the Fruition it self.   14

[229ᵛ]

The like you are to observe in poynt of gaming, and be sure to 230ʳ make your winings and losses 'greater then they are; this will much 'A' enhance the opinion of your wealth being affirmd with Oaths, and Storys of your Cheating of Rookes, and Gamsters of fortune though the very same way they pasd upon you. Loosers may hav leave to talke.   20

Be sure to give out all your Mistris[ses] to be great Ladys and persons of Honor though they are as common as the pitt in a Play-house, any mans for half a Crowne—A Hackney-coach any mans for 12 pence an houre, and 18 pence the first.

Your negligance is most judiciously exprest in a reservd way of 25 singing to your selfe out of tune, and seeming not to minde what is sayd to you, as if you were diverted with your owne better imaginations. But be sure to have a Care of the Choyce of your Oaths and to use none but such as are in present vogue with persons of Quality, these if you give them the Right tone will wonderfully 30

---

6 *GR's paragraph*   [229ᵛ] *Only notes written by Longueville in vertical lines in top right-hand corner:* Hudibras / Character of the Long Parliament. *B*   16
winings] wining / *B*   are;] are *B*   18 Rookes,] Rookes. *B*   Gamsters]
Gamster / *B*   19 Loosers] loosers *B*   20. 1–4 *Very rough notes interlined:*
maledicto / Ile tel it you plainly and with a Fescue. / Dr S Dr Dr Cha / Mated
of   Decis *B*   22–3 Playhouse,] Playhouse *B*   23 Crowne—] Crowne *B*
23–4 A . . .] *interlined B*   27 diverted] *altered from* am *B*

distinguish you from meane conversations. Example is the Soule of Galantry and therefore you are to doe nothing that is not done by others, nor omit any thing that is, how ill soever it become's you, but follow your Leader in the fashion with a perfect resigna-
5   tion of your selfe to whatsoever is in present request, and profound abhomination of the Contrary.

An old fashion is more gracefull then the new one that succeeds it at first, untill by time and custome it has insinuated it selfe into our likinge.

10   The Italians call any long and tedious Story Bibia, a Bible.

Vesinanza' è un mezo Parento. Vecinanza è mezzo Parentado.

The Master of the Revels would have brought him within his Patent of Jocorum Mascarum et Revellorum, and have shewne him.

15   The Duke of Biron at his Death, Sayth De Serres, Il prioit en commandant et commandoit en priant.

[A Covetous Man]

A Covetous man is a Slave that digs in a Mine, he gets a great deale of Gold and Silver together, but none for his owne use, for he is more afeard to touch it then a Thiefe, and knowes noe use of it
20   but that which his Debtors pay. He hoords up money as a Jack Daw doe's, and to just as much purpose. His Desires are like Hel to which they tend that has no Bottome or Damnation that has noe endes

His wishes like Damnation hav noe end
25   Nor bottom like to hell to which they tend.

230ᵛ His Wealth is like a Witches feast that never satisfies, and he

1 Example] example *B*   3 thing] thing⟨s⟩ *B*   4 you,] you. *B*   5 request,] request. *B*   5–6 profound abhomination] *altered from* hourly renouncing
B   6 abhomination of] abhomination ⟨of whatsoever is⟩ not of *B*   7
gracefull then] gracefull ⟨at fi⟩ then *B*   succeeds] succeed / *B*   19 a Thiefe]
altered from if it were not his owne *B*   21–2 to which they tend] *interlined B*

keepes it as evell Spirits are sayd to doe hidden Treasure under 'A'
grownde. He had rather save twopence then his Soule, and If the
Devill would give money for it he would be sure to be his Customer
but because men have found out ways enough of their owne Invention to damne themselves to get money, he always keep's his 5
witches poore. He differs only from the Madmen in Bedlam, that
they are maintaind at the publique chardge and he at his owne,
which if he understood he would give over his Trade immediatly
and retire himself to save chardges, for though Gayning be his
delight Saving is much more. He mistake's his ends, for by striving 10
by his riches to make himself Master of the world, he render's
himself the greatest Slave in it. He is the Devils martyr and penitent; for by denying himselfe all the pleasures of this world he
store's up Damnation for the next. He cannot be sayd to have
money but his money has him and he is possest of it as men are 15
with evill Spirits, never to be cast out. He is the Platonique Lover
of his money, confine's his desires to contemplation only, but dare's
not thinke of enjoyment. He is the greatest Idolator in the World
and puts his trust in Images. He is but an Iron chest that holds
money, rather then owne's it, and death is the Key that unlocks 20
him, a Leatherne Pouch, a Canvace Money bag. All that he enjoys
is only in the Imagination, in which a mad man, or one that
believe's he has the Philosophers Stone may be as rich.

He Swallows Wealth as unsatisfyd as the Sea, and make's as
little use of it. He love's the largest money and will willingly take 25
none but such as he may clip himselfe. He is a true votary to his
Pagod Goddes money and serves her like a zelot with perpetuall
fasting and praying for more. For this he suffers persecution
willingly, and endures the Scorne and Hatred of the World with
the obstinacy of a Quaker. His Conscience is as lardge as his 30
Desires and will straine at nothing but parting with money. He
feare's Death, but do's not care to be Buried because Money was
digd out of the earth and hath beene often buried in it. He keepe's
his Conscience Seald up in his Bags, and never carry's it about him,

2 grownde.] grownde B   Soule,] Soule. B   and] *interlined B*   3 it] *altered
from* Soules B   would be . . . his] *altered from* were his only B   5 damne]
or damme B   to get money] *interlined B*   6 witches] wretches W   8 he
understood] he be understood B   16 out.] out B   18 Idolator] Idolat[ ] B
19 puts . . . in] *altered from* worships B   puts] put B   20–1 and . . . him]
interlined B   21 him,] him. B   27 Pagod] *interlined B*   serves] serve B
28 For] for B   32 Buried]Bured B   33 in] [ ] B   34 carry's] crry's B
about] [   ]t B

because he find's it troublesome, and a great hindrance to [a]
thriving man. He believes money to be the Soule of the World,
because it was lodgd in the Bowels of the earth, as the Soule doe's
in man, so it gives lawes to all the outward Parts, and is all in all,
and all in every part; That this being the universall Soule ought to
be preservd before the Particular. He is a kinde of Our Lady of
Loretto, that has inestimeable Wealth, but know's not how to use
it.

To looke a little nearer into him He is one that put's out his
money to Nurse but like a tender Parent, is very carefull into
whose handes he trusts it, where he may be sure to see it thrive and
grow apace. He lets out money at Livery as men doe Hackneis but
take's security to have it returnd safe againe and sound winde and
Limbe. Wax is his Birdlime with which he hampers men, as foulers
doe Birds with lime twigs, and make's em leave their feathers behind,
if they scape soe. He makes a mans name serve for a Spell to catch
him with, as Conjurors doe Spirits, and keep him in hold untill he
hath given Satisfaction, for Hand and Seale and Act and Deed, are
but introductions to Prisons. He makes a Decoy of his Coyne, and
let's it fly abroad to bring home more with it. He farme's out his
money and his Tenants are his Villanies, all they get revert's to
him, and their Person too, if they be behinde hand with him.

He spends nothinge but time which is his Worke or Occupation,
and his tooles Money Wax and Parchment. He is a Spider that
Spins his Wealth out of his owne Bowells by Pinching and Sparing
his Guts. He is a Crocodile that lives by rapine and grow's as longe
as he live's. He is like a great overgrowne Firr Tree that parts with
nothing but dead leavs and Drops of Raine, that kill all plants that
grow under it. His Death is a kinde of Treasure-Trove, and his
Buriall the Resurrection of his money, which he commonly leave's
in a litiguous Condition of purpose that his memory, which would
otherwise rot from the face of the earth may live in old Records,
and orders of Chancery. After his Death the first Sally of his money

---

3 was lodgd] *altered from* lives B   4 so it] *altered from* and B   gives] give
B   5 part;] part B   7 has] ha B   inestimeable] inestieable *or possibly* un-
estieable B   9 *Editor's paragraph*   11 where . . . sure] *altered from* and is
very carefull B   12 apace] apacce B   13 againe] agane [*interlined*] B
15 with] wᵗ B   feathers] feather B   17 Conjurors] Conurors B   19 Prisons.]
Prisons, B   22 behinde] behonde B   23 time] *or* times B   26 lives
. . . and] *interlined* B   26-7 as longe as] as longe [*altered from* while] B   27 Firr]
interlined B

is in Burnt Wine Deaths-head-Rings, and long Clokes Tristitiæ
Imitamenta, which his counterfet mourners have need of to cover
their Inward Joy. But we will follow him noe further, for noe man
knowe's which way he is gone, unlesse his Ghost walke to discover where he hid his money or left some debt unpayd, after he 5
hath beene abhominably belyd in a funerall Sermon. He is like a
Lobster all Claws and belly. He is like a Spaniell that will hunt and
set partridges, but not eate soe much as a bone of them.

Though Lawyers are in a perpetuall State of Civill Warre always **231ᵛ**
wrangling with one another, yet they are ever found to continue **'A'**
True to their generall Interest, and from the Judge to the Petti- 11
fogger to conceale the Mysteries of their Profession from the Common enemy. All their Quarrells are but as they are Seconds to
John a Nokes, and John a Stiles as Hectors are to Chiauses.

A Wel[sh] Farme is to be let furnishd or unfurnishd that is 15
Stockd or unstocked in which the Tenant take's all the Paynes and
the Landlord halfe the Profit.

Where noe Religion is, but all Religions.

A whore is like a Crocodile that fastens upon her Prey with her
Tayle.   20

A Prodigal like an Elke that goes backwards when he feedes.

The Spanyards use to present their friends when they are let
bloud (Sangriá).

He committed a Tub-preching Botcher to prison for sowing
Sedition.   25

When Princes treat about Peace or War they doe as the Gaul did,
put their Swords into the Ballance of Justice.

For what prerogative has Greatness left, but that its wants are
greate.

     2 mourners] mourner / *or possibly* murner / *B*   5 unpayd,] *altered from* un-
payd. *B*   15 Wel[sh]] Wel: *B*   16 unstocked] unstocke / *B*   23 (Sangriá)] Sangriá [*interlined*] *B*   26 did,] did *B*   29 greate] greater *W*
     812728   I

He prays perpetually like an Aldermans Image on a Tombe and in the night will now and then assume a Cloake or Hat, but not rob nor steal by noe meanes.

Eate no cheese toasted in the Candle it is like a Soul broyld for the Devills Break-fast.

The Devil is like a Cheating Gamster that trust's his false dice (the wicked) to themselves, but never ventures a Saint without fingering and slurring.

Noe false religion in the World can ever prosper but by putting men out of their play of Reasoninge.

Levellers would have all men like Spanish Swords, to be all of a length.

One that got an estate in the late times, and came of with the Act of Oblivion.

Tis fair play to enter your man before you binde him.

The Hollanders have hired the Lapland witches to put forth a whole fleet of eg-shell against the English, and engagd them to serve their State with soe many dozen bottles of Winde, from time to time to run away with as oft as they shall have occasion to be worsted at Sea.

A great noyse devowre's all lesser and convert's them into it selfe.

For as the sturdy youth of North and West
On Lincolns-In Olympique Plaines contest.

Must I then have patience a whole week?
An everlasting weeke.

He had issue one Brother and 2 Sisters.

1 Aldermans] *interlined B*   and] *new paragraph B*   3 steal] stea / *B*
4–5 *Interlined B*   7 themselves,] themselves. *B*   13–14 *Interlined B*
21 convert's] convert's: *B*   23–4 *Underlined B*   25 Must] ⟨Must I then
forbeare⟩ / Must *B*   27 Brother] Brothe[ ] *B*

[Inconsistant Opinions]

Ἰνκονσισταντ οπινιονς 114 Octobri 10 65

The Hobbists will undertake to prevent Civill wars by proving
that Mankind was borne to nothing else, To reduce men to
Subjection and obedience, by maintaining that Nature made them
all equall, Secure the Rights of Princes, by asserting that whosoever
can get their Power from them has right enough to it, and perswade 5
them and their Subjects to observe imaginary Contracts, by affirming that they are invalid as soone as made.

Princes whose office is to govern others are commonly more
governd then the meanest of their Vassalls, as generally there are
more Servants that governe their Masteres, then Maisters that 10
governe their Servants.

Lawyers that make Justice the object of their Studys, in their
Practice endeavor nothing more then to make Just and Unjust all
one.

Heroique Poets magnify Feates of Armes and those Virtues in 15
others which they are the most averse to them selves of all men
Living.

Strada in the Proem of his Decads endeavors to perswade his
Readers That he is the fittest man to write the Truth of that History, because he was utterly unconcernd, and of neither Partie, and 20
yet immediatly after say's that warre of which he was to write,
being for the most part upon the accompt of Religion, he believe's
himselfe professing Religion (that is being concernd) the fittest
person to describe the Truth of it.

Philosophers and Divines have many fierce Disputes whether 25
the world begun in the Spring or not, as if that æquinox Line were

---

[232ʳ] *Heading* Octobri] *or possibly* Octobre *B*   1–17 *Underlined roughly*
B   4 equall,] equall. *B*   Rights] Right *C*   5 it,] it. *B*   8 *Editor's*
paragraph   9 Vassalls,] Vassalls. *B*   are] *om. B*   12 *Editor's para-*
graph   12–14 Studys . . .] *underline om. B*   15 *Editor's paragraph*   16 them
selves] themselves *W*   17. 1–3 *See p. 138, ll. 12–13*   18 *Editor's paragraph*
25 *Editor's paragraph*   26 Spring] *altered from* Vernall æquinox *altered from* S *B*
that] *possibly altered from* the *B*   æquinox] *interlined B*   were] wee *or possibly*
wer / *B*

not always vernall to one part of the Globe, or all the 4 Seasons were not always at the same time in being in severall parts of the world.

Aristotelians say Materia appetit Formam, which Matter being only Passive and haveing noe Action nor motion of it self, is most ridiculous.

Solomon calls a whore a Strange woeman which is more strang having soe many of them himselfe.

In France the People are much more subject to Diseases then they are with us, and yet Physitians are much lesse esteemd there then here.

Men admire Cloaths and yet dispise Taylers that make them.

In Rome the fountaine of Catholique Religion, Atheisme and Irreligion [most] of all abounds.

232ᵛ
'Aa'

[Incongrue and Inconsistant Opinions]

Ἰνκονγρυε & Ἰνκονσισταντ οπινιονς Octobri 1[4] 65

It is not unpleasant to observe how inconsistant the Opinions of the world are, to them selves, and how all Sorts of men doe not only act but say, things cleane Contrary to what they pretend and meane. Aristotle undertake's to prove the world to be eternall, and without Beginning, and presently after strive's to maintaine Materia prima, which supposes a beginning of all things. Democritus and Epicurus acknowledg it to have a Begininge yet make the Principles of it æternall.

Plato banishd Poets out of his Republique, and yet forgot that that very Commonwealth was merely Poeticall.

---

1 all] *interlined B*   3. 1–4 *See p. 126, ll. 4–8 Different ink B*   4–6 *Different ink B Editor's paragraph*   7 *Editor's paragraph*   9–11 *Different ink B Editor's paragraph*   12 *Editor's paragraph*   13 *Editor's paragraph*   14 Irreligion] Irreligi / B   [most]] *MS. damaged B*   18–p. 229, l. 9 Aristotle . . .] *underlined roughly B*   23 *Editor's paragraph*

The Stoiques would by noe meanes allow of any Passion in a wise man, and yet were soe Passionate in maintaining that opinion, That hundreds of them in Tumultuous Frays lost their Lives in Defence of their Doctrine, and kill'd as many that opposd it.

The Mathematicians admit and lay the foundation of their Art in Body abstract, without Quantity, and yet never after Consider any thing but Quantity: The Philosopher will not endure to heare of Body without Quantity, and yet never after meddles with Quantity any further.

Lucretius begins his excellent Poem of Nature with a Solemne Invocation of Venus to assist him and Pacify Mars, and grant the Romans Peace, That Memmius might be at leasure to minde his reasons and immediatly after deny's the Gods to have any consideration, or take any Notice at all of humane affayres.

Papists and Arminians maintaine Free-will, and yet will allow noe use of it in the Affayres of the world, but place all Piety in obedience to the wills of others. The Presbyterians and Fanatiques utterly deny Free-will, and yet assume all Freedome and Liberty to oppose their Governors at their owne will and pleasure. The Former of these erect Religious houses and Monasteries, where men may live free from the Diversions of the world and wholly at leasure to apply themselves to Divine Contemplations, which yet they never doe but spend the greatest part of their time in singing and saying prayer's by Rote. The later dissallow of these and betake themselves to Trades, and occupations, and yet place all the Duties of Religion and Piety merely in Contemplation, which they call New-light.

[Inconsistant Opinions]

Ινκονσισταντ οπινιονς 114 Feb 4 66

Decrepit old men are most covetous of welth that have noe time nor will to enjoy it, but only store it up to leave behind them, while

---

1 *Editor's paragraph*   1–2 in . . . man] *interlined B*   5 *Editor's paragraph*
10 *Editor's paragraph*   15–27 *Underlined roughly B Editor's paragraph*   27. 1–3
[fo. 233ʳ] *See p. 174, l. 35–p. 175, l. 2*   28–p. 230, l. 10 *Underlined roughly B*
28 *Editor's paragraph*   29 it,] it. *B*

Youth that has soe many days to come, and winters of Adversity to expect, makes noe provision for it self against them.

When Learning was at the lowest, in the most meane and contemptible Quality, in the Barbarous monkish Ages, it was most
5 highly esteemd reverencd, and advancd: Colledges and Schooles built evry where to improve it, and great preferments always open to those that were but meanly skilful in it; But since it is arrivd at soe great perfection, it is despisd, and scornd as Pædantry; and noe provision nor encouradgment left for those whose inclinations, and
10 naturall abilities might prove a great advancment to it.

The Rabbins interpret Chammes Discovery of his fathers Nakedness to signify he guelt him, and if that be true, he did it, to prevent his getting more Children, which was very unreasonable when he had but three Sons to inherit the whole world.

15 Nature ha's given Beasts leasure and opportunity enough for contemplation, by the easines of life she ha's provided for them, but noe capacity to apply themselves to it; But man that ha's abilities for it, she has denyd those advantages by the unavoydable encumbrances of human Affayres. And among men those that have
20 the greatest conveniencies, have always the least inclinations to it.

We cannot remember any Laws made in our times for rectifying of some Publique Abuse, but advantage has afterwards beene taken from the very words of that Law, to encouradg the Practice of that abuse to greater extravagancies then were usd before.

25 The falser and more Ridiculous any Religion is, the more actions of Piety it produce's, and the violenter zeale in the Professors; As appeare's by the Mahometans, among whom soe many thousands devote themselves, in their Armies against the Christians, to sacrifice their lives as voluntere Martyrs for the Mussle-man-
30 cause, others to put out their eies after they have seene Mahomets Tombe; And the Indians that out of Devotion throw their Bodys

2 provision] provsion *B*   3 *Editor's paragraph*   8 soe] *interlined B*
11 *Editor's paragraph*   12 guelt] *altered from or possibly to* gueld *B*   15–p. 231,
l. 5 *Underlined roughly B Editor's paragraph*   21 *Editor's paragraph*   We] we
B   in our times] *interlined B*   22 has] hes *B*   25 *Editor's paragraph*   is]
interlined B   29–30 for the Mussle-man-cause] *interlined B*

under the wheeles of the Pagods chariots to be crushd to death, actions of Zeale and Devotion that are never found among soberer Religions. Soe the Jewish Idolaters cut their flesh, and sacrificd their Children to Moloch, while the Orthodox Jewes had noe such fire in their Zeale.   5

Men that professe honor for the most part practice least, and esteeme that Patents of their Titles but Dispensations for not doing things honorable, As Lawyers that profes Justice endeavor to perswade men that they are obligd to be Just noe further then the Law can compell them, and the one Halfe of all their Practice 10 is to make that good.

Chyrurgians are lesse esteemd then Physitians though their Paines are greater then the others and their Knowledg more certaine.

Men commonly judg of the events of things, not as they are in 15 Probability like to succeed, but as they desire to have them: As Bowlers screw and force their bodys that way they would have their Bowles run.

There are many that delight to talke of nothing but Religion and the Service of God, and yet will rather renounce both, then 20 loose one penny in defence of their fayth, though they have got never soe much by it: while others whom noe man would guess by their lives and Conversation to have any Sense of Religion at all, will venture to loose all they have rather then not professe what they really believe.   25

Men covet those things most, which Nature or Fortune has **233ᵛ** denyd them, and dispise those (though better) that are in their '**A**' power to enjoy.

Noah had noe sooner escapd the waters, but he presently found out wine, which has drownd and destroyd as many people since, as 30 the Deluge did before.

4. Children to] Children, ⟨while⟩ to B   6 *Editor's paragraph*   7 es-
teeme] esteene *B*   8 honorable,] honorable,. *B*   12 *Editor's paragraph*
15 *Editor's paragraph*   19–28 *Underlined roughly B*   19 *Editor's paragraph*
24. venture] *altered from* loose *B*   28. 1–4 *See p. 138, ll. 4–6*   29 *Editor's
paragraph*

Tully say's in one place Rei Militaris virtus præstat cæteris omnibus: and in another Cedant Arma Togæ.

Nature has turnd Man into the world worse provided for then any other Creature, made him have need of more things, and furnishd him with lesse, Given him a Capacity to understand Truth, and Desire to persue it, but hid it from him, as wee doe things from Spaniels when wee teach them to fetch and carry, as if shee tooke Delight in our Industry.

The nearest way to honor is to have none at all.

Fooles invent fashions, and wise men are faine to follow them.

Honor and advanc'ment are only Due to merit, but for the most part fall into the hands of undeservers, as tall woemen are most fit and proper for tall men, but are always affected, and taken up by little low ones.

Men never understand the world, and advantages of life untill they are Past the use of both.

Wicked and ungodly Men have much the Advantage of the Righteous and holy both in this world, and the next: For the Righteous are involv'd and suffer in all publique Calamities for the Sins of those, who (according to the Church of Rome) may if they please share with them in the merits of their owne holinesse and Piety.

Children in their play doe their owne Busnes (without knowing or regarding it) more wisely then the prudentst men, that thinke they understand what they doe, and proceed with all convenient Caution: for with perpetuall exercise and agitation of all the Parts of their bodys, they distribute the Nutriment to evry one, and

1 *Editor's paragraph*   3–8 *Underlined roughly B Editor's paragraph*   3 Man into] *possibly* Man ⟨out⟩ into *B*   8 Industry.] Industry *B*   9 *Editor's paragraph*   10 *Editor's paragraph*   11 *Editor's paragraph*   14. 1–3 *See p. 176, ll. 1–7*   15 *Editor's paragraph*   17–p. 233, l. 10 . . . expose] *underlined roughly B*   17 *Editor's paragraph*   21 holinesse] *possibly altered from* holinesse. *B*   23 *Editor's paragraph*   25 convenient] *altered from* manner of *B*   26 Caution:] Caution; *B*   agitation] *altered from* motion *B*   the] *interlined B*

assist Nature in contributing to their owne Growth, while the wisest men by mistaking their ends, or ill Judging in the manage of their Designes, bestow a great deale of Paines and labour to noe purpose unless it be to render them selves worse then they were. Soe Children when they first begin to speake learne Languages 5 without minding much sooner and with more ease and facility then afterwards when they are growne up and understand what they would doe they can possibly attaine to by the best Methods and instructions.

Souldiers expose themselves to almost certaine Death, to obteine 10 the Conveniences of life, and sometimes the inconveniences: And those that in a right nick, and lucky occasion, are able to contemne and disdaine life, doe afterwards become Masters of all the advantages of it.

Men persue their Pleasures till they turne to paine's, and like the 15 Reprobates, for a little transitory tickling Delight damne themselves to longe and lasting Torments, for pleasures like money stay longest where they are most moderatly and sparingly usd, and he that enjoy's them temperatly enjoys most at long-running: But 19 in this Nature her selfe seeme's to take part against us, in / making 234ʳ those things pleasent that betray and ruine us, and those that 'A' preserve us (like Medcines) both harsh and ungratefull to Sense.

The more Ignorant men are, the more obstinate they are allways in their Opinions, for Implicite fayth is ever more pertinatious then that which can give an accompt of it selfe, And as men in the Darke 25 endeavor to tread firmer then when they are in the light, the Darknes of their understandings make's them apt to lay hold on any thing, and hold faster wheresoever [it] happen to be though it be out of their way; or as Cowards that are wel backd appeare boldest soe he that believe's as the Church believe's (though he 30 know's not what it is) is more Confident, and obstinate then he that can give a reason for his fayth.

1 Growth,] Growth. B   2 Judging] Juding B   6 without minding] *interlined B*   10 *Editor's paragraph*   16 tickling] ticklng [*altered from* itching] B   19 enjoys] [   ]oys B   23–p. 234, l. 13 *Underlined roughly B* 23 *Editor's paragraph*   25 selfe,] selfe B   27 lay hold] *altered from* hold fast *altered from* lay hold B   28 hold faster] *altered from* stand firmer B   wheresoever] *probably* wheresoev / B   to be] *interlined B*   29 way;] way. B   31 is)] is, B

Men derive their Bravery from the remedy of their Defects, and glory in their Cloaths that doe but cover and disguise their naked-nesses, and had never beene used nor needed, had it not beene for the unhappinesse of their falne condition, as if they gaind not lost
5 by it, and had made themselves finer then ever God meand they should bee, like Trees that grow the better for being cropd.

Those that are envious make them selfs miserable because they see others happy, and switch, and spur them selves because they see others outgoe them; and very foolishly torment themselves to
10 render those they envy never the worse.

Lyers are commonly the most credulous of all People, and though they know that they seldome speake Truth themselves, yet they are apt to believe that evry man else doe's.

The Proverb says A burnd Child dread's the fire, but a burnt
15 person that should be at yeares of Discretion will never regard it.

The easiest way to understand Truth, is by Fables and Apologues that have nothing at all of Truth in them, For Truth ha's little or nothing to doe in the Affayres of the world, although all things of the greatest weight and moment are managed in her Name, like
20 a weake Princesse, that has the Title only and Pretence and falshood all the Power. For they are her Ministers (and ministers seldom prove true) that act by her Authority, while shee like Prester-Jone seldome suffers her face to be seene.

Those that perjure themselves to delude others by æquivocation
25 doe it (as they belive) to save their Consciences harmelesse, where the Sin is much greater, then if they forswore themselves plainly without any tricks, for in that they doe but deceive the world, and may be thought to make somewhat too bold with God's Mercy, which the other disclame and doe their Indevors to deceive God
30 and the world, and their owne Consciences too.

1 *Editor's paragraph*   3 it] in B   7 *Editor's paragraph*   envious]
evnious B   10 worse.] worse B   11 *Editor's paragraph*   14 *Editor's paragraph*   16 *Editor's paragraph*   easiest . . . Truth] *underlined B*   20 and
Pretence] *interlined B*   21 and ministers] *altered from* who B   22 that] *altered
from* and B   24 *Editor's paragraph*   27 without] without, B   world,]
world. B   28 Mercy,] *possibly altered from* Mercy. B

As men are more glad to meet with their Friends and acquaintances in a Forraine Cuntry then at home, Soe they are more delighted to finde wit, and Sense in a Strange language then their owne mother Tongues, though the worth of the thing exprest be the same, and they come easier to understand it. 5

Small Fountaines are the Originalls of mighty Rivers: and Great Lakes but of petty rivolets.

Persius who only of all the Roman Poets came nearest to the Fustian and Bumbast ways of expression used in the declining Age of that Language, Is yet the only Author that take's Notice of it 10 as a vice in others, and indeavors to render it Ridiculous in a way almost as vicious as it selfe.

Thinges not True ought to be finer sayd then those that are, else they would never be preferd before Truth, if Ephæstion had not beene finer then Alexander he had never beene taken for him. 15

The Flourishes of Arts (which are only to amuse and cheat the 234ᵛ Ignorant) require more paines and time then the usfull part of 'ᴀ' them, as writing Masters bestow more labour in practicing to make Knots and Dashes, then letters. Soe the most necessary and usefull of all Seedes wheate, creepe's out of the plaine Stalke with- 20 out any flourish at all, while all the Gaudy Bravery of Tulip's serve to noe purpose but an empty shew.

The Subtletys of the Stoiques were most ridiculous, who held good and wisdom were bodys but to be wise was neither Good nor Body, That Justice and fortitude were living Creatures. Seneca Ep. 25 113.

Fooles have always the strongest fayths, as we see in madmen who believing themselves Princes will not be Confuted with whipping, nor the severest discipline of Bedlam though it be a very unusuall manner of treating Princes. 30

6 *Editor's paragraph*   mighty] *altered from* mighty, B   Rivers:] *interlined* B
7. 1–3 *See p. 10, ll. 16–18*   8–9 . . . and] *underlined* B   14 before] bef[ ] B
18 practicing] *altered from* making B   23 *Editor's paragraph*   25 living] lving B
27 *Editor's paragraph*   madmen] madme / B   29 discipline] disc / pline B
30 manner] *altered from* way B

All Guifts presents and offices of friendship are commonly done to those that need them not: never where they are necessary or seasonable. Those that want are to expect noe more then the mere hire of their Labour (if that) which is never rated according to the merit of their Paines but the necessity of their Condition, for the poorer men are, the Cheaper their Imployments are always esteemd.

Among Religious People of the ordinary rate evry man almost is an Hypocrite to him selfe, and does not only dissemble with others, but his owne Conscience and understanding.

They that tell us we must lay by reason in matters of Fayth, forget that nothing but reason can tell them soe, and there they deceive them selves; and while they thinke they lay it by they use it: and they may with the same sense perswade us when we take up a perspective, to lay by our eies; for there is noe beliefe in the world, that hath not either reason, or some implicit thing like reason (that supplys the place of it) which is the Ground and foundation of it, else noe man living can give an accompt why he is rather of one fayth then another.

The Imagination of man is as Naturally delighted with a prospect of knowledg as the eie is with the Landscap of a Cuntry, and therefor as when we get upon a mountaine, where the farthest thing we can see is but another Mountaine, we are more pleasd with a faint and languishing appearance of that which at such a distance, does but appear otherwise then it is, then with a certaine and perfect view of that which ly's neare to us, and to which we ow all the discovery we have of the other.

Men take up any thing that make's for them upon any account and nothing that makes against them upon any.

All great and extraordinary Actions of Friendship favour and Affection have for the most part ever beene conferd where they were least deservd and (with allowance for the envy such things

<hr />

1 *Editor's paragraph*   8 *Editor's paragraph*   11 *Editor's paragraph*
28 *Editor's paragraph*   30 *Editor's paragraph*   32 and (with] (and with
[*probably altered from* and with] B

always bring with them) noe man could imagine the true reason
how they came about.

Critiques and commentators use comonly to passe over that
which is hard, and make that which is plaine obscure.

The Common-wealth of Lawyers is a Government that subsists 5
by Civill warre, for they are at perpetuall Controversy with one
another, and yet noe Society of men in the world is better united
then they are to their owne generall Interest.

Civity was never found in any Nation, where Learning was not
before, and yet it is soe farre otherwise in Persons; that there is 10
scarse any thing more rare then a profest Scholler Civill.

Immateriall and Vacuum are all one and yet some Philosophers
deny the one and acknowledg the other.

The opac body of the earth is much more the Cause of day then
of night, for if there were noe earth there would be night [but] if 15
there were noe earth there could be noe Day.

[Bankrupt]

Βανκ-ρυπτ *202*. Oct. 6. 67

Is made by breaking, as a Bird is hatch'd by breaking the Shel.
For he gaine's more by giveing over his Trade then ever he did by
dealing in it. He drives a Trade as O Cromwel did a Coach, til
it broke in Pieces. He is very tender and careful in Preserving his 20
Credit, and Keepe's it as methodically as a Race-Nag is dieted that
in the end he may run away with it. For he observ's al punctual
Curiosity in performing his word, until he ha's improv'd his Credit
as far as it can go; and then he has catch'd the Fish, and throw's
away the Net, as a Butcher when he has fed his beast as fat as it can 25
grow, cut's the Throat of it. When he ha's brought his Designe to
perfection, and disposd of all his Materials, He lay's his Traine

3 *Editor's paragraph*   5 *Editor's paragraph*   9 *Editor's paragraph*
10 soe] foe *B*   otherwise] otherw[   ] *B*   12 *Editor's paragraph*   14 *Editor's*
paragraph   15 of night,] of night.   *B* would] *altered from* night *or* might *B*
[but]] *MS. damaged B*   21 is dieted] *interlined B*   22 observ's] observ' / *B*
24 as far] af far *B*   25 Net,] Net. *B*

(like a Powder-Traytor) and get's out of the way while he blow's
up al those that Trusted him. After the Blow is given, there is no
manner of Intelligence to be heard of him for some Months, until
the Rage and Fury is somewhat disgested, and al hopes vanishd
5 of ever Recovering any thing; of Body or goods, for Revenge, or
Restitution. And then Propositions of Treaty and accommodation
appeare like the Signe of the hand and Pen out of the Cloudes, with
Conditions more unreasonable then Thievs are wont to demand
for restitution of stolen Goodes. He shoote's like a Fouler at a
10 whole Flock of Geese at once, and stalke's with his Horse to come
as neare, as he possibly can without being perceivd by any one, or
giving the least suspicion of his Designe, until it is too late to
prevent it, and then he fly's from them, as they should have done
before from him. His way is so commonly usd in the City that he
15 rob's in a Rode like a High-way-man, and yet they wil never
arrive at wit enough to avoyd it; for it is don upon Surprise and
as thievs are commonly better mounted then those they rob, he
very easily makes his escape and flys, beyond Persuite of Huon-
Crys, and there is no possibility of ever overtaking him.

235ᵛ
'Aa'

[War]

ὦαρ 206 Octobri *13 67*

20   Is a Cessation of humanity, a Demurrer to al Civil Justice and
Appeal to the Sentence of the Sword, a Tryal by the Balloting of
Guns, and the Supreme Court of Judicature in the whole world, to
which al Nations equally Submit, and put them selves upon God
and their Cuntry. It is a kinde of Inferior Day of Judgment only the
25 proceedings are different, for as the Trumpets sound, and the Dead
rise in the one, so the Trumpets sound, and the Living fal in the
other, so contrary are the ways of Divine, and humane Justice, for
Gods Judgments commonly hang halfe and save half without any
appearing consideration of Particulers, which among men is the
30 most unequal way in the world, though the Justest to him that
understands al things. It is like a Clerkes-case where the Judges
themselves argue, only it is not carryd by most voyces, but the

16 wit] *or possibly* wil *B*   it;] it. *B*   18 makes] ma[   ] *B*   [**235ᵛ**] *Heading*
Octobri] *or possibly* Octobre *B*   25 proceedings] proceeding / *B*   30 though]
thoug / *B*   31 Clerkes-case] Clockes-case *W*

strongest and most powrful, for he that can make the most preva-
lent Party is always Judg'd to have the right. But that side that is
worsted ha's as hard a fate as the Gallique Orators that lost their
lives with their Causes. It is a Disease contracted by the Surfets
and Disorders of Peace, a Burning Feaver, and Runing Gout which 5
the world always has in some Part or other. An evil Spirit that
posses[ses] it, and remov's from one Limbe to another, makes it
mad and raving and is not to be cast out but by fasting, that is,
until it ha's Destroyd and consumd al that which went to maintaine it. For as al Creatures are nourishd by the Dams that breed 10
them, soe is war supported by the Disorders that brought it
forth, and do's not degenerat from the Breed it came of for it put's
al things out of order where ever it comes. It is a Monster in a
Labyrinth that feeds upon mans flesh, For when it is once engagd
it is a matter of exceeding difficulty to get out of it agen. It destroys 15
al the Productions of Peace that bred it, like the eldest son and heir
of the Ottoman Family, and Plants nothing but Barbarisme where
ever it prevayles. It determines al Controversys in the world
Divine and humane, without understanding what they are, and
cleares al Doubts as the Sun do's darknes, without seing what it is, 20
the only way they are capable of Resolution. For the General of an
Army is more infallible then al the General Councels, and interprets
more solidly without understanding, then they could doe with al
their Subtletys. It is sayd to be the last Reason of Kings, because it
should be kept as a Reserve when al others fayl. It is a Storme 25
raysd by Statesmen the Conjurers of the world that beare's down
al before it like a Hurricane, and is not so easily allayd, as raysd.
It is never so barbarous as when it is Civil, for in Civil wars Parties
are inflamd with Particular animosities, and provocations given
and receivd in the Quarrel, which never happens in Forraine wars. 30

[Horse-Courser]

῍Ορσε-κυρσερ *204* Oct 8 67

Is one that has read Horses, and understands al the Virtus, and
Vices of the whole Species by long Conversation with them, and

7–8 makes . . . raving] *interlined B*   8 fasting,] fastin / *B*   9 consumd]
comsumd *B*   which went] which it went *B*   12 forth,] forth *B*
17 the] t[ ] *B*   Family,] Family. *B*   20 is,] is *B*   23 could] cou[ ] B
27 Hurricane,] Hurricane. *B*   30 the] th *B*

how to make his best advantages of both. He make's his first applications to a Horse as some Lovers do to a Mistres, with special regard to her eies and legs, and passes other Parts with lesse severe, and curious Scrutiny. He understands al Diseases incident to the
5 body of Horse, and what to abate in the Price for every one, according as it is capable either of Cure or disguise. He has more ways to hide Defects in Hors-flesh, then women have Decays in faces, among which, oaths and Ly's are the most general, for when they are applyd warm, they serve like an Universal Medcine, to cure al
10 Infirmitys alike, For he that affirme's or Deny's any thing confidently, is sure to gaine some beliefe, though from an equal Obstinacy, as two stone's of equal hardnesse rubd together, wil teare something from one another, and false wares wil not be put of but by false meanes, as al things are maintaind, and nourishd by that which
15 is agreeable to their own Nature. All his other Operations are nothing to that of Quacking, with which he wil put of Diseases as fast as a Mountebank do's Cures. He understands the Cronologie of a horses mouth most critically, and wil finde out the yeare of his Nativity by it, as certainly as if he had been present at the Mares
20 Labour, that bore him. All his Arts wil not serve to Counterfet a Horses Paces but he has a lere trick that serves instead of it, and that is to cry down al those Paces which he want's, and magnify those he has. When he is lame of one foot, he has a very fine expedient by pricking the other over against it, to make him go right
25 againe. He is a strict observer of al Saints days only for the Fayrs that are kept on them, and knows which is the best Patron for buying, and which for Selling. For Religion having always been a Traffique, the Saints have in al Ages been esteemd the most fit and proper to have the Chardg of al Fayres where al Sorts of Trades
30 are most usd, and always where a Saint ha's a Fayre he has a church too, as St Peters at Westminster, St Bartholmew in Smithfield, &c.

236ᵛ
'Aa'

[Churchwarden]

ΚὑρX ὡαρδην 203 Oct. *8 67*

Is a Publique Officer intrusted to rob the Church by Virtue of his Place, as long as he is in it. He has a very great care to eate and

7 faces,] faces B   13 another,] *altered from* another. B   20 him.] him.. B
23 of] *altered from* on B   30 usd,] usd. B   31 Smithfield,] Smithfield. B

drinke wel upon al Publique occasions that concern the Parish, for a good Conscience being a Perpetual feast, he believes the better he feeds, the more Conscience he use's in the Discharge of his trust: and as long as there is no Dry-money-Cheat usd al others are allowd according to the Tradition and Practice of the Church in the purest Times. When he lay's a Tax upon the Parish he commonly rayses it a fourth part above the account to supply the Default of Houses that may be burnt, or stand empty, or men that may breake and run away, and if none of these happen his Fortune was the greater and his hazard never the lesse, and therefore he devide's the over-plus between himselfe and his colleagus, who were ingag'd to pay the whole, if al the Parish had run away, or hangd themselvs. He over-reckons the Parish in his Accounts, as the Taverns do him, and keep's the od money himselfe instead of giving it to the Drawers. He eates up the Bel-ropes like the Asse in the Emblem, and convert's the broken glass-windores into whole Bere-glasses of sack: and before his yeare is out, if he be but as good a fellow, as the Drinking Bishop was, pledge's a whole Pulpit-ful. If the Church happen to fal to decay in his time, it prove's a Deo-dand to him for he is Lord of the Manor, and do's not only make what he pleases of it: but ha's his Name, recorded on the wals among Texts of Scripture, and Leathern-buckets, with the yeare of his Office, that the memory of the unjust as wel as the Just may last as long as so transitory a thing may. He Interprets his Oath as Catholiques do the Scripture, not according to the Sense and meaning of the words, but the Tradition, and Practice of his Predecessors, who have always been observd to sweare what others please and do what they please themselves.

Court-wit must be very slight, when evry man Professes it, and that Trade very trivial which every man learn's of himself and ha's a Stock to set up with. Tis not unlike the subtle mystery of Linck-boys, whose Busnes ly's in the Dark, and to obtrude themselves upon al men that are in it, and to walk before them with more smoke and vapour then light.

5 Tradition] Tadition *B*   7 above the account] *interlined B*   12 run away] *or possibly* run-away *B*   13 themselvs.] themselvs / *B*   14 himselfe] *or* him / selfe *B*   16 Emblem,] Emblem. *B*   24 so . . . thing] *altered from* it *B*   29–34 *From 'A Court Wit', See Appendix B*   30 and] [ ] *B*   31 the subtle mystery] *probably* ⟨the subtle mystery⟩ *B*   33 and] [ ] *B*

Our modern Reformers handle their matters just like those who usd to debauch in Taverns heretofore on humiliations and Sundays, when the Heaven-drivers were Comeing, remove their Pots and Glasses out of the way, and sit as innocently as if they had
5 not been drinking at al. But as soon as the visitation was over, produce their affayrs again, and fal to the Busnes of the Day with more freedom then before.

They deal with the Church, in being severe to Papists, as we doe with Children when they are angry with som body, Ah naughty
10 man; did he hurt the child? give me a Stroke and I wil beat him.

They have usd the —— like the Prodigal child, made him take money of his Freinds to forsake them, and put himself into the hands of Strangers, who when they had spent al he had, have left him to feed with hogs (like King Dor) and now he has noe way but
15 to return home again to his Friends, who wil kil for him the fatted calf.

The Court now apply's to the Parlament as Cuntry people when they have lost their Goods or Cattle by thievs, goe to Conjurers and Cunning-men to finde them out agen.

20 If there ever were a Mystery of Iniquity it is now, though knavery was never more foolish in any Age, for indeed Mysterys though they looke wise seldom prove So.

I wil follow you as Cheap as your Shadow.

[Letters]

1ʳ Dear Sir
'A'   I am very Sensible of the exceedinge great favour I receivd from
26 you by your letters to Mr Bernard, wherein you are pleasd to let me know, I have the happines to live in your memorie, then which nothinge but (that which came with it) the knowledge of your health and Safety, could have beene more dearely welcome to mee,

---

6 their affayrs] *altered from* them *B*   15 Friends,] Friends. *B*   15. 1–3
See p. 115, ll. 3–5   18 their] th[ ] *B*   21 Age,] Age. *B*   23 *Under-lined B*

But I am further obligd to you for your kinde concernment, and
care of my good Successe which indeed Sir I shall ever believe I owe
rather to the good wishes of such excellent persons as your selfe
then any desert or industrie of mine owne. I beseech you commend
my most humble Service to your noble father, and if you doe not   5
thinke your last favour misplacd, for bringinge you this trouble,
indeed Sir there is noe man livinge, to whom the knowledge of
your happinesse (when you shall please to thinke me worthy of it)
can be more really welcome then to

Your most affectionate   10
and faythfull Servant

Junii 28°

ℬutler

[1ᵛ
blank]

Deare Sister   86ʳ
  I have read your letter, that you sent to my wife, In which you   'A'
Desire my Advice about breeding of your Son, and although I have   16
considerd much and long of it, and not only conferd with my
Cussen Kemish, but severall others of my Friends about it I know
not what to say to you. For not knowing the Naturall Parts and
Inclination of the youth I know as little what to Propose to you in   20
it, For if he doth not naturally take a Delight in his Booke, it
wilbe in vain to think by any other meanes to Prevayl upon him to
do it. And therefore All I can say to you concerning that, is to Put
him to some Grammar school among which there is no great
Difference that I could ever observe especially to those who have not   25
extraordinary Inclinations of their owne Tempers to it: where with
little Industry they may easily attaine to so much as will serve them
in their Ordinary Occasions of Busnes, which is the Common Rate
of all Mens Educations, and sometimes more Prosperous to themselves, then it provs to those who indeavor to go further. As for   30
your breeding him to the Law, whether he be fit for it or not: is
much more Difficult to Determine. For as in all that Profession,
There are many hunderds that make no Advantage at all, for one
that dos, So there is nothing certaine but th'expence and Danger,
where youth being left to it self without so much as a Tutor Or   35

---

  5 father,] father. *B*   [86ʳ] *Written in a column along the top edge:* 7 5 0 / 3 6 0 /
Ale 2 10 / Ba 0 9 / Self 0 4 *B*   19 you.] yo *B*   24 among] *altered from*
Of *B*   34 dos,] dos. *B*

Governor, shall meet with so many that make it their Trade and
Busnes to Corrupt, and if they have any thing undo them. This I
have sene in a Friend of mine an Eminent Lawyer of the Temple,
who bred up 3 or 4 Sons in his own Profession, and under his own
5 eie, and yet could not with all his Care Possibly preserve them
from being utterly ruind by the ill Company that perpetually lay
in wayt for them.

But if you have a mind to send him to any Schoole in this Towne
I need not tell you how careful your Sister wilbe to her Power of
10 him, nor shall I be wanting in any thing that is in mine. But the
lease of the House where we live, being neare expiring, wee shall
be necessitated to Remove, I suppose the next Quarter, where wee
shall indevor to finde better conveniences for him then this Place
14 can afford.

[Lists of Synonyms]

[87ᵛ]   Calamity. Distress, Misery. Affliction, want, Need, Indigence,
'B' Poverty. Penury. Suffering. Care Necessity. Tribulation Perse-
cution, Trouble, Molestation, Contrition. Anxiety. Anguish,
Torment Grief, Sorrow. Melancholy. Sadnes. Dejection. Dis-
content. Paine. Displeasure, Vexation. Remorse. Humility.
20 Meaneness. wretchedness. Disrespect. Rancor. Regret. Hardship.
Difficulty. Disparagment uneasines.4[o] Unhappines, Infelicity,
Disaster. Misfortune, Il fortune, hard fortune, Bad fortune Torture
Disquiet. Dispair. Dispite. Grievance. Pressure. Oppression, wrong.
Injury. Affront. Baffle. Scorn. Shame Infamy. Ruine. Cark and
25 Care.

Empire. Reign, Authority. State, Power, Command. Govern-
ment. Rule. Prerogative. Soverainty, Controll Magistracy.
Majesty. Dominion. Principality. Supremacy. Throne. Crown,
Scepter. Dignity. pre eminence Grandure. Greatnes. Kingship.
30 Presidence, Superiority. Monarchy. Signiory. Sultany. Dynasty.
Province Palatinate; Prelacy. Regality. Regence. Kingdom.
Democraty. Aristocratie. Oligarchy Tyranny. Usurpation Juris-

---

4–14 under . . .] A anser *written across text in large ornamental letters B*   8
Schoole] Shoole *B*   10 mine.] mine *B*   [87ᵛ] *No punctuation at end of most*
MS. lines B   22 Torture] Tortur / *B*   24 Shame] Sham / *B*   29 pre
eminence] pre eminenc / *B*

diction. Royalty. Governance. Arbitration. Priority. Precinct.
District.

Inact. establish. Confirme. Ratify. Ordaine. Order. Over-rule.
Settle. Passe. Decree. Determine. Resolve. Control. Seale.
Command. Injoyn. Rescribe. Prescribe. oblige. Binde. Pass a Fine. 5
Give Livery and Seasin. Signe. Act. Vote.

Long. Tedious. lasting. Everlasting. Incessant. Indefatigable.
untyr'd. laborious. Endless Infinite. Large. Plentifull. Abundant.
Copious. exceeding. Innumerous. universall. Incomprehensible
overgrowne. vast. Unlimited. uncircumscribd. Superfluous. over- 10
don. Impetuous. Immense shallow.

Bondage, Bondes, Slavery, Captivity. Yoake. Chaines Fetters,
shackles. Manacles. Guives. Locks Bolts. Vassalage. Villanage.
Subjection. Thrall. Thraldom. Ægypt. Babilon. Prison Dongeon
Jayl, Goale. Bridewell. Counter. Cage. Roundhouse. Stocks. 15
Pillory. whipping. Scourge.

To Nul. Voyd. Cancell. Abrogate. Repeal. Disanull. Revoke.
Disoblige. Abolish. Rescind. Expunge Retract. Re[set]. Reverse.
Abjure. Deny. Renounce. Abdicate. Disclame. Redress. Forsweare
Recall. Dissolve. inlarge. Dischargd. Quit. Quit clame. Recede. 20
Renege. Disowne. Disavow. Extirpate. cashere. Resigne, exter-
minate. Suppress.

[List of Anecdotes]

The Mayd of Honor, and the Dog. Dr Charltons verberation, **89ᵛ**
Anatomy, and Ecclips, Father Mores and F Ms Dispute About **'B'**
Religion. The Italian Cut-purse with wooden Hands. T Mason 25
and Sir T Not. The welch like to be Hangd. Pish Nick her wits
making Love. The Quaker, and Milkmayd. The old Parson that
could not Remember nor Repeat, Common Prayer without his
Spectacles. The Rats that would hang a Bell about the Cats neck.
Paytons beating T L. The Gamster that Quarreld because his Flat 30
was Black. The Parson Cookolded by the Bride. Jasper M. and

18 Re[set]] Re[ ] *B*

Pilgarlique The Serpent, and the Rock. Revelations and Revolutions. D Givillim and the King of France   Lord Scudamor Embasador in France, his wife and Secretary Sir R Brown. Presbitor of the Nature of a Cat. Foxes story of the Eg-chariot   Terence his
5 Epistles. Dr Gerrards universal Medcine. Scarbrow upon the Glandules. Mr Pecks singing of Psalmes. Dr Glissons Reason why Nature has the Inward Parts of all Men in the same Position. Love and Honor in a Sowgelder   Pagan Fisher at Olivers Funeral. Frienda's making Gallantery. King Fucusar. Their Interpretation
10 of Feet and Garden for Pudenda. Lawyer and Long-lane Pint of wine. Dr Dorchester Reading with Grass. W Egerton and Hostess. The Doctor of Clarkenwel and his Daughter and Son in Law. The Reverent Man that had his Prick burnt with a Candle which he took for a Clap. The Button-seller Pawnd. Busbys taking of Physick
15 cun exercitio. B Blandford learning of wops and Squint Ferran Story of the Earl of Sandwitch his Travelling in Spaine. Sir P witches making of Love. An hous visitation. The Charecters of Nile for Cataracti. Sir James Bag and his Chambermayd.

1 Pilgarlique] Pilgarlque *B*

PROSE AND VERSE FROM WILLIAM LONGUEVILLE'S COMMONPLACE BOOK

Notes on Upper Endpapers

Fides Nominum est salus proprietatum. Tertull: [1ʳ]

Aglets, any dangling thing in ear, or points. fr: aiguillettes. In old English poets, as Spencer &c.

Debander l'arc, ne gueri pas la plaie.

           Garde chaud le pie et teste.   [2ʳ]
           Et au reste vive en beste.   6

Gulae substructa lascivia est, et in salacitatem Voracitas transit. Tertull:

Men pay no Toll in France for a Horse with 4 white Feete.   [2ᵛ]

The french call one that is over-officious; Valet du Diable.   10

           4 throws of Rome
Ternio.
Senio.
Canicula. worse of all. damnosa canicula
Venus. best.   15

1–8 *Written in Butler's hand C*   1 proprietatum] [   ]rietatum *C*   1.1–5
Rough notes in Butler's hand: habilis / h — abilis – able / Axes. ιλι'σ. Achilles [?vide]
totus Homerus. / Ileum εἴλω. ἔλο. εἴλον. Ιō must be taken. / Ansata superbè dextra
[?vide] Anulus. *C*   2 In] in *C*   3. 1–2 *Verse draft, in Longueville's hand, from*
B 98ᵛ *or* 121ʳ *C*   4. 1–2 *Verse draft, in Longueville's hand, from B* 75ᵛ *C, with*
S Butler *added at end C*   9–10 *Written in Longueville's hand C*   11 Rome]
Rom *C*   11–15 *Written in Butler's hand C*

France and the French

[i^r]   The French use so many words upon all occasions, that if they did not cut them so short in pronunciation, that they are allmost Inarticulate, They would grow tedious and insufferable.

They infinitely affect Rhime, though it becomes their Language
5 the worst in the World, for pronouncing words otherwise then They are written, they make the most confounded stuffe in the world read; and though they spoile the little Sense they have to make way for it, yet they are often forced to make the same Syllable serve to Rhyme with Itselfe; which is worse then mettle upon met-
10 tle in Heraldry. They have not yet redeemd themselves (nor are they ever like to doe) from the Pedantry of Quibble (which they call equivoc and highly admire) and Poeticall Gods and Goddesses, which passe with them for Wit and learning: and are esteemd more modish then Sense and Reason; which renders their Compositions
15 (for they write nothing else) exceeding Flat, and insipid.

They are naturally so Incontinent of their Tongues; that there is nothing so uneasy to Them as to bee Silent. This Loquacity is so naturall to them, that whosoever has to doe with any of them; tho' in the smallest matter Imaginable shall never come off without a
20 long Dispute and Wrangling; For rather then bate a Souse markée in any Cheat they will talk an Houre.

In Paris they gaine most by Cheating of Strangers either in the Price of whatsoever they have occasion for, or the fantastique value of their money which they reckon by livers, Though they have no
25 such Coine in the World.

[i^v]   To talk perpetually with Them is an universall Remedy or medecine against all Paines; for like Dogs they cure all their wounds with their Tongues: and when they are once Speechlesse they are given over as past all hope of Recovery. I never came among Them
30 but that verse of the Poett was allwaies in my Head

Raucàque Garrulitas, studiumque immane loquendi.

France and the French] *Editor's heading*   7-8 and . . . it] *underlined C*
8-9 make . . . Itselfe] *underlined C*   15. 1-5 *See p. 138, ll. 1-5 (C reads:* They
find it much easier . . .)   16 so . . . Tongues] *underlined C*   20 a Souse
markée] *underlined C*   24-5 by . . .] *underlined roughly C*

For they talk so much they have not time to Thinke: and if they
had all the witt in the world their Tongues would runn before It:
For they [are] always in Chorus, as a kennell of Hounds opens
alltogether; And every man has a speciall Regard to what Hee
sayes Himselfe; but none at all to what hee heares from others: 5
And by these meanes They are all better pleased, then if they talkd
ever so much to the purpose.

The French Nation is like a Tavern to the English that drink up
their wines and are ever wrongd and Cheated by Them.

Their women are so Ill-favourd and deformd that they have 10
great Reason to call one another Bougers: for it is a kind of unnaturall sin to have to doe with any of them and if ever the Presbiterian Hugonots possesse themselves of the Gouvernment There
will bee no end of Hanging Witches.

They have one Incurable disease and that is they admire them- 15
selves so much that they Scorne to take notice of what others doe:
And since some of their foolish Neighbours study their Language
out of Mode and affectation impute It to their Extraordinary Merit
and Believe they ought to give them Lawes and instruct them in All
things else. And because some of the English Nobility and Gentry 20
out of mere fashion, that send their Children to travaile, put Them
to learne to Ride and fence in their Academies, become Confident
like Pedants that they are Able to teach them All things Else. And
to This the Vanity and Basenesse of some English Scriblers does
contribute very much; who to acquire themselves a little false and 25
Ridiculous Reputation among the Rabble, are not ashamd to
Dishonour their Native Countrey by Translating their paltry
writings into our Language who have farr Better of our owne.

When they meete in Conversation They all (like Jackdaws and
Rookes) chatter rather then talk together and no man mindes what 30
another saies because hee knows before Hand, that It is not worth
his Attention.

The present King is building a most Stately Triumphall Arch [ii^r]
(which one calld a Triumvirall arch) in memory of his victories and
the great actions which hee has performd; But if I am not mistaken 35
Hee is; in the Reason of those Erections, which tho they beare the
names at Rome of those Emperours to whom they were dedicated
(as Titus &c) were never raysed by themselves, but decreed

(like triumphs) by the Senate and built at the Charges of the people;
For that Glory is lost which any man designes to consecrate to
Himself. Hee takes a very good Course to weaken the Citty of paris
by adorning of It and to undoe It, by making It appeare Greater
5 and more Glorious; for hee pulls down whole streetes to make
roome for those pallaces and publick structures: which hee is
allready Building or pretends to doe. That if they should at any
time attempt to act any of their Old tragedies of Rebellion over
againe They may bee the lesse able to prevaile. For hee hates the
10 Citty and by taking all occasions to bee Absent from It endeavours
to keep It as poore as hee cann. Hee is now building a magnificent
fabrick upon a Hill without the towne which hee pretends to bee a
Colledge for Astronomers and builds It high that they may have a
freer prospect of the Heavens from all parts But the Strength and
15 fortification of the designe of It makes It plaine that hee intends it
for a Castle to overtop and command all parts of the Citty and to
have a free view of all the Houses in that Rather then those in the
Heavens: And indeed it is Wonderfull to what a great Quietnesse
hee has reduced the one half of it i.e the filous That used to gouvern
20 as freely in the night; as the Magistrates did in the day: for there is
no Citty in the world that is freer from that people nor any Countrey in which the High wayes are Safer.

There is nothing Great nor magnificent in all the Country (That
I have seen) but the building and furniture of the Kings houses and
25 the Churches; All the rest is mean and paltry The shops little and
dark and poorely furnished with wares.

They have very few publick Inns and those nasty and only for
the reception of Carryers For every house allmost is an Inn and
has a stable as well as Lodgings to bee lett which makes all the
30 Roomes stinck most unsufferably tho they did not thro down all
the filth of severall familyes into the yard which is the common
house of office to Them all.

[ii^v]   The King is necessitated to lay heavy taxes upon them in his
own defence and to keepe them Poore to keep them Quiett for if
35 they were suffered to enjoy any plenty They are naturally so
Insolent that they would become ungovernable and use him as

2–3 For . . . Himself] *underlined* C   4 undoe It, by] undoe [*altered from* render]
It lesse, by C   5 more] mor / C   make] mak C   10 by taking] ⟨by
tak[ ]⟩ *partially altered to* seat *or* set C   21 from that] *or possibly* from those C
32. 1–2 Vide al fine de Dr Lockey's Geography. beaucop de mr Butlers notes
sr France C

they have done his predecessors. But hee has renderd himself so
secure that they have no thoughts of attempting any thing in his
time.

Hee indeavours to lessen the authority of the pope daily in his
Dominions and makes what hee pleases passe for the priviledges of ₅
the Gallican Church and if hee continue it but a short time his
Holinesse will have as little power in france as hee has in England.
And there is now a Controversy between them whither the fryers
of any order may bee allowd to preach without license from the
Bishops which the pope has absolutely enjoind and the King has ₁₀
peremptorily forbidden upon paine of Death.

The Churchmen over-looke all other people as haughtily as the
Churches and steeples doe private Houses.

All people use to bee kind and good Natur'd when they take
their leaves.   ₁₅

The Lawyers seeme to bee more Numerous then ours at London
For tho in the vacation of the parlement the pallace was fuller
upon a small Court day then ever I saw Westminster hall in a full
terme. They walk the streetes in great state and Every man has
his Lacquay or Two to beare up the taile of his Gowne. They plead ₂₀
at the Barr in the same fashiond Capes that priests weare in Procession. Both they and their Clyents must of necessity bee admirably
Litigious That doe so naturally abound with words and their own
sence. All trades sett up among them as they doe with us to shew
that Justice Itselfe is but a Commodity and to bee bought and sold ₂₅
to Him that will give most.

Their witts and virtuosoes alwaies goe in Couples like Fryers and
upon all occasions magnify and extoll one another. They apply to
Great persons unknown to shew their witts with the same confidence that tradesmen use to putt of their wares.   ₃₀

The players set up no Bills in the Streetes but only on the Houses
where they act; tho all other sorts of people are so naturally
inclined to It that a small student seldom does his Exercise without
vapouring Bills to publish what rare Feates hee is to performe and
all shopkeepers wrap up the wares they sell in printed papers – – – ₃₅
and generally they are All the Kings servants.

They doe nothing without ostentation and the King himselfe [iii^r]
is not behind with his Triumphall Arch consecrated to Himselfe

and within and without his Impresse of the Sun with, hoc pluribus
Impar.

The French doe not use to conceale the virtues of any thing that
has relation to Themselves.

5   If the Citty of Paris were far more Beautifull then It is; It wants
one ornament with which London abounds; Beautifull women,
that are the Greatest rarities in the world in P. and make It looke
like a great fair House Ill furnished: For those that have not seen It
cannot fancy How unpleasant it is to find a perpetuall defect of
10 those objects which all men naturally take delight to looke upon;
and which are so common with us that wee take no notice of Them,
untill by the want of them, wee find how uncomfortably a Great
Citty appeares without Them. For the same things that Excellent
Pictures are to Galleryes Bewtifull women are to Streetes. Theirs
15 decay so soone; that after 20ty, Age and Youth appeares mixt
together in the same face. Quære, the Climate kind to nothing
that It produces, but Corne and Fruite.

The French are so greedy of money that they use more Conscience when they are trusted with the meate, then the Reckon-
20 ing; for they will treate by the Head better for 2. 3ds. (where they
have no possibility of over-Reckoning) then they will when they
are to Account.

The French King having Coppies of the best pieces from Rome
is as a great prince wearing Cloathes at 2d Hand.

25 The King in his prodigious Charge of Buildings and furniture
does the same thing to himselfe, that hee indeavours to doe by
Paris; Render himselfe weaker by endeavouring to appeare the
more Magnificent; let's goe substance for shadow.

[iiiᵛ]   Nothing does more demonstrate their Poverty then the Base-
30 nesse of their money, the most common being of Alloyd and debasd Brasse. And that difference that is between the Coyn (which
is the common measure of all things) of the 2 Nations seemes to
bee the very same in every thing else.

Their Theaters and stages and Actors are most intollerable, in

1–2 hoc pluribus Impar] *underlined* C   13–14 For . . . Streetes] *underlined* C
14 Streetes.] Streetes C   16 Quære,] Qᵃ C   16–17 the Climate . . .
underlined C   27–8 Render . . . Magnificent] *underlined* C   28 Magnificent;] Magnificent. C   28. 1–2 *Written by Butler at the top of* [iiiᵛ] *facing
Dictionary* What is that to You? Que souciez vous in cela. / tant qu'il est Prisonier,
il le seroit ausi C   28. 3 *Written in the same ink as ll.* 29 *ff.* S Butler. C
30 money] *underlined* C

Comparison of ours: and their musick much worse then punchinello's.

Their Pitts are made shelving, like ours: but without seates, which makes them stand very uneasily: and to save their money, Buy pleasure with paine.   5

They have no manner of passion in their pronunciation, nor change of their voyces according to the Sence: But run on as they use to doe in speaking: and make a short stop at every Rhime which is most lewd and ridiculous For without Cadence and Accent in pronunciation the best Sence cannot but loose much of 10 It's grace and elegance, in any language. But the french who use to pronounce a whole Line without any distinction, as if it were all but one word; loose that Advantage of Humouring Sence (if they had It) which other more Sober and significant Languages, never omitt. When they pronounce any Latin word which they have not 15 yett melted down into their own Language, They never observe the proper Accent and Quantity: but make every Syllable of an equall Length, which appeares very sillily.

> For they that Love to feed on meats that stinke
> Must bee as lewd in all they doe or thinke.   20

[English–French Dictionary in Butler's Hand]   [ivr-lxxxivr]

1–2 punchinello's.] *then interlined* qᵃ talk all / C   4–5 to . . .] *underlined* C

Passages under Various Headings

[lxxxiv^r] The things blyth martiall only make
Mans life more sweet then plum in Cake
Then lick of Sirrup, Rhime in Meeter
Or whatsoe're It is that's Sweeter.
5 A free Estate and smooth soft hand;
For tender Palm and good free land
Are tye'd with thred of blood, and from
The selfe same Rugged Parent come.
For one would hardly give a Straw
10 For Ground that's gott with proper Paw:
Next willing ground; for Lands are willing
As well as women to bee Tilling:
And both are with rough Share ploughd upp
E're they can yeeld desired Cropp.
15 So like in this that It may b'avowd
Land's got with Child and woman ploughd.
A field not base; for fields as well as
Men may bee said to bee base fellows
For if they yeeld not 10 for one
20 Of Pease or of obligation sown;
They are so base 'tis hard to tell you
Which is the field, and which the fellow.

A Gown unbusied hanging by
For Gowns and Gown-men too that lye
25 Unbusied may goe hang; unlesse
They had rather ly in Beggars presse.

A Constant flame that never tires
For that's the nature of good fires.
For flames and horses that are Good
30 Will never tire, tho made of wood.
The Græcian horse was both that burnd

1–p. 255, l. 7 *Written in r.h. col.* (*Dictionary in l.h.*) C   5 A free Estate] *underlined* C   hand;] hand C   8 Rugged Parent] *underlined* C   16 *Underlined* C
20 or...] *underlined* C   23 A Gown unbusied] *underlined* C   27–8 *Underlined* C

And all Troy-town to Ashes turnd.
For when within the walls h'had gott
The horse did burne; the flames to trot.

By thy side a lovely toy
That's sometime Kind and sometime Coy   5
For shee that's alwayes kind or Coy
Will quickly either tire or Cloy.

Blest in your selfe and in your husband too;
The Glory of our Roman dames are you:
N[i]grina, whilst so kindly you impart   10
Your fortune, where you wisely Gave your Heart.
E[v]adne and Alcestis wee Admire
Who martyrs of Chast wedlock did expire:
Wheras in life your merits shine so cleare
You need not dye to make your Love Appeare.   15

Private, unimployd, unpreferd, out of office, out of Powr. Reducd,   [lxxxivv]
reformado'd, cashierd, unobeyd, neglected, unregarded Cast out
of Authority, exauthorized. Debasd. uncommanding. Repulsd.
disobeyd, unimpowrd. unadvancd. ²⁰ Impotent. humbled. wretched. low. deposd. turnd out. Degraded. Disrespected. undomin-   20
ering. undervalewd. uninterested. Depriv'd. dispoyld. Retrench'd.
lowrd. unactive. expeld prostrated. Banishd. proscribd. ⁴⁰ Displac'd.
dishonourd. vayld. depresd. undon. Ruind. puld downe. overthrown.
unhorsd. Dismounted. overturnd. stripd. bereft. Ungouverning.
Uncontrouling.   25

Martial li. 10. Ep. 32.

Ars utinam Mores, Animumque effingere posset
Pulchrior in terris Nulla tabella feret.

If Art could draw her minde and lovely manners,
The World ne're saw a Sweeter Picture, then Hers.   30

If Art her minde or manners could expresse,
Never was Picture of such Lovelynesse.

If Art her manners and her minde could draw,
The world so sweet a picture never saw.

6–7 *Duplicated* B 43ᵛ   8–15 *Written into space at bottom of both cols.* C
10 N[i]grina] *uncertain reading*   15 Love] Lov / C   28 feret.] feret. Mart.
l. 10. Ep. 32. C

If art her mind or manners could designe
The world ne're saw a Picture so Divine.

Fallit enim vitium Specie virtutis et umbra
Cum sit Triste habitu vultuque et veste Severum.

5   Vice cheats in virtue's shape, if it appeare
In habit Grave and Countenance Severe.

Goe hunt the orange-tawny Colourd Fox
And to my Mistresse give her skin: whose locks
Are shorter and more orange tawny farr
10   Then H[ai]rs that grow on Tayles of Foxes are.

1ʳ   Creation

Some suppose that at the Creation Light dispelld a moist vapour
that filld the Vast extent of Space which cannot bee; For light does
not dispell moisture, but attract It; nor does the Sun disperse a
Fogg but by Exhaling It.

15   When God had created Man in Paradice Hee gave him no
command (that wee heare of) to Worship Him; but only enjoynd
him to bee Obedient to a Small Negative Order not to Eate of the
Fruite of one Tree (for it is plaine Hee was not forbidden to Eate
of the tree of life) tho' hee were after banishd out of paradice; That
20   hee might not Doe It; For God would not trust to his Obedience
any more when hee had once violated It. All the rest of his Duty
was only to increase and multiply, and possesse and Enjoy &c. The
Dri'd up Nipples of the Breasts of all men may seeme to inferre,
That man was at first Created both Male and Female as the Scrip-
25   ture sayes. Tho afterward for his greater Convenience the femall
parte was taken out of Him, for his Conversation only and Assistance. But that provd so unhappy to Him, that his Helper helpt
the Serpent to betray Him.

6 Grave] *altered from* Solemn *C*   Countenance] *altered from* in face *C*
10 H[ai]rs] Hers *C*   11 Light] *underlined C*   16 to Worship Him] *underlined C*
18–19 for … life] *underlined C*   19–21 That … Duty] *underlined C*   22 The]
the *C*   27 that his Helper] *underlined C*

Antiquity and Antiquary 2ʳ

Hee is more mad and silly in his implicit Admiring of the Ancients then any of the Moderns can bee in being but pleased with Themselvs.

Understanding 3ʳ

Men glory in that that is their Infelicity Learning of Greek and 4ʳ Latin to understand the Sciences conteind in Them, which hardly 5 countervaile the Paines and industry and time that is layd out upon Them and commonly prove no better a Bargaine then hee makes who breakes his Teeth to crack a Nutt that has nothing but a Maggott in It. For the greatest advantages they acquire by It, is (for the most part) nothing but to unriddle difficult and far-fet 10 Curiosities that serve to no purpose but to passe upon the Account of learning and knowledge to which they are really but Warts and Cornes or Sencelesse Excrescencies. For what could any man gaine in the Improvement of his understanding by expounding the true meaning of—Jura per Anchialum (upon which so vast Industry has 15 been thrown away) if it could have been attaind but only to please himselfe and some few others of the same humour with a difficult Trifle. For the variation of Languages at the Building of Babell was but a 2d Curse upon the fall of man And as the first brought him knowledge at the Charge of Labour and Drudgery in tilling 20 the Earth that was renderd Barren of purpose only to find him worke and in the End to devoure Him, So do's this 2d of learning Languages afford him a very pittifull Returne of Knowledge in comparison of the intollerable Paines and Industry that is spent upon It; for which hee would have nothing but his Labour for 25 his Paines, if hee did not Divert himselfe with setting false Values 4ᵛ upon some little Things, that light in his Way, tho utterly imperti-nent to his designe and purpose. As pretious stones were perhaps at 1st found out by those who digd into the Earth to another End,

---

3. 1–82 *Verse drafts from B* 18ʳ *C*   3. 83–4 [3ᵛ] *See* 'The Obstinate Man', *sent.*
10; *GR* ii. 423–4 *His Wits . . . is*   3. 85–8 *Verse draft from* 'Satyr upon Human
Learning', ll. 123–6; *GR* i. 209   4–18 . . . *Trifle*] *duplicated C* 7ᵛ   4 *that*
that] *that which C* 7ᵛ   12–13 *and knowledge . . . Excrescencies*] *om. C* 7ᵛ
15 *Jura per Anchialum*] *underlined C* 4ʳ   22 *Him,*] Him. *C*

to which altho they were unusefull yet the Caprich of mankind has renderd them a Costly and vainglorious Trouble. For if the antient and forrain Authors exceed the modern in any thing It was because they came Easier to their Knowledge and were not com-
5 pelld to endure the slavery of studying more Languages then their own Mother tongues which now take up the greatest part of that time in mans age that is fittest and most proper for study and does but render him the more unready at his owne language And therfore It is no wonder that the antient Grecians were and are still so
10 much Admird for their Eloquence when they had but one language to lay out their witt and Ingenuity upon and the Moderns so many.

5^r   Wisdome

5^v   Fooles and Knaves are but Vehicles to convey the Affaires of the World upon, and keepe it allwayes in Motion which if all men were Wise or Honest would meete with inevitable obstructions.
15 Nor are they Impertinent or unnecessary in Great Councells, if rightly managed for they will serve to doe that which wiser or Honester men would never bee obligd to Endure. And all publick Societyes and bodyes politique must as well as the Naturall have feete to tread upon and Hands to Act as well as Heads and Hearts
20 to Judge and Resolve: For a Councell of all Wisemen would bee as unusefull, as a man that is All Head. Concurrers are alwayes more usefull to wise men, and lesse troublesome, then those that delight to Object and many times much wiser, for an objection is obligd to bee true and pertinent or else It is Intollerable to those that under-
25 stand Better, which no Concurrence is Subject to. For most men object out of Ignorance or too subtle and over-understanding (which is not much Better) more often then out of certaine and Right Judgment.

6^r   [Assent]

15 Nor] nor C   20–1 For . . . Head] *underlined* C

Writing   6^v

As men would have better Memories (Seneca sayes) if they did not trust to Writing; So they would have better fancies if They did not use to Reade.

Learning   7^r

One that has made a Hasty March through most Arts and 7^v
Sciences: but like an Ill Captaine left the Garrisons and Strong 5
townes behind him untouch'd.

To a living Tongue New words may bee Added; but not to a dead tongue as Latin Greeke Hebrew.

Qui ultra facultates Sapit desipit.

Ad odorum differentias nondum excogitantur verba.   10

Sence and Reason is too Chargeable for the ordinary occasions of Schollars in universities to doe their Exercises withall and Few are able to goe to the price of It; And therfore Metaphisicks are better to those purposes as being Cheap and slight which any Dunce may easily beare the Expence of and make a better noyse in the Eares of 15 the Ignorant then that which is true and Right.

Non Qui plurima sed Qui Utulia legerunt, Eruditi Habendi.

Hee is a foole that has nothing of philosophy in Him But not so much as hee who has nothing else but philosophy in Him.

The Antients left the World much Learneder then the Moderns 20
found It for many of their writings were lost and some no doubt that wee never heard of; Beside the great numbers of impertinent and Ignorant Errors which the Barbarous Ages produced; which

3. 1–16 *Verse drafts from B* 132^r *and* 132^v C   5 but . . . the] *underlined* C
7–8, 9, 10 *Interlined in a different ink* C   13 And therfore Metaphisicks] *underlined* C   17 *Interlined in a different ink* C   20–p. 260, l. 3 *Written in the
different ink of ll.* 7–8, 9, 10 C   22–p. 260, l. 3 Beside . . .] *underlined* C

prove no lesse Impediments to the Increase of true and reall Knowledge then the unhappy losse of those things that were good and
usefull.

8ʳ   The Soule

  The Soule is so environed with faculties, Affections, Passions and
5 Inclinations, which flow in upon it; like so many waves And tosse
it; And as either Gett Prædominance It carries the Soule away with
a Strong Currant; Sometimes Revenge, sometimes Hate, Envy or
Malice; Another while Pride then hope, then Griefe, Joy feare or
earthly love take their turnes; so that Divine Charity had need of
10 many eyes to watch so many Enemies; much Constancy not to bee
Discouraged And much Patience to Endure such Assaults.

10ʳ   [Poetry]

12ʳ   [Sin]

13ʳ   [Content]

13ᵛ   [Anger]

14ʳ   Cheating

  Cheates are like Witches that have no Power over a Gull untill
they have Gotten Something from Him and then have a perfect
Hanke to dispose of all the Rest.

15ʳ   [Flattery]

  3. 1–13 See p. 257, ll. 4–18 . . . Trifle   4–11 Written in a large hand C
11. 1–26 [9ʳ] Verse drafts from B 18ᵛ C   11. 27–68 [9ᵛ] Verse drafts from B 17ʳ C
11. 69–92 [10ʳ] Verse drafts from B 50ʳ and 50ᵛ C   14. 1–20 [14ᵛ] Verse drafts
from B 78ʳ C

Misfortunes   16ʳ

Optimè miserias ferunt, Qui abscondunt.

Old age is misery enough of Itselfe without the Additionall
Calamity of Want.

Confidence,   17ʳ

is but the wit of the Face; like Painting, it may impart an Artificiall Flourish to the outside: but cannot alter lineaments, nor 5
mend those Features which nature has contrived amisse.

His Tongue's a two edgd sword in Lawyers Hand;   18ᵛ
Whose double stroakes no Innocence can withstand.

Truth will to both bee Just: Angels that fell
The 1st distinction made of Heaven and Hell.   10

Of bloody slanders who undaunted can
The deadly stroke endure; is more then man:
Nothing of sublunary growth or Make
Of that immortall temper can partake.
Wee learn this lesson only from that Chaire   15
Where God and man the Joynt Professors are.

Their only Crimes they were, who swore them so,
And who these oaths so lightly did allow.

They ran at Ease and hardly did blow for 't,
For a false Oath did never yett sweare short.   20

Lawyer   19ʳ

rates his abilities by his Eating: and so long as hee hath been in
Commons, So much hee is presum'd to understand of the Common
Law. And though hee has never studyed, yet having Eaten so
many yeares towards the Law; It is sufficient to enable Him to bee

3. 1–6 *See 'Case of King Charles I', par. 4; GR* i. 333. *C reads* Hands *for* Hand
6. 1–35 [**17ᵛ**] *See 'A Court Wit', T* 94ʳ⁻ᵛ, *and Appendix B below for C variants*
18 *Underlined C*   19 *Interlined* i.e. the lawyers *C*   20 *Underlined C*
21 ff. *For omitted passages (p. 262, ll. 3. 1–11, etc.) see 'A Lawyer', GR* ii. 168–70, *and
Appendix B below for C variants*

calld to the Barr: And so many yeares as hee hath been in the Butler's booke, So much hee is supposed to understand of the year-
bookes.

Hee is bound to eate in Commons like a horse that's tyd to the
5 manger.

19ᵛ A Lawyer serves the King in his Gouvernment as his Servants
doe in his family, steales and imbezzles his power and authority
from Him and takes a great deale more from Him then hee is allowed in Reason and Justice.

10 All officers that are employd about the execution of the Lawes
have something of the Hangman in their Natures and Conversations and ought to bee avoyded by Those who have no Necessary
businesses to doe with them, as much as Butchers are and soldiers
ought to bee forbidden to bee of Juryes.

15 A Lawyer that has been used to Speake for or against any thing
and has made It his Constant practice when hee has followed the
trade long enough to bee made a Judge, cannot bee so Reverendly
Dull as not to bee Able to make Justice appeare to Incline (like
victory ever in great Battles) to which side hee pleases; like the
20 old great Justice who is sayd to have Directed Juryes by only
Handling of his Beard for a man that is constantly usd to one kind
of study shall find It allwayes running in his Head of Itselfe and
which way soever his Inclination tends, It sweighs that way with
all It's weight, as Bowles runn according as the Bias is turnd and
25 only goes true by being made false and Partiall and fitt to Comply
with all Sorts of Grounds: As those that have no Byas are the Hardest to bee manag'd and made Goe Upright.

As labouring Men their hands, Cryers their lungs
Porters their backs, lawyers hire out their Tongues.

3. 1–11 'A Lawyer', sent. 23–7   3. 12–13 'A Lawyer', sent. 28   4 in
Commons like] underlined C   5. 1–4 'A Lawyer', sent. 30   5. 5–10 'A
Lawyer', sent. 32, 31   5. 11–13 'A Lawyer', sent. 34   6–9 . . .] under-
lined C   14. 1–6 Verse draft from B 67ʳ   14. 7–10 Verse draft from B 44ʳ or
46ᵛ or 77ʳ C   22 and] superimposed on semicolon C   24–6 as Bowles . . .
Grounds] underlined C

A tongue to gaine and Hire Accustomed long
Grows quite insensible of Right and wrong.

Law   20^r

His hands are gor'd with blood like vultur's Claws
The engine of his Murders are the Laws.

Tis true the Gospell and the Law reveal   5
The waies of future Blisse and present weale.
But when all Arts convert them to a Trade
They guard not But our Happinesse invade.

The Breath of Lawyers and the peoples minds
Are as the yeilding waves, and blustring winds.   10

Where there is No rule of Law All ought to bee entertained 21^v
with Jealousy.

[Dueller]   23^v

Thoughts   24^r

   are subject to the same order which other naturall things are, for
they come to perfection by Degrees, and afterward decay by the
same, for as the 2d and 3d. Thoughts are better then the first, so   15
the 4th and 5th. are commonly worse unlesse the Judgment bee
extraordinary, which in most men is so easily discompos'd, that It
will hardly endure beyond the first Thought, and therfore such
men usually speake better then They write, and better suddainly
then after premeditation.   20
   Such men are very unhappy if they fix their minds upon any
thing, for the further they pursue It, It still becomes the worse.

   The minde of man in her Conceptions observs the same order

---

2. 1–3 [20^r] 'A Lawyer', sent. 29   2. 4–7 'A Lawyer', sent. 33   2. 8–15
Verse drafts from B 67^v and 77^v C   11–12 *Possibly two lines of verse* (. . . bee /
entertained . . . *C*)   12. 1–23 *See* 'A Dueller', *sent. 5–10; T* 102^{r–v}, *and Appendix B below for C variants*

that God did in the Creation For as the first production was but a
Chaos or Confusd Masse of things informd and disposd into order:
so the first Thoughts are rude and discomposd which the 2d digest
into Forme and order.

25ʳ   Life and Death

5   The world accounts 7 yeares to bee the ordinary standard for
the life of a Man; But God Almighty enlarges It to 70: though Hee
gives him no security for one minute; That hee might not venture
upon any wicked Attempt; being so neare (for any thing hee knowe-
es) to his End.

26ʳ   [Death]

27ʳ   [Charity]

28ʳ   Nature

28ᵛ   Mr Hobs de Cive. That man is not born fit to society, which is
11   Contrary not only to All Ages and experience: But so Inconsistent
with Sence that it agrees not with his owne. For 1st. hee sayes, if
man lovd man Naturally (that is As man) no Account can bee
given, why every man should not Love every man alike.

29ʳ   Censure

29ᵛ   Whosoever has not outgrown the Censure of the World is in his
16   Minority and unfitt to meddle with any Thing that belongs to
Him; for th'end of that Censure being to render every thing
Contemptible that lights in It's way; whatsoever is Ill done, is so

8 upon . . . Attempt] *underlined in a heavier hand* C   9. 1–50 [28ʳ⁻ᵛ] *Verse
drafts from B* 15ᵛ C   10 That] that C   society,] society. C   13 Account]
underlined C   14. 1–13 [29ʳ] See *p. 302, ll. 12–22*   17 Him;] Him C

allready; and does not need It's assistance; and therfore It reserves
that for those Things only, that are Good and Excellent.

Schoolmaster   30ᵣ

is a kind of Lord of Misrule that has Absolute Dominion in his
Territories and (like the King of Macassa) is Party Judge and Executioner Himselfe. Authority is a great Corrupter of good manners 5
and his perpetuall Dominion over Children makes him not know
How to conteine Himselfe in a private condition and as Countrey
squires become stark fooles by being alwayes the wisest in the
Company So does hee among his Pupills. The utmost of his Jurisdiction extends but to the Breech only and hee does Justice on 10
that part for the whole outward Boy. Hee carryes his Rod before
Him like a Roman Consull and is both magistrate and Lictor himselfe and is no lesse proud and Cruell then both together. His
perpetuall concernments in Boys play makes him never Serious but
in Trifles and alwayes a Truant in serious things. Hee never take's 15
down a Boy but hee takes him upp as a Grave statesman sayd of
the Army that was preferd to Disbanding. Hee finds that to say the
same thing over and over ever so many times is not so dangerous
as the Ancients held it &c. Hee is a small magistrate in the Common
Wealth of letters, that has his office for terme of life and never rises 20
Higher. Hee practices oratory as Demosthenes did, who is sayd to
put stones in his mouth to mend his Pronunciation, and hee is
very Industrious to use words every way as Hard. For hee teaches
his Schollars as they doe Birds to sing by Keeping them Darke
with his insignificant terms that they may not understand what 25
they are Doing.

King and People   30ᵛ

For who false oathes too Easily believe
Their Crime resemble, who stoln Goods receive.

Shall oaths for Goods and land bee layd aside,
And all receivd; when men for life are tryde?   30

13 His] *possibly new paragraph C*   19 &c.] &c *C*

31ʳ   The People

Whatsoever is well done of many can no more bee rewarded;
then the offences or Crimes of many punish'd: which is but Justice;
Because in great multitudes Every Particular is not Equally Capable
of contributing to the Good or Bad of what has been done; And
5 therfore not fit to have an Equall share either in the Reward or
punishment.

There is no Sort of people so Magicall as the Rabble; whose
perpetuall practice it is by Charmes, and Superstitious observations, to cure Diseases, and foretell events; They cann rout evill
10 spirits with a Hot spitt and a   , a Flint with a Hole in't; a
sickle and an Hors-shoe; Divine with the oracle of a Sive and sheares; foretell mischiefs by the Running of an Hare, the flying of a
Crow, or the falling of Salt; and Good by a spider or the Itching of
their noses; with their severall Interpretations of all sorts of
15 Dreames and infinite Devices to foreknow Husbands and wives:
and which shall dye first; They have charms to cure Agues, the
toothach, Cramps warts, sore-eyes and the Itch: Then their
observations of dayes, not to begin any businesse on a friday: nor
to paire their nayles on a tuesday; to rise with the —— forwards
20 and put on the Right stockin first; with innumerable vanities of
this Kinde; which they faithfully believe in; practice and observe;
professing a knowledge of that which learned men confesse they
understand Nothing of: That this Sort may justly seeme to owe
Its originall to the vanity and Inconsiderate lightnesse of the
25 Credulous Rabble; and the imposture of Others; rather then to the
Invention and discovery of wise and knowing men.

31ᵛ   All Ceremony and pompe and State was at first intended to no
other purpose but only to Entertaine Them, for whose Service the
Wisdome of the law has in all Ages been wholy taken upp and all
30 the formalityes of Courts of Justice Solely Dedicated. For their
Sakes is all the wisdom of the World perpetually engag'd, to
observe their Humours and apply to every one with eternall
slavery and subjection. For their Interest is all Warr and Peace

---

3 Because in] *underlined C*   11 Hors-shoe;] Hors-shoe. *C*   11–12 sheares;]
sheares. *C*   15 and infinite . . . wives] *underlined C*   22 professing a know-
ledge] *underlined C*   26. 1–16 [**31ᵛ**] *See p. 42, l. 36–p. 43, l. 12, and apparatus*
30 For] for *C*

made and all the greatest Actions of Both designd and managd. By
their Judgments are most Religions establisht orthodox and alterd
as Idolatrous and Superstitious. By their voyces the greatest
difficulties are easily Decided; for they being the greatest numbers
have alwaies the most voices which is the only Ballance to deter-   5
mine Right and wrong and true and false that the world is Capable
of. By their Authority is allmost all the Businesse of the Civill life
perpetually manag'd and nothing past but what they please to
approve of. And tho they seeme to bee as much or more in Subjection then others; yet It is to Those that doe but manage the   10
Gouvernment for Them: and such as they made As the people of
Rome made their magistrates to bee gouvernd by and yett kept the
Supreme Power still in their own Hands. Nay they have Dominion
over the very Thoughts of the wisest of men who dare not speake
freely what they think and know for Feare of giving them offence.   15
Hence it is that no Sort of men are so naturally Ambitious to have
a Share in all Gouvernments; as those that are the most unfitt to
manage them: as if they did but strive to obteine that which they
have a naturall Right unto and believd themselvs unjustly deprivd
of.   20

Next o're his shoulders dangled to his Knee   **32ʳ**
A Cloake of Presbiterian loyaltye
This safely covers Hell Itselfe; and drawes
The peoples Admiration and applause.

—And for his Safety sake his power lay downe;   25

Thrice happy they who with clean hands and Heart
Act in this tragedy, the victims part.

Who dying feel no Other grief or paine
But for the guilt of Those by whom they're Slaine.

It will bee sayd of thy owne norfolk line   30
Some with thy blood are stain'd; and others shine.

And yet the weaknesse of our lives past Race,
Exalt the power and victory of Grace.

4 Decided;] Decided. *C*   18 as if] *underlined C*   27 the . . .]
underlined C   29 by . . .] *underlined C*   30 norfolk line] *underlined C*
33 *Underlined C*

32ᵛ   the King

The Lawes of the land that give the King power to make warr
doe by Consequence give him power to Raise money to mainteine
It; otherwise They only give him power to doe that, which is not
in his power to doe.

33ʳ   Incongruous and Inconsistent Opinions

35ᵛ   His opinions are a kind of Mosse that grows upon Rocks and
6 sticks fast although It have no Rooting.

Glasse is but the Ice of Fire, and cold Iron in Greenland burns as
grievously as Hot.

35ᵛ   As all Countries are sayd to bee the Same to a Wiseman; So
10 ought all Gouvernments to bee. It is not only a Cleanlinesse but
ornament to have shifts of opinions and Judgment and Sense as
well as Cloaths and to put on none, but those that are newest in
the fashion; for a man lookes as Ridiculous in an old fashion fayth
and loyalty, as in an Antique Habit and thinks hee is in the mode,
15 'Cause solomon sayes; nothing's new under the Sun.

Why should not the Sceptique Statesman bee wiser then all
others as well as the philosophers of that sect are justly esteemd to
bee so? or to bee positive in faith and Integrity lesse Sottish then
in any thing Else?

20   All Knowledge and understanding is Attaind not by a Dull and
obstinate adhæring to any one opinion or perswasion; but by
Advancing still farther and farther and renouncing those tenents
which It once thought Infallible.

36ʳ   Marriage and Women

Princes before they enter into a warr with a powrfull Enemy are
25 wont to make Peace, and enter into Leagues and alliances with all

1–4 *Duplicated* C 68ᵛ   1 The C 68ᵛ: SB. the C 32ᵛ   3–4 which . . .]
underlined C 32ᵛ   13 fashion;] fashion. C   15 'Cause solomon sayes]
underlined C   18 or . . . Integrity] *underlined* C   22 renouncing those
tenents] *underlined* C

their Neighbours: So Women that use to quarrell and contest with
their Husbands allwayes indeavour to ingage (by their civility
and Complacence) the good opinion of as many as they can to
take their Parts; and believe the best on their Sides.

Women that love their Husbands too fondly are more Apt to 5
pick Quarrells with them upon Punctilioes of Kindnesse or unkind-
nesse (as lovers doe in Romances) then those who are Indifferent
or have no Affection for them at All.

A good woman is infinitely more to bee Valued then a good Man
because they passe through farr greater Difficulties to become 10
Such, then Men; who are not naturally Subject to so many Infirmities, nor tyed to Such strict Rules of Virtue; as Women are bound
to observe; and for that very reason have the Stronger Inclinations
to breake Them, according to the perpetuall Current of Humane
Nature, that alwayes grow's (like other Streames) more Violent; 15
when It meetes with opposition; especially such as it is Able to
breake through. And yett virtue in Women in the ordinary Sence
of the world signifies nothing else but Chastity; and vice the Contrary; as if they were Capable of neither Good nor Bad above the
Middle; and that Part were the / Seate where their Soules resided **36ᵛ**
and the Same thing with the Heart and Braine in Men: For all 21
their wit and Ingenuity is for the most part derived from thence
and relates to nothing else, as being the onely End of their Creation
and their Province to bee the Seminary of mankinde for which they
are better qualifyed then any thing Else.   25

Great Persons very seldome marry happily Because they are
deprivd of the freedome of their Choice and [too] diverted by the
Wealth and other Advantages of offerd Matches, to make use of
their own Discretion (if they have any) to fitt or please themselves
with the other no lesse reall conveniences of Personall liking and 30
naturall Inclination; which are supposd to signify nothing in the
affaires of the World; though there can bee no true and naturall
Marryage contracted without Them; And all Love and Honour in

8. 1–2 See 'A Cuckold', sent. 9; GR ii. 373 His wives Faults . . .   8. 3–10
Verse drafts from B 37ʳ C   13–14 for . . . Them] underlined C   18 but Chastity]
underlined C   19–20 above the Middle] underlined C   24–5 for . . .] underlined
C   31–2 which . . . World] underlined C

Romances would immediately become voyd and of none effect; And
yett there are seldome any other Considerations used by one side
at least, in all matches that are made especially on the womans part
who are either forc't by their Parents or betrayd and Sold by their
5 Friends; when they are left Rich, to fall to the share of Such who
regard nothing but their Fortunes; if they chance to escape the
greater Danger themselvs that they are generally destind like
Andromeda to bee Chaynd to Rocks and devourd by Monsters.

The Scripture in many places brands Idolatry with the name of
10 Whoredome and calls AntiChrist the whore of Babilon to let us
know That nothing is so like a false Religion as a false Woman that
prostitutes her Body as Idolaters doe their Soules to Pride, Avarice,
and Ambition; the originalls of all false Religions in the world.

Such a remedy as the Stoiques found out against Cuckolding, to
15 have all women Common to all men.

He hath endowed Her with all his worldly Detts and diseases.

It is much better for an old woman to marry a yong Man then an
old man to marry a yong woman for very good Reasons.

37ʳ   [Beliefe]

37ᵛ   [Oath]

38ʳ   [Obstinacy]

39ʳ   [Faith]

41ʳ   Drunkennesse

Vespasian turned Urine into Silver; but Drunkards turne Silver
20 into urine.

Serpents lay by their Poyson when they drinke.

Fishes that drinke perpetually, never pisse.

Dutchmen have not only Liberty of Speech in all their Consulta-
tions But freedome to bee Drunck that they may speake the freer
when their Braines are Hott.   5

[Idolatry]   42ʳ

Reputation   43ʳ

No man can injure his Attempts more then by raysing an
expectation of them; For whosoever takes upp Reputation upon
Credit shall bee sure to pay deare for it, and the performance
commonly how good soever becomes but a foyle to the expectation.   10

It is more noble for a man to vindicate himselfe by his Deeds then
his words, for men cure their wounds with their hands, and Doggs
with their tongues.

A vaine glorious man does not gaine so much Reputation with
himselfe as Hee looses with others.   15

There is no way so easy and certain to attaine to Honour as by 43ᵛ
the open practice and profession of those things that are most
infamous and dishonourable.

Honour   44ʳ

All the titles and Priviledges of Honour may bee easily bought;
or idly disposd of; but Honor it Selfe never: and therfore they are 20
never to bee sold by the Buyer, as having no Intrinsique value;
altho' the Sottish world is apt to believe They have, after an

---

7–8 For . . . it] *underlined* C   18. 1–6 [**44ʳ**] *Verse drafts from B* 98ᵛ (*or* 127ʳ
or 135ʳ *or* 137ʳ) *and* 137ʳ *C*

invisible manner, like the Reall presence in the Church of Rome; for both are supposd to bee performd by the Power of Words.

44ᵛ   The greatest honour that can bee given to an excellent prince is to bee styled the Father of his people; and the greatest Dishonor
5   that can bee chargd upon a private person is to bee Call'd the Son of the People, that is, the Kings Grandchild.

All Tombs and inscriptions can only preserve the names (and that but for a short time) not the memory of those for whom they were erected; for they that have Fame of their owne, need them not:
10   and those that have none can never bee Rememberd by Them farther then that there were once Some persons living that bore Such names and Characters; and the better and more noble those titles of vertue and Honour are, they are for the most part the lesse True: and if they were not, can never bee so considerable to their
15   Posterity as the worst gotten Wealth, that they left behind; For that may bee Inherited But vertue and Honour were never Entayld and if they bee not continued in the Race which at first they raysd are but a Shame and infamy to It.

For there was never yet Intaile
20   Of Vertue upon Heires Male.

45ʳ   Gratitude

——Hee that is ungratefull
Is all things that are Base and Hatefull.

46ʳ   [Patria]

46ᵛ   [Pleasure]

47ʳ   [Punishment]

47ᵛ   [Parents]

---

1 like . . . Rome] *underlined C*   13–14 the lesse True] *underlined C*
15 as . . . Wealth] *underlined C*   18 but . . .] *underlined C*   20. 1–6
Verse drafts from B 17ʳ *and* 68ʳ *C*

[Power]

[Pope]

God

Arguments from the will of God are very ill grounded; For if wee cann understand nothing of Him but by his Actions; wee shall never understand any Thing of his will; which must of necessity bee before his Actions.

That vulgar Opinion and Saying of inconsidering persons; that 5 the more men pry into the Secretts of Nature, the lesse they believe of Religion; is not only false; but as Atheisticall as to say; the more men have of Reason and Judgment the lesse they believe in God. For that very Inquiry into Nature; the further It goes, will at length bring the most obstinate in spight of their Hearts to an 10 acknowledgment of a first Intelligent Cause: and that is God. And if it has not that effect upon some men; It is an argument of nothing but their Ignorance and smattering.

There is no Atheist comparable to an Hipocrite; for as the Apostle sayth; Men's faith is known by their workes; much more is 15 their Infidelity: And hee that out of the strength of his unbeliefe and Contempt of God is able to abuse and defy him to his Face, and thinks to impose upon him, and come off only by giving him Good Words (as there is no doubt but there are some that doe it between Hauke and Buzzard, Jeast and Earnest and against their own 20 Consciences) is much more Condemnd out of his own mouth, then Hee that sayes but what hee thinkes; when hee has not witt enough to thinke better. By all which It appeares, that those Ideots think that to believe in God, tho' but as the Devill does, to doe Him all

2–4 wee . . .] *underlined C*   5–p. 274, l. 2 *Duplicated C* 90ᵛ   5–7 that . . . say] *underlined C* 50ʳ   7 Atheisticall *C* 90ᵛ: Atheisticall; *C* 50ʳ   9 further] farther *C* 90ᵛ   11 acknowledgment *C* 90ᵛ: acknowledgment, *C* 50ʳ   God. *C* 90ᵛ: God *C* 50ʳ   11–12 And . . . men] *underlined C* 50ʳ   13 Ignorance and smattering] smattering and Ignorance *C* 90ᵛ   14 . . . Hipocrite] *underlined C* 50ʳ   15 sayth] sayeth *C* 90ᵛ   Men's] Man's *C* 90ᵛ   their] his *C* 90ᵛ 15–16 much . . . Infidelity] *underlined C* 50ʳ   16 their] his *C* 90ᵛ   21 much . . . mouth] *underlined C* 50ʳ   23–p. 274, l. 2 By . . . *C* 90ᵛ: om. (*available space already filled*) *C* 50ʳ   24 tho' . . . does] *underlined C* 90ᵛ

the Disservice they can, is sufficient to perswade Him, They are of
his Party.

50ᵛ   Hee that has so good a perswasion of his own witt (that Hee
believes it will lead him to the understanding of God doe's but put
5   to sea in a Sculler; For as Hee cannot speake of Him with proper
words so wee cannot think of him with competent Thoughts And
therfore when they that believe they know most of him have told
us of entity, infinite, omnipotent, and æternall into which the
sharpest witt of man can no more penetrate; then a worme can
10   creepe through the Globe of the Earth; if they goe further There is
little difference between their subtlest Notions of Him and the
wild Apprehensions which the most Barbarous Religions have of
Him; For I cannot tell whither it bee more Rude to believe Him
to bee an old man or the Sun; or to say that before the Creation;
15   Hee was weary of being Alone; a thing which can seldome bee
sayd of a wiseman.

All that wee can understand of God (for in this discourse I alway
except Believing) is but only as hee is a Creator; for in that Sence
only does hee descend to our Capacities in which hee has relation
20   to us (all other being unnecessary if not improper) but this is
nothing to his Essence; for hee was a God before hee was a Creator;
and had been so still tho the world had never been made: nor can
wee understand more of his being by the Creatures; then wee can
of the being of man by any of his Actions; if wee will venture
25   farther (as wee can hardly conteine ourselves within the province
of nature) wee cheate ourselves with negatives: and Believe wee
can discover what God is by telling what hee is not; And therfore
not content with saying, Hee is light wee proceed farther and call
Him Immateriall, Immortall, Infinite, &c: forgetting that the diff-
30   erence between the purest matter and immateriall is Infinite; as
the disproportion between the Creator and the Creature must bee;
and therfore though Light bee the excellentest part of the Creation
from which the immediate motion of all the Rest proceeds: It is
infinitely different from the nature of God to whom wee can with no
35   more Reason suppose It to have any Resemblance then wee can
say that the Spring of a Watch upon which the whole movement

1–2 They . . .] *underlined C* 90ᵛ   10 if . . . further] *underlined C*   21 for . . .
before] *underlined C*   26 with negatives] *underlined C*

depends, is more like the watchmaker; then the wheeles that are stirred by It.

Hee that thinkes to arrive at the Knowledge of God by Nonsence, 51ᵛ does but like Mohomet ride to Heaven on a Mule.

Popery   52ʳ

The Introduction of the Popish Religion tends to nothing; but 5 to promote the Interests of a forrein Prince; in opposition to our owne; and to advance the trade of priests heere, like the French manufactures, to undoe and ruine our owne Artificers. To remove the Staple of Religion, so well settled heere, into the Dominions of Forreiners; that by their Interests are obliged to bee our Enemies, 10 and can gaine nothing fairely by It; But only by imposing and putting tricks upon us. For Reformation was not a thing produced upon the suddain or a vaine novelty that sprung up in the world without Reason: But had for many Ages before been the designe and endeavour of the whole Christian world: And grew up equally 15 with the Restoration of learning and knowledge; that together with Religion was at the Same time overrun by Barbarisme. For while the Church enjoyed the Prudence and learning of the antient fathers It kept within some Compasse of Reason and moderation but after in the Sottish times of Ignorance (which they therfore 20 call the mother of Devotion) It broke out into all those prodigious extravagancies, which now passe in the world for Catholique and Apostolicall; For Christianity began when the world was at the heigth of learning and knowledge; But Popery when it was, at the Depth of Ignorance and Sottishnesse: of which it was but the 25 naturall effect.

It is impossible to speake with any Ingenuity in Defence of the Church of Rome, or to prevaile any way, but with Tricks and fallacies; For there is a great deale of difference between Reason that comes plainely and naturally of Itselfe; and That which is forced 30

1 watchmaker] *or* watch-maker *C*   6 of . . . Prince] *underlined C*   9–10 into
. . Forreiners] *underlined C*   12 For] *underlined C*   16–18 that . . . while]
underlined C   21 the . . . Devotion] *underlined C*   22–6 For . . .]
underlined C   28 Tricks] *altered to* Tricks: *C*   29–30 Reason . . . Itselfe]
underlined C

and vext, against it's naturall Tendency: As wine that runs freely
with It's own weight is better; then that which is trodden and
prest with labour and Drudgery.

52ᵛ   Popery was attempted to bee Reduc'd by the Emperors and All
5   Christian princes for at least 500 yeares before It was brought to
passe in Germany and England &c. but still diverted by the Bishop
of Rome Sometimes by Publishing of Croysados to send them a
santering to the Holy land; and sometimes by making of Quarrells
and setting them together by the Eares with one another or raysing
10   of warrs among Them. For popery was introduced into All nations
by the Same meanes and expedients, that Tiranny was in France
that is Suppressing of Generall Councells, as that nation, was
inslaved by being Depriv'd of their Congregations of Estates; that
preserv'd their liberty Inviolable while They were injoyed. But
15   they owe their present Slav'ry to the English, who reduc'd them
to that Condition, that to bee free from their Dominion they were
forc'd to submitt to the Arbitrary Insolence and Tiranny of their
own Princes, who by Providence seeme to Revenge the Implacable
malice, they naturally beare us and all the Cheats and injuries they
20   have ever done us or ever shall.

The Church of Rome is call'd the Catholick Church for noe
reason so much as because It has something of All Religions in It;
as the Ceremonies of the Jewish, the Eating what They worship
with the old Ægiptians: the Adoring Gods of inferiour Quality
25   designd to all occasions with the antient Pagans.

53ʳ   It was not Queen Elizabeth that introduced the Reformation so
much as the Cruelty of her sister Queen Mary that confirmd and
settled It and by her Breach of Faith ha's taught the most Ignorant
how farr They are to trust to all obligations and promises of that
30   Kinde which has noe meane Influence upon the Nation to this very
day. And allthough They suppose the People of England sottish
enough to bee Impos'd upon, by the meane and contemptible
esteeme that other nations have of them, that is but a vulgar Error

---

2–3 better . . .] *underlined* C   11–14 that . . . injoyed] *underlined* C
18–20 who . . .] *underlined* C   22 something . . . It] *underlined* C   25. 1–8 *Verse
drafts from* B 127ʳ C   26–31 . . . day] *duplicated* C 89ʳ   30–1 to . . .
day] *underlined* C 53ʳ

in them, who take measure of all the nation by the Prodigious weaknesse of those, who only have the favour to bee trusted and imployed in Publick affaires whose Ignorant sottishnesse and the effects of It, Dishonesty; are notoriously known to all the world. No doubt a very just and Ingenious way to make a nation Contemp- 5 tible by their own examples and lay it upon the nature of the People; who are more sensible of the folly and extravagance of it, then Forrainers have either Reason or opportunity to bee.

The popish Religion is the most advantagious of any other to 53ᵛ weake Princes but the most inconvenient in the world to those who 10 are able and excellent For the pope having the Conduct of the common peoples Consciences is a very usefull partner to Those who doe not understand How to gouvern them Alone, But who has once possest himselfe of that Power what prince shall presume to dispute his Right with Him, as no Active and valiant prince 15 can forbeare where his Incroachments are so insufferable Hee is sure to have the worst of It, unlesse hee can deale with Him as our H. 8. did, before whose time the Clergy tooke upon Them the disposing of the Crowne; and were perpetually vexatious to all those that vindicated their Right; but very Indulgent to those 20 [that] gave way to Them to doe what they please.

Priests

54ʳ

The levites among the Jewes had no Share in the lands of the Countrey they were to Divide by lott and possesse: For if they usd so much Injustice afterwards in Feeing of their Sacrifices they were not to bee trusted with matters of greater Importance to the 25 Commonwealth, Cities and townes. As when they gott Jerusalem in their Hands (though besieged by the Romans) Three of them (that undertooke to defend It) by their mutuall divisions made a greater Destruction of the People then the enemy that beleagured It; And as their Imployment was but a kind of Butchery to kill 30 Beasts &c in Sacrifice; So they were found to bee the Executioners of all their owne Prophetts to Christ himselfe.

1–2 who . . . those] *underlined* C   18–19 before . . . Crowne] *underlined* C
19 vexatious] *or possibly* vexations C   27 Three of them] *underlined* C

54ᵛ
[Preaching]

55ᵛ As the motions of the Heavens can never bee reduc'd to any
certaine Accompt; but still there is reason enough left to make the
wisest doubt; whither the Earth moves or They; So those heavenly
motives of Zeale and Holinesse can never bee plainely Demonstra-
5 ted to bee free from all Earthly considerations.

56ᵛ Fleas never dung in wollen. Nutmegs grow no where but in an
unwholsome Aire.

57ʳ
[Oppressor]

57ᵛ
Virtue and Vice

Vertues and vices are very neare of Kin and like the Austrian
family beget one Another.

10 Jubemur in Evangelio ab officiis Christianæ pietatis in publico
abstinere puta Erogatione in Pauperes, longis orationibus &c
Quanto magis à vitiis et operibus tenebrarum in Conspectu Hominum Cavendum?

58ʳ
Example

The examples of princes have the same Power that their proc-
15 lamations have to Declare their wills and Pleasures And the
worse they are, are generally the better obeyed, and passe for the
most naturall, faythfull wayes of flattery, For the more Sharers
there are in Infamy, the lesse falls to every one's dividend and is
esteem'd more considerable then any Reall Services a man can
20 possibly performe by exposing his life or fortunes to the Greatest
Hazards.

The power of example is so Great that It reconciles us to those

---

o. 1–6 [**55ᵛ**] *Verse draft from B* 127ʳ *C*   1–5 *Duplicated C* 84ᵛ   5. 1–14
Verse draft from B 60ᵛ–61ʳ *C*   7. 1–27 *See* '*An Oppressor*', *T* 127ʳ⁻ᵛ, *and Appendix*
B below for C variants   13 Cavendum?] Cavendum? SB. *C*   15–16 And . . .
obeyed] *underlined C*

things that wee have a naturall aversion to and compells us to delight in that which was Odious to us before, renders those Habits and fashions which at first appeard Deformd and ridiculous Becoming and Gracefull by seeing them commonly worne, and makes us dislike as much what wee liked before, in so much that 5 when a man becomes Constant to any mode that is given over by others, Hee is esteemd as Fantastique and vaine as those that study to bee the foremost in new ones. It alters our very Appetites gives us new Senses of things and makes us change those againe for newer; as if nothing were good or evill in itselfe but as It is received 10 and valued; for the time being, enforces us to reject those Customes which wee have been ever so long usd to as senselesse and absurd and after a while embrace them againe as zealously as wee cast them / off before.   58ᵛ

It reconciles us to Death Itselfe for wee dye as well as live by 15 example; for no man could ever dispose of his body to bee Buryed in perfect mind and memory; if hee did not know that hee has the example of all mankind for It. Whatsoever is said or written for or against any thing is allwaies interpreted by that opinion which the world had of it before, without any consideration at all whither 20 It bee true or false as the Church of Rome would have Doctrines of faith determined. And therfore all the Preaching in the world cannot reclaime men from those sins which they see daily committed before their eyes for they take the Tradition and perpetuall practice of all Ages to bee the most orthodox Interpretation of 25 any thing that can bee sayd against them. Example is the shortest and readiest Compendium of all ways of teaching; it is so easy that wee learn by It insensibly before wee are aware as Children doe languages. It instills itselfe into us without our knowledge and wee doe not learn by It but catch It like a Contagion. It is a Tutor that in- 30 structs in Good and Evill with the Greatest authority of any other; for every man believes himselfe if not obligd, at least licens't to doe that which hee sees others doe, and therfore where It prevailes tho in the most foolish and ridiculous things Imaginable, It easily overthrows all the Strength of Reason that can bee oppos'd against It; 35 for men doe not consider nor regard what the world sayes but what It does; and believe actions to bee the best Interpreters of words. Man is of all Creatures most affected with Imitation; for to see a

---

2 before,] before *C*   16–17 for . . . memory] *underlined C*   18 Whatsoever] whatsoever *C*   27 teaching;] teaching *C*

thing done, is not halfe so delightfull as to behold It well represented. Whole nations and provinces doe not only use the same Tone
in their Pronunciations, but seem to learne their very lookes of one
another.

59ʳ   Witt

5   is a thing, that so few men in the world have any occasion for,
that It becomes a meere Drugg and is perishable according to the
Humour and fashion of the times which It allwayes complyes
with, and leaves as the Devill do's witches when they are in the
Hands of Justice, Hence It is that no witt is now in mode but
10 Ribaldry, which as Soone as the fashion alters will bee Burnt by
the Hand of the Hangman.

Poetry is a thing that passes in the world upon It's good behaviour. It is like taking of Tobacco or Drinking of Coffee which
men doe at first for Company and retaine afterwards by Custome.
15 It is no staple Commodity but passes only among Those that take
it and meetes with as Few that judge rightly of it as all those things
doe that have no measure nor weight but fancy to bee examined
by.

60ʳ   [Tragedy of Nero]

63ʳ   History

63ᵛ   The Lord Bacon was not so much a Naturall Philosopher as a
20 Naturall Historian: who of all others is the most fabulous, especially
if hee takes up what hee writes upon Tick.

64ʳ   Madnesse

Nulli mortalium magis Strenuè insaniunt quàm Sapientes: ubi
eos semel Insania Corripuit, dum enim Ingenio fulcire delicia
student, Conspicuam magis reddunt Dementiam.

12–13 behaviour.] behaviour C   18. 1–32 [**59ᵛ**] *Verse drafts from B 127ᵛ and*
38ʳ *C*   24 Dementiam.] Dementiam. SB. *C*

[Words]

Gouvernment disorderd

The more disorders any Gouvernment runs into, the harsher
must the Councells bee that are prescribd for It's Recovery till
the remedy becomes at last more uneasy then the disease. For when
the malady is habituall, the medecine will appeare as odious untill
it is too late. And hee that apply's it, too overwise and politiquely 5
timorous or disaffected; who fancies things worse then they are
only because Hee would have them So.

Gouvernment like an Ill-going Watch, is allwayes out of order.
Whither the fault bee in the thing Itselfe or in the Ignorant management of It; is not easy to determine; though in the small Accompt 10
which the world has of a very few good Princes, It plainely appeares
the thing has been done in severall ages with admirable Successe
and as great Ease; But never by any who wanted either Reason or
Integrity. For though Dissembling bee by some statesmen esteem-
ed the greatest mastery of it; Yett where It is often or dully prac- 15
ticd 'tis impossible to bee long undiscovered And then 'tis as silly
as if it were profest then which nothing can bee more Ridiculous.
Solomon only hitt upon the Right, that it is Justice that establishes
the Throne of a Prince. For though Justice bee the untowardest
way in the world to acquire Crownes, yet it is the best and wisest 20
course to establish and secure them; For being the only finall
Cause, for which all Gouvernment was designd; the more Princes
vary from it or give others but occasion to pretend they doe, the
sooner and easier They are supplanted. The most common enemyes
of It are all Sorts of malefactors thieves, murtherers, and magis- 25
trates; For Cheats and Impostors that are not done in open defy-
ance of It are corrected with milder punishments; For a small
matter taken by force is punishd with Death; when ever so many
times as much obteind by fraud and delusion extends but to the

5–7 And . . .] *underlined C*   8–9 order. Whither] order whither *C*   13–14
But . . . Integrity] *underlined C*   15 mastery] *altered in a different ink to* mistery
C   15–17 Yett . . . Ridiculous] *underlined C*   19 Justice] *underlined C*
23 or . . . doe] *underlined C* doe,] *altered in a different ink to* doe; *C*   27–p. 282, l. 1
For . . . Whipping] *underlined C*

Pillory and Whipping: But the most pernicious of all private enemyes to the publick Peace are Zealots and fanatiques: and especially tender Consciences that like Plague Sores infect the soundest, that come within their Reach tho they preserve those
5 that have them &c.

66ᵛ   Those who talk of the —— Prerogative to Adjorne, prorogue, or Dissolve Parliaments as oft as hee pleases doe not consider, That the late King did not part with that Power as long as Hee could possibly avoyd It; But when hee had reduc'd himselfe to that
10 Necessity that could by no other imaginable meanes bee provided for, Hee was forc'd though against all Reason of State, as well as his own Interest, to passe that Act of Continuance which after proved his Utter Ruine. And if one Prince could bee brought to those Inconveniences (I will not say by his owne fault) It is more
15 then possible, that another may; upon the same and perhaps a more desperate Accompt. Especially when there is a president for It, so fresh in the memoryes of all men, which was then wanting; as well as Circumstances to aggravate those Reasons into matter of Fact; which were then only in Pretence.

67ʳ   The Interests of the King and his Parliament (though they are
21 really the Same) yet by Factions are renderd so different; that hee is constraind in Reason rather to trust to a Treaty with his most Implacable Enemyes: then Venture a Conference with his great Councell. For though they are sayd to meete to consult with Him
25 about the weighty affaires of the Nation, It is really nothing else but to contrive How to impose upon one another.

> The King's Advising with his Parliament
> Is how the one may th'other Circumvent.

67ᵛ   The Power and Interest of our House of Commons cannot but
30 bee greatly encreast when elections are become so strangely deare and chargeable: For evry new member is but a kind of Merchant Adventurer; that would never lay downe so great a Stock if hee

---

1 Whipping:] *altered in a different ink to* Whipping; *C*   4–5 tho . . . them] *underlined C*   11 Hee was forc'd] *underlined in pencil C*   12 that . . . Continuance] *underlined C*   15–16 upon . . . Accompt] *underlined in pencil C*   18–19 as well . . .] *underlined C*   19. 1–4 *See* 'Observations upon the Long Parliament', *par. 1; GR* i. 420 Moderation . . . Extremities   19. 5–14 *Verse drafts from* B 35ʳ *C*   28. 1–30 *Verse drafts from* B 67ʳ, 87ʳ, *and* 67ᵛ *C*   31–2 Merchant Adventurer] *underlined C*

did not expect a Suiteable Returne. And this swelling greatnesse
can proceed from no other Cause then an Equall Decrease of power
and Authority in the King and house of Peeres, Some of whom are
no lesse greedy then the Commons to bee sharing the Remainder
of his decaying Interest; if they had power to effect It: which is   5
no meane Cause of their violent Contests and Quarrels.

And if the members of the House of Commons had but the
priviledge of the Lords That no parliament could bee summoned
without the same persons (for the Lords are never dissolvd but
only prorogud) they would immediately render themselves as   10
absolute as they did when they had an Act of Continuance: For
[though] they sitt but at the will and pleasure of the King, They
allwaies act at their owne And as time do's both make and Repeal
Lawes, the longer they sitt, they believe They have the greater
Right to doe so; and assume an Arbitrary power to Increase their   15
priviledges accordingly; by rendring them as Nice and Peevish as
tender Consciences that will not endure to bee touched ever so
gently without the violation of all lawes Divine and humane which
they will allow no power on Earth the license to doe, But only their
owne; which though it may bee Spirituall enough is very un-   20
christian; To doe that to others which they would not have done
to themselves: and when it prevailes never misses to introduce
Tiranny. But the greatest of all their priviledges is, that they are
not Accountable to the people; by whom they are entrusted for any
abuse or breach of Trust; tho' they have voted a King to bee So,   25
and made him severely Answere for It; Right or wrong and directly
against the Intention of those by whom they were Trusted and
pretended to Represent; So Injust is all power where It is It's own
Judge and is accomptable in Its own opinion, to nothing But
Conscience and the day of Judgment; which is not so dreadfull as a   30
tryall heere by God and the Countrey: They presume when the
Gouvernment begins to Decline, they stand fairest for It; though
they know not what to doe with It when they have It. The equality
of their voyces among men of so strangely different talents, estates
and Qualities is but a Kind of Levelling and contrary to all just   35
Reason and yett their Businesse is not possibly to bee managd any

4-5 of . . . Interest] *underlined C*   5 It:] It. *C*   11 an . . . Continuance]
underlined C   19-20 But . . . owne] *underlined C*   21-2 To . . . themselves]
underlined C   23-4 that . . . people] *underlined C*   25 tho' . . . So] *underlined C*
28-30 So . . . Judgment] *underlined C*

other Way; which shews they were never meant to advise princes
in matters of State the which such Numbers are as Incapable of
understanding as managing and if the same voyces that chose them
might once more prevaile They should (like malefactors) bee
5 returned to the places from whence they came, with all the other
Circumstances. Their priviledges or prerogatives are whatsoever
68ʳ they are pleased to Call so; for they are meerely Traditionall / and
therfore are the more proper to serve all occasions, as wax which
the world has made choice of to confirm and Seale all writings is
10 the easiest to bee Counterfeited and receive new Impressions of all
other things; But that the Impression signifyes nothing &c.

Besides this Calamity at Home, the proper and naturall Interests
of the Nation abroad must bee layd by and those embraced that
are unprofitable and pernicious to the Common Good; for Tyranny
15 the Enemy at home can no way so well secure Itselfe as by Being
alwayes in League and confederacy with that forrein enemy which
must bee purchased by granting large Concessions to those whose
friendship is Hurtfull to us and that is advantageous to the particular Interest and Support of the present usurpation. And this
20 wee have lately seen practicd and felt too by a Gouvernment which
these men condemn now But must bee feine to imitate to the
intollerable losse and dammage of the whole nation and finall Ruine
of All Trade and Commerce.

68ᵛ   Warr

Soldiers are said to bee Voluntiers when they take up Arms out
25 of necessity; and have none other way in the world to live.

70ʳ   Princes

Those Princes that liv'd nearest to the Ruine and destruction
of their predecessors have been the least concernd in the unfortunate Destruction and the most averse to take example by their

---

7 so;] so. *C*   8 occasions,] occasions. *C*   11–12 &c. Besides] &c /
Besides *C*   14 Good;] Good. *C*   16 with . . . enemy] *underlined C*
18 and] *followed by one or two-word space C*   21–3 But . . .] *underlined C*   23. 1–4
[68ᵛ] *See p. 268, ll. 1–4*   23. 5–24 *Verse drafts from B* 40ʳ *C*   24 Volun-
tiers] *underlined C*   25. 1–2 [70ʳ] *Verse draft from B* 65ᵛ *C*

Ruines and avoyd Doing those things that provd so fatall to Them:
As the fearfull and miserable murther of our Ed. 2. could not deterr
his Grand Child from doing the Same things and worse, and consequently Suffering the Same Fate.

Princes who are sayd to give Laws to their Subjects, sell them **70^v**
at their own Rates and make the Dearest Commodities of Them 6
in the world.

Great Princes that are not Naturally of a martiall temper themselves, seldom prosper in their warrs, though managd by Captaines
ever so able in their own Persons; as if the Genius of him under 10
whose ensigns they fight, did infuse something of It's own avers-
nesse into all those that ingage in his undertakings. Whither They
use lesse Judgment in the choice of under officers, or take lesse
care in providing Necessary Supplyes of Ammunition and constant
recruites; or pay ill and reward and punish worse, or whither 15
because few men prosper that undertake any thing against their
own Inclinations It is hard to Determine.

All Princes are more Stupid then ordinary Animalls that have
some presense of foule weather before it comes and nature has so
ordered it that men feele paine in their Corns before Raine, though 20
never in It.

No man can oblige a Prince more then hee that kills his father.

No princes are buryed in greater state then those that are
murtherd.

Princes that have most of all Things else have least of themselvs, **71^r**
for though they have to Doe with all men; they converse with 26
none; and are as much debarrd and diverted from themselvs, as
others, by their very Guards: For though All men stand bare before
them; their private thoughts are no where so coverd, and they
speake with none, but in masquerade where no man appeares 30
openly in his own person, nor plays his part, but like Scaramuch

---

7. 1–8 *Verse drafts from B* 127^v *and* 121^r *C*   16–17 because . . . Inclinations]
underlined C   20–1 though . . .] *underlined C*   27–8 as others . . .
Guards] *underlined C*   30 but in masquerade] *underlined C*

behind a vizard: which is one reason why they commonly know lesse of men then Those of any other condition; and are easier discovered themselves being perpetually exposd to the Scruteny and observation of all others: and their Defects (like Eclipses) more
5 gazd upon then when they shine with their greatest splendour.

For really a prince is but a kind of sight or shew, not made for his owne Sake, but the Entertainment of others; and therfore every one believes, Hee has an Equall Right to judge and censure; How hee pleases; nor has hee more power and prerogative over all,
10 then every private man in his own Dominions in his thoughts assumes over him; and uses more Arbitrarily; For as a Prince is sayd to bee the Father of his Countrey, Every man that consequently must bee his son, cannot but believe Himselfe concernd, How hee manages his estate: and if it bee Ill ordered, takes It to
15 Himselfe; and supposes It to bee his own losse, and his Duty to endeavour a Reformation and if hee can, have a Hand in carrying It on. For most men when they find a Gouvernment in disorder doe as those who live upon the seacosts are sayd to Doe, when they see a ship at Sea in a Storme; Watch and pray for a wreck;
20 that they may share in the Goods, It carryes: and oftentimes betray the wretched vessell to fall upon the Rocks, by setting up false lights in the darkest nights, to draw them into their own Destruction; which if any escape with life they dispatch them on shoare to make the wreck sufficient and lawfull. Yet there are more
25 Treasons committed by princes against themselves then by all their spightfullest and most subtle Enemies: and they would bee
71ᵛ better preservd from Poyson by taking the Assay / of their own Actions; then All their Meats and Drinks; that are used only as formalities of state and no Reall meanes of their preservation. So
30 if they could by touching cure Themselves of the Kings evill, they would not need Miracles to support Reasons of State, nor bee at the Charge of paying Ignorant people for Believing in them; by hanging the Price about their necks, which is no mean symptome of the disease, in the Judgment of all those who best understand It.
35 For a Princes distempers are epidemicall and never faile to infect all those whose Constitutions are of the same Inclination and fright

---

1 is one reason] *underlined C*   2–3 and . . . themselves] *underlined C*   4–5 and their . . . upon] *underlined C*   10 in his thoughts] *underlined C*   11–14 and . . . estate] *underlined C*   17 For most men] *underlined C*   19 Watch . . . wreck] *underlined C*   24–5 more . . . themselves] *underlined C*   27–8 of . . . Actions] *underlined C*   31–2 nor . . . them] *underlined C*

others as farr off from them as they can convey Themselves possibly, with as naturall an Aversion; which is no more to bee Reconcild then the Plague and Health are in the same person. For Reputation in the Affaires of the world is an engine by which those who have it may with ease manage any weight tho many 5 times Heavier then their naturall strength is able to performe; and those who have lost or never had It no more (like beasts) then what they are Able to beare and others are pleasd to lay upon them. But that which is lost is the most desperate to recover; For as Wealth (which is many times the same thing with reputation) is 10 more difficult to begin then increase when it is in a way: Reputation has all that difficulty and a greater, For when It is lost though hee that finds It is never the better for It; Yet none was ever known to restore It. And as Bankrupts when they have once stood out the statute loose all they have beside the Debts they owe, So 15 hee that is a Bankrupt in Reputation has nothing to begin againe with and no body will trust him untill Hee has recovered that which hee has no way left to attaine to.

The King of France his Conquests are like the Danes hunting of Sheepe.   20

His going to —— before Councell like King Phys his—
          But first let's have a Dance.

—— will owe his —— to his French education as his father did to his French matrimony.

Tho St Lewis was one of the most virtuous and pious princes 72ʳ
that not only France but perhaps any Nation ever had yett his 26
Gouvernment was as pernicious to his subjects as any of their worst Kings, and if his miscarriages had not been past upon the accompt of piety and zeale for Religion as they were really intended, had left as bad a Character upon his memory to Posterity, as the 30
lesse Devout mistakes of some other Princes have done upon Theirs. For his Imprisonment in Egipt was no lesse a Calamity and dammage to his people then King Johns was in England; and incurrd upon a more unwise accompt of which hee was so farr from being Sensible

3–6 For . . . performe] *underlined C*   3 For] for *C*   11 more . . .
increase] *underlined C*   21 His] — his *C*   25 the] *om. C*   26–8 his
. . . Kings] *underlined C*

and more Cautious That it was not long before hee engagd upon
a 2d Adventure as Imprudent and unfortunate; in which beside
his Charge and labour hee lost his life. That tho the frenzies of
Charles the 6th. brought his kingdome into greater slavery (by
5 the faults of others) St Lewis's fits of zeale, to propagate Religion,
by invading Infidells, were more destructive to Himselfe, besides
the miseries they brought upon the nation. So that unlesse the
Cause makes saints as it is said to do Martyrs, the Pope had little
Reason to inrowl him in the Kalender, beside his old Interest to
10 ingage Christian princes to expose themselves and their people to
the most desperate attempts only to promote his Reason of state;
and to conferr a title of Honour in the Kingdome of Heaven costs
him much lesse, then to make a Bastard an Italian Duke or marry
a niece (his Sister) to a Souveraine prince. For tho the Saints are
15 the nobility of the other world, and some of them have great
revenues heere; the Clergy are their Receivers and tenants, who
pay them nothing but Suite and Service; For to make a trade of
Adoring the Names and Images of men is more Roman and of
greater Antiquity then the Christian religion or Christ himselfe
20 and more Authentique then any other Tradition of the Church of
Rome, which has only changd the name; but preservd the thing
entire as they received it from hand to hand long before those
times, which they now call the most Christian and Primitive and
indeed is the truest Character of Its Antiquity and universality:
25 for It has been used in all Ages by allmost all Nations and Religions;
but only the originall of the Christian, the Jewish.

72ᵛ CR came to the Crowne by the Right of two Women and therfore
has the more Reason to bee Kind to Them.

Reges nostri Quibus Angiæ matres Cæteris præstantiores semper
30 fuisse observatum est.

One Brother ruind another by forcing Him to marry a Whore
and was after ruind himselfe by whores. For Gods Judgments
commonly pay men's Crimes in Kind And like that fundamentall

5 St . . . zeale] *underlined C*   7–8 the Cause] *underlined C*   11 his . . .
state] *underlined C*   14–15 the . . . world] *underlined C*   16–19 who
. . . then] *underlined C*   21–2 which . . . entire] *underlined C*   26 but
. . .] *underlined C*   26. 1–12 [**72ᵛ**] *Verse drafts from B 67ʳ C*   29–30 *Interlined*
C   30 est.] est. SB. C

Law of all Justice; Doe unto others as they have done unto [them],
and returne by the Same measure by which they have received.
And though wee doe not presently perceive th'effect of Bad Actions,
more then every moment the Growth of a plant; yett they never
stand still but evry minute ads something to their encrease; untill 5
at length they produce the fruites to which they were by the
Lawes of nature at first condemnd.

Riches   73ʳ

Gold is made of Earth as man was, which is one Reason why
hee has so great a naturall affection for It. It is the Soule of all the
Civill life, that can resolve all things into Itselfe; and turn Itselfe 10
into all things.

Those who are supplyed by usurers are fed like the Prophets by 73ᵛ
Ravens.

A Tubb was bigger to Diogenes then the whole world to Alexander
for I never heard that the one cryed Because hee had but one tubb, 15
as the other did because Hee had but one world to conquer.

The World   74ʳ

The World complaines that only bad men are Happy and fortunate when it is commonly their prosperity that makes Them so.

All good people are but Aliens in this World of which the Devill 74ᵛ
is Prince, and therfore are incapable of those priviledges and 20
Immunities, which the wicked being natives and Freeborne subjects
as freely enjoy.

If the Earth run Round in 24 houres the motion must of necessity
bee more Rapid then any thing that wee can imagine: But if the
Sun move about the Earth the Swiftnesse must bee infinitely more. 25

4 more . . . plant] *underlined* C   7. 1–12 *Verse drafts from B 6ᵛ* C   7. 13–14
Verse draft from B 134ᵛ C   8 Gold is] *underlined* C   11 things.] *then interlined in a different ink* This not well. as I thinke C

75^r   [Conversation]

76^r   [Patience]

76^v   Pride

Pride wants the best Condition of vice; that is, Concealment.

There is so little Reason for the pride and insolence of this world that the difference between Great and mean Persons in It, is no more then between two malefactors that ride to the Same Gallows, one in a Cart and the other on a Sledge: And hee in the Cart should scorne and despise the other as his inferior that is drawn through the Durt, while hee rides in State and is more eminently Gazed upon by the Rabble then the poore obscure wretch; that is, drag'd too low, to bee taken notice of.

77^r   Lying

Lyers are commonly very good natur'd and doe their feates as well to please others as Themselves; and require no more of any man, But his Beliefe; for which they will returne Reall courtesies.

In our English State wee have no Lawes for any Sort of Lyars and yett their Sin is against a flat Divine law. Quære why It should bee thus tolerated.

A ship-board They have a punishment for lyars—in Sea discipline ubi.

Hee who is able to lye to Those confidently who hee knowe's doe not Believe one word is arrivd at a great perfection.

78^r   Love

If Love bee only desire of union with the thing beloved no man would give his life for the thing hee loves, being a course contrary to his ends.

0. 1–2 [**76^v**] *Verse draft from B* 97^v *or* 107^r *or* 121^v C   4 two malefactors] *underlined C*   16 A] a C   lyars—] lyars. C   16–17 in . . .] *interlined C*
22. 1–4 *Verse draft from B* 68^v C

As quarrelsome as love and honour and as peevish.

Although Love is said to overcome All things, yet at long
Running; there is nothing allmost, that does not overcome Love;
Whereby It seemes Love does not Know how to use It's victory.

[Honesty]   78ᵛ

Truth   79ʳ

Speculative Truths have little to doe in the Affaires of the world 80ʳ
and if they were reduced to practice; would bring Things to 6
greater Disorder (supposing the generall Temper and Talent of
most men to bee of the Same condition as they naturally prove
to bee) then they are in this confusd mixture of True and false and
wise and foolish and Right and wrong &c For beasts of the same 10
Species, that have no Notion of Truth at all, live quieter among
themselves then men who for the most part are not much better
furnish'd; and yet have more then they know how to make Good
use of. And yet all the affaires of the world (how false soever) are
managd in the name of Truth, as the late usurpation and slavery 15
heere was in the name of the Keepers of the liberties when there
were no such persons nor things in Being.

Long discourses may and Doe commonly Stirre or excite men to 81ʳ
Action But not Gouverne them in It: for the understanding is by
the flame of the passions never enlightned; but Dazled. 20

Cato Cared; That the publick might neither Doe nor suffer 81ᵛ
wrong.   Dyed at 48.

Athenodorus alwaies Refused the Acquaintances of Great men;
and Cato valued It more then the highest exploit; That hee won
him to Himselfe.   25

---

1. 1–6 *Verse drafts from B 68ᵛ C*   17. 1–10 [80ᵛ] *Verse draft from B 15ᵛ C*
18–25 *Written in a large hand C*   22 Dyed] dyed *C*   24–5 That . . .]
underlined roughly C

82^r   ## Talke

> Eternall Talking's but an overheat
> O'th' Braine, as some put wine in parrots meate;
> For still the more men are in want of Sense
> They have it out and more in Confidence.

5   In dressing of a Calfes head the Braines and Tongue are wont to
goe together.

The french have a publick officer whom they call Langageur
whose businesse is to Search the tongues of all Mercat-hogs to
discerne whither they bee Sound or not: but they want one much
10 more necessary, to inspect the Tongues of men whither they have
not more Dangerous Symplements of worse infirmities then worms
and meazles.

83^r   ## Prophesy

I could never understand what purpose Prophecy can pretend to;
unlesse It bee to Satisfy the Curiosity of those who delight in
15 Novelty: which this is the earliest way to forestall and anticipate
for as diseasd Appetites long for green fruite and desire things
before they are in Season so sickly minds commonly affect the
Knowledge of Events before their Time, which at such a distance
are alwayes so Raw and incertaine that they can never give any
20 tast of Sence Satisfaction to a Sound and healthfull understanding:
Beside (granting them to bee true) they are alwaies Impertinent
to the present Age and unnecessary to the future; for like the Clay
of China Potters they are always prepard for the use of an Age to
come in which the present is not at all concernd: and (the time to
25 which they are destind being never plainely determined) the Future
has as little Advantage of Them: For though they are sent out long
before, the Successe commonly arrives [before] them, nor are they
ever truly understood, untill that interprets Them and that is
always too late: Then, whither they foretell Good or Bad they are

---

12. 1–16 [82^v] *Verse drafts from B* 132^v *C*   18 Time,] Time. *C*   18–19 which
. . . Raw] *underlined C*   21 Beside . . . true] *underlined C*   24 and (the]
and the *C*   25 destind being] destind (being *C*   28–9 untill . . . late]
underlined C

of bad use or none at all; for if they presage Good that Good will not come the sooner by being foretold; unlesse the Successe depend upon the Beliefe of the prediction and then it ceases to bee a prophesy and becomes a Cause of such an Event; which it might as well have been; tho It had been false. But if they threaten Evill to come either that evill may bee prevented by being foreknown, or it may not; if it may, then the prediction will become false; if it may not, the foreknowledge of evill that cannot bee avoyded does but Aggravate it; So that whither they are true or false or Good or Bad they are either unnecessary or Pernicious. And truly hee that considers what an unhappy province a mere prophet designes Himselfe, will never expect much Judgment from such a person: For as no prophet was ever esteemd in his owne Time, more then in his owne Countrey So hee that can bee Content to bee accounted Foole and madman while hee lives, to bee reverently thought upon by the world perhaps some 100s. of yeares after hee is Dead makes but an unwise Choice And therfore some that have been thrifty of their Creditt have imparted their Revelations only to the walls of Religious Houses, to bee found in their future Ruines: for in such places they are commonly found or sayd to bee So.

Prophets and Alchimists use to call things by other names then they are commonly known by, that when they miscarry they may have the liberty of Evasion, and in the meane time may not bee contradicted because they are not understood.

Clergy-men should bee like Buckets; that are hangd up in their churches; to quench burning houses; But they directly contrary use to sett houses on fire with Them; as eliah burnt his Sacrifice with water.

Clergy men calling themselves Pastors doe not improperly expresse the truth of their own Conditions; and that of their Congregations: For as a shephard does not take Care of his flock for It's own sake; but to Cloath Himselfe with their fleeces; and to Eate or Sell their Flesh: No more doe they Labour to convert and preserve

2–3 unlesse . . . prediction] *underlined C*   3–5 then . . . false] *underlined C*
7 may,] may; *C*   11–12 what . . . Himselfe] *underlined C*   15 to . . . upon]
underlined C   16–17 makes . . . Choice] *underlined C*   21 . . . Alchimists]
underlined C   26–8 But . . .] *underlined C*   29 Pastors] *underlined C*   31–2 for
. . . sake] *underlined C*

mens Soules, but to enrich themselves with the profitts of their Livings: and conversion of their purses; and the Advantages that they make of Them.

84^r   Religion

84^v   Most men in their professions of Religion Act as if they thought
5   the best and safest way to Heaven; were to get a Pass from the Devill, to travaile securely upon their Occasions through his Dominions, without any molestation, or further restriction, then being obedient to the lawes, and paying the usuall duties and Customs of all Places they are to passe through.

85^r   Presbiterians condemn whom they please by the Eternall Decrees
11   of providence; And independents execute the Sentence upon them by a warrant under the Hand and seale of providence; So that the one makes himselfe Judge and the other a Sheriffe (or rather executioner) to Destiny.

15   Independents cannot abide to have the trade of preaching regu-
lated; but would have all opinions true or false left at large, for all sorts of Interpreters to make their best of.

For to say It is fatall; meanes no more then that It is Something which wee doe not understand the Reason of.

20   Phanaticks believe all Religion consists in Words and Devotion; nothing else; Praying and preaching without any regard of their actions; as the lives of the old Philosophers were nothing, but their Sayings.

85^v   There is no Religion in the world so averse to warr as the
25   Christian in the primitive Institution of it; untill of late times It has been Adulterated with the Doctrines and practices of the Jewish: with which It is apparently Inconsistent: and therfore was Impos-sible to bee propagated by the Sword; as the mahometans and

5–6 a . . . Devill] *underlined C*   7–8 then . . . lawes] *underlined C*   9. 1–5
See p. 278, ll. 1–5   15 Independents] *underlined C*   27–8 therfore . . .
Sword] *underlined C*

before the Pagan were; Nor could It more probably bee contrivd
against the Interest of Gouvernment; being Inconsistent with the
most necessary part of all Gouvernments; Warre: without which
no monarchy nor free State in the world can either increase or
defend and preserve Itselfe; that the wonderfull increase and pro- 5
pagation of It may seeme as great a miracle, as any of those upon
which our Saviour layd the foundation of It.

In the Primitive times of the pagan Religion, the world made
Deities and Saints of none, but Great Conquerors, mighty princes
and Heroes; as they calld the Sturdiest and most desperate fighters: 10
But when that humor grew out of fashion; the world (that
naturally inclines to run into extreames) tooke a quite contrary
Course and admitted none to those Cælestiall dignities, but only
those who were before the most Contemptible; that could with
greatest patience indure to bee the most humble wretched and 15
miserable of all others. And when the suffering of Injury and affliction was renderd the shortest way to the greatest Glory; which
others before went to purchase by Imposing: It is no wonder that
the most wretched and miserable of all ages have ever since abounded
with the greatest Gluts of Saints; as when the Northern Barbarians 20
overrun Civility and the Christian Religion, as well as the Roman
empire; one age producd greater numbers of Holy saints then All
others have done ever since: For Sanctity like Miracles is Ceast;
and though both were frequent in the Primitive time; yet now
appeare so seldome unlesse in Disguise and masquerade to abuse 25
and cheat the world; That some Believe there is many a Saint in
the Rubrique, that will bee found but an Hypocrite at the day of
Judgment: For the Lives of Saints are no more True, and drawn by
the life; then their pictures that are made meerely out of the fancy
of a Bungling Artificer; though both are equally Reverenc't and 30
ador'd by the duller World.

Christ delivered his Doctrines in parables and Allegories as the 86ʳ
antient Prophets had done their predictions of his life and Death.

2 against . . . Gouvernment] *underlined* C   3 without which] *underlined* C
12 into extreames] *underlined* C   13–14 but . . Contemptible] *underlined* C]
14 Contemptible] Contemtible C   15 patience] *underlined* C   17–22 which
. . . empire] *underlined* C   23 Sanctity . . . Ceast] *underlined* C   27 but an
Hypocrite] *underlined* C   28–9 and . . . pictures] *underlined* C   30–1 though
. . .] *underlined* C   32–3 as . . . predictions] *underlined* C

That there might bee a Conformity in Both and all promisses performd punctually the same way, they were made.

The Jewish Religion never extended to Forrein Nations (as the Christian has done) nor converted any (that wee heare of) but Single proselites: but was confin'd within the narrow limits of their own Countrey; and not able to secure a 3d part of that from Revolting in All ages; to the Idolatry of their bordering neighbours: nor is it profest by any at this day, but by those of their own Tribes; not because they will admit of no others, but none will indure to bee admitted. Whenas many daily fall from them; And they are not able to produce above one Learned man in their Law in an Age; nor have been for many yeares.

86ᵛ   It is not to bee Imagin'd that the multitude should use the Christian Religion better or otherwise, then they did Christ himselfe; when hee would have planted It among them; that is, so foolishly and incertaine, like Themselves, that Sometimes they would follow Him into the wildernesse to heare his Doctrine and see his Miracles; untill they were allmost stervd; at another time for the Same Reasons endeavour to stone Him; at one time take his part so farr that the High priests durst not meddle with Him; for feare least they should rescue Him out of their Hands: and within 2 or 3 dayes after, when It was referrd to them by pilate, to resolve what they would have done unto Him; to cry out, Crucify Him &c To bee eye witnesses of all his miracles that were done before their faces: and yett bee unconvinc'd; and believe lesse then the Devill, in Them; and in a few months after when the same things, were but only told them; bee Satisfyed and converted to the number of 4000 at a Clap. And when they had put him to Death with all the Cruelty of Zeale and Ignorance; voluntarily Offer themselves to suffer the Same for his sake; rather then deny

87ʳ   what They / had Zealously done, to bee Barbarous and Inhumane.

There is no Heard of wild Beasts that is not a more prudent Corporation then any ungouvernd multitude of Men; for there is no one kind of Savage Creatures, but doe naturally agree better among Themselves in all things that concerne their own preservation; and destroy none; but those of other specieses; then man; who being a little World has something of all other Sorts of Beasts (wild and Tame) in his nature: and uses the same Ferity against those of his owne Species; which the most brutish of all other wild Beasts never doe; but against such as are of a different Kinde; that if hee bee (as hee is calld) Lord of all other Creatures; hee is a naturall prince fit and proper for such subjects; and the lyon that is his Lord lieutenant over foure leggd Beasts, is as much Inferior to Him, in the savagenesse of his nature, as hee is in politiques and Reason of state. How is it possible that Religion (which naturally tends to Dissention and Division) should subsist without order and Gouvernment; more then the Civill state can doe; when the very Gouvernment of Hell (our saviour sayes) would ruine; if It were but Divided? For the perpetuall Consequence of disorder and Confusion is submission to as lawlesse and extravagant a Tyranny. And it is as silly to suppose the Multitude Capable of Judging rightly of any thing; as to make the Hands Leggs and feet of men able to think and determine; and the Head to goe and Act and the bus'nesse of any one member to performe and execute the proper office and function of any other. For the Scripture does no more command those who have no Sence nor Reason to understand; then It do's such as have no ears, to Heare and altho' they may believe they have as much as the wisest; no conceited foole ever thought otherwise of Himselfe and It is probable; their Riddle of Knowing without using the Meanes is; but a Dispensation to bee above understanding, as well as Ordinances. For if knowledge were to bee acquird by only making an Ignorant Distinction between Carnall and spirituall, Men might arrive at the topp of all understanding, as easy as Jackdaws are taught to speake; and much after the same Rate: for if unnaturall distinctions introduc'd errors and mistakes among the learned; why should they not doe so, and much more among the Ignorant?

1 then man] *underlined* C   2–3 has . . . nature] *underlined* C   5 Kinde;] Kinde. C   6–7 hee is . . . lyon] *underlined* C   10–15 How . . . Tyranny] *underlined* C   20–1 For . . . understand] *underlined* C   23 no conceited foole] *underlined* C   24–6 their . . . Ordinances] *underlined* C   28–9 Men . . . understanding] *underlined* C   30 for . . . distinctions] *underlined* C   31 among the learned] *underlined* C

87^r ## [Christian Religion]

88^v # Jews

The Reason why the Heathens objected to the Christians in the primitive Church the Worshipping of an Asses head, may seem to bee This: To a Heathen a Jew and a Christian were all one; the Vulgar not understanding the difference, the one growing out of 5 the other. Now by the Jews law all the firstlings of Cattle were to bee offerd to God (except a yong Asse) which was to bee Redeemd. A heathen being present at these Sacrifices and seeing yong Calves and lambs killd only yong Asses redeemd, might very well thinke, They had that silly Beast in great estimation: and thence might 10 imagine, They worshipt It as a God.

89^r # Reformation

Reformation is a poore little Foolish thing, that has not liv'd long enough in the world to understand the tricks of It; and therfore out of mere Simplicity, for a few uselesse Speculative truths runs Itselfe into a thousand Inconveniences: and never knows when 15 any Thing is too much or too little. But having broke loose from the Greatest Slavery in the world, is so wanton of It's liberty: that It considers nothing else; and therfore never knowes what It would have. For Religion that was first planted among the Rabble, can never so perfectly and naturally agree with any thing else.

90^r ## [An Atheist]

91^r # Man

91^v The very being of Humane events depends upon our Ignorance 21 of Them, for man has so free a disposition of his own Actions and so naturall a regard of his own Good That if hee have Notice of

0. 1–22 [87^v] *See 'A Proselite', sent. 5–9; GR* ii. 200–2, *and Appendix B below for C variants*   2 an Asses head] *underlined C*   3 To . . . one] *underlined C*   6 except . . . Asse] *underlined C*   10. 1–22 [88^v] *Verse draft from B* 131^r *C*   10. 23–8 [89^r] *See p. 276, ll. 26–31*   16 is] is, *C* liberty] *underlined C*   19. 1–31 *See 'An Atheist', GR* ii. 261–2, *and Appendix B below for C variants*   19. 32–53 [90^v] *See p. 273, l. 5–p. 274, l. 2*   19. 54–9 [91^r] *Verse drafts from B* 127^r *C*

any evill to befall Him hee can easily prevent It For hee that by
the meere observation of other mens Harms can avoyd his owne
of which hee has but a probable Guesse (which is the chief businesse
of Civill Prudence) might doe much more upon a certaine foreknowledge And in those Events Good and Bad are so mixt and 5
intangled that It is impossible to divide them For they many times
become the Causes and Effects of one another For many mens misfortunes have been the only way to their happinesse And if they
had foreknown or prevented the Evill the Good had never succeeded as wee may observe in the story of Themistocles who used 10
to say Periissem nisi periissem, and in the Earle of Somersetts
breaking of His Legg.
So the happinesse of others hath been the only Cause of their
Ruine as all histories doe sufficiently testify.

A Man lookes as ridiculously in an old fashion'd fayth and 15
loyalty as an Antique Habit.

Men baite with little fishes to catch Great ones.

Men of great Witts differ from those that are Dull as the Hand
do's from the Foote; for tho the fingers of the one are no more then
the toes of the other and the Senses of both Equall, yett the one 20
is fitted by nature for all the uses of Life Whereas the other is good
only to beare the Burthen of the Body and bee trodden upon.

Every man's Reason is but the naturall effect of the Temper of 92r
his Body; as all Waters differ only according as they are qualifyed
by the Aire or Earth they runn through. 25

It is one of the greatest flaws in human Nature, that most men
ignorantly mistake the ends which they doe or should propose to
themselves; and when they are in a faire way of obteining them are
so possest and delighted with the prosperous meanes they have
used, that they believe those to bee the only things, they proposd 30
to themselvs at first; and like the Prisian that swallowed his Knife
instead of his Meate, mistake the Instruments they use to bee the
very worke they are to bee imployed upon. And that is the Reason
why they are never Satisfyed; for mistaking the End of their

19 Foote;] Foote. C   20 Equall,] Equall. C   32 Instruments] underlined,
and interlined above: his Bow to bee the mark hee aimes at C

designe, they are perpetually out of the way and the further they
goe are but the farther off from the end of their Journey; and as
preposterously delight to labour in vaine and drudge to no purpose;
For a Covetous Man that believes mony to bee the only purpose
5 of Humane life and applyes himselfe to Nothing else layes heavier
loads upon Himselfe and is content with lesse Allowance; then a
Carman gives his Horse that gets his Living for Him. For a Carman
feeds and dresses his Horse and when hee is Sick is at the Charge
of a Farrier: But an Avaritious man is a Beast to a more Barbarous
10 owner, that takes no Care of him at All, but turns him up after
hard labour to Grase like an Asse upon Thistles: and which is the
greatest Curse of all, the Beast takes delight in It; and takes paines
so wretchedly to no purpose, that hee dares not so much as think
who It is for.

92ᵛ   There are as many Children begotten against the Wills of their
16 Parents as with them and that may bee one Reason why a great
part of Mankind is generally so Idle and vaine for being Designd
in their Generation to no purpose; It is no wonder, if they prove
so afterwards in their Lives: for although nothing can bee Done
20 without the Consent of the Parents yet very little else is left to
their disposing: For if Children or no Children, or male or female
were in their free Choice, the world would bee but meanly and
that unequally stockd with Mankind, But nature has wisely kept
that power in her own Hands, else the world would bee worse
25 ordered, then It is; and while the one parent is for one Sex and the
other for another; They would produce nothing but Hermephra-
dites; But in the greatest numbers considering the paine or Shame
of Bearing Them and the trouble and charge of Keeping and
breeding Children, none at All; for all Bastards are but Intruders
30 and come confidently into the world before they are invited; and
therfore are commonly more bold then Welcome.

93ʳ   Knowledge

All the Knowledge mankind is Capable of is not considerable
enough to damne any man that wants It when that want itselfe
is too severe a punishment.

2–3 as . . . purpose] *underlined* C   13–14 that . . .] *underlined* C

There is no Ignorance so Impertinent as that which proceeds from Curiosity and over-understanding of any thing For beside the lost labour It rather argues Defect of Judgment which is more desperate to bee Cured then any want of Industry or lesse considerable parts. Those men as Terence says of his poetasters Faciunt nec intelligendo ut nihil intelligant and is much worse then understanding lesse then the thing will beare for that may bee supplyed, but that which is over-done is spoyld, as more men perish by excesse then want of necessaries And monsters are seldome renderd such by a naturall defect of members, but for the most part by having two or three too much. And no Number can bee sayd to bee more times lesse then it is, then just so many as it really conteins But is Capable of being falsly extended to [in]finite times more. For Error is Copious and men are apter to fall into It by over-doing then performing lesse then They might.

[Passion] 93ᵛ

Reason 94ʳ

Ebbs and flowes.

For sober Reason takes to Compleasance
No lesse then pertinacy t'ignorance.

Sence and Reason need no Tradition; because they are Originalls. 95ʳ

There is nothing more perishable then an Army; which wasts 96ʳ every day whither It bee in Action, or not; and melts away like Snow in the Sun, especially upon long and difficult Marches to forrain remote Parts: in which the way Itselfe is enemy enough. And the Alps cost Hanniball more paine to overcome; then all the power of Italy and Rome.

Holland that is of itselfe the nastiest place in the world, do's for 96ᵛ that very Reason produce the most cleanly Inhabitants, while other Countries of wholsome and cleare Ayre render the people negligent and consequently Slovenly.

17–18 *Interlined alongside heading C*   23 the . . . enough] *underlined C*

Ice swims upon the Top of water, by Being Compact; as naturally as Froth does by being loose and spungy.

> Know Truth's the greatest wit of All mankind
> And Those that know It best the most Refind;
> 5 And vaine Credulity the worst of Folly;
> Altho It passe for Reverend and Holy.

97ʳ   When Adam by disobedience had opend a Gap for Sin to enter
into paradice; Zeale and murther were the next in order that
followed It; And that very method is exactly continued by those
10 Sins to this day: for Rebellion is allways either introduced or
seconded by Zeale and murther.

98ʳ   Conscientia

98ᵛ   The proper duty of Conscience is to forbeare and abstaine from
doing such things as wee judge unjust and Criminall; and while It
keepes within that Compasse; It can never doe amisse. But when
15 It changes It's nature and becomes Active and Pragmaticall It turnes
to a kind of zeale and being out of it's naturall Element is apt to
runn into all the Barbarous inhumanities in the world. For as it is
but a negative virtue It has no Power at all to impose; no more
then a negative Voice has to prescribe: and when It assumes that
20 and transgresses It's bounds, there is no wickednesse in the world
that It will not make It's Duty. Nor any inhumanity so horrible
that It will not render the whole duty of man.

Those that stand most for liberty of Conscience have no reason
so considerable for It; as that they have alwaies been found to have
25 the largest Consciences of all men and therfore require the greater
Roome: altho a large Conscience and none at all in the publick
sense signify the Same Thing: And that Liberty they pretend to,
is so extravagant; that It knows not what It would have; nor
within what limitts It can endure to bee confind; unlesse It bee

   8 Zeale and murther] *underlined* C   12–22 *Duplicated* C 29ʳ   17–18 For
. . . virtue] *underlined* C 98ᵛ   17 as C 29ʳ: *om.* C 98ᵛ   19 prescribe]
present C 29ʳ   20 there is] there's C 29ʳ   20–1 in . . . that] *om.* C 29ʳ
21 It's] a C 29ʳ   21–2 Nor . . .] *underlined* C 98ᵛ; *om.* C 29ʳ   22 man.]
man. NB. C 98ᵛ   26 altho . . . all] *underlined* C   28 that . . . have] *underlined* C

a Conjurers Circle, in which It may safely raise the Devill when It pleases; and imploy Him upon what occasions It shall find necessary or usefull to It's own affaires.

Conscience   99ʳ

It is better Sleeping in a whole Conscience then a whole Skin.

Conscience is an obligation and though It bind ever so much; 99ᵛ
yet every man has It, in his own Keeping, and can dispose of It   6
how hee pleases: can compound and dispence and commute at his
own Rates: and if hee finds himselfe too hardly prest Can hire a
priest to doe It for Him, at a very easy price: And as hee is both
plaintiffe and Defendant Himselfe, can easily deferr the suite, as   10
long as Hee pleases; being secure (as hee believes) from paying any
Costs or dammages, or loosing any thing by default in this world:
and therfore being his own Sollicitor hee often cheats and abuses
himselfe; As others doe their Clients; and making his Case better
then it is; is overthrown when hee comes to Tryall. And altho' It   15
has naturally no Jurisdiction, but in Its owne limits; yet like other
Courts it is always encroaching; for Conscience, that has nothing
to doe but in It's own Affaires, never meddles with Itselfe, But is
alwaies zealously busy in All publick concerns, and intruding Itselfe
into all men's businesse; to divert and forgett It's owne. For Con-   20
science is nothing but an internall Account; which all men keepe,
or ought to keep: of their own Actions, and has nothing to doe
with Those of other men; and yet It is perpetually busy in assuming
an Arbitrary power, over those of all others; and prescribing It's
owne Rules to Those, over whom It has no Authority at All.   25

And as all usurpers are naturally Tyrannicall; So it is allwayes
most Severe; where It has least Right to pretend: and omits no
sort of Cruelty, to mainteine that power; which It is unjustly
possest of. And that which at first was nothing but Tendernesse
and selfe preservation in time becomes the Greatest Inhumanity in   30
the world to all others; like all other sins which the more they are
Indulgd become the more destructive.

5 Conscience] *underlined* C   8–9 if . . . price] *underlined* C   10 can . . .
suite] *underlined* C   14–15 As . . . Tryall] *underlined* C   18 never . . .
Itselfe] *underlined* C   19–20 intruding . . . owne] *underlined* C   22 or . . .
keep] *underlined* C   24 an Arbitrary power] *underlined* C   25–6 prescribing . . . usurpers] *underlined* C

COMMENTARY

p. 1, l. 1. *Travellers are allow'd to Lye*. Cf. the proverb 'A traveller may lie with authority' (*ODEP* 836; Tilley, T476).

p. 1, ll. 14–16. *Christians that travel, etc.* Sir Henry Blount reports the Turks' 'confidence, to catch or buy up for *Slave*, any *Christian* they finde in the *Countrey; nor* can hee escape unlesse where he bee a setled knowne *Merchant*, or goe with some *Protector*' (*Voyage into the Levant*, 1636, p. 102).

p. 1, ll. 17–18. *The Mahometan Religion, etc.* 'They abhorre *bloud*, and things strangled, and care little for *fish*, or *fowle*, but often buy them alive, to let them goe; whereto they pretend no *Metempsuchosis*, or any other reason, but that of naturall compassion; wherein they are so good, as to let *fowle* feede of their *Granaries*' (idem).

p. 2, ll. 10–18. *It was Queen Mary, etc.* Cf. p. 276, ll. 26–31.

p. 2, ll. 32–3. *Wine had no Share, etc.* Cf. p. 231, ll. 29–31, and note.

p. 3, l. 11. *Tu es Petrus.* Matt. xvi. 18.

p. 3, l. 17. *cry down Morality for Dirt.* Cf. Ralpho's antinomian arguments in *Hudibras*, II. ii. 233–50. Wilders cites Clement Walker, *Compleat History of Independency*, 1661, iii. 29: 'Their [the Independents'] fourth Principle is, *That they may commit any sin, and retain their Sanctity in the very Act of sinning: For what is sinfull in other men, is not so in the Saints; who may commit any crime against the Law of God, and yet it cannot be imputed to them for sin.*' Cf. p. 44, ll. 10–14.

p. 3, ll. 21–2. *commit Iniquity upon the Tops of Houses.* See 2 Sam. xvi. 22.

p. 3, l. 25. *a Painted Sepulchre.* Cf. Matt. xxiii. 27 ('whited sepulchres').

p. 3, l. 31. *O. C.*: Oliver Cromwell. He intended a thorough reformation of the law, and his Chancery Ordinance (21 August 1654) 'beat' the most notorious of the courts (D. Veall, *The Popular Movement for Law Reform 1640–1660*, Oxford, 1970, pp. 225, 180–3). But Cromwell's supervision of the courts is more probably in Butler's mind: the trial of Charles I or the administration of justice in the eleven districts of the major-generals.

p. 4, l. 1. *Charity does not, etc.* An allusion to the proverb 'Charity begins at home' (*ODEP* 115; Tilley, C251).

p. 4, l. 6. *a wise Child, etc.* Proverbial (*ODEP* 899; Tilley, C309).

p. 4, ll. 13–14. *They who study Mathematicks, etc.* 'So if a man's wit be wandering, let him study the mathematics; for in demonstrations, if his wit be called away never so little, he must begin again' (Bacon, 'Of Studies', in *Works*, vi. 498).

p. 4, l. 27 n. *as the Jewes did, etc.* See Exod. xxxii.

p. 5, l. 1 n. *Not only over all this World, etc.* Ovid, *Metamorphoses*, xv. 840–50, describes the ascent of Julius Caesar's soul ('luna volat altius illa / flammiferumque trahens spatioso limite crinem / stella micat'). For such flattery of later Caesars see: Suetonius, *Augustus*, c. 4; Lucan, *Pharsalia*, i. 45–7; Statius, *Thebaid*, i. 24–31.

p. 5, l. 3 n. *as monkies are, etc.* 'The CEPUS, or *Martine Munkey*' is described by Edward Topsell as having 'a long tail, the which such of them as have tasted flesh wil eat from their own bodies' (*History of Four-footed Beasts and Serpents*, 1658, p. 6).

p. 5, ll. 8–9. *So Thousands dye, etc.* See note to p. 168, ll. 1–2.

p. 6, ll. 7–12. *No man can possibly, etc.* Cf. p. 236, ll. 11–19.

p. 6, l. 24. *the Modern Way of Test.* The Test Act of 1673 required that all office-holders under the Crown take the oaths of supremacy and allegiance, 'receive the sacrament of the Lord's Supper according to the usage of the Church of England', and declare disbelief in transubstantiation (25 Car. II, c. 2).

p. 6, l. 25 n. *that of lead and Bone Ashes.* 'Let *Knuckle-Bones*, or other *Bones* be burnt very white . . . stamp them fine, and grind them upon a *Grind stone* fine as flower, then mosten such subtile bone-ashes . . . with *strong Beer*, and of this make *Copels*' (*Assays of Lazarus Ercken*, trans. Sir John Pettus, in *Fleta Minor*, 1683, I. i. vi. 21–2). These cupels hold the precious metal and the lead with which it is 'proved' (ibid. I. i. xxi. 57).

p. 7, l. 18. *by the eares*: 'a proverbial phrase, originally used of animals fighting' (Wilders, note to *Hudibras*, I. i. 4). See *ODEP* 716; Tilley, E23.

p. 7, l. 27. *collection*: 'the act of deducing consequences; ratiocination; discourse' (Johnson, *Dictionary*).

Consequence: 'proposition collected from the agreement of other propositions; deduction; conclusion' (ibid.).

p. 8, l. 19. *discourse.* 'A judgement takes in two severall simple terms, and upon them passeth the sentence of their agreement or disagreement. A discourse takes into consideration two of the judgements already past . . . and from those two draws forth a third' ([Seth Ward,] *Philosophicall Essay*, 1652, ii. 58–9).

p. 8, ll. 29–31. *who say the Ancients, etc.* 'But there remaineth yet another use of Poesy Parabolical, opposite to that which we last mentioned: for that tendeth to demonstrate and illustrate that which is taught or delivered, and this other to retire and obscure it: that is when the secrets and mysteries of religion, policy, or philosophy are involved in fables or parables' (Bacon, *Advancement of Learning*, II. iv. 4, in *Works*, iii. 344). See also Sprat, *History of the Royal Society*, 1667, p. 5.

p. 8, ll. 33–5. *For as (Seneca say's), etc.* 'I know that all those men, who will admonish any man, beginne with precepts and end in examples; yet must I alter this course. For some are to be handled in one sort, some other in an other. Some there are that will be perswaded by reason, to some we must oppose the names and authoritie of great persons to stay their mindes, that are astonished at the lustre of things' (*Dialogues* VI. ii. 1, in *Works*, trans. Thomas Lodge, 1614, p. 712). See also *Epistolae Morales*, xciv–xcv.

p. 9, l. 4. *neare kin to a Ly.* Cf. p. 65, ll. 8–21.

p. 9, ll. 14–24. *It is very probable, etc.* Cf. Rom. ix. 20–1.

p. 10, l. 5. *streining of Knats, etc.* Matt. xxiii. 24.

p. 10, l. 7. *penny-wise, and Pound-foolish.* Proverbial (*ODEP* 620; Tilley, P218).

p. 10, l. 15. *De Coercendis Imperii Terminis.* In Augustus' *breviarum totius imperii*: 'addideratque consilium coercendi intra terminos imperii' (Tacitus, *Annales*, I. xi).

p. 11, l. 7. *Sale-work*: work of inferior quality, ready-made for sale. See p. 59, ll. 1–2.

p. 12, l. 9. *Occasion of*: need, or opportunity, for.

p. 12, l. 28. *Present*: attentive.

agreable: 'answering to the circumstances' (*OED*).

p. 13, ll. 13–17. *Wit is like Science, etc.* The emphasis on poetic universality, as opposed to the particularity of history, is ultimately Aristotelian (*Poetics*, ix. 1451^b 5–7), but a more immediate concern is with the currently unfashionable particularity of early seventeenth-century writers. Cf. Sprat, *History*, p. 413:

It is requir'd in the best, and most delightful *Wit*; that it be founded on such images which are generally known, and are able to bring a strong, and sensible impression on the *mind*. The several subjects from which it has bin rays'd in all Times, are the *Fables*, and *Religions* of the *Antients*, the *Civil Histories* of all *Countries*, the *Customs* of *Nations*, the *Bible*, the *Sciences*, and *Manners* of *Men*, the several *Arts* of their hands, and the works of *Nature*. In all these, where there may be a resemblance of one thing to another, as there may be in all, there is a sufficient Foundation for *Wit*.

p. 13, ll. 13–15. *as Arguments . . . Science.* Locke refers to '*the improvement of Knowledge*: which though founded in particular Things, enlarges it self by general Views; to which, Things reduced into sorts under general Names, are properly subservient' (*Essay concerning Human Understanding*, 1690, III. iii. 4).

p. 13, ll. 21–2. *to instruct, etc.* Horace, *De Arte Poetica*, ll. 333–4 (discussing poetry in general):

> aut prodesse volunt aut delectare poetae
> aut simul et iucunda et idonea dicere vitae.

Among the Renaissance theorists, Guarini had had reservations about tragedy's 'delight' and preferred tragicomic release from melancholy to tragic purgation through terror, 'percioche gli effetti del purgare son veramente oppositi infra di loro. l'un rallegra, & l'altro contrista. l'un rilascia & l'altro ristinge' (*Compendio della Poesia Tragicomica*, p. 22, app. to *Il Pastor Fido*, Venice, 1602).

p. 13, ll. 23–5. *the Ancient Romans cald, etc.* Latin: *ludus.* Greek: παιδιά (amusement) and παιδεία (education); see Plato's quibbling in *Laws* 656c.

p. 13, ll. 25–7. *if any man should, etc.* The standard defence of the heroic was to assert its exemplary value, as Spenser had done in his letter to Raleigh. Thus Davenant believes 'I have usefully taken from Courts and Camps, the patterns of such as will be fit to be imitated by the most necessary Men' (*Gondibert*, ed. D. F. Gladish, Oxford, 1971, Preface, p. 13).

p. 13, ll. 29–30. *Images . . . Virtues.* Hobbes uses these terms in his Answer to Davenant, ibid., pp. 49–50: Where the precepts of true philosophy fail, 'as they have hetherto fayled in the doctrine of Morall vertue', the philosopher's part devolves upon him 'that undertakes an Heroique Poeme (which is to exhibit a venerable and amiable Image of Heroique vertue)'.

p. 13, ll. 32–3. *the best end of Tragedy, etc.* This psychological argument, familiar from Lucretius, ii. 1–6, had not yet entered written discussions of tragedy, except that of Lorenzo Giacomini Tebalducci Malespini, 'Dela Purgatione dela Tragedia' (1586), in *Orationi e Discorsi*, Firenze, 1597, p. 30. Hobbes, to whom it would be congenial, comes closest to applying it to theatre in *Human Nature*, ix. 19. See Baxter Hathaway, 'The Lucretian "Return upon Ourselves" in Eighteenth-Century Theories of Tragedy', *PMLA* xlii (1947), 672–89.

p. 14, l. 10. *The Stoicall Necessity.*

The Destinies maintaine their right precisely, there is neyther prayer that moveth them, nor misery or favour that altereth them. They observe their irrevocable course, they passe onward in an assured and unaltered order. Even as the water of violent streames neither turneth backe, nor stayeth, but every wave is forcibly driven one by an other that beateth at his backe: so the order of Destiny is governed by an eternall succession, the decree whereof is, not to change that which hath beene ordained and destinated.

But what meanest thou by this word Destiny, I thinke it to be an invincible and immutable necessity of all things and actions (Seneca, *Quaestiones Naturales*, xxxv–xxxvi, in *Works*, trans. Lodge, p. 793).

p. 14, ll. 24–5. *That which the wise man, etc.* The words of Agur in Prov. xxx. 8 (but compatible with Eccles. iv. 1, 6; vii. 7, 11–12; ix. 16; and *passim*).

p. 15, ll. 5–6. *being . . . discontinu'd*: having ceased to be frequented or occupied.

p. 15, l. 16. *if his eies had been open.* Gen. iii. 7.

p. 15, ll. 18–19. *the Devil and his wife, etc.* Woman's complicity with the devil was proverbial in such sayings as 'the devil and his dam' (*ODEP* 179; Tilley, D225).

p. 16, l. 8. *standing Measure*: standard of measurement.

p. 17, l. 4. *Declinations*: declensions.

p. 17, ll. 4–5. *Anomula's*: anomalies; deviations from its grammatical rules.

p. 17, ll. 14–15. *what the Levellers, and Quakers, etc.* Typically, the Leveller William Walwyn, *The Power of Love*, 1643, p. 44, asks, 'as learning goes now adaies, what can any judicious man make of it, but as an Art to deceive and abuse the understandings of men, and to mislead them to their ruine?' The most forceful Quaker critic of learning was the Oxford M.A. Samuel Fisher, author of *Rusticus ad Academicos*, 1660.

p. 17, l. 33. *Dispensations, and Gifts, and Lights*: divine interventions, and inspirations, and revelations. Cf. *Hudibras*, I. i. 473–6, where the fanatic Ralpho is said to have acquired his knowledge by 'Gifts' and 'New light', and see ibid. I. iii. 1337–58 for his attack on Hudibras's scholarship.

p. 18, l. 14. *make a virtue of Necessity.* Proverbial (*ODEP* 861; Tilley, V73).

p. 18, l. 34. *Conversation*: acquaintance, society.

p. 19, l. 4. *design'd; as.* In C Longueville interlines 'Eccles. c. 8'.

p. 19, ll. 18–19. *as the earth, etc.* Gen. iii. 18.

p. 21, ll. 15–19. *that shield that fell, etc.* See Plutarch, *Numa*, xiii. The story goes that in time of plague this heaven-sent shield came into the hands of Numa for the salvation of Rome. The original shield, and the copies which the king had been told to have made, were kept in the Curia Saliorum.

p. 21, ll. 22–4. *the Devil of Error, etc.* 2 Cor. xi. 14.

p. 21, ll. 25–7. *that Mistake, etc.* Alexander, 'with *Hephestion*, one of the trustiest of his Friends', visited the mother of Darius. 'When they entred, in regard they were both habited alike, *Sisygambres* taking *Hephestion* for the King (because he was the more comely and taller Man) fell prostrate at his Feet' (Diodorus, XVII. xxxvii. 5, trans. G. Booth, 1700, p. 537). Cf. Arrian, *Anabasis*, II. xii. 3–8.

p. 21, l. 26. *braver*: more splendid in appearance.

p. 21, ll. 28–30. *Truth is, etc.* Cf. *Hudibras*, I. i. 147, Butler's note, and p. 65 below, ll. 1–8, and note.

p. 22, l. 14. *the Legend*: the *Golden Legend* or *Lombardica Historia*, compiled by

Jacobus a Voragine between 1255 and 1266, and consisting mainly of saints' lives and commentaries on Church festivals.

p. 24, ll. 8–10. *Can any thing, etc.* 'Avaritia vero senilis quid sibi velit non intellego: potest enim quicquam esse absurdius quam quo viae minus restet eo plus viatici quaerere' (*De Senectute*, xviii. 66).

p. 24, ll. 28–9. *the Ægyptian Conjurers.* '[The Egyptians'] Priests were their Judges, the eldest of which was chiefe in pronouncing sentence. He wore about his necke a Saphire Jewell, with the Image of *Truth* therein engraven' (Purchas, *Pilgrimage*, 1626, VI. IV. ii. 642). See also Exod. vii. 11–12. *Conjurers*: sorcerers, mystics.

p. 25, l. 2. *to the third or fourth Generation.* Exod. xx. 5; xxxiv. 7; Num. xiv. 18; Deut. v. 9.

p. 25, l. 3. *the other unto thousands.* Deut. vii. 9.

p. 25, l. 5. *God see's no Sin in the Saints.* 1 John iii. 9–10.

p. 25, ll. 7–8. *When the Devil tempted Christ, etc.* Matt. iv. 5; Luke iv. 9.

p. 25, ll. 13–14. *clean and unclean Beasts.* Gen. vii. 2, 8–9. Cf. Lev. xi.

p. 25, l. 14. *Sacrifices of Cain, and Abel.* Gen. iv. 3–5. Cf. Exod. xiii. 12; xxxiv. 19; Lev. xxvii. 26.

p. 25, ll. 14–16. *Josephs refusing, etc.* Gen. xxxix. 7–9. Cf. Lev. vi. 2 ff.

p. 25, l. 21. *and not be Ignorant.* In *C* Longueville interlines 'Vide Chillingw. c. 6. p. 290. aut', which would make a significant parallel in *The Religion of Protestants*, '3rd Impression', 1664; on p. 290 Chillingworth argues that 'faith is not knowledge, no more then three is foure, but eminently contained in it, so that he that knowes, believes, and something more, but he that believes many times does not know, nay if he doth barely and meerely believe, he doth never know' (edn. Oxford, 1638, p. 325).

p. 26, l. 6. *The Turkes accompt mad men Saints.* '[The Turks] have such as have lost their wits, and naturall Idiots, in high veneration, as men ravished in spirit, and taken from themselves, as it were to the fellowship of Angels. These they honour with the Title of Saints, lodge them in their Temples, some of them going almost starke naked; others clothed in shreds of severall colours, whose necessities are supplyed by the peoples devotions, who kisse their Garments as they passe through the streets, and bow to their benedictions' (Purchas, *Pilgrimes*, 1625, II. VIII. viii. ii. 1292).

p. 26, l. 9. *David complaine's, etc.* Ps. lxix. 9.

p. 26, ll. 12–13. *Repentant Teares are, etc.* 'God in some sort complaines against *Samuel*, when hee saith, *How long wilt thou mourn for Saul?* God could not (if one may say so) endure his lamenting, and not hearken to his suit. These are those waters which in a manner offer violence to heaven: The spirit of God moveth upon such waters, and they make a river of oblivion in Paradise' (Virgilio Malvezzi, *Il Davide Perseguitato: David Persecuted*, trans. Robert Ashley, 1647, p. 15).

p. 26, l. 14. *States*: republics, commonwealths.

p. 26, ll. 14–16. *as the King of France, etc.*

This Gabell is, indeed, a Monopoly, and that one of the unjustest and unreasonablest in the World. For no man in the Kingdom . . . can eat any Salt, but he must buy of the King and at his price, which is most unconscionable; that being sold at *Paris* and elsewhere for five Livres, which in the exempted places is sold for one. . . . This Salt is . . . imposed on the Subjects by the Kings Officers with great rigour, for though they have some of their last provision in the house, or perchance would be content (through poverty) to eat meat without it, yet will these cruell villaines enforce them to take such a quantity of them; or howsoever they will have of them so much money (P[eter] H[eylin], *A Full Relation of Two Journeys*, 1656, V. v. 265).

p. 26, l. 21. *obedience is better then Sacrifice*. 1 Sam. xv. 22.

p. 26, l. 24. *Ostentation of Gifts*: the display of personal inspiration which set prayers in the Anglican liturgy precluded (cf. 1 Cor. xii. 1, 4).

p. 27, ll. 4–5. *as the Bishops did King James, etc.* At the Hampton Court Conference, 1603, '*Whitgift* Arch-Bishop of *Canterbury* . . . with a *sugred bait* (which *Princes* are apt enough to swallow) said, *He was verily perswaded, that the King spake by the Spirit of God*' (Arthur Wilson, *History of Great Britain, Being the Life and Reign of King James the First*, 1653, p. 8). *The Canons of 1604* assert 'that the Kings Majestie hath . . . the same authority in causes Ecclesiasticall that the godly Kings had amongst the Jews, & Christian Emperors in the Primitive Church' (Canon II). *Persona mixta* is a concept in patristic discussion of the Incarnation. 'Ergo persona hominis, mixtura est animæ et corporis: persona autem Christi, mixtura est Dei et hominis' (Augustine, *Epistolae*, cxxxvii. 11). For a concise historical account, see C. Dodgson, ed., in *Library of the Fathers*, x (Tertullian, i), Oxford, 1842, p. 48, note h. The Definition of Chalcedon (451) finally rejected the mixture of human and divine natures in the Person of Christ and affirmed One Person in Two Natures.

p. 27, ll. 20–1. *those things*: i.e. which pertain to the Church.

p. 27, ll. 29–31. *It is no lesse Idolatry, etc.* Cf. p. 174, ll. 10–13.

p. 27, l. 32–p. 28, l. 2. *Æquivocation, etc.* Cf. p. 234, ll. 24–30.

p. 28, ll. 6–8. *Christ himself, etc.* John xiii. 27.

p. 28, ll. 10–11. *our Richard the third, etc.* 'King *Richard* now by his wives death, having made himselfe way to marry another; useth all the alluring means he can devise, to win the love of the Lady *Elizabeth* his Neece [and sister of Edward V]' (Sir Richard Baker, *Chronicle*, 1653, p. 333).

p. 29, ll. 4–6. *Livy Dec. 3. L 4. Prodigia, etc.* Livy, XXIV. x. 6.

p. 29, ll. 10–12. *when our Savior, etc.* Matt. iv. 2.

p. 29, ll. 12–13. *St Peter denyd, etc.* Matt. xxvi. 69–74; Mark xiv. 66–72; Luke xxii. 54–60; John xviii. 15–27.

p. 29, ll. 23–4. *The Judaicall and Levitical Law, etc.* The Law's delivery to Moses, Exod. xii, xx, etc.; Lev. i, etc.; Moses' civil magistracy, Exod. xviii. 13–16, etc.; delivery to Aaron, Exod. iv. 28, etc.; Aaron's priesthood, Exod. xxviii. 1–3.

p. 30, l. 14. *Mythologies*: interpretations.

p. 30, ll. 18–19. *If any man, etc.* Matt. v. 40.

p. 30, ll. 22–6. *The one of things, etc.* For a more detailed account see Cicero, *De Natura Deorum,* II. xxv. 65–xxvii. 68.

p. 30, ll. 24–5. *when Ixion made love, etc.* See Pindar, *Pythian Odes,* ii. 21–40.

p. 30, ll. 26–7. *The other of Notions, etc.* See Cicero, *De Natura Deorum,* II. xxiii. 61, III. xxiv. 61.

p. 30, l. 32. *Porrum et cæpe, etc.* Juvenal, *Satires,* xv. 9.

p. 31, ll. 4–11. *It was the Profuseness, etc.* 'Pope *Julius* was now dead, and succeeded by *Leo* the Tenth [1513–21], of the House of *Medici.* This Pope being over-munificent, endeavour'd to recover his *Exchequer* by a plenary *Indulgence.* These Favours of the Court of *Rome* used to be publish'd by the *Hermites;* but the *Dominicans* being look'd on as the best Managers, the Matter was put into their hands. These Men, it seems, flourish'd extravagantly upon the Virtue of *Indulgences,* and told the People they wou'd wipe out the Blemish of any Crime whatever' (Jeremy Collier, *Ecclesiastical History of Great Britain,* 1708–14, II. ii. 7ᵇ). Cf. p. 41 below, l. 31–p. 42, l. 10.

p. 31, ll. 23–4. *He that give's to the Poore, etc.* Cf. Sir Thomas Browne, *Religio Medici,* ii. 13: 'He that giveth to the poor lendeth to the Lord: there is more rhetoric in that one sentence than in a library of sermons.'

p. 31, ll. 29–32. *such a Stile as the great Turke, etc.* '[While lists of his dominions are not favoured by the Sophy,] the prolixity of Titles and Epithites is no less redundant in another kind, adorning his Letters and Dispatches with hyperboles of his resemblance to the Sun; his affinity to the Stars; and agreement with the sweetest and rarest sorts of fruits, flowers, gems, *&c.* As also with the Epithites of wise, famous, sweet, victorious, mercifull, just, beautifull, couragious, *&c.*' (Sir Thomas Herbert, *Some Years Travels into Divers Parts,* 1665, p. 226). For Turkish examples see Purchas, *Pilgrimes,* I. IV. i. ii. 344–5, II. IX. xv. xii. 1612; Richard Hakluyt, *Principal Navigations,* 1598–1600, II. i. 137–8, 192–3.

p. 32, l. 14. *Originall*: 'the fact of arising or being derived from something' (*OED*).

p. 32, ll. 18–19. *Cattle (of which the first Money, etc.* 'Moreover Theseus coyned money, which he marked with the stampe of an oxe, in memorye of the bulle of Marathon, or of Taurus the captaine of Minos, or els to provoke his citizens to geve them selves to labour. They saye also that of this money they were since Hecatombœon, and Decabœon, which signifieth worth a hundred oxen, and worth tenne oxen' (Plutarch, *Theseus*, xxv. 3, trans. North, 1895–6, i. 54).

p. 32, ll. 20–1. *Keepers of Parkes, etc.* ' . . . as the keeper of a park claims the skins of all bucks he kills as his fee' ('A Broker', *T* 86ʳ).

p. 32, l. 29. *Circumstance*: 'That which is not of the essence or substance: . . . what is adventitious or casual'; or perhaps simply 'a detail' (*OED*).

p. 33, l. 1. *faith and hope, etc.* See p. 149, ll. 8–10, and note.

p. 33, l. 2. *the Devils believe and tremble.* Jas. ii. 19.

p. 33, ll. 13–14. *his mercy is above all his workes.* Ps. cxlv. 9.

p. 33, ll. 25–33. *They that believe God dos not foresee, etc.* Cf. Robert South, on Prov. xvi. 33: 'Things are not left to an *æquilibrium*, to hover under an indifference whether they shall come to pass or not come to pass; but the whole train of events is laid beforehand, and all proceed by the rule and limit of an antecedent decree . . . The reason why men are so short and weak in governing is, because most things fall out to them accidentally, and come not into any compliance with their preconceived ends . . . But now there is not the least thing that falls within the cognizance of man, but is directed by the counsel of God . . . whose influence in every motion must set the first wheel a going. He must still be the first agent' (*Sermons Preached upon Several Occasions*, 7 vols., Oxford, 1823, i. 205–7).

p. 34, ll. 9–10. *Error as wel as Devotion, etc.* Alluding to the proverbs 'Ignorance is the mother of devotion' (*ODEP* 396; Tilley, I117) and 'Ignorance *the Mother of presumption, and of errors*' (Giovanni Torriano, *Piazza universale di proverbi italiani: or A Common Place of Italian Proverbs*, 1666, i. 116, no. 14). Cf. 'Impudence is the Bastard of Ignorance' ('An Impudent Man', *GR* ii. 213).

p. 34, ll. 22–4. *When Absolom, etc.* 2 Sam. xv. 7.

p. 35, l. 4. *Hoc est Corpus meum.* Matt. xxvi. 26; Mark xiv. 22; Luke xxii. 19.

p. 35, ll. 5–6. *to whom all times are present.* Cf. South, *Sermons*, i. 204: 'God, by reason of his eternal, infinite, and indivisible nature, is, by one single act of duration, present to all the successive portions of time; and consequently to all things successively existing in them: which eternal, indivisible act of his existence, makes all futures actually present to him; and is the presentiality of the object which founds the unerring certainty of his knowledge.'

p. 35, ll. 7–8. *Joseph is say'd, etc.* Matt. i. 19.

p. 35, ll. 8–9. *Justice only, etc.* Perhaps Heb. xii. 23.

p. 35, l. 15. *occasions*: personal needs.

p. 35, l. 32. *Rebellion is sayd to be, etc.* 1 Sam. xv. 23.

p. 36, ll. 7–9. *St Paul was glad to appeale, etc.* Acts xxv. 11.

p. 36, ll. 10–11. *The Israelites, etc.* Exod. i. 6–14.

p. 36, ll. 12–13. *for being Poore, etc.* Gen. xlvii. 1–6.

p. 36, ll. 15–16. *50000 Bethshemites were destroyd, etc.* 1 Sam. vi. 19.

p. 36, ll. 27–8. *Charity that can only, etc.* See p. 149, ll. 8–10, and note.

p. 37, l. 11. *Gathering of Churches*: the process of voluntary association by which the Independent congregations came into being.

p. 37, ll. 11–12. *Gathering of Grapes, etc.* Matt. vii. 16; Luke vi. 44.

p. 37, l. 17. *their Deliverance . . . by the Plagues.* Exod. vii. 14–xii. 36.

p. 37, ll. 17–18. *their second Captivity in Babilon.* 2 Kgs. xxiv–xxv.

p. 37, l. 29. *depraving*: debasing (coinage).

p. 37, ll. 31–4. *as this unnaturall Mixture, etc.* Acts xv. 1–31.

p. 38, ll. 18–21. *Pharo who was Destroyd, etc.* Exod. iv. 21–xiv. 31, esp. xiv. 4.

p. 38, ll. 26–8. *They became so unsatisfy'd.* Exod. xiv. 11–12; xvi. 3; xvii. 3.

p. 39, ll. 1–2. *Christ commanded the Devil, etc.* Luke iv. 8.

p. 39, ll. 5–26. *The Religion of the Pagans, etc.* See p. 30, ll. 22–6, and note.

p. 39, l. 27. *David put on Sauls Armour.* 1 Sam. xvii. 38–9.

p. 40, ll. 12–17. *An Excomunicate Jew, etc.*

Ex iam ostensis liquet quid sibi velint Causæ . . . ob quas apud Judæos Talmudicos quis posset rite Excommunicari, id est eo usque pristina libertate consortii inter suos civilis privari ut nec intra quatuor cubitorum distantiam eorum cuiquam assidere ei fas esset, nec legitimi seu civilis hominum numeri pars aliqua, etiamsi præsens, interdum haberetur (John Selden, *De Anno Civili et Calendario Veteris Ecclesiæ seu Reipublicæ Judaicæ*, 1644, xviii. 82–3).

In locis ab Hierosolymis decem amplius dierum itinere dissitis perpetuo ut ante (quoniam illuc Apostoli seu Neomeniæ nuntii, maxime . . . *Apostoli Tisri* mensis, cuius dies 10 erat festum Expiationum illud Magnum, tempestive satis pervenire tunc nequibant) festa agunt duplicia (ibid. xvii. 82).

p. 40, ll. 18–22. *Great Prilates, etc.* 'That [formality] of adding DEI GRATIA in stiles, is now more proper to supremacie. . . . [Yet] heretofore those curious differences of *Providentia* or *Clementia Dei*, which are now usd by Bishops and inferior Princes, were not so distinguisht from *Dei Gratia*, as later times (whose beginning I know not) have made them' (John Selden, *Titles of Honor*, 1614, I. vi. 116–17).

p. 41, l. 5. *Single Money*: small change.

p. 41, ll. 9–12. *when Adam, etc.* Gen. iii. 11–15.

p. 41, ll. 13–17. *The Inhabitants of the City, etc.* Many believed that the disasters of 1665–6 were God's judgements: 'All the king's enemies and the enemies of monarchy said, here [in the Plague] was a manifest character of God's heavy displeasure; as indeed the ill life the king led, and the viciousness of the whole court, gave but a melancholy prospect' (Gilbert Burnet, *History of his Own Time*, i. 39–10). For further discussion of this attitude, and of the monarchists shifting the blame on to rebellious Londoners, see E. N. Hooker, 'The Purpose of Dryden's *Annus Mirabilis*', HLQ x (1946), 49–67.

p. 41, ll. 20–3. *Vasa περιρραντήρια, etc.* Transcribed from Lipsius' comment on 'aqua perluere' (Tacitus, *Historiae*, IV. liii, in *Opera*, Geneva, 1619, ii. 527). For the derivation of 'delubra' Lipsius is deleting as spurious 'mortuorum' in 'Alii delubra dicunt ea templa, in quibus sunt labra corporum abluendorum mortuorum, ut Dodonæi Iovis aut Appolinis Delphici, in quorum delubris lebetes tripodesque visuntur' (which he quotes from pseudo-Asconius, comment on 'delubris' in Cicero, *In Caecilium Divinatio*, i. 3).

p. 41, ll. 24–6. *as the Turkes Janizares, etc.* In the time of Amurath, third king of the Turks, 'it was ordained that for the augmentation of this Militia [the Janizaries], every fifth Captive taken from the Christians, above the age of 15 years, should be the dues of the *Sultan* who at first were to be distributed amongst the Turkish Husbandmen in *Asia*, to learn and be instructed in the Turkish Language and Religion. . . . In former times this Militia consisted only of the Sons of Christians, educated in the Mahometan Rights; but of late that politick Custom hath been disused' (Sir Paul Rycaut, *Present State of the Ottoman Empire*, 1668, III. vii. 190–1).

p. 41, ll. 31–2. *our King Harry's Codpiece.* The writer of '*The* Court *Burlesqu'd*' observes of 'Old *Harry's* C – – piece in the *Tower*':

> Besides, it brought into this Nation,
> So Great a thing as Reformation;
> And therefore, to our Lady's Eyes,
> Can be of no disdainful Size.
>
> (*Posthumous Works . . . by Mr Samuel Butler*, 1715, p. 23.)

p. 42, l. 1. *Pope Leo the tenth.* See p. 31, ll. 4–11, and note.

p. 42, ll. 5–6. *his Mistrises and Favorites.* 'Non caruit etiam infamia, quod parum honeste non nullos e cubiculariis (erant enim e tota Italia nobilissimi) adamare, & cum his tenerius atque libere iocari videretur. Sed quis vel optimus atque sanctissimus princeps in hac maledicentissima aula lividorum aculeos vitavit? & quis ex adverso tam maligne improbus ac invidiæ tabe consumptus, ut vera demum posset obiectare, noctium secreta scrutatus est?' (Paulus Jovius, *De Vita Leonis Decimi*, Florence, 1549, iv. 98–[99].)

p. 42, ll. 7–9. *untill the oppression grew Intollerable, etc.* 'This shame, and dishonor was increased in the Country of *Saxony*, and other parts of *Germany*, when it was known, that the proceed, and benefit of those Indulgences, extorted with great rigor and avarice by the Bishop of *Arembauld*, . . . was not to be paid in to the Apostolical Chamber at *Rome*, but given to *Magdalen*, Sister to the Pope, and devoted to the avarice of a Woman; for then the matter became detestable, and the cries and exclamations lowed in all parts of *Germany*' (Sir Paul Rycaut, Pt. ii to Platina, *Lives of the Popes*, p. 36).

p. 42, l. 8. *improve*: enhance in monetary value (*OED*).

p. 42, ll. 12–14. *writing (or owning) of Polemique Bookes, etc.* 'On the second of *February* [1522], king *Henry* . . . received a Bull from the Pope, whereby he had the Title given him to be defender of the Christian Faith, for him and his successors for ever; which Title was ascribed to him, for writing a Book [*Assertio Septem Sacramentum*] against *Luther* as it was given out: but thought to be written, by Sir *Thomas Moor*, or by *Fysher* Bishop of *Rochester*' (Baker, *Chronicle*, p. 384).

p. 42, l. 23. *The Councell of Trent.* This Council (1545–63) held meetings during the pontificates of Paul III, Julius III, and Pius IV.

p. 42, l. 33. *Gibellins*: an Imperial, opposed to the Papal, faction in the Italian states.

p. 43, ll. 27–8. *Preaching masters perpetually Cry down Nature.* For instance, John Webster, *The Saints Guide*, 1654, p. 2: '*The Natural man receiveth not the things of the Spirit of God, for they are foolishness unto him: neither can he know them because they are spiritually discerned.* A natural man cannot know them by any natural power or acquisition. But the man of the most and greatest acquired knowledg in the World is no more then a natural man: *For that which is born of the flesh is but flesh*, not spirit. Therefore can he not understand the things of the Spirit of God; they are otherwise discovered, that is, spiritually, not carnally.'

p. 43, l. 31. *holding forth*: sermonizing. See Wilders, note to *Hudibras*, II. iii. 353.

p. 44, ll. 4–5. *brand's with the Names of Hypocrites.* Matt. xxiii. 13, 14, 15, 23, 25, 27, 29.

p. 44, ll. 10–14. *The Godly, etc.* Cf. p. 3, l. 17, and note.

p. 44, ll. 16–17. *Mandates to inable them, etc.* Royal dispensation, in letters mandate, could relieve a candidate of the exercises required for a degree.

p. 44, l. 20. *Chapmen*: men whose business is to buy and sell.

p. 45, ll. 3–7. *The First Quarrell, etc.* Gen. iv. 3–8. Cf. Dryden, *Hind and the Panther*, i. 279–81.

p. 45, ll. 12–13. *Jewes that sacrific'd their Children.* 2 Kgs. xvii. 17; Ps. cvi. 37–8.

p. 45, ll. 31–2. *as St Peter, etc.* Matt. iv. 18–22; Mark i. 16–20; Luke v. 2–11.

p. 45, ll. 33–4. *as St Mathew, etc.* Matt. ix. 9.

p. 45, l. 35–p. 46, l. 1. *Our Savior commanded, etc.* Matt. xix. 21; Mark x. 21; Luke xviii. 22.

p. 46, l. 3. *St Paul was stricken Blinde.* Acts ix. 3–9.

p. 46, ll. 7–14. *The originall of worshipping Images, etc.* Cf. Browne, *Pseudodoxia*, I. v, ix.

p. 46, ll. 12–14. *their Adoration of Crocodiles, etc.* 'Even the so much undervalu'd *Ægyptians* themselves never yet decreed divine Honours to any *Creature* from which they received not some considerable Benefit. Their *Ibes* destroy multitudes of Serpents. . . . I could shew the advantages they reap by *Ichneumons, Cats,* and *Crocodiles*' (Cicero, *Nature of the Gods,* I. xxxvi. 101, trans. 1683, p. 57).

p. 46, l. 17. *the smaller Numbers are always prefer'd.* Cf. Matt. xx. 16: 'many be called, but few chosen.'

p. 46, l. 19. *universality, and Generall Consent.* '[Catholics believe] That the true notes of the Church are, Universality, Antiquity, Continuance, Multitude, succession of Bishops, from the Apostles Ordination, Unity in Doctrine, Unity among the members themselves, and with their head' (Alexander Ross, πανσεβεια: *Or, a View of All Religions,* 1653, xiii. 464).

p. 46, l. 21. *Roman Immolation.* 'The Priest having brought the sacrifice to the Altar, used to pray, laying his hand on the Altar; Musick in the mean time sounding. Then he layeth on the head of the beast, Corn or a Cake, with Salt and Frankincense, this was called *Immolatio* from *mola* the Cake' (ibid. iv. 104).

p. 46, l. 24. *Without a Parable he spoke nothing.* Matt. xiii. 34; Mark iv. 34.

iv. 46, ll. 26–7. *killing a Slave, etc.* See Jonson, *Catiline,* i. 483–6:

> I'have kill'd a slave,
> And of his bloud caus'd to be mixt with wine.
> Fill every man his bowl. There cannot be
> A fitter drinke, to make this *sanction* in.

Sallust's sceptical report (which omits mention of a slave) continues, 'post exsecrationem' all tasted it, 'sicuti in sollemnibus sacris fieri consuevit' (*Catiline,* xx. 2), which could be mistaken to include the blood as customary. Cf. Dio Cassius, XXXVII. xxx. 4, and (for a similar incident) Diodorus, XXII. v. 1. Oldham, *Satires upon the Jesuits,* i. 8–15, uses the same allusion.

p. 46, ll. 27–9. *both the old Law, etc.* Gen. ix. 4; Acts xv. 29.

p. 46, l. 30. *Christ (who cald himself life).* John xi. 25; xiv. 6.

p. 46, l. 34–p. 47, l. 2. *So the Jewes, etc.* John ii. 19–21; Matt. xxvi. 61; Mark xiv. 58.

p, 47, l. 13. *Officer.* Judas was the Apostles' treasurer (John xiii. 29).

p. 47, l. 17. *believd in him, etc.* Jas. ii. 19.

p. 47, ll. 18–22. *the Devill tempted him, etc.* Matt. iv. 5–11; Luke iv. 5–13.

p. 48, ll. 1–2. *they Bent the knee.* 1 Kgs. xix. 18.

p. 48, l. 8. *divided the Empire.* Presumably the (re)division of the Imperial administration on the death of Constantine in 337.

p. 48, ll. 22–3. *by their Assistance, etc.* While the Eastern emperors retained land in Italy (up to 1071), it was Charlemagne who crushed, but never drove out, the Lombards. '*Charles* receiving from *Adrian* Intelligence of the injury which had been done him, sends Ambassadours to *Desiderius* to persuade him to restore what he had wrongfully taken from the Pope . . . [The Lombard king refuses, so Charles invades] *Itely,* where encountring *Desiderius,* he vanquishes and puts him to flight, and then takes and spoils his whole Countrey. . . . Thus ended the Kingdom of the *Lombards,* in the two hundred and fourth year after their coming into *Italy,* and in the year of our Lord seven hundred seventy six' (Platina, *Lives of the Popes,* pp. 146–7).

p. 48, ll. 37–8. *as they did to our Will: 2, etc.* William II and Henry I both succeeded despite the claim of their elder brother, Duke Robert of Normandy; Stephen despite Henry I's daughter Maude; John despite his brother Geoffrey's son Arthur (Baker, *Chronicle,* pp. 46–7, 55–6, 66 ff., 99 ff.).

p. 49, ll. 17–18. *who in Charity, etc.* An allusion to the proverb 'Charity begins at home' (*ODEP* 115; Tilley, C251).

p. 49, l. 19. *this Treasury of the Church.* See p. 49, l. 29–p. 50, l. 3, and note.

p. 49, ll. 23–6. *The Church of Rome, etc.* '[Catholics] say Christ is the meritorious cause of our justification, but the formal cause is either intrinsecal, & that is the habit of infused grace; or extrinsecal, to wit, the righteousness of Christ; or actual, which are our good workes; so that heer is a threefold formal cause: they teach that justification consisteth not in the bare remission of sins, but also in the inward renovation of the mind. That we are not onely justified, but also saved by good works, as efficient causes' (Alexander Ross, πανσεβεια, xiii. 457).

p. 49, l. 29–p. 50, l. 3. *they found out another expedient, etc.*

But after the Tenth Century . . . the Popes . . . called it [indulgence] a plenary Remission, and the pardon of all Sins: which the World was taught to look on as a thing of a much higher nature, than the bare excusing of Men from Discipline and Penance. Purgatory was then got to be firmly believed, and all Men were strangely possessed with the terror of it: So a deliverance from Purgatory, and by consequence an immediate admission into Heaven, was believed to be the certain effect of it. And to support all this, the Doctrine of *Counsels of Perfection*, of Works of *Supererogation*, and of the *Communication* of those Merits, was set up; and to that, this was added, That a Treasure made up of these, was at the Pope's disposal, and in his keeping' (Gilbert Burnet, *Exposition of the Thirty-Nine Articles*, 1699, Art. xiv, p. 137).

p. 50, ll. 2–3. *as the Spanish Friers, etc.* 'Barbarie and chiefly therein *Algier* ... holdeth captive in miserable servitude, one hundred and twentie thousand *Christians*, almost all subjects of the King of *Spaine* ... To the Redemption of Captives by the Orders of the *Trinitie*, and of Saint *Marie de Mercede* in *Spaine* and *Italy*, are yeerly gathered about one hundred and fiftie thousand Duckets' (Purchas, *Pilgrimes*, II. ix. xii. vi. 1565).

p. 50, l. 19. *Actions*: supplies relative to demand.

p. 50, l. 25. *at so little in the Hundred*: at so low a percentage premium.

p. 50, l. 31. *lick up it's old vomit.* Proverbial (*ODEP* 196; Tilley, D455).

p. 50, l. 32. *eversince the Church-lands were Sold.* On 19 October 1646 'An Ordinance for appointing the Sale of the Bishops Lands, for the Use of the Commonwealth, was this day read the First and Second time' (*Commons Journals*, iv. 699). 'By the State of the Accompt of the late Bishops Lands, bearing the Date the Fourth of *March* 1650, delivered into the Parliament, it appears, that ... there was then discharged, and to be discharged, by Purchases made before that Time, to be paid for in ready Money and *Goldsmiths-Hall* Bills, the Sum of 371,669*l*. 8*s*. 7*d*.' (ibid. vii. 22).

p. 51, ll. 3–7. *in the late Contest, etc.* The contest in 1673 lasted from 5 February to 7 March, when Charles cancelled his Declaration of Indulgence. A part of the episcopate was often credited with Catholic sympathies, notably Peter Gunning, Bishop of Ely (Burnet, *History of His Own Time*, i. 321), but the bishops worked to arouse antipapal feeling against the Declaration: 'The bishops, he of London [Henchman] in particular, charged the clergy to preach against popery, and to inform the people aright in the controversies between us and the church of Rome' (ibid. i. 555). See also Marvell, *Rehearsal Transpros'd*, ed. D. I. B. Smith, Oxford, 1971, p. 119. The truth is that assemblies of Protestant dissenters threatened conformist congregations, and it was hardly the bishops' 'certaine Interest' to have them freed by the same Indulgence. On 27 February the Commons resolved upon a bill for the relief of Protestant dissenters alone, which in the words of George Morley, Bishop of Winchester, 'would have bin an establishment of Schisme by a Law' (Bodl. MS. Tanner 42, fo. 7). In manœuvring against this bill the bishops might have looked pro-catholic, for the Lords amendments not only acknowledged the king's dispensing power, but omitted doctrinal tests, whereby, the Commons objected, 'Liberty might be given to Popery, and all Heresies and Sects whatsoever' (*Lords Journals*, xii. 580). The bill was abandoned. See Frank Bate, *The Declaration of Indulgence*, 1908, pp. 125–7.

p. 51, l. 6. *Stales*: decoy birds, persons 'made use of . . . as a cover for sinister designs' (*OED*).

p. 51, ll. 11–16. *the generall Il will, etc.* 'The truth is our *Bishops* slipt the occasion; since had they held a steady hand upon his Majesties restauration, as easily they might have don, The Church of England had emerg'd & flourish'd without interruption; but they were then remisse, & covetous after advantages of another kind, whilst his Majestie suffer'd them to come into an harvest, which without any injustice he might have remunerated innumerable gallant Gentlemen with for their services, who had ruin'd themselves for him in the late rebellion' (Evelyn, *Diary*, 12 Mar. 1672; ed. de Beer, 6 vols., Oxford, 1955, iii. 609). Cf Clarendon, *Continuation*, pars. 189–90.

p. 51, ll. 29–30. *a Ballance, etc.* Cf. p. 159, ll. 23–4, and note.

p. 51, ll. 30–1. *Fishers of Men.* Matt. iv. 19; Mark i. 17.

p. 51, ll. 33–4. *the Fox in the Fable, etc.* 'I will conclude with a famous tale of one of these crafty animals [foxes]; that having killed a goose on the other side of the river, and being desirous to swimme over with it, to carry it to his denne . . . (least his prey might prove too heavy for him to swimme withall, and so he might loose it) he first weighed the goose with a piece of wood, and then tryed to carry that over the river, whiles he left his goose behind in a safe place' (Sir Kenelm Digby, *Treatise of Bodies*, xxxvi. 3, in *Two Treatises*, Paris, 1644, p. 308). Cited by Wilders, comment on *Hudibras*, III. i. 672, where the same allusion occurs.

p. 52, ll. 7–8. *as a Thief is, etc.* Proverbial (*ODEP* 810; Tilley, T110).

p. 52, ll. 13–14. *as the best saints, etc.* Cf. Sir Thomas Browne, *Religio Medici*, ii. 10: '*Magnæ virtutes nec minora vitia*, it is the posie of the best natures, and may bee inverted on the worst; there are in the most depraved and venemous dispositions, certaine pieces that remaine untoucht; which by an Antiperistasis become more excellent . . . For it is also thus in nature. The greatest Balsames doe lie enveloped in the bodies of most powerfull Corrosives.'

p. 52, ll. 15–16. *of their Conversations*: for dealings with them.

p. 52, l. 21. *Conversations*: conduct in society.

p. 52, l. 22. *discerning of Spirits.* 1 Cor. xii. 10.

p. 52, l. 27. *Purchaces*: (irregular) profits.

p. 52, ll. 31–2. *Compassing of widdows Houses.* Matt. xxiii. 14 ('devour widows' houses'), 15 ('compass sea and land'). The sense 'grasp physically' could attach to 'compass'.

p. 52, l. 32. *tithing of Mint.* Luke xi. 42.

p. 53, l. 4. *turne*: convert.

p. 53, ll. 6–7. *the virtuoso's Trick, etc.* See illustration overleaf.

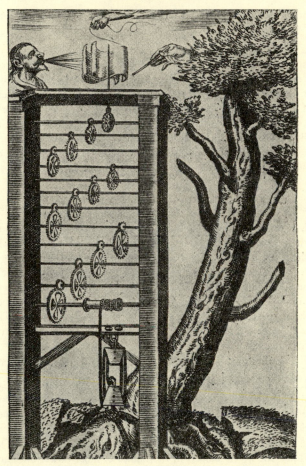

The whole force of this engine doth consist in two double Pulleys, twelve wheels, and a sail. One of these Pulleys at the bottome will diminish half of the weight [of 4,000,000,000 lb., supposed equivalent to uprooting an oak], so that it shall be but as 2000000000, and the other Pulley will abate ¾ three quarters of it: so that it shall be but as 1000000000. And because the beginning of the string being fastned unto the lower Pulley, makes the power to be in a subquintuple proportion unto the weight, therefore a power that shall be as 1000000000, that is, a subquadruple, will be so much stronger then the weight, and consequently able to move it. Now suppose the breadth of all the axes and nuts, to be unto the Diameters of the wheel as ten to one; and it will then be evident, that to a power at the first wheel, the weight is but as 100000000. To the second as 10000000. . . . To the twelfth as $\frac{1}{1000}$. And to the sails yet lesse. So that if the strength of the straw, or hair, or breath, be but equall to the weight of one thousandth part of a pound, it may be of sufficient force to pull up the Oak (John Wilkins, *Mathematicall Magick*, 1648, I. xiv. 99–100; plate, p. 98).

p. 53, ll. 19–21. *Our Savior calls, etc.* Matt. xxi. 13; Mark xi. 17.

p. 54, l. 5. *as the Devill, etc.* Matt. xiii. 25.

p. 54, ll. 16–17. *The Day that thou eatest, etc.* Gen. ii. 17.

p. 54, l. 17. *he liv'd some Hundreds, etc.* Gen. v. 5.

p. 54, ll. 19–21. *But the Serpent, etc.* Gen. iii. 14–15.

p. 54, ll. 24–5. *when their very prayers, etc.* Matt. vi. 6.

p. 55, l. 1. *docible*: tractable.

p. 55, ll. 4–5. *the bloud of the Martyrs, etc.* Proverbial (*ODEP* 69; Tilley, B457).

p. 55, l. 8. *impost*: ?compost. Not in *OED*.

p. 56, l. 1. *chargeable*: burdensome (financially).

p. 57, l. 19. *Island Shocks*: shag-haired lap-dogs, said to have come from Iceland. See *OED*, s.v.'Shough'.

p. 57, l. 22. *Caprich*: 'an humor, a fancy, a toy in ones head, a giddy thought' (Blount, *Glossographia*).

p. 58, l. 13. *Jump*: act in concord; respond to one another. Cf. *Hudibras*, I. iii. 1239–40. 'Good wits jump' is proverbial (*ODEP* 326; Tilley, W578).

p. 58, ll. 20–1. *wit and Fancy are, etc.* 'Time and education begets experience; Experience begets memory; Memory begets Judgement, and Fancy; Judgement begets the strength and structure; and Fancy begets the ornaments of a Poeme' (Hobbes, 'Answer to the Preface', in Davenant, *Gondibert*, p. 49).

p. 58, ll. 25–7. *those silly Indians, etc.* The Indians of Virginia who captured Capt. John Smith in 1607 *'brought him a b[a]gge of Powder, which they carefully preserved till the next spring, to plant as they did their Corne, because they would be acquainted with the nature of that seede'* (Purchas, *Pilgrimes*, IV. IX. iv. ii. 1709).

p. 59, l. 4. *a Cheat is worse, etc.* Cf. the proverbs 'A liar is worse than a thief' (*ODEP* 457; Tilley, L218) and 'A tale-bearer is worse than a thief' (*ODEP* 803; Tilley, T55).

p. 59, l. 9. *Tuition*: custody of a ward. In law the victim, being 'out of his Reason, and Senses', is a ward of the king, from whom his guardianship should be begged. See Sir William Blackstone, *Commentaries on the Laws of England*, 1765–9, III. xvii. 258, xxvii. 427; Joel Hurstfield, *The Queen's Wards*, 1958, pp. 72–6.

p. 59, l. 18. *Humorists*: persons 'subject to "humours" or fancies' (*OED*).

p. 59, l. 26. *taken by violence, etc.* On heaven taken by violence see Matt. xi. 12.

p. 59, l. 29. *who was truth it self*. John xiv. 6.

p. 60, l. 1. *si Natura, etc.* Juvenal, *Satires*, i. 79 (. . . indignatio versum).

p. 60, ll. 6–10. *He who first, etc.* The Greek poet Archilochus (probably eighth century B.C.) developed in its early form the iambic metre, especially suited to satire. Tradition has it that both the father Lycambes and his daughter Neobule hanged themselves as a consequence of Archilochus' verses. See Horace, *Epistles*, I. xix. 23–31, and cf. *De Arte Poetica*, l. 79: 'Archilochum proprio rabies armavit iambo.'

p. 60, ll. 36–7. *though a Copy, etc.* Gen. i. 26–7.

p. 61, ll. 2–3. *forty Days, etc.* Gen. vii. 12.

p. 61, ll. 4–5. *whose Punishments, etc.* Exod. xx. 5–6.

p. 61, l. 9. *Statute of Stabbing.* This statute 1 Jac. I. c. 8 enacted that 'every person and persons which . . . shall stab or thrust any person or persons, that hath not then any weapon drawn, or that hath not then first stricken the party which shall so stab or thrust, so as the person or persons so stabbed or thrust, shall thereof die within the space of six moneths then next following, although it cannot be proved that the same was done of malice forethought, yet the party so offending . . . shall be excluded from the benefit of his or their Clergy, and suffer death as in case of wilful murder' (Joseph Keble, *Statutes at Large*, 1676, p. 964). Hence stabbing weapons were in effect more 'illegal' than shooting or cudgelling weapons. See Blackstone, *Commentaries*, IV. xiv. 193–4.

p. 61, ll. 18–22. *He who in a Rage, etc.* Protogenes (late fourth century B.C.) in painting Ialysus' dog 'could not satisfie and please himselfe in expressing the froth which fell from his mouth as hee panted and blowed almost windlesse with running . . . At the last, falling cleane out with his own workmanship, because the art might be perceived in it, in a pelting chafe he flings me the spunge-full of colors that he had wiped out, full against that unhappie place of the table which had put him to all this trouble: But see what came of it! The spunge left the colours behind, in better order than hee could have laid them, and in truth, as well as his heart could wish. Thus was the froth made to his full mind, and naturally indeed by meere chaunce, which all the wit and cunning in his head could not reach unto' (Pliny, *Nat. Hist.* XXXV. xxxvi. 102–3, trans. Holland, 1601, ii. 542).

p. 61, l. 25. *Spirits*: 'The faculties of perception or reflection; the senses or intellect; mental powers' (*OED*).

p. 61, l. 32. *Temper*: elemental balance (of heat, coldness, and other physical qualities).

p. 62, l. 7. *height*: full growth.

p. 63, ll. 34–5. *In all Mutations, etc.* As Cardan explains, 'cum necesse sit materiam primam semper sub aliqua iacere forma, . . . in transmutationibus par materiae quantitas requirenda fuit, cum maior aut minor opportuna esse non possit. Atque ea ratione ex consimilibus consimilia magis fiunt, quam ex dissimilibus' (*De Subtilitate*, i, in *Opera*, iii. 359ᵇ).

p. 64, l. 4. *Prepossession is more, etc.* An adaption of the proverb 'Possession is nine . . .' (*ODEP* 640; Tilley, P487).

p. 64, l. 12. *prevayl'd*: prevailed upon.

p. 64, ll. 18–19. *the madman in the Acts, etc.* Acts xix. 13–16.

p. 65, ll. 1–8. *Reason | Is, etc.* Cf. Locke, *Human Understanding*, IV. v. 2: '*Truth* then seems to me, in the proper import of the Word, to signifie nothing but *the joining or separating of Signs, as the Things signified by them, do agree or disagree one with another*'. For general discussion of Butler's epistemology see pp. xxix–xxxiv above.

p. 65, ll. 6–8. *she sometime miscarry, etc.* Locke gives five instances of reason's failure in *Human Understanding*, IV. xvii. 9–13.

p. 65, l. 7. *Subtlety*: inherent impediment to perception or ordering. Cf. subtlety of mind: 'Est autem subtilitas ratio quædam, qua sensibilia a sensibus, intelligibilia ab intellectu, difficile compræhenduntur' (Cardan, *De Subtilitate*, i, in *Opera*, iii. 357ᵃ).

p. 65, l. 8. *Betweene this, and Truth.* Butler may derive the concept of a middle ground between truth and falsehood from Aristotle, *Metaphysica*, Γ. vii. 1012ᵃ4–9.

p. 65, l. 10. *Intelligence*: intelligibility.

p. 65, l. 12. *deliver's*: expresses.

p. 65, ll. 13–17. *by rendring them, etc.* Complex ideas of substances lacking equivalents in Nature are discussed by Locke in *Human Understanding*, II. xxxi. 18–26.

p. 65, ll. 15–17. *some other Condition, etc.* Cowley, 'The Muse', note to ll. 30–3, explains that '*Poetry* treats not onely of all things that are, or can be, but makes *Creatures* of her own, as *Centaures, Satyrs, Fairies*, &c. makes *persons* and *actions* of her own, as in *Fables* and *Romances*, makes *Beasts, Trees, Waters*, and other irrational and insensible things to act above the possibility of their natures, as to *understand* and *speak* . . .'

p. 66, ll. 13–20. *The Original of Reason, etc.* According to Bacon, *Advancement of Learning*, I. vi. 2, in *Works*, iii. 295, 'in the work of the creation we see a double emanation of virtue from God; the one referring more properly to power, the other to wisdom; the one expressed in making the subsistence of the matter, and the other in disposing the beauty of the form.' Glanvill,

Vanity of Dogmatizing, 1661, p. 104, defines reason as 'the Image of the Creators Wisdom copyed out in the Creature'. Sprat, *History*, p. 82, explains that 'they [the Royal Society] meddle no otherwise with *Divine things*, than onely as the *Power*, and *Wisdom*, and *Goodness* of the *Creator*, is display'd in the admirable order, and workman-ship of the Creatures'.

p. 66, l. 13. *Original*. See note to p. 32, l. 14.

p. 66, l. 24. *Religion*: devotion to some principle (in this case the laws governing the several causes independently).

p. 67, ll. 20–4. *The very being of fayth, etc.* Two points are maintained by Butler in this sentence: (i) a man must have enough reason to understand what an unverifiable message is about before he can have faith in that message specifically; (ii) if he can go further and verify the message, then his faith in it is superseded by knowledge of it. So some reason is a prerequisite for faith, and some ignorance a co-requisite. The construction of the sentence is confusing because with the words 'for no man' Butler shifts his ground from (i) to (ii). Cf. William Chillingworth's insistence that 'as Opinion so Faith, is alwaies built upon lesse evidence then that of sense or science' (*Religion of Protestants*, p. 35). Cf. also p. 25 above, ll. 19–23, and note.

p. 68, l. 18. *beside*: 'beyond the range or compass of (L. *præter*); utterly apart from; *hence* sometimes approaching the sense of "contrary to" ' (*OED*).

p. 69, l. 2. *Discretion*: separation or distinction (from the original Latin meaning of *discretio*), as well as discernment or judgement (in a late Latin sense).

p. 69, l. 22. *sequitur Corvos testaque lutoque*. Persius, *Satires*, iii. 61 ('an passim sequeris . . .').

p. 70, ll. 14–15. *30 of the Best Popes, etc.* Platina, *Lives of the Popes*, describes twenty-three pontiffs as martyred under the pagan emperors, but the figure has varied. Butler perhaps concludes from the canonization of all early popes that they had all been put to death.

p. 71, l. 12. *dislike*: 'disapproval, displeasure' (*OED*).

p. 71, ll. 14–15. *Men in the upper Region, etc.* Cf. Boyle, *Touching the Spring of the Air* (1660), in *Works*, ed. Thomas Birch, 5 vols., 1744, i. 68: 'And it may not irrationally be doubted, whether or no, if a man were raised to the very top of the atmosphere, he would be able to live many minutes, and would not quickly die for want of such air as we are wont to breathe here below.'

p. 72, ll. 4–5. *Conscience*.

But there is one species of courts, constituted by act of parliament, in the city of London and other trading and populous districts, which in it's proceedings so varies from the course of the common law, that it may deserve a more particular consideration. I mean the courts of requests, or courts of conscience, for the recovery of small debts. . . . The constitution is this: two aldermen, and four commoners, sit twice a week to hear all causes of debt not exceeding the value of forty shillings; which they examine in a summary way, by the oath of the parties or other witnesses, and make such order therein as is consonant to equity and good conscience (Blackstone, *Commentaries*, III. vi. 81).

p. 72, ll. 24–5. *the Curse of the earth.* Gen. iii. 17–18.

p. 73, ll. 19–20. *as Men of Politiques affirme.* The most famous statements of this theory were published (1705–29) by Bernard Mandeville; for the seventeenth-century background see F. B. Kaye, Introduction to *The Fable of the Bees*, by B. Mandeville, 1924, I. xxxviii ff.

p. 74, l. 25. *humorous*: peevish, capricious.

p. 75, ll. 10–11. *the Curse of God is, etc.* Jer. xxv. 15–16, 27–8; Isa. li. 17, 22.

p. 76, ll. 25–6. *Conversation*: company, society.

p. 76, ll. 28–9. *In the Scripture, etc.* Isa. v. 20.

p. 77, l. 17. *mysteries of Iniquity.* From 2 Thess. ii. 7: 'For the mystery of iniquity doth already work.' The phrase was variously applied (e.g. Edward Bowles, *The Mysterie of Iniquitie, Yet Working . . . for the Destruction of Religion Truly Protestant*, 1643). Butler puns on 'mystery' in another sense: 'a trade guild or company' (*OED*).

p. 78, ll. 15–18. *like flat Noses, etc.* 'They of *Guinea*, their Noses are flat, which they make so when they are young; for they esteem a flat Nose a great ornament unto them . . . Flat Noses seem also most comely unto the *Moores*' (John Bulwer, *Anthropometamorphosis*, 1650, vii. 81–2). 'In *Casena* a Region of *Afrique* neer *Ethiopia*, there are men who have Lips of a monstrous shape and thicknesse. . . . [And] the *Egyptian Moores*, and those of *Afrique* have all thick lips' (ibid. xi. 107).

p. 80, ll. 10–17. *They who suppose, etc.* Cf. Swift, *Tale of a Tub*, ix, in *Works*, ed. Herbert Davis, 14 vols., Oxford, 1939–68, i. 105: '*Epicurus* modestly hoped, that one Time or other, a certain Fortuitous Concourse of all Mens Opinions, after perpetual Justlings, the Sharp with the Smooth, the Light and the Heavy, the Round and the Square, would by certain *Clinamina*, unite in the Notions of *Atoms* and *Void*, as these did in the Originals of all Things.' Cf. also Dryden, 'To My Honored Friend, Sir Robert Howard', ll. 25–34.

p. 80, ll. 12–14. *all things to fall, etc.* See Lucretius, v. 187–94:

> Namque ita multa modis multis primordia rerum
> Ex infinito iam tempore percita plagis,
> Ponderibusque suis consuerunt concita ferri,
> Omni' modisque coire, atque omnia pertentare,
> Quæcunque inter se possint congressa creare,
> Ut non sit mirum si in taleis disposituras

Deciderunt quoque, & in taleis venere meatus,
Qualibus hæc rerum genitur nunc summa novando.

(Ed. cit. by Butler below, Leyden 'ex Officina Plantiniana', 1611, p. 117.)

p. 81, ll. 4–5. *Conversations*: conduct in society.

p. 81, l. 13. *in Order to*: in regard to.

p. 82, l. 2. *Breed*: offspring. Cf. 'brood'.

p. 82, ll. 11–14. *as in the Mathematiques, etc.* Cf. Locke, *Human Understanding*, IV. xi. 6: 'And though mathematical demonstrations depend not upon sense, yet the examining them by Diagrams, gives great credit to the Evidence of our Sight, and seems to give it a Certainty approaching to that of the Demonstration it self.'

p. 82, ll. 14–17. *And in cases, etc.* Cf. Bacon's contention that 'the Senses . . . are very sufficient to certify and report truth, though not always immediately, yet by comparison, by help of instrument, and by producing and urging such things as are too subtile for the sense to some effect comprehensible by the sense' (*Advancement of Learning*, II. xiii. 4, in *Works*, iii. 388–9).

p. 82, ll. 19–22. *for there is nothing, etc.* 'Concerning the Thoughts of man, . . . The Originall of them all, is that which we call SENSE; (For there is no conception in a mans mind, which hath not at first, totally, or by parts, been begotten upon the organs of Sense.) The rest are derived from that originall' (Hobbes, *Leviathan*, 1651, i. 3).

p. 82, ll. 21–2. *collection and Consequence.* See note to p. 7, l. 27.

p. 82, l. 26. *That is made by the Sun.* See note to p. 98, l. 1.

p. 83, ll. 20–4. *Nature ha's planted, etc.* 'Man is a political creature and one whose nature it is to live with others' (Aristotle, *Ethica Nicomachea*, 1169ᵇ18–19).

p. 83, ll. 25–33. *It is not improbable, etc.* Cf. p. 93, l. 21–p. 94, l. 1.

p. 83, ll. 27–8. *those Parts of the Sun, etc.* Cf. Aristotle, *De Plantis*, 817ᵇ40–818ᵃ3: 'In every kind of plant there is natural heat and moisture, and, when these are consumed, the plant will become weak and grow old and decay and dry up.' Similarly flesh is a compound of fire and water (*De Generatione et Corruptione*, II. vii). The idea of a mutable sun emitting particles that are incorporated in living organisms is at variance with Aristotelian theory, where the sun operates through the medium of air as efficient cause, water being the responsive element; see note to p. 84, ll. 28–9.

p. 83, l. 29. *forc'd*: 'artificially made or prepared; as opposed to *natural*. Chiefly of soils' (*OED*).

p. 83, l. 34–p. 84, l. 4. *The Virtuosi affirme, etc.* Sprat, *History*, p. 127, commends Hugenius for 'applying the Motion of *Pendulums* to Clocks, and Watches . . . For thereby there may be a means found out, of bringing the

measures of *Time*, to an exact *Regulation*: of which the benefits are infinite.'
At a Royal Society meeting on 14 March 1667 'Mr. HOOKE produced . . .
a contrivance to make a motion of a clock to go along with the shadow on
a wall, for which he offered a demonstration; affirming withal, that . . . upon
the same principle he would make an instrument to solve the inequality
of days both from the sun's excentricity and his right ascension upon the
elliptical as well as circular hypothesis' (Thomas Birch, *History of the Royal
Society*, ii. 156). See also *Philosophical Transactions*, IV. xlvii. 937–53 (in which
pp. 940–1 contain a table of solar variations from 'the *Equal* or *Mean* day').
Cf. Locke, *Human Understanding*, II. xiv. 21.

p. 84, ll. 5–6. *The Ignorance of Naturall Causes, etc.* 'How manie things doe
we name miraculous and against Nature? Each man and every Nation doth it
according to the measure of his ignorance' (Montaigne, *Essayes*, trans.
Florio, 1603, II. xii. 304). 'It is certain that many things, which now seem
miraculous, would not be so, if we come to be fully acquainted with their
compositions, and *operations*' (Sprat, *History*, p. 214). Cf. p. 84, l. 30–p. 85, l. 6.

p. 84, l. 15. *wider*: i.e. per day; see p. 92, ll. 1–5.

p. 84, ll. 18–19. *The Braine is sayd, etc.* 'For the brain, or in creatures without
a brain that which corresponds to it, is of all parts of the body the coolest'
(Aristotle, *De Somno et Vigilia*, 457^{b}29–31).

p. 84, l. 20. *Sagacity*: keen discernment, here (in the original Latin sense) of
scent.

p. 84, l. 21. *A Fig-tree, etc.* The early spring fruit of fig trees is described in
Pliny, *Nat. Hist.* XVI. xl. 95, trans. Holland, i. 471–2: 'The Figge trees . . .
both tame and wild, make no shew of flowers: for they are not to soone
bloomed (if they bloome at all) but they bring forth their fruit.'

p. 84, ll. 22–4. *A whale, etc.* Pliny, *Nat. Hist.* IX. lxxxviii. 186, trans. Holland,
i. 270, reports 'examples of freindship among fishes, . . . and namely, betweene
the great Whale Balæna, and the little Musculus. For whereas the Whale
aforesaid hath no use of his eies (by reason of the heavie weight of his eie-
browes that cover them) the other swimmeth before him, serveth him in
steed of eies and lights, to shew when hee is neere the shelves and shallowes,
wherein he may be soone grounded, so big and huge he is.' Cf. Browne,
Pseudodoxia, II. iii.

p. 84, ll. 25–6. *A Load-stone, etc.* According to Pliny, *Nat. Hist.* XXXVII. xv.
61, trans. Holland, ii. 610, 'there is such a naturall enmitie between Diamants
and Loadstones, that if it be laid near to a peece of yron, it will not suffer it
to be drawn away by the loadstone: nay, if the said loadstone be brought
so near a peece of yron, that it have caught hold therof, the Diamant, if it
come in place, will cause it to leave the hold & let it go.'

p. 84, ll. 27–8. *some Philosophers have believd otherwise.* See Plato, *Republic,* 546a–c; Jean Bodin, *Methodus, ad Facilem Historiarum Cognitionem,* Paris, 1566, vi. 262–80.

p. 84, ll. 28–9. *heat and moysture govern most.* Cf. Aristotle, *Meteorologica,* 346^{b}21–3: 'For the sun as it approaches or recedes, obviously causes dissipation and condensation and so gives rise to generation and corruption.' See also *De Longitudine et Brevitate Vitae,* 465^{a}14–18.

p. 85, ll. 23–4. *which Pidgeons in the East, etc.* 'They which dwell heere [Bagdad], and travell from hence to Balsara, carrie with them Pigeons, whom they make their Letter-posts to Bagdad, as they doe likewise betweene Ormuz and Balsara' (Purchas, *Pilgrimage,* V. XIV. ii. 580). See also Peter Heylin, *Cosmography,* 1670, iii. 786.

p. 85, l. 32–p. 86, l. 2. *Phancy and Memory, etc.* Cf. the proverb 'great wits have short memories' (*ODEP* 335; Tilley, W577) and Halifax, 'Miscellaneous Thoughts and Reflections', in *Complete Works,* ed. J. P. Kenyon, Harmondsworth, Middx., 1969, p. 237: 'Though memory and invention are not upon good terms, yet when the first is loaded, the other is stifled.'

p. 86, ll. 11–13. *Snayles and Fleas, etc.* 'Of the great Black Snail. In this slimy Animal . . . are very many rare and excellent Observables. The first is his Eyes, which are four in number, (like black atramentous Spots) fixed to the end of their horns; or rather to the ends of those black filaments or optick nerves, which are sheathed in her horns which she can retract or protrude, through the hollow trunck of her horns, as she pleaseth' (Henry Power, *Experimental Philosophy,* 1664, p. 36). According to Robert Hooke, fleas have two 'feelers, or rather smellers' and 'a small *proboscis,* or *probe*', but there are no eyes there (*Micrographia,* 1665, liii. 210–11).

p. 86, ll. 16–19. *The Specificall Principles, etc.* Cf. Aristotle's view of matter as the principle of individuation only within the formally differentiated species: 'And when we have the whole, such and such a form in this flesh and in these bones, this is Callias or Socrates; and they are different in virtue of their matter (for that is different), but the same in form; for their form is indivisible' (*Metaphysica, Z.* viii. 1034^{a}5–8). See also ibid. *Δ.* vii. 1016^{b}31–5. If the 'infinite variety' of matter is a considered philosophical assertion, Butler follows Anaxagoras, Leucippus, and Democritus (Aristotle, *De Generatione et Corruptione,* I. i); but cf. the objections of Lucretius, *De Rerum Natura,* ii. 478–521.

p. 86, ll. 19–21. *For wee see the same clod, etc.* According to Aristotle, the seasons impart that heat and movement which causes the spontaneous generation of animals and plants from decomposing earth or organic tissue. See *De Generatione Animalium,* 715^{b}25–8, 743^{a}35–6.

p. 86, l. 29. *For the English most comonly.* Butler does not complete this sentence.

p. 87, ll. 1–2. *all the Light wee see is by Reflection.* Cf. Sir Kenelm Digby, *Treatise of Bodies*, viii. 7, in *Two Treatises*, p. 61: '[It is objected against his theory of light's corporeity] that the light which goeth from the fire to an opacous body farre distant without interruption of its continuity, should seeme to be jogged or putt out of its way, by the wind that crosseth it. Wherein the first fayling is, that the objectour conceiveth light to send species unto our eye from the middest of its line: whereas with a litle consideration he may perceive, that no light is seene by us but that which is reflected from an opacous body to our eye: so that the light he meaneth in his objection, is never seene att all.' Alexander Ross, *Philosophicall Touch-Stone*, 1645, p. 12, asks Digby, 'I pray, from what opacous bodie is the light of the Sun, Moon and Stars reflected, when we look upon these *luminaries*?'

p. 87, l. 6. *not heat, etc.* Cf. Bacon, *De Calore et Frigore*, in *Works*, iii. 646.

p. 87, ll. 7–8. *the Coldnes of the upper Regions, etc.* Cf. Bacon, op. cit. iii. 645: 'The middle region of the air hath manifest effects of cold, notwithstanding locally it be nearer the sun; commonly imputed to antiperistasis, assuming that the beams of the sun are hot either by approach or by reflexion, and that falleth in the middle term between both; or if, as some conceive, it be only by reflexion, then the cold of that region resteth chiefly upon distance. The instances shewing the cold of that region are, the snows which descend, the hails which descend, and the snows and extreme colds which are upon high mountains.' See also *French Virtuosi I*, vi. i. 35; *II*, clxxxiv. 301.

p. 87, ll. 10–12. *The Intelligible world, etc.* 'There is a three-fold World, Elementary, Celestiall, and Intellectuall, and every inferior is governed by its superior, and receiveth the influence of the vertues thereof, so that the very original, and chief Worker of all doth by Angels, the Heavens, Stars, Elements, Animals, Plants, Metals, and Stones convey from himself the vertues of his Omnipotency upon us, for whose service he made, and created all these things' (Cornelius Agrippa, *Three Books of Occult Philosophy*, trans. J[ohn] F[rench], 1651, I. i. 1; cited by Wilders, note to *Hudibras*, I. i. 530). See also *Hudibras*, II. iii. 225–34, and 'An Hermetic Philosopher', par. 5; *GR* ii. 234 ff.

p. 87, ll. 13–14. *The most probable way, etc.* Lucretius, *De Rerum Natura*, ii. 1048–89, is a likely influence here. The atomists believed in a plurality of worlds, unlike Plato, Aristotle, and the Stoics. See also Bacon, *Description of the Intellectual Globe*, trans. in *Works*, v. 519, 534–7. Cf. p. 188, ll. 17–19.

p. 87, ll. 14–15. *the reason of the Peripatetiques, etc.* According to the Aristotelian Alexander Ross, *Philosophicall Touch-Stone*, pp. 24–5, 'we deny that the matter of the celestiall bodies is *univocall* to that of elementary, for then . . . It should be the subject of corruption, and of transmutation into sublunary bodies'. Cf. Aristotle, *Metaphysica*, H. v. 1044^{b}27–9.

p. 87, ll. 16–18. *where there is no corruption, etc.* Bacon, *History of Dense and Rare*, trans. in *Works*, v. 399–400, explains that 'in no transmutation of bodies is there any reduction either from nothing or to nothing . . . Therefore the sum total of matter remains always the same without addition or diminution; but that the sum of matter is variously distributed among different bodies cannot be doubted.'

p. 87, l. 29. *she*: the mind of man (more explicitly in *B* 182ʳ version).

p. 87, ll. 30–1. *All things were hidden, etc.* William Harvey, *Anatomical Exercitations concerning the Generation of Living Creatures*, 1653, lxxii. 462–3, calls 'the Radical and Primigenial moisture . . . evident in an *Egge*, . . . the most simple, pure, and sincere body imaginable: wherein all the *parts* of the *Chicken* do abide *in potentia*, but none, *actu*: nature seeming to have afforded to it the same priviledge which men commonly ascribe to the *materia prima*, or first *Matter*, [from] which all things spring; namely, to be *capable of all formes, potentially*, but to *possess none, actually.*'

p. 88, ll. 1–2. *The Beames of the Sun, etc.* Cf. Digby, *Treatise of Bodies*, x. 2, in *Two Treatises*, pp. 76–7.

p. 88, l. 2. *exhalations.* 'When the sun warms the earth the evaporation which takes place is necessarily of two kinds, not of one only as some think. One kind is rather of the nature of vapour, the other of the nature of a windy exhalation. That which rises from the moisture contained in the earth and on its surface is vapour, while that rising from the earth itself which is dry, is like smoke' (Aristotle, *Meteorologica*, 341ᵇ7–10).

p. 88, ll. 2–5. *as water in the Inside, etc.* According to Julius Caesar Scaliger, *De Subtilitate ad Cardanum*, Paris, 1557, xlvi, 'cum pars aquæ plurima sit extra locum suum [the sphere of water], . . . & terra multis pervia specubus eo in loco, qui & aquæ debebatur, & a terra occupatus est: [this water] in terræ cava loca sese induit. Quæ cum sint angusta, neque tantam maris molem capere queant: compressa ea aquæ portio ab extrinsecus incumbente mari, suasque, iure loci, repetente sedes, egredi quaqua via possit, quærit: quemadmodum aqua illa per tubulos faciebat. Qua impressione fiunt aquarum exitus, atque exilitiones, quæ Græca origine Scatebræ appellantur. Atque hæ in suo loco quia non sunt, deorsum evoluuntur.' Butler may be influenced by reports of mountain-top streams on Tenerife in Sprat, *History*, p. 203.

p. 88, l. 8. *Functions*: i.e. of the soul. 'The *Animal faculty* is that which sends feeling and motion to all the body, from the brain by sinews; and nourisheth Understanding; The *Vital faculty* gives life from the heart by Arteries to all the body' (Blount, *Glossographia*, s.v. 'Faculty'). Cf. Walter Charleton, *Immortality of the Human Soul*, 1657, pp. 171–2); Harvey, *Generation of Living Creatures*, lxxi. 448.

p. 89, l. 14. *a double Penis*. Possibly a misreading of Pliny, *Nat. Hist.* XI. cx. 263, trans. Holland, i. 352: 'Fishes and Serpents have none [testicles] at all; but in stead therof there be two strings or veines reach from their kidnies to their genitall member.'

p. 89, ll. 14–16. *The Femall is sayd, etc.* 'That the young Vipers force their way through the bowels of their Dam, or that the female Viper in the act of generation bites off the head of the male, in revenge whereof the young ones eat through the womb and belly of the female, is a very ancient tradition. In this sense entertained in the Hieroglyphics of the Egyptians; affirmed by Herodotus, Nicander, Pliny, Plutarch, Ælian, Jerome, Basil, Isidore, seems countenanced by Aristotle, and his Scholar Theophrastus . . .' (Browne, *Pseudodoxia*, III. xvi).

p. 89, ll. 28–9. *The smallest Sands, etc.* I have found no other mention of this phenomenon.

p. 90, ll. 1–2. *So in the Bloud, etc.* At a Royal Society meeting on 6 July 1664 'Mr. HOSKYNS desired, that some physicians, upon occasion, might be appointed to examine the truth of what KIRCHER affirmed, that little worms were found in the blood of pestiferous persons. Dr. MERRET related, that Dr. HARVEY had sometimes found the blood full of worms in malignant fevers' (Birch, *History*, i. 449). On 8 April 1663 'Mr. HOOKE . . . was desired . . . to have ready, the microscopical appearance of the little fishes in vinegar' (ibid. i. 216). For description of *'the Eels in Vinegar'* see Hooke, *Micrographia*, lvii. 216–17.

p. 90, l. 8. *Cold Iron, etc.* 'Take a wedge of Iron . . . and heating it red-hot, you shall, according to the Laws of its refrigeration, endue it with a polary verticity . . . [But] though it hath but acquired a feeble virtue by its refrigeration, yet if you take it up cold, and with a few smart strokes of a great Mall, or Hammer, you beat the one end of it, setting the other against some hard resisting matter, . . . you shall thereby give it a most powerful Magnetisme . . . [Moreover,] you may by inverting and repercussing the Extremes, alter the polarity of the Iron at your pleasure . . .' (Henry Power, *Experimental Philosophy*, pp. 160–1).

p. 90, ll. 11–15. *There is in Oxfordshire, etc.* Robert Plot, *Natural History of Oxford-Shire*, Oxford, 1677, iv. 75, describes '*Lapis arenarius*, commonly called *Free-stone*, and used in Building; of which we have as great plenty and variety in *Oxford-shire*, peradventure as in any other part of *England*. The Quarry at *Heddington* . . . supplies us continually with a good sort of *stone*, and fit for all uses but that of *fire*; in which, that of *Teynton* and *Hornton* excel it. In the Quarry it cuts very soft and easie, and is worked accordingly for all sorts of Building; very porous, and fit to imbibe lime and sand, but hardening continually as it lies to the *weather*.' The stone of Burford will not endure fire like Teynton stone, though even that should be surbedded, '*i.e.* set it edg-ways, contrary to the posture it had in the bed' (ibid., p. 76). Plot, *Enquiries to be Propounded to the Most Ingenious of Each County*, [1679], iv. 7, asks 'What *Quarries* of *Free-stone* are there in this *County*, . . . in what order do the *beds* lye? do they *dip*, or lye in *plano Horizontis?* whether better *surbedded* in work, or laid as they *grew* in the *bed?*' See also John Morton, *Natural History of Northampton-Shire*, 1712, II. i. 45. 116, and Gilbert White, *Natural History of Selborne*, 1789, iv. 9.

p. 90, ll. 16–17. *the Lord Cravans house at Causham, etc.* William, Earl of Craven (1606–97), son of Sir William Craven, Lord Mayor of London. *Causham* is Caversham; see Margaret Gelling, *The Place-Names of Berkshire*, Pt. i (*English Place-Name Soc.* xlix), Cambridge, 1973, p. 175. The house is described by Thomas Campion in 1613, '*fairely built of bricke, mounted on the hill-side of a Parke within view of* Redding' (*Works*, ed. Walter R. Davis, Garden City, N.Y., 1967, p. 235). I have found no evidence of Lord Craven's building at Caversham Lodge during the Restoration; indeed it was occupied between 1665 and 1672 by a relative, Sir Anthony Craven, Bt. See *Complete Baronetage*, ed. G. E. C., 5 vols., Exeter, 1900–6, ii. 204. Lord Craven did build a large house at Hampstead Marshall, Berks. See *VCH Berkshire*, 4 vols., 1906–24, iv. 179.

p. 90, ll. 17–19. *And the New Theater, etc.* The accounts for the building of the Sheldonian Theatre, 1664–7, show what stone was purchased (MS. Bodl. 898, fos. 15ᵛ, 20ᵛ, 25ᵛ, 26ᵛ, 36ʳ, 37ʳ, 40ʳ, etc.). 'The external walls were . . . principally Headington freestone; but some "Burford" stone was used' (*Oxford Stone Restored*, ed. W. F. Oakeshott, Oxford, 1975, p. 41). See also *VCH Oxfordshire*, 1907– , iii. 51.

p. 90. ll. 26–8. *Those Sparkes of Fire, etc.* 'It is a very common Experiment, by striking with a Flint against a Steel, to make certain fiery and shining Sparks to fly out from between those two compressing Bodies. . . . I spread a sheet of white Paper, and on it, observing the place where several of these Sparks seemed to vanish, I found certain very small, black, but glistering Spots of a movable Substance, each of which examining with my *Microscope*, I found to be a small round *Globule*; some of which, as they looked pretty small, so did they from their Surface yield a very bright and strong reflection on that side which was next the Light . . .' (Robert Hooke, *Micrographia*, viii. 44).

p. 90, l. 29–p. 91, l. 1. *If pease, etc.* Transcribed from Sir Christopher Heydon, *Defence of Judiciall Astrologie*, Cambridge, 1603, p. 43.

p. 91, ll. 1–6. *The Reason is, etc.* 'Whether the sap of Trees runs down to the roots in Winter, whereby they become naked and grow not; or whether they do not cease to draw any more, and reserve so much as sufficeth for conservation, is not a point indubitable. . . . But that the sap doth powerfully rise in the Spring, . . . he that hath beheld how many gallons of water may in a small time be drawn from a Birch-tree in the Spring, hath slender reason to doubt' (Browne, *Pseudodoxia*, II. vii). Cf. John Evelyn, *Sylva*, 1664, p. 91.

p. 91, l. 4. *mortifyd*: 'transf. Of plants: Decayed' (*OED*).

p. 91, ll. 7–8. *Chronical Diseases, etc.* Heydon, *Defence of Judiciall Astrologie*, 'Table of the Principall Matters', characterizes 'Diseases, sharp' as 'governed by the moone', and 'Diseases, chronical' as 'first governed by the sunne for a yeare, ever after by *Saturne*'. See further ibid., pp. 472–3.

p. 91, ll. 12–15. *Some men Suppose, etc.* Thomas Vaughan observes from the ashes of vegetables that

although their weaker, exterior elements expire by violence of the fire yet their earth cannot be destroyed but vitrified. The fusion and transparency of this substance is occasioned by the radical moisture or seminal water of the compound. This water resists the fury of the fire and cannot possibly be vanquished. . . . These two principles [of earth and water] are never separated, for Nature proceeds not so far in her dissolutions. When death hath done her worst there is an union between these two and out of them shall God raise us at the last day and restore us to a spiritual constitution (*Anthroposophia Theomagica*, 1650, in *Works*, ed. A. E. Waite, 1919, pp. 30–1).

Blount, *Glossographia*, defines radical moisture as 'the natural moysture spread like a dew in all parts of the body, wherewith the parts are nourished'. Sir George Ent, *Apologia pro Circulatione Sanguinis*, 1641, pp. 81–3, identifies this with the spirit exhaled in chemical distillations (which is, for the greatest part, 'sal volatilis, in quo virtus rei præcipua continetur') and with the natural saline exhalations that condense and fall as life-giving dew. There are those, says Ent, who affirm, '*ab ipsis plantarum salibus terræ commissis, easdem denuo plantas repullulare. Et hinc forte orta est fabula de phœnice: Aiunt namque e cineribus combustæ palmæ . . . novam arborem exurgere.*'

p. 92, ll. 1–5. *Those Philosophers, etc.* Butler rightly detects an optical illusion—lunar parallax—but this cannot affect observation by more than one degree. Astronomers explained that the moon will either go beyond or fail to reach the tropics (by up to five degrees) according as the nodes (the points at which her apparent orbit intersects the ecliptic) move around the ecliptic. According to Thomas Blunderville, *Theoriques of the Seven Planets*, 1602, pp. 59–60, 'The latitude of the Moone is none other thing but her distance from the Eclipticke line, which distance is never above five degrees. And her latitude is twofold, that is, Northerne and Southerne. For the deferent of the Moone [the circle that carries her] in the space of one moneth cutteth the Eclipticke in two places right opposit one to another, and thereby the one halfe of her deferent enclineth towards the North, and the other halfe thereof enclineth towards the South.' But their positions on the ecliptic, and hence the relative angle to the earth of the moon's circle, are not constant. 'This circle is equally moved, contrary to the succession of the signs, about the centre and poles of the Eclipticke, making his revolution almost in 19 yeares: and by the moving of this circle, the poles of the deferents of the

Auge [or apogee] are carried about the poles of the eclipticke' (ibid., p. 35).

p. 92, l. 12. *the first being turnd into witches*. G. L. Kittredge,*Witchcraft in Old and New England*, 1929, p. 177, gives instances of 'the cat-witch, injured in that shape and suffering the same wounds *in propria persona*'. Cf. note to p. 131, ll. 25–6.

p. 92, l. 13. *Possest by the Devil*. Matt. viii. 28–32; Mark v. 1–13.

p. 92, l. 14. *Iron is an extraction of Clay*. 'Succus igitur est ex quo formatur metallum: quem pariunt varii motus. quorum proximi sunt aquæ fluxus terram molliens aut secum rapiens: terræ cum aqua permistio: vis caloris agens in misturas ut gignat id genus succos' (Georgius Agricola, *De Ortu et Causis Subterraneorum*, Basle, 1558, v. 71–2). 'Iron because the earthy part is gross and impure, and exceeds the humid . . . burns and consumes as often as it is heat[ed] in the fire, and will not melt of it self without extraordinary great violence' (Albaro Alonso Barba, *First Book of the Art of Mettals*, trans. [Edward Mountagu], 1670, p. 85. Cf. John Webster, *Metallograph[i]a*, 1671, pp. 62–3, 66; Birch, *History*, i. 247.

p. 92, ll. 17–18. *whether Timber do shrink, etc*. Robert Hooke, *An Attempt to Prove the Motion of the Earth*, 1674, p. 8, observes of a wooden instrument 'that moyst weather will make the frame stretch, and dry weather will make it shrink'.

p. 92, ll. 21–3. *the Antients usd to cullour, etc*. I have found no other mention of this practice.

p. 92, ll. 29–32. *The Sun drawing neare, etc*. Cf. Walter Charleton, *Physiologia Epicuro-Gassendo-Charltoniana*, 1654, III. xv. ii. 351, for the hypothesis that, 'when the Sun hath made some sensible advance in the lower world, beyond the Nadir point or midnight circle, and hasteneth toward our East; He moves and drives along before him into our horizon, the (formerly) quiet and cold Aer of the Night'. See also *French Virtuosi II*, cliii. 204–5.

p. 93, ll. 10–11. *The Tradition, etc*. 2 Pet. iii. 10. For other sources see Thomas Burnet, *Theory of the Earth*, 2 vols., 1684–90, III. iii.

p. 93, l. 12. *Decay'd*: decreased in volume.

p. 93, l. 21–p. 94, l. 1. *Nor is it improbable, etc*. Cf. p. 83, l. 25–33.

p. 93, ll. 23–5. *as the greatest Part, etc*. See notes to p. 83, l. 27–8, and p. 84, ll. 28–9.

p. 93, l. 29. *resolv'd into earth*: i.e. by elemental transmutation. 'Fire, air, water, earth, we assert, originate from one another, and each of them exists potentially in each, as all things do that can be resolved into a common and ultimate substrate' (Aristotle, *Meteorologica*, 339^{a}36–339^{b}2). Birch, *History*, ii. 68, records an experimental conversion of water into earth.

p. 94, l. 6. *the Spirits of the world.* Cf. note to p. 224, l. 2.

p. 94, ll. 11–16. *causd by the Motion of the Earth, etc.* Cf. John Wallis, 'Hypothesis about the Flux and Reflux of the Sea', 1666, *Philosophical Transactions*, I. xvi. 268–9:

> . . . supposing the Sea to be but as a loose Body, carried about with the Earth, but not so united to it, as necessarily to receive the same degree of *Impetus* with it, as its fixed parts do; The acceleration or retardation in the motion of this or that part of the Earth, will cause (more or less, according to the proportion of it) such a dashing of the Water, or rising at one part, with a Falling at another, as is that, which we call the Flux and Reflux of the Sea: Now this premised, . . . suppose the Earth carried about with a double motion . . . [so that] the *Diurnal* motion, in that part of the Earth, which is next the Sun, . . . doth abate the progress of the *Annual*, . . . and in the other part, which is from the Sun, . . . it doth increase it, . . . that is, in the day time there is abated, in the night time is added to the *Annual* motion, about as much as is . . . the Earths *Diameter.* Which would afford us a Cause of two Tides in twenty four hours; the One upon the greatest Acceleration of motion, the Other upon its greatest Retardation.

To explain why 'the Time of Tides, moves in a *moneths space* through all the 24. hours', Wallis hypothesizes that 'the Line of the *Annual* motion . . . will be described, not by the Center of the Earth, . . . But by the *Common Center of Gravity of the Bodies, Earth and Moon,* as one Aggregate' (ibid. I. xvi. 270–3). See also *French Virtuosi II*, cxlvii. 188–9.

p. 94, l. 17. *collected:* inferred, deduced.

p. 94, ll. 31–2. *that appeare's at any Distance, etc.* Cf. p. 131, ll. 1–4, and notes.

p. 95, ll. 12–14. *though our Fire, etc.* Cf. Digby, *Treatise of Bodies,* vi. 6, in *Two Treatises,* p. 44, arguing for atomism that 'flame is a much grosser substance then pure fire, (by reason of the mixture with it, of that viscous oyly matter, which being drawne out of the wood and candle, serveth for fewell to the fire, and is by litle and litle converted into it)'.

p. 95, l. 36–p. 96, l. 1. *the Rootes of the Nerves, etc.* Cf. Aristotle, *De Partibus Animalium,* $686^{a}33$–$686^{b}2$: 'Thus [moving down the scale of nature] the animal becomes a plant, that has its upper parts downwards and its lower parts above. For in plants the roots are the equivalents of mouth and head, while the seed has an opposite significance, for it is produced at the extremities of the twigs.' See also Plato, *Timaeus,* 90a.

p. 96, ll. 24–9. *So the Antients were of opinion, etc.* For a collection of such opinions see Burton, *Anatomy of Melancholy,* I. II. iii. 12.

p. 96, l. 30. *the Mines of Potosy.* 'At the foot [of the Cerro Rico] is the Citie *Potosi,* inhabited by twentie thousand *Spanish* men, and ten thousand women, as many *Negroes,* and foure thousand *Indians.* . . . The entrance and Myneworkes are so dangerous, that they which goe in, use to take the Sacrament of the Altar, as if they went to their death, because few returne. The Earle of *Villar* made a proclamation, that all the *Indians* should have leave and libertie to labour in this Myne, and to have foure Rialls a day for each mans worke, which they were before forced to doe for nothing' (Purchas, *Pilgrimes*, IV. VII. ix. 1420–1). For a description of mining the silver see ibid. III. v. ii. iv. 946–7.

p. 97, ll. 4–7. *And when the Jewes, etc.* Judg. iii. 5–8, 12–14; iv. 1–3; vi. 1; x. 6–8; Ezek. xxxix. 23–4.

p. 97, ll. 7–9. *It was the worst part, etc.* Gen. iii. 17–19.

p. 97, ll. 19–20. *That Cyprus, etc.* 'In the time of *Constantine* it was forsaken of the Inhabitants, as before forsaken of the Elements, which refused to water with any drops of raine that Iland (sometime called Macaria or *happy*) the space of seventeene yeeres together, or as others have it, sixe and thirtie' (Purchas, *Pilgrimage*, V. XIV. iii. 585).

p. 97, ll. 21–2. *And in Ægypt, etc.* 'It is affirmed by many, and received by most, that it never raineth in Egypt, . . . but this must also be received in a qualified sense, that is, that it rains but seldom at any time in the Summer, and very rarely in the Winter' (Browne, *Pseudodoxia*, VI. viii). See also Purchas, *Pilgrimes*, II. VII. iv. i. 988.

p. 97, ll. 22–3. *nor were there ever, etc.* 'Numquam ita caelum nubilum est ut in sole Rhodos non sit' (Solinus, *Collectanea Rerum Memorabilium*, xi. 32). Cf. Pliny, *Nat. Hist.* II. lxii. 153.

p. 97, ll. 24–5. *in the Ilands of the west Indies, etc.* According to a report of 1668, 'the *Sea-brise* comes not into *Jamaica* till 8 or 9 of the clock in the morning, and ordinarily ceaseth about 4 or 5 at night. . . . The Clouds (he saith) begin to gather about 2 or 3 of the clock in the afternoon at the Mountains, and do not embody first in the Air, and after settle there, but settle first, and embody there; the rest of the Skie being clear till Sun-set; so that they do not pass near the Earth in a body, and only stop where they meet with parts of the Earth elevated above the rest; but precipitate from a very great height, and in particles of an exceeding rarified nature, so as not to obscure the Air or Sky at all' (*Philosophical Transactions*, III. xxxvii. 718).

p. 98, l. 1. *the Sun makes all things in Nature*: i.e. as efficient cause, so that 'coming-to-be occurs as the sun approaches and decay as it retreats' (Aristotle, *De Generatione et Corruptione*, 336^{b}17–18).

p. 98, l. 12. *like Balaams Ass.* Num. xxii. 22–7.

p. 98, l. 16. *ridden by Hags in the Stable.* John Aubrey, *Miscellanies*, 1696, xiii. 111–12, describes 'a Flint with a hole in it (naturally)' hung as a charm 'to prevent the Night-mare (*viz.*) the Hag from riding their Horses, who will sometimes sweat all Night.' See also G. L. Kittredge, *Witchcraft in Old and New England*, pp. 219–20.

p. 98, l. 17. *Poster. Lib.* 1us: *Analytica Posteriora*, 78ᵃ38.

p. 99, ll. 1–3. *Pope Paul the 2d, etc.* 'Paul II. natif de Venise auparavant nommé Pierre Barbo, Cardinal du titre de S. Marc, fut subrogé. Sa premiere vocation fut le trafic . . . Grossier & de lourd esprit, n'aimant ni les lettres ni les lettrez, si qu'il declaria heretiques ceux qui par jeu ou serieusement pro-fereroyent ce mot d'Academie ou d'Un[iv]ersité' (de Serres, *Histoire*, i. 920).

p. 99, ll. 8–10. *Guicciardine write's, etc.* 'At last the mine was accomplished, & the [papal] army standing in order of battell to go forthwith to thassalt, . . . *Peter* of *Navarre* caused fire to be put to the mine, which with so great noyse & fury blew up so high the wall and chappell [in the wall], that in that space and division was made open to those without, the intralls of the Citie within together with the maner of the souldiors prepared to defende it: But falling eftsones downe agayne, the whole wall tooke the same place . . . as if there had not bene any separation or removing at all' (Francesco Guicciardini, *Historie . . . Conteining the Warres of Italie and Other Parts*, trans. Sir Geffray Fenton, 1579, x. 569).

p. 99, ll. 22–5. *In Persia, etc.* Transcribed from Sir Paul Rycaut, *Present State of the Ottoman Empire*, 1668, I. xi. 46.

p. 99, ll. 26–7. *Quære whether, etc.* Perhaps a camletted paper with wavy veins like marble. Herbert, *Travels*, p. 224, describes a Turkish firman 'upon paper very sleek and chamletted with red and blew, agreeable to the mode of *Persia*'. Bacon, *Sylva Sylvarum*, par. 741, in *Works*, ii. 578, explains camletting.

p. 100, ll. 1–2. *As in Constantinople, etc.* The relevant periods of French rule would presumably be 1204–61 in Constantinople (the Latin empire), 1266–82 in Sicily, 1501–4 in Naples, 1499–1525 in Milan, and 1659 onwards in Flanders.

p. 100, ll. 3–6. *The Spaniards overcame, etc.* I have not found this detail in accounts of the conquest. The familiar facts are collected in Montaigne's reference to 'the just astonishment which those [Indian] nations might justlie conceive, by seeing so unexpected an arrivall of bearded men; divers in language, in habite, in religion, in behaviour, in forme, in countenance; . . . mounted upon great and unknowne monsters; against those, who had never so much as seene any horse, or lesse any beast whatsoever apte to beare, or taught to carry eyther man or burthen; covered with a shining and hard skinne, and armed with slicing-keene weapons and glittering armor' (*Essayes*, III. vi. 545). Cf. Purchas, *Pilgrimes*, III. v. viii. 1118; Joseph Acosta, *Naturall and Morall Historie of the East and West Indies*, trans. E. G., 1604, p. 69.

p. 100, ll. 7–9. *Childeric, etc.* 'Ainsi mourut Childeric [d. 673], n'ayant regné que deux ans, & laisant une detestable memoire à la posterité, d'avoir bien commencé & mal fini tout au contraire de son predecesseur Chilperic premier [d. 481], qui commença mal & finit bien' (de Serres, *Histoire*, i. 88).

p. 100, ll. 10–11. *Charles Martel, etc.* 'Mais . . . Pepin se mesconneust en sa prosperité. Car ne se contentant pas de Plectrude sa femme legitime, s'amourachea d'une Damoiselle nommee Alpayde, de laquelle it eut un bastard, qui se sera fort renommer en la suite de ceste histoire, sous le nom de Charles Martel Et comme le mal croissoit, il repudia Plectrude, & espousa Alpayde' (ibid. i. 91–2).

p. 100, ll. 12–15. *In France those great Lords, etc.* A paraphrase of Cotgrave's gloss, which explains that '*the gibbet of the* (*simple*) *high* Justicier *hath but two pillers; the Lord Chattelaines, three; the Barons, foure; the Earls, six; and the Dukes, eight*' (Randle Cotgrave, *Dictionarie of the French and English Tongues*, 1611).

p. 100, ll. 25–7. *Queene Elizabeth, etc.* Transcribed (slightly abridged) from John Stow, *Annales, or Generall Chronicle of England*, cont. Edmond Howes, 1615, p. 869. The proclamation was made on 12 February 1580.

p. 100, ll. 26–7. *a Nayl of a yeard*: one-sixteenth of a yard, $2\frac{1}{4}$ inches.

p. 100, ll. 28–9. *Buck a Herald, etc.* Sir George Buc (d. 1623), Master of the Revels and not a herald. His *History of the Life and Reign of Richard III* was published in 1646 as the work of 'Geo: Buck Esquire', a nephew of Sir George's, who pretended to have written it. See Mark Eccles, 'Sir George Buc, Master of the Revels', in *Thomas Lodge and Other Elizabethans*, ed. Charles J. Sisson, Cambridge, Mass., 1933, p. 499. The *History* makes a spirited defence of Richard's person and conduct; see esp. pp. 78 ff.

p. 100, l. 29. *he founded the Heralds Colledg.* 'Let us look upon his charitable, religious and magnificent works. . . . He also first founded the Colledge and Society of Heralds, and made them a Corporation . . . (A taste of his love to Honour, and his Noble care for the conservation of Nobility, Chevalry and Gentry)' (ibid., p. 138).

p. 100, ll. 30–2. *Charles the 5t, etc.* 'Voilà quelle fut la desolation de Rome par l'armée de Charles-Quint, . . . pendant que ce Prince faisoit cesser toutes sortes de réjoûissances en Espagne, & faire par toutes les Eglises des priéres publiques pour la delivrance de celuy qu'il tenoit prisonnier' (Louis Maimbourg, *Histoire du Lutheranisme*, Paris, 1680, i. 163–4).

p. 100, l. 32–p. 101, l. 3. *So our H: 7th, etc.* 'There is a strange tradition, that the King . . . for the better credit of his espials abroad with the contrary side, did use to have them cursed at Paul's (by name) amongst the bead-roll of the King's enemies, according to the custom of those times' (Bacon, *Historie of the Raigne of King Henry the Seventh*, in *Works*, vi. 144).

p. 101, ll. 7–9. *As the Veneti, etc.* 'Venetiæ olim quidem erant locus quispiam desertus, non habitatus, & palustris; qui vero nunc Veneti appellantur

Franci erant ab Aquileia & cæteris Franciæ locis: & inhabitabant terram, quæ e regione Venetiarum [iacet]. Veniente autem Avarum rege Attila, & Franciam universam depopulante ac perdente, Franci Aquileiam cum reliquis Franciæ urbibus deserere cœperunt, & ad Venetiarum insulas habitatoribus vacuas venerunt, & tuguria illic fecerunt, metu Attilæ regis' (Constantine Porphyrogenitus, *De Administrando Imperio*, trans. Joannes Meursius, Leiden, 1611, xxviii. 69–70).

p. 101, ll. 13–14. *to send their Children, etc.* 'The English Saxons also in that age conflowed & resorted from all parts into Ireland, as it were to the mart of good learning: and hence it is, that we read so often in our writers, concerning Holy men thus; *Such a one was sent over into Ireland for to be trained up in learning*' (Camden, *Britannia*, trans. Philemon Holland, 1610, sect. 'Ireland', p. 68).

p. 101, ll. 15–17. *The Roman Emperors, etc.*

> Il grande Imperio, ch'era un corpo solo,
> Havea dui capi, un ne l'antica Roma,
> Che reggeva i paesi occidentali,
> E l'altro ne la nuova, che dal volgo
> S'appella la città di Constantino;
> Questa era capo a tutto l'oriente;
> Onde l'aquila d'oro in campo rosso
> Insegna Imperial poi si dipinse,
> E si dipinge con due teste anchora.

(Trissino, *Italia Liberata da Gothi*, 3 vols., Rome–Venice, 1547–8, I. ii. 22ᵛ.) See also C. F. Menestrier, *Origine des Armoiries et du Blason*, Paris, 1680, pp. 538–49.

p. 101, ll. 18–20. *The Story of Godfry of Bullen, etc.* At Ascalon, 12 August 1099. According to Dodechinus, app. to Marianus Scotus, *Chronica*, Basle, 1559, cols. 459–60, 'miro videlicet modo: quum in exercitu nostro non ultra 5000 militum, & 15000 peditum fuissent: & in exercitu hostium 100000 equitum, & 400000 peditum esse potuissent. Tunc mirabilis in servis suis Dominus apparuit, quum antequam confligeremus, pro solo impetu nostro hanc multitudinem in fugam vertit . . . Ceciderunt ibi Maurorum ultra 100000 gladio.' Such figures indeed exaggerate the Egyptians' strength; W. B. Stevenson, *Crusaders in the East*, Cambridge, 1907, p. 35 n., reckons 20,000 to have been 'about the maximum possible'.

p. 101, ll. 24–5. *those . . . destroyd by Charles Martel.* At Poitiers, 10 October 732. As to Saracen casualties: 'Les histoires asseurent qu'il y demeura sur le champ Trois cens soixante & quinze mille personnes' (de Serres, *Histoire*, i. 99).

p. 101, l. 28–p. 102, l. 2. *When a Turk, etc.* Paraphrased from Rycaut, *Present State of the Ottoman Empire*, II. vi. 111. The Turks, knowing most emirs' pedigrees to be dubious, are the less inclined to respect the sanctity of their persons. The 'deep Sea-green' of their turbans is the colour of the Prophet (ibid. II. vi. 110–11).

p. 102, ll. 3–6. *William Marise, etc.* Transcribed (with slight alterations) from Baker, *Chronicle*, p. 129.

p. 102, ll. 7–13. *Brunhault wife to Sigebert, etc.* 'Brunehault trouvee coulpable d'une infinité d'horribles crimes, . . . fut liée à la queuë d'une jument indontee, & trainee par pays difficile & raboteux. Ainsi deschiree à diverses pieces, mourut à diverses fois . . . Brunehault, seulement louee par les historiens, d'avoir fait bastir beaucoup de Temples, & fondé de grands revenus pour faire le service, pendant qu'elle servoit à ses passions. S. Gregoire a inseré quelques epistres siennes à Brunehault où il la louë en termes fort avantageux pour sa pieté & prudence singuliere' (de Serres, *Histoire*, i. 80–1). Brunehaut (543–614) married Sigebert, King of Metz or Austrasia, in 568 (ibid. i. 67).

p. 102, ll. 14–27. *The little kingdom, etc.* Translated (slightly rearranged and abridged) from de Serres, *Histoire*, i. 65.

p. 102, ll. 28–31. *Although the Tribunes of the People, etc.* According to Jean Bodin, *Methodus, ad Facilem Historiarum Cognitionem*, vi. 215, 'tanta potestas erat Tribuniplebis, ut non modo Senatus, sed etiam magistratuum & collegarum, ipsiusque plebis acta unus sua intercessione impediret: nec ulterius progredi poterant, nisi prius imperium illi a plebe solenni iure suffragiorum abrogaretur. . . . Postremo creato Dictatore soli Tribuni imperium retinebant, cum cæteri magistratus abdicarent. Igitur si regia potestas in Consulibus; multo certe maior in Tribunis.' Yet this was essentially power to veto and to impeach; in raising levies initiative rested with the consuls, who worked through the military tribunes (Polybius, *Histories*, VI. xix–xxi). The personal dangers Butler greatly exaggerates, assuming perhaps that the well-known fates of the Gracchi and of Appuleius Saturninus were typical. See Livy, *ep.* lviii, lxi, lxix.

p. 102, l. 32–p. 103, l. 12. *The Popes of Rome, etc.*

John [VIII], of English Extraction, but born at *Mentz*, is said to have arriv'd at the Popedom by evil Arts; for disguising her self like a Man, whereas she was a Woman, . . . upon the death of *Leo* [IV], (as *Martin* says) by common consent she was chosen Pope in his room. But suffering afterward one of her Domesticks to lie with her, she hid her big-belly a while, till as she was going to the *Lateran* Church between the *Colossean* Theatre . . . and S. *Clement*'s, her travail came upon her and she died upon the place . . . Some say, the Pope for shame of the thing does purposely decline going through that street when he goes to the *Lateran*, and that to avoid the like Error, when any Pope is first plac'd in the Porphyry Chair, which has a hole made for the purpose, his Genitals are handled by the youngest Deacon (Platina, *Lives of the Popes*, p. 165).

p. 103, ll. 13–16. *The Ægyptian Dervises, etc.* Transcribed (slightly abridged) from Rycaut, *Present State of the Ottoman Empire*, I. xiii. 139.

p. 103, l. 15. *the Seaven Sleepers*. The koranic account of these youths, who awoke after three hundred years immured in a cave at Ephesus, adds the dog, not mentioned by Gregory of Tours or other Christian hagiographers (*The Koran*, xviii, trans. George Sale, 1734, pp. 239–40 and note g).

p. 103, l. 25. *Metaposcopie*: i.e. metoposcopy, 'the art of judging a person's character or of telling his fortune by his forehead or face' (*OED*).

p. 103, ll. 32–4. *The Shepherds of England, etc*. The Pastouraux, who swept through France in 1251, vowed to liberate Louis IX after his defeat at Mansourah; they were suppressed for their lawlessness. See Matthew Paris, *Chronica Majora*, ed. H. R. Luard, 7 vols., 1872–83, v. 246–54. One of their preachers came to England, and 'in brevi plus quam quingentos pastores, aratores, porcarios, et bubulcos, et hujusmodi plebem suis nutibus mancipavit' (ibid. v. 253).

p. 104, ll. 1–11. *Constantine, etc*. Cf. p. 48, ll. 4 ff.

p. 104, ll. 12–16. *Osporco, or Hogsface, etc*. '*Sergius* the second, a *Roman*, . . . came to the Popedom at the same time that *Michael* Emperour of *Constantinople* died. 'Tis said that this *Sergius* was surnamed *Bocca di Porco* or *Hogsmouth*, which for shame of it he changed for *Sergius*, and that from thence came the Custom down to our times, that when any one is made Pope he laid by his own name and took one of some of his Predecessours; though all have not observ'd it' (Platina, *Lives of the Popes*, p. 160). Cf. Browne, *Pseudodoxia*, VII. xvi.

p. 104, ll. 17–19. *Cato uticensis lent his wife, etc*. 'Then Hortensius . . . stucke not to tell him his mind plainly, and to desire his wife of him, which was yet a young woman, and Cato had children enough. . . . In fine, Cato seeing the earnest desire of Hortensius, he did not deny him her' (Plutarch, *Cato Utican*, xxv. 4–5, trans. North, v. 132). 'Now, because he was to provide a stay and governor of his house and daughters, he tooke Martia againe, which was left a widowe and verie riche, for that Hortensius dying, made her his heire of all that he had' (ibid. lii. 3, v. 160).

p. 104, ll. 20–4. *A Græcian Prince, etc*. 'Un tal Principe Greco, chi si vantava della stirpe di Costantino Magno; e mostrava privilegi di carta pecora vecchia, veggendo l'ambizione de gli Italiani, dava loro titoli a decine senza risparmio, per ogni minima mercede; e a Ferrara sè gran profitto dove infeudò le terre del Turco' (Alessandro Tassoni, *La Secchia Rapita . . . Con le Dichiarazioni del Signor Gasparo Salviani*, Bologna, 1651, VII. xxi. 8 n., pp. 165–6).

p. 104, ll. 25–30. *Diogenes, etc*. See Diogenes Laertius, vi. 29, 67, 77. 'Cowsheel' ($\beta o \grave{o} s \ \pi \acute{o} \delta a$) is the old reading (cf. $\pi o \lambda \acute{u} \pi o \delta a$), 'bovis pedem' in the translation (Paris 'apud Jacobum Nicole', 1585) suggested by Butler's notes to *Hudibras*, II. ii. 15, and II. iii. 737.

p. 104, ll. 32–3. *the Seditions, etc.* '[The Popes] were a long time chosen by the People, as we may see by the sedition raised about the Election, between *Damasus*, and *Ursicinus*; which Ammianus Marcellinus [XXVII. iii. 12–13] saith was so great, that *Iuventius* the Præfect, unable to keep the peace between them, was forced to goe out of the City; and that there were above an hundred men found dead upon that occasion in the Church it self' (Hobbes, *Leviathan*, III. xlii. 291).

p. 105, ll. 3–8. *The Turkes are wont, etc.* 'For the Turks are very liberal in giving titles to the new slaves, calling one a Cavalier, another, a Count's Son, and saying the others are very rich, by that means to get the greatest ransom out of them' (Emanuel de Aranda, *Historie of Algiers and It's Slavery*, trans. John Davies, 1666, p. 165).

p. 105, ll. 9–14. *The Tartarian women, etc.*

[In the province of Tibet] when the mothers meane to marrie anye of their damsels, the mother dothe carrie them neere the high way side, and with mirth and cheere procureth those that do travell, to sleepe with hir, and sometimes there lyeth with her ten, and with some other twenty. And when the stranger or traveller goeth his wayes from any suche Damsell, hee must leave unto hir some jewell, the whiche jewell, the saide damsels or wenches do hang at their neckes, in token and signe that they have lost their virginitie wyth strangers. And she that hathe used hir selfe with moste strangers, it shall be knowen by the most quantitie of jewels that she weareth aboute hir necke, and she most soonest shall finde a mariage, and shall be most praysed and loved of hir husband (Marco Polo, *Most Noble and Famous Travels*, trans. [J. Frampton], 1579, p. 77).

p. 105, ll. 19–20. *Mem: Henry the 4th, etc.*

Comme le Roy chassoit en la foreste de Fontainebleau, voici qu'il oit environ á demi lieüe de lui l'aboi de plusieurs chiens, le cor & le cri de gens qui chassent; & tout soudain ce bruit s'approche fort pres de sa personne. . . . Il commande au Comte de Soissons, & à quelques autres d'aller recognoistre ces chasseurs. Ils s'avancent, & oyent le bruit, mais n'en voyent ni les auteurs ni l'endroit. Un grand homme noir parle à eux du profond des halliers, mais comme les choses inopinees & nonpreveües donnent du trouble à l'esprit, ils ne peurent distinctement entendre sa voix pour l'affinité des vocables que les uns rapporterent avoir ouy, *M'attendez-vous*? ou, *M'entendez-vous*? & les autres peut-estre avec plus de vraisemblance, *Amendez-vous*. Mais ce que le phantosme disparut aussi tost que la parole fut ouye, leur fit juger qu'il n'estoit pas expedient de poursuivre plus outre. . . . Les manœuvres, charbonniers, buscherons, les pastres & paisans d'alentour rapportent qu'ils voyent aucunefois un grand homme noir, qui mene une meute de chiens, & chasse par la forest, sans leur faire neantmoins aucun mal. & appellent cest esprit errant, *Le grand veneur* (de Serres, *Histoire*, ii. 760–1).

p. 105, ll. 29–31. *That whensoever they are worsted, etc.* '[The Gauls] at the beginning, fight more fiercely than men, but in the end more faintly than women' (Livy, *Romane Historie*, X. xxviii. 4; trans. Holland, 1600, p. 372). Cf. Caesar, *De Bello Gallico*, III. xix. 6; Tacitus, *Agricola*, xi. 3.

p. 105, l. 34. *in the Crowd*: as one of the canons in the Confession of Faith directed against the errors of the Albigenses.

Brevint p 169: Daniel Brevint, *Missale Romanum, Or the Depth and Mystery of the Roman Mass Laid Open and Explained*, 2nd edn., Oxford, 1673, xiv. 169.

p. 106, ll. 4–5. *Caligula had a Statue, etc.* See Suetonius, *Caligula*, xxii. 3.

p. 106, ll. 7–8. *as Chaucers Friers did Hell.* 'The Summoner's Prologue', *Canterbury Tales* (*D*), ll. 1693–6.

p. 106, l. 15. *Statute of vagabonds.* This statute 27 Hen. VIII. c. 25. enacted: 'A valiant beggar, or sturdy vagabond, shall at the first time be whipped, and sent to the place where he was born, or last dwelled by the space of three years, there to get his living: And if he continue his roguish life, he shall have the upper part of the gristle, or his right ear cut off: And if after that he be taken wandring in idleness, or doth not apply his labour, or is not in service with any Master, he shall be adjudged and executed as a felon. No person shall make any open or common dole, nor shall give any money in alms, but to the common boxes, and common gatherings in every Parish, upon pain to forfeit ten times so much as shall be given' (Joseph Keble, *Statutes at Large*, p. 470).

p. 106, ll. 20–1. *Epistles Dedicatory, etc.* For 'Demetrius exhortatory letter to Ptolomey as touching his library', 'Ptolomeis epistle to Eleazar for interpreters to translate the Bible', and 'Eleazars letters in aunswere to Ptolomey' see Josephus, *Antiquities of the Jewes*, XII, ii (*Works*, trans. Thomas Lodge, 1602, pp. 290–1).

p. 106, ll. 25–7. *No man was capable, etc.* 'Imperoche se i Magi, col configlio de' quali si governavano, erano cosi ben nati, come si sapea, che à quel grado non potea essere assunto chi non fusse generato da un figlivolo con la propria madre, si potea pensar, che religione, & che costu mi dovessero cercar d'imprimer ne gli animi de gli altri' (*I Compassionevoli Avvenimenti di Erasto*, Venice, 1556, xvii. 144–5). I have not been able to identify the edition to which Butler's page-reference applies.

p. 107, l. 7. *Parens Historiæ.* Bodin, *Methodus, ad Facilem Historiarum Cognitionem*, iv. 63.

p. 107, ll. 8–11. *when commending his Ingenuity, etc.* '*Another argument of his integrity and unpassionate disposition, was his refutation of* Paulus Jovius *his Oration* de morbo gallico, *in favour of the* French ... Reason it is (*saith he*) to disburden the *French* of the infamy of this disease, when as the *Spanish* brought it into *Italy* from the westerne Islands. *Such was his love, such his care, to write nothing but truth!*' (ibid. iv. 80, trans. [Thomas Heywood], in Sallust, *Two Most Worthy and Notable Histories*, 1608, Preface, sig. ¶3ᵛ).

p. 107, l. 11. *the Neapolitans.* 'It hapned as an infection to the french men whilest they were at *Naples* ... [It] was transported out of *Spaine* to *Naples*, & yet not proper or natural of that nation, but brought thether from the yles, which in those seasons began to be made familiar to our regions by the navigacion of *Christofer Colonus*' (Guicciardini, *Historie*, ii. 128).

p. 107, l. 21. *know nothing of the Longitude*. Sprat, *History*, p. 382, claims that to accomplish the discovery of another new world 'there is only wanting the *Invention of Longitude*, which cannot now be far off. . . . This if it shall be once accomplish'd, will make well-nigh as much alteration in the World, as the invention of the *Needle* did before.' See also ibid., p. 183, and Dryden, *Annus Mirabilis*, clxiii and note.

p. 107, ll. 24–9. *The Scripture set's, etc.* 1 Kgs. xi. 3–4.

p. 107. ll. 30–2. *The 70 Disciples, etc.* When 'the Lord appointed other seventy also, and sent them . . . into every citie and place, whither hee himselfe would come', he in fact said, 'Cary neither purse nor scrip, nor shoes' (Luke x. 1, 4); but cf. Mark vi. 8, and Luke xxii. 36.

p. 108, ll. 4–6. *William the Conqueror, etc.* William landed at Pevensey in East Sussex; but it is probably the origin of the New Forest which Butler recollects:

Along the East banke of this river [Avon] in this Shire [Hants], King William of Normandie pulled downe all the townes, villages, houses, and Churches far and neere, cast out the poore inhabitants, and when he had so done brought all within thirty miles compasse or thereabout into a forrest and harbour for wild beasts, which . . . we now call *New forrest*. . . . And this did he, either that the Normans might have safer and more secure arrivall into England, (For it lieth over against Normandie) in case after that all his wars were thought ended any new dangerous tempest should arise in this Iland against him (Camden, *Britannia*, p. 259).

p. 108, ll. 9–10. *Those 7 Cities of Greece, etc.*

Smyrna, Rhodos, Colophon, Salamis, Chios, Argos, Athenae,
Orbis, de patria certat, Homere, tua.

See *Greek Anthology*, xvi. 297–8.

p. 108, ll. 14–15. *The Indians of Moabar, etc.* '[The inhabitants of Moabar] are good men of warre, and verye fewe of them drinke wine, and those that doe drinke it, are not taken to be as a witnesse, nor yet those that go unto the Sea, saying, that the Marriners are dronkards' (Marco Polo, *Travels*, p. 117).

p. 108, ll. 16–17. *The Rabbins interpret, etc.* Judg. xvi. 21. It is commonly suggested that this was a heavy mill normally turned by oxen, but I have failed to locate Butler's rabbinical interpretation.

p. 109, ll. 11–12. *Christ told the woman, etc.* Mark v. 34.

p. 111, ll. 13–15. *as among the Antients, etc.* The Romans frequently sacrificed cattle in their expiations of monstrous births. See Livy, XXIII. xxxi. 15 (when a cow calved a colt); XXVII. iv. 11–15; XXX. ii. 9–13; XXXI. xii. 5–9; XXXII. i. 10–14; etc.

p. 112, ll. 4–5. *as all things, etc.* See note to p. 240, ll. 14–15.

p. 112, ll. 17–19. *The kings of Great Britaine, etc.* From Edward III to Elizabeth the arms of France were borne in the first quarter; from James I onwards in the first place quarterly. Coins of 1663 introduced four distinct shields, which gave precedence to the arms of England. Early coins of James I were inscribed ANG SCO FRAN ET HIB REX; later coins substituted MAG BRIT for ANG SCO. See Stephen Martin Leake, *Historical Account of English Money*, 2nd edn. enl., 1745, pp. 362–3.

p. 112, ll. 29–32. *their keeping of Publique Ovens, etc.* See Cotgrave, *Dictionarie*: 'Seigneur bannier. *A Lord that hath the royaltie, or priviledge of a common mill, oven, presse, etc*'; 'Subjects banniers. *Such as are bound to grind at a Mill, or to bake in an Oven belonging to another*'; 'Taureau bannier. *A common, or town, bull; for whose leacherie the Lords of France . . . exact a fee of their poore tenants.*'

p. 113, ll. 10–11. *Wo to that Kingdom, etc.* Eccles. x. 16.

p. 113, l. 14. *Keepers of Liberties.* After the execution of Charles I 'it was declared by the Parliament that they were fully resolved to maintain and uphold the fundamental laws of the nation, in order to the preservation of the lives, property, and liberty of the people, notwithstanding the alterations made in the government for the good of the people: and the writs were no more to run in the King's name, as they had always done, but the name, style, and test, to be "*Custodes libertatis Angliæ, authoritate Parliamenti*" ' (Clarendon, *History*, xi. 246). See also p. 164, ll. 15 and 23.

p. 114, l. 1. *That Justice, etc.* Isa. ix. 7.

p. 115, ll. 3–5. *Rebels have been used, etc.* Luke xv. 7 ('ninety and nine' persons, as in variant *B* 193ᵛ); 'forty' may be suggested by Gen. xviii. 29.

p. 115, ll. 12–13. *It is Safer, etc.* Cf. Samuel Parker, *Discourse of Ecclesiastical Politie*, 1670, Preface, pp. liv–lv: '*I think I have proved enough to satisfie any man of an ordinary understanding, That Indulgence and Toleration is the most absolute sort of Anarchy, and that Princes may with less hazard give Liberty to mens Vices and Debaucheries, than to their Consciences.*' See also Marvell, *Rehearsal Transpros'd*, pp. 54–6.

p. 115, ll. 20–1. *The worst Governments are the Best, etc.* See p. 118, ll. 28–33.

p. 115, l. 22. *chargeable*: burdensome, expensive.

p. 115, l. 26. *as their Predecessors the Pagans very wisely did*: i.e. in the capacity of *pontifex maximus*.

p. 116, ll. 1–3. *The two best of all, etc.* As for Titus's mother, '[Vespasian] espoused FLAVIA DOMITILLA, the freed woman of STATILIUS CAPELLA, a Romane gentleman of *Sabraca*, and an Africane borne, committed unto him sometime upon trust, and enfranchised in the freedom of *Latium*' (Suetonius, *Vespasian*, iii, in *Historie*, trans. Holland, 1606, p. 241). As for Marcus's wife, the *Historia Augusta* speaks of Faustina's 'impudicitiae fama' and specifies her relations with pantomimists and with sailors and gladiators (*Marcus*, xxvi. 5; xxiii. 7; xix. 7). See also ibid. xxix. 1–3.

p. 116, ll. 4–5. *The Emperor Vitellius, etc.* '[Vitellius] devided repast into three meales every day at the least, and sometime into foure . . . Now his manner was to send word that hee would breake his fast with one (freind) dine with another, &c. and all in one day' (Suetonius, *Vitellius*, xiii. 1, trans. Holland, p. 235).

p. 116, ll. 11–30. *When our Edward the 4th, etc.*

[Edouard] pouvoit reserver une bonne partie de l'argent qui se leveroit pour ce traiet (car les Rois d'Angleterre n'exigent rien outre leur domaine, sinon pour la guerre de France) Mais voici l'une des accortises d'Edouard. Il avoit à desseing amené dix ou douze bons sires de ville, lesquels avoyent parmi les communes, voix en chapitre, & qui le plus soigneusement avoyent procuré ceste levee. Ceux-cy ne sçachans ce que c'estoit que de loger à la haye furent bien tost las des fatigues militaires, ayans presumé que d'abordee une bataille advantageuse decideroit tout le differend. Et pour leur faire vivement favourer les douceurs de la paix au prix des aigreurs de la guerre: Edouard les alarmoit tantost de doutes, tantost de craintes, pour dissiper en Angleterre les murmures de son retour (de Serres, *Histoire*, i. 859).

p. 117, l. 18. *Rate*: i.e. of return.

p. 118, ll. 10–14. *The Chineses, etc.* On the inhospitality of the Chinese (latterly more amenable to trade), see Barnadino de Escalante, *Account of the Empire of China*, trans. John Frampton (1579), in *A Collection of Voyages*, ed. Thomas Osborne, 1745, II. x. 48, xiv. 73; Purchas, *Pilgrimage*, IV. XIX. x. 475; [Juan Gonzalez de Mendoza], *Historie of the Great and Mightie Kingdome of China*, trans. Robert Parke, 1588, I. III. vii. 71, xvii. 72.

p. 118, ll. 14–16. *The Jewes disdain'd, etc.* Acts x. 28. Cf. Tacitus, *Historiae*, V. v.

p. 118, ll. 19–20. *But when the later began, etc.* Roman citizenship was granted to the Italian peoples after the Social War, and its extension to the provinces began in the time of Caesar. In A.D. 212 the *constitutio Antoniniana* of Caracalla made all free inhabitants of the Empire citizens.

p. 119, ll. 4–5. *had not Power to make, etc.* Such power was given first to Caesar, by a *Lex Cassia*, 44 or 45 B.C., at which time only 14 of the original 50 patrician *gentes* survived.

p. 119, ll. 6–8. *That if a great or Rich Plebeian, etc.* This is apparent in Cicero, *De Domo Sua*, xiii. 35; xiv. 37, 38. The conditions and procedures of adoption are described in Aulus Gellius, *Noctes Atticae*, V. xix, and Gaius, *Institutes*, i. 98–107, 134.

p. 119, ll. 23–7. *one of the most Antient Religions, etc.* I cannot tell which religion Butler intended. Lord Herbert of Cherbury, *De Religione Gentilium*, 1673, ch. xi, provides a general account of men worshipped by the Romans and older nations.

p. 119, ll. 27–8. *the Romans built Temples, etc.* See note to p. 126, ll. 2–3.

p. 120, ll. 12–21. *The ill Constitution, etc.* See also p. 161, ll. 20–9.

p. 121, ll. 9–10. *though Solomon say's, etc.* Prov. xi. 14 and xxiv. 6: '. . . *there is safetie*'.

p. 121, ll. 23–6. *For it is an ill Signe, etc.* See the proverb 'Never had ill work-man good tools' (Tilley, W858). Cf. *ODEP* 26; Tilley, W857.

p. 122, ll. 17–18. *whose Death he tooke, etc.* 'King *Edward* besides his being old, and worn with the labours of war, had other causes that hastened his end: his grief for the losse of so worthy a son, dead but ten moneths before [in July 1376] . . .' (Baker, *Chronicle*, p. 192).

p. 123, l. 3. *Coronation-Cunduit.* When Charles II before his coronation went in procession from the Tower to Whitehall, 'the Streets in the City were Rayled & Gravelled; . . . the Windowes & houses were beautifyed with rich Carpetts & hangings, the Conduits rann with wine' (Sir Edward Walker, *Circumstantial Account of . . . the Coronation of His Majesty King Charles the Second,* 1820, p. 76).

p. 123, l. 26 n. *2 Instit.*: Sir Edward Coke, *The Second Part of the Institutes of the Lawes of England,* 1642.

p. 124, ll. 1–13. *He that believes, etc.* Cf. Hobbes, *Leviathan,* III. xxxii. 196:

When God speaketh to man, it must be either immediately; or by mediation of another man, to whom he had formerly spoken by himself immediately. How God speaketh to a man immediately, may be understood by those well enough, to whom he hath so spoken; but how the same should be understood by another, is hard, if not impossible to know. For if a man pretend to me, that God hath spoken to him supernaturally, and immediately, and I make doubt of it, I cannot easily perceive what argument he can produce, to oblige me to beleeve it. . . . For to say that God hath spoken to him in the Holy Scripture, is not to say God hath spoken to him immediately, but by mediation of the Prophets, or of the Apostles, or of the Church, in such manner as he speaks to all other Christian men.

p. 124, ll. 28–30. *Guevara, etc.* 'The letters of one of these stamped mettals doth saye, *Phoro. dact. Leg.* Your Majestie hath to understand, that this stampe is the most auncient that ever I sawe or read . . . This *Phoroneus* was king of *Egipte* before that *Joseph* the sonne of *Jacob* was borne. . . . This was he that first gave lawes in *Egypte,* and also (as it is thought) in all the worlde, wherof it doth proceed, that all Counsellours and lawyers of *Rome* did call the lawes that were juste, and moste just *Forum,* in memory of king *Phoroneus.* And so the letters of this mettall would thus much saye: *This is Kinge Phoroneus, which gave lawes to the Egyptians*' (Antonio de Guevara, *Familiar Epistles,* trans. Edward Hellows, 1574, p. 22). Guevara's 'most auncient' could be taken in the limited context of Roman coinage, to which preceding discussion has been confined.

p. 124, l. 30–p. 125, l. 2. *Much like the Stagg, etc.* Wyatt's sonnet 'Whoso list to hunt I know where is an hind' concludes,

> And graven with Diamondes in letters plain
> There is written her faier neck rounde about:
> 'Noli me tangere for Cesars I ame,
> And wylde for to hold though I seme tame.'

Butler's story could derive from this or some other version of the Petrarchan original; but an actual report of a stag killed in France having a collar inscribed 'Hoc me cæsar donavit' is given by Robert Gaguin, *Compendium super Francorum Gestis*, Paris, 1500, ix. 93ᵛ. Cf. Pliny, *Nat. Hist.* VIII. l. 119.

p. 125, ll. 32–3. *For Torva Mimaloniis, etc.*

> cludere sic versum didicit 'Berecyntius Attis'
> et 'qui caeruleum dirimebat Nerea delphin,'
> sic 'costam longo subduximus Appennino.' . . .
> quidnam igitur tenerum et laxa cervice legendum?
> 'torva Mimalloneis inplerunt cornua bombis,
> et raptum vitulo caput ablatura superbo
> Bassaris et lyncem Maenas flexura corymbis
> euhion ingeminat, reparabilis adsonat echo.'

(Persius, *Satires*, i. 93–102.)

'Hi versus [99–102] Neronis sunt, et huic sunt compositi' (ibid., *Scholia Antiqua*).

> 'quorsum haec? aut quantas robusti carminis offas
> ingeris, ut par sit centeno gutture niti?'

(Ibid. v. 5–6.)

p. 126, ll. 2–3. *for the Antients never gave, etc.* From Claudius to Diocletian deceased emperors judged worthy of apotheosis were given the title *divus* by the Senate. When it was proposed to build a temple of *Divus Nero* during his lifetime, 'ipse prohibuit, ne interpretatione quorundam ad omen malum sui exitus verteretur: nam deum honor principi non ante habetur quam agere inter homines desierit' (Tacitus, *Annales*, XV. lxxiv).

p. 126, ll. 4–8. *No less mistake, etc.* Among 'queries concerning epitaphs' Sir Thomas Browne asks, 'Whether *siste viator* bee not improperly used in church epithites, that forme being proper unto sepulchres placed of old by highwayes & where travellers dayly passed' (Addition to *Miscellany Tracts*, in *Works*, ed. Sir Geoffrey Keynes, 4 vols., 1964, iii. 226). See J. M. C. Toynbee, *Death and Burial in the Roman World*, 1971, p. 73.

p. 126, ll. 9–11. *The like error may be observd, etc.*

> Præterea quamvis solidæ res esse putentur:
> Hinc tamen esse licet raro cum corpore cernas:
> In saxis, ac speluncis permanat aquarum
> Liquidus humor, & uberibus flent omnia guttis.

(*De Rerum Natura*, i. 346–9, edn. Leyden 'ex Officina Plantiniana', 1611, p. 11.)

p. 126, ll. 13–15. *Persius also, etc.*

> 'Rem populi tractas?' (barbatum haec crede magistrum
> dicere, sorbitio tollit quem dira cicutae)
> quo fretus? dic hoc, magni pupille Pericli [i.e. Alcibiades]. . . .
> fert animus calidae fecisse silentia turbae
> maiestate manus. quid deinde loquere? "Quirites,
> hoc puta non iustum est, illud male, rectius illud." '

> (*Satires,* iv. 1–9.)

p. 126, l. 15. *Quirites*: the Romans (in their civilian, as opposed to political and military, capacity).

p. 126, l. 18. *praeposterous*: having last and first (here end and means) in inverted order.

p. 126, l. 21. *Perspective*: 'an optical instrument for looking through or viewing objects with; a spy-glass, magnifying glass, telescope, etc.' (*OED*).

p. 127, ll. 6–8. *They are much mistaken, etc.* Cf. Butler's verse-draft criticisms of Descartes's separation of soul and body (*B* 21ᵛ, 109ʳ). Descartes 'cannot believe, that what I seem to perceive in my *sleep* proceeds from *outward Objects*' (*Meditations,* trans. William Molyneux, 1680, vi. 92). On sleep see also *French Virtuosi I,* xxi. i. 130: '[Man's] superior part being then (according as *Trismegistus* saith) . . . freed and loosned from the senses and corporeal affections, it hath more particular converse with God and Angels, and receives from all parts intelligence of things in agitation. . . . [Another virtuoso] said, That he as little believ'd that the Species and Images of things come to the Soul, as that the Soul goes forth to seek them during sleep, roving and wandring about the world.'

p. 127, ll. 14–18. *Among so many Millions of Errors, etc.* Cf. Bacon, *Advancement of Learning,* II. xiii. 4, in *Works,* iii. 388–9, on the sceptics: 'But here was their chief error; they charged the deceit upon the Senses; which in my judgment (notwithstanding all their cavillations) are very sufficient to certify and report truth . . . But they ought to have charged the deceit upon *the weakness of the intellectual powers, and upon the manner of collecting and concluding upon the reports of the senses.*' Cf. Locke, *Human Understanding,* IV. xi. 1–9.

p. 127, ll. 19–24. *When the Rude Antients, etc.* Lucretius explains the process,

> quo pacto per loca sola
> Saxa pares formas verborum ex ordine reddant . . .
> Haec loca capripedes satyros, nymphasque tenere
> Finitimi fingunt, & Faunos esse loquuntur:
> Quorum noctivago strepitu, ludoque iocanti
> Affirmant volgo taciturna silentia rumpi . . .

> (*De Rerum Natura,* iv. 573–83, ed. cit., p. 95.)

The provision of the nymphs is Butler's addition.

p. 127, ll. 29–30. *Lucretius is mistaken, etc.*

> Præterea meminisse iacet, languetque sopore,
> Nec dissentit, eum mortis, letique potitum
> Iampridem, quem mens vivum se cernere credit.

(ibid. iv. 765–7, p. 100.)

p. 128, ll. 1–7. *Men of the quickest apprehensions, etc.* Cf. Sprat, *History*, p. 85: 'This [lack of persistence] is the wonted constitution of *great Wits*: such tender things, are those exalted actions of the mind; and so hard it is, for those imaginations, that can run swift, and mighty Races, to be able to travel a long, and a constant journey.'

p. 128, ll. 7–11. *Hence it is that Virgil, etc.* Dryden, Preface to *An Evening's Love*, in *Works*, x. 206, refers to '*the superfluity and wast of wit . . . in some of our predecessors: particularly we may say of* Fletcher *and of* Shakespear, *what was said of* Ovid, In omni ejus ingenio, facilius quod rejici, quàm quod adjici potest, invenies. *The contrary of which was true in* Virgil *and our incomparable* Johnson.' See also Dryden, *Essay of Dramatick Poesie*, in *Works*, xvii. 58; Richard Flecknoe, 'Short Discourse of the English Stage', in Spingarn, *Critical Essays*, ii. 93–4; Sir Thomas Pope Blount, *De Re Poetica*, 1694, ii. 106, 147, 148–9, 152–3.

p. 128, ll. 16–17. *a Virtuoso's watch, etc.* See p. 83, l. 34–p. 84, l. 4, and note.

p. 128, ll. 28–9. *The Sceptique Philosopher, etc.* I have not identified the philosopher. For a possible example of the argument, see Davenant, *Gondibert*, Preface, pp. 18–19.

p. 129, ll. 8–20. *The Invention of the Vibration, etc.* John Wilkins, *Essay towards a Real Character, and a Philosophical Language*, 1668, II. vii. 191–2, gives a full account of the pendulum experiment and derives the various units of measurement from the $39\frac{1}{4}$ inch 'standard'. The Royal Society was showing a continuing interest in the scheme. See Birch, *History*, i. 70, 74, 500, 505–7, 508–9, 510–11, etc.

p. 129, ll. 23–4. *Tis Strange that the Lacedemonians, etc.* See Plutarch, *Lycurgus*, xix–xx, trans. North, i. 146–7, for an account of 'long speache [being] much disliked, and reproved among the Lacedæmonians'.

p. 129, ll. 28–9. *Cæsars dexterity in dictating, etc.* 'For vigor and quicknesse of spirit, I take it, that C. *Cæsar* Dictatour, went beyond all men besides. . . . I have heard it reported of him, that hee was wont to write, to read, to endite letters, and withall to give audience unto suiters and heare their causes, all at one instant. And being emploied, as you know he was, in so great and important affaires, hee ordinarily endited letters to foure secretaries or clearkes at once: and when he was free from other greater businesse, he would otherwhiles find seven of them worke at one time' (Pliny, *Nat. Hist.* VIII. xxv. 91, trans. Holland, i. 168).

p. 130, ll. 1–4. *they provided not only Common Places, etc.* Seneca, *Controversiae*, i, Preface, 23, describes an orator rehearsing 'has translaticias quas proprie sententias dicimus, quae nihil habent cum ipsa controversia implicitum, sed satis apte et alio transferuntur, tamquam quae de fortuna, de crudelitate, de saeculo, de divitiis dicuntur; hoc genus sententiarum supellectilem vocabat. Solebat schemata quoque per se, quaecumque controversia reciperet, scribere.' Cf. Cicero, *De Oratore*, I. xiii. 56; xxxi. 141; xxxvi. 165.

p. 130, l. 10. *like Caligula.* It was said of him 'nec servum meliorem ullum nec deteriorem dominum fuisse' (Suetonius, *Caligula*, x. 2).

p. 130, ll. 16–17. *because Trees and all Plants, etc.*

> Et sursum nitidæ fruges, arbustaque crescunt,
> Pondera, quantum in se 'st, cum deorsum cuncta ferantur.
>
> > (*De Rerum Natura*, ii. 189–90, ed. cit., p. 33.)

p. 130, l. 25. *Dr Sp:s Dedication, etc.* I have found no book by a Dr. Sp... dedicated to Clarendon or any other Cl.... Sprat's *History*, for example, is dedicated to Charles II.

p. 130, ll. 25–7. *what Marco Polo relate's, etc.* 'When they thinke it dinner tyme, then they . . . do poure out the broath upon the floore, saying, that theyr Idols, their wives, and children doe fill themselves with it' (*Travels*, p. 42).

p. 130, ll. 28–30. *Ja: Howell write's, etc.* 'Thereupon the great Bell of *Lorenzo* rung out to give notice that every one should be ready in Arms, which had not been done a hundred years before' (J[ames] H[owell], *Second Part of Massaniello*, 1652, p. 14). '*Porto* was offended by some of the Canons; whereupon they set up the Kings Picture in a high Balcone, but a Cannon bullet shot it through and through' (ibid., pp. 65–6). Howell's *Second Part* continues Alexander Giraffi, *Exact Historie of the Late Revolutions in Naples*, trans. Howell, 1650.

p. 131, ll. 1–4. *Lucretius is mistaken, etc.*

> hæc [corpuscula rerum] puncto cernuntur lapsa diei
> Per totum cæli spatium diffundere sese . . .
> Hoc etiam in primis specimen verum esse videtur,
> Quam celeri motu rerum simulacra ferantur,
> Quod simul ac primum sub divo splendor aquai
> Ponitur: extemplo cælo stellante, serena
> Sidera respondent in aqua radiantia mundi.
>
> > (*De Rerum Natura*, iv. 200–13, ed. cit., p. 87.)

p. 131, l. 4. *a perpetual . . . emanation*: i.e. light will not travel suddenly all the way from the stars; only from the height of the dispersing clouds, above which there is 'perpetual' starlight. Cf. Sir Kenelm Digby on 'that vast body of shining light . . . that filleth all the distance betweene heaven and earth' (*Treatise of Bodies*, vii. 7, in *Two Treatises*, p. 50).

p. 131, ll. 11–14. *Dr Don's writings, etc.* Cf. Philip King, *Surfeit to A B C*, 1656,
i. 10: 'For Bishop *Andrews* and Dr. *Donne*, I could never conceive better of
them, then as a voluntarie before a lesson to the Lute, which is absolutely the
best pleasing to the eare; but after finished absolutely forgotten, nothing to
be remembered or repeated.' If Butler has Donne's poetry in mind, his concern for over-all 'Designe' is unusual; other critics (notably Dryden, in
Works, iv. 6–7, 78; xvii. 30) were preoccupied with Donne's versification and
diction.

p. 131, l. 13. *moode*: mode.

p. 131, ll. 15–17. *They that write Plays, etc.* Dryden, *Essay of Dramatick Poesie*,
in *Works*, xvii. 74, defends the verisimilitude of rhymed plays 'by distinguishing betwixt what is nearest to the nature of Comedy, which is the imitation of common persons and ordinary speaking, and what is nearest the
nature of a serious Play: the last is indeed the representation of Nature, but
'tis Nature wrought up to an higher pitch'. Yet he had used rhymed couplets
in two comedies, *The Rival Ladies* and *Secret Love* (if only in places where the
serious side of the action was being 'raised').

p. 131, ll. 18–22. *Our moderne Authors, etc.* Thyer compares Pope, *Epilogue to
the Satires, Dia. II*, ll. 171–80.

p. 131, ll. 25–6. *like witches to cast, etc.* 'Paul affirmeth that the Galatians were
deluded, when he saith, *O foolish Galatians, who hath bewitched you?* Gal. 3. 1.
Where he useth a word [*margin*: ἐβάσκανε] borrowed from the practise of
witches and sorcerers, who use to cast a miste (as it were) before the eies, to
dazle them, and make things appeare unto them, which indeede they doe not
see' (William Perkins, *Discourse of the Damned Art of Witchcraft*, Cambridge,
1608, I. iv. 23). Cf. Joseph Glanvill, *Philosophical Considerations about Witchcraft*, 4th edn. enl., 1668, iii. 17.

p. 131, l. 26. *Owles of Athens.* Owls are emblems of wisdom, but also of solemn
stupidity. For their association with Athena see A. B. Cook, *Zeus*, 3 vols.,
Cambridge, 1914–40, III. i. 776–836.

p. 133, l. 1. *Artificiall*: 'skilfully made or contrived' (*OED*).

p. 133, ll. 20–3. *So Scaliger, etc.* Scaliger, *De Subtilitate*, Preface, enumerates
those qualities which make up the excellence of Cardan's *De Subtilitate*—'ut
nihil in universa natura præterea requiri posse videatur'—and remedy the
defects of Philo, Cicero, Apuleius, and Aristotle. Cardan, *De Vita Propria*,
xlviii, in *Opera*, i. 47ᵃ, comments: 'Nam Scaliger, & Dunus, & Ingrassias, &
Gauricus, & Solnander sibi nominis comparandi gratia contradixerunt.'

p. 133, l. 34. *over-curious*: too elaborate, intricate, abstruse.

p. 134, ll. 1–6. *They are in an Error, etc.* See note to p. 127, ll. 6–8.

p. 134, l. 8. *Tincture*: 'specious or "colourable" appearance' (*OED*). It may be
significant that alchemists used 'tincture' to mean the 'quintessence' of a thing.

p. 134, l. 18. *Principles*: chemical elements (supposedly mercury, sulphur, salt, water, and earth).

p. 134, l. 24. *project*: in alchemy, throw the elixir 'or powder of projection into a crucible of molten metal' (*OED*); here used figuratively for the animals' ejaculation of sperm.

p. 134, ll. 34–5. *Raymond Lully interpret's Kabal*, etc.

. . . Kabbala. cum sit nomen compositum ex duabus dictionibus videlicet abba, & ala. abba enim arabice: idem est quod pater latine, & ala arabice idem est quod Deus meus, & cum Deus meus nomen nihil aliud importet nisi Christum dominum nostrum benedictum qui vere filius Dei est: & filius Dei nihil aliud importet nisi sapientiam divinam. Propterea dicimus quod hoc vocabulum kabbala, quod scribitur per litteram k. nihil aliud est arabice importans latine præter superabundans sapientia. Est igitur kabba habitus animæ rationalis ex recta ratione divinarum rerum cognitivus. Propter quod apparet quod est de maximo etiam divino, consequutive divina scientia vocari debet. (Ramón Lull, *De Auditu Kabalistico*, Preface, in *Opera*, ed. Lazarus Zetzner, Strasburg, 1598, p. 45.)

p. 135, ll. 1–4. *His Ars Brevis*, etc. The nine letters (B–I, and K) have six sets of meanings: *absoluta* (B=*bonitas*, C=*magnitudo*, etc.), *relata*, questions (. . . K=*quomodo*), subjects for study (B=*deus*, and so down the *Scala Natura*), virtues, and vices. The letters are manipulated, in the *Ars Brevis*, through four geometrical figures. See Frances A. Yates, 'The Art of Ramon Lull', *Journal of the Warburg and Courtauld Institutes*, xvii (1954), 115–73. Lull does promise rapid instruction, but not to the ignorant: 'Homo habens optimum intellectum & fundatum in logica & in naturalibus, & diligentiam: poterit ipsam [scientiam] scire duobus mensibus' (*Ars Magna Generalis et Ultima*, XIII, in *Opera*, p. 681). A mere 'subtle and good mind' will need six months (ibid., loc. cit.).

p. 135, l. 2. *Paire of Twises*: set of small instruments kept in a little case.

p. 135, ll. 5–10. *This his Commentator Cornelius Agrippa*, etc. 'Ea insuper huius scientiæ est promptitudo & facilitas, ut etiam pueri impuberes, hac arte freti, in omnibus ferme facultatibus docte disserere possint: multi etiam qui in extrema senectute se ad literas contulere, hac arte paucis mensibus in viros doctissimos evasere, ita hæc ars omnem temporis indigentiam vincit & inopiam. Quod ne fabulosum videatur, extant nostræ memoriæ testes' (Cornelius Agrippa, *In Artem Brevem Raymundi Lullii Commentaria*, Dedication, in Lull, *Opera*, p. 808). Unlike Lull, Agrippa demands no prerequisites for a study of the Art—'se sola sufficiente nulla alia scientia præsupposita' (ibid., p. 807).

p. 135, l. 6. *Vanity of Science*. Alluding to Agrippa's *De Incertitudine et Vanitate Scientiarum*, 1530.

p. 135, ll. 11–16. *the Story of Cardan, and Nicholas Flamell*, etc.

Quis fuit ille qui mihi vendidit Apuleium iam agenti annum ni fallor xx. Latinum, & statim discessit, ego vero qui eousque neque fueram in ludo literario nisi semel, qui nullam haberem Latinæ linguæ cognitionem, cum imprudens emissem quod esset auratus, postridie evasi qualis nunc sum in lingua Latina . . . (Cardan, *De Vita Propria*, xliii, in *Opera*, i. 38ᵃ).

. . . there fell by chance into my hands a Guilded Book, very old and large, [costing two florins. It explained] in plain words the *transmutation* of Metals [but concealed the *prima materia* in cabalistic symbols] . . . I made a Vow to God, to demand their interpretation of some *Jewish* Priest, belonging to some Synagogue in *Spain* . . . [and went to] S. *James*, where with much devotion I accomplished my Vow. This done in *Leon*, at my return, I met with a Merchant of *Boloign*, who brought me acquainted with a Physician one M. *Canches*, a *Jew* by Nation, but now a *Christian* . . . [and] he most truly interpreted unto me the greatest part of my *Figures*, in which, even to the points and pricks, he could decypher Great Mysteries which were admirable to me. (Nicholas Flammel, *Hieroglyphicks*, trans. in William Salmon, *Medicina Practica*, 1692, III. xxiv–xxv. 524–31.)

p. 135, ll. 16–19. *his 12 Principles in a Circle, etc.* The twelve principles are 'forma, materia, generatio, corruptio, elementatio, vegetatio, sensus, imaginatio, motus, intellectus, voluntas, & memoria' (Lull, *Duodecim Principia Philosophiae*, Introduction, in *Opera*, p. 118). There is no diagram of these principles

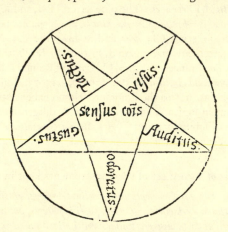

in a circle, though such arrangement would be consistent with Lull's practice. Butler may be confusing the twelve principles with the nine letters B–K; those appear in many circular diagrams. The diagram of five senses appears in *De Auditu Kabalistico*, III. vi G, in *Opera*, p. 109.

p. 135, l. 20. *Pyramids and Alters in verse.* A variety of shaped poems is displayed in George Puttenham, *Arte of English Poesie*, 1589, II. xi, and the fashion persists in the seventeenth century with such examples as Herbert's 'The Altar' and 'Easter Wings' in *The Temple*, 1633. Butler's contempt, more fully expressed in 'A Small Poet', par. 17 (*GR* ii. 120), is shared by Dryden in *Mac Flecknoe*, ll. 207–8, and later by Addison in *Spectator* 58.

p. 135, ll. 22–3. *such as Cardan saw, etc.* Probably meaning the images of people and things which Cardan as a young child saw moving in the air at the foot of his bed (*De Vita Propria*, xxxvii, in *Opera*, i. 27).

p. 135, ll. 24–8. *The Author of the History, etc.* 'A Relation of the Pico Teneriffe' explains that the town of Guimar is 'inhabited for the most part by such as derive themselves from the old *Guanchios*' (Sprat, *History*, p. 209). They use 'Butter of Goats Milk' as the base of a hardening agent, which they apply to dead bodies, then dried in the sun (ibid., p. 211). 'Antiently when they had no knowledge of Iron, they made their Lances of Wood hardned as before' (ibid., p. 212). See ibid., p. 213, for the description of their whistling 'so loud as to be heard five miles off'.

p. 135, ll. 29–32. *Scaliger say's, etc.* Scaliger, *De Subtilitate*, xci, condemns Cardan's interpretation of Anaxagoras' saying 'in omnibus esse omnia': 'Non enim ubique omnem dicebat esse substantiam: sicut tu. Nunquam putasset ille, in acu Balænam inesse. Sed aiebat, nullam imponi formam novam: quia commistæ essent omnes. Ita artificem, puta sculptorum, ablatione superfluæ materiæ formam detegere, quam falso imponere sese dicat: suberat enim.' See Cardan, *De Subtilitate*, v, in *Opera*, iii. 435.

p. 135, ll. 33–4. *Figure being, etc.* Scaliger, ibid. ccclix. 4, makes a distinction: 'Est enim figura, non extremitas corporis, ut veteres dixere, sed dispositio extremitatis.' See also ibid. lxi. 1. Yet Butler need not have this in mind; cf. Walter Charleton, *Physiologia*, III. X. i. 265: 'The Figure of a Body is really nothing but the *Body it self*; at least, the meer *Manner* of its Extreme parts, according to which our sense deprehends it to be smooth or rough, elated or depressed.'

p. 136, ll. 1–2. *the wonders, etc.* Most obviously the hypothesis that '*a streight Line continued grows a Circle*' (Marvell, *Rehearsal Transpros'd*, ii. 199). Marvell cites Nicolaus of Cusa, *De Docta Ignorantia*, I. xiv–xv, in *Opera*, 3 vols., Basle, 1565, iii. 10–11.

p. 136, l. 8. *Priviledg*: sole right to print a text.

p. 136. ll. 13–14. *Dicere quæ puduit, etc.* Ovid, *Heroides*, iv. 10.

p. 137, ll. 3–7. *Ben: Johnson, etc. Volpone*, Prologue, ll. 33–4. Browne, *Pseudodoxia*, VI. xii, explains that 'writing Ink [is] commonly made by copperose cast upon a decoction or infusion of galls. . . . [For] no other salt that I know will strike the colour with galls.'

p. 137, ll. 8–10. *Cambden, etc.* Camden reads 'Trinobantes' for the Yorkshire 'Brigantes' in Tacitus, *Agricola*, xxxi. 4 (*Britannia*, pp. 687–8); I have found nothing closer to Butler's anecdote. The Trinobantes, from Middlesex and Essex, betrayed their country to Caesar (ibid., p. 417).

p. 137, ll. 11–12. *Dr Bates, etc.* 'Redeo ad *Cromwellium*, cuius Victorias non ea erant *Brigæ* fluenta quæ suis ripis terminarent. Nam ponte sublicio e cymbis asseribusque contabulatis, ad *Rossium* coniungit utramque ripam' (George Bate, *Elenchi Motuum Nuperorum in Anglia*, Amsterdam, 1663, ii. 39). '*Priorex* [of Ireland, Lord Ormonde], *Episcopos & Primores* conveniens, hortatur serio, ut . . . *Sin minus ad salivam faceret ipsius regimen, obessetque patriæ defensioni, maturaret ille discessum lubens, alteri onere commendato*' (ibid. ii. 53).

p. 137, ll. 15–21. *Glanvile of Witchcraft, etc.* 'I have endeavoured . . . to remove the main prejudices I could think of, against the existence of *Witches* and *Apparitions*: and I'm sure I have suggested much more against what I defend, than ever I heard or saw in any that opposed it' (Glanvill, *Philosophical Considerations about Witchcraft*, xvi. 74–5). 'For he that saith, *That if there are* WITCHES, *there is no way to prove that* Christ Jesus *was not a Magician, and Diabolical Impostor*, puts a *deadly* Weapon into the *hands* of the *Infidel*, and is himself next door to the *SIN AGAINST THE HOLY GHOST*' (ibid. xiv. 70).

p. 138, l. 4. *Coyne*: the device stamped upon money.

p. 138, l. 6. *Mr. D.*: unidentified. I have found nothing resembling the statement in Dryden.

p. 138, ll. 12–13. *Juvenal proposes, etc.*

> quidquid agunt homines, votum, timor, ira, voluptas,
> gaudia, discursus, nostri farrago libelli est.

> > (*Satires*, i. 85–6.)

p. 138, ll. 14–16. *He commits as great a fault, etc.*

> Clytemestram nullus non vicus habebit.
> hoc tantum refert, quod Tyndaris illa bipennem
> insulam et fatuam dextra laevaque tenebat;
> at nunc res agitur tenui pulmone rubetae,
> sed tamen et ferro, si praegustarit Atrides
> Pontica ter victi cautus medicamina regis.

> > (Ibid. vi. 656–61.)

p. 138, l. 16. *Methridate*: 'a strong Treacle or preservative against poison, devised at first by the *Pontian* King *Mithridates* [131–63 B.C.], from whom it took name' (Blount, *Glossographia*). Immune to poison, the king had to persuade a guard to kill him with a sword (Appian, *Historia Romana*, XII. xvi. 111).

p. 138, l. 19. *Dent riant*. 'Dents riantes' is a term for the fore-teeth, 'because in laughing they are commonly seene' (Cotgrave, *Dictionarie*). I have not found it applied to satire.

p. 138, l. 21. *Incogitance*: thoughtlessness.

p. 139, ll. 1–3. *as Hippocrates says, etc.* See note to p. 280, ll. 22–4.

p. 140, ll. 9–10. *Play a Prize*: 'engage in a contest or match' (*OED*).

p. 143, ll. 7–9. *So Mr Hobs believd, etc.* In the Preface to his English translation Hobbes recalls that national anxiety '*concerning the rights of Dominion, and the obedience due from Subjects*' had precipitated his publication of *De Cive*. '*I have not yet made it out of a desire of praise . . . but for your sakes Readers, who I perswaded my selfe, when you should rightly apprehend and throughly understand this Doctrine I here present you with, would rather chuse to brooke with patience some inconveniences under government . . . then selfe opiniatedly disturb the quiet of the publique*' (*Philosophicall Rudiments concerning Government and Society*, 1651, sigg. B6ᵛ–7ʳ).

p. 143, ll. 9–11. *the Anatomist, etc.* Francis Glisson, *Anatomia Hepatis*, 1654, v. 67, writes of bodily organs etc. 'partes istæ situm suum uno perpetuoque tenore servant, ut tam in vivis, quam demortuis, facta corporum dissectione, de partium omnium situ indubitate constet'. Cf. p. 246, ll. 6–7.

p. 143, ll. 12–14. *Or he who durst never, etc.* Presumably Roger Bacon's gatehouse at the northern end of Grandpont, or Folly Bridge, described in Wood, *Antiquities of the City of Oxford*, ed. Andrew Clark, 3 vols., Oxford, 1889–99, i. 425–6. '*There is a tradition, that the study of friar Bacon, built on an arch over the bridge, will fall, when a man greater than Bacon shall pass under it*' (Johnson, *Vanity of Human Wishes*, l. 140 n., in *Collection of Poems*, ed. Robert Dodsley, 4 vols., 1755, iv. 161).

p. 143, l. 34–p. 144, l. 2. *The Rabins interpret, etc.* '[Eve told Adam,] If I must die thou shalt die with me; but when her perswasions prevailed not over his constancie, she brake off a branch from the tree, and beat him till he did eat; as it is expressed in *Genesis* 3. [1]2. *The Woman which thou gavest to be with me, she gave me of the Tree*, (that is, she pluck'd off a bough from the Tree, and with it beat me) *and I did eat*; so it is expounded in the Book *Chajim* (that is, the way of Life)' (Lancelot Addison, *Present State of the Jews*, 1675, xvi. 135).

p. 144, l. 26. *Figuræ Dictionis, et Figuræ Sententiæ*. 'The garnishing of speech in words, called *figura dictionis*, is wherein the speech is garnished by the pleasant and sweet sound of words joined together. This is either in the *measure* of sounds [as in verse]; or in *repetition* of sounds' (Pierre Ramée, *Art of Rhetoric Plainly Set Forth*, iii, trans. in Hobbes, *English Works*, ed. Sir William Molesworth, 11 vols., 1839–45, vi. 519). 'Garnishing of the frame of speech in a *sentence*, is a garnishing of the shape of speech, or a figure [by exclamation, revocation, apostrophe, prosopopœia, etc.]' (ibid. vii; vi. 524). Cf. George Puttenham, *Arte of English Poesie*, III. x.

p. 144, ll. 29–34. *Of this Mr Waller, etc.* 'He haz often sayd that way (e.g. Mr. Edmund Waller's) of quibling with sence will hereafter growe as much out of fashion and be as ridicule as quibling with words—quod N.B.' (John Aubrey, 'Samuel Butler', in *Brief Lives*, i. 136).

p. 144, l. 31. *Heroiques*: heroic couplets; 'the *English* Heroick of five feet' (Dryden, *Sylvæ*, Preface, in *Works*, iii. 17).

p. 144, l. 34. *Trotto d'Asino dura poco*. Proverbial (Giovanni Torriano, *Italian Proverbes*, i. 291, no. 1).

p. 145, l. 19. *instructs with Pleasure.* See note to p. 13, ll. 21–2.

p. 146, l. 26. *Clinching*: making clinches or puns.

p. 146, l. 28. *the Devills Oracles.* Raleigh, *History of the World*, 1614, I. I. vi. viii. 96, refers to 'the Trade of riddles in Oracles, with the Devils telling mens fortunes therein', and specifies 'the Temple of *Apollo* at *Delphos* (one of his chiefe Mansions)'. See also Milton, *Paradise Regain'd*, i. 430–59.

p. 147, l. 7. *Summum Jus, Summa Injuria.* Proverbial (Erasmus, *Adagia*, I. x. xxv). Cf. *ODEP* 235; Tilley, R122.

p. 147, l. 9. *as Hippocrates say's. Aphorisms*, I. iii.

p. 147, ll. 12–14. *Simon Magus was destroyd, etc.* Acts viii. 18–24; v. 1–10.

p. 147, l. 16. *Impostures*: impostors.

p. 148, ll. 3–4. *Antiquity abrogate's Laws, etc.* See p. 207, ll. 26–30, and note.

p. 148, ll. 20–1. *The Proverb say's, etc.* See *ODEP* 352; Tilley, C305.

p. 148, ll. 21–2. *But he that visits, etc.* Exod. xx. 5; xxxiv. 7; Num. xiv. 18; Deut. v. 9.

p. 148, ll. 23–32. *I have known, etc.* Cf. p. 231, ll. 19–25.

p. 149, ll. 7–8. *Charity is the chiefest, etc.* 1 Cor. xiii. 1–3, 13.

p. 149, ll. 8–10. *For Faith and Hope, etc.* Butler would appear to conclude from 1 Cor. xiii. 8–10 that charity alone is infallible and enduring, and that all other things—including faith and hope—must therefore pass away. Cf. p. 33, l. 1.

p. 150, l. 17. *The Curse upon the Jews.* Deut. xxviii. 25, 63–5.

p. 151, ll. 28–9. *ingendred by equivocall Generation.* See *Hudibras*, III. ii. 1–12.

p. 151, l. 32. *as some believd*: especially William Prynne. See John Miller, *Popery and Politics in England 1660–1688*, Cambridge, 1973, pp. 85–7.

p. 152, ll. 3–9. *The Pagan Religion, etc.* See p. 30, ll. 22–6, and note.

p. 152, ll. 23–5. *Our Bishops, etc.* Cf. p. 194, ll. 22–6. *Bishop'd*: confirmed in faith (the rite of confirmation).

p. 153, l. 3. *manage*: go through its paces.

p. 153, ll. 16–20. *Geometry, etc.* Transcribed, with minimal alteration, from *Leviathan*, I. iv. 15, and I. iv. 14.

p. 153, ll. 21–2. *Germans Authors of Gentry, etc.* 'Scutchions, and Coats of Armes hæreditary, where they have any eminent Priviledges, are Honourable; otherwise not: for their Power consisteth either in such Priviledges, or in Riches, or some such thing as is equally honoured in other men. This kind of Honour, commonly called Gentry, has been derived from the Antient

Germans. For there never was any such thing known, where the German Customes were unknown. Nor is it now any where in use, where the Germans have not inhabited' (ibid. 1. x. 45).

p. 153, l. 29–p. 154, l. 4. *His Grandfather, etc.* In *C* Longueville interlines 'H 4. of France   Ja–2ᵈ'. The Duke of York, whose Catholicism was clearly apparent when he resigned the admiralty in 1673 rather than take the test, was indeed proceeding in 'a way quite Contrary'. Burnet noted, 'He has a strange notion of government, that everything is to be carried on in a high way and that no regard is to be had to the pleasing the people' (*Supplement to History of His Own Time*, ed. H. C. Foxcroft, Oxford, 1902, p. 51).

p. 154, l. 9. *Water's the clepsydra, etc.* See p. 93, ll. 10–21.

p. 154, l. 13. *Grimoires*: books 'of conjuring, or exorcising, much in use among Popish Priests' (Cotgrave, *Dictionarie*).

　　　　　Bead rols: rolls or lists 'of such as Priests were wont to pray for in Churches' (Blount, *Glossographia*).

p. 154, l. 16. *Monsters, etc.* In fact *monstrare*, 'to show', is in another line of derivation from the common source, *monere*, 'to warn'. 'Monster' is derived via *monstrum*, 'an omen'. See Eric Partridge, *Origins*, 1966.

p. 154, l. 18. *to go into them.* 2 Sam. xvii. 25; 1 Kgs. xi. 2; 1 Chr. ii. 21; vii. 23; etc.

p. 154, ll. 19–22. *in the little French Lawyer, etc.* In Act II, sc. i, of Beaumont and Fletcher's comedy the lawyer La-Writ is persuaded to take the place of an absent combatant in a duel, and after his victory (II. ii) he grows incorrigibly quarrelsome. Eventually he is beaten by a lame old gentleman (IV. vi), and then foreswears violence.

p. 154, l. 22. *So the last Duke of Burgundy, etc.* Charles's early victory at Montlhery, 1465, quite changed his character, 'for after this he never followed any mans devise but his owne, and whereas before he had hated the wars, and loved nothing that appertained thereunto: his thoughts were after this so cleane altred that he continued in the wars till his death, in them ended his life, & by them desolated his house' (Phillippe de Commines, *Historie*, trans. Thomas Danett, 1596, 1. iv. 18).

p. 155, ll. 1–3. *The Fortunes of Sir W. C., etc.* Presumably they allowed their homonymous benefactor to pass as a relative. I can find no occasion for this anecdote in the lives of Sir William and Henry Coventry or of other, less prominent, candidates.

p. 155, ll. 13–14. *Banish'd all Philosophers, etc.* Tacitus, *Agricola*, ii. 2, notes the fact, 'expulsis insuper sapientiae professoribus atque omni bona arte in exilium acta, ne quid usquam honestum occurret'. See also Suetonius, *Domitian*, x. 3; Pliny, *Epistles*, III. xi. 2; Aulus Gellius, XV. xi. 4.

p. 155, ll. 14–16. *As the Lady*, etc.

> Nunc igitur qui res Romanas imperat inter,
> non trabe sed tergo prolapsus et ingluvie albus,
> et studia et sapiens hominum nomenque genusque
> omnia abire foras atque urbe excedere iussit.
>   'Quid facimus? Graios hominumque relinquimus urbes,
> ut Romana foret magis his instructa magistris.
> Nunc Capitolino veluti turnante Camillo
> ensibus et trutina Galli fugere relicta,
> sic nostri palare senes dicuntur et ipsi
> ut ferale suos onus exportare libellos.'

(Sulpicia, *Queritur de Statu Rei Publicae et Temporibus Domitiani*, ll. 35–44.)

> Haec ego. Tum paucis dea [Calliope] me dignarier infit:
> pone metus aequos, cultrix mea: summa tyranno
> haec instant odia et nostro periturus honore est.

(Ibid., ll. 63–5.)

p. 155, ll. 17–18. *The Historian of Gresham Colledge*, etc. Sprat, *History*, pp. 111–13, emphasizes the Society's abhorrence of luxury in language. 'The ill effects of this superfluity of talking, have already overwhelm'd most other *Arts* and *Professions*; insomuch, that when I consider the means of *happy living*, and the causes of their corruption, I can hardly forbear ... concluding, that *eloquence* ought to be banished out of *civil Societies*, as a thing fatal to Peace and good Manners' (p. 111).

p. 155, ll. 20–1. *which were sayd to be*, etc. 'Has [statuas] primum Tusci in Italia invenisse referuntur, quas amplexa posteritas paene parem populum urbi dedit quam natura procreavit' (Cassiodorus, *Variarum*, VII. xv. 3).

p. 155, ll. 23–5. *which the French virtuosi*, etc. '*Let two contrary extremities never touch each other*, &c. . . . This rule obliges us to know those Colours which have a Friendship with each other, and those which are incompatible, which we may easily discover in mixing together those Colours of which we would make trial. . . . *Green*, for example, is a pleasing Colour, which may come from a *blue* and a *yellow* mix'd together, and by consequence *blue* and *yellow* are two Colours which *sympathize*: and on the contrary, the mixture of *Blue* with *Vermillion*, produces a sharp, harsh, and unpleasant Colour; conclude then that *Blue* and *Vermillion* are of a contrary Nature' (Roger de Piles, obs. ¶ 361, in C. A. du Fresnoy, *De Arte Graphica*, trans. Dryden, 1695, pp. 174–5).

p. 156, ll. 1–2. *Red Lattices, and Dogs turds Proper*. Butler alludes to the trellis-work and, probably, the drops which heralds would have called 'frett(ee)' and 'gutt(ee)' respectively. See Randle Holme, *Storehouse of Armory and Blazon*, Chester, 1688, pp. 55 (figs. 56–68, 89–96), 59–60, 62–3.

p. 156, ll. 9–11. *The holy Ghost*, etc. Acts ii. 3–4.

p. 156, ll. 13–15. *as the Division of Tongues, etc.* Gen. xi. 6–8.

p. 156, l. 16. *weapon-Salve.* Walter Charleton quotes recipes for this sympa-thetic ointment, as for example: '*Of the Mosse grown on a humane skull 2. ounces: Mumie half an ounce: Human fat depurated 2. ounces: Oyle of Line seed 12. drachmes: Oyle of Roses, and Bole Armeniack, ana one ounce. Mix them, and by frequent agitation incorporate them into an Unguent. Into which a splinter of wood, or the weapon stained with the patients blood, is to be immersed*' ('Translators Supplement' to J. B. van Helmont, 'Magnetick Cure of Wounds', in *Ternary of Paradoxes*, 1650, p. 103). Cf. *Hudibras*, III. ii. 1031–2.

p. 156, l. 18. *Morisco*: 'the Moorish language' (*OED*).

　　　Fingalian. According to Sir William Petty, *Political Anatomy of Ireland*, 1691, p. 106, 'the *Fingallians* [near Dublin] speak neither *English, Irish,* nor *Welch*'.

p. 157, l. 13. *Evidences*: title-deeds.

p. 157, l. 17. *Publique Registers.* Petty, *Treatise of Taxes and Contributions*, 1662, ii. 27, predicts many less lawsuits 'if Registers were kept of all mens Estates in Lands, and of all the Conveyances of, and Engagements upon them'. See *Commons Journals*, viii. 480, 482, 545–6; ix. 436, 445; Sir Josiah Child, *Brief Observations concerning Trade*, 1668, p. 6; Petty, *Political Arithmetic*, i *ad fin.*

p. 157, ll. 23–4. *the only man of their Profession, etc.*: i.e. Bacon.

p. 157, l. 26. *Sufficient*: sufficiently.

p. 158, l. 17. *Aio te Æacida Romanos, &c.* This line from Ennius, *Annales*, is quoted in Cicero, *De Divinatione*, II. lvi. 116: 'Quis enim est qui credat Apol-lonis ex oraclo Pyrrho esse responsum

　　　　　　　aio te Aeacida Romanos vincere posse.

. . . [Pyrrhus] hanc amphiboliam versus intellegere potuisset, "vincere te Romanos" nihil magis in se quam in Romanos valere'.

p. 158, l. 28. *Fustian*: 'belonging to cant or made-up jargon' (*OED*).

p. 158, l. 30. *Intention*: 'meaning, significance, import' (*OED*).

p. 159, ll. 1–3. *like Lullys Ars brevis, etc.* See p. 134, l. 34–p. 135, l. 10, and notes.

p. 159, ll. 12–14. *The English, etc.* Paraphrased from Baker, *Chronicle*, p. 518.

p. 159, ll. 23–7. *Dryden weighs Poets, etc.* Butler most probably refers to Dry-den's comparing Shakespeare, Beaumont and Fletcher, and Jonson in *Essay of Dramatick Poesie*, in *Works*, xvii. 55–8.

p. 159, ll. 23–4. *the Virtuoso's Scales, etc.* The Royal Society virtuosi had in-vented 'A very exact pair of *Scales*, for trying a great number of *Magnetical Experiments*' (Sprat, *History*, p. 247).

p. 159, ll. 26–7. *Committit vates, etc.* Juvenal, *Satires*, vi. 436–7.

p. 159, l. 28. *He complaynd of B Johnson, etc.* Dryden is most critical of Jonson in the Epilogue to the Second Part of *The Conquest of Granada*, 1672, and in the appended 'Defence of the Epilogue', p. 170, he explains that Jonson, 'when at any time, he aim'd at Wit, in the stricter sence, that is Sharpness of Conceit, was forc'd either to borrow from the Ancients, as, to my knowledge he did very much from *Plautus*: or, when he trusted himself alone, often fell into meanness of expression'. Butler may recall '40' from an unrelated quotation in Dryden's next paragraph.

p. 159, l. 29. *Set a Thief, etc.* Proverbial (*ODEP* 810; Tilley, T110). '*There is another crime with which I am charg'd. . . . I am tax'd with stealing all my Plays, and that by some who should be the last men from whom I would steal any part of them*' (Dryden, *An Evening's Love*, Preface, in *Works*, x. 210). For such charges see R. F., *A Letter from a Gentlemen to the Hon. Ed. Howard*, 1668, p. 2, and Gerard Langbaine, 'Dryden', in *Lives and Characters of the English Dramatick Poets*, Oxford, 1691, pp. 130–77.

p. 160, l. 1. *without a Seame.* John xix. 23.

p. 160, l. 3. *tore their Garments.* Josh. vii. 6; 2 Kgs. xix. 1; Esther iv. 1; etc.

p. 160, l. 4. *left his Mantle behinde.* 2 Kgs. ii. 13.

p. 160, l. 11. *as Plato from Epichamus.* According to Diogenes Laertius, *Plato*, iii. 9, trans. E. Smith, in *Lives of Philosophers*, 2 vols., 1688–96, i. 205, '[Plato] was also beholding to *Epicharmus* the *Comedian*, most of whose Writings he transcrib'd, as *Alcimus* assures us . . . It is apparent, says he, that *Plato* took many things out of *Epicharmus*. As for Example . . .'

p. 160, ll. 12–13. *Homer stole his Poems, etc.* The source of this story is in fact Naucrates, in Eustathius, *Commentarii ad Homeri Odysseam*, Preface *ad fin.* Vulcan's temple was at Memphis, and the name of the supposed authoress was Phantasia.

p. 160, l. 14. *from him and Ennius Virgil, etc.* 'Iam vero Aeneis ipsa nonne ab Homero sibi mutuata est errorem primum ex Odyssea, deinde ex Iliade pugnas?' (Macrobius, *Saturnalia*, v. ii. 6). See ibid. v. ii–xvi. '[As for] those Fopps, who . . . would put off to us some *French* Phrase of the last Edition: . . . at best they are onely serviceable to a Writer, so as *Ennius* was to *Virgil*. He may. *Aurum ex stercore colligere*' (Dryden, *Conquest of Granada*, Defence of the Epilogue, p. 168). See Macrobius, op. cit. vi. i–v.

p. 160, ll. 16–17. *Charlton excepted, etc.* Charleton, *Physiologia*, I. i. i. 4, classes himself amongst those 'ELECTING' philosophers, who, 'reading all with the same constant Indifference, and æquanimity, select out of each of the other Sects, whatever of Method, Principles, Positions, Maxims, Examples, &c. seems in their impartial judgments, most consentaneous to *Verity*'. Apologies for copying are habitual in his prefaces—for example, *Darknes of Atheism*

Dispelled, 1652, sigg. b3ʳ–c2ʳ; *Natural History of the Passions*, 1674, sigg. bb5ᵛ– 6ʳ, cc1ʳ⁻ᵛ.

p. 160, ll. 22–3. *One that can raise, etc.* Cf. 'A Republican', par. 1 *ad fin.* (*GR* ii. 56), who 'has a mind to be a Piece of a Prince, tho' his own whole Share of *Highness* will not amount to the Value of *a Pepper Corn yearly if it be demanded*'.

p. 160, ll. 31–2. *the Law of selve-preservation.* 'Therefore the first foundation of naturall *Right* is this, That *every man as much as in him lies endeavour to protect his* life and members' (Hobbes, *Philosophicall Rudiments concerning Government and Society*, 1651, i. 11). See also ibid. i. 10; v. 1; *Leviathan*, II. xxvii, xxx.

p. 161, ll. 5–6. *Mr Hobs his Doctrine, etc.* '[*Nosce teipsum* is meant to teach us that] whosoever looketh into himself, and considereth what he doth, when he does *think, opine, reason, hope, feare,* &c, and upon what grounds; he shall thereby read and know, what are the thoughts, and Passions of all other men, upon the like occasions' (*Leviathan*, Introduction, p. 2).

p. 161, ll. 9–10. *Club-Caballers*: fellow members of political cliques.

p. 161, ll. 20–9. *There is no Question, etc.* See also p. 120, ll. 12–21.

p. 162, l. 3. *Presbytery is, etc.* ' For never was there a plainer Parallel than of the Troubles of *France*, and of *Great Britain*; of their Leagues, Covenants, Associations, and Ours; of their *Calvinists*, and our *Presbyterians*: they are all of the same Family' (Dryden, Dedication of *History of the League*, in *Works*, xviii. 7). See also Dryden, op. cit., Postscript, and *Religio Laici*, Preface, in *Works*, xviii. 396; ii. 105–6.

p. 162, ll. 17–18. *as he has illegitimate.* Six bastard sons are mentioned in Wood, *Life and Times*, ed. Andrew Clark, 5 vols., Oxford, 1891–1900, i. 208; ii. 46, 53, 192–3, 237; iii. 8. The *DNB* article on Charles names eight.

p. 163, l. 4. *Great Counsels*: parliaments, by analogy with 'Privy Council' (but historically in England an assembly of peers alone, last convened by Charles I at York in 1640).

p. 163, l. 13. *Mutiners*: 'turbulent, rebellious, or mutinous' persons (*OED*).

p. 163, l. 17. *under the Rose.* Proverbial (*ODEP* 854; Tilley, R185).

p. 163, ll. 30–3. *This Parliament, etc.* Possibly in reference to the session 18 September 1666 to 8 February 1667, when Parliament became much involved with accounts of money spent, and the propriety of its proceedings was a matter of argument. See *Cal. Treasury Books*, ii, Introduction, pp. xxxiv–l. On 19 December 1667 the Parliamentary Commission of Accounts was set up, for the history of which see ibid., pp. l–lxxxvi. But *B* 211's hand seems to be late.

p. 164, l. 3. *distrain'd*: constrained or forced 'by the seizure and detention of a chattel or thing, to perform some obligation' such as payment of money;

punished 'by such seizure and detention for the non-performance of such obligation' (*OED*).

p. 164, ll. 6–7. *as the Saxons did, etc.* Faced with invasions by the Picts and Scots, the British king Vortigern 'fled to the *Saxons* for aide, a warlike people of *Germany*, and who had greater swarmes then their hives would well hold. And here we may plainly see how dangerous a thing it is for a Nation, to call in strangers to their aide, and especially in any great number; for though they come at first but Mercenaries, yet once admitted, and finding their own strength, they soon grow Masters, as here it proved with the *Saxons*' (Baker, *Chronicle*, p. 3). The Saxons, under Hengist and Horsa, landed in 449.

p. 164, l. 15. *Keepers of the Liberties.* See note to p. 113, l. 14.

p. 164, l. 17. *the Safty.* On 26 October 1659 the officers of the army agreed 'that a number of persons should be chosen, who under the style of a *Committee of Safety* should assume the present entire government, and . . . consider and determine what form of government was fit to be erected to which the nation should submit' (Clarendon, *History*, xvi. 90). This committee, in which the officers had control, was suppressed in January 1660 (ibid. xvi. 91–5, 109–11).

p. 164, l. 18. *Sejanus:* Gnaeus Seius, put to death by Mark Antony. For the story of his wonderful horse see Aulus Gellius, III. ix: subsequent owners were Dolabella, Cassius, and Antony, and it became proverbial to say of unfortunate men, 'Ille homo habet equum Seianum.'

p. 165, l. 10. *Organum Animatum.* Aristotle's definition of a slave *qua* slave, the corresponding definition of a tool being 'inanimatus servus' (*Ethica Nichomachea*, viii. 1161ᵇ4–5).

p. 165, l. 12. *Jument:* 'a laboring beast, a horse' (Blount, *Glossographia*).

p. 165, ll. 15–16. *Colebert might better, etc.* 'Le nom de **Colbert** n'a rien de commun avec celui de la couleuvre (*coluber*); on dit que ce reptile avait été adopté comme armes prétendues parlantes par un courtisan qui se faisait gloire de se réchauffer aux rayons du symbolique soleil de Louis XIV. On appelait *colibertus* en b. lat. (*colonus libertus*), *colibert* et *collebert* en v. franc., des colons libres, attachés comme ouvriers ou laboureurs aux domaines de leur seigneur' (Baron de Coston, *Origine, Etymologie & Signification des Noms Propres*, Paris, 1867, pp. 407–8).

p. 165, l. 19. *Dutch Reconning:* 'or *Alte-mall*, a verbal or Lump-account without particulars' (B.E., *New Dictionary of the Terms . . . of the Canting Crew*, 1699).

p. 165, ll. 26–7. *Charecters Languages, etc.* Wilkins, *Essay towards a Real Character*, IV. i–iii. 385–420, sets out, and transliterates into, universal characters. For universal language see ibid. IV. iv. 421–34. For universal medicines see ibid. II. viii. 219–25; for measures see ibid. II. vii. 190–4, and also p. 129, above, ll. 8–20, and note.

p. 166, l. 1. *Aristotle says they prove nothing*. For Aristotle universals have no independent existence, nor can they be grasped except through induction from particulars; yet the concept is important in logic (*Analytica Posteriora*, 81ᵃ40–ᵇ6). His unequivocal criticism is limited to the Platonic Forms, which contribute neither to the being of sensible things, nor to an understanding of them (*Metaphysica*, M. 1079ᵇ12–18).

p. 166, l. 15. *Shipmoney*: 'a writ is framed in form of law, and directed to the sheriff of every county in England, to provide a ship of war for the King's service, . . . and with that writ were sent to each sheriff instructions that, instead of a ship, he should levy upon his county such a sum of money' (Clarendon, *History*, i. 148). For the opposition to ship-money see S. R. Gardiner, *History of England, 1603–42*, 10 vols., 1883–4, viii. 92–4, 102–3, 200–3, etc.

p. 166, ll. 15–16. *the vast Sums brought in, etc.* On 10 June 1642 Parliament published 'Propositions for the bringing in of money or plate to maintain horse, horsemen and arms, for the preservation of the public peace' (Clarendon, *History*, v. 336). 'And it is hardly credible what a vast proportion of plate was brought in to their treasurers within ten days; there being hardly men enough to receive it, or room to lay it by in' (ibid. v. 338).

p. 166, ll. 27–8. *new lights*. For an ironic account of these divine revelations see *Hudibras*, I. i. 473–514.

p. 167, l. 6. *Estimation*: repute, prestige.

p. 167, l. 24. *by thousands at a time*. Acts iv. 4. Cf. p. 296, ll. 13–31.

p. 167, ll. 25–8. *If the Thiefe, etc.* See Luke xxiii. 39–43. Cf. Matt. xxvii. 38; Mark xv. 27.

p. 168, ll. 1–2. *for thousands dy, etc.* 'My first Observation is, That few are *starved*. This appears, for that of the 229250 which have died, we find not above fifty one to have been *starved*' (John Graunt, *Natural and Political Observations . . . upon the Bills of Mortality*, 1662, iii. 1). Butler makes the same observation on p. 5, ll. 8–9, and p. 301, ll. 8–9.

p. 168, ll. 3–4. *Noe men are more unsatiable, etc.* Cf. p. 148, ll. 12–19.

p. 168, l. 14. *dispence with*: excuse.

p. 169, l. 5. *Roote and branch*. Londoners petitioned the Commons, 11 December 1640, to end episcopal government, beseeching '*That the said Government with all its Dependencies, Roots and Branches, may be abolished*' (John Rushworth, *Historical Collections*, 8 vols., 1659–1701, III. i. 93). For 'An Ordinance for the abolishing of Archbishops and Bishops', 1646, see Firth and Rait, *Acts and Ordinances of the Interregnum*, ii. 879–83.

> *They set up Presbytery.* Parliament, 'having abolished the Prelaticall Hierarchy by Archbishops, Bishops, and their Dependants, and instead thereof laid the foundation of a Presbyterial Government in every Congregation, with Subordination to Classical, Provincial, and National Assemblies, and of them all to the Parliament', established Presbyterianism by the Ordinance of 14 March 1646 (Firth and Rait, i. 833–8).

p. 169, l. 19. *the Engagement.* In January 1650 it was enacted that 'all men whatsoever . . . of the age of eighteen years and upwards shall as is hereafter in this present Act directed, take and subscribe this Engagement following; viz. I do declare and promise, That I will be true and faithful to the Commonwealth of England, as it is now Established, without a King or House of Lords' (Firth and Rait, ii. 325). This Act was subsequently repealed in January 1654 (ibid. ii. 830–1). Bulstrode Whitelock, *Memorials of the English Affairs*, 1682, p. 428, reports opposition in March 1650: 'Letters from *Chester*, of the Ministers in that Country, bitterly exclaiming against the Ingagement, and condemning all that take it *to the Pit of Hell.* . . . From *Exeter*, Letters of the averseness of the Citizens to the *Ingagement.* . . . That all the Magistrates, except two Constables, refused to take the *Ingagement.*'

p. 169, l. 24. *the Covenant.* In September 1643 Parliament subscribed to the 'Solemn League and Covenant' between England and Scotland, and directed that the nation do likewise. Subscribers undertook to preserve the reformed religion of Scotland and to reform that of England; they concluded, 'And this covenant we make in the presence of Almighty God, the searcher of all hearts, with a true intention to perform the same, as we shall answer at that great day when the secrets of all hearts shall be disclosed . . .' (Clarendon, *History*, vii. 259).

p. 169, l. 30–p. 170, l. 4. *Some write that Apelles, etc.* Zeuxis painted 'a boy carying certaine bunches of grapes in a flasket, and seeing . . . that the birds flew to the grapes, he . . . sayd, Ah, I see well ynough where I have failed, I have painted the grapes better than the boy, for if I had done him as naturally, the birds would have beene afraid and never approched the grapes' (Pliny, *Nat. Hist.* XXXV. xxxvi. 66, trans. Holland, ii. 535).

p. 170, ll. 8–12. *The Turkish Historys report, etc.*

> [To kill Mustapha] seven Muts (these are strong men bereft of their speech, whom the Turkish tyrants have alwaies in readinesse, the more secretly to execute their bloudy butchery) . . . cast a bow-string about his necke, he poore wretch stil striving, and requesting that he might speake but two words to his father before he died. All which the murtherer . . . both heard and saw by a travers from the other side of the tent: but was so far from being moved with compassion, that thinking it long till he were dispatched, with a most terrible and cruell voice he rated the villains enured to bloud; saying, *Will you never dispatch that I bid you?* . . . Which horrible commanding

speeches, yet thundering in their eares, those butcherly Muts . . . strangled him (Richard Knolles, *Generall Historie of the Turkes*, 1638, p. 763).

p. 170, ll. 13–14. *Lucullus his Lamprys, etc*. I have found no report of this in connection with Lucullus. He cut through mountains to let the sea into his fish-pools at Baiae (Plutarch, *Cimon and Lucullus*, xxxix. 3; Pliny, *Nat. Hist.* IX. lxxx. 170; Varro, *Res Rustica*, III. xvii. 9). Fish there later came to the hand of Domitian (Martial, *Epigrams*, IV. xxx. 1–7). Cf. Pliny, *Nat. Hist.* X. lxxxix. 193, XXXII. vii. 16. On lampreys in particular see Macrobius, *Saturnalia*, III. xv; Pliny, *Nat. Hist.* IX. lxxxi. 172. Cf. Varro, *Res Rustica*, III. xvii. 5–8.

p. 170, ll. 14–15. *Arion in the Fable, etc*. Arion, when his servants conspired to throw him overboard, asked to sing a lament, and, 'cithara sumpta, suam coepit deflere mortem; quo sonitu ducti delphines e toto mari pronatant ad Arionis cantum. Itaque . . . super eos se deiecit; quorum unus Ariona exceptum pertulit ad Taenarium litus' (Hyginus, *Astronomica*, ii. 17). Cf. idem, *Fabulae*, 194; Herodotus, i. 24; Ovid, *Fasti*, ii. 83–116.

p. 170, l. 26. *Gods Servants Servant*. 'Servus Servorum Dei' is 'a title of the Pope employed in official documents. It was first used by St. Gregory the Great (590–604) and has been in general use since the time of Gregory VII (1073–85)' (*Oxford Dictionary of the Christian Church*, ed. F. L. Cross).

p. 170, l. 30. *Cain slew his brother Abel*. Gen. iv. 8.

p. 172, ll. 5–6. *And those times cald, etc*. See p. 185, ll. 1–6, and note.

p. 172, ll. 9–10. *The Scripture says, etc*. Matt. xxvi. 3–5; Mark xiv. 1–2; Luke xxii. 2.

p. 172, l. 9. *President*: 'the appointed governor or lieutenant of a province' (*OED*).

p. 172, l. 13. *Crucifige*: crucify (him). 'At illi succlamabant dicentes crucifige crucifige illum' (Luke xxiii. 21). Cf. Mark xv. 13.

p. 172, l. 23. *in Querpo*: with the body not concealed by overgarments or armour.

p. 173, ll. 2–5. *For Knight and Squire, etc*. 'Knight or Cniht or Cnyht (as it was writen in the *Saxon*) signified as *puer, servus*, or an attendant' (Selden, *Titles of Honor*, 2nd edn. enl., 1631, II. v. xxxiii. 769). 'Esquire signified one that was attendant, and had his employment as a servant, wayting on such as had the Order of Knighthood in matters that conduced to Armes, bearing their Shields, and helping them to Horse and such like' (ibid. II. III. xxvii. 555). Cf. Latin 'scutarius', a shield-wright. 'But doubtlesse both in *Persius* and *Cicero, Baro* is taken for a stupid or contemptible and blockish fellow. . . . [The Germanic root] signifying a man came by application to be restraind to a dignitie, as *Dux* and *Comes* from their common significations did' (ibid. II. I. lii. 428.) '*Count* or *Comes* (which wee now call EARLE) is, in notation of the word, only as much as a *Follower*' (ibid., edn. 1614, II. iv. 219). Butler takes 'dux' in the sense of 'one who leads or shows the way; a guide' (*Oxford Latin Dictionary*).

p. 173, l. 8. *Curious*: 'intricate, abstruse, subtle' (*OED*).

p. 173, ll. 15–16. *Navigation the only Art, etc.* God told Noah how to build the ark (Gen. vi. 14–16).

p. 174, l. 32. *the Princes of Parma.* Margaret of Austria, Duchess of Parma, was regent of the Netherlands from 1559 to 1567.

p. 175, l. 8. *Palmerins*: sixteenth-century Spanish romances, of which the original hero was Palmerin de Oliva, a legendary prince of Byzantium.

p. 175, l. 28. *of the skins of Beasts.* Gen. iii. 21.

p. 176, ll. 8–10. *No Sect of Philosophers, etc.* Besides the ancient Mediterranean cults, there were the Brahmins of modern India. Herbert, *Travels*, pp. 54–5, shows 'in how many things they concurr with *Pythagoras*, (to this day famous among them.)'

p. 176, ll. 11–14. *There is a Trick, etc.* Cf. p. 65, ll. 10–21, and notes.

p. 176, ll. 30–1. *St Paules Doctrine, etc.* 1 Cor. vii. 14.

p. 177, ll. 9–10. *the whore of Babilon.* Rev. xvii. 1–5.

p. 177, l. 17. *Intrepidity.* The noun was new in French (1665—Robert, *Dictionnaire*); it did not enter English until the end of the century (first *OED* quotation, 1704).

p. 178, ll. 1–2. *Some outlying whimsy, etc.* Cf. 'A Humorist', *GR* ii. 324, who applies himself 'to some particular Kind of Folly . . . 'Tis commonly some out-lying Whimsie [etc.]' A beast is said to be 'outlying' that 'makes its lair outside a park or enclosure' (*OED*).

p. 179, ll. 11–14. *Mr Wray and Coleman, etc.* Burnet, *History*, ii. 105, recounts how the 'zealous protestant' wife of Sir Philip Tyrrwhit, 'a papist', invited Edward Stillingfleet and himself to a discussion, 3 April 1676, 'with some that her husband would bring'. These included Edward Coleman, secretary to the Duchess of York, subsequently executed, December 1678, for complicity in the Popish Plot. Coleman 'took the whole debate upon him', and Burnet afterwards published *A Relation of a Conference, Held about Religion*, 1676, in which he identifies another of the Catholics present as 'Mr. W.' (p. 1). Edward Wray of Barlings Abbey, Lincs., was associated with his neighbour Tyrrwhit in estate matters (*Cal. State Papers Dom.*, 1672, pp. 46, 226). In September 1673 he had argued religion with Richard Baxter: 'The Lady *Clinton* having a Kinswoman (wife to *Edward Wray*, Esq;) who was a Protestant, and her Husband a Papist (throughly studied in all their Controversies, and oft provoking his Wife to bring any one to dispute with him) desired me to perform that office of Conference . . .' (*Reliquiæ Bax-terianæ*, ed. Matthew Sylvester, 1696, iii. 107. 244). For family relationships see *Complete Peerage*, ed. G.E.C., 14 vols., 1910–59, VII. 698; XII. ii. 259, 569–70; *Complete Baronetage*, ed. G.E.C., i. 97; Charles Dalton, *History of the Wray Family*, 2 vols., 1880–1, II. 84.

p. 179, l. 21. *Ragust*: ragout; specifically, the sauce or relish of the stew.

p. 179, ll. 21–2. *The Parish clearks, etc.* Sir Edmund Chambers, *Mediaeval Stage*, 2 vols., Oxford, 1903, II. 118–19, ascribes cycles of miracle plays at Clerken-well, *c.* 1400, to 'a guild of St. Nicholas, composed of the "parish clerks" attached to the many churches of the city. At a later date the performances of this guild seem to have become annual and they are traceable . . . to the beginning of the sixteenth century.' See also ibid. II. 379–82. Clerkenwell derives its name from a much earlier association with scholars. See J. E. B. Gover *et al.*, *Place-Names of Middlesex* (*English Place-Name Soc.* xviii), Cambridge, 1942, p. 95.

p. 179, l. 24. *the Devill with two Loggerheads*. Double heads for devils are a common medieval stage property. See, for example, *York Records*, ed. Alexandra F. Johnston and Margaret Rogerson (*Records of Early English Drama* i), Toronto, 1978, i. 55. As a child, Bulter might have seen them in plays at Worcester. The connection with the Jesuits eludes me.

p. 179, l. 25. *Dutch Roderigos*. Probably the 'Rederijkers' or 'Cameren van Rhetorica'. These medieval dramatic societies had survived into the seventeenth century, most notably in Amsterdam. See *Penguin Companion to Literature: Europe*, ed. A. Thorlby, 1971, p. 643.

p. 179, ll. 29–30. *he that can belive, etc.* John Wilkins, *Discovery of a New World... in the Moone. With a Discourse concerning the Possibility of a Passage Thither*, enl. edn., 1640. In adding the 'Discourse' (I. xiv. 203–42) Wilkins was prob-ably influenced by Francis Godwin, *The Man in the Moone*, 1638.

p. 179, l. 31. *of Gotham, as wel as Gresham*. Gotham College was 'an imaginary institution for the training of simpletons' (*OED*). Wilkins was a founder of the Royal Society.

p. 180, ll. 2–3. *He that undertook, etc.* John Bulwer, *Pathomyotomia, Or a Dis-section of the Significative Muscles of the Affections of the Minde* [i.e. the head muscles nearest the brain], 1649.

p. 180, ll. 3–4. *the modern French Virtuosos, etc.* 'The end of *Portraits* is not so precisely as some have imagin'd, to give a smiling and pleasing Air together with the resemblance; this is indeed somewhat, but not enough. It consists in expressing the true temper of those persons which it represents, and to make known their *Physiognomy*' (Roger de Piles, obs. ¶ 393, in du Fresnoy, *De Arte Graphica*, p. 182). Cf. ibid., obs. ¶ 233, pp. 152–3.

p. 181, l. 16. *in Sober Sadnes*: 'in earnest, not joking' (*OED*).

p. 181, ll. 23–4. *by the Grant*. 'Grants, *concessiones*; the regular method by the common law of transferring the property of *incorporeal* hereditaments, or, such things whereof no livery can be had' (Blackstone, *Commentaries*, II. xx. 317).

p. 182, ll. 1–2. *make mens opinions the Standart, etc*. The *Confession of Faith of the Westminster Assembly of Divines* (1646) emphasizes doctrine as determining the purity of particular churches (xxv. 1) and acknowledges Church officers' 'power respectively to retain and remit sins, to shut that kingdom [of heaven] against the impenitent, both by the Word and censures; and to open it unto penitent sinners' (xxx. 2). See also Firth and Rait, i. 789–91; Roger L'Estrange, *Interest Mistaken*, 1661, pp. 59, 102, 114.

p. 182, ll. 15–22. *The Spanish Souldiers, etc*. When in July 1575 they had forced their commander to flee, 'almost three thousand of the old souldiers, after the manner of seditions, created them a Generall, whom they called the *Electo*, casting their *Militia* into a new model; and dividing the Offices of Warre among themselves, in order of battell marched to *Antwerp* . . . [There] they all bound themselves by oath to obey the *Electo*, and not to lay down arms till they had their pay to a *Maravedi*. Which very Act passed not tumultuously in that tumult, but orderly and gravely, as if there had been no sedition. . . . Nay, they set up a Gallows on the place, and made Proclamation in the *Electo's* name, That whosoever for the future stole or plundred, should be immediately hanged: which was so punctually observed by the souldiers, two of them being instantly trussed up, that *Antwerp* heard of no more such offences' (Famianus Strada, *De Bello Belgico*, trans. Sir Robert Stapylton, 1650, viii. 5). For further mutinies see ibid. viii. 8, 17 ff.

p. 183, ll. 13–14. *The Richest, etc*. Cf. Montaigne, *Essayes*, II. xii. 280: 'Whereas in other creatures, there is nothing but we love, & pleaseth our senses: so that even from their excrements & ordure, we draw not only dainties to eat, but our richest ornaments and perfumes.'

p. 183, ll. 23–4. *The Goths, etc*. Cf. p. 164, ll. 28–9.

p. 185, ll. 1–6. *believe the Best Modern, etc*. 'Those times are the ancient times, when the world is ancient, and not those which we account ancient *ordine retrogrado*, by a computation backward from ourselves' (Bacon, *Advancement of Learning*, I. v. 1, in *Works*, iii. 291). See also Hobbes, *Leviathan*, Conclusion, p. 395; Glanvill, *Vanity of Dogmatizing*, xv. 141; Swift, *Battle of the Books*, in *Works*, i. 147.

p. 185, l. 10. *Imagines et Spectacula Humanæ vitæ*. 'Tragedy is essentially an imitation not of persons but of action and life, of happiness and misery' (Aristotle, *Poetica*, 1450ª16–17).

p. 185, l. 11. *Persone mezzane*. Lodovico Castelvetro, *Poetica d'Aristotele*

Vulgarizzata, et Sposta, Vienna, 1570, III. xiii. 153^r, expounds *Poetica*, 1452^{b}30–1453^{a}17: 'Divide le persone in tre parti in ottime, in pessime, & in mezzane, & mostra come trapassando l'ottima persona o la pessima da felicita a miseria o da miseria a felicita non generano compassione ne spavento nel commune popolo, & come solamente la mezzana il sa trapassando da felicita a miseria. Laonde conchiude che la mezzana persona è la persona tragica quando trapassa da felicita a miseria.'

p. 185, l. 20. *are Incapable of Pitty*: cannot be pitied.

p. 185, l. 24. *for their own Sakes*. 'Griefe, for the Calamity of another, is PITTY; and ariseth from the imagination that the like calamity may befall himselfe; and therefore is called also COMPASSION, and in the phrase of this present time a FELLOW-FEELING: And therefore for Calamity arriving from great wickedness, the best men have the least Pitty; and for the same Calamity, those have least Pitty, that think themselves least obnoxious to the same' (Hobbes, *Leviathan*, I. vi. 27).

p. 185, ll. 29–30. *some Mistake or oversight of their Ancesters*. This may be found in the families of Alcmeon, Oedipus, Orestes, Meleager, Thyestes, and Telephus, which are specified as pre-eminent sources for tragedy in Aristotle, *Poetica*, 1453^{a}18–21.

p. 185, l. 30. *the Jews eating of Sour Grapes*. Jer. xxxi. 29; Ezek. xviii. 2.

p. 186, ll. 12–14. *though tru History be, etc.* A falsification of Aristotle's argument that 'the poet's function is to describe, not the thing that has happened, but a kind of thing that might happen, i.e. what is possible as being probable or necessary' (*Poetica*, 1451^{a}36–8).

p. 186, ll. 15–18. *the Tragedy of Pyramus and Thisbe, etc.* Shakespeare, *Midsummer Night's Dream*, III. i. 34–43. 'Flute the Bellows mender' is an error for Snug the joiner.

p. 187, ll. 6–7. *who are the Only Persons, etc.*

Mediocribus esse poetis
non homines, non di, non concessere columnae.

(Horace, *De Arte Poetica*, ll. 372–3.)

p. 187, ll. 25–6. *Davids Tongue, etc.* Ps. xlv. 1.

p. 188, l. 5. *Curious*: studious, heedful.

p. 188, l. 6. *Pricks*: points.

p. 188, ll. 17–19. *All the Stars, etc.* Cf. p. 87, ll. 13–14, and p. 98, l. 17.

p. 189, l. 12. *Comfortable Importances*. See Samuel Parker, Preface to John Bramhall, *Vindication of Himself and the Episcopal Clergy*, 1672, sig. A2^r: He has agreed to write this preface even though he is much concerned '*in Matters of a closer and more comfortable importance to my self and my own Affairs*'. Marvell,

Rehearsal Transpros'd, i. 6, wonders 'what this thing should be of a *closer importance*; But being *more comfortable* too, I conclude it must be . . . either his Salvation, or a Benefice, or a Female.' As Parker can have no worries about the first two, 'Why, then it must of necessity be a Female.'

p. 189, ll. 20–4. *One that could tell, etc.* Cf. p. 151, ll. 27–9.

p. 189, l. 27. *Complexions*: dispositions, natures.

p. 190, l. 3. —— *that bring him Children*. Most notably Barbara Villiers, Charles's 'first and longest mistress, by whom he had five children' (Burnet, *History*, i. 168). See note to p. 162 above, ll. 17–18.

p. 190, ll. 4–15. *And this unhappines, etc.* In 1667 Edward Hyde, Earl of Clarendon, was dismissed from the chancellorship, in which capacity he had directed national policy since his return from exile with the King. He died in banishment at Rouen in 1674. Burnet, *History*, i. 450–1, comments on his dismissal: 'The king was grown very weary of the queen: and it was believed, he had a great mind to be rid of her. The load of that marriage was cast on the lord Clarendon, as made on design to raise his own grandchildren. Many members of the house of commons . . . were brought to the king, who all assured him that upon his restoration they intended both to have raised his authority and to have increased his revenue, but that the earl of Clarendon had discouraged it'. See also ibid. i. 176; Evelyn, *Diary*, i. 289, iii. 493; Wood, *Life and Times*, i. 335, 337, 440. Compliance with circumstances by a sometimes reluctant Clarendon had become in popular retrospect his 'plots': his daughter's marriage to the Duke of York, Charles's match with Catherine of Braganza, the sale of Dunkirk, the second Anglo-Dutch war, and that Restoration settlement to which Butler probably alludes, whereby the old Royalists who had sold their lands to Civil War 'wolves' received no compensation. See p. 197, ll. 1–12. In Aesop the 'guardians' are sheepdogs.

p. 190, ll. 8–10. *For when he had enterd, etc.* The metaphor is from backgammon. Divisions on the board are called 'points', and when a player enters a point with a single man he lays it open to possible hits from the opponents' men, this vulnerability being called a 'blot'. But if he then binds his man by entering another on that same point he denies the opponent access.

p. 190, l. 18. *his Gout*. Clarendon recounts his having suffered from gout since 1645 (*Life of Edward Earl of Clarendon . . . Written by Himself*, iii. 68, vi. 7; *Continuation*, par. 1215).

p. 190, ll. 19–29. *The old Greek Poets, etc.* Cf. p. 39, ll. 5–26.

p. 190, ll. 26–9. *And Ovids Metamorphosis, etc.* Cf. p. 6, ll. 13–15.

p. 191, ll. 22–3. *whose very imaginations, etc.* 'And yet the effects of the force of the Mothers Imagination in the signing of the *Fœtus* is very wonderful . . . Signatures of less extravagance and enormity are frequent enough, as the similitude of Cherries, Mulberries, the colour of Claret-wine spilt on the woman with child, with many such like instances. . . . [Thomas Fienus] does acknowledge that the Imagination of the Mother may change the figure of the *Fœtus* so as to make it beare a resemblance, though not absolutely perfect, of an Ape, Pig, or Dog, or any such like Animal' (Henry More, *Immortality of the Soul*, III. vi. 3). See further ibid. III. vi–vii.

p. 192, l. 3. *weather glass*: 'a kind of thermometer, used to ascertain the temperature of the air, and also to prognosticate changes in the weather' (*OED*).

p. 192, ll. 10–11. *In the Scotch translation, etc.*: unexplained. No such departures from the received English text are found in Scottish editions (Geneva Version, 1579, 1601, 1610; King James, 1633, etc.). The *editio princeps* of the Old Testament in Scottish Gaelic was not until 1801 (Irish Gaelic, 1685).

p. 192, ll. 24–5. *as all Empire, etc.* For example, [Dudley Digges], *An Answer to a Printed Book, Intituled, Observations upon Some of His Majesties Late Answers and Expresses*, Oxford, 1642: 'Those long lived Patriarchs had this advantage, by begetting a numerous posterity, they might people a Nation out of their own loynes, and be saluted *Patres patriæ* without a metaphor; the same being their subjects and their children. In relation to this, it was properly said by the Ancients, a Kingdome was but a larger family . . . Thus Regall power sprang first from Paternal'. See also Hobbes, *Leviathan*, II. xx. 102–3; Sir William Temple, 'Essay upon the Original and Nature of Government', in *Miscellanea*, 1680, pp. 63–8; Sir Robert Filmer, *Patriarcha*, 1680, i. 8.

p. 193, ll. 7–8. *Angels converse by Intuition, etc.* 'But if any speak at a distance to another, he must use a louder voice; but if neer, he whispers in his ear: and if he could be coupled to the hearer, a softer breath would suffice; for he would slide into the hearer without any noise, as an image in the eye, or glass. So souls going out of the body, so Angels, so Demons speak: and what man doth with a sensible voyce, they do by impressing the conception of the speech in those to whom they speak, after a better manner then if they should express it by an audible voyce' (Cornelius Agrippa, *Occult Philosophy*, III. xxiii. 413). See also Aquinas, *Summa Theologica*, Ia. cvii. 1.

p. 193, l. 9. *In St. John's time*. Rev. viii. 1.

p. 193, l. 12. *Truth can be no older, etc.* Cf. the proverb 'Truth is time's daughter' (*ODEP* 844; Tilley, T580; *Hudibras*, II. iii. 663–4).

p. 193, l. 14. *the Father of Lyes*. John viii. 44.

p. 194, ll. 1–2. *who are more, etc.*: of whom there are more to each just and grateful person than can easily be reckoned.

p. 194, l. 6. *on Free-cost*: 'cost-free, gratis' (*OED*).

p. 194, l. 8. *Occasions*: 'affairs, businesses' (*OED*).

p. 194, ll. 22–6. *The Bishops, etc.* Cf. p. 152, ll. 23–5.

p. 194, ll. 29–30. *Adam and Eve believd, etc.* Gen. iii. 5–6.

p. 194, l. 30–p. 195, l. 1. *Lucifer fell from Heaven, etc.* Isa. xiv. 12–15.

p. 196, ll. 11–13. *Adam after his Fall, etc.* Gen. iii. 7–10.

p. 197, ll. 1–12. *The Chanceler Hide, etc.* See note to p. 190, ll. 4–15.

p. 197, ll. 10–11. *Dispensations and outgoings*: Puritan terms for Providential intervention. 'An Hypocritical Nonconformist', *GR* ii. 41, 'does not care to have any thing founded in Right, but left at large to *Dispensations* and *Outgoings* of Providence, as he shall find Occasion to expound them to the best Advantage of his own Will and Interest'.

p. 197, ll. 13–14. *The Cruelty of the Grand Signor, etc.* According to Rycaut, *Present State of the Ottoman Empire*, 1. xvi. 74, 'the Grand Signior hath scarce performed the ceremonies of his inauguration before he hath seasoned his entrance to his Throne with the bloud of his Brothers; which barbarous custom began in the time of *Sultan Bajazet*'.

p. 197, ll. 23–5. *where Merit is so much Regarded, etc.* There were greater opportunities on account of the Turks 'admitting no succession to Offices or Riches, but only in the direct *Ottoman* Line' (ibid. 1. xvi. 69). Blount, *Voyage into the Levant*, p. 63, contrasts with Christian practice examples of the Turks' 'choice, and *education* of *persons*, apt to each use, [which] must needs make it excellently performed'. Yet cf. Rycaut, op. cit. 1. i. 2, on favouritism.

p. 197, l. 30. *having more sons, etc.* Five sons survived to adulthood: Edward, the Black Prince; Lionel, Duke of Clarence; John of Gaunt, Duke of Lancaster; Edmund, Duke of York; Thomas, Duke of Gloucester.

p. 198, l. 1. *occupyd*: practised, employed. The construction with an adverb is not in *OED*.

p. 199, ll. 6–8. *For as there is no Folly, etc.* Cf. p. 280, ll. 22–4.

p. 199, ll. 11–12. *that Devill that assume's, etc.* 2 Cor. xi. 14.

p. 199, l. 24. *as Diogenes was.* See Seneca, *Epistulae Morales*, xc. 14; Lucian, *Historia*, 3; Diogenes Laertius, vi. 23, 43.

p. 199, l. 28. *Sir P. Neal*: Sir Paul Neile, *c.* 1613–86, scientist and F.R.S. In his verse draft of ll. 4–6 Butler changes the name to 'Sidrophel'. Cf. Joseph Toy Curtis, 'Butler's Sidrophel', *PMLA* xliv (1929), 1066–78, and Wilders, Appendix B to *Hudibras*, p. 454. Neile was a Commissioner for Appeals in Excise, first appointed 1673 (*Cal. Treasury Books*, iv. 143). I have been unable to trace Butler's two stories about him.

p. 200, ll. 1–3. *This Pope, etc.* Presumably Clement X, 1670–6, who left all business to Cardinal Altieri. 'This manner of dealing gave occasion to many witty Men at *Rome* (according to their custom) to publish *Pasquils* . . . one of which was affixed on the Pope's Picture, hanging over the door of his Bed-Chamber, and was this, *Qui stô, per Insegna*, that is, I am here for a Sign; alluding to the person of the Pope, who served onely for a shadow' (Rycaut, Pt. ii to Platina, *Lives of the Popes*, p. 362).

p. 200, l. 2. *Pasquill*: 'an old Statue or Image in *Rome*, whereon Libels, Detractions, and Satyrical invectives are fixed, and on him fathered, as their Author' (Blount, *Glossographia*). See also *OED*, s.v. 'Pasquin'.

p. 200, l. 12. *Lipsius his Dogge*. Lipsius' dog would bring his master as much meat from the market as he carried forth money to pay for, but 'other lesse doggs, snatching as he trotted along, part of what hung out of his basket (which he carried in his mouth) he sett it downe to werry one of them; whiles in the meane time, the others fedde at liberty and at ease upon the meate that lay there unguarded; till he coming backe to it, drove them away, and himselfe made an end of eating it up' (Digby, *Treatise of Bodies*, xvii. 1, in *Two Treatises*, p. 320).

p. 200, ll. 23–4. *to aske Leave, etc.* See Job i. 8–19.

p. 201, ll. 16–17. *Dr. Wil: has set up, etc.* I have found no occasion for this comment in John Wilkins or other likely writers.

p. 201, l. 19. *wars with the Græcians*: the two Illyrian Wars (229–228, 219 B.C.) and the three Macedonian Wars (214–205, 200–196, 172–168/7 B.C.).

p. 202, l. 4. *Cross-knave*: perverse knave.

p. 202, l. 16. *a burnt Child, etc.* Proverbial (*ODEP* 92; Tilley, C297).

p. 203, ll. 6–7. *as the Roman Velites, etc.* 'The youngest and poorest soldiers became *velites* or light-armed troops; those next in age composed the *hastati* or front-line troops; the soldiers in their prime made up the *principes* or second line; while the oldest men were assigned to the third line and called *triarii*' (H.M.D. Parker, *Roman Legions*, Oxford, 1928, p. 14).

p. 203, ll. 9–10. *that Sottish Story, etc.* See Aulus Gellius, X. xvii. 1.

p. 203, ll. 17–18. *Socrates his Dying, etc.* Socrates was indicted for refusing to recognize the state gods and for introducing other new deities (Diogenes Laertius, ii. 40). See also Plato, *Apology*, 24b, and *passim*; Xenophon, *Memorabilia*, 1. i. 1, and *passim*. See Diogenes Laertius, ii. 37, on Xanthippe's beating her husband.

p. 203, ll. 22–3. *that Paralel, etc.* Florus divides the Romans' history into 'foure degrees, or maine progressions', each of 250 years. '*The first revolution was under Kings . . . in which space they wrestled and strove about their Mother-citie with their neighbours. This may be the time of their infancie. The following period, from the Consulship of Brutus, and Collatinus, to the Consulship of Appius Claudius, and Quintus Fulvius, . . . in which they subdued Italy . . . was a time most famous for*

*manhood, and deeds of Chevalry. It may well bee therefore termed their youthfull
age. From hence, to* Augustus Cæsar, . . . *in which he setled peace thorow all the
World . . . is the very Mans estate, and as it were the strength & ripenesse of the
Roman Empire. From* Augustus Cæsar, *to our dayes,* . . . *through the unworthinesse
of Emperours, the force* of the Roman people *waxt old, as it were, and wasted it
selfe*' (*Roman Histories*, i, Introduction, 4–8, trans. E[dmund] B[olton], Oxford,
1636, sigg. A10ᵛ–11ᵛ).

p. 203, ll. 28–32. *But when the world, etc.* Godfrey Goodman, *Fall of Man,
Or the Corruption of Nature*, 1616, iii. 348–82, contended 'now is the olde age
or decay of this world'. Cf. Lucretius, ii. 1150–74. This was opposed by
George Hakewill, *Apologie of the Power and Providence of God in the Government of
the World*, 1627; see esp. bk. iii. In 'A Romance Writer' (*GR* ii. 275) Butler
refers to the world as 'grown old'.

p. 204, ll. 14–15. *when they had the Management, etc.* 'And where before the
Bishop and the Alderman were the absolute Judges to determine all businesse
in every Shire, and the Bishop, in many Cases, shared in the benefit of the
Mulcts with the King; now he [William I] confined the Clergie within the
Province of their own Ecclesiasticall Jurisdiction' (Baker, *Chronicle*, p. 38).

p. 205, l. 23. *the good old Cause*: a Puritan phrase for the interests of their party.
Butler's Character, 'An Hypocritical Nonconformist' procures 'fresh supplies
for the *good old Cause and Covenant*, while they are under Persecution' (par.
1; *GR* ii. 36).

p. 205, l. 27. *carry on the work*: a phrase used by Puritans for the furtherance
of their cause. See *Hudibras*, I. i. 201; II. i. 919; II. ii. 50.

p. 206, l. 19. *Burnt wine*: wine warmed by immersing a hot poker. *OED* cites
Steele, *Tatler* 36: 'I'll lay Ten to Three, I drink Three Pints of burnt Claret
at your Funeral'.

p. 206, l. 20. *mortality-Rings*: rings with the figure of a skull, worn in memory
of one dead; death's-head rings. Cf. p. 225, l. 1.

p. 206, l. 29. *Legall Interest*: currently limited by statute 12 Car. II, c. 13,
to a maximum of 6 per cent. See Blackstone, *Commentaries*, II. xxx. 463.

p. 207, l. 16. *as Mahomet was.* '[Mahomet] was made over-seer of the businesse
of *Abdalmutalif* his Master, or (as some say) his Grand-father: and traded for
him in Soria, Egypt, and Persia, and after his death, inherited his goods'
(Purchas, *Pilgrimage*, III. III. i. 241).

p. 207, ll. 26–7. *Customes that are made, etc.* According to Blackstone, *Commentaries*, Introduction, iii. 67, 'the goodness of a custom depends upon it's
having been used time out of mind; or, in the solemnity of our legal phrase,
time whereof the memory of man runneth not to the contrary. This it is

that gives it it's weight and authority; and of this nature are the maxims and customs which compose the common law, or *lex non scripta*, of this kingdom.'

p. 209, l. 34. *Artificiall*: systematic, logically contrived.

p. 210, ll. 14–20. *Renegades are always, etc.* Sir Henry Blount 'generally . . . found them Atheists, who left our cause for the *Turkish* as the more thriving in the Wor[l]d, and fuller of preferment: these hate us not otherwise than in shew, unlesse where they finde themselves abhorred for their Apostacy; then take heed, for in your ruine they get both revenge, and reputation of zeale' (*Voyage into the Levant*, p. 112). Cf. Marvell, *Rehearsal Transpros'd*, i. 42.

p. 210, l. 23. *Agnition*: 'recognition, acknowledgement' (*OED*). *Sir T N* cannot be identified; possibly the royalist Sir Thomas Nott, mentioned p. 245, l. 26. Butler may refer to Nott's Civil War dealings with Parliamentary committees (see *DNB*) or to his expulsion from the Royal Society in 1675 for non-payment of his subscription.

p. 211, ll. 25–6. *Boyling a kid, etc.* Exod. xxiii. 19; xxxiv. 26; Deut. xiv. 21.

p. 211, l. 26. *Muzzling the Ox, etc.* Deut. xxv. 4; 1 Cor. ix. 9; 1 Tim. v. 18.

p. 211, ll. 28–9. *the Divine Nature, that is, etc.* Jas. iii. 17; Exod. xxxiv. 6.

p. 212, ll. 3–4. *the Husband and wife are one Flesh*. Gen. ii. 24.

p. 212, ll. 5–6. *condemnd to keep hogs*. Luke xv. 15. Cf. vv. 13, 30 ('devoured thy living with harlots').

p. 213, l. 4. *upon the Place*: 'on the spot' (*OED*).

p. 213, l. 17. *Restringences*: retentions (produced by the astringency of cold).

p. 214, ll. 1–2. *Socrates was wont, etc.* See Plato, *Symposium*, 220c–d (cf. §§ 174e–175d); Aulus Gellius, II. i. 1–3; Diogenes Laertius, ii. 23.

p. 214, ll. 2–3. *some Indian Fanatiques, etc.* 'Within the Temple [at Ahmedabàd] continually stand many naked *Gioghi* . . . There is, no doubt, but these are the ancient Gymnosophists . . . who then went naked, and exercis'd great patience in sufferings' (Pietro della Valle, *Travels into East India and Arabia Deserta*, trans. George Havers, 1665, I. xv. 52). See further ibid. I. xv. 52–3; I. xvii. 55–6.

p. 214, l. 5. *God made Man in his own Image*. Gen. i. 27.

p. 214, l. 27. *Disaffected*: a term applied by Puritans to those not sympathizing with their cause. See *Hudibras*, III. ii. 553.

p. 214, ll. 28–9. *the Naturall Priviledg of wormes, etc.* A reference to the proverb 'Tread on a worm and it will turn' (*ODEP* 837; Tilley, W909).

p. 215, l. 1. *all extreames use to meet*. Proverbial (*ODEP* 235).

p. 215, ll. 6–8. *the Antient Greek Philosophers, etc.* Butler may have in mind the Greek συμπόσιον, nominally a drinking-party, first used as a setting in works, so titled, by Plato and Xenophon; later used by Plutarch and Athenaeus. German skill in mechanical arts was proverbial (*ODEP* 300; Tilley, G88); so was German drinking (Tilley, G86; Burton, *Anatomy of Melancholy*, I. II. ii. 2, III. III. i. 2).

p. 215, l. 12. *the Bishop of Munster*: Christoph Bernhard von Galen (1606–78). He engaged in numerous wars, latterly against the Turks (1664), against the Dutch (1665–6 and 1672–4), and against the Swedes (1675–8). His making peace with the Dutch in April 1666 was considered a betrayal by his English allies. See Dryden, *Annus Mirabilis*, ll. 145–8.

p. 215, ll. 18–20. *The Prince of Conde, etc.* Louis de Bourbon, Prince of Condé (1530–69), fought in Piedmont, at Metz, and at St. Quentin; then, with Coligny, he led the Huguenots in the first three religious wars, and was killed at the battle of Jarnac. 'On tenoit ce Prince de son temps plus ambitieux que religieux; car le bon Prince estoit bien aussi mondain qu'un autre, & aymoit autant la femme d'autruy que la sienne, tenant fort du naturel de ceux de la race de Bourbon, qui ont esté fort d'amoureuse complexion' (Brantôme, *Memoires, Contenans les Vies des Hommes Illustres*, 4 vols., Leyden, 1666, iii. 211).

p. 216, l. 2. *the Laws against vagabonds*. These date from the 'Act for Punishment of Rogues, Vagabonds, and sturdy Beggars' (39 Eliz. c. 4), in which all earlier legislation was repealed. Offenders were to be whipped, then escorted to the parish of their birth. See further Acts of 43 Eliz.; 1 and 7 Jac. I; 14 and 19 Car. II. (See further note to p. 106, l. 15.)

p. 216, l. 3. *Scandalum Magnatum*: 'the utterance or publication of a malicious report against any person holding a position of dignity' (*OED*).

p. 216, l. 11. *the* ——: the king of England, Charles II.

p. 217, l. 13. *Drinke of this Cup*. 1 Cor. xi. 28. Cf. Matt. xx. 22–3; xxvi. 27.

p. 217, ll. 23–4. *the Devill has his Chappell, etc.* Cf. the proverb 'Where God has his church, the devil will have his chapel' (*ODEP* 309; Tilley, G259).

p. 217, ll. 23–4. *Metropolitan*: metropolis, chief centre.

p. 217, ll. 24–5. *those very Oracles, etc.* See note to p. 146, l. 28.

p. 217, ll. 26–7. *Sandwitch was burnt, etc.* The body of Edward Mountagu, Earl of Sandwich, was recovered from the sea after the battle of Solebay, 28 May 1672, in which his ship the *Royal James* had been burnt. See Evelyn, *Diary*, 31 May 1672; iii. 616. In 1656 Mountagu had shared Blake's command when the Spanish West Indian treasure fleet was intercepted at Cadiz (in fact by a squadron under Captain Richard Stayner). The Marquis de Baydes, governor of Peru, was travelling with his family in the vice-admiral, which was fired. 'In the fire the marquesse's lady, and one of his daughters fell downe in a swownd, and were burned. The marquesse himself had opportunitye to have escaped, but seinge his lady and his daughter, whom he loved exceedingly, in that case, said he would die where they died, and embracinge his lady, was burned also with them' (letter from Mountagu, in *State Papers of John Thurloe*, ed. Birch, 1742, v. 433). See also ibid. v. 399; Clarendon, *History*, xv. 26; Waller, 'Of a War with Spain, and a Fight at Sea', ll. 75–88.

p. 217, ll. 27–9. *So Cromwels and Bradshaws Heads, etc.* On 30 January 1661 the remains of Cromwell, Bradshaw, and Ireton were removed to Tyburn. There 'they were pull'd out of their Coffines and hang'd at the several angles of that Triple Tree, where they hung till the Sun was set; after which they were taken down, their heads cut off, and their loathsome Trunks thrown into a deep hole under the Gallows' (*Mercurius Publicus*, 1661, iv. 64). 'The Heads . . . are set upon Poles on the top of *Westminster-hall* by the common Hangman: *Bradshaw* is placed in the middle, (over that part where that monstrous High Court of Justice sate,) *Cromwell* and his Son in Law *Ireton* on both sides of *Bradshaw*' (ibid. v. 80).

p. 218, l. 5. *Self-preservation.* See note to p. 160, ll. 31–2.

p. 218, ll. 12–13. *which he take's up of himself*: i.e. as beneficiary of his own self-love.

p. 218, l. 35. *to blinde*: i.e. with blinkers attached to the bridle.

p. 219, l. 17. *Ingineres*: plotters, schemers.

p. 219, l. 35. *give aime to*: make a target for.

p. 220, ll. 8–9. *take place of*: 'take precedence of; go before' (*OED*).

p. 220, l. 9. *Dependences*: dependants.

p. 220, l. 16. *a worme in his Tongue.* 'There is a certaine little worme in doggs tongues, called by a Greeke name Lytta, which if it be taken out when they be young whelps, they will never after proove mad' (Pliny, *Nat. Hist.* XXIX. xxxii. 100, trans. Holland, ii. 363).

p. 220, l. 18. *set*: wager.

p. 220, l. 22. *Pudding*: jack pudding, attendant buffoon.

p. 221, ll. 19–20. *Loosers, etc.* Proverbial (*ODEP* 485–6; Tilley, L458).

p. 221, l. 23. *Hackney-coach.* 'Hackney' was in fact a slang term for a prostitute. Cf. *Hudibras*, III. i. 892.

p. 222, l. 11. *Vesinanza, etc.* Cf. Boccaccio, *Decameron*, i, Introd., par. 49: 'Tutte l'una all'altra, o per amistà, o per vicinanza, o per parentado, congiunte.'

p. 222, l. 13. *Jocorum Mascarum, etc.* Royal patents conferred 'officium Magistri iocorum revelorum et mascorum omnium et singulorum nostrorum vulgariter revelles and Maskes' (*Documents relating to the Office of the Revels in the Time of Queen Elizabeth*, ed. A. Feuillerat, Louvain, 1908, p. 53, and *passim*).

p. 222, ll. 15–16. *Il prioit, etc.* '[It was reported] que ses prieres sentoyent plus l'homme de guerre que le Chrestien, plus un grand Capitaine qu'un bon Religieux, Il prioit en commandant & commandoit en priant' (de Serres, *Histoire*, ii. 999). Charles de Gontaut, Duke of Biron, who had fought with distinction against the League, intrigued with Spain and Savoy, and suffered death for treason in 1602.

p. 222, l. 26. *a Witches feast that never satisfies*: i.e. 'where nothing feeds but only the Imagination' ('The Luxurious', *GR* ii. 357). In antiquity the magician Pases 'incantamentis quibusdam efficiebat, ut repente convivium omnibus instructum partibus adesse videretur: rursum ubi libuisset, omnia protinus evanescebant' (Erasmus, *Adagia*, II. VII. xxxi). See Suidas, s.v. Πάσης; also Bodin, *Demonomanie des Sorciers*, Paris, 1580, II. iv. 85ᵛ, for a similar description of the feasts of a recent Count of Aspremont.

p. 223, l. 27. *Pagod.* See p. 230, l. 31–p. 231, l. 1, and note.

p. 224, l. 2. *the Soule of the World.* '*The Spirit of Nature* [or Universal Soule of the World] . . . is, *A substance incorporeal, but without Sense and Animadversion, pervading the whole Matter of the Universe, and exercising a plastical power therein according to the sundry predispositions and occasions in the parts it works upon, raising such Phænomena in the World, by directing the parts of the Matter and their Motion, as cannot be resolved into meer Mechanical powers*' (Henry More, *Immortality of the Soul*, 1659, III. xii. 1).

p. 224, ll. 4–5. *all in all, and all in every part.* A common scholastic formula: 'anima est tota in toto, et tota in qualibet parte' (Milton, *De Doctrina Christiana*, in *Works*, New York, 1931–40, xv. 46). For further citations see Arnold Williams, 'A Note on *Samson Agonistes*, ll. 90–94', *MLN lxiii* (1948), 537.

p. 224, ll. 6–7. *Our Lady of Loretto, etc.* Loretto, near Ancona, is described in Heylin, *Cosmography*, p. 97: 'The Church here being admirably rich, and frequented by Pilgrims from all parts to pay their devotions to our Lady of *Loretto*, and behold her Miracles. Concerning the removal of whose Chamber hither, in our description of *Palestine* [p. 722], you shall meet with a very proper Legend.'

p. 224, l. 17. *as Conjurors doe Spirits.* According to Agrippa, *Occult Philosophy*, III. xxiv. 414–15, the names of spirits 'obtain efficacy and vertue to draw any spirituall substance from above or beneath, for to make any desired effect'. Agrippa discusses at length the calculation and use of spiritual names or 'characters' (ibid. III. xxiv–xxxiii). Perhaps more pertinent is the process whereby a conjuror, having raised a spirit, can 'bind and tye him with the bond of obligation . . . that he will attend him constantly at his thrice repeating [his name]' (Additions to Scot, *Discovery of Witchcraft*, 1665, XV. viii. 226).

p. 224, l. 21. *Villanies*: villeins—who 'could not leave their lord without his permission; but, if they ran away, or were purloined from him, might be claimed and recovered by action, like beasts or other chattels. . . . A villein could acquire no property either in lands or goods; but, if he purchased either, the lord might enter upon them, oust the villein, and seise them to his own use' (Blackstone, *Commentaries*, II. vi. 93).

p. 224, ll. 26–7. *grow's as longe as he live's*. 'Now a Crocodile . . . layeth an Egge no greater then a Gooses Egge, and from so small a beginning ariseth this monstrous Serpent, growing all his life long, unto the length of fifteen or twenty cubits' (Topsell, *History of Four-footed Beasts and Serpents*, p. 683).

p. 225, l. 1. *Burnt Wine Deaths-head-Rings*. See p. 206, ll. 19–20, and notes.

p. 225, ll. 1–2. *Tristitiæ Imitamenta*. Tacitus, *Annales*, III. v; XIII. iv.

p. 225, ll. 9–14. *Though Lawyers, etc.* Cf. p. 237, ll. 5–8.

p. 225, l. 14. *John a Nokes, and John a Stiles*. 'Fictitious names for parties in legal actions' (*OED*).

         Chiauses: gulls, dupes.

p. 225, ll. 15–17. *A Wel[sh] Farme, etc.* 'He hires the public money, as they do farms in *Wales*, for half the profits, pays the one moiety to the collectors and receivers, and keeps the other himself' ('A Banker', *T* 83ʳ).

p. 225, ll. 19–20. *a Crocodile, etc.* 'The tail of a Crocodile is his strongest part, and they never kill any beast or man, but first of all they strike him down and astonish him with their tails' (Topsell, *History of Four-footed Beasts and Serpents*, p. 685).

p. 225, l. 21. *an Elke, etc.* '[The elk's] upper lip is so great, and hangeth over the neather so far, that he cannot eat going forward, because it doubleth under his mouth, but as he eateth he goeth backward like a Sea-crab, and so gathereth up the grass that lay under his feet' (ibid., p. 167). Cf. Pliny, *Nat. Hist.* VIII. xvi. 39.

p. 225, l. 22. *present*: give presents to.

p. 225, l. 23. *Sangriá*: a present made to one who bleeds.

p. 225, ll. 26–7. *as the Gaul did, etc.* When Rome was occupied by Brennus' Gauls in 390 B.C., and a ransom—'a thousand pound weight of gold'— had been agreed on, 'the Gaules brought forth false weights and uneven ballance. And when the Tribune refused them, behold, the insolent and prowd Gaule would needs have his sword weighed too for vantage' (Livy, v. xlviii. 8, trans. Holland, p. 211).

p. 226, l. 8. *slurring*: sliding the die out of the box without turning it.

p. 226, l. 11. *like Spanish Swords*. The Spaniards retained the old long rapier throughout the seventeenth century, whereas in England there was a transition to the short sword and swords carried therefore varied in length. See Egerton Castle, *Schools and Masters of Fence*, 1892, pp. 242–7, 317–19, 334–5.

p. 226, l. 14. *Act of Oblivion*. This enacted, 12 Car. II, c. 11, s. 48, that 'any manors, lands, tenements or hereditaments, not being the land or hereditaments of the late King, Queen, Prince or of any of the archbishops, bishops, deans, deans and chapters, nor being lands and hereditaments sold or given for the delinquency or pretended delinquency of any person . . . shall be held and enjoyed by the purchasers'.

p. 226, l. 15. *Tis fair play*, etc. See note to p. 190, ll. 8–10.

p. 226, ll. 16–19. *the Lapland witches, etc.* It was popularly believed that witches could 'saile in an egge shell, a cockle or muscle shell, through and under tempestuous seas' (Reginald Scot, *Discoverie of Witchcraft*, 1584, I. iv. 10); also that 'the Sorcerers neare the North sea use to sell the winde to saylers in glasses' (Sir John Harrington, notes to Ariosto, *Orlando Furioso*, xxxviii, ed. R. McNulty, Oxford, 1972, p. 447). The Royal Society 'Inquiries' to be sent to Iceland in 1662 include: 'Whether it be true, that they sell winds, or converse with spirits, or often see them?' (Birch, *History*, i. 166). According to Glanvill, *Philosophical Considerations about Witchcraft*, xviii. 90, ''tis confidently reported by sober intelligent men that have visited those places, that most of the *Laplanders*, and some other *Northern* people are *Witches*.' John Scheffer, *History of Lapland*, Oxford, 1674, xi. 58, discusses the Laplanders' supposed control of winds.

p. 226, ll. 23–4. *For as the sturdy youth, etc.* Probably a reference to the wrestling, for which sport in particular Lincoln's Inn Fields were well known. See H. B. Wheatley, *London Past and Present*, 3 vols., 1891, ii. 394.

p. 226, ll. 25–6. *a whole week, etc.* Cf. Terence, *Eunuchus*, 223–4: 'hui univorsum triduom'.

p. 226, l. 27. *He had issue, etc.* Oedipus, to whose situation this would apply, is usually said to have had four children by Iocasta.

p. 227, ll. 1–7. *The Hobbists, etc.* Hobbes argues that the only alternative to political submission is a primal anarchy in which there can be no security whatever because all men are equal in ability to destroy one another (*Leviathan*, I. xiii, II. xvii). The rights of a prince cannot be extinguished but, in cases where he lacks power of enforcement, the obligations of subjects may be; the commonwealth being in effect dissolved, men are at liberty to seek other protection (ibid. II. xxix. 174). If they submit to one who already has the power, that is 'sovereignty by acquisition'; if they contract to establish a ruler, and covenant their rights to him, that is 'sovereignty by institution' (ibid. II. xvii. 88). This contract is invalid as soon as made inasmuch as by transferring all rights to him they cease to be a party. It is further imaginary in that Hobbes did not regard a multitude as a legal entity; individuals can agree among themselves to cede rights to a ruler, but only in him, when he assumes power, do they become a corporate body (ibid. II. xviii; *De Cive*, v–vi).

p. 227, ll. 15–17. *Heroique Poets, etc.* Cf. p. 13, ll. 18–34.

p. 227, ll. 18–24. *Strada in the Proem of his Decads, etc.*

And indeed, since there is such weight in the truth of History, from which nothing takes off more then affection in the writer; whence should we rather fear the faith of a relation, from one that is a party and hardly dispenses with love and hatred? or from one that centred in the middle, and professing holiness of life, either untouched with any factious desires, or above them; and either keeps at distance the occasions of a lie, or beats it from him? That I may speak something of my self, I hold not the subject of this Warre inconsistant with my course of life, Religion being the cause of both; nor do I conceive my self unfit either to report the matter of fact, or to find out the causes (Strada, *De Bello Belgico*, i. 2).

p. 227, l. 25–p. 228, l. 3. *Philosophers, etc.* Browne, *Religio Medici*, i. 21, declines to dispute 'whether the world was created in autumn, summer or spring, because it was created in them all; for whatsoever sign the sun possesseth, those four seasons are actually existent'. Browne's proof of this, *Pseudodoxia*, VI. ii, depends on the various heights of the sun at various latitudes, an absolute comparison of which could suggest that one part of the globe is always on the same plane as the 'æquinox line' or celestial equator.

p. 228, ll. 4–6. *Aristotelians say, etc.* 'Nec tamen sequitur, si in materia est potentia passiva tantum, quod non sit generatio naturalis: quia materia coadiuvat ad generationem, non agendo, sed inquantum est habilis ad recipiendum talem actionem, quae etiam habilitas appetitus materiae dicitur et inchoatio formae' (Aquinas, *Scriptum super Sententias*, II. XVIII. i. 2c). Cf. Aristotle, *De Generatione et Corruptione*, 324^{b}18–19; Cardan, *De Subtilitate*, i, in *Opera*, iii. 358^b–359^b; Scaliger, *De Subtilitate*, lxi. 1. See also note to p. 87, ll. 14–15.

p. 228, l. 7. *Solomon calls a whore, etc.* Prov. ii. 16; v. 3, 20, etc.

p. 228, l. 8. *having soe many, etc.* See p. 107, ll. 24–9, and note.

p. 228, ll. 18–19. *Aristotle undertake's, etc.* Aristotle's analysis, *De Caelo*, i. 10–12, establishes 'that the heaven as a whole neither came into being nor admits of destruction, as some assert, but is one and eternal, with no end or beginning of its total duration, containing and embracing in itself the infinity of time' (ibid. ii. 1, 283^{b}26–30).

p. 228, l. 20. *Materia prima.* 'Our own doctrine is that although there is a matter of the perceptible bodies (a matter out of which the so-called "elements" come-to-be), it has no separate existence, but is always bound up with a contrariety. . . . We must reckon as an "originative source" and as "primary" the matter which underlies, though it is inseparable from, the contrary qualities' (*De Generatione et Corruptione*, 329^{a}29–31). Cf. *Physica*, I. vi–ix.

p. 228, ll. 20–2. *Democritus and Epicurus, etc.* See Diogenes Laertius, ix. 44, x. 43–5; Lucretius, v. 416–31.

p. 228, l. 22. *Principles*: sources, those things from which it originates (viz. atoms moving in the void).

p. 228, l. 23. *Plato banishd Poets, etc. Republic*, 398a–b, 607e–608b.

p. 228, l. 24. *Poetical*: fabulous, fictional, ideal.

p. 229, ll. 1–2. *The Stoiques, etc.* '[The Stoics] say, That a wise man always keeps himself in a sedate and quiet Temper, free from Passion' (Diogenes Laertius, *Zeno*, vii. 117, trans. R. M., in *Lives of Philosophers*, i. 533). Cf. ibid. vii. 110.

p. 229, ll. 3–4. *That hundreds, etc.* Zeno, going to the Stoa or Portico at Athens, and 'designing it a Place of Peace and Quiet, that had been a Place of Sedition; he there began to teach his Philosophy, and read upon several Subjects. For in that Place, during the Government of the Thirty Tyrants, no less than fourteen hundred of the *Athenians* had been put to Death' (ibid. vii. 5, trans. in *Lives*, i. 466). Butler is misinterpreting a Latin version which he quotes in his note to *Hudibras*, II. ii. 15: '*In Porticu (Stoicorum Scholâ Athenis) Discipulorum seditionibus, mille Quadringenti triginta Cives interfecti sunt.*' Cf. 'An Hermetic Philosopher', par. 6; *GR* ii. 241–2.

p. 229, ll. 10–14. *Lucretius, etc.* The invocation, which makes this request for peace (i. 29–43), is shortly followed by an attack on religion (i. 62–126). Cf. ibid. v. 165–9; ed. cit., p. 116:

> quid enim immortalibus, atque beatis
> Gratia nostra queat largirier emolumenti,
> Ut nostra quicquam causa gerere adgrediantur?
> Quidve novi potuit tanto post ante quietos
> Inlicere, ut cuperent vitam mutare priorem?

p. 230, ll. 11–12. *The Rabbins interpret, etc.* '[With respect to Gen. ix. 24, Rab and Samuel differ,] one maintaining that he castrated him, whilst the other says that he sexually abused him. He who maintains that he castrated him, [reasons thus:] Since he cursed him by his fourth son, he must have injured him with respect to a fourth son' (*Babylonian Talmud, Sanhedrin*, viii. 70ᵃ, trans. H. Freedman, 1935, p. 469).

p. 230, ll. 28–30. *devote themselves, in their Armies, etc.* '[The] Voluntiers or Adventurers, called by the Turks *Gionullu*, . . . are often very hardy, and ready to attempt the most desperate Exploits, moved by a desire of the reward, and by the perswasion, that at worst dying in a War against Christians, they become Martyrs for the Mahometan Faith' (Rycaut, *Present State of the Ottoman Empire*, III. iv. 181).

p. 230, ll. 30–1. *to put out their eies, etc.* See Purchas, *Pilgrimes*, II. IX. ix. 1503, on the Prophet's tomb at Medina: 'The *Mosleman* Pilgrimes . . . throng hither, and with great Veneration kisse and embrace the grates (for none have accesse to the Urne of stone) and many for love of this place leave their Countrey, yea, some madly put out their eyes to see no worldly thing after, and there spend the rest of their dayes.'

p. 230, l. 31–p. 231, l. 1. *the Indians, etc.* 'In the Kingdome of *Narsinga*, or the Coast called *Choramandel*, there standeth a *Pagode*, that is . . . drawne forth, with great Devotions and Processions: there are some of them, that of great zeale and pure devotion doe cut peeces of flesh out of their bodies, and throw them downe before the *Pagode*: others lay themselves under the wheeles of the Cart, and let the Cart runne over them, whereby they are all crushed to peeces, and pressed to death, and they that thus die, are accounted for holy and devout Martyrs' (ibid. II. X. viii. xliv. 1769).

p. 231, ll. 3–4. *the Jewish Idolaters, etc.* 1 Kgs. xviii. 28; Lev. xviii. 21; 2 Kgs. xxiii. 10.

p. 231, ll. 19–25. *There are many, etc.* Cf. p. 148, ll. 23–32.

p. 231, ll. 29–30. *Noah had, etc.* Gen. ix. 20–1.

p. 232, ll. 1–2. *Rei Militaris, etc. Pro Murena*, ix. 22.

p. 232, l. 2. *Cedant Arma Togæ. De Consulatu Suo*, in *De Officiis*, I. xxii. 77.

p. 232, l. 20. *according to the Church of Rome.* See p. 49, l. 29–p. 50, l. 3, and note.

p. 232, l. 25. *convenient*: due, requisite.

p. 233, l. 12. *in a right nick*: at a critical juncture (cf. *ODEP* 565; Tilley, N160).

p. 234, ll. 14–15. *A burnd Child, etc.* See *ODEP* 92; Tilley, C297.

p. 234, l. 22. *Prester-Jone*: the Emperor of Ethiopia. It was reported that the Emperor 'shewed his face but once in the yeere, having at other times his face covered for greater state, and therefore also spake to none, but by an Interpreter' (Purchas, *Pilgrimage*, VII. iv. 742). Cf. Herbert, *Travels*, p. 228.

p. 234, ll. 26–30. *Those that perjure, etc.* Cf. p. 27, l. 32–p. 28, l. 2.

p. 235, ll. 8–12. *Persius, etc.* For Persius' attack on abuse of language see *Satires,* i. Cf. p. 125, ll. 30–3, and note.

p. 235, ll. 14–15. *if Ephæstion, etc.* See note to p. 21, ll. 25–7.

p. 235, ll. 23–6. *The Subtletys of the Stoiques, etc.* 'It is the opinion of our sect, that that which is good is a bodie, because that which is good acteth. . . . They say that wisedome is good, it followeth then of necessitie that it is corporall. But they thinke that to be wise is not of the same condition. It is a thing incorporall, and accidentall unto wisedome, and therefore it cannot produce any action, neyther profite any wayes' (Seneca, *Epistulae Morales,* cxvii. 2–3, in *Works,* pp. 467–8). Ep. cxiii deals with the question 'so much canvassed amongst Stoicks, whether justice, fortitude, prudence, and the rest of the vertues are living creatures' (sec. 1; p. 454). A virtue is defined as the soul (an animal) in a certain attitude.

p. 236, ll. 11–19. *They that tell us, etc.* Cf. p. 6, ll. 7–12.

p. 236, l. 15. *perspective.* See note to p. 126, l. 21,

p. 237, ll. 5–8. *The Common-wealth of Lawyers, etc.* Cf. p. 225, ll. 9–14.

p. 237, l. 9. *Civity:* (perhaps a scribal error for) civility. This sense is not in *OED.*

p. 237, ll. 12–13. *some Philosophers, etc.* Lucretius, who denies the immaterial and makes the soul substance, acknowledges vacuum (*De Rerum Natura,* iii. 94–135, i. 329–417). Plato, who acknowledges the immaterial and ideal, denies vacuum (*Timaeus,* 80c).

p. 237, ll. 14–16. *The opac body, etc.* Cf. p. 87, ll. 1–4, and note.

p. 237, ll. 19–20. *as O Cromwel, etc.* On 29 September 1654 Cromwell drove his coach in Hyde Park, 'but at last provoking the horses too much with the whip, they grew unruly, and run so fast, that the postillion could not hold them in; whereby his highness was flung out of the coach-box upon the pole . . . and afterwards fell upon the ground' (Thurloe, *State Papers,* ii. 652). Cf. Denham, 'A Jolt', in *The Rump: or a Collection of Songs and Ballads,* 1660, pp. 15–18.

p. 237, l. 27. *disposd of:* put in place, made ready.

p. 238, l. 7. *the hand and Pen, etc.* In signs and emblems concerning a hand it was conventional to draw a cloud around the forearm, as it would otherwise look to be severed. It is this convention to which Butler alludes, not to the subject-matter of some particular hand-and-pen emblem. See illustration on p. 320 above.

p. 238, ll. 25–6. *the Trumpets sound, etc.* 1 Cor. xv. 52.

p. 239, ll. 3–4. *the Gallique Orators, etc.* Presumably an allusion to the fates of leaders chosen at councils, most prominently Vercingetorix: '*The next day*

Vercingetorix *having called a Councell, told them, that he had not undertook that warre for his own occasions, but for the cause of a common liberty: and forasmuch as they were necessarily to yield to fortune, he made offer of himself unto them, either to satisfie the* Romans *with his death, or to be delivered unto them alive*' (Caesar, *De Bello Gallico*, vii. 89, in *Commentaries*, trans. Clement Edmonds, 1655, i. 195). Cf. Scipio Dupleix, *Memoires des Gaules*, Paris, 1627, I. ix. 31: 'Leur coustume estoit de venir armés en leurs conseils de guerre: & celuy qui arrivoit le dernier estoit cruellement meurtri en pleine assemblée.'

p. 239, ll. 16–17. *like the eldest son, etc.* See note to p. 197, ll. 13–14.

p. 239, l. 24. *It is sayd, etc.* I have failed to locate the saying; the sentiment is in Livy, IX. i. 10: 'iustum est bellum . . . quibus necessarium, et pia arma, quibus nulla nisi in armis relinquitur spes' (quoted by Grotius, *De Jure Belli et Pacis*, II. xxiv. 7, in an extensive discussion of causes of war).

p. 239, l. 32. *Conversation*: involvement, preoccupation.

p. 240, l. 2. *applications*: approaches, addresses.

p. 240, ll. 14–15. *al things are maintaind, etc.* According to Harvey, *Generation of Living Creatures*, lxxii. 464, 'an *Animal* is *nourished* by the same thing whereof it is made; and augmented by that out of which it is *generated*.'

p. 240, l. 21. *lere*: 'sly, underhand' (*OED*).

p. 240, ll. 30–2. *where a Saint ha's a Fayre, etc.* John Brand records that in ancient times 'upon any extraordinary Solemnity . . . Tradesmen used to bring and sell their Wares, even in the Church-yards, especially upon the Festival of the Dedication; as at Westminster, on St. *Peter*'s Day; at London, on St. Bartholomew' (*Observations on Popular Antiquities*, Newcastle upon Tyne, 1777, Appendix, p. 361). The well-known Westminster fair of Butler's day was St. Edward's, or Magdalen's. Granted to the Abbot of Westminster by Henry III in 1248, it was at first held in St. Margaret's churchyard, and from 1542 up to the nineteenth century in Tothill Fields. Bartholomew Fair, chartered 1133, was finally suppressed in 1855. See Wheatley, *London Past and Present*, i. 110–15, iii. 387; William Addison, *English Fairs and Markets*, 1953, pp. 51, 95.

p. 241, l. 2. *a good Conscience, etc.* Proverbial (*ODEP* 318; Tilley, C605).

p. 241, l. 4. *Dry-money-Cheat*: i.e. involving hard cash.

p. 241, ll. 15–16. *the Asse in the Emblem.* See Geffrey Whitney, *Choice of Emblemes*, Leyden, 1586, p. 48: The ass's being allowed to eat a laboriously made rope can represent 'those, that lewdely doo bestowe / Suche thinges, as shoulde unto good uses goe'.

p. 241, l. 18. *the Drinking Bishop.* Unidentified; but cf. Sir William Temple, *Letters . . . from 1665 to 1672*, [ed. Jonathan Swift], 2 vols., 1700, i. 58–9, on 'the most Episcopal Way of Drinking that could be invented' out of 'a formal Bell . . . that might hold about two Quarts or more', at the Castle of the Bishop of Münster (for whom see note to p. 215, l. 12).

p. 241, l. 23. *the memory of the unjust, etc.* Cf. Prov. x. 7; Matt. v. 45.

p. 242, l. 2. *humiliations*: 'days of prayer and fasting. From time to time, Parliament set aside special days of humiliation, on which the nation was to acknowledge its errors or seek the assistance of God for the accomplishment of His will' (Wilders, note to *Hudibras*, II. iii. 712).

p. 242, ll. 11–16. *the Prodigal child, etc.* Luke xv. 11–24. The initial parallel is with the prodigal son's taking his portion from his father and forsaking him to go into a far country.

p. 242, l. 14. *King Dor.*

Partendosi da Pianfu andando verso Ponente, si truova un grande, & bel castello nominato Thaigin, qual dicesi haver edificato anticamente un Re chiamato Dor. . . . [Un-Khan, called Prester John, had this rebellious vassal brought to his court.] Dove giunto, per ordine di quello, vestito di panni vili, fu posto al governo dell' armento del Signore, per volerlo dispregiare, & abbassare. Et quivi stette in gran miseria per due anni . . . [Then Un-Khan] li perdonò, & fece vestir lo di vestimenti regali, & con honorevole compagnia lo mandò al suo regno. Qual d'indi innanzi fu sempre obediente, & amico ad Umcan. (Marco Polo, *Viaggi*, II. xxxi, in Gian Battista Ramusio, *Navigationi et Viaggi*, 3 vols., Venice, 1563–1606, ii. 32–3.)

p. 242, l. 19. *Cunning-men*: 'wise men', wizards. Cf. *Hudibras*, II. iii. 106.

p. 243, l. 14. *Deare Sister*: more likely the sister of Butler's wife, through whom the request had been made and whom Butler refers to as 'your Sister' (p. 244, l. 9). The tone of the letter too would be more suited to a sister-in-law. Of Butler's wife and her family there is no certain knowledge. Butler himself had four sisters (b. 1602, 1605, 1610, and 1621), and if the letter is in fact to one of them, the youngest, Margaret, would be most likely to have this son of grammar-school age in the latter part of the century.

p. 244, l. 9. *to her Power*: as far as she is able.

p. 244, l. 24. *Cark*: trouble, anxiety (usually coupled with 'care').

p. 245, l. 15. *Counter*: the prison attached to the city court of a mayor, 'the name of certain prisons for debtors, etc. in London, Southwark, and some other cities and boroughs' (*OED*).

p. 245, l. 23–p. 246, l. 18. *The Mayd . . . Chambermayd.* The identity of the following may be, at least, conjectured. *Dr Charlton*: much ridiculed for his scientific pretensions and perhaps in these instances for his use of inappropriate words; see p. 160, ll. 16–17, and 'On Dr. Charlton's Feeling a Dog's Pulse', *GR* i. 404–10. *Father More*: Henry More (1586–1661), Jesuit; but no record of the dispute. *Sir T Not*: Sir Thomas Nott; see note to p. 210, l. 23. *The Rats*: in the fable of 'The Mice in Council' (Perry, *Æsopica*, 613). *Payton*: Sir Edward Peyton (1558?–1657), anti-royalist, involved in violent incidents. *The Gamster*: his 'Flat' being his broad and thin false die. *D Givillim*: Butler's variant of 'Guillim' and possibly an error for John Guillim, author of *A Display of Heraldry*, 1610. *Lord Scudamor*: ambassador 1634–9; petitioned his recall after Lady Scudamore had been refused, in May 1638, the *tabouret* or right of being seated on a ceremonial visit to the French queen; his petition negotiated in England, in November 1638, by his secretary *Sir Richard Browne* (subsequently English resident in France, 1641–57). *Dr Gerrard*: Peter Gerrard, M.D. (Oxon.) 1669, admitted College of Physicians 1671; but no publications. *Scarbrow*: Sir Charles Scarborough, F.R.S., physician to Charles II, author of *Syllabus Musculorum*, 1676. *Mr Peck*: possibly Thomas Pecke (*fl.* 1664), verse writer. *Dr Glisson*: see p. 143, ll. 9–11, and note. *Pagan Fisher*: Payne (or, in his Latin, 'Paganus') Fisher, poet-laureate to Cromwell, author of *Threnodia Triumphalis in Obitum Olivari Protectoris*, 1658 (trans. 1659). *Dr Dorchester*: Henry, Marquis of Dorchester, F.R.S., a close student of physic and anatomy, elected Fellow of the College of Physicians 1658 (ridiculed in the pamphlet *Lord Roos His Answer to the Marquesse of Dorchester's Letter* [1660], attributed to Butler by Aubrey and Ashmole). *W. Egerton*: possibly Sir William Egerton, K.B., son of Earl of Bridgewater. *Busby*: Richard Busby, headmaster of Westminster School 1638–95. *B Blandford*: B[ishop] Walter Blandford (1619–75), bishop of Worcester; 'wops' (? blows) uncertain. *Squint Ferran*: Captain Ferrers, attended Sandwich on his embassy to Spain (1666–8); on their travelling see F. R. Harris, *Life of Edward Montagu*, 1912, ii. 52–6, 126–7, 142–3, 152–3. *Sir P witche*: Sir Peter Wyche, jun. (1628–99?), F.R.S., traveller and translator, or possibly Sir Peter Wyche, sen. (d. 1643), ambassador to the Porte. *Sir James Bag*: Sir James Bagge, of Plymouth, knighted 1625, creature of Buckingham's and enemy of Sir John Eliot.

p. 247, l. 1. *Fides Nominum, etc.* Tertullian, *De Carne Christi*, xiii. 11 (slightly misquoted).

p. 247, l. 3. *as Spencer*. See *Faerie Queene*, VI. ii. 5 ('aglets'), II. iii. 26 ('aygulets').

p. 247, ll. 5–6. *Garde chaud, etc.* Proverbial. Cf. Montaigne, *Essayes*, II. xii. 271 ('Tenez chauds les pieds et la teste, / Au demeurant vivez en beste'), and Jan Gruter, *Florilegium Ethico-Politico*, Frankfurt, 1610, ii. 220 ('Le pied sec, chaut la teste; au reste, vivez en beste').

p. 247, ll. 7–8. *Gulae substructa, etc.* 'Prior venter, et statim cetera saginae substructa lascivia est; per edacitatem salacitas transit' (Tertullian, *De Ieiunio*, i. 2.).

p. 247, ll. 11–15. 4 *throws of Rome.* 'Iactus quisque apud lusores veteres a numero vocabatur, ut unio, trinio [*or* ternio], quaternio, senio. Postea appellatio singulorum mutata est, et unionem canem [*or* canicula], trionem suppum, quaternionem planum vocabant' (Isidorus, *Origines*, XVIII. lxv)

The highest throw, Venus, was when each of the dice showed a different number. See further Oystein Ore, *Cardano the Gambling Scholar*, Princeton, 1953, pp. 168–9, 232–40.

p. 247, l. 14. *damnosa canicula*. Persius, *Satires*, iii. 48.

p. 248, l. 9–10. *mettle upon mettle*. Proverbial: 'metal upon metal is false heraldry' (*ODEP* 529; Tilley, M906).

p. 248, l. 20. *Souse markée*: 'Sou marqué, ancienne pièce de cuivre valant quinze derniers' (Littré, *Dictionnaire*).

p. 248, l. 31. *Raucàque Garrulitas, etc.* Ovid, *Metamorphoses*, v. 678 ('Nunc quoque in altibus facundia prisca remansit / raucaque . . .').

p. 249, l. 12–13. *Presbiterian Hugonots*. See p. 162, l. 3, and note. Butler refers to Presbyterian witch-hunting in *Hudibras*, II. iii. 139–44, and footnote.

p. 249, l. 33. *a most Stately Triumphall Arch*. 'The arch was unquestionably the Arc de Triomphe du Trône set up in the Faubourg S. Antoine to celebrate the victories of Louis XIV in Flanders and la Franche-Comté in 1666–1667. Designed by Claude Perrault, it was partially erected between 1668 and 1680 when construction finally stopped altogether; very little work, however, was done after 1670' (Norma E. Bentley, '*Hudibras* Butler Abroad', *MLN* lx. 255). 'The *Triumphal Arch* out of the Gate of *St. Antoine* is well worth seeing; for in this the *French* pretend not only to have imitated the Ancients, but to have out-done them. They have indeed, used the greatest Blocks of Stone that could be got, and have laid them without Mortar, and the least side outward, after the manner of the Ancients; but I am afraid their Materials are very short of the *Roman*, and their Stone is ill chose, though vastly great. Indeed the *Design* is most Magnificent; it is finisht in *Plaister*, that is, the *Model* of it, in its full Beauty and Proportions' (Martin Lister, *Journey to Paris*, 1699, p. 54). Cf. John Northleigh, *Topographical Descriptions*, 1702, ii. 62–3; [Germain Brice], *New Description of Paris*, trans. [James Wright], 1687, i. 128–9.

p. 249, l. 38. *as Titus &c.* The Arch of Titus was erected 'in honour of Titus and in commemoration of the siege of Jerusalem *in summa Sacra via* . . . but not finished and dedicated until after his death' (S. B. Platner, *Topographical Dictionary of Ancient Rome*, 1929, p. 45). Other famous arches were those of Constantine (A.D. 312; victory over Maxentius) and Septimius Severus (A.D. 203; the Parthian victories).

p. 249, l. 38–p. 250, l. 1. *decreed (like triumphs), etc.* 'Concerning the rewards which were bestowed in war, some were by the *Senate* conferred upon the L. Generall . . . [As last of these] they honoured him at his comming home also with a Triumph. . . . Moreover for a perpetuall memory of this their triumph in some publique place certaine trophies were erected. . . . Sometimes there were statues, columns, and arches built in token of triumph.

These arches . . . were known by the name of *Arcus triumphales*' (Thomas Godwin, *Romanæ Historiæ Anthologia*, Oxford, 1614, IV. vi. 190–1).

p. 250, l. 7. *pretends*: intends, plans.

p. 250, l. 8. *their Old tragedies of Rebellion*. Most recently of the Fronde: the First Fronde (of the Parlement) in 1648–9, the Second Fronde (of the Princes) in 1649–53.

p. 250, ll. 11–12. *a magnificent fabrick upon a Hill*. 'The Observatory—so it was actually called—was also designed by Perrault. On a site selected by the most prominent astronomers in Paris, the building was begun in 1667 and completed five years later' (Bentley, *MLN* lx. 255–6). Lister visited the completed '*Observatoire Royal*, built on a rising Ground just without the City Walls . . . In all this Building there is neither Iron nor Wood, but all firmly covered with Stone, Vault upon Vault. The Platform a-top is very spacious, and gives a large and fair view of all *Paris*, and the Countrey about it' (*Journey to Paris*, p. 52). Cf. Brice, *New Description of Paris*, ii. 64–7; Northleigh, *Topographical Descriptions*, ii. 51–2.

p. 250, l. 19. *filous*: thieves.

p. 250, l. 32. *house of office*: latrine. Cf. p. 216, ll. 5–9.

p. 251, ll. 5–6. *priviledges of the Gallican Church*. The *libertés de l'Église gallicane* constituted an historical claim to administrative autonomy by both king and bishops. In 1663 the Sorbonne had published a declaration to this effect (reiterated in the Four Gallican Articles of 1682). Louis XIV claimed that right to nominate senior ecclesiastics which derived from the Pragmatic Sanction of Bourges (1438) and the Concordat of Bologna (1516).

p. 251, ll. 8–11. *a Controversy between them whither the fryers, etc.*

Si Clément IX avait pu croire que le roi, en renonçant aux commissaires apostoliques, entendait reconnaître les droits du saint-siège et la liberté des religieux, il fut bientôt tiré de son illusion par un arrêt du Conseil d'État qui, même pour le spirituel, soumettait les réguliers aux évêques français, et ceux-ci à la couronne: c'est le célèbre *arrêt d'Agen*, ainsi nommé parce qu'il fut rendu à l'occasion d'un différend entre l'évêque d'Agen et certains religieux de son diocèse (4 mars 1669). . . . Clément IX ne se laissa pas abuser par ces hypocrites excuses [Louis's claim to act within Gallican rights], et le cardinal Rospigliosi, en ordonnant au nonce de réclamer sans délai la rétractation de l'arrêt, chargea Lionne d'avertir le roi que de pareils attendats n'étaient pas moins périlleux pour l'État que pour la religion . . . Aux plaintes répétées de Clément IX, Louis XIV se contenta de répondre que, 'si Sa Sainteté voulait bien expédier une bulle qui contînt les mêmes réglements portés dans l'arrêt . . ., il la ferait recevoir dans son royaume en l'autorisant de ses lettres patentes (Charles Gérin, *Louis XIV et le Saint-Siège*, 2 vols., Paris, 1894, ii. 379–81).

p. 251, ll. 16–19. *The Lawyers, etc.* Northleigh, *Topographical Descriptions*, ii. 48–9, describes 'their *Palais*, [so called] from its having been antiently the Palace and Residence of their Kings . . . There is in it a great Hall arch'd and vaulted, with the several Chambers of Justice about it . . . Their Parliament opens at a set Day, call'd St. *Martin* [11 November]; when all the

Members of it attend in that great Hall in their scarlet robes . . . They keep a Court of Aids here, a separate Jurisdiction from the Parliament; and also a Chancery for the Tryal of Points of meer Equity. They have here also what they call their Chamber of Accounts, the same with our Court of *Exchequer*.' Northleigh also stresses the number of 'Court Officers and Ministers of Justice, Advocates and Proctors'; the Palais 'is more crowded than our *Westminster Hall*' (ibid. ii. 106).

p. 251, l. 19. *in great state*. 'Amongst the Living Objects to be seen in the Streets of *Paris*, the Counsellors and Chief Officers of the Courts of Justice make a great Figure; They and their Wives have their Trains carried up; so there are abundance to be seen walking about the Streets in this manner' (Lister, *Journey to Paris*, p. 18).

p. 251, l. 24. *All trades sett up among them*. 'This Hall [of the Palais] is all Vaulted with Freestone, with a row of Arches in the middle, supported with great Pillars, round which are several Shops employed by divers Tradesmen' (Brice, *New Description of Paris*, ii. 169–70).

    as they doe with us. 'Besides the Law Courts, a part of Westminster Hall was taken up with the stalls of booksellers, law stationers, sempstresses, and dealers in toys and small wares' (Wheatley, *London Past and Present*, iii. 484).

p. 252, ll. 29–30. *the Basenesse of their money, etc.* Petty, *Treatise of Taxes*, xiv. 6, includes the French 'Soulz' among base moneys 'for the most part consisting [of] great pieces, though of small value'.

p. 254, l. 1–p. 255, l. 7. *The things, etc.* See Martial, *Epigrams*, x. xlvii:

> Vitam quae faciant beatiorem,
> iucundissime Martialis, haec sunt:
> res non parta labore sed relicta;
> non ingratus ager, focus perennis;
> lis numquam, toga rara, mens quieta;
> vires ingenuae . . .
> non tristis torus et tamen pudicus . . . .

p. 254, ll. 1–22 are based on 'Vitam . . . ager' (ll. 17–22 alluding to 'vires ingenuae'); ll. 23–6 are based on 'lis numquam, toga rara'; l. 27–p. 255, l. 3, are based on 'focus perennis'; p. 255, ll. 4–7 may be prompted by 'non tristis torus et tamen pudicus' (ll. 6–7 being used in *Hudibras*, III. ii. 907–8).

p. 254, l. 10. *Paw*: hand.

p. 254, l. 26. *presse*: (1) cupboard; (2) crowded conditions, or (possibly) straits.

p. 254, l. 31. *that burnd*: i.e. with the rest of the city.

> arduus armatos mediis in moenibus adstans
> fundit equus victorque Sinon incendia miscet
> insultans.
>
>   (Virgil, *Aeneid*, ii. 328–30.)

p. 255, l. 5. *Kind*: sexually compliant.

p. 255, ll. 8–15. *Blest in your selfe, etc.* A free translation of Martial, *Epigrams*, IV. lxxv.

p. 255, l. 12. *E[v]adne and Alcestis*. Evadne burned herself on her husband's funeral pyre; Alcestis volunteered to die on behalf of her husband, who had omitted to sacrifice to Artemis at the bridal feast.

p. 255, l. 17. *reformado'd*: of an officer, left without a command, owing to the 'reforming' or disbanding of his company.

p. 255, l. 18. *exauthorized*: deprived of authority.

p. 255, l. 21. *uninterested*: without a personal share or stake in anything.

p. 255, l. 23. *vayld*: humbled, fallen.

p. 255, ll. 27–8. *Ars utinam Mores, etc.* Lines 5–6 of the epigram. Martial's subject is Marcus Antonius Primus.

p. 256, ll. 3–4. *Fallit enim vitium, etc.* Juvenal, *Satires*, xiv. 109–10.

p. 256, ll. 7–10. *Goe hunt, etc.* A parody of Davenant, 'For the Lady, Olivia Porter', ll. 1–4:

> Goe! hunt the whiter Ermine! and present
> His wealthy skin, as this dayes Tribute sent
> To my *Endimion's* Love; Though she be farre
> More gently smooth, more soft then Ermines are!
>
> (*Shorter Poems*, ed. A. M. Gibbs, Oxford, 1972, p. 43.)

p. 256, ll. 11–12. *Some suppose, etc.* The exposition of 'waters' in Genesis i. as watery vapour was congenial to alchemical and hermetic authors. Interpreting Jacob Boehme, *Three Principles* [iv. 19], Thomas Vaughan writes in *Cœlum Terræ*, 'This first something was a certain kind of cloud or darkness, which was condensed into water, and this water is that one thing in which all things were contained'; and in *Aula Lucis* he specifies 'concerning the chaos itself . . . it is not rain-water, nor dew, but it is a subtle mineral moisture' (*Works*, pp. 213, 318). Anaxagoras' primitive humidity may also be relevant; see 'Plutarch' (Aëtius), *De Placitis Philosophorum*, III. xvi. 896–7.

p. 256, l. 19. *the tree of life*. Gen. ii. 9; iii. 22. Cf. Gen. ii. 16.

p. 256, ll. 22–5. *The Dri'd up Nipples, etc.* See *Hudibras*, III. i. 761–70, and Browne, *Pseudodoxia*, III. xvii: 'Plato and some of the Rabbins . . . conceived the first Man an Hermaphrodite; and Marcus [Angelus] Leo the learned Jew, in some sense hath allowed it; affirming that Adam in one *suppositum* without division, contained both Male and Female.' See Plato, *Symposium*, 189e ff.

p. 256, ll. 24–5. *as the Scripture sayes*. Gen. i. 27; v. 2.

p. 257, l. 6. *countervaile*: 'make an equivalent return for' (*OED*).

p. 257, l. 10. *far-fet*: far-fetched.

p. 257, l. 15. *Jura per Anchialum.* Commentators on Martial (*Epigrams*, XI. xciv. 8) offer various interpretations of 'Anchialum': a (supposed) Hebrew deity, Martial's boy, the town Anchiale, etc.

p. 257, l. 18. *the Building of Babell.* Gen. xi. 1–9.

p. 257, ll. 19–22. *as the first, etc.* Cf. p. 97, ll. 7–9, and note.

p. 257, ll. 25–6. *his Labour for his Paines.* Proverbial (*ODEP* 438; Tilley, L1).

p. 259, l. 1. *Seneca sayes.* According to Marcus Seneca, *Controversiae*, i, Preface, 18, 'quorumcumque stilus velox est, tardior memoria est'. This principle is alluded to by Lucius Seneca (*Epistulae Morales*, lxxxviii, *ad fin.*), and explicitly stated in Plato, *Phaedrus*, 275a; Caesar, *De Bello Gallico*, vi. 14; Quintilian, *Institutiones Oratoriae*, XI. ii. 9.

p. 259, l. 11. *Chargeable*: expensive.

p. 260, ll. 12–14. *like Witches, etc.* '[Witches] might try to obtain something personal belonging to their victims—a tooth, nail clippings, hair, or bits of clothing—for use in working evil' (Rossell Hope Robbins, *Encyclopedia of Witchcraft and Demonology*, 1959, pp. 322–3).

p. 260, l. 14. *Hanke*: 'restraining or curbing hold' (*OED*). Cf. Thomas Potts, *Wonderfull Discoverie of Witches*, 1613, sig. P4[r]: '[The witches] had then in hanck a child of *Michael Hartleys* of Colne.'

p. 261, l. 5. *Flourish*: complexion. Cf. Shakespeare, *Sonnets*, lx. 9.

p. 261, l. 21–p. 262, l. 3. *rates his abilities, etc.* Sir William Dugdale, *Origines Juridiciales*, 1666, lxx. 321[a], quotes Judges' Orders of 1630, 'That none be admitted to the Barr, but only such as be at the least of eight years continuance, and hath kept his Exercises within the House, and abroad in *Innes of Chancery*, according to the orders of the House.' For the pertinent orders see ibid. lvii. 159[a] (Inner Temple), lxi. 202[b] (Middle Temple), lxvii. 288[b] (Gray's Inn). To retain his inn-chamber a Middle Temple student had to be in commons—i.e. eat at the common table—for six weeks in every year, a Gray's Inn student eight weeks (ibid. lxi. 202[a], lxvii. 287[a]).

p. 262, ll. 1–2. *the Butler's booke.* In the Middle Temple 'the *Chief Butler* is to keep a Buttry-book, and to enter therein all such Orders as are made by the Bench, at the Table . . . He is likewise to enter the names of such as are admitted into Commons . . . He also entreth the names of all such as perform any Moot or Exercise, either within the House or abroad, to the end he may give a true accompt thereof when he is thereto called' (ibid. lxi. 198). Cf. ibid. lxvii. 275[b] (Gray's Inn).

p. 262, ll. 13–14. *Butchers are, etc.* Dryden, Second Prologue to *Secret Love*, ll. 28–31, makes the same allusion. It has yet to be explained.

p. 263, l. 11. *entertained*: treated, considered, received.

p. 264, ll. 1–2. *For as the first production, etc.* 'This Masse, or indigested matter, or Chaos created in the beginning was without forme, that is, without the proper forme, which it afterwards acquired, when the Spirit of God had separated the Earth, and digested it from the waters' (Raleigh, *History of the World*, I. i. v. 5).

p. 264, ll. 5–6. *The world accounts 7 yeares, etc.* 'A lease for a single life is generally valued at seven years Purchase' (Stephen Primatt, *City and Country Builder and Purchaser*, 1667, p. 21). Cf. Petty, *Treatise of Taxes and Contributions*, iv. 20.

p. 264, l. 6. *God Almighty enlarges It to 70.* Ps. xc. 10.

p. 264, l. 10. *man is not born fit to society.* See *De Cive*, Paris, 1642, i. 2.

p. 264, ll. 12–14. *For 1st. hee sayes, etc.* A literal translation from *De Cive*, loc. cit.

p. 265, l. 3. *Lord of Misrule*: 'one chosen to preside over Christmas games and revels' (*OED*). See Stubbes, *Anatomy of Abuses*, 1877–82, I. xii. 146–8; Stow, *Survey of London*, ed. C. L. Kingsford, 2 vols., Oxford, 1908, i. 97; Wood, *Athenæ Oxonienses*, ii. 239.

p. 265, l. 4. *like the King of Macassa.* See *An Historical Description of the Kingdom of Macasar* [trans. from the French of N. Gervaise], 1701, ii. 98–9: 'When the ordinary Justice has seiz'd upon an Offender, the Court refers him to be judg'd by the King, if he be not too far off: and . . . if he deserve death, the King makes him serve in some public Place for a Divertisment to the People, by proposing a Reward to such of the Souldiers as shall first hit the Offender in such a part of the Body, as he shall direct 'em: and sometimes to make tryal of his own Activity, he will shoot at the fatal Mark himself.' Macassar is a district in the Indonesian island of Celebes.

p. 265, l. 5. *Authority is a great Corrupter of good manners.* Cf. the proverb 'Honours change manners' (*ODEP* 383; Tilley, H583).

p. 265, l. 7. *conteine Himselfe*: confine himself; remain.

p. 265, ll. 11–13. *Hee carryes his Rod, etc.* The lictors' office was to carry before the consul 'certaine bundles of birchen rods with an axe wrapped up in the middest of them: the rods in latin were called *Fasces*, the axe *Securis*. The reason why they carryed both axes and rods was to intimate the different punishment that belonged unto notorious and petty malefactors' (Godwin, *Romanæ Historiæ Anthologia*, III. ii. ii. 111).

p. 265, l. 16. *but hee takes him upp*: 'except by interrupting and correcting what the boy is saying'.

p. 265, ll. 16–17. *as a Grave statesman, etc.* Clarendon, in his eulogy on the army, addressed to the Lords and Commons on 13 September 1660: 'The King will part with them, as the most indulgent Parents part with their Children, for their Education, and for their Preferment: He will prefer them to Disbanding; and prefer them by Disbanding' (*Lords Journal*, xi. 173–4; *Commons Journal*, viii. 172).

p. 265, ll. 17–19. *to say the same thing, etc.* 'Occidit miseros crambe repetita magistros' (Juvenal, *Satires*, vii. 154).

p. 265, ll. 21–2. *as Demosthenes, etc.* See Plutarch, *Demosthenes*, xi. 1.

p. 266, l. 3. *Particular*: individual.

p. 266, l. 7. *Magicall*: 'addicted to magic' (*OED*).

p. 266, l. 10. *with a Hot spitt, etc.* Cf. perhaps *Hudibras*, I. ii. 233–8, or Aubrey, *Miscellanies*, xiii. 112: 'In the *Bermudas*, they use to put an Iron into the Fire when a Witch comes in.'

 a Flint, etc. See note to p. 98, l. 16.

p. 266, l. 11. *an Hors-shoe.* 'It is a thing very common to nail Horse-shoes on the Thresholds of Doors: Which is to hinder the power of Witches that enter into the House' (Aubrey, *Miscellanies*, xiii. 112).

p. 266, ll. 11–12. *a Sive and sheares.* 'To discover a thief by the sieve and sheers: Stick the points of the sheers in the wood of the sieve, and let two persons support it, balanced upright, with their two fingers: then read a certain chapter in the Bible, and afterwards ask St. Peter and St. Paul, if A. or B. is the thief, naming the persons you suspect. On naming the real thief, the sieve will turn suddenly round about' (Francis Grose, 'Superstitions', pp. 54–5, in *Provincial Glossary*, 1787).

p. 266, l. 12. *the Running of an Hare.* 'If an *Hare* or the like creature crosse the way where one is going, it is (they say) a signe of very ill luck' (Nathaniel Homes, *Dæmonologie*, 1650, vi. 60). Cf. Browne, *Pseudodoxia*, V. xxii. 1.

p. 266, ll. 12–13. *the flying of a Crow.* 'If a Crow fly but over the house and Croak thrice, how do they fear, they, or some one else in the Family sha[l]l die?' (William Ramesey, Ελμινθολοτια. *Or, Some Physical Considerations . . . of Wormes*, 1668, VI. vi. v. 271.) John Gaule, Πῦς-μαντία, *The Mag-Astro-mancer*, 1652, xx. 181, specifically mentions among omens 'a crow lighting on the right hand, or on the left'.

p. 266, l. 13. *the falling of Salt.* See Browne, *Pseudodoxia*, V. xxii. 3; Brand, *Popular Antiquities*, ix. 87, 95; Grose, 'Superstitions', pp. 65–6, in *Provincial Glossary*.

 a spider. '[Some] have thought themselves secure of receiving Money, if their Hands itched, or, by chance, a little Spider fell upon their Cloaths' (Defoe, *Secret Memoirs of the late Mr. Duncan Campbel*, 1732, vi. 60). This is the 'money-spider' or 'money-spinner' (*Aranea scenica*). It was proverbially unlucky to kill spiders (*ODEP* 819).

p. 266, ll. 13–14. *the Itching of their noses.* This usually presages the appearance of a guest or stranger. See Tilley, N224.

p. 266, l. 18. *not to begin, etc.* 'Some days . . . are commonly deemed unlucky: among others, Friday labours under that opprobrium; and it is pretty generally held, that no new work or enterprize should be commenced on that day' (Grose, 'Superstitions', p. 65, in *Provincial Glossary*). Cf. Tilley, F679, and Gaule, Πῦς–μαντία, xx. 181.

p. 266, ll. 18–19. *nor to paire, etc.* See Browne, *Pseudodoxia*, v. xxii. 10, on 'the set and statary times of paring of nails' (Tuesday not being mentioned). Saturday was proverbially unpropitious (*ODEP* 288, 54; Tilley, F682, N10).

p. 266, l. 19. *to rise, etc.* Butler's Character, 'An Undeserving Favourite . . . came to Preferment by unworthy Offices, like one that rises with his Bum forwards, which the Rabble hold to be fortunate' (*GR* ii. 366). Cf. Foresight, in Congreve, *Love for Love*, II. i.

p. 266, l. 20. *put on the Right stockin first.* Cf. *Hudibras*, II. iii. 701–4:

> *Augustus* having, b'oversight,
> Put on his *left*-shoo, 'fore the *right*,
> Had like to have been slain that day,
> By *Souldiers* mutining for pay.

p. 266, l. 23. *Sort*: i.e. of 'knowledge'.

p. 266, l. 24. *originall.* See note to p. 32, l. 14.

p. 267, ll. 11–13. *As the people of Rome, etc.* Magistrates were elected through the *comitia* (*curiata, centuriata*, or *tributa*), to the vote of which assembly they had then to bring their proposals. 'Constat autem et ambos Consules et Magistratus omnes obtemperare Senatui semper debuisse, quoties id è repub. esse, patribus et plebi visum est' (Milton, *Defensio Prima*, in *Works*, vii. 370).

p. 267, ll. 21–33. *Next o're his shoulders, etc.* Lines 30–1 suggest a source later than Butler: some unidentified panegyric upon William Howard, Viscount Stafford, beheaded 29 December 1680. It was observed at his trial 'that all his owne Relations, & of his Name & family Condemn'd him, excepting onely his *Nephew* the *Earle* of *Arundel*' (Evelyn, *Diary*, 7 December 1680; ed. de Beer, iv. 234). Stafford had, however, been imprisoned since October 1678, and the drawn-out preliminaries to impeachment could have suggested to Butler these (albeit uncharacteristic) reflections on the fate of a Catholic peer.

p. 268, ll. 1–4. *The Lawes of the land, etc.* Until the Customs and Excise yield began to increase after 1674, revenues fell short even of peace-time expenditure. For details of Charles's finances see W. A. Shaw, introductions to *Cal. Treasury Books*.

p. 268, l. 9. *As all Countries, etc.* Proverbial (*ODEP* 900; Tilley, M426). See also *Hudibras*, III. ii. 1293–4, and Wilders's note.

p. 268, l. 15. *'Cause Solomon sayes, etc.* Eccles. i. 9 (Solomon being the supposed speaker).

p. 268, l. 22. *tenents*: tenets.

p. 269, l. 24. *Seminary*: 'seed plot, a place where plants are set to be removed' (Blount, *Glossographia*).

p. 270, ll. 7–8. *like Andromeda, etc.* See Ovid, *Metamorphoses*, iv. 668–90; Apollodorus, II. iv. 3.

p. 270, ll. 9–10. *brands Idolatry with the name of Whoredome.* Most frequently in Ezekiel (vi. 9; xliii. 7–9; and *passim*).

p. 270, l. 10. *calls AntiChrist, etc.* The identification of Antichrist (1 John ii. 18, 22; iv. 3; 2 John 7) with the Whore of Babylon (Rev. xvii. 1–5) is not explicit in Scripture.

p. 270, ll. 14–15. *Such a remedy, etc.* Diogenes Laertius records the Stoics' opinion 'That Wives should be in common; so that a man might make Use of the first he met by accident; for thus *Zeno* and *Chrysippus* both ordain'd in their *Common-Wealths*; for that they will all have the same Charity and Affection for their Offspring; and by that means Adultery and Jealousie will be remov'd out of the World' (*Zeno*, vii. 131, trans. in *Lives*, i. 542).

p. 270, l. 17. *He hath endowed, etc.* See 'Solemnization of Matrimony', in *Book of Common Prayer*, 1662: 'With my body I thee worship, and with all my worldly goods I thee endow.'

p. 270, l. 19. *Vespasian turned Urine into Silver.* See Suetonius, *Vespasian*, xxiii. 3: 'When his sonne TITUS seemed to finde fault with him for devising a kinde of tribute, even out of urine: the monie that came unto his hand of the first paiment, hee put unto his sonnes nose: asking withall, *whether he was offended with the smell, or no*, and when he answered *No: and yet* quoth he, *it commeth of Urine*' (trans. Holland, p. 251).

p. 273, l. 15. *Men's faith, etc.* Jas. ii. 18.

p. 273, ll. 19–20. *between Hauke and Buzzard.* Proverbial (*ODEP* 359; Tilley, H223).

p. 274, l. 14. *an old man.* Cf. Dan. vii. 9: 'the Ancient of dayes'.

p. 274, ll. 14–15. *before the Creation, etc.* Cf. du Bartas, *Devine Weekes*:

> Shall valiant *Scipio*, thus himselfe esteeme,
> *Never lesse sole then when he sole doth seeme:*
> And could not God (O Heav'ns! what frantike folly)
> Subsist alone, but sinke in melancholy?

('First Day of the First Weeke', ll. 45–8, trans. Sylvester, 1605, p. 3.) Scipio's saying is proverbially applied to a wise man (*ODEP* 900; Tilley, A228).

p. 274, ll. 32–3. *though Light bee, etc.* Gen. i. 3. Cf. 1 John i. 5: 'God is light'.

p. 275, l. 4. *like Mohomet, etc.* The elmparac or alborach, said to have carried Mahomet to heaven, was 'of nature betweene a Mule and an Asse' (Purchas, *Pilgrimage*, III. III. ii. 245). See also Topsell, *History of Four-footed Beasts*, p. 26.

p. 275, ll. 7–8. *like the French manufactures.* According to the 1674 'Scheme of the Trade, as it is at present carried on between England and France' (*Somers Tracts*, 1809–15, viii. 30–1), English imports totalled £1,136,150, exports only £171,021, leaving a £965,129 'balance gained by the French from us yearly, besides the toys, gloves, laces, &c.'

p. 275, l. 19. *Compasse*: proper limits.

p. 275, ll. 20–1. *which they therefore, etc·* See note to p. 34, ll. 9–10.

p. 276, ll. 4–6. *Popery was attempted, etc.* Butler would have in mind the fourteenth-century English statutes of Provisors and Praemunire (see Blackstone, *Commentaries*, IV. viii); the French Pragmatic Sanction of Bourges (1438); the Council of Constance (1414–17, convened at the instigation of the Emperor Sigismund); the Council of Basle (1431–49).

p. 276, l. 8. *santering*: wandering. 'To *Santer . . .* is derived from *Saincte terre*, *i.e.* The Holy Land, because of old time. . . many idle persons went from place to place, upon pretence that they had taken, or intended to take the Cross upon them, and to go thither' (John Ray, *Collection of English Words Not Generally Used*, 1691, p. 111).

p. 276, l. 9. *by the Eares.* See note to p. 7, l. 18.

p. 276, l. 13. *Deprivd of their Congregations of Estates.* The French States-General had last met in 1614–15, and was not to meet again until 1789.

p. 276, ll. 23–4. *Eating what They worship, etc.* Cf. p. 30, ll. 30–2.

p. 276, ll. 26–31. *It was not Queen Elizabeth, etc.* See p. 2, ll. 10–18.

p. 276, l. 28. *her Breach of Faith.* Mary initially proclaimed that, while she much desired her subjects to embrace Catholicism, 'her highness mindeth not to compel any her said subjects thereunto unto such time as further order by common assent may be taken therein' (*Tudor Royal Proclamations*, ed. Hughes and Larkin, 1964–9, ii. 5–6).

p. 277, ll. 18–19. *the Clergy tooke upon Them, etc.* Cf. p. 48, ll. 35–8, and note.

p. 277, ll. 22–3. *had no Share, etc.* Josh. xiv. 1–4.

p. 277, l. 24. *in Feeing of their Sacrifices.* By the law of Moses the tenth of all produce, as well as flocks and cattle, must be offered to the Lord (Lev. xxvii. 30, 32); this tenth was assigned to the Levites as the reward of their services

(Num. xviii. 21, 24). 'How the payment of these Tenths was either observed or discontinued, partly appeares in holy Writ [2 Chr. xxxi; Neh. xiii; Mal. iii], partly in their institution of more trustie Over-seers [some thirty years] after the new dedication of the Temple by *Judas Machabæus*' (John Selden, *Historie of Tithes*, 1618, II. vi. 18). Malachi deals explicity with the Levites' unjust 'feeing': they sacrificed as the Lord's part of the offerings what was polluted or corrupt (i. 6–ii. 9; iii. 7–12).

p. 277, ll. 26–30. *As when they gott Jerusalem, etc.* According to Tacitus, *Historiae*, V. xii, 'pervicacissimus quisque illuc [Jerusalem] perfugerat eoque seditiosus agebant. tres duces, totidem exercitus: extrema et latissima moenium Simo, mediam urbem Ioannes, templum Eleazarus firmaverat. multitudine et armis Ioannes ac Simo, Eleazarus loco pollebat; sed proelia dolus incendia inter ipsos, et magna vis frumenti ambusta.' Cf. Josephus, *Wars*, V. i. 2–5.

p. 277, ll. 30–1. *to kill Beasts &c.* The Levites 'shall slay the burnt offering, and the sacrifice for the people' (Ezek. xliv. 11).

p. 277, ll. 31–2. *the Executioners, etc.* Best taken in the same general sense as Christ's lament over Jerusalem (Matt. xxiii. 37; cf. vv. 29–35). The Old Testament is deficient in recording such executions; furthermore, the authority to judge false prophets 'belonged onely to the *seventy in Ierusalem*', in the supposed composition of which 'onely *foure* were chosen' out of 'the *Tribe of Levi*' (Thomas Godwin, *Moses and Aaron*, 1625, V. iv. 235, 233). At the trial of Christ, however, the priests were also of the assembly (ibid. V. i. 221–2; Matt. xxvi. 3, 57 ff.).

p. 278, ll. 8–9. *like the Austrian family.* Most prominently in the case of the ruling emperor Leopold I: himself the child of first cousins, he married in 1666 his sister's daughter Margaret of Spain.

p. 278, ll. 10–11. *Jubemur in Evangelio, etc.* Matt. vi. 1–7.

p. 279, l. 38–p. 280, l. 2. *Man is of all Creatures, etc.* Cf. Aristotle, *Poetica*, 1448[b] 5–19.

p. 280, ll. 22–4. *Nulli mortalium, etc.* See Butler's translation of Hippocrates, *Aphorisms*, VI. liii: 'Madness of Study and Consideration are harder to be cured than those of lighter and more fantastic Humour' ('An Affected Man', GR ii. 335). The next entry in *C* is a Latin version of the aphorism.

p. 281, ll. 18–19. *Solomon only, etc.* Prov. xvi. 12. Cf. Isa. ix. 7.

p. 281, l. 26. *Impostors:* an error for 'impostures'.

p. 282, l. 3. *Plague Sores.* Probably the deep, ragged, slow-healing ulcers left by the broken buboes of those who have recovered from the fever. But none of the plague's skin lesions is infectious; in its bubonic form the disease cannot spread directly from man to man. See J. F. D. Shrewsbury, *History of Bubonic*

Plague in the British Isles, Cambridge, 1970, pp. 4–5; W. G. Bell, *The Great Plague in London in 1665*, rev. edn., 1951, pp. 126–8.

p. 282, l. 12. *Act of Continuance*. This enacted, 'That this present Parliament now assembled, shall not be dissolved, unless it be by Act of Parliament to be passed for that purpose; nor shall be, at any time or times, during the continuance thereof, prorogued or adjourned, unless it be by Act of Parliament to be likewise passed for that purpose' (Rushworth, *Historical Collections*, III. i. 264). Charles gave his assent on 10 May 1641.

p. 282, l. 16. *president*: precedent.

p. 282, ll. 22–3. *a Treaty with his most Implacable Enemyes:* i.e. with the French. See pp. xxvii–xxviii.

p. 282, ll. 23–4. *great Councell*. See note to p. 163, l. 4.

p. 282, ll. 31–2. *Merchant Adventurer*: historically 'a merchant engaged in the organization and despatch of trading expeditions over sea' (*OED*).

p. 283, ll. 13–14. *as time, etc.* See p. 207, ll. 26–30, and note.

p. 283, ll. 21–2. *To doe that to others, etc.* Cf. Luke vi. 31.

p. 283, l. 25. *voted a King to bee So*. By 'An Act of the Commons of England . . . for the Trying and Judging of Charles Stuart, King of England' (6 January 1649; Firth and Rait, ii. 1253–5).

p. 283, l. 31. *the Countrey*. Trial by jury is 'called also the trial *per pais*, or *by the country*' (Blackstone, *Commentaries*, III. xxiii. 349).

p. 284, ll. 4–6. *They should (like malefactors), etc.* See note to p. 216, l. 2.

p. 284, l. 19. *present*: current, existing.

p. 284, l. 27. *concernd in*: mindful of; affected by.

p. 285, l. 15. *recruites*: reinforcements.

p. 285, l. 19. *presense*: presentiment, foreboding.

p. 285, l. 28. *bare*: bare-headed.

p. 285, l. 31. *Scaramuch*. The part of the braggart Scaramouch was created by Tiberio Fiorelli, whose Italian company made triumphant visits to London under the patronage of Charles II, April–September 1673 and June–October 1675. See Eleanore Boswell, *Restoration Court Stage*, Cambridge, Mass., 1932, pp. 118–22.

p. 286, ll. 14–15. *takes It to Himselfe*: takes it personally.

p. 286, ll. 16–17. *carrying It on*. See note to p. 205, l. 27.

p. 286, l. 24. *to make the wreck sufficient and lawfull*.

Wreck . . . Is, where a Ship is perish'd on the Sea, and no man escapes alive out of it, if any part of the Ship, or any of the Goods that were in it are brought to Land by the Waves, they belong to the King by His Prerogative, or to such other person to whom the King has granted *Wreck*. But, if a man, a Dog or a Cat escape alive, so that the owner come within a year and a day, and prove the Goods to be his, he shall have them again by provision of the Statute of *Westm. 1. ca. 4. & 17 Ed. 2. ca. 11.* (Thomas Blount, Νομο-λεξικον, *A Law-Dictionary*, 1670, s.v. '*Wreck*'.)

p. 286, l. 27. *Assay*: foretaste (made by a subordinate to test royal food).

p. 286, l. 30. *the Kings evill*: scrofula. It was believed curable by the royal touch, and 'it has been estimated that Charles II touched in all as many as 100,000 persons' (Cross, *Dictionary of the Christian Church*). The 'touch piece' of gold or silver (at first an angel coin), pierced for hanging round the neck, dates from the reign of Edward III. See Shakespeare, *Macbeth*, IV. iii. 141–65.

p. 287, l. 11. *in a way*: established.

p. 287. ll. 14–15. *stood out*: undergone the process prescribed by.

p. 287, l. 21. *His going to* ——. Before the morning Council, 'Le Roi alloit à la messe, où sa musique chantoit toujours un motet' (Saint-Simon, *Mémoires*, ed. A. de Boislisle, Paris, 1879–1930, xxviii. 342).

p. 287, ll. 21–2. *King Phys his, etc.* See Buckingham, *The Rehearsal*, v. i:

> 1 *King*: Come, now to serious counsel we'l advance.
> 2 *King*: I do agree; but first, let's have a Dance.

These are in fact the 'rightful kings' of Brentford. The usurpers, King Phys-[ian] and King Ush[er], have just 'stolen away'.

p. 287, l. 32. *his Imprisonment in Egipt*. Louis left France in 1248, and in 1249 took the Egyptian port of Damietta. 'Le dessein de Louys estiot sans laisser refroider la victoire, & donner moyen à son ennemi de se recognoistre, d'attaquer le Caire, . . . mais l'ignorance des lieux estrangers où il estoit . . . [gave Sultan Melexala means] de desfaire l'armee de Louys, & de le prendre prisonnier. . . . Les conditions furent fort dures en une grande extremité. Que Damiete seroit remise entre les mains du Sultan: tous prisonniers rendus, & huict mille livres d'or. . . . Mais à son retour il ne retrouva ni son Royaume en si bon ordre qu'il avoit laissé, ni les Estats voisins en meilleure paix' (de Serres, *Histoire*, i. 315–17). Captured and released in 1250, Louis returned to France in 1254.

p. 287, l. 33. *then King Johns was in England*. Presumably an error for 'King Richard's'. Cœur de Lion was imprisoned at Durrenstein (1292–4), having been captured while attempting, more 'wisely', to return home from the Holy Land. 'But in *England* Duke *John* took upon him as king, perswading the people that his brother king *Richard* was not living; and indeed it was easie to remove, they knowing him to be a prisoner, to the affirming him to be dead' (Baker, *Chronicle*, p. 94).

p. 288, ll. 1–3. *hee engagd upon a 2d Adventure, etc.* 'Louys donc ne pouvant vivre sans servir à l'avancement des affaires de la Chrestienté, ne peut estre retenu de se resoudre au voyage de la Barbarie: contre l'advis de ses Estats,

& contre sa propre experience. Zele qui lui succedera mal, & à tout son Royaume. Ainsi il se croisa pour la seconde fois' (de Serres, *Histoire*, i. 319). He embarked on 1 July 1270, and died of dysentery at Tunis on 25 August.

p. 288, ll. 3–5. *tho the frenzies of Charles the 6th., etc.* Charles VI (1380–1422) regna treze ans, ou avec ses oncles, ou seul, jouyssant de son bon sens, & vingt et [neuf] en phrenesie, non regnant, mais regi ou plustost ravi de la diverse passion d'autrui. . . . En la premiere Scene de ce theatre, nous verrons les oncles du jeune Roy en mauvais mesnage l'un contre l'autre. Louys Duc d'Anjou declaré Regent, comme premier Prince du sang, traversé par ses freres, les Ducs de Berry & de Bourgongne, & luy abusant imperieusement de son autorité. Le Duc d'Anjou estant forti de quartier par la mort, Louys Duc d'Orleans frere du Roy Charles VI. prendra sa place, comme premier Prince, & viendra aux Prinses avec Philippes le Hardy, Duc de Bourgongne son oncle: lequel en mourant laissera Ian son fils successeur de sa jalousie contre Louys Duc d'Orleans son cousin. Ian passera outre, car il le tuera. mais la haine ne sera pas morte, estant provignee en Charles Duc d'Orleans fils de Louys massacré: & esmouvera infinis troubles. . . . Ian qui avoit tué, sera tué par Charles Dauphin, qui sera Roy à son tour. mais de Ian naist au autre Philippes de Bourgongne, qui rallume un nouveau feu pour se vanger de la mort de son Pere. L'estranger meslé parmi ces guerres civiles, les femmes y entassent leurs fureurs. (ibid. i. 489, 455–6.)

p. 288, l. 8. *as it is said to do Martyrs.* 'It is not the suffering, but the cause which makes a martyr' (*ODEP* 785; Tilley, S956).

p. 288, ll. 13–14. *to make a Bastard, etc.* Alexander VI made an agreement with Louis XII, whereby '*Cæsar Borgia* who was the Popes bastard Son, having renounced his Cardinals Cap, and taking *Carlotta de Alebretto*, Daughter to the King of *Navar*, and Kinswoman to the King of *France* for his Wife, should be invested in *Romagna*, *Marca*, and *Umbria* . . . [Alexander] gave his Daughter *Lucretia* in Marriage to *John Sforza*, Lord of *Pesaro*, . . . then he took her from *Sforza*, and gave her to *Lewis* of *Aragon*, Bastard Son of *Alfonso* King of *Naples*; who being killed, she was given to *Alfonso da Esté* Duke of *Ferrara*, with whom afterwards she ended her days' (Rycaut, Pt. ii to Platina, *Lives of the Popes*, p. 15).

p. 288, l. 17. *Suite and Service.* See Blount, *Law Dictionary*: '*Sute of Court*, or *Sute-service*, is an attendance which a Tenant owes to the Court of his Lord, (*Anno 7 Hen. 7. ca. 2.*)'.

p. 288, l. 27. *by the Right of two Women.* Margaret Tudor, Henry VII's eldest daughter, who married James IV of Scotland, and her granddaughter Mary Queen of Scots, mother of James I of England.

p. 288, l. 31. *by forcing Him to marry a Whore.* The Duke of York, contracted to Anne Hyde at Breda on 24 November 1659, secretly married her on 3 September 1660, and their first child was born seven weeks later. Charles was against the match, but reconciled himself to it. See Burnet, *History*, i. 293–5, 298–9, and notes. Cf. Marvell's attack on Anne's character in *Last Instructions to a Painter*, ll. 49–78.

p. 289, ll. 1–2. *Doe unto others, etc.* Lev. xxiv. 19; Matt. vii. 1–2.

p. 289, ll. 6–7. *they produce the fruites, etc.* Cf. Matt. vii. 17–18.

p. 289, l. 12. *like the Prophets.* Elijah was fed by ravens (1 Kgs. xvii. 6).

p. 289, ll. 14–16. *A Tubb was bigger, etc.* See *Hudibras*, I. iii. 18–21, and Wilders's notes: 'On being told of Democritus' opinion that there were an infinite number of worlds, Alexander cried out in despair that he had only conquered one of them. See Valerius Maximus, VIII. xiv; Plutarch, *De Tranquilitate Animi*, iv. 466. According to Cicero (*Tusculan Disputations*, V. xxxii. 92), Diogenes frequently told Alexander that he himself was superior to the King, for whereas he had no needs, Alexander was never satisfied.'

p. 289, ll. 19–20. *of which the Devill is Prince.* See John xiv. 30, and cf. Matt. iv. 8–9.

p. 290, l. 5. *on a Sledge.* Blackstone, *Commentaries*, IV. vi. 92, describes the punishment of high treason: 'That the offender be drawn to the gallows, and not be carried or walk; though usually a sledge or hurdle is allowed, to preserve the offender from the extreme torment of being dragged on the ground or pavement.'

p. 290, l. 7. *eminently*: conspicuously.

p. 290, l. 14, *a flat Divine law.* Lev. xix. 11.

p. 290, ll. 16–17. *A ship-board, etc.* 'Seamen convicted of Lying, to be corporally punish'd, by being hoisted up upon the Main Stay, *&c.* and others to forfeit half a Day's Pay' (*Laws, Ordinances, and Institutions of the Admiralty of Great Britain*, 2 vols., 1746, ii. 297). See ibid. ii. 296–7 for relevant statute 13 Car. II. c. 9.

p. 291, l. 1. *as love and honour*: i.e. in heroic plays. Butler parodies such emotional conflicts in 'Repartees between Cat and Puss' (*GR* i. 91–7).

p. 291, l. 16. *Keepers of the liberties.* See note to p. 113, l. 14.

p. 291, l. 21. *Cato*: Cato Uticensis (95–46 B.C.). For praise of his character see Plutarch, *Cato Minor, passim*.

p. 291, ll. 23–5. *Athenodorus, etc.*

When Cato understoode that Athenodorus surnamed Cordylion, a Stoicke Philosopher, excellently well learned, dwelt at that time in the city of Pergamum, being a very old man, and one that stiffely refused the friendship of kings, Princes, and noble men, desirous to have him about them: to write to him, he thought it was but lost labor. Wherefore . . . he tooke sea, and went into Asia to him, hoping he should not lose his jorney, for the great vertues he knew in him. So when he had spoken with him, and talked of divers matters together: at length he brought him from his first determination, and caried him to the campe with him, esteeming this victorie more, then all the conquestes of Lucullus or Pompey, who had conquered the most parte of the world. (Plutarch, *Cato Utican*, x, trans. North, v. 117.)

p. 292, l. 7. *Langageur*: i.e. langayeur, 'an *Officer that searches the tongues o*

Market-Hogs, thereby to discerne whether they be sound or no' (Cotgrave, *Dictionarie*). Cf. langayer, *'to worme, or search the root of the tongue of a Hog'* (ibid.).

p. 292, l. 11. *Symplements*: symptoms.

p. 292, l. 12. *meazles:* a disease produced in swine by tapeworm larvae.

p. 292, ll. 22–3. *like the Clay of China Potters.* See Brownes's discussion (*Pseudodoxia*, II. v. 7) 'concerning Porcellane or China dishes, that according to common belief they are made of Earth, which lieth in preparation about an hundred years under ground'.

p. 293, ll. 11–12. *designes Himselfe*: maps out for himself; assigns himself.

p. 293, ll. 13–14. *more then in his owne Countrey.* Matt. xiii. 57; Luke iv. 24; John iv. 44.

p. 293, l. 27–8. *as eliah burnt his Sacrifice with water.* 1 Kgs. xviii. 30–8.

p. 294, l. 2. *Livings*: livelihoods.

conversion: in law 'the action of (illegally) converting or applying something to one's own use' (*OED*).

p. 294, l. 6–7. *his Dominions.* See p. 289, ll. 19–20, and note.

p. 295, l. 4. *free State*: republic.

p. 295, l. 23. *like Miracles.* It was a common belief among Protestants that miracles had ceased to occur after apostolic times. See Shakespeare, *Henry V*, I. i. 67, and *All's Well*, II. iii. 1; Scot, *Discoverie of Witchcraft*, 1584, VIII. i. 156; Perkins, *Discourse of Witchcraft*, I. iv. 13–17.

p. 296, ll. 16–18. *they would follow Him, etc.* Matt. xv. 29–33; Mark viii. 1–4.

p. 296, l. 19. *for the Same Reasons endeavour to stone Him.* 'Then the Jewes tooke up stones againe to stone him. Jesus answered them, Many good workes have I shewed you from my Father; for which of those workes doe ye stone me? The Jewes answered him, saying, For a good worke we stone thee not, but for blasphemy, and because that thou, being a man, makest thy selfe God' (John x. 31–3).

p. 296, ll. 19–21. *take his part, etc.* Matt. xxi. 46; Luke xx. 19.

p. 296, ll. 22–4. *within 2 or 3 dayes after, etc.* Luke xxiii. 13–23.

p. 296, ll. 24–5. *To bee eye witnesses, etc.* John x. 24–5.

p. 296, ll. 25–6. *lesse then the Devill.* See Matt. iv. 3–6; Luke iv. 3, 9–11.

p. 296, ll. 26–8. *when the same things, were but, etc.* Acts iv. 4 ('about five thousand'). Cf. Acts ii. 41 ('about three thousand').

p. 296, l. 28. *at a Clap*: at a stroke; all at once.

p. 297, l. 3. *Ferity*: 'cruelty, fierceness' (Blount, *Glossographia*).

p. 297, l. 6. *Lord of all other Creatures.* Gen. i. 26, 28.

p. 297, ll. 12–14. *the very Gouvernment of Hell, etc.* Matt. xii. 26; Luke xi. 18.

p. 297, l. 22. *such as have no ears, to Heare.* See Matt. xi. 15; xiii. 9, 43; Mark iv. 9, 23; vii. 16.

p. 297, l. 26. *as well as Ordinances.* See Hudibras, II. ii. 250 (A saint should be above Conscience, 'As far, as above *Ordinances*'), and Wilders's note: 'Clarendon describes this phrase as "peculiar to that time". He applies it to the younger Vane, whom he describes as "unlimited and unrestrained by any rules or bounds presecribed to other men by reason of his perfection. He was a perfect enthusiast and without doubt did believe himself inspired" ' (Clarendon, *History*, xvi. 88). Cf. Evelyn, *Diary*, 25 December 1657; ed. de Beer, iii. 204.

p. 298, ll. 1–2. *the Heathens objected, etc.* 'I heare that amongst all filthy beasts, from what perswasion I know not, they worship an Asses head, like worship like manners' (Minucius Felix, *Octavius*, ix. 3, trans. Richard James, Oxford, 1636, p. 29). See also Tertullian, *Apologeticus*, xvi. 1–2; *Ad Nationes*, I. xi, xiv; and cf. Tacitus, *Historiae*, v. iii–iv; Josephus, *Contra Apion*, II. vii.

p. 298, l. 3. *a Jew and a Christian were all one.* See Suetonius, *Claudius*, xv. 4; Dio Cassius, LXVII. xiv. 1–2; LXVIII. i. 2; Tertullian, *Apologeticus*, xvi. 3.

p. 298, ll. 5–6. *all the firstlings, etc.* Exod. xiii. 12–13.

p. 299, l. 11. *Periissem nisi periissem*: i.e. he would not have enjoyed the prosperity he did (in Persia) had he not fallen from power in Greece (Plutarch, *Themistocles*, xxix). Cf. Thucydides, i. 136.

p. 299, ll. 11–12. *the Earle of Somersetts breaking of His Legg.* According to Wilson, *Life and Reign of King James the First*, p. 54, 'Sir *James Hayes*, some say the Lord *Dingwell*, at a Tilting . . . made choice of Mr. *Car* (according to the custom) to present his *Shield*, and *Device* to the King; and as he was descending, the Horse . . . threw him down before the King, and broke his *leg*. This accident gave the King occasion to take notice of him.' Robert Carr was created Earl of Somerset in 1613.

p. 299, ll. 31–2. *like the Prisian, etc.* Browne, *Pseudodoxia*, II. iii, cites the case of 'a young man of Spruceland [i.e. Prussia] that casually swallowed a knife about ten inches long, which was cut out of his stomach, and the wound healed up'.

p. 300, l. 10. *turns him up*: turns him loose.

p. 300, l. 29. *breeding*: bringing up.

p. 301, ll. 5–6. *Faciunt nec intelligendo, etc. Andria*, Prologue, l. 17.

p. 301, ll. 8–9. *as more men perish, etc.* See note to p. 168, ll. 1–2.

p. 301, ll. 24–5. *the Alps cost Hanniball, etc.* Polybius writes of Hannibal's completed crossing that 'although a little before hee had parted from the River of *Rhone* with thirty eight thousand Foote, and eight thousand Horse, hee had scarce then halfe his Army entire' (*History*, III. lx. 5, trans. Edward Grimestone, 1633, p. 137). Cf. Livy, XXI. xxxviii. 2–5.

p. 301, ll. 26–9. *Holland that is, etc.* Cf. p. 184, ll. 13–17, above.

p. 302, ll. 6–7. *When Adam by disobedience, etc.* Rom. v. 12.

p. 302, l. 15. *Pragmaticall*: busy; doctrinaire; officious.

p. 302, l. 22. *the whole duty of man.* Eccles. xii. 13; also the title of an enormously popular devotional work, published 1658, probably by Richard Allestree. Wing, *Short-Title Catalogue . . . 1641–1700*, i, New York, 1972, lists 39 editions.

APPENDIX A

Passages from Butler's Manuscript which occur in Longueville's Commonplace Book and Thyer's *Genuine Remains*

NOTE. Thyer marked his selected passages in the B.L. manuscript with a marginal **X**. A few passages so marked do not appear in his printed text; they are here denoted '**X** *Thyer*'. They are (with a single exception) in the 'Virtue and Vice' section of the manuscript, and one may see from Thyer's sequence that they would have been printed at the very end of his volume, where the printer would have needed a new sheet to include them.

1: 9–11   *GR* ii. 474
1: 13–16   *GR* ii. 475
1: 20–1   *GR* ii. 474
2: 1–6   *GR* ii. 473–4
3: 1–5   *GR* ii. 475
3: 20–2   *GR* ii. 475
3: 23–4   *GR* ii. 475
3: 28–31   *GR* ii. 474–5
4: 4–5   *GR* ii. 474
4: 8–12   *GR* ii. 474
4: 13–16   *C* 24[r]
4: 17–22   *C* 66[v], *GR* ii. 478
4: 23–5: 3   *C* 86[r], *GR* ii. 473
5: 4–9   *C* 73[v]
5: 23–4   *C* 46[v]
6: 7–12   *C* 92[v]
6: 16–28   *C* 37[v], *GR* ii. 485
7: 1–6   *GR* ii. 490
7: 9–15   *GR* ii. 490–1
7: 22–5   *GR* ii. 491
9: 14–24   *C* 1[r]
9: 25–7   *C* 37[r]
10: 4–18   *GR* ii. 485–6
10: 8–11   *C* 3[v], 7[v]
10: 12–18   *C* 4[r]
10: 16–18   (*B* 234[r] *version*) *C* 93[r]

10: 31–11: 3   *C* 6[v]
11: 8–14   *C* 74[r], *GR* ii. 486–7
11: 15–21   *C* 3[v]
11: 22–12: 2   *GR* ii. 487–8
11: 24–7   *C* 75[r]
11: 28–31   *C* 8[r]
12: 3–7   *C* 5[v]
12: 11–34 . . . disposing] *GR* ii. 488–9
13: 5–12   *C* 95[v]
13: 35–14: 3   *C* 95[v]
14: 12–17   *GR* ii. 489–90
14: 18–23   *C* 5[r]
14: 24–9   *C* 75[r], *GR* ii. 490
15: 3–9   *C* 7[r], *GR* ii. 489
15: 15–19   *C* 97[r]
15: 20–33   *C* 5[r]
16: 6–14 . . . can] *C* 5[r]
17: 11–30 . . . Physique] *C* 7[r]
17: 37–18: 6   It . . . Paines] *C* 7[v]
18: 6–11   if . . . to] *C* 3[v]
18: 29–19: 32 . . . easy] *C* 3[r–v]
21: 1–7   *C* 82[r]
21: 8–27   *C* 79[r]
21: 12–14   *GR* ii. 499
22: 29–32   *C* 95[r], *GR* ii. 499

22: 33–23: 5   C 14ʳ
23: 16–18   GR ii. 485
24: 11–30   C 80ᵛ
25: 1–3   C 50ᵛ
25: 7–11   GR ii. 505
25: 7–9   C 54ʳ
25: 10–11   C 53ʳ
25: 12–16   C 21ʳ
25: 19–23   C 39ʳ, GR ii. 466
26: 14–16   C 85ʳ, GR ii. 505
26: 17–20   C 53ʳ
26: 26–31   C 53ʳ
26: 26–8 . . . it in] GR ii. 505
27: 1–2   C 27ʳ
27: 7–19   GR ii. 506
27: 29–31   C 51ʳ
27: 32–28: 2   C 77ʳ, GR ii. 506–7
28: 3–8   C 25ʳ
28: 9–11   GR ii. 507
29: 10–14   C 73ʳ
29: 15–18   C 35ʳ, 51ʳ; GR ii. 469
29: 23–4   GR ii. 507
29: 29–30: 6   GR ii. 507
30: 7–12   C 44ᵛ
30: 13–15   C 54ᵛ
31: 20–2   GR ii. 505
32: 6–8   GR ii. 501
32: 14–21   C 54ʳ
32: 22–33   C 86ᵛ
32: 34–33: 2   C 37ʳ
33: 7–12   C 25ʳ
33: 13–17   GR ii. 508
33: 18–24   C 39ʳ, GR ii. 466–7
33: 25–33   C 51ʳ, GR ii. 467–8
34: 4–8   he that . . .] GR ii. 467
34: 22–4   GR ii. 508
34: 25–33   C 54ᵛ
35: 1–3   GR ii. 508
35: 4–6   C 53ᵛ
35: 7–9   C 36ʳ
35: 10–20   GR ii. 508–9
35: 32–36: 3   GR ii. 509
36: 14–18   GR ii. 467

36: 19–21   GR ii. 468
36: 22–6   C 54ᵛ
36: 22–4 . . . it] GR ii. 471
36: 31–37: 15   GR ii. 509–10
37: 16–36   GR ii. 468–9
38: 1–6   C 54ᵛ
38: 15–17   GR ii. 506
38: 18–30   C 38ʳ, 88ʳ
39: 5–26   GR ii. 471–2
40: 3–11   GR ii. 510
40: 12–17   C 88ʳ
40: 23–31   C 86ᵛ
40: 32–41: 3   C 54ᵛ
41: 4–7   C 27ʳ
41: 31–42: 15   C 89ᵛ
42: 16–22   C 25ᵛ
42: 36–43: 12   C 31ᵛ
43: 13–21 . . . Pretences] GR ii. 502–3
44: 2–9   Our . . .] GR ii. 503
44: 10–17   GR ii. 502
44: 18–26   GR ii. 500–1
44: 27–30   (B 223ᵛ version) C 84ʳ
45: 3–9   C 55ᵛ, GR ii. 503–4
45: 26–8   C 84ʳ
45: 29–35 . . . money] GR ii. 502
51: 19–25   C 54ʳ
54: 8–14   C 90ᵛ, GR ii. 501
54: 15–22   C 97ʳ
56: 1–13   C 59ʳ
57: 17–19   GR ii. 491
58: 1–10   C 4ʳ
58: 13–20   There . . . Judgment (B 222ʳ version)] C 95ʳ
58: 20–7   wit . . . (B 222ʳ version)] C 95ʳ
58: 28–30   X Thyer
59: 12–16 . . . Pound] GR ii. 500
59: 24–30   So . . . (B 222ʳ version)] C 79ᵛ
65: 1–69: 4 . . . distinctions] GR i. 393–401
65: 1–25   C 94ʳ⁻ᵛ

67: 8–27   *C* 94^v

68: 22–9   *C* 14^r

68: 30–7   Instinct . . . *C* 94^v

69: 7–33   *GR* i. 401–3

70: 1–11   *GR* ii. 511–12

70: 1–7   *C* 57^v

70: 14–15   30 . . .]   *C* 53^r

  70: 16–24   **X** *Thyer*

70: 25–9   *C* 43^r, *GR* ii. 512

  71: 9–13   **X** *Thyer*

71: 18–21   *GR* ii. 512

71: 22–4   *C* 82^r, **X** *Thyer*

  71: 28–31   **X** *Thyer*

71: 32–72: 3   *C* 74^v, **X** *Thyer*

72: 9–11   *C* 14^r

72: 31–73: 3   *C* 92^r, **X** *Thyer*

73: 9–10   *C* 16^r, 92^r, **X** *Thyer*

  73: 11–36   **X** *Thyer*

74: 1–5   *C* 91^r, 92^r, **X** *Thyer*

74: 6–9   *C* 14^v

  74: 12–32   **X** *Thyer*

74: 33–75: 4   *C* 57^v, **X** *Thyer*

  75: 5–6   **X** *Thyer*

75: 7–11   *C* 41^r

  75: 20–4   **X** *Thyer*

  76: 3–5   **X** *Thyer*

76: 6–9   have . . . one *and* 76: 19–21
  such . . . Evill] Such . . . Evill:
  Who have . . . one *C* 29^r

76: 21–8   as . . . Cure] *C* 29^r

77: 2–15   if . . . reduc'd] *C* 29^r

78: 22–3   *GR* ii. 500

78: 24–6   *C* 15^r

78: 27–79: 3   *C* 80^r

79: 12–14   *C* 15^r

79: 20–7   *GR* ii. 500

79: 28–80: 9   *C* 85^r

81: 3–17   *C* 89^r

81: 3–12   . . . world] *GR* ii. 470

82: 24–83: 8   *C* 25^v

85: 7–12   *C* 25^v

86: 22–6   *C* 25^v

87: 19–21   *C* 74^r

87: 31–2   *C* 74^r

89: 20–5   *C* 25^v

90: 20–2   *C* 28^v

93: 10–94: 5   *C* 74^v

94: 6–10   *C* 91^v

97: 7–12   It . . . (*B* 223^v *version*)] *C*
  97^r

99: 12–21   *C* 63^r

100: 12–15   *C* 44^v

101: 4–14   *C* 63^r

101: 28–102: 2   *C* 41^r

102: 3–6   *C* 47^r

102: 7–13   *C* 47^r

102: 28–31   *C* 48^v

102: 32–103: 12   *C* 49^r

103: 17–19   *C* 31^r

104: 20–4   . . . money] *C* 44^v

104: 31–105: 2   *C* 49^r

105: 2–8   *C* 41^v

105: 17–18   *C* 56^v

106: 20–1   *C* 56^v

107: 6–11   *C* 63^r

107: 16–19   *C* 63^r

107: 20–3   *C* 56^v

107: 24–108: 3   *C* 56^r

108: 9–13   *C* 56^v

111: 12–15   *GR* ii. 483

111: 16–20   *GR* ii. 476

111: 21–6   *GR* ii. 476

112: 24–6   though . . .] *C* 20^r

112: 33–113: 5   *GR* ii. 476–7

113: 6–33   . . . of] *GR* ii. 480–1

114: 1–10   *GR* ii. 479–80

114: 22–32   *GR* ii. 481–2

115: 3–5   . . . Repentance (*B* 193^v
  version)] *GR* ii. 476

115: 12–24   *GR* ii. 482–3

116: 6–10   *GR* ii. 483

116: 31–4   *GR* ii. 483

118: 24–33   *GR* ii. 484

119: 9–16   *GR* ii. 484

120: 25–32   *GR* ii. 477

121: 1–11   *GR* ii. 477–8

APPENDIX B

Variant Readings in the Commonplace Book Characters

NOTE. To facilitate the use of any edition printing Thyer's texts the numerical reference is to the sentence in the Character where the words appear.

Sentence	Thyer's Reading	Commonplace Book Reading
	'THE OBSTINATE MAN', sent. 10; *GR* ii. 423–4 His Wits . . . is	*C* 3ᵛ. *No variants.*
	'A COURT WIT', *T* 94ʳ⁻ᵛ	*C* 17ᵛ
1	Certainly	*om.*[1]
	must be	must needs be
	one	man
2	subtle	*om.*
3	betters	better
	dependants . . . amiss	dependants: and out, For nothing
4	out; while	else was expected from Him while[2]
	true	*om.*
6	Beside	Besides
	to pay	*om.*
6–9	For . . . vayles	*om.*
10	has	hath
11	as dull discerners	——
	'A LAWYER', sent. 23–7; *GR* ii. 168 He is an *Apprentice* . . . Jugler	*C* 19ʳ
23	Master, is	Master; and is
	Fool	——
24	wrest Law	wrest his Law
26	it . . . it	'em . . . 'em
	Client	*possibly* Clients
	itself	themselves

---

[1] *For a further, holograph, version of the first two sentences see p. 241 ll. 29–34.*

[2] *In T the additional words* nothing . . . Him *are written and deleted earlier in the sentence after* lose;

Sentence	Thyer's Reading	Commonplace Book Reading
	——, sent. 28; *GR* ii. 169 He Strife	*C* 19^r
28	never . . . that it	prunes businesses that they
	——, sent. 29; *GR* ii. 169 The Wisdom . . . out	*C* 20^r (*headed* Law)
29	the Law	it
	——, sent. 30; *GR* ii. 169 His Client . . . Men	*C* 19^r. *No variants.*
	——, sent. 31–2; *GR* ii. 169 and that which *Horace* . . . Hands. He values . . . Scoundrels	*C* 19^r. *Sentences transposed*: He values . . . Scoundrels; and that which *Horace* . . . Hands
31	of his Mouth	of Mouth
	——, sent. 33; *GR* ii. 169–70 The Law . . . again	*C* 20^r
33	Men's	Man's
	——, sent. 34; *GR* ii. 170 He has . . . Reason	*C* 19^r. *No variants.*
	'A DUELLER', sent. 5–10; *T* 102^{r-v} There . . .	*C* 23^v
6	in a more	in more
7–8	He is . . . part	*om.*
9	business with	business readily with
10	prepense	prepensed
	'AN OPPRESSOR', *T* 127^{r-v}	*C* 57^r
1	because	'cause
2	and . . . for	*om.*
3	that rests . . . ease	*om.*
5	He is as . . . voyage	*om.*
10	Tis . . . and	*om.*
	wines are	wine is
	money.	money. The Head of any Bird or Beast eraced or pulld off by force is held by Heralds a more Honourable Bearing then two of the same kind; but cutt off or alive. Hee over layes those that have Dependance upon Him; as a

Sentence	*Thyer's Reading*	*Commonplace Book Reading*
		Sow does her Piggs. [*Last sentence underlined.*]
	'A PROSELITE', sent. 5–9; *GR* ii. 200–2 Change of Religion being . . . Stocks	*C* 87ᵛ
6	Religion	It
7	He imposes	He that changes oft imposes
8	were	are
9	Ignorance	Interest
	for if . . . gains	and Some gaine
	his	their
	'AN ATHEIST', *GR* ii. 261–2	*C* 90ʳ
1	whole	*om.*
4	without Regard	without any Regard
	the Position of	those mathematicall Lines and measures in
5	the World	this World

INDEX OF TOPICS

NOTE. This index is of selected general topics. Most passages dealing with persons, books, or other particulars may be located in the text by way of the corresponding entries in the Commentary, which is covered by the second index. Italic type denotes material classified by Butler or Longueville under the given keyword.

INDEX TO INTRODUCTION
AND COMMENTARY